THE STRENGTH OF THE PACK

The Personalities, Politics and Espionage
Intrigues that Shaped the DEA

Douglas Valentine

D1205297

THE STRENGTH OF THE PACK
The Personalities, Politics and Espionage Intrigues that Shaped the DEA

Published by Douglas Valentine

Print ISBN: 9781625361479
Ebook ISBN: 9781625361462

This book is dedicated to Mitch Climan and Mike Privitello: Old friends, may you rest in peace.

And to Alice, my wife, the love of my life: I see you now in a more beautiful light.

TABLE OF CONTENTS

AUTHOR'S NOTE

I STARTED RESEARCHING *THE STRENGTH of the Pack* 20 years ago. I had recently completed a book about the CIA's Phoenix Program in Vietnam, and I knew that several Phoenix Program veterans had moved into the Drug Enforcement Administration (DEA) and the DEA's predecessor organization, the Bureau of Narcotics and Dangerous Drugs (BNDD). I was curious to know how these CIA officers were put to use in the war on drugs, and for whom they were really working.

I knew there had been hearings before a Senate committee in 1975, and that one of the sensational allegations was that a CIA assassination squad, staffed by former Phoenix Program personnel, existed inside the DEA's Special Operations Unit. I wanted to know if those allegations were true. Andrew Tartaglino was the first DEA agent I approached in this regard. Andy had served as the BNDD's chief of inspections, and as the DEA's first deputy administrator. He knew as much as anyone about the CIA's infiltration and subordination of the DEA.

Andy agreed to help, within strict limits, but he stressed that in order to fully understand the DEA problems, I had to learn how those problems originated in the Federal Bureau of Narcotics (FBN). The prospect of researching and writing another book before I wrote this one was daunting, but I did it. My book about the FBN, *The Strength of the Wolf,* was published by Verso in 2004, and offers a treasure-trove of information about many of the people and intrigues that occur in this book.

The Strength of the Wolf introduced a new cast of characters onto America's historical stage. It is the only book to thoroughly document the history of the FBN from its birth in 1930 until its wrenching termination in 1968. As with *The Strength of the Pack*, it is based largely on interviews with agents, although their recollections are set within the context of the full extent of documentary sources on the subject of federal drug law enforcement. I refined both books by focusing on the most outstanding agents and cases.

The moral to the story of federal drug law enforcement is simple: in the process of penetrating organized crime, case-making agents invariably stumble upon the CIA's involvement in drug trafficking, along with the CIA's political protectors. One of the reasons the FBN was abolished, was that its case-making agents uncovered these political and espionage intrigues. Adapting to this reality is perhaps the primary reason the DEA survives. It certainly has not come close to winning the War on Drugs.

Agent integrity is another of the main themes of *The Strength of the Wolf* and *The Strength of the Pack*. Indeed, the need to modify agent behavior was a major reason why, in the wake of Andy Tartaglino's epic corruption investigation in 1968, the BNDD was created to replace the FBN. Ironically, Tartaglino's corruption investigations of the BNDD and DEA featured a number of agents he had investigated while they were in the FBN, and who had risen to prominent positions in the organization.

Both books deal with the subordination of FBN executives and case-making agents by spies and politicians, and occasionally by influential drug traffickers. This is very heavy stuff, and the CIA did its best — albeit unsuccessfully — to prevent me from succeeding. In particular, it tried to prevent several agents from talking to me.

With the publication of *The Strength of the Pack*, my work is finished. Although you do not need to read *The Strength of the Wolf* to understand or enjoy this book, I recommend that you do so. It can only help.

I would like to take this opportunity to thank three agents in particular: Tony Pohl for his editorial assistance; John Warner for providing me with a copy of *Project Pilot III*, the joint CIA-DEA history of the French Connection; and Jerry Strickler for the many hours he spent helping me. Several other agents, including Vic Maria, Bob DeFauw, Fred Gregory, and Ralph Barber, remain my friends as well.

I am very grateful to all the agents who openly told me about their hassles with one another, as well as with the CIA and the political establishment. I'd like to think that everyone owes them a debt of gratitude. Much of our history is hidden behind a wall of national security, and that sad fact prevents America from realizing its potential as a force for truth and justice. The agents who contributed to this book have given us back a portion of our rightful heritage.

Douglas Valentine
September 2009

CAST OF CHARACTERS

ACAMPORA, COLONEL TULIUS — US Army Counter-Intelligence officer assigned to the CIA in Rome and Saigon, friend of Andy Tartaglino, Jack Cusack and Fred Dick; helped several CIA officers enter the BNDD/DEA.

AMBROSE, MYLES J. — Commissioner of Customs, 1969-1972; Director of ODALE and Advisor on Narcotics to President Nixon 1972-1973; architect of DEA.

BARTELS, JOHN R., JR. — Administrator of DEA 1973-May 1975; his rivalry with Andy Tartaglino would lead to Congressional investigations and his dismissal from office.

BELK, GEORGE M. — Veteran FBN Agent, member of The Purple Gang, BNDD Chief of International Operations and DEA Chief of Intelligence, target of Andy Tartaglino's corruption investigation.

BENSINGER, PETER B. — DEA Administrator 1976-1981.

BOLTEN, SEYMOUR: CIA Special Assistant for the Coordination of Narcotics 1972-1975, Advisor to DCI William Colby and DCI George H.W. Bush.

BONNER, ROBERT C. — DEA Administrator 1990-1993.

BOYD, JAMIE: US Attorney, Western District Texas, 1977-1981, aligned with Customs against the DEA, involved in the murder investigation of Judge John Wood, an event that precipitated the FBI takeover of DEA management in 1981.

BROSAN, GEORGE B. — Acting Chief Inspector, DEA, July 1973-December 1974, ally of Andy Tartaglino against John Bartels.

BURKE, TERRENCE — Former CIA officer, Acting DEA Administrator 1990.

BUSH, GEORGE H.W. — As US Vice President 1981-1989 and President 1989-1993 fully integrated the FBI, military and CIA in federal drug law enforcement.

CASEY, DANIEL P. — Veteran FBN Agent, BNDD Regional Director in Los Angeles and New York, held numerous senior staff positions in the DEA, involved in Tartaglino battle with Bartels.

COLBY, WILLIAM E. — Executive Director CIA 1971-1973, Director of Central Intelligence, 1973-1976, brought CIA more deeply into drug law enforcement.

COMPTON, JACK — BNDD Agent in Mexico and Customs Agent in Texas aligned with Jamie Boyd against the DEA, involved in Wood murder investigation.

CONEIN, LUCIEN E. — Former CIA Officer, DEA Chief of Special Operations Group comprised of former CIA officers (aka "The Dirty Dozen").

CUSACK, JOHN T. — Veteran FBN Agent, BNDD Director of European Office, 1969-1971; ODALE executive 1972-1973; DEA chief of Foreign Operations 1973-1977. Ally of Myles Ambrose and rival of Anthony Pohl.

DAYLE, DENNIS — Veteran FBN Agent, member of The Purple Gang, head of the DEA's CENTAC Program 1976-1981, target in Andy Tartaglino's corruption investigation, involved in Tartaglino's battle with John Bartels.

DICK, FRED T. — Veteran FBN Agent, BNDD Director Saigon Office 1969-1972, DEA Director Bangkok Office 1972-1975, target of Andy Tartaglino's corruption investigation.

DURKIN, WILLIAM J. — Veteran FBN Agent, member of The Purple Gang, BNDD Director of New York Office 1969-1971, DEA chief of Enforcement 1973-1975, target of Tartaglino's corruption probe, involved in Tartaglino's battle with Bartels.

ELLIS, DAVID C. — Assistant Commissioner of Customs for Operations, rival of Myles Ambrose and the BNDD.

EVANS, JOHN G. — Veteran FBN Agent, member of The Purple Gang, DEA Chief Inspector 1976-1977, Chief of Enforcement 1977-1978, involved in the Wood murder investigation.

FLUHR, ARTHUR J. — Veteran New York FBN Agent, target of Andy Tartaglino's integrity investigation, Director of EPIC 1976-1981.

FULLER, PATRICK W. — DEA Chief Inspector 1969-1973, managed secret-CIA staffed inspection program in the BNDD.

GREENE, STEPHEN H. — DEA Agent in Saigon under Fred Dick, Acting DEA Administrator 1993-1994.

HELMS, RICHARD — Director of Central Intelligence, 1967-1973, authorized secret-CIA staffed inspection program and covert intelligence program in the BNDD.

INGERSOLL, JOHN — Director, BNDD 1969-1973, worked with Helms and Colby, opened the BNDD to CIA infiltration.

KNIGHT, PAUL E. — CIA officer under FBN/BNDD/DEA cover, opened BNDD office in Afghanistan 1969, DEA Agent in Charge of European Operations 1972-1975.

KROGH, EGIL — Deputy to John Ehrlichman, Nixon Administration liaison to the BNDD and co-creator of the White House Special Investigations Unit, primary force in politicization of Nixon's war on drugs.

LAWN, JOHN C. — Veteran FBI Agent, involved in Wood murder investigation, DEA Administrator 1985-1990, involved in Iran-Contra scandal.

LEUCI, ROBERT — SIU Detective, in 1971 became the main informant for Andy Tartaglino against corrupt SIU officers and public officials in New York City.

LOGAY, WILLIAM J.: CIA Officer under Tully Acampora in Saigon, worked with Fred Dick in Saigon, asked to join Fuller's secret CIA inspections program, overt DEACON Agent.

LUDLUM, JAMES H. — CIA liaison to the BNDD 1969-1972, member of ONNI, Senior Intelligence Agent in DEA

MATTOCKS, GARY — CIA Officer in Vietnam, covert DEACON I Program agent, testified at the trial of CIA protected drug trafficker/asset in the DEACON I Program.

McDONNELL, CHARLES — Veteran FBN Agent arrested for heroin trafficking, turned government informant, central character in Tartaglino's corruption investigation.

MEDELL, ROBERT — Cuban exile CIA officer, member of Fuller's secret CIA inspections program, covert BUNCIN agent.

MINNICK, WALTER: Staff Director, Cabinet Committee on International Narcotics.

MITCHELL, JOHN — US Attorney General 1969-1972, Ingersoll's primary backer in Nixon White House, facilitated secret CIA inspections unit in BNDD.

MONASTERO, FRANK V. — Assistant to Tartaglino in the BNDD, involved in Tartaglino's corruption investigation in New York 1971-1973, DEA Operations Chief 1980-1985.

MULLEN, FRANCIS M., JR: Veteran FBI Agent, involved in Wood murder investigation, DEA Administrator 1981-1985, involved in Iran-Contra scandal.

POHL, ANTHONY S. — Veteran FBN Agent, head of New York's International Division 1969-1972, architect of Franco-American Agreements, creator of DEA's CENTAC Program, rival of Jack Cusack, ODALE and Myles Ambrose.

PROMUTO, VINCENT — ODALE prosecutor, Deputy Public Relations Officer for John Bartels, focus of Tartaglino corruption investigation 1974, focus of battle between Bartels and Tartaglino.

SALMI, RICHARD E. — Veteran FBN Agent, BNDD Agent in Turkey, DEA Inspector involved in MKULTRA investigation and Iran-Contra scandal

SHACKLEY, THEODORE — CIA Station Chief Miami, Laos, South Vietnam 1964-1972, Chief Western Hemisphere Division 1972-1974, Chief East Asia Division, Associate Deputy Director for Operations 1976-1978, involved in exile Cuban, Nugan Hand and Iran-Contra drug scandals.

SMITH, PHILLIP R. — Veteran FBN Agent, member of the Purple Gang, Chief of Special Projects in BNDD, Domestic Intelligence Division Chief and Acting Chief Inspector in DEA, arch rival of Andy Tartaglino.

STRICKLER, LAWRENCE J. — Head of Latin America Division in BNDD and DEA, played a major role in smashing the French Connection in Latin America.

TARTAGLINO, ANDREW C. — Veteran FBN Agent, Chief Inspector and Deputy for Enforcement of BNDD, Acting Deputy Administrator of the DEA, managed several corruption investigations; his clash with the Purple Gang and John Bartels led to his departure from the DEA in 1975.

TRIPODI, THOMAS — CIA Officer 1961-1968, BNDD Agent and assistant to Andy Tartaglino in the Charlie McDonnell and New York City corruption probes, helped form CIA secret inspections unit, investigated Frank Waters in 1974.

WARNER, JOHN — Executive Director to John Ingersoll, then BNDD Director of Office of Strategic Intelligence; DEA Chief of Foreign Intelligence 1973-1976.

WESTRATE, DAVID L. — Assistant to Tartaglino in BNDD, DEA Operations Chief 1985-1990; did much to shape the DEA's operations and procedures.

WATERS, FRANCIS E. — Veteran FBN Agent in New York, said by Charlie McDonnell to have stolen and sold heroin from the 1962 French Connection case, target of Andy Tartaglino.

1

THE SHADOW OF THE WOLF

IN APRIL 1968, THE JOHNSON Administration combined the Federal Bureau of Narcotics (FBN) with the Bureau of Drug Abuse Control (BDAC) to create the Bureau of Narcotics and Dangerous Drugs (BNDD).[1] With that action, the age of the freewheeling federal narcotics agent came to a close. The strength of federal drug law enforcement would thereafter reside in the Pack, not the Wolf.

But for all its sophistication, the newfound BNDD would still require extraordinary people to lead its 670 agents scattered in some 100 field offices, most in the United States.[2] The preeminent personality would be the director of the organization. The odds-on favorite for the job was Henry L. Giordano, the ultra-conservative commissioner of the FBN. Also in the running was John Finlator, the iconoclastic director of the BDAC.[3] Both were appointed acting associate directors of the BNDD upon its creation, with the tacit understanding that one would be chosen director.[4]

Instead, when the day of reckoning came Attorney General Ramsey Clark announced the appointment of thirty-eight year old John E. Ingersoll as the BNDD's director. Clark never even considered Giordano because of "widespread corruption among FBN agents at the time."[5] Other candidates were considered, Clark said, but Ingersoll "offered a clean break with a past that had ended in corruption and, I hoped, a new progressive, scientific based approach to drug control in a time of deep social unrest."[6]

Ingersoll would be the organization's only director throughout its brief and tumultuous five-year existence.

Clark's decision stunned and humiliated Giordano, and knocked many a proud FBN agent to his knees. Indignities were heaped upon insults. To begin with, the FBN, with its 38-year tradition of hunting down the world's top heroin traffickers, had been forced into a shotgun wedding with the two-year old BDAC, which focused on "kiddy" drugs like LSD and pot, and enforced federal regulations on the medical use and abuse of prescription drugs. One wit described the merger of the two outfits as "a wedding between a drunken sailor and an old maid."

The hardest pill to swallow for Giordano and some FBN agents was that Ingersoll had never made an undercover drug buy or bust. How could a man with no hands-on experience lead the nation's top drug law enforcement agency? To make matters worse, Ingersoll came across as a "stiff bureaucrat" and made no effort to court the affections of his subordinates. This standoffish style was an affront to the FBN's "Goodfellows" culture. Street work was steeped in violence and deception, and agents often relied on one another for their lives. As a way of dealing with the stress, they bonded by drinking and socializing together after hours.

That was not Ingersoll's style. He wasn't eager to socialize, nor was he daunted at the prospect of commanding the FBN's legendary wolf pack. With a chuckle, Ingersoll recalled his first meeting with John J. Rooney, Chairman of the House Appropriations Committee. Rooney greeted Ingersoll by saying, "So, you're the guy who got the job Giordano was supposed to get."[7]

In another telling instance, Ingersoll approached Rooney for a budget increase that would allow him to spend almost $20,000 to arrest top drug traffickers. Rooney noted that in the 1930s, the FBN had sent Lepke Buchalter to the electric chair for mere pennies. Rooney asked Ingersoll if he had heard about this infamous drug trafficker.[8] He hadn't. Rooney was aghast, but Ingersoll didn't care. His job was to break away from the past. His objective was to drag federal drug law enforcement — kicking and screaming — into the present.[9]

Ingersoll's main qualification was his reputation as an effective manager. A native of Northern California, his philosophy was shaped by the internment of a Japanese friend during the Second World War.

Ingersoll was determined to make the American justice system more equitable. A career in law enforcement seemed an appropriate mechanism for achieving this goal. After serving two years in the US Army Counter Intelligence Corps (CIC), he enrolled in the criminal justice program at the University of California, Berkeley. While earning his degree, Ingersoll studied under criminology guru Orlando W. Wilson, whose progressive approach to law enforcement emphasized prevention, deterrence, and training. Wilson took an interest in Ingersoll's career, and in 1956 Ingersoll joined the Oakland police department. He served as a patrolman, as an administrative assistant to the police chief, and as commander of the planning division.[10]

One manifestation of Ingersoll's independence was his membership in the "Cell," which he joined while on the Oakland police force. The Cell's origins are obscure, although member Richard Blum said it was formed as a response to the repression of the McCarthy era.[11] Ingersoll was the group's youngest member and least senior in rank. Blum described it as "a group of people, all life time friends, all law enforcement, all progressive professionals." One famous Cell member was Wesley A. Pomeroy. As under-sheriff of San Mateo County, Pomeroy deftly handled security for the 1964 Republican Party presidential convention in San Francisco. His unique approach to crowd control included sharing police communications systems with protestors, and helping demonstrators set up barricades. Pomeroy, to the horror of hard-core law enforcement officials, was a member of the American Civil Liberties Union (ACLU) and a proponent of the decriminalization of marijuana; but he was the kind of guy Ingersoll could relate to.

Ingersoll stepped onto the fast track in 1961, when he became a consultant for the International Association of Chiefs of Police (IACP) in Washington, DC. Two years later he was the IACP's director of field operations, touring the country with a staff of experts and surveying the operations of big city police departments, including New York. The IACP job gave Ingersoll senior management experience and put him in contact with the country's top law enforcement officials, including Deputy Attorney General Ramsey Clark, who shared Ingersoll's commitment to Civil Rights, and appreciated his innovative approach to law enforcement at a time when the nation was wracked by race riots and war protests.

"Ingersoll was trying to grapple with the problem on an intellectual level," a colleague explained.[12] That intellectual approach, though heresy in the minds of many law enforcement officials, enabled him to achieve results. While director of IACP's field services, Ingersoll conducted a study of the segregated Charlotte, North Carolina police department. He recommended that the City Council hire a new police chief who would recruit and promote Afro-Americans, to promote racial harmony in the community. Despite fierce opposition within the 450-member police force, the City Council offered Ingersoll the job. Excited by the challenge of putting his philosophy into practice, he accepted in July 1966.

Ingersoll's experiment in desegregating the Charlotte police department, and his hiring of the first women into the force, became a model for modernizing big city police departments around the nation. He proved he could change the nature of an organization; and that accomplishment, along with his belief in "management by objective," combined to convince Attorney General Ramsey Clark that Ingersoll, not Giordano or Finlator, was the best man to lead the BNDD.

Ingersoll in the Saddle

IN MID-1968, JOHN INGERSOLL WAS in his prime. Standing five-feet ten-inches, he had the stout, rugged build and the poker face of a jack-booted motorcycle cop. He was confident he could unite federal, state, and local agencies in an enlightened, systematic approach to drug law enforcement. In preparation for this task, Attorney General Clark assigned Ingersoll to his personal staff for approximately six months. From this relatively secure vantage point, Ingersoll had time to learn how the BNDD fit within the federal government. He tracked the merger of the FBN and BDAC, and met with staff officers and field supervisors from both organizations. He also toured the BNDD's foreign outposts.

At the end of this incubation stage, in November 1968, the BNDD was divided into two major divisions. Ingersoll named Henry Giordano as manager of the Enforcement Division, which was composed of three offices: domestic investigations; foreign operations and intelligence; and investigative services. Former BDAC director John Finlator oversaw the Scientific and Regulatory Division, which had offices for training, compliance, science and education.[13] Giordano and Finlator obstructed Ingersoll, each in his own fashion. Finlator cooperated "superficially," but spent most of his time outside the office making public speeches that often contradicted Ingersoll's stated policies. Giordano was an "obstacle" and sat in his office with a permanent pout on his face.[14]

Ingersoll accepted this unpleasant reality, primarily because he felt capable of reaching past his petulant deputies into their divisions to find people who were willing to get the job done. He tried to establish relationships based on cooperation. Rather than surround himself with outsiders, he decided to trust in the goodwill and professionalism of the people he inherited — not counting Giordano and a few other diehard opponents who, he felt, would weed themselves out.

Perry Rivkind and John Warner were the only friends Ingersoll brought into the BNDD. A wealthy Illinois Republican, Rivkind had met Ingersoll while teaching law enforcement at a college in Charlotte. Rivkind became Ingersoll's first executive assistant, handling his correspondence, and gladhanding dignitaries in a way that did not come naturally to Ingersoll.

John Warner had met and befriended Ingersoll while he was in the California state narcotics bureau and Ingersoll was in the Oakland Police Department. They remained friends, and in 1969 Ingersoll made Warner his liaison to state and local narcotics enforcement bureaus. In that capacity Warner formed the BNDD's Metro Enforcement Groups, using Law Enforcement Assistance Administration (LEAA) funds to bring together federal, state and local narcotics units.[15] The ultimate purpose was to free BNDD agents from having to arrest street addicts so they could develop interstate and international cases. Well respected and known as a loyal assistant who would never embarrass or backstab his boss, Warner became Ingersoll's executive assistant when Rivkind became the BNDD's chief of training.

Many BNDD agents accepted Ingersoll and his progressive outlook, in hopes of obtaining key positions. After decades of dealing with Harry J. Anslinger (the FBN's reactionary commissioner from 1930-1962), and then Anslinger's clone, Henry Giordano, officials from other government agencies generally considered Ingersoll a breath of fresh air. Anslinger and Giordano had resisted change, and they jealously guarded their power, but Ingersoll reached out and sought cooperation.

A focal point of change was the organization's legal department, which consisted of about ten attorneys involved in a variety of matters, including forfeiture law. Chief Counsel Donald Miller was a throwback from the FBN. Miller handled internal legal issues, including agent wrongdoing, and worked with Ingersoll forging agreements with foreign nations.

Miller's deputy, Michael R. Sonnenreich, was representative of the younger attorneys that gravitated into Ingersoll's circle. A Harvard graduate, Sonnenreich had worked in the Justice Department's criminal division before transferring to the BNDD. Sonnenreich would work closely with Ingersoll and Justice Department attorney John W. Dean III, crafting the Controlled Substances Act of 1970.[16] Sonnenreich and Dean also wrote the Model State legislation that brought state drug laws into synch with federal laws. Sonnenreich, Ingersoll and Dean would become friends, and Sonnenreich would serve as Ingersoll's legal advisor until his departure from the BNDD to head a controversial marijuana commission in 1972.

Ingersoll's most important personnel decision was awarding Andrew C. Tartaglino the job of chief inspector. Tartaglino had joined the FBN in New York in 1952, and had become intimately familiar with the drug underworld while making undercover buys from Mafiosi in Brooklyn and the Lower East Side.[17] (Tartaglino made a case on Joseph "Piney" Armone, who thirty years later would achieve notoriety as John Gotti's underboss.) Tartaglino served in Rome from 1956-59 and in Paris from 1959-60. He was a supervisor in the FBN's liaison group at the US Attorney's office until 1963, when he became a field inspector with the unenviable job of investigating agent wrongdoing.

In 1964, in what proved to be a major turning point in FBN history, George H. Gaffney, the FBN's Deputy Commissioner, assigned Tartaglino to David Acheson, the Treasury Department's assistant secretary for law enforcement. Gaffney ostensibly sent Tartaglino to help Acheson on an issue regarding Interpol.[18] In reality, Gaffney was an enemy of Tartaglino's mentor, legendary FBN agent Charlie Siragusa. And when Siragusa retired in 1963, Gaffney exiled Tartaglino to Treasury as a way of getting "Siragusa's man" out of his hair.[19]

Gaffney's decision would come back to haunt him. Acheson came to rely on Tartaglino and when the Interpol assignment ended, Acheson asked Tartaglino to initiate, with Anthony Lapham (said by Tartaglino to be a CIA officer working undercover as Acheson's deputy) an integrity investigation that spanned three years and resulted in the resignation of dozens of FBN agents, including some of Gaffney's inner circle.[20] In January 1968, at the request of Acheson's replacement James P. Hendricks, Tartaglino formed a special task force that expanded the corruption investigation and sealed the FBN's doom.

By his own account, Tartaglino met with Ingersoll in April 1968 and asked to be transferred back from Treasury to the BNDD "with status." Ingersoll felt that several corrupt FBN agents had slipped into the BNDD, so he agreed. Then, using Tartaglino as his filter, he began the critical task of selecting 17 regional directors. As Tartaglino recalled, "Ingersoll made every decision himself, in consultation with Giordano and Finlator." Behind the scenes, however, Ingersoll asked Tartaglino about each candidate's "lifestyle" before the interview.

When the process was over, former FBN agents held the most important regional directorship jobs in the BNDD. The most prized positions, New York and Los Angeles, were awarded to veteran FBN agents William J. Durkin and Daniel P. Casey. Two members of Tartaglino's anti-corruption task force became regional directors, and a third became the deputy regional director in Miami.[21] Ingersoll's relocation of regional headquarters from Atlanta to Miami acknowledged Miami's new prominence as the cocaine capital of the drug world. The fourth member of Tartaglino's anti-corruption group, John G. Evans, became chief of general investigations under Giordano's assistant, John R. Enright. With Giordano sulking in his office, Ingersoll relied heavily on Enright to manage enforcement matters. Walter Panich, a twenty-eight year FBN veteran, ran Ingersoll's policies and procedures staff, which effectively organized the BNDD. Working closely with Panich was Phillip R. Smith, a veteran FBN agent with 18 years service.[22]

BDAC veterans and outsiders fared well in securing headquarters positions: Edward Anderson became chief of intelligence and foreign operations, and Edward Mullin became Anderson's deputy in charge of intelligence. As former FBI agents, Anderson and Mullin worked diligently to organize the BNDD's intelligence files and create a central register of informants. Anderson, however, quickly earned a reputation as a nitpicker who kept his staff bogged down in unnecessary paperwork.[23] In particular he aggravated Henry L. Manfredi, his deputy in charge of foreign operations. A veteran FBN and CIA agent with 20 years experience overseas, Manfredi had recently suffered a heart attack, and was driven to despair and debilitating angina attacks by Anderson's petty demands.

One veteran FBN agent, with many years experience in France, said that Mullin and Anderson "didn't have a clue" about managing the BNDD's foreign or intelligence operations. When they were there, he said, "We didn't know who was in charge."[24]

The BNDD was a relatively small organization, and Ingersoll's personnel decisions had a tremendous impact on agent morale. In this particular instance he placed Manfredi under Anderson because Manfredi, though better qualified and held in high esteem by FBN agents, had spent twenty years overseas and had few official contacts in Washington. Anderson on the other hand was well known to many Washington law enforcement officials. Ingersoll made his decision at a critical moment when he was expanding the foreign and intelligence operations crucial to federal drug law enforcement. It was a good decision, insofar as Manfredi's presence as chief of foreign operations provided operational continuity during the BNDD's overseas expansion. But it was a poor decision in that Anderson's inexperience enabled the Nixon régime to more easily meddle in BNDD affairs. Instead of coasting to retirement, Manfredi found himself knee-deep in Nixonian dirty tricks and, having suffered physically from the mismanagement, he died in January 1970 of a massive heart attack at a White House press conference, less than an hour after meeting with CIA officials complicit in Nixon's political subterfuges.[25]

A similar though less dramatic dilemma confronted Paul E. Knight, a CIA officer who, like Manfredi, worked under the cover of the FBN. Knight joined the FBN in 1950 and served in Rome from 1952 until 1955, when he opened the FBN's office in Beirut, Lebanon. In 1962 he joined the CIA, while maintaining his FBN job as a cover.[26] He knew Andy Tartaglino well, and in 1968 Tartaglino brought Knight into the BNDD as a staff assistant to Ingersoll. According to Knight, his job was to prepare policies and procedures for the BNDD's expanding stable of overseas agents. Knight claims he taught incoming agents how to work with foreign policemen and the diplomatic corps; how to acquire and handle the mercenary soldiers of fortune who served as informers overseas; and how to differentiate between "fascinating, accurate, and useless intelligence." No one, however, remembers seeing Knight at headquarters. Indeed, Knight was still a CIA officer and, for reasons unknown to Ingersoll, spent a considerable amount of time meeting with notorious CIA officer Edwin P. Wilson at his sprawling farm in Virginia.[27]

In 1971 Wilson ostensibly retired from the CIA, serving with Naval Intelligence for the next five years, and forming a network of arms supply, freight-forwarding and computer companies. During this period he employed a number of Cuban exiles and former US Army Special Forces personnel. In 1982 he was convicted of arranging assassinations and selling 20 tons of plastic explosives to Libya. That conviction was overturned 21 years later when it was established that he had been working for the CIA all along.[28]

After his conviction, Wilson's shadow empire was expanded into "The Enterprise" by Major General Richard Secord (deputy assistant secretary of defense for international security affairs from 1981 to 1983) and several of Wilson's CIA associates, including Thomas Clines and Theodore Shackley. These Enterprise players figured prominently in the Iran-Contra Affair, one of the US Government's most notorious drug dealing/espionage intrigues, which is discussed at the end of the book.[29]

The nature of Paul Knight's relationship with Ed Wilson remains unknown, but in 1969 Knight opened a BNDD office in Kabul, Afghanistan, partly to locate hashish suppliers, but essentially as a cover for CIA operations directed against the Soviet Union.

Cleansing the System

THE JOB SELECTION PROCESS, AS overseen by Ingersoll and Tartaglino, caused considerable resentment. Three cases involving FBN agents serve as examples. Ernest M. Gentry, an FBN agent since the Second World War and a member of the Justice Department task force that created the BNDD, was so upset by Ingersoll's appointment that he retired. Another veteran from the Second World War, Charles "Pat" Ward, was serving as the FBN's district supervisor in Chicago. He had just purchased a house, but was summarily transferred to Detroit. Ward retired rather than move.[30] And Ross B. Ellis, an agent since 1940 and the founding father of the "Purple Gang" (a powerful clique of FBN agents within the BNDD) became despondent after a demeaning transfer to Seattle. Ellis took a demotion in order to remain in Detroit as a group supervisor, and then quit in despair.

The indignities heaped upon Gentry, Ward, Ellis and other colleagues did not sit well with many old FBN agents. They blamed Andy Tartaglino, whom they felt was using his clout as chief inspector to persecute his old enemies, especially a number of New York agents who had avoided Tartaglino's 1968 purge, some by joining the BDAC.

This conglomeration of freewheeling former FBN agents from New York, Detroit, Chicago and elsewhere was referred to as the Purple Gang, and was thought to secretly manage BNDD affairs. The most prominent members were George Belk, William Durkin and Phillip R. Smith. Smith and Belk had been close friends from the time they met and became partners in Detroit in 1952. Durkin had started his FBN career in Chicago in 1951, and in 1959 had been Belk's enforcement assistant while Belk was the district supervisor in Chicago. Belk had been an agent since 1948, and had nine years experience in top management positions, as district supervisor in Chicago (1959-1963) and New York (1963-1968).[31] Many agents held him in high regard, and Ingersoll had high hopes for Belk, who after a year's study at the Industrial War College at Fort McNair had become Ingersoll's special assistant. Again, Ingersoll's philosophy was one of trust, and even though he felt that Belk was an egotist, he selected him to plan and manage his innovative "systems approach" to drug law enforcement.[32]

It's questionable that a Purple Gang conspiracy really existed. Tartaglino certainly believed it did, and told a Senate Committee in 1976 that the Purple Gang conspired "to profit illegally from their employment in drug enforcement; to insure their own professional success, and that of their colleagues, in matters such as promotions and preferred and influential assignments; and to exercise their power within Government to stop or undercut integrity investigations that might expose them."[33]

The dynamic created by the tension between Tartaglino's clique and the Purple Gang cannot be understated when analyzing the history of the BNDD.

Management By Objective

IN HIS EFFORT TO MODERNIZE drug law enforcement through "management by objective," Ingersoll appointed professional administrators to head the BNDD offices of management analysis, personnel, and finance. He also assigned accountants and financial experts as staff officers to the regional directors. Ingersoll also emphasized training and tried to cultivate a new breed of agent. The ideal recruit was a Marine captain with Vietnam War combat experience and a college degree. Accelerated promotions and incentive payments became standard procedure. Recruits were trained for six weeks, rather than two, in an expanded curriculum that included courses in how to work with the public, and also local and foreign law enforcement agencies. In 1970, the training program was expanded to include a course for foreign police officers.

All of this stood in stark contrast to the FBN tradition of on-the-job training, in which recruits were assigned to a senior agent and taught how to make cases "on the street." BNDD agents underwent

THE STRENGTH OF THE PACK

a rigorous four-week Treasury Agent training course in Washington. Institutional bias made it difficult for women, and the first female agent, Heather Campbell, was not hired until 1971. Promoting Afro-American and Hispanic agents also took tremendous effort, despite their excellent performance as undercover agents and, later, as supervisors and managers.

The training facilities were rudimentary. The BNDD leased a building with a gym and firing range next door to its headquarters. The trainers wanted to see how well recruits performed while tired, confused, and about to encounter "the unexpected."[34] So the trainers made the recruit, carrying weights in each hand, run up several flights of stairs while Led Zeppelin blared in the hallway. When they got to the top of the steps, the recruits entered a room, drew their sidearms, and decided which (if any) targets ought to be shot.

Another one of Ingersoll's major concerns was internal security. Ingersoll believed that several corrupt FBN agents had slipped into the BNDD. As a result, he gave Tartaglino permission to pick up where his anti-corruption task force had left off. The BNDD's inspections staff consisted of only a handful of agents, and Tartaglino quickly added several more. His focus was still on New York agents, where he worked closely with inspectors Thomas P. Taylor and Ivan Wurms, and IRS and Justice Department inspectors.

Not everyone was happy with this arrangement; and when John Finlator learned what was happening, he contacted criminal division chief Henry Petersen at Justice, and complained that Tartaglino "operated alone," was "obsessed," and should not be left unsupervised.[35]

"To resolve the problem of fairness," Tartaglino recalled, "an assistant chief of the criminal division, Robert Rostall, was assigned to oversee the establishment of the inspections staff." To further satisfy Finlator, BDAC agent Richard A. Callahan, now the BNDD's regional director in Boston, monitored the process. "Callahan," said Tartaglino, "was a Finlator confidant whom I briefed before the merger."

With Callahan watching from the wings, Rostall reviewed Tartaglino's performance and declared it a success. Rostall then joined the BNDD's legal staff and traveled with Tartaglino to make cases on agents around the country.

2

THE MCDONNELL CASE

TARTAGLINO'S GREATEST TRIUMPH WAS THE case he and Justice Department attorney Robert Rostall made on Charles R. "Charlie Mac" McDonnell, a sharp Afro-American undercover agent with experience in New York and San Francisco. Described as "affable" and "a gentleman," McDonnell was always dressed in a jacket and tie, and never let a partner buy turkey. (fake drugs). Alas, Charlie Mac was as wrong as a three-dollar bill.[1]

The case on McDonnell began in New Orleans in 1967, when FBN Agent Jack Compton busted Marvin Sutton with a quarter-kilo of heroin.[2] Sutton flipped and named Joe "Louis" Miles as his source. A former heavyweight boxer from Baltimore, Miles sold heroin in New Orleans and New York, where for years he had been an informant for several FBN agents. In 1967, Miles was sharing an apartment and dealing narcotics with Charlie McDonnell, who had transferred to the BDAC and was serving in Baltimore. Miles was also employed as an informant by Edward "Russ" Dower, a former FBN agent in New York who had followed McDonnell into the BDAC.[3]

In a statement given to US Attorney John E. Clark in Texas in August 1975, Compton told how he developed a typical conspiracy case against Miles.[4] Compton said he wasn't ready to "pull the plug," nor was the local US Attorney, but Tartaglino preemptively arrested

Miles in New Orleans in March 1968. After his arrest, Miles made the astonishing allegation that New York agents were hijacking heroin shipments. The agents were also diluting ten-pound seizures of narcotics with baking soda. The agents would turn in the weaker seizure as evidence, and let Miles sell the other half as a way of keeping him in business. "They were actually peddling narcotics," Compton said incredulously, "but it wasn't coming fast enough, so the New York agents bought their own Italian connection."

In order not to go to prison, Miles agreed to set up a buy from Charlie Mac. To help make the case on McDonnell in Baltimore, Tartaglino called on Thomas C. Tripodi, Hank Manfredi, and Joseph M. Arpaio, the head of the Washington field office.[5] Tripodi had been an FBN agent from 1960-1962, when he transferred to the CIA's security office. He returned to the BNDD specifically for the McDonnell bust. CIA agent Hank Manfredi, whom Tartaglino was then officially bringing into the BNDD, was an expert in interrogation and surveillance. Manfredi had yet to assume his post as chief of foreign operations at headquarters and, as part of the McDonnell case, interviewed the infamous Mafia informant, Joe Valachi, at La Tuna Prison in Texas, about suspected New York agents.

In April 1968, Tartaglino and Arpaio watched while Joe Miles bought two kilograms of heroin from McDonnell on a golf course in Maryland. A second buy was made in June in the Baltimore apartment that Miles and McDonnell shared. McDonnell (who resigned from the BDAC in May) was arrested on a hot afternoon in July, while working on the pants press machine at his brother's dry cleaning company.[6]

Then came a series of unexpected setbacks. Though no longer an agent, McDonnell had information in some 200 pending drug cases, and on that basis he was able to cut a deal with the local US attorney. He also bought some breathing room by claiming to have purchased heroin from Francis E. Waters, a former FBN agent who had resigned in December 1967. McDonnell agreed to set up Frankie Waters and BDAC Agent Russ Dower. He helped himself further by naming more than two-dozen current and former agents involved in illegal activities.[7]

Tartaglino jumped at the bait. He intended to build his strongest case against Waters, but he wanted to make a case on Dower and have him testify against Waters as well. Tartaglino obtained an arrest warrant for Dower but, mistakenly, did not execute it right away. Instead, he put it in his "back pocket" with the consent of the US attorney. Then he had Miles call Dower to arrange a meeting. When Dower refused to talk on the phone, Tartaglino realized that Charlie Mac had managed to sound the alert. Dower was aware that he was being set up.

Faced with an impasse, Tartaglino asked Dower's boss in Boston, Dick Callahan, to order Dower to meet Miles in Washington. Callahan instructed Dower that he was to wear a "wire" during the meeting. It was an order he could not refuse without projecting consciousness of guilt, so he went. But when Miles started talking about McDonnell's allegations about Frankie Waters, Dower turned the transmitter off. He later claimed it had malfunctioned. Not easily outflanked, Tartaglino had wired Miles on another frequency and caught his conversation with Dower anyway.

"We arrested Dower in DC," said Tartaglino. "We showed him the warrant and the tape, and he talked for about three hours. He admitted some things, and laid other things out. But then he went and hired attorney Ed Rosnor, who told him to retract everything. Which he did. And when the case went to court, the judge said the tapes were inadmissible, because we had not advised him of his rights."

With Dower's flawed arrest, making a case against Frankie Waters became harder than ever. Waters, aka Frankie Black, was one of the FBN's most successful and notorious agents. He was instrumental in making the famous "French Connection" case in 1962, and in 1965 he established a link between labor leader Irving Brown and Corsican drug trafficker Maurice Castellani. Castellani, who will appear throughout this book, was bringing money to (and receiving instructions from) one of the defendants incarcerated in the 1962 French Connection case. In December 1965, Waters and Agent Francis J. Selvaggi made the seminal Nebbia case in Georgia, seizing nearly 200 pounds of French Connection heroin from a US Army warrant officer who had been hired by the mob as a courier. Mafioso Frank Dioguardia was arrested, along with several Corsican traffickers. The Nebbia case was so important it would provide the basis for several of the BNDD's biggest successes.

A short, stocky, incredibly tough agent with unorthodox methods, Frankie Waters made many significant contributions to federal drug law enforcement. But Charlie Mac claimed that Waters was his heroin source, and that the heroin was part of a stash Waters kept from the famous 1962 French Connection bust. Tartaglino forged ahead. Wasting no time, he ordered McDonnell to call Waters and arrange a meeting at the Eastern Airline lounge at La Guardia Airport. Tom

Tripodi wired Charlie Mac in Washington, and two BNDD agents accompanied him aboard the plane. Other agents set up surveillance in the airport lounge. Inspectors Ike Wurms and Tom Taylor sat in a van in the parking lot, hoping to tape the conversation between Waters and McDonnell over the airport static.[8]

According to Taylor, he and Wurms saw an Afro-American pull up to the terminal in a Lincoln Continental with DC plates. Waters got out of the Lincoln and went inside. "Frankie's a bad ass," Taylor said, "and when we tell Charlie Mac that he's coming, we could feel the tension over the wire. Frankie sat down at the bar, and the first thing Charlie said to him was, 'I'm going back on the next flight, so we only have a few minutes.'"

"Waters could tell by McDonnell's demeanor that something was wrong. 'Wait a minute,' Frankie said, 'I gotta talk to you.' At which point Charlie mumbles, 'They got one of your prints.'

"'We better lay low,' Frankie whispers back. Then Charlie says out loud, 'I need a quarter-key [meaning a quarter kilogram of heroin].' At which point Frankie invites him for a ride. Then the reception breaks apart. Frankie fades into the night, and Charlie Mac goes back to DC."

When told of Taylor's account, Frankie Waters got visibly upset.[9] "It's totally untrue that I went to meet Charlie in someone else's car. I went from my house in Hempstead in my Buick and returned the same way. I didn't want to talk to Charlie, and he never said to me anything about my prints. Pure fiction."

When asked why he met with McDonnell, Waters said, "When Charlie was the BDAC boss in Baltimore, he made a lot of calls to me about cases. Even after I quit we talked a lot. But when we met at La Guardia, he was acting weird. So I excused myself and went to the men's room, and when I got there, Bob Williams [a known narcotics violator and the man driving the Lincoln] was standing at the urinal. We go to have a drink, and he tells me funny stories."[10]

Some of the funny stories concerned the allegations Charlie Mac was making to Andy Tartaglino. It must be stressed that based on those allegations, Frankie Waters was tried in February 1975 for selling heroin to Charlie McDonnell. Waters was acquitted, and McDonnell served a mere eleven months in prison for selling Miles several pounds of heroin.

"Don't you think it's significant that Charlie Mac was let out of jail after eleven months?" Waters asked rhetorically. "It's because he testified against me!"

Likewise, Miles served no time in exchange for having worked as an agent provocateur for Tartaglino. As Jack Compton stated in his affidavit, "My informants were telling me that Miles was selling narcotics, so I called Tartaglino and Company and told them. But they said, 'Leave him alone.' They came down on one occasion and busted his pad, with him in it."[11] Compton noted that Miles somehow got away, apparently with a kilogram of heroin that "never surfaced anywhere. He did it twice," Compton said, "and my informants were starting to get the message. They started thinking that I was taking payoffs from Miles, because they could make him, and they wanted to make him. But [the inspectors] wouldn't touch him."[12]

Compton also said that shortly after Waters was charged in 1974, "Miles got seriously dead in New Orleans, and I don't think anybody has ever bothered to look very damned far in that case."[13]

Summary

THE CHARLIE MCDONNELL CASE HAD repercussions that lasted for the next eight years, during which time Andy Tartaglino would earn a reputation as a zealot whose integrity investigation destroyed the good, along with the bad and ugly. The tactics Tartaglino used also set a dangerous precedent. Tartaglino believed that in order to make a case on a bad agent, an inspector must use the same tactics an agent uses to set up drug dealers. Alas, that included the same crime for which suspected agents were being investigated — enabling an informer to sell drugs that were not recovered and used as evidence.

In the short term, Tartaglino rode a wave of success. He and Rostall generated an average of two indictments per month until November 1968 when, in an attempt to preempt the incoming Nixon Administration, Attorney General Ramsey Clark held a news conference to proclaim the Johnson Administration's success in cleansing the BNDD of any lingering corruption. "32 Narcotics Agents Resign in Corruption Investigation Here," screamed the page-one headline in the December 14, 1968 *New York Times*. Clark noted that five of the bad agents had been indicted, and that additional prosecutions and resignations would soon be forthcoming.

"After Clark made his announcement," Tartaglino said dejectedly, "our informers were no good anymore. The integrity investigation was called off, but the job was only half done."

Tartaglino's probe was eventually revived and targeted some of the BNDD's highest Purple Gang executives. Indeed, in 1975,

Tartaglino's vendetta would nearly kill the BNDD's successor organization, the Drug Enforcement Administration, in its cradle. But that calamity was yet to come. With the corruption purge swept under the carpet, the fledgling BNDD turned its attention to Nixon's escalating, deeply political war on drugs — and to its own bureaucratic battles.

3

CONNOISSEURS OF CHAOS

DURING THE FIRST YEAR OF its existence, the BNDD was in great disorder. Its job was to enforce the laws, but the laws kept changing. Change and uncertainty were the order of the day, and the BNDD was struggling to adapt.

Part of the problem was that public attention had turned from heroin to more "dangerous" drugs. LSD was thought to be the greatest menace to society, even by Ingersoll, and in October 1968 the government made it a felony to manufacture, sell, or distribute the potent hallucinogenic drug. Colleges and research institutes experimenting with LSD were required to turn their supplies over to the BNDD.[1] The head of the BNDD's laboratory, John Gunn, recalled CIA officers coming over to make sure it was all there. This is ironic, insofar as the CIA had been surreptitiously sprinkling LSD around America since 1952, and some of the BNDD's top agents had been involved in the program.[2] Code-named MKULTRA, it began in 1952 when the CIA hired FBN Agent George H. White to set up a safe house and test LSD on unsuspecting American citizens in New York. In 1955, White became district supervisor in San Francisco and opened three new MKULTRA safe houses in the Bay Area. White and his assistant, Ira "Ike" Feldman, sprinkled so much acid in the Bay Area that they helped spawn America's psychedelic generation.

Several New York agents were involved as well. In 1961, Andy Tartaglino helped Charlie Siragusa set up an MKULTRA safe house in downtown New York.[3] It consisted of two apartments with a two-way mirror in between, so the CIA could film LSD-addled dupes, even Congressmen, in compromising positions.[4] George Gaffney, John Enright and George Belk managed the "pad" in succession until 1966, when the CIA told Tartaglino to shut it down. Henry Giordano knew about it, as did many other agents who used it as a place to make cases or debrief informants.[5] The "pad" was so well stocked with liquor that the FBN wolf pack gang celebrated the French Connection case there in 1962.[6]

Ike Feldman opened a second MKULTRA safe house at 212 East 18th Street when he was transferred to New York in 1962.[7] One of the most notorious agents in FBN history, Feldman stood five-feet two-inches and was famous for wearing a fedora pulled down over his eyes and a full-length Chesterfield overcoat with velvet collars, and for smoking humongous Winston Churchill cigars. According to Feldman, he used a German prostitute named Ursula in sexual blackmail schemes aimed at East German diplomats, who were working at the United Nations. When not working for Feldman, Ursula labored for Vivienne Nagelberg, wife of Gerson Nagelberg, a Harlem nightclub owner, drug trafficker, and informant for several FBN agents.[8]

Feldman spoke pidgin Chinese and was the FBN's agent in Chinatown, where he moved from one establishment to another, taking payoffs in exchange for not causing the owners trouble with the INS.[9] Eventually caught in a trap set by Andy Tartaglino, Feldman ratted out several agents and got bounced out of the BNDD as part of the general house cleaning.[10]

Two agents in Feldman's group, Howard Safir and Peter M. Scrocca, played prominent roles in the BNDD. Safir quit the DEA to join the US Marshall Service and later became famous as New York's police commissioner under Mayor Rudy Giuliani. According to Safir, drug law enforcement in New York was "exciting, terrifying, weird and dangerous" in the early days of the BNDD.[11] Blond and prematurely balding, Scrocca was considered the best undercover agent in the New York office. Scrocca, notably, was Safir's senior partner in Feldman's group.

Their first day working together, Safir saved Scrocca's life. Scrocca was pretending to be a taxi driver/heroin addict. He was making an undercover buy when the dope dealer grabbed his "buy money" and hit him on the head with a gun. Safir was covering the buy across the street when he saw Scrocca dash out from behind the cab, shouting, "Howie! He got a gun!" As the dope dealer aimed his gun at Scrocca's back, Safir drew and shot the guy in the chest. As the man lay bleeding to death on the street, Safir asked the older, wiser agent, "What do we do now?"

"Put him in the cab," Scrocca replied. Then they drove him to a nearby hospital and dropped him off at the emergency room entrance. Such was the rough and tumble nature of federal drug law enforcement agents in those days. In return for saving Scrocca's life, Safir got a $500 reward, and Scrocca, out of gratitude, taught him many valuable lessons. The most important was never to tell anyone, especially the bosses, what they were really doing. In those days, even the straight agents weren't expected to talk about colleagues who were stealing money, guns and drugs from dope dealers. The agents had a code of silence that covered everything from unauthorized "gypsy" wiretaps, to planting evidence, and worse, such as adulterating seized drugs, as Jack Compton asserted.

Drug law enforcement in New York was different from everywhere else in the country. New York had the most addicts and traffickers, and was the place where the most cases could be made. It was also where the rules were most frequently broken. In one instance, Safir traveled with an informant to San Francisco to make an LSD case on a distributor. While Safir was occupied elsewhere, his informant, a felon on parole in New York, checked into the BNDD office. When the agents patted him down, they found a gun. "We told him he had to give it up," one of the agents recalled. The guy was genuinely hurt. 'But why?' he said. 'Howie [Safir] lets me carry one!'"[12]

Street work in New York, and everywhere else, only got weirder and more dangerous during the early years of the BNDD.

Playing For Positions

INGERSOLL DID NOT IMMEDIATELY APPOINT any Afro-Americans to regional director posts, though FBN Agent Arthur Lewis would get the job in Philadelphia in 1970. Ingersoll did, however, direct the regional directors to start upgrading blacks to group supervisors, and Bill Durkin in New York immediately named Clarence Cook supervisor of Group 7.[13] It was the first time in 38 years of federal drug law enforcement that an Afro-American had achieved a management position.

Born in Alabama, Cook graduated from Michigan State with a degree in psychology. He joined the FBN in Chicago in 1960. At the time, Durkin was Belk's enforcement assistant and Ben Theisen was Cook's group leader. Cook was the first black to have a white partner in Chicago. But it was not all peace, love and flowers. While in training in Washington, DC, he was told by the FBN's deputy assistant for enforcement, Wayland L. Speer, that black agents were nothing more than "informants with a gun."[14] That attitude hadn't mellowed much by 1968. The unreconstructed white supremacists said they couldn't find any "qualified" Afro-Americans to promote, and the Afro-Americans had, by design of the supremacists, no sponsors at headquarters to support them.

The situation improved in 1968 when Cook, then a group supervisor in New York, went to Bill Durkin and posed a simple question: Why were white agents rewarded for being aggressive, but blacks considered uppity? Durkin said he'd never thought of it that way. Then he made a leap of faith: he gave Cook permission to tour several Southern colleges to recruit Afro-Americans into the BNDD. The following year Cook put together a team of agents to do the same thing, and more Afro-Americans agents joined the BNDD. But even after Arthur Lewis was appointed (regional director (RD) in Philadelphia, most Afro-American agents still had to claw their way up the ladder of success. The white supremacist mentality has never been shattered, and tokenism is still the order of the day.

The late Sixties brought about other changes, including a mass migration of Americans to the Southwest. As a result of a barroom brawl and shooting incident in New York in 1967 in which Frankie Waters shot out the window of his car, Agent Arthur J. Fluhr was demoted and transferred to the one-man Phoenix office in 1968.[15] Other New York agents quit rather than accept such an indignity, but Fluhr, an agent since 1954, found plenty of action in Arizona. By the time he was promoted and assigned to Dallas two years later, the Phoenix office had increased to fifteen agents and had made a string of big cases. The reason was the flood of drugs pouring across the Mexican border. "When I first arrived," Fluhr recalled, "Phoenix was a one-man office covering the whole state of Arizona. So I called up [RD] Dan Casey in San Francisco and asked him, 'What do I do?' Casey said, 'Do what the guy before you did: talk to Joe Bananas in Tucson.'"

"Bananas" was Joe Bonanno, retired Don of one of New York's fabled five Mafia families. Long a government informant, Bonanno fed Fluhr information that put Southwest drug smuggling in its proper context. "There was as much organized crime in Arizona as New York," Fluhr explained. "Snow Birds from the north. I found thirty-six organized crime figures in Arizona alone."

Along with the Miami area, BNDD operations in the Southwest increased dramatically as a result of traffickers in South America using Mexico as a transit point. Escalating, as well, was the age-old conflict between the BNDD and Customs for informants, cases, arrests, and seizures along the border.

Organized Crime

FOR DECADES THE ITALIAN MAFIA and its financiers from the Jewish underworld had a monopoly on drug distribution in America, but by the 1960s, their Afro-American and Hispanic associates were also involved. Together, with their Anglo and other ethnic associates, they were called "Organized Crime."

In 1969 Edward Mullin headed the FBN's organized crime division. As a counter-intelligence expert at the FBI, he had worked on Mafia cases in Cleveland and, in 1966 and 1967 was the FBI's liaison to a Justice Department task force investigating Mafia operations from upstate New York into Canada. US Attorney Robert Peloquin headed the task force in Buffalo.[16] Purple Gang member Phil Smith was the FBN's representative to Peloquin's task force until January 1968, when Smith became the FBN's chief inspector. Knowing that Peloquin, Mullin and Smith had worked well together in Buffalo, Ingersoll selected Mullin to manage organized crime cases at headquarters. Ingersoll placed Smith in Mullin's unit as liaison to the Justice Department's new drug task forces.

Mullin's unit also served as the BNDD's point of contact with the Senate's Permanent Subcommittee on Investigations.[17] Walter Fialkewicz, an FBN agent since 1950, had been with the subcommittee since 1967, when it focused on Black Power groups and domestic terrorism. When Senator Henry Jackson (D-WA) became chairman in 1970, the subcommittee began to emphasize organized crime and would conduct two hearings relevant to the BNDD: one on fraud and corruption in military clubs in Vietnam, the other on organized crime's use of stolen securities to finance legitimate and illegitimate enterprises. Fialkewicz reported once a week to Mullin and Smith on the subcommittee's discoveries.

Mullin, however, was accustomed to advanced FBI technology, and was frustrated to find that the BNDD did not have intelligence files or a central register of informers. Lacking those support systems, and having little drug law enforcement experience, he soon quit the BNDD to join a private security company formed by Peloquin.

Luckily, veteran FBN agents were accustomed to acting independently and were making cases anyway. Picking up where the Buffalo task force left off, they carefully monitored the New York Mafia's connection in Montreal. The breakthrough occurred in late 1968 when members of Clarence Cook's group, led by Agent John O'Brien, arrested a major drug trafficker crossing over the Canadian border with five kilos of heroin.[18] Based on this investigation, the BNDD established that Canada's Cotroni Mafia family was dealing with America's Gambino family through Carlo Gambino's emissary, Guido Penosi. Penosi's syndicate was linked to the Lucchese family through Teamster Johnny Dioguardia, and to the Genovese family through Salvatore Di Pietro in Miami. By mid-1969, BNDD agents were making cases out of Montreal on three of the five New York Mafia families. And Ingersoll had started an initiative to bring the Canadians into an accord with the French, with the object of establishing a BNDD office in Montreal.

Foreign Operations

INGERSOLL'S MAIN "FOREIGN OPERATIONS" OBJECTIVE was to convince French officials that it was to their political advantage to arrest French traffickers and destroy their clandestine heroin conversion laboratories. He was also trying to persuade the Turks to stop their criminal underground from growing opium, converting it into morphine base, and selling the morphine base to French traffickers. But, Ingersoll said, the French were still in "a state of denial." So that early effort failed.[19]

While Ingersoll dealt with strategic issues, BNDD agents posted overseas took direct tactical action. Their accomplishments during this chaotic start-up period are too extensive to chronicle; but it's safe to say that they, not agents at headquarters, carried the organization. William Wanzeck was in Bangkok running operations in the Far East, with agents in Hong Kong, Korea and Singapore. George Emrich was in Mexico City, covering South America and the Caribbean. And Michael G. Picini was the boss in Rome, overseeing Europe and the

Middle East. All overseas agents worked with foreign counterparts and were usually prohibited, by the laws of the host country, from conducting undercover operations.[20] Overseas agents didn't have the same degree of control over informers as in the States, and some of their informers, who were often arms traffickers, carried weapons. Sometimes their best sources of information were policemen, which was the best way of gathering intelligence on host country traffickers. Very quietly, BNDD agents also gathered unilateral intelligence on corrupt police officers and officials assisting the traffickers.

BNDD agents were greatly assisted by the US military's criminal investigations branches when making cases on American military personnel overseas. Employees of the Agency for International Development's Public Safety Program helped too. AID, for example, provided the funds and aircraft for the BNDD's marijuana eradication program in Mexico.[21] The problem with Public Safety, according to George Belk, was that we "could never tell who we were talking to,"[22] meaning the CIA routinely placed its officers in Public Safety slots for cover purposes. Foreign policemen and intelligence officers were painfully aware of this, as well as the fact that some BNDD personnel (like Paul Knight) were mainly CIA agents working under BNDD cover.

There is no small irony in the CIA using BNDD credentials to cover its officers; for some highly motivated BNDD agents possessed NYPD detective shields, which they used to cover their extra-legal activities, such as breaking into apartments without search warrants.[23] In any event, as we shall see, the CIA would contribute mightily to the BNDD's undoing, by hiring as assets both the drug traffickers BNDD agents were working against, and the corrupt policemen and politicians the BNDD agents were working with abroad. As one agent notes rather dryly, "This caused us problems, particularly in Bolivia and Mexico."

The French Obsession

MANY BOOKS HAVE BEEN WRITTEN about various aspects of the French Connection, yet some of the main chapters in its history will never be told, and some of its main characters never known. This shroud of mystery is what makes this underworld element so fascinating and worthy of study, as federal narcotics agents had been doing since 1919. Based on fifty years of research, the BNDD had a substantial body of knowledge to work with, though much was outdated, and there was no easy means of accessing the current, correct information. Two old FBN cases provided the most promising leads: the 1965 Nebbia and 1967 Oscilloscope cases. Both pointed to the Joseph Orsini organization in Madrid and Marseille, and transit points in Latin America and Canada. These cases also led to French army Captain Michel Victor Mertz and his associate Jean Bousquet, a "wealthy French contractor" and a "representative" of notorious Corsican drug trafficker Paul Damien Mondoloni.[24]

The BNDD's Paris office asked the French to investigate Mertz and Bousquet, and the Sûreté Nationale recruited an informant in their organization. Bousquet was arrested in France in June 1968 after arranging the delivery of 112 kilos of heroin to America. He would not name his customers, but he named his couriers. Bousquet also revealed that in 1967, he and Mertz had shipped 730 kilos of heroin to the US in Citroens.[25] Mertz, an agent of the French intelligence agency SDECE (*Service de Documentations Exterieure et de Contre-Espionage*) was not arrested until November 1969, in the first of several intelligence-related cases that would strain Franco-American relations. Convicted in July 1972, Mertz was released in February 1973. His only remark at the time was, "It's a good thing that Bousquet doesn't know where the merchandise is coming from."[26]

The FBN believed that Santo Trafficante was the evil Mafia genius behind the Nebbia and Oscilloscope cases. A Frenchman convicted in the Nebbia case, Louis Douheret, lent credence to that belief by naming Arnold Romano and Benjamin Indiviglio as his Mafia contacts.[27] Romano and Indiviglio were known to purchase heroin from Trafficante in Miami. Douheret also named Joseph Luccarotti and Achille Cecchini as Orsini's top assistants in France.

Corruption and Customs

WHILE FBN AGENTS WERE CLOSING in on top Mafia and French traffickers in 1967, Andy Tartaglino's integrity investigation went into overdrive and sent many talented agents running for the exits. Bereft of this irreplaceable pool of talent, the BNDD was seizing less heroin at a time when more was coming into the country than ever before. To make matters worse, Customs Service port inspectors were making more heroin seizures, and Customs agents were questioning the couriers and opening investigations apart from the BNDD into important facets of the French connection.

This disruptive trend started in earnest in May 1967, when Customs agents arrested Joe Luccarotti's brother Ange for bringing heroin to a Cuban receiver in New York.[28] The intrepid Customs agents did their homework and discovered that Corsican traffickers in Latin America were sending shotgun style deliveries into the US. Through July 1968, Customs seized around 200 kilos of French connection heroin and developed leads the BNDD did not have on American Mafia traffickers in Mexico and Montreal, their wholesalers and customers in the US, and Italian, Corsican and French traffickers in Europe and South America.

Most significantly, Customs learned that a French criminal of Corsican origin, Auguste Ricord, ran a sprawling drug trafficking organization in Buenos Aires. A trafficker since the late 1930s, Ricord was wanted in France as a Nazi collaborator during the German occupation.[29] In 1947 he fled to Buenos Aires and established prostitution rings in several South American countries. The FBN had known about Ricord since 1951, when it made a huge conspiracy case in New York on Ricord and his fellow Corsican traffickers (and Gestapo informants) Joseph Orsini and Francois Spirito, as well as several major Mafiosi. The case revealed the French connection and its associates in Canada, Mexico, South America, the Middle East, Far East, and Europe. American authorities deported Spirito to France in 1953 and Orsini in 1958, but the French granted them amnesty. As the FBN knew, Orsini and Spirito had reunited in Madrid and revived their important facet of the French connection.

Ricord also purchased protection from Argentina's police commissioner, and by 1966 was managing a hugely profitable drug trafficking organization composed of "Corsican thugs hired by the French secret service during the Algerian crisis to combat terrorist cells."[30] By early 1968, Customs knew the identities of the major traffickers in Ricord's so-called "Group France," but wasn't telling the BNDD everything.

The BNDD was wounded by the Customs Service's lack of cooperation. Fortunately, it was generating its own leads into Ricord's Group France. Some came from Douheret, others from Alberto Larrain Maestre, a Puerto Rican fugitive in the Oscilloscope case; other leads came from contacts in various South American police forces.[31] Unfortunately, the Argentine police force learned about the Customs investigation of Ricord, and prematurely arrested Group France member Dom Orsini and several associates in February 1968.[32] Many of the Corsicans bribed their way to freedom, and Ricord dropped from sight.

The BNDD blamed Customs for this mistake, and asserted that Customs agents had little if any authority to conduct investigations overseas. But Customs agents knew they were on the verge of making the most glorious case of their careers. Upstaging the BNDD was an added bonus, so the Customs agent in charge, Albert W. Seely, told the Customs Commissioner that Ricord was responsible for "50 to 75 percent" of the heroin entering the US.[33] Although the statistics were wildly overblown, Seely was given permission to continue his investigation, and fired the first shot in what would become a debilitating war with the BNDD.

The next shot was fired in July 1968, when a cleaning person at Washington's Dulles Airport accidentally found a bag of heroin hidden in the lavatory of a plane that had arrived from Frankfurt and was preparing to depart for St. Louis and Denver.[34] The ground crew notified Customs. A Customs agent found eleven more packages hidden in the walls of the lavatory. The bags of heroin were returned to their hiding place, and the Customs agent took a seat where he could keep an eye on the lavatory. In St. Louis, the Customs agent watched while a Belgian courier subsequently identified as Willie Wouters removed the heroin. When the plane reached Denver, Wouters went to the toilet and removed the heroin. He then boarded a flight to New York, where Customs Agent Al Seely arrested him with six kilos of heroin.

Up to that point it was a classic Customs case, but the Wouters case raised two issues. First was the practice of granting bail to defendants in major narcotics cases. Wouters named Argentine Jack Grosby as his contact man with the Belgian suppliers. Grosby, who had been named in the 1967 Oscilloscope case, was arrested. But the judge allowed a Mafia lawyer to post Grosby's bail, and Grosby fled to Argentina to join his Group France contact, Louis Bonsignour.[35] The other problem was jurisdictional. The problem was not simply that Customs had dared to allow the heroin to circulate around the country as a way of identifying and arresting the receiver. Customs had been doing that for years, through what it called "convoy cases." The problem with the Wouters case was that Customs refused to share the leads it developed in Europe with the BNDD, thus impeding BNDD investigations into these same groups. The Wouters arrest had (like the premature arrest of Dom Orsini) forced several European gangs to suspend operations while they reorganized. Even Customs noticed the difference: starting in July 1968, the amount of heroin it seized at ports of entry "dwindled dramatically."[36]

Enter Tony Pohl

IN AUGUST 1968, JOHN INGERSOLL and William Durkin gave BNDD Agent Anthony S. Pohl in New York the task of streamlining the BNDD's French connection investigation by reviewing cases and debriefing defendants. To this end, Pohl went to the Atlanta Penitentiary to interview Jean Nebbia, Joseph Luccarotti and Louis Douheret. At the insistence of William Tendy, the assistant US Attorney in charge of narcotic cases in New York's Southern District, Pohl was "assisted" by Al Seely.[37]

An extraordinary individual about whom much more will be said, Pohl was born in New York City but educated in Lyon, France during the Second World War. He joined the US Army CID afterwards and transferred to the FBN in 1960. Fluent in French, Pohl questioned the three French drug traffickers at Atlanta while rough, gruff Seely, who had joined Customs in 1962 after twenty years with the NYPD, twiddled his thumbs. The rivalry between Pohl and Seely would become the stuff of legends.

Pohl questioned Nebbia first, who revealed the existence of a new smuggling operation in France and Puerto Rico. He also named members in the Bousquet group in Nice. At Seely's request, Pohl asked Nebbia about Ricord. Nebbia said only that Ricord controlled the operation in Argentina, with the help of Bonsignour. Then he made the intriguing observation that the South American traffickers "could not operate if they did not pay off the Mafia."[38]

Neither Pohl nor Seely had any idea just how important Nebbia's comment was, but Pohl had carefully recorded it. They also didn't know that Sicilian Mafioso Tomasso Buscetta, on behalf of Carlo Gambino, had been financing Ricord's organization since 1966, and was meeting regularly with its members.[39] Nor did they know that Buscetta and his partner, Giuseppe "Pino" Catania, were shipping heroin to Carlo Zippo in New York through Jorge Asaf y Bala in Mexico, Mafia contacts in Texas and California, and the Canadian Mafia in Montreal. Bousquet always shipped heroin directly to the US in automobiles.

Next Pohl questioned Luccarotti, who offered nothing. What Pohl didn't know, and what slick Al Seely didn't say, was that Joe Luccarotti's brother Ange had been providing Customs with some of its most important leads into the Ricord organization since his arrest in May 1967.

Louis Douheret, the last person interviewed at Atlanta, was the most helpful. Douheret told Pohl that the Orsini organization had moved ninety kilos of heroin a month directly to the US from 1959 until 1964![40] The 1965 Nebbia and July 1968 Bousquet cases confirmed that Orsini was still engaged in massive deliveries directly to the US. The BNDD did not have the resources to pursue every lead, and Pohl rightfully considered these direct shipments a "slap in the face," so he began to dismantle the Orsini organization and smash what the evidence indicated was the biggest facet of the French connection — which left Seely free to concentrate on Ricord.

The Fish Can Case

THROUGH WILLIE WOUTERS, SEELY LEARNED that Andre Hirsch was laundering money through Panama to a bank in Geneva, Switzerland.[41] The Swiss agreed to help, and in November 1968 they notified Seely that Hirsch was planning to smuggle a quantity of heroin in fish cans from Spain to a front company established by Serge Hysohion in New York. Through an informer he was not sharing with the BNDD, Seely knew that Hirsch was in touch with the Mafia receiver, Armando Gagliani.

But, unknown to Seely, Pohl was investigating Hirsch and his supplier, Ange Simonpierri, from another angle. Pohl's investigation led to the arrest in France in November 1968 of Louis Bonsignour, a fugitive in the Oscilloscope case.[42]

The fish cans were delivered in December 1968, but, due to a longshoremen's strike, were not unloaded until February 1969. During this period, Customs received permission to place a wiretap on everyone involved in the case, but only on condition that the BNDD have access to the tap.[43] Having to share his secrets with Pohl was a hard pill for Seely to swallow, and his resentment grew.

While they waited for the longshoremen's strike to end, Gagliani and Hysohion grew impatient. Here the situation gets complicated. Gagliani felt he was losing money, so he started negotiating with Edouard Rimbaud, a controller for Corsican traffickers Jean Croce and Joseph Mari. Hysohion knew that Rimbaud was also supplying Antonio Flores, a Puerto Rican in New York. Demand for heroin in New York was increasing, and whatever he could provide would be bought, so Hysohion set up a parallel arrangement with Flores.

On March 7, 1969, Customs agents allowed the fish cans to be delivered to Hysohion's company. Unknown to Seely, the delivery was made by one of Pohl's informants. The next day Rimbaud arrived and told Flores that he would soon have some heroin for him. Rimbaud then went to Hysohion's apartment to unpack the fish cans. Showing how complex the situation was, Corsican trafficker Jean-Claude Kella was in the apartment at the time, negotiating yet another deal with Gagliani.[44]

Rimbaud and Hysohion delivered the heroin to Gagliani, and the three of them were arrested by Customs and BNDD agents. Flores was arrested as well, but was released after Rimbaud denied knowing him. Rimbaud also turned over his sources to Flores for five percent of his future profits. Flores fled to Europe, where he had plastic surgery and continued to buy from the Croce/Mari organization.

From a law enforcement perspective, things had worked out well. Allowing the BNDD access to the wiretap enabled the bust to go down; for while listening to the French speaking traffickers, Pohl realized that another phone in Brooklyn needed to be tapped. It was over that phone that the traffickers were making their deals. By tapping that second phone, the evidence needed for conviction was obtained. But Seely felt that Pohl had "stolen" the case from him, and decided to withhold critical leads provided by Wouters and the two dozen other couriers Customs held in custody. Those leads would take Seely and his partner Edward T. Coyne to Europe, and exacerbate the worsening relations between Customs and the BNDD, particularly in view of the fact that US prosecutors decreed that Pohl would accompany Coyne and Seely as their advisor, to ensure it would be a joint operation and not a competition between rival agencies.

Leads from the Fish Can case would put the BNDD on the trail of Kella in Miami.[45] The manhunt for Kella was of epic proportions and would lead to Louis Cirillo, perhaps the biggest distributor in New York. Made in 1971, the Cirillo case was one of the BNDD's greatest triumphs. The hunt for Kella would also lead to two traffickers the BNDD was never able to corral: Maurice Castellani, leader of the CIA-connected Trois Canards gang, and Paul Mondoloni, the grand architect of Corsican drug trafficking in Mexico.[46]

The BNDD's foreign operations would take another giant step forward on April 29, 1969, when Alberto Larrain Maestre, the main fugitive in the Oscilloscope case, met in Madrid with agent Bob DeFauw. According to DeFauw, Maestre offered to become a paid informant and, in return for free passage, "He told us about Mondoloni, Sarti, and Ricord, how Dom Orsini arranged the delivery of heroin from Marseille to Madrid, and Frank Mari's role as the money man in the US." Maestre also provided leads to Dr. Joseph Mengele and, at the other end of the cultural spectrum, Meyer Lansky, who in February 1970 was meeting with Paul Mondoloni in Acapulco to set up new trafficking routes through Mexico.

All in all, by mid-1969, the BNDD was making headway in the burgeoning war on drugs. All that was needed was a coherent strategy, more money, and cooperation from Customs.

4

TURNING TO TARTAGLINO

BY EARLY 1969 IT WAS evident to John Ingersoll that the BNDD's enforcement effort was not properly coordinated at headquarters. His enforcement chief, Henry Giordano, was an obstacle, and Ingersoll could not rely on agents in the field forever. He desperately needed new blood at headquarters. The break came in April 1969, when Giordano decided to retire. Some say Ingersoll fired him. In either case Ingersoll jumped for joy, and when he came back down to earth, he made Andrew Tartaglino an offer Andy couldn't refuse.[1]

Throughout 1968, Tartaglino as chief of inspections had continued to investigate agents he suspected of corruption. The purge was undermining morale, and Ingersoll felt that by getting Tartaglino out of inspections, the organization could make a fresh start. At the same time, Tartaglino's management skills, drive, and experience with international drug trafficking made him a perfect replacement for Giordano.

As Tartaglino recalled, Ingersoll called him into his office in May 1969 and said that he had recommended to Attorney General John Mitchell that Tartaglino fill Giordano's spot.[2] Mitchell agreed and got Tartaglino a waiver to jump from a GS-15 to a GS-18, the equivalent of a general in the army. This extraordinary decision placed Tartaglino above everyone else in the organization except John Finlator, the only other GS-18 in the BNDD at the time. Finlator and a number of agents were unhappy with the decision, but Ingersoll, in his own words, had "absolute confidence in Andy."[3] Knowing this, Tartaglino accepted the offer and became the BNDD's chief of enforcement. In June 1969 he moved into a spacious corner office with a beautiful secretary, lots of chairs and even a comfortable sofa for his steady stream of guests.

Tartaglino named former BDAC agent Frank Monastero as the chief of his policy and planning staff. Monastero's staff, including Agent David Westrate from Detroit via Los Angeles, energized and expanded the office that Walter Panich had initially organized and managed. Monastero and Westrate prepared the budget, wrote the agent's manual, handled Tartaglino's correspondence, and worked closely with administrative chief Nelson "Bill" Coon.[4]

Monastero was Tartaglino's neighbor and knew him as well as anyone. He described him as a gentle person who "liked shooting the breeze, growing roses, and sharing a glass of red wine with friends."[5] Tartaglino hated staff meetings and paperwork, preferring to manage the organization's major operations.

According to Monastero and several other agents, Tartaglino also had a secret life that included a bad marriage, a brother and son who committed suicide, and a seething desire for revenge. Tartaglino was tormented by the fact that several "corrupt" FBN agents had slipped through his grasp, and he longed for the day when he could resume his uncompleted corruption investigation. That is why, as a condition for accepting the job as chief of enforcement, Tartaglino insisted that Ingersoll give him permission to travel "as necessary" to New York to monitor the Justice Department's investigation of corrupt agents.[6] Ingersoll agreed and then passed the chief inspector job to Patrick Fuller. A former colleague of Ingersoll's at the Oakland PD, Fuller had been a career IRS inspector and BDAC's regional boss in Los Angeles.

Tartaglino's secret plan began to unfold on November 21, 1968, when he presented Ingersoll with the first of four reports. The November 1968 report was titled "Integrity Investigation — New York Office, History, Recommendations and Conclusions."[7] The history was extensive, dating back to the fatal heroin overdose of Agent Crofton Hayes in 1953, and the role FBN Agents Fred Dick and Bill Durkin had played in papering over a failed integrity investigation of New York agents in 1961. Dick and Durkin recommended procedural reforms, such as better control of informant files and better ways to conduct searches. They advised that excessive drinking not be tolerated. But they had also recommended that no one be fired, and Tartaglino found Dick and Durkin's reports insufferably self-serving.

Tartaglino submitted three other reports: a May 1969 memorandum on resolved cases of wrongdoing by BNDD agents, a June 1, 1969 memorandum on unresolved cases on agents charged with wrongdoing; and a June 23, 1969 memorandum listing negative reports on about eighty current and former agents.[8] Of these, forty-five agents had resigned, eight had been indicted, twelve were cleared of wrongdoing, and twenty cases were, like the one against Frankie Waters, still under investigation. As Tartaglino coolly recalled, these reports became "very important later on." Indeed, in 1975 these reports helped launch Senate hearings that nearly paralyzed the DEA.

Before relinquishing his position as chief inspector, Tartaglino also assigned Inspector Robert Goe the task of conducting an "in-house" study to determine if the Purple Gang, as noted in Chapter 1 was conspiring "to profit illegally from their employment in drug enforcement; to insure their own professional success, and that of their colleagues, in matters such as promotions and preferred and influential assignments; and to exercise their power within Government to stop or undercut integrity investigations that might expose them."[9]

Goe's job was a document search, not an investigation involving interviews or surveillances, and what he discovered is unknown. Goe is deceased, and his final report was lost or destroyed. What remains is a synopsis that straddled the issue: Goe did not find a conspiracy, but he found enough evidence to warrant a full-scale investigation. The radical and potentially embarrassing idea of an investigation was summarily dismissed by Ingersoll's old friend and protector, Chief Inspector Pat Fuller, and by the Nixon Administration's protector William Ryan, chief of the Justice Department's narcotics and dangerous drugs unit.[10]

The Johnson Administration had formed Ryan's narcotics and dangerous drugs unit specifically as an adjunct to the BNDD. It was designed to assist the BNDD in legal proceedings, such as issuing wiretap authorizations. It also worked with the BNDD and Justice Department strike forces building cases in federal courts against major drug violators. And, as in the case above, it allowed the attorney general to squash any politically embarrassing actions the BNDD might undertake.

Tartaglino certainly felt that Ingersoll and Mitchell, through Ryan, forced Fuller to shut down the investigation.[11] Indeed, instead of continuing Tartaglino's investigation, Fuller instructed Irwin Greenfield, chief of the field inspections division, to send a memo to Ingersoll, which officially closed the 35 investigations that were ongoing in 1968.[12] A copy of the memo was put in each of the 35 case files.

Tartaglino also felt that pressure from the Purple Gang had influenced Ingersoll to shut down his investigation, for the good of the organization. "Only half of the job was done," he bitterly complained. "But it was a done deal, and thirty-five cases go down the tubes."

One That Got Caught; One That Got Away

As ENFORCEMENT CHIEF, TARTAGLINO WORKED closely with Ingersoll's special as sistant George Belk developing a "systems approach" to federal drug law enforcement. Based on the theory of management by objective, the systems approach was the cornerstone of BNDD enforcement policy. In the reorganization of June 1969, Ingersoll placed Belk in charge of criminal investigations so Belk could directly manage the systems apparatus.

Working with chief administrator Nelson Coon, Tartaglino and his staff also established the policies and procedures that would advance the BNDD's organizational interests. However, having vaulted over every GS-16 and 17 in the outfit, Tartaglino's elevation was not universally admired by his colleagues. John "Ray" Enright thought he should have gotten the job as enforcement chief, but, as noted, he instead became Tartaglino's deputy.[13] Enright was hurt. He felt his job was a duplication of Tartaglino's, and that he was there solely as a buffer between Tartaglino and Purple Gang leader George Belk. To make matters worse, the regional directors reported to Enright on the organizational chart, but in reality they communicated directly with Belk or Tartaglino. As Enright plainly admits, "Belk had a huge staff and I had none, and I didn't know what I was supposed to do."

According to one agent, Enright didn't do much of anything. Meanwhile, Belk was secretly harboring a grudge against Ingersoll for not promoting him to chief of enforcement. Like many senior agents in management positions, Belk deeply resented the fact that Tartaglino was responsible for every promotion on the enforcement side. Tartaglino, meanwhile, began to shape the BNDD in his image, using his new position to settle old scores in ways he could not have done as chief of inspections. Here are two examples, for now.

Tartaglino in particular harbored an abiding hatred for George Gaffney. The animosity began in the early 1950s when they worked together in New York in different cliques — one Italian, the other Irish. The ill feelings festered over the years until Gaffney replaced Tartaglino's mentor, Charlie Siragusa, as deputy commissioner of the FBN. Although Tartaglino possessed a Machiavellian knack for out-foxing his enemies, Gaffney was equally shrewd. And as a special advisor to Ingersoll, he had more clout — until Andy's promotion to GS-18. Then the tables turned.

By his own account, Gaffney's fatal mistake was testifying for Agent Eugene Marshall at Marshall's trial in March 1965. Marshall was the FBN agent-in-charge of Miami, and was arrested for accepting bribes. At the trial, Gaffney was asked about Marshall's work history. Gaffney played it by the book and said there was nothing adverse in Marshall's personnel files.[14]

"Marshall was convicted and sent to prison, but Andy wanted more," Gaffney said bitterly. "Finally Ingersoll calls me into his office. [Chief Counsel] Don Miller's there. They ask me why I testified for Marshall." Furious at being grilled about an event that had happened over three years earlier, Gaffney said, "I told them I could only speak about what was in the files, and everything in Marshall's files was favorable."

Gaffney believed until his dying day that Tartaglino used the Marshall incident to turn Ingersoll against him. Speaking through clenched teeth, he described his three years at the BNDD as "pure hell." Only a conference room separated his office from Ingersoll's, but the director "never" approached him for advice, despite the fact that he had been the FBN's most successful district supervisor in New York, a position he held from 1958 until August 1962, when Bobby Kennedy asked him to serve as the FBN's enforcement assistant.

"Coming back from an Interpol conference in Mexico, Ingersoll and I were sitting on a plane," Gaffney recalled. "So I took the opportunity to tell him that one of the big problems I saw in BNDD was that no one really understood how to make a conspiracy case. But he didn't listen. He relied on Andy, totally."

Gaffney clung to his job until he turned fifty and then retired in early 1971.

Dennis Dayle was a top-notch FBN agent who also felt the sting of Andy Tartaglino's wrath. Early in his career, Dayle had been an agent in Chicago while Belk was district supervisor of the office.[15]

In 1963, Dayle was assigned to Lebanon and served throughout the Middle East. But in 1966, headquarters accused Dayle of submitting a false sample of opium. In frustration he quit the FBN and joined the BDAC, where his investigative skills were welcomed with open arms. Handsome, tough and charming, Dayle served as chief of BDAC's organized crime unit until March 1968, when he became its agent-in-charge in Miami. When the BNDD was created, and Miami replaced Atlanta as the region's headquarters, Dayle fully expected to be named regional director. But Dayle had disobeyed one of Tartaglino's edicts: he had worked on a marijuana case in 1968 with Sal Vizzini, a black-balled former FBN agent then serving as police chief in South Miami. Before resigning under a cloud from the FBN in 1966, Vizzini had been assigned to Miami and had worked closely with the aforementioned Eugene Marshall.

Dayle had disobeyed Tartaglino, plus he was one of the FBN agents whom Tartaglino suspected of jumping to the BDAC as a way of avoiding his 1967-1968 integrity investigation. So, Tartaglino convinced Ingersoll to make Dayle a group supervisor under William Logan, a lesser light from the BDAC with little narcotics experience, who became regional director in Miami.

"I liked Andy," Dayle said, "and as chief inspector he knew all the secrets, the big one being that Henry Giordano was under the CIA's yoke. Then Andy replaced Henry and it was the same thing. But unlike Henry, Andy changed after his promotion. He came off as a nice little guy, but he had a Napoleon complex, and once he got power, he abused it. The true Andy emerged and he ran rampant over everybody."

Dayle's conflict with Tartaglino and the CIA was amplified by his independent style. The archetypal lone wolf, Dayle single-handedly initiated a narcotics conspiracy case in Nicaragua in October 1969; at the same time CIA asset Anastasio Somoza and his drug dealing anti-Castro Cuban allies were waging a brutal counter-insurgency against Nicaragua's farmers and labor leaders. At the center of Dayle's case were Somoza's immigration chief, José Pepe Alegret, and Pedro Luis Rodriguez Y Paz, the manager of the Somoza-Alegret drug ring. The ring, alas, had CIA protection, as Dayle discovered when he asked Tartaglino for permission to go to Managua to cause the arrest of Y Paz, a rabid anti-Castro Cuban fugitive. Dayle knew that Y Paz and Alegret co-owned a chic nightclub on a cliff overlooking Lake Nicaragua.[16] He knew their distributor in Miami, Fernando Acostor, sent naïve young women on all-expenses-paid pleasure trips to Managua, where they were enticed by Y Paz into smuggling drugs back to Miami. And he also knew that Y Paz was flying a chemist back and forth from Managua to a cocaine lab in Ecuador.

Dayle had a warrant for Y Paz, but it was about to expire. "Time was running out," Dayle recalled. "So Logan called headquarters, and I talked to Andy's assistant, Dave Westrate. Westrate talked to Andy, and Andy said to wait while he talked to State."

Certain that Tartaglino, whom Dayle refers to as "the screen," was stalling on the CIA's behalf until the warrant expired, Dayle flew without authorization on a tourist visa to Managua and petitioned Ambassador Kennedy Crocket to have Y Paz arrested. Crocket said that was a fine idea, but that Nicaragua had no extradition treaty with America. Pressed by Dayle, Crocket promised to come up with something, and three weeks later he summoned Dayle back to Managua, where he had arranged for him to meet Somoza — thinking that would bring an end to the problem.

"Crockett, Somoza and I sat around a conference table," Dayle recalled, "and Somoza laughed when I said that I wanted Y Paz. But when I told him that I would name Alegret as a defendant in the case, unless I got Y Paz, his demeanor changed and he accused me of blackmail. After I repeated my threat for the third time, Somoza told me to return to Miami and that he would contact me on Thursday — which just happened to be the day of Andy's big mobile task force conference.

"We're at the hotel having dinner when a waiter comes over with a phone. It's Somoza. 'Take some men and go to the cargo area of Miami International Airport,' he says. As we arrive, we see an Electra plane land and taxi over to our bay. The Electra feathers one prop. A door opens and a ladder comes down. Three men in mufti descend with a mailbag with legs sticking out of it. The legs belong to Y Paz."

Dayle savored the recollection, and then continued his epic tale of woe. "After the conference, Andy went back to Washington and one of the first things he did was call me up and chew me out for showing ingenuity and initiative. Within weeks I was transferred from Miami, where I had a brilliant record on the Organized Crime Task Force in Detroit."

Dennis Dayle was the first BNDD agent to recognize the massive cocaine problem in Miami, and its connection to the anti-Castro exile Cuban community through CIA assets like Somoza in Latin America.[17]

For that he was punished. But every dog has his day, and seven years later, after Tartaglino's fall from grace, Dennis Dayle would have his revenge.

Meanwhile the BNDD was girding its loins, preparing for battles on several fronts: it was about to abandon the streets in pursuit of international conspiracies; Customs was about to launch a broadside; and Tartaglino was about to allow the CIA to infiltrate the BNDD ... and forever poison its soul.

5

SYMBOLIC STRATEGIES

NINETEEN SIXTY-EIGHT WAS A BAD year for Democrats. In March, overwhelmed by the fact that the Vietnam War was unwinnable, President Johnson announced his decision not to seek re-election, throwing the Party into chaos. In April, the Civil Rights movement lost its heart and soul when Dr. Martin Luther King, Jr. was assassinated in Memphis. Any hopes of winning the presidency vanished in June, when Senator Robert F. Kennedy was assassinated in Los Angeles. And for several days in August, protestors battled Mayor Richard J. Daley's rampaging police force at the Democratic Party convention in Chicago. As the election drew near, the shameless Republicans gleefully exploited the situation, blaming America's social unrest on the liberal policies of Johnson's Great Society. Permissiveness, they said, fostered crime in general, and drug abuse in particular.

With the Democrats leaderless and their rank and file in disarray, villainous Richard M. Nixon did what he had failed to do eight years earlier and was elected President of the United States. Upon occupying the White House, he turned to four men for guidance: chief of staff H. R. "Bob" Haldeman; legal counsel John D. Ehrlichman; national security advisor Henry Kissinger; and attorney general John N. Mitchell. Each had an impact on federal drug law enforcement. But, ironically, it was Democrat Daniel "Pat" Moynihan who initially took the lead role in formulating drug policy, largely because, traditionally, drug addiction had been a big city issue. As Nixon's special assistant on urban affairs, Moynihan pressed the President's inner circle to address the heroin issue in all its complexity; starting at its source in the faraway poppy fields of Turkey, through French chemists and traffickers to Mafia distributors, and finally into the veins of addicts, many of them disenfranchised minorities.

Dealing with the root causes of drug addiction or racial issues was not standard Republican fare. But Nixon had made a campaign promise to restore law and order, so his advisers decided to use their formidable public relations powers to devise "symbolic strategies" for showing success in the war on drugs, no matter how ephemeral or fleeting those successes were.[1] In this way, the issue of drug abuse was transformed from a public health and law enforcement matter into a statistical shell game played for partisan political purposes. Nixon's advisers also turned federal drug law enforcement into a bureaucratic battlefield where powerful personalities, rather than coherent policies, were the driving force. This crisis erupted in full force when Nixon's advisers turned to Republican scion Myles Ambrose, the newly appointed Commissioner of Customs, to show instant success in the war on drugs.

Under normal circumstances, Nixon would have relied upon Ingersoll, but Ingersoll was otherwise engaged. By his own estimate, half his time was spent building the BNDD's administrative capabilities; everything from acquiring cars, radios, agents and office space to developing operational plans, including drug abuse prevention programs.[2] A quarter of his time was spent traveling abroad on international initiatives. The other quarter was spent, often with assistant deputy attorney general John W. Dean III, working on new legislation like the Controlled Substances Act. Submitted to Congress in July 1969, the Controlled Substances Act completely revamped the outdated 1914 Harrison Narcotics Act.[3] It regulated all drugs into one of five schedules, with Schedule I reserved for the most dangerous and Schedule V for the least. This law would form the basis of federal drug control for decades to come.

Ingersoll's early work with the Justice Department paid dividends. By convincing the states to join federal task forces, he was able to move his agents off the streets and onto major conspiracy cases. More importantly, Ingersoll formed a close relationship with attorney general John Mitchell, who thereafter served as Ingersoll's advocate in the Nixon Administration. This was good news for the BNDD, for Mitchell was Nixon's most trusted adviser and the Administration's front man in the war on drugs.

Unfortunately, while Ingersoll was pursuing long range strategies, Customs Commissioner Myles Ambrose was convincing White House officials that Customs was doing a better job at drug interdiction than the BNDD, and was better qualified to lead the war on drugs. Conditions at the time, though fleeting, seemed to support this blather. More narcotics than ever were pouring into the country, enabling Customs port inspectors to make more seizures than ever. BNDD agents were making cases, yes, and Ingersoll would report 4,192 arrests in fiscal year 1969.[4] But most were of street level pushers, users of pot and other "kiddy" drugs that were popular at the time. As Treasury Enforcement Assistant Eugene Rossides testified to a Senate panel, the BNDD seized only 115 pounds of heroin that year, while Customs seized 311.[5]

The statistics hurt Ingersoll and helped Ambrose. Plus, with the help of CIA psychologists, Customs port inspectors were learning how to better profile couriers, and that too meant more seizures.[6] More seizures translated into more arrests, more arrests meant more informants, more informants meant better intelligence, and better intelligence meant more cases. Bolstered by early successes, Ambrose claimed that Customs had the jurisdiction to pursue cases it initiated, and was not obligated to share information with the BNDD. And that meant trouble.

The Ascent of Myles Ambrose

TURNING TO AMBITIOUS MYLES AMBROSE was not altogether unsound. His expertise was as a political opportunist, but he also had the qualifications to lead Customs to the forefront of federal drug law enforcement. Having prosecuted narcotics cases as an assistant US attorney in New York from 1954-1957 (including Andy Tartaglino's first big case in 1955), he understood the nuts and bolts of federal drug law enforcement.[7] He understood it in its broader context too. In 1957, at the tender age of thirty-one, he became the Treasury Department's assistant secretary for law enforcement and chief coordinator of Treasury's law enforcement agencies: FBN, Customs, Secret Service, Alcohol/Tobacco/Firearms, Coast Guard and IRS intelligence divisions. In this pivotal position, Ambrose worked with Attorney General William Rogers (Nixon's Secretary of State) on the seminal

Appalachian case, in which dozens of top Mafiosi were arrested in upstate New York and prosecuted in one of the government's first organized-crime conspiracy cases. This meant that Ambrose knew, by name and pedigree, most of the nation's top drug traffickers better than Ingersoll.

Ambrose also had a firm grasp of the espionage aspects of drug law enforcement. As assistant secretary for law enforcement, he was Treasury's representative to the National Security Council. He also supplied the CIA with cover for its officers under FBN, Customs and other Treasury Department posts in Rome, Paris, London and Tokyo, and he helped the CIA place officers in the six Treasury coordinator positions in the continental US. Ambrose was an observer at the 1958 Geneva Commission on Narcotic Drugs, and, with James Rockefeller, he co-chaired the first US-Mexico Narcotics Conference in 1960.

Charismatic and flamboyant, Ambrose was a man the Republicans could trust to do their bidding. He had served in a patronage position as head of New York's Waterfront Commission in the early 1960s and later campaigned, unsuccessfully, for a seat in the New York State Legislature. Well-connected at all levels of government, he could call upon almost any Republican governor, senator, bureaucrat, or Wall Street lawyer. He was a powerhouse, and upon being named Customs commissioner in 1969, Ambrose merrily began making and effecting drug law enforcement policy in accordance with White House wishes, apart from and at odds with Ingersoll and the BNDD.

The Perfect Scapegoat

AMBROSE IS A LARGE MAN with an imperious air. Leaning back in a black leather swivel chair, puffing on a big cigar, he explained the origins of the rivalry between Customs and the BNDD. "In the early days," he said, "Customs was confined to gathering narcotics intelligence overseas. But that wasn't a problem because Anslinger had no intentions of expanding his outfit … and because Customs did not conduct investigations overseas."

The problem, he claims, began with Ingersoll.

As Ambrose explained, Customs had legal jurisdiction along the border and within the United States for twenty-six kilometers. Within that area, Customs agents can stop and search any person or vehicle without a warrant. They also developed informant networks among hotel clerks and the like, and conducted surveillances of drug traffickers so they could arrest them when they tried to smuggle drugs across the border. However, when the BNDD was created, Ingersoll broke with tradition and sent his agents into this nohunting zone reserved for Customs agents; soon the Customs agents, through informers and surveillances, discovered, to their horror, that BNDD informers were smuggling drugs across the border so BNDD agents could make busts in the States.

"Well," Ambrose said with righteous indignation, "Customs alone was authorized to allow drugs into the country, so Customs agents began stopping and searching BNDD cars. Next thing you know, Mexico becomes the focus, not just of the rivalry, but of the war on drugs in general."

Ambrose expounds with artful sincerity: In 1968, Nixon gave a campaign speech in California in which he promised to clean up the drug problem along the border. After his election, Nixon gave the text of the speech to Martin Pollner, the director of his advisory committee on crime, and told Pollner to make it happen. By 1969, Pollner was an assistant to Eugene Rossides, the Treasury Department's assistant secretary for law enforcement. Rossides was serving in the position Ambrose had once held, and was now his boss. A Columbia University graduate and former all-American football player, Rossides was a die-hard Republican and had managed Nelson Rockefeller's successful gubernatorial campaign in New York. Like Ambrose, he was eager to promote the Treasury Department and the Customs Services at the expense of the Justice Department and the BNDD.

Ambrose explained that Martin Pollner, with the blessings of Eugene Rossides, wrote a paper that proposed to solve the drug problem along Southern California's border by tripling the number of Customs agents from 333 to 1000. Upon hearing about Pollner's plan, deputy attorney general Richard Kleindienst went to Mexico in a brazen attempt to preempt Treasury and protect the BNDD. Kleindienst, according to Ambrose, had an axe to grind. A native of Arizona, Kleindienst had served as director of field operations for Nixon's campaign in 1968. He had worked arduously, some say unscrupulously, against Rockefeller, the preferred candidate of the North-eastern branch of the Republican Party, of which Ambrose and Rossides were members. This personal animosity between Kleindienst and Ambrose created more bureaucratic and political stumbling blocks in the quest for a concerted federal enforcement effort.

"Kleindienst asked the Mexicans to stop smuggling," Ambrose growls. "So the Mexicans asked him, 'What's in it for us?' The answer was, 'Enough money to boost the Mexican Federal Judiciary police from 250 to 400 agents; money and equipment for the Mexican army and aircraft; and sensory devices for the Mexican Air Force.'"

But the Mexicans used the largesse for self-serving ends and smuggling proliferated. The problem, Ambrose asserts, was corruption. "We couldn't involve the Federal Police too early in a case, because they'd inevitably find some way to delay us. In Mexico City, their Customs Chief was actually taking bribes."

It is customary for American politicians to blame our drug problem on corrupt or antagonistic foreign officials, rather than the unique social conditions that create America's insatiable craving for drugs. This self-serving rationale also deflects attention from the inability of US officials to stop its own citizens from dealing drugs. In any event, Ambrose chose Mexico as the target of the first battle in Nixon's symbolic war on drugs.

Operation Intercept

MEXICO WAS THE PERFECT SCAPEGOAT. Mexican students staged impressive anti-American riots during the 1968 summer Olympics, and more in October. The riots were blamed on Communist agitators, and the Mexican police dutifully killed dozens of demonstrators.[8] But the unrest persisted and quickly led to a deterioration of relations with the hairy-chested macho men in the Nixon regime. The Mexican problem demanded immediate action, and the White House got involved through John Ehrlichman and his understudy, Egil "Bud" Krogh.[9]

A World War II veteran and graduate of Stanford Law School, Ehrlichman had helped manage Nixon's 1968 presidential campaign and was rewarded with an appointment as Nixon's chief counsel. When he went to Washington, Ehrlichman brought along Bud Krogh, a family friend and junior member of his law firm in Seattle. Krogh was a thirty year old, former Naval officer with no law enforcement experience. But he hated hippies with a purple passion, and that alone qualified him to become Nixon's deputy assistant on law enforcement. According to John Finlator, "Krogh was the man who gave day-to-day advisories to the agencies and to whom they looked for guidance and decisions."[10]

Krogh's first assignment was to clean up Washington DC, which Nixon (devoid of irony) considered the crime capital of the country. While researching the problem, Krogh read a report on the correlation between drug addiction and crime. He immediately grasped its partisan political potential and began to replace Moynihan as the White House's point man on drug policy. The real experts were at the BNDD, of course; but the White House needed someone to manage its symbolic strategies. Which is how, through happenstance and zealotry, Krogh got the job of bashing Mexico.

Through Krogh, the White House in the summer of 1969 created Task Force One under the co-chairmanship of rivals Eugene Rossides and Richard Kleindienst.[11] The purpose of Task Force One was to plan and put into effect a huge drug interdiction operation along the Mexican border from Brownsville, Texas, to San Diego, California. They called it Operation Intercept. According to Myles Ambrose, the unstated purpose was political; "to fulfill Nixon's pledge to improve the interdiction of drugs from Mexico." Unlike the spectacular seizure of a large shipment of French connection heroin, Intercept would not be a flash in the pan, but would grab headlines over a period of weeks.

Ambrose chose senior Customs Agent Harold Smith to head the Intercept Task Force. Phil Smith was the BNDD's representative along with George Emrich, the BNDD agent-in-charge in Mexico City.[12] The BNDD provided support to Task Force One by gathering intelligence about smugglers and their secret airfields deep inside Mexico. This job fell to about thirty Spanishspeaking agents, all of whom were in Mexico clandestinely. During Intercept, the BNDD also worked overtly with the Mexican Federal Police to increase air surveillance along the border. But, as Ambrose stresses, "It was Customs' job to stop and search cars at the border crossings, which we started doing in September 1969."

Launched on September 22, one day after Mexican officials were notified, Intercept created the largest traffic jam in history and prevented thousands of Mexican farmers from delivering their perishable produce to market. Never mind that it did nothing to stop drug smuggling. Or that by the time it ended in October, it had humiliated Mexican officials from Tijuana to Mexico City. All it did, according to Mexican President Diaz Ordaz, was erect "a wall of suspicion" between the US and Mexico.[13]

But for that very reason it accomplished its symbolic mission. Intercept was a perfect expression of the nativist aspect of American politics. It appealed to the mean streak in Nixon's conservative political base and was hailed by strutting White House officials as a smashing success.

Behind the scenes, the State Department viewed Intercept as a huge failure in foreign relations. It also prompted Henry Kissinger to involve the National Security Council more deeply in White House drug war policies, largely through his deputy General Alexander Haig, as well as through NSC narcotics advisors Arthur Downey and Arnold Nachmanoff and their staff. But Nixon was willing to pay the price, because Operation Intercept proved he was "tough on crime."

Fallout From Intercept

OPERATION INTERCEPT WAS A COUP for Myles Ambrose. As a result, Customs obtained an $8.5 million supplementary appropriation from Congress.[14] Ambrose devoted seventy-five percent of the money to fighting drugs. "We bought airplanes and boats, and added six hundred seventy new agents," he said with smug satisfaction.[15]

Many of these new Customs agents were assigned to narcotics units in Washington, San Pedro, Houston, New Orleans, and Chicago. The command post unit in New York, working closely with the NYPD's Special Investigations Unit, increased from six to sixteen agents. Many new hires became Customs Inspectors, and armed with the well-established legal right to check any crossborder traveler's baggage without a warrant, were posted at some 400 major sea and air ports of entry. All in all, Customs vastly improved its position, and began to rival the BNDD as America's lead drug law enforcement agency.

Another disastrous result of Intercept was the ascent of former FBI agent G. Gordon Liddy. Based on an April 1966 raid on Timothy Leary's LSD commune in Milbrook, New York, Liddy achieved notoriety as a law and order zealot. On that basis, he campaigned in New York State's Republican Party primary. His opponent, however, was a normal human being and the Party's first choice, and in exchange for dropping out of the race, Liddy was made a special assistant on drug issues to Eugene Rossides. In that position, for his kindred spirits Egil Krogh and Myles Ambrose, Liddy wrote the Intercept operational plan, and served as its representative in El Paso.[16]

During Intercept, Liddy worked with David Ellis, the Customs Service's chief of field operations. A World War II hero from Texas, Ellis had years of enforcement experience along the Mexican border. By Ellis' account, Liddy was a native New Yorker, so Ambrose trusted him to write the Intercept proposal, rather than someone (Ellis, for example) from the Southwest, who was in tune with the subtleties of the situation.

Tensions already existed between Customs and the BNDD, between Justice and Treasury, and between the White House, State Department and NSC. But with the decision to allow Liddy to write the Intercept proposal, tensions *within* Customs were inflamed. The point of contention was between Ellis and Ambrose. Ellis had been promised the commissioner's job, and was devastated when Ambrose, who had never served a day in the Service, got it instead. Thereafter, Ellis and a clique of loyal Customs agents stood by helplessly while Ambrose handed out sensitive assignments to integrity-challenged but politically obedient pals like Liddy.

"I had friends in Mexico," Ellis recalled, "and I knew we were going to lose our heads over Intercept. I'd read the proposal and I knew that Liddy's sole purpose was to abuse the Mexicans. I told Ambrose it was absurd, which is why he assigned *his boy* Harold Smith to head it."

Like everyone who got involved with Liddy, Ambrose would regret it. He knew during Intercept that Liddy was "doing things he wasn't supposed to do," and that Rossides thought Liddy was nuts and was going to fire him.[17] But Krogh disliked Rossides, and Ambrose knew that Krogh, as Nixon's adviser, had more clout than Rossides. Krogh's position was further strengthened in December 1969 when Ehrlichman became Nixon's chief advisor on domestic affairs — which encompassed the war on drugs. So Ambrose convinced Krogh to bring Liddy onto the White House staff. Which explained how the Nixon Administration got saddled with the bald-headed zealot who would help bring about its demise.

There was nothing that Ingersoll could do to alter the fact that Ambrose had maneuvered Customs into a preeminent position on the Southwest border. Adding to his problems was the mysterious death of George Emrich, the BNDD agent-in-charge in Mexico City, on September 19, 1969, three days before Intercept began.

Phil Smith was the BNDD representative to the Intercept task force. As Agent Rick Dunagan recalled, Smith summoned him from Monterey (where he was stationed) to the Princessa Hotel in Acapulco on the night of September 19.[18] Dunagan arrived to find Smith sitting at a table littered with empty bottles of booze. Smith mumbled that he and Emrich had argued. Emrich had accused Smith of usurping his authority in Mexico, and then stormed out of the room in a drunken rage. Emrich went for a walk along the beach and was not seen again until early that morning, when his body was found floating face down in a tidal pool. The Mexicans said he had gotten caught in the undertow and drowned. But when Dunagan examined the body at the morgue, he saw a gash in Emrich's head and a pool of blood on the floor. Hank Manfredi conducted an investigation and determined that the gash had occurred when the Mexicans accidentally dropped Emrich's body while lifting it onto the slab in the morgue. But, as Dunagan notes skeptically, bodies with rigor mortis don't bleed; a fact that suggested the possibility of foul play.

Manfredi was slated to replace Emrich as the agent-in-charge in Mexico City.[19] But after he completed the Emrich investigation, with its sinister loose ends, Manfredi turned the job down. A few weeks later in January 1970, after meeting with CIA officials about intrigues in Mexico, Manfredi died of a massive heart attack during a White House press conference.[20] Manfredi's death was a tremendous blow to the BNDD, and further complicated Ingersoll's dilemma about what to do in Mexico.

Andy Tartaglino recommended Joe Arpaio as regional director in Mexico City, as a reward for his assistance in making the integrity case on Charlie McDonnell. A veteran agent who had served in Chicago and Turkey, Arpaio was not the best choice. According to his deputy, Arpaio knew the Mexicans were corrupt, "but took the attitude that it didn't interfere." Arpaio "was easily stroked" and more concerned that his agents were loyal to him, as opposed to being ethical.[21] One BNDD agent fathered two illegitimate children while in Mexico under Arpaio; others were involved in deadly shootouts; and one agent in Guadalajara took money — all without repercussions.[22] Arpaio's complacent attitude led to greater abuses and generated even more serious problems in Mexico.

Intercept impacted the BNDD in other subtle ways. In a positive sense, it forced John Mitchell — who did not want to see Justice upstaged by Treasury — to cement his relations with Ingersoll. Within the BNDD, Intercept also galvanized the agents against Customs. The Purple Gang in particular was loath to stand on the sidelines and watch while Ambrose and goons like Gordon Liddy stole their thunder. The FBN had battled Customs since 1930, and its ascendancy was something the BNDD simply could not suffer.

The Heroin Committee

BY LATE 1969, A COMBINATION of factors in federal drug law enforcement — including Intercept, John Ingersoll's French and

Turkish initiatives, the Vietnam War, and the BNDD's battle with Customs — were of concern to national security advisor Henry Kissinger. Unwilling to let the wrangling bureaucrats at Customs and the BNDD negatively impact his diplomatic and espionage operations, Kissinger formed the cabinet level Ad Hoc Committee on Narcotics, otherwise known as the Heroin Committee.

The formation of the Heroin Committee marked the end of Pat Moynihan's commanding influence over drug policy. Ehrlichman and Kissinger wanted him out of their hair, and sent him to Europe to push Cusack's plan to get the Turks to stop producing opium.[23] Moynihan's departure opened the door for Egil Krogh to step in as the White House representative to the Heroin Committee, which became the focal point of Nixon Administration drug-war policy. It was formally composed of cabinet members, but those eminent individuals were usually represented by deputies at Committee meetings. Kissinger's deputy, Alexander Haig, often chaired the meetings.

James Ludlum represented the director of the CIA, Richard Helms. Medium built, with fair hair and features, Ludlum had served in the FBI until 1955, when he joined the CIA as a counter-intelligence officer on James J. Angleton's staff. In 1962, Ludlum became Angleton's liaison officer to all federal law enforcement agencies, except the FBI. Ludlum met about once a month with FBN Commissioner Giordano or Deputy Commissioner Gaffney, and was well aware of the issues involved.[24]

"When Kissinger set up the Heroin Committee," Ludlum said, "Angleton sent me there as a way of keeping the narcotic function within the counterintelligence staff. It wasn't really a counterintelligence function, but Angleton was still on his Great Mole hunt, looking for the double agent [KGB defector Anatoly] Golitsin had prophesized. That was the context in which he lived. He never gave up power, which is why narcotics came under his realm, even though it didn't belong there.[25] Anyway, I was sent to the Committee with Charlie Frost as my deputy, and we started dealing with directly with Helms and his deputy for operations, Tom Karamessines, and the division chiefs.

"The Heroin Committee was a group of forceful people," Ludlum explained, "whose bosses didn't take responsibility. The CIA certainly didn't take it seriously, because it wasn't part of their mission. I remember Helms calling me in and asking, 'Who the hell are Ehrlichman and Krogh?'

"The Committee had a Working Group at the Assistant Secretary level, which met at the Executive Office building. The principle player there was Bob Andrews, representing the Defense Department. His concern was addiction among troops in Vietnam. Harry Schwartz was from State and his only interest was in maintaining good relations with the target countries, Turkey and France. The person representing AID [the State Department's Agency for International Development] from the Turkey desk was Mary Walmpers, and her interest was minimal too — to make sure that Cusack's opium eradication program squared with the long-term interests of the government.[26] Customs went along with AID. But the BNDD, represented by Hank Manfredi, was interested only in making arrests. I remember that Hank was working closely with Jack Caulfield [formerly a detective with the NYPD's intelligence unit] from the White House and," Ludlum rolls his eyes, "Gordon Liddy from Treasury."

Ludlum refers to an "implementation" meeting on November 3, 1969, attended by Ehrlichman; Roger Key from the Office of Management and Budget (OMB); Alexis Johnson from State; Dr. Eagleberger from the Department of Health Education and Welfare (HEW); Gene Rossides ("a Greek who hated the Turks," according to Ludlum) from Treasury; Arthur Downey and Richard Blumenthal from the National Security Council (NSC); and Helms and Ludlum from the CIA. At this meeting, Lebanon and the Far East were declared off-limits for national security reasons. The focus of the meeting was the flow of Turkish opium to heroin labs in Marseille. Present was William Handley, the American Ambassador to Turkey.[27]

According to Ludlum, Handley confused the Committee by claiming, contrary to BNDD statistics, that most diverted opium went not to France but to Iran, which had recently announced its intention to cultivate 20,000 hectares of poppies in economic "self-defense" against Turkey and Afghanistan.[28] In order to get the Turks to control opium production, thus eliminating Iran's incentive to grow it, Handley presented Cusack's proposal for a $50 million loan to the Turks, to cover its losses. Mary Walmpers gagged at the figure, Ludlum said, and Moynihan blurted out, "You're putting me on!"

Even Myles Ambrose thought Cusack's payoff idea was ridiculous. When John Mitchell asked him what he thought of it, Ambrose said, "It's Alice in Wonderland." He explained to Mitchell, with whom he later became friends, that one square mile of opium could produce enough heroin to supply every addict in the world. The idea being that someone will always find a spare hectare somewhere.[29]

"Drugs were not Kissinger's priority," Ludlum explained. "Drugs were a no-win situation. State and the CIA saw the larger interests that were at stake in Turkey and they wanted a less aggressive policy. They were all trying to offset Moynihan, who wanted to buy the 1970 crop and plow under seventy-one and seventy-two — but for less money. The cash payment was to buy up the ten percent that was leaked from legal production. Manfredi and his deputy John Parker had all the statistics from Cusack: they knew where the farms were and who ran them, and they wanted to give fifty bucks to each farmer and to use the rest of the money to offset the loss to the Turkish pharmaceutical companies. AID's agriculture and economic experts said the money wouldn't cover the black market loss to farmers, so they only agreed to provide police and lab testing equipment through Public Safety people reassigned to BNDD. But the Turkish Ministry of Agriculture wasn't interested in crop substitution, and their enforcement was weak, and the whole Turkish program eventually failed."[30]

The next item on the agenda, raised by NSC official Art Downey, was France. Ludlum described it as being a "touchy" subject. "Nixon and Pompidou were scheduled to meet in January 1970 to restore Franco-American relations," he explained, "which had been badly damaged during the de Gaulle era, and we were told to re-energize BNDD's Paris office."

One result was the replacement of Ambassador Shriver by Thomas Watson (an executive officer at IBM, which sold computers to the CIA), and the assignment of CIA officer Paul Van Marx as Watson's special assistant.[31] Van Marx was a banking expert who'd spent most of his career in Switzerland. His job was to ensure that BNDD conspiracy cases did not compromise CIA assets in foreign governments. As an agent explained, "If we had an informer, Van Marx would know if he or she also worked for the Air Force, or someone else. He had intelligence on foreign nationals in thirty-one countries. He'd check out informers for us too. For example, the CIA in Germany would hang a wire on a potential recruit, to find out if the guy was, as he professed, a corrupt cop, or actually an East German spy."[32]

Lebanon and Vietnam were the unspoken problems facing the Heroin Committee.[33] When it came to Vietnam, there was disagreement on how to proceed. Nixon launched his Vietnamization program, which was designed to return management of the war to the hapless government of Vietnam. Without telling the South Vietnamese, Kissinger approached the North Vietnamese through a French banker in July 1969. The North Vietnamese rejected the overture, but continued to parlay with Kissinger in a Paris suburb, where SDECE had installed eaves-dropping equipment.[34] To facilitate this crucial deal, Kissinger needed the assistance of SDECE, despite the fact that James Angleton and others believed it was involved in drug smuggling (like the CIA) and penetrated by the Soviets (perhaps like the CIA). Angleton didn't like the fact that SDECE was involved, but it wasn't his call. For Kissinger, those considerations were far less important than reaching a settlement in Vietnam.

The problem for the BNDD was that it could not show success in the drug war without smashing the Far East Asian connection.

6

THE BIG PICTURE

GEORGE BELK WAS A BIBLE-QUOTING native of North Carolina who joined the FBN in 1948 in Atlanta. A tireless worker and two-fisted drinker known for reciting catchy phrases to make his point, Belk was gruff but fair. He had a way with words and on one Monday morning in New York, while he was district supervisor in the mid-1960s, he assembled all the agents in the office. In his silky smooth Southern drawl he said: "I have eighty-five agents here under my command, and the City of New York has thirty-two thousand policemen. Last month my eight-five men killed more people than the entire police force of New York City." Then, even slower for emphasis, he said, "Don't you ever think of giving these people a chance to surrender?"[1]

Belk believed in giving subordinates a free hand, but he kept tabs on everyone and did not accept laziness or ineptitude. It was not uncommon to see Belk chewing out an agent, or telling an agent to write up his own bonus. No manager in the BNDD commanded more respect.

"As enforcement assistant and a GS-18," one agent notes, "Andy [Tartaglino] had tremendous power. But within an organization there are bosses, and there are leaders. Andy was the boss, but Belk was the leader."

Unlike Tartaglino, Belk had commanded troops in the field, as a district supervisor in Chicago and New York.[2] For many agents, that made all the difference. Having attended the War College at Fort McNair and having managed an MKULTRA safe house in New York, Belk also had his own CIA and military contacts. Ingersoll knew all this and felt that Belk had "great potential." Alas, he never rose to Ingersoll's level of expectation.[3]

After returning from the War College, Belk served as Henry Giordano's special assistant until June 1969, when Giordano retired and Ingersoll made Tartaglino his enforcement chief. Belk felt that he, not Tartaglino, deserved the job. He was also one of the GS-17s that Tartaglino had vaulted over, and he resented Ingersoll for not giving him a promotion too. Instead, Ingersoll moved Belk laterally into the planning division and then to chief of the criminal investigations division, reporting to Tartaglino's deputy John Enright. While in the planning division, Belk played the lead role in organizing the BNDD's "systems approach."[4] The systems approach was designed to take BNDD agents off the streets, where they were making small "buy and bust" cases on heroin addicts, pot heads and pill poppers, and focus them on immobilizing major heroin conspiracies. It was an idea with merit, but would ultimately prove incompatible with Nixon's political need for immediate statistical and symbolic successes.

The issue of informants was at the heart of the systems approach. Previously, agents "owned" their informants, often without entering their names in the office file. Under the systems approach, agents would still recruit informants, but they would be owned by the organization. Informants could be paid at much higher rates, too, sometimes in excess of $50,000.[5] Theoretically, this readjustment would galvanize the organization. The systems approach also brought into vogue the "controlled delivery," in which loads of narcotics were allowed into the US — at the risk of being lost — in order to entrap everyone involved. And it engendered the tactic of "letting it walk," in which BNDD informants generated drug deals but BNDD agents, in order to set up a bigger bust, did not make arrests or confiscate narcotics — which were distributed by middlemen to addicts on the street.

FBN agents understood the venal nature of drug law enforcement. Their catch phrase was, "In order to make narcotic cases, your inform-ant has to deal drugs." The systems approach amplified that theory to a grand scale that compromised the integrity of the BNDD to its core. As Agent Bowman Taylor said, "I used to think we were fighting the drug business. But after they formed the BNDD, I realized we were feeding it."[6]

Planning of the systems approach was done at Airlie House, a bucolic estate in Warrenton, Virginia, where Belk's team had all of their creature comforts met by an ever-present staff of waiters and bartenders. Belk and his team, featuring Walter Panich and Phil Smith, spent several months eating, drinking, and debating the systematic approach of "management by objective."[7] Once they determined what the objectives were and how to achieve them, they returned to headquarters to gather, analyze, assemble, and "machine process" the extant bits and pieces of information in BDAC and FBN files.[8] A file room was established and an efficient method of indexing names and cases was devised for cross-referencing. The file room was managed by retired Air Force officer Don Angel with a female staff composed of one group of closely-knit older white women, and another group of young Afro-American women from the same town in Virginia. The file room was computerized and became the institutional library of enforcement operations.[9]

Having organized the available information, Belk and his team established nine major drug trafficking systems — nine being a number large enough to engage the entire organization, but small enough to be managed by desk officers at headquarters. One system focused on cocaine out of Central and South America; another on Mexican cartels; three were focused on US organized crime systems tied to groups in Canada, Italy and France; one was global in nature and responsible for more heroin being introduced into the US than any other source; and the others involved non-narcotic drugs like LSD.[10] The systems incubation period lasted until September 1969, at which point Belk established a "war room" in the office of investigations.[11] Desk officers were assigned to monitor each system and its sub-systems, provide money to regional directors, and work with agents to develop targets of opportunity.

At the same time Ingersoll and Tartaglino placed Phil Smith in charge of the Office of Special Projects in the criminal division. The Office of Special Projects built the BNDD's air wing, conducted research programs with the CIA and the military, provided technical aids and documentation to agents, handled fugitive searches, served as the point of contact with other agencies, and established mobile task forces in major cities.[12] It also linked headquarters with regional directors. In one special project named Operation Flanker, Smith and RD John Evans in Chicago targeted 20 Mafia drug lords dealing with the Herrera crime family. Flanker climaxed in February 1971, when 54 traffickers were arrested in raids in New York, Chicago, Detroit, and New Orleans. Ingersoll would boast that the case "partially immobilized four of nine worldwide narcotics distribution systems that have been identified by the Bureau."[13]

Partially as a result of Flanker, the BNDD would receive a supplemental appropriation that increased its 1971 budget to $43 million and enabled Ingersoll to expand his force to 1600 agents.[14] Smith's Office of Special Projects grew so powerful that Tartaglino viewed it as a threat to his power base, and eventually took it away from Belk and put it under operations chief John Enright.[15]

Growing Controversies

NOT EVERYONE WAS AWED BY the systems approach. One agent described it as, "a publicity stunt developed with the knowledge that no one became a system you couldn't reach." Another called it a "... concoction. They picked the nine most promising conspiracy cases already going, so they didn't need new informers. Then they played off the lesser cases, and relied on wiretaps. It was a legacy of Tartaglino's integrity investigation." Yet another called it an intelligence function, not an enforcement function.

New York regional director Bill Durkin opposed the systems approach on the basis that the BNDD's strength was having agents on the street, not making conspiracy cases at headquarters.[16] This led Durkin to a falling-out with Belk, who wanted each regional director to tell him, in writing, how many traffickers in each system were being investigated in his region. Durkin felt this was a waste of time and did not comply for nearly a year. "The systems concept was predicated on the assumption that we knew the name of every violator," a Durkin supporter explained. "But we didn't. Durkin knew this, and he didn't abide by it. Otherwise, we would have lost touch with the streets. We wouldn't have known what the price of heroin was."[17]

As head of the premier office in the BNDD, Durkin's opinion meant a lot. But, according to another agent, Durkin placed his personal advancement over the welfare of the agents. "He was a good man, but a poor leader," the agent said.[18]

Durkin's career had not prepared him to run the BNDD's premier New York office. Tall, husky, blond-haired Bill Durkin began his career in Pennsylvania, through a family connection to FBN Commissioner Harry Anslinger. He worked as a street agent in New York in the mid-1950s; as Belk's enforcement assistant in Chicago;

as Anslinger's aide-de-camp in 1961; and as the agent-in-charge in Mexico from 1962-1968, where he worked closely with the CIA managing a small force of three or four men. Like Belk, Durkin resented Ingersoll and, behind his back, called him "that motorcycle cop." But for some unexplained reason, Ingersoll gave him the New York job, which Durkin lacked the management and leadership skills to handle. Thus he appreciated anyone who helped him, which is why he gave full support to Tony Pohl to organize and operate the International Division. New York's International Division would rival Belk's systems operations at headquarters.

Durkin's big problem was that he was besieged by Andy Tartaglino and Pat Fuller's constant probes into issues of agent integrity. According to one agent, Durkin was so intimidated he actually advised his agents to lay low rather than stir up trouble by using the standard operating procedures required to make cases.[19] This was very important, for the number of BNDD arrests fell to such an extent that in late 1969, New York Mayor John Lindsay and John Mitchell decided to form a task force specifically to reduce the number of heroin addicts in New York.[20] The Joint Task Force consisted of a small group of BNDD agents hand-picked by Andy Tartaglino to work with state and city police forces. Under the direction of Agent Theodore Vernier, the Joint Task Force went into business in January 1970.[21]

Something else needs to be said about Bill Durkin. At six feet four inches tall, with rugged good looks and the build of a football player, Durkin was the antithesis of diminutive Andy Tartaglino. He also let it be known that he disapproved of Tartaglino's sweeping corruption investigation. "Durkin didn't believe that everyone in New York was wrong," a group supervisor recalled. "The first day on the job he got everyone together and said the slate was clean."[22]

There is no small irony in this, for Durkin was Andy Tartaglino's main target.

The French Connection Takes Precedence

JOHN INGERSOLL'S STRATEGY WAS TO go to the source of America's drug problem: Those places where opium was grown, converted into morphine base and heroin, and routed to America. Ingersoll wanted to open offices in all these countries, and he knew that success would come not through unilateral undercover operations, but by forging diplomatic relations and treaties with foreign governments. The

French connection was his major preoccupation, and in this regard he turned to formidable Tony Pohl.

Tony Pohl is an example of the extraordinary person found in the old FBN. A cultured individual, Pohl was born in New York and raised in France. His mother was a concert pianist and his father conducted the Strasbourg symphonic orchestra.[23] Pohl's entry into law enforcement came through his older brother Leon, a chief inspector of the 10th Criminal Police Brigade in Lyon, France, who worked with the US Army Criminal Investigations Division (CID). Shortly after the war, Tony Pohl joined the US Army and was assigned as a Special Agent to the CID in Heidelberg, Germany. At the time, counterfeiting of US dollars was a major problem and the CID functioned as a stand-in agency for the US Secret Service, which had no agents in Europe.

Tony Pohl worked with high-placed contacts in the French, German, Dutch and Belgian police forces on counterfeiting cases. One of his most important contacts was Emil Benhamou, director of the anticounterfeiting division of the French National Police and head of its financial section. In the late 1950s Pohl was transferred to the CID's Central Detachment in Washington, DC. Based on Pohl's contacts in European police forces and fluency in several languages, Charlie Siragusa recruited Pohl into the FBN in 1960. Pohl worked in New York, Paris and Marseille until his transfer to Chicago in 1963. He arrived in New York in 1968.

By January 1969, Pohl's International Division encompassed three enforcement groups, and Pohl was Durkin's official advisor on the French drug trafficking underworld. In April 1969, having completed a review of old cases, he wrote a memo critical of the BNDD's foreign operations. Durkin was impressed and sent it to Ingersoll, who summoned Pohl to BNDD headquarters in Washington. Based on Pohl's recommendations, Ingersoll contacted Jean Dours, Director of the French National Police, and Pierre Epaud, Director of the French Criminal Police (Police Judiciaire), with the objective of enlisting their formal assistance in smashing the French connection.

On May 5, 1969, Pohl and Ingersoll met with Epaud and Marcel Carerre, chief of the French National Police's Central Narcotics Office (CNO), in Paris. Ingersoll took a hard line at this meeting. He accused the French of being primarily responsible for America's drug problem.[24] He said that 80 percent of the heroin entering the US was refined in clandestine laboratories in or near Marseille. He asked the

French authorities to organize special narcotic enforcement squads to deal with the problem because, at the time, the CNO had only about 15 detectives. Those 15 detectives, apart from four assigned to Marseille, were responsible for all of France. To assuage the French and assure them of their importance in the joint venture, Ingersoll added that he was relocating the BNDD's regional headquarters in Europe from Rome to Paris.

Epaud's reaction was predictable. He was so offended by the 80 percent figure that he politely said, "qui," then let the matter drop. This meant that Pohl had to call on his old friend Emil Benhamou in order to get the French bureaucrats to go along with the deal. As head of the Sûreté's financial section, Benhamou had access to Interior Minister Raymond Marcellin. Benhamou was also aware that French Prime Minister Jacques Chaban-Delmas supported Ingersoll's proposal. Knowing this, he contacted Pohl and said that Epaud would be in Mexico for an Interpol meeting in October 1969. Pohl knew that Ingersoll was scheduled to attend a regional directors meeting in Miami that month. Together they decided that if Benhamou could steer Epaud to Miami, Ingersoll might repair relations and revive the negotiations.[25]

Pohl explained the plan to Bill Durkin. He showed Durkin an itinerary he and Benhamou had prepared, in which Ingersoll and Epaud would travel to Washington to meet Attorney General John Mitchell. Durkin and Tartaglino agreed it was worth a try, and in early August 1969 they proposed to Ingersoll that Epaud be invited to visit the US and that Pohl be the official interpreter.

In mid-August 1969 the BNDD moved its Rome office — lock stock and barrel — to Paris. Jack Cusack arrived as regional director, replacing Michael G. Picini, a veteran FBN agent who had been running European and Middle Eastern operations in Rome since 1963. Cusack was a Fordham grad and FBN agent since 1948. His claims to fame were arresting jazz saxophonist Charlie Parker, and helping Charlie Siragusa open the Rome office in 1951. Cusack returned to New York in 1953 to run the FBN's conspiracy squad. In 1957, after switching his loyalty from Siragusa to Giordano, Cusack became district supervisor in Atlanta, managing FBN operations in Cuba. He returned to Rome in 1959 and ran European and Middle East operations until 1963.[26]

Cusack had vast knowledge of the drug trafficking underworld. He was ambitious and smart, with close ties to the CIA, at times using

FBN investigations as cover for CIA missions.[27] He had never been a good undercover agent and spoke few words of French; but he could write English well and blow with the political winds. He grasped the big "national security" picture and while at FBN headquarters, as chief of foreign operations from 1965 until 1967, he routinely buried reports that implicated the CIA's proprietary airline, Air America, in large-scale drug smuggling.[28]

Also during this period, Cusack developed a plan for reducing the amount of illicit opium produced in Turkey. Farmers in Turkey were paid to grow opium for the government, but they secretly diverted a portion of their crop into the black market where the profit margin was considerably wider. In 1968, approximately 5,000 kilograms of opium and 800 kilograms of morphine base were seized in Turkey.[29] It was a big problem and a top priority for the Heroin Committee.

Cusack established a correlation between opium output in Turkey and addiction in the US. He also produced statistics showing that Turkish opium was the raw material for 80 percent of the heroin emanating from clandestine labs in Marseille. His statistics impressed the White House and certain Congressmen, and by 1969 Cusack was Ingersoll's special assistant on Turkey. By late 1969, the Heroin Committee had adopted his proposal that the US buy the surplus opium grown by Turkish farmers, pay the Turks to reduce the number of provinces authorized to grow opium, and have them grow peanuts instead.[30]

Cusack was popular in US political circles, but was not warmly welcomed in Paris. While serving as the FBN's district supervisor in Rome, he frequently sent agents into France on unilateral undercover operations, several of which were blown.[31] CNO Chief Carerre mistrusted Cusack and strenuously objected to his appointment. But Ingersoll wanted to assert his authority, and felt that Cusack had the "ugly American" approach needed to offset Pohl's cultured style.

Then in September, Myles Ambrose threw a monkey wrench into Ingersoll's sensitive diplomatic initiative. Aware that relations between the CNO and BNDD were strained, Ambrose had the Customs agent-in-charge in Paris ask CNO chief Marcel Carrere if US Customs could form official relations with his organization. Carrere was outraged and complained that Ambrose's initiative would contravene the "Agreement" between Ingersoll and Epaud. The Agreement specified that the CNO and BNDD would work exclusively with one another, specifically to avoid the confusion and cross-purposes engendered by multi-agency contacts.[32] By October, as a result of Ambrose's initiative, the French were "vituperative," and started to doubt that Ingersoll's initiative had the approbation of the US Government.[33]

But Pohl and Benhamou came to the rescue again. They reassured their bosses that the other party was negotiating in good faith, and in October 1969, French and Americans officials did meet and reach a breakthrough agreement in Miami. Ingersoll and Epaud (assisted by Pohl as their interpreter) discussed the pertinent issues: resolving the BNDD/Customs conflict; organizing well-staffed special enforcement groups in Paris and Marseille, conducting joint operations under French direction, posting French narcotic agent Claude Chaminadas in New York as liaison to Pohl's International Division, and bringing Turkey as well as Canada into the planned agreement on narcotics enforcement.

The timely exchange of intelligence was the most divisive issue, primarily as a result of Paris RD Jack Cusack's opposition. Cusack believed that French officials protected several clandestine labs in Marseille, and that French police and customs officers in Marseille were untrustworthy. In one case in 1967, BNDD agents watched while French Customs Officer Thomas Megozzi absconded with 86 kilograms of morphine base from the Turkish ship, S/S Karadeniz. Megozzi was arrested but merely transferred to another dock area.[34] Thus, when Cusack arrived in Paris in August 1969, he refused to share intelligence with CNO Chief Marcel Carerre in Paris, on the assumption it would fall into the hands of corrupt French police officials in Marseille. Negotiations in Miami advanced only after Cusack agreed to communicate directly with Epaud, and share BNDD intelligence with Carerre. In return, Epaud and Carerre agreed to replace the unreliable French cops in Marseille. With that, the Agreement went forward.[35]

Reaching the Presidential Level

As CIA OFFICER JIM LUDLUM recalled, a Heroin Committee meeting on November 6, 1969 was devoted almost entirely to finding a way to diminish international drug smuggling without offending French officials. "The question was, 'Should we raise the diplomatic exchange to the Presidential level? Does the President want to be in the forefront?'

"The answer was yes," said Ludlum, "and the decision was made to send Ingersoll with Tony Pohl as his interpreter to Paris, with Kissinger's blessings."

On November 8, an embassy official in Paris delivered a letter from Nixon to French President Georges Pompidou. Two days later, Ingersoll met with Interior Minister Marcellin and proposed an Inter-Governmental task force. Marcellin agreed, and discussions began about how to smash the Orsini organization; how to stop the movement of acetic anhydride legally manufactured in Lyon to clandestine labs in and around Marseilles, and the need to involve Turkey. Behind the scenes, the arrest of SDECE Agent Michel Mertz (see Chapter 3) was seen as a positive development. As a further sign of good faith, Epaud, in liaison with Pohl, drafted the first Protocol of Understanding.[36]

On November 21, Pompidou sent a letter to Nixon, expressing high hopes for their upcoming conference in February 1970. Pompidou expressed confidence in Ingersoll and promised that his proposals would be studied. But, he said, the 80 percent figure did not coincide with French information, and opium producing nations like Turkey were more of a problem than France.

Establishing the facts was an important step in achieving a formal Agreement, and on December 3, 1969 in Marseille, BNDD Agent Bob DeFauw presented a report to Ingersoll and Pohl on the French connection system.[37] DeFauw unveiled a wall map (which became a fixture in Belk's war room) that tracked known smuggling routes from Turkey and Lebanon to labs in France and Belgium. The map indicated transit points in Spain, Canada and Mexico, and identified the major importers in America. "Each system had a different colored yarn," DeFauw recalled, "including one that detailed the AM-1 Alberto Larrain Maestre system, which led to Claude Pastou and Lucien Sarti [ranking members of the Ricord Group]."[38]

DeFauw's information was based largely on information provided by Maestre, a US citizen, after his arrest in 1967. During a April 29, 1969 interview with DeFauw, Maestre mapped out the AM-1 system. Maestre revealed that all his narcotics transactions were negotiated in Spain by Domingo Orsini, that French traffickers delivered the heroin to Orsini in Madrid from Marseille, and that Domingo hired couriers to fly the narcotics to New York City.[39] Maestre provided leads to Louis Bonsignour, and other members of Ricord's Group France, to the Jewish mobsters in Miami, Norman Rothman and Meyer Lansky, who were financing many of the transactions, as well as to their Mafia associate Santo Trafficante. In exchange for this information Maestre, married to a wealthy French wine heiress, received a free pass and thereafter worked for the BNDD and DEA for many years.[40]

DeFauw's report, titled "International Committee on Narcotics," identified ten heroin conversion labs in France, and credited the French with seizing labs in March and October 1969. The lab seized in March had the capacity to produce 120 kilos of heroin a month. DeFauw identified the main lab operators (Jean Baptiste Croce, Antoine Restori and Honore Beyson), and traced their heroin through traffickers in Montreal to Guido Penosi and other Mafiosi in New York.

The eighteen articles in Epaud's "protocol of understanding" were accepted on December 4, 1969 at the first meeting of Ingersoll's Inter-Governmental task force (the Commission for the Study and Coordination in Narcotic Control). When the task force met again on December 11, Krogh was present as Nixon's representative. Plans were made for the Sûreté and BNDD to organize mobile task forces in Paris and Marseille; and for the Sûreté to form official relations with the Turkish police. On 7 January 1970, the *New York Times* reported that the US had reached an agreement with France, and that twenty-four French special police officers were to be sent to Marseille to handle the problem.[41]

Franco-American relations got another boost on February 3, 1970, when the Inter-Governmental Committee held its first plenary session at the White House. Krogh arranged lunch. Ambrose of Customs was not invited. *Au contraire*; on February 5, Nixon granted the BNDD "sole responsibility for representing the US Government in dealings with foreign law-enforcement officials on matters pertaining to narcotics and dangerous drugs."[42] Customs was not included. The following day Ingersoll awarded Pohl a step increase as a bonus "for advising me on diplomatic protocols in our negotiations with top officials of the Government of France and others over the past six months or more."[43]

On February 24, Nixon and Pompidou met to restore Franco-American relations, amid anti-Pompidou protests by Jewish organizations over France's sale of Mirage jets to Saudi Arabia. Nixon's agreement to the sale was what reportedly convinced the French to sign off on the proposed drug enforcement accords.[44]

In May 1970, IBM executive Arthur Watson replaced Sergeant Shriver as Ambassador to France. Joint BNDD and Central Narcotics Office operations went into gear and Nixon's war on drugs overcame its biggest hurdle, for only the French could smash the French connection. The Agreement between the BNDD and the General

Directorate of the French National Police was officially signed by
Attorney General John Mitchell and Interior Minister Raymond Marcellin on February 6, 1970, in a formal ceremony at the French Ministry of Interior attended by Ingersoll and Pohl as his interpreter.[45]

Branching Out

IN MARCH 1970, TURKEY SIGNED onto the Agreement and Ingersoll
sent a contingent of temporary duty (TDY) agents to Ankara to join a
task force under the direction of Galip Labernas, chief of the Central
Narcotics Bureau in Ankara, and BNDD Agent Jim Daniels, a loyal
subordinate of Jack Cusack.

Cusack could trust Daniels to send him positive reports from
Ankara. His problem was Agent Dick Salmi in Istanbul. Cusack hated
Salmi for writing a February 1970 report that criticized the Turkish
National Police for its rampant corruption and reliance on torture.[46]
In his report, Salmi quoted a letter Cusack wrote in 1962, saying
that Labernas "extorted kick backs from informants on reward payments."[47] Salmi said that American aid was being misused, and that
Turkish cops were selling out cases. Worst of all, Salmi described the
eradication program as unnecessary and contradicted Cusack's assertion that only ten percent was being diverted. "Fifty percent was more
like it," Agent Bob DeFauw said.[48]

The report was not well received in Washington, and Cusack
responded by trying to get Salmi transferred. He said Salmi was
trigger-happy, and cited a gunfight Salmi had with Gary Bouldin, an
American hashish trafficker. Bouldin had killed three Turkish cops
with an automatic rifle before Salmi arrived on the scene and blew
Bouldin away, Dirty Harry style, in a gunfight in downtown Istanbul.
Cusack also expressed concern about Salmi's safety. Mustafa Dincer, a
major trafficker Salmi had arrested, had escaped from prison and was
publicly vowing to murder Salmi. But Salmi refused to run away, and
the Turkish cops (who loved Salmi) pleaded with Ingersoll to let him
stay. Ingersoll agreed and Salmi, as the Istanbul agent-in-charge, made
a string of spectacular cases.[49]

Cusack's biggest battle was fought with Tony Pohl, who had a low
personal opinion of "Q-sack." He considered Cusack's reliance on
illegal unilateral undercover operations "counter productive," and
his Turkish opium plan "a statistical substitute for genuine investigations." Ingersoll also allowed Pohl to exercise considerable influence
over Cusack's operations in Europe, much to Cusack's dismay.

Cusack pressed the American line, whatever the cost. But his over-all impact was negative. His deputy, Bob DeFauw, considered him a poor manager. De-Fauw said that Cusack "alienated everyone" from the secretaries, who "were always in tears," to the agents, "especially Dick Salmi in Istanbul." DeFauw felt that Cusack's promotion was political and had been engineered by Senator Thomas Dodd (D-CT). Then guiding Nixon's draconian "No-Knock" anti-drug legislation through the Senate, Dodd, like Treasury Secretary Eugene Rossides, was an avid supporter of Greece and was looking to score points by bashing the Turks. So he backed Cusack and his plan.

While Cusack concentrated on his ambitious Turkish plan, DeFauw handled the region's day-to-day operations and gradually opened 18 new offices in the region, the first in London, Frankfurt and Madrid. Agent Albert Habib (having returned from a four year tour in Bang-kok) replaced DeFauw in Marseille. Agents Jacques Kiere and John Coleman were assigned to Brussels, and Michael Antonelli took charge in Rome.

In the Far East, offices in Singapore and Seoul were closed and the agents transferred to Kuala Lumpur and Tokyo. A new office was opened in Saigon in March 1969 and in November, CIA agent Paul Knight opened a BNDD office in Kabul, Afghanistan.[50] According to Knight, "The idea was to chart the flow of heroin from Iran and Afghanistan, although France and Turkey remained the focus. To facilitate international commerce, Transit International (TIR) license plates were being issued by European governments, enabling trucks to cross borders without inspection. Turkish TIR trucks were going back and forth to Iran, then on to the Tarraballo Dam project in Pakistan. Turkish traffickers used this system to obtain opium in Pakistan. But they were also moving in the other direction, to France and Germany. I'd been reading the intelligence reports, and after talking with CIA, it was decided that for political reasons it was better to start tracking the traffic from the West, not the East."

The BNDD signed an Accord with Mexico in May 1970, and by the end of the year, BNDD agents were popping up everywhere. The big cases had yet to be made, but the pieces were in place for that to happen. As Bob DeFauw recalled, "The few of us who had served overseas with the FBN had been gathering intelligence for years, and we'd laid the groundwork. We were ready to go for the throat; the rest was just picking them off. We started making hits by land and sea," he said with pride, "seizing labs and large amounts of morphine base."

But there were still several obstacles to overcome, not least of which was Myles Ambrose.

The Memo Of Understanding

IN 1970, HEROIN COMMITTEE MEETINGS degenerated into a juris-dictional dispute between Customs and BNDD. "Treasury enforce-ment," Jim Ludlum explained, "was more aggressive than Kleindienst and Ingersoll. Rossides and that lunatic Liddy were leading the charge. They wanted to know who was in charge in Mexico, and then they started a fight over foreign operations everywhere."

The problem was Ingersoll's failure to use Nixon's edict, giving the BNDD "sole responsibility" overseas, to its full advantage. He also failed to respond forcefully when, in early 1970, the incorrigible Myles Ambrose unilaterally met with law enforcement officials in sev-eral Western European nations to form Custom task forces like the one the BNDD had with France. Only after Congressman Rooney challenged Ingersoll on the issue in March 1970 did Ingersoll com-plain to Attorney General John Mitchell.

By then, Rossides had already complained to Treasury Secretary David M. Kennedy about Nixon's edict. Mitchell and Kennedy argued over the issue at a cabinet meeting, at which point Nixon told John Ehrlichman to resolve the dispute. Ehrlichman sided with Mitchell, as Mitchell was closer to Nixon than anyone else. The result was a presidential directive, promulgated in May, that subordinated Cus-toms entirely to the BNDD in all areas of narcotics law enforcement, especially controlled delivery.[51]

As a knowledgeable agent recalled, "Mitchell signs it and BNDD takes over. Then Ambrose calls up Ingersoll and asks for 'a minor role.' Myles said the executive order had demoralized his agents, and that several high ranking Customs officials had threatened to resign as a result. He said that everyone knew BNDD had the authority, but it was to everyone's advantage to allow Customs to assist. He reminded Ingersoll that Customs alone had the power of search and seizure [without warrants] along the border, where the majority of seizures were made. He promised that Customs would not conduct 'lead' drug investigations overseas. And he promised that Customs would notify BNDD whenever a seizure was made."

On June 29, Ambrose reached into his bottomless bag of blar-ney and convinced Congressman Claude Pepper that Nixon's May directive allowed "persons engaged in the crime elsewhere to escape investigation and prosecution." Ambrose said: "under our present system, we detect blindly and prosecute partially."[52]

Testifying before Pepper's Select Committee on Crime were Customs Agents Ed Coyne and Al Seely. With tears welling up in his eyes, Coyne explained how, in December 1969, Rossides sent him and Seely to Europe to gather evidence (emanating from the Wouters and Fish Can cases) from Swiss, Spanish, and French officials. Coyne said, "we weren't treated too cordially by these people."[53]

Customs agents were posted around the world to collect transfer taxes and detect illegal cross-border commerce into the US. But Coyne and Seely's European excursion was the first time Customs agents had followed a narcotics case overseas in almost twenty years. Inspired by Ambrose, the agents went with a confrontational attitude. "While we were there," Coyne recalled, "we go to give evidence to the French and they say, 'Give it Pohl.' So we give it to Pohl and he'd hand it to them."[54]

Ed Coyne, notably, had been an FBN agent from 1953 until 1961, when he blew the whistle on corruption in the New York office. Shortly thereafter, for health reasons, he transferred to Customs. Coyne was an honest cop, but he hated narcotics agents to a fault; thus when he testified to Congress he forgot to mention that Tony Pohl had actually accompanied him and Seely on their trip, and that the French had cordially welcomed them with champagne. Instead, when Pepper pressed him, Coyne said: "They were insulting to us in the way they treated us."[55] Coyne said that he and Seely didn't even know if the traffickers they had identified in Spain and Switzerland had been tried.

Pepper was appalled that the word of an American cop wasn't good enough for foreign officials. There had to be something sinister going on behind the scenes to make them behave so badly. Having been prepped by Ambrose, the Committee members knew exactly what the problem was — Tony Pohl! Congressman Wiggins asked Coyne if the rivalry between Customs and BNDD was over. Coyne deferred to his superior Al Seely, who replied, "You are putting us on very thin ice." Unable to restrain himself, Coyne blurted: "All we want is what belongs to us, and to be able to investigate them to the best of our ability and I feel that definitely if we have a smuggling case and its goes overseas, that we should be able to pursue our own investigations."[56]

The Committee members recoiled in horror. How could this be? The Customs agents explained that they had discovered a secret bank account in Switzerland and that the Swiss had told them where the money was going. They did not mention that the bank account had been discovered by Emile Benhamou; instead they complained that the French insisted that all Customs inquiries be funneled through the BNDD — meaning Pohl. The Customs agents did not mention that the French were acting in strict accordance with the protocols being negotiated with the BNDD. They did say they had to wait for Pohl to get back to them with the replies, and that (gasp) Pohl was using the hard-earned Customs information to start investigations against defendants in the Wouters and Fish Can cases.[57]

Horrified, Pepper convinced the Ways and Means Committee that Nixon's May 1970 directive canceled out the $49 million supplemental appropriations given to Customs that year. It hadn't, and Ingersoll could have explained why. But Ingersoll felt it was beneath his dignity to engage Ambrose in a public debate. Taking the high road, he agreed to allow Customs to pursue narcotic cases overseas. "As a result," a knowledgeable agent adds ruefully, "Ingersoll drafted general guidelines and put them in a memorandum of understanding, which gave Myles the leverage he needed to undercut the BNDD." The agent sighed. "Ingersoll claimed it was the gentlemanly thing to do. But — truth be told — he was intimidated by Myles, who promptly put Nixon's directive under his ashtray, where he could smash his cigars on it."

Appeasing Ambrose was a big mistake, and that summer the cutthroat Customs Commissioner gleefully announced the discovery of a "new system" that the BNDD had overlooked. As Ambrose recalled, "Seely discovered that the South American mules contacted their bosses from pay phones at Grand Central Station. They'd have the woman behind the desk place the calls, so we monitored the calls, and isolated about half a dozen pertinent calls. That's what starts the investigation through which we found another major system through South America, which led us to Auguste Ricord."[58]

Having just announced his vaunted "systems approach," Ingersoll was badly embarrassed. The BNDD was quietly, not publicly, developing its own leads to Ricord, and once again tensions between Customs and the BNDD flared.

Meanwhile, Egil Krogh had returned from Vietnam with a new appreciation of the level of addiction among US troops — and the political dangers that problem posed to Nixon's re-election prospects in 1972. Thus, in the summer of 1970, a new front was opened in the burgeoning war on drugs.

7

A NEW YORK NARCOTIC AGENT IN SAIGON

THE DEMOCRATS HAD PINNED THEIR November 1968 election hopes
on a settlement of the Vietnam War. But South Vietnam's president,
General Nguyen Van Thieu, had to agree with Johnson's plan, and
that sad fact gave Nixon's merry pranksters the opening they needed.
They simply told Thieu that he'd be richly rewarded if he didn't settle.[1] LBJ found out about the deal through an FBI wiretap on Nixon's
campaign manager, John Mitchell, soon to be America's top cop. But
the discovery came too late and the Republican's first "October Surprise" helped Nixon to win the presidency.

While Kissinger began secret peace talks with the North Vietnamese in Paris in early 1969, Nixon publicly pursued a contradictory
plan called Vietnamization, in which US troops would fight the Communists until South Vietnam could fend for itself. The forked-tongue
plan would allow US troops to be withdrawn and bring "Peace with
Honor."[2] More importantly, the troop withdrawal nudged China into
relations with American businessmen, at the expense of the Soviets.

While Nixon and Kissinger were holding the so-called China Card
up their sleeve, morale among beleaguered US troops was falling and
heroin addiction was rising. The military had no intention of broad-
casting the fact, but it did ask that a BNDD agent be assigned to
Saigon. This was risky business, as the agent would surely discover

that the three main factions in South Vietnam's drug trade were: the air force under General Nguyen Cao Ky; the police and customs services under Prime Minister Tran Thien Khiem; and the army, navy and National Assembly, under Thieu's auspices.[3]

Fred T. Dick was the agent John Ingersoll sent on this suicide mission to Saigon. An FBN agent since 1951, Dick had served in New York and Kansas City until his patron, Henry Giordano, brought him to headquarters as an inspector in 1959. In 1961, Giordano gave Dick the unenviable task of assisting the FBN's enforcement chief, Wayland Speer, in an integrity investigation in New York. With Dick's help the wily New York agents subverted Speer's investigation, and after Speer was demoted, Dick and Anslinger's aide-de-camp Bill Durkin concluded the investigation in a way that made it palatable for Treasury Department officials whose sole interest was avoiding a scandal. Fred Dick was trustworthy that way.

Dick earned further credits by backing Giordano over Charlie Siragusa in the battle to replace Harry Anslinger as Commissioner of the FBN. Giordano rewarded Dick by giving him the plush San Francisco district supervisor's job in 1965. There was a downside however, for backing Giordano over Siragusa earned Dick the eternal enmity of the Grand Inquisitor, Andy Tartaglino. Tartaglino kept Dick in his gun sights and was about to pull the trigger in 1968, when Giordano came to the rescue and got Dick appointed to the Industrial College of the Armed Forces.[4] Dick lingered there until early 1969, after the chaos of the BNDD's creation, but concurrent with Henry Giordano's retirement and replacement by Andy Tartaglino as enforcement chief.

Fred Dick was the archetypal FBN agent, the kind Tartaglino hated. His lone wolf methods were strictly old school. It is said that on a frigid February night in the early 1950s, while holding an informant by the ankles over a pier, Dick lost his grip and the unlucky fellow plunged into the Hudson River, never to be seen again.[5] That experience taught Dick the golden rule of federal drug law enforcement, which all senior agents thereafter imparted to their junior partners: informants don't float.

FBN folklore aside, Fred Dick knew that Tartaglino had nothing pleasant in store for him in Washington, and he saw Saigon as a relatively safe haven. Nor was Ingersoll's decision to send him there ill-advised. Despite having the thickest Internal Affairs file in the BNDD, Dick was one of the few agents capable of running the Saigon office. Having spent three years as district supervisor in San Francisco, which handled Far East Asian cases, he was familiar with the scene. Before he left for Saigon, he read all reports in the BNDD library and had discussions with all the agents he could find who had served in the Far East.[6] Dick even prepared a dossier on an American trafficker he intended to turn into an informant. He compiled files on the two traffickers then known to have a French connection in the Far East, Ralph Schmoll (later identified as Ange Simonpierri, a SDECE agent and source for US mobsters since 1955) and Michel Libert.[7]

Dick wanted to succeed and attended meetings the military arranged at the Pentagon, where he received several pledges of help. When he arrived in Saigon, however, he learned that as far as the military was concerned, "Out of sight was out of mind."[8] His next rebuff came from his civilian boss, deputy ambassador Sam Berger, the embassy's narcotics attaché and chairman of its Irregular Practices Committee, which was responsible for investigating corruption within the Government of Vietnam (GVN). Berger made it clear that President Thieu's regime could not survive a narcotics investigation. The problem, Berger said, was opium out of the Golden Triangle, not heroin in Saigon. When Dick stated his intention to follow the trail wherever it led, Berger retaliated. Dick had been staying at a hotel, and when it came time for him to be assigned his official quarters, Berger placed him in a sergeant's billet. Dick was a GS-15 with the rank of a colonel, so this wasn't just a personal insult — it had the effect of stigmatizing Dick within the diplomatic corps.

Dick discovered just how invisible he was when he paid a courtesy call on William Colby, a senior CIA officer and deputy ambassador in charge of pacification. Colby was the US embassy's liaison with Prime Minister Tran Thien Khiem, manager of one of three major drug trafficking factions. After cooling his heels in Colby's outer office for forty-five minutes, Dick departed in disgust. "I never met him personally" he said, "nor did I ever see him at any social or business functions."

Dick turned to AID's Office of Public Safety. In 1969, Public Safety had one officer, Major (not a military rank, an unusual first name) McBee, advising the Judicial Police, which oversaw the corrupt Narcotics Squad within the National Police Command.[9] An Afro-American, McBee had been with the California Narcotics Bureau while Dick was district supervisor in San Francisco. They were bitter rivals and McBee — a shadowy figure who had worked in Ecuador and Iran, and was likely a CIA agent — did not conduct investigations or work with the military. To improve the situation, BNDD agent Charles Vopat joined Public Safety in late 1969, after working as a shoofly for Andy Tartaglino (and making an integrity case on Ike Feldman).[10] Vopat became the Narcotics Squad's sole American advisor, with the job of ridding it of corruption.

It was "a chaotic scene," Dick explained. "Public Safety advisors were not on the streets conducting investigations. The Army's CID units were avoiding the National Police, whom they did not trust. The Navy and the Air Force had their own operations, but there was no exchange of drug intelligence and a dim view, at best, of what was going on in the field."

Dick's big break was meeting Colonel Walter Sears, the Marines Corps' Narcotics Control Officer. Sears had been Ingersoll's escort officer in the summer of 1969, and, according to Dick, "knew more than all the others combined." As a favor for Ingersoll, Sears extended his tour to help Dick.[11] "And that's when the logjam began to break," Dick said. "Walt went to General [Creighton] Abrams, who was kind enough to provide me with one of his back-up choppers, and for a number of months we flew all over that damn country to find out what was going on. We learned a lot: some good, some bad."

Apart from the heroin problem, tons of marijuana was being cultivated in South Vietnam and lots of US troops were smoking it. "So we decided to do something about it," Dick said. "We found that if we flew at about three hundred feet we could pinpoint the marijuana fields. Then we either landed and pulled them up, or burned them with the aid of a helmet full of chopper fuel. I remember on one excursion the Black door gunner shaking his head and saying, 'They wouldn't believe this back in Detroit.'"

But there were problems. The Hoa Hao was a large and powerful religious sect in the Delta. Dick spotted acres of marijuana growing in their fields, but they fought the Communists and so he did nothing about it, "in the interest of diplomacy." That was his style. He carefully picked his battles, fighting only when he might win. He didn't lie, either. Despite the CIA's disappointment, Dick disproved the rumor that North Vietnamese regulars used drugs and then went into battle in a ferocious frenzy. The one case he investigated "turned out to be foot powder." He also found no evidence to support the claim that the Vietcong were trafficking in order to finance the insurgency. "MACV did capture large stores of narcotic drugs in tunnels, medical supplies from Hungary and other East Block countries. But most of it was old and useless."

A Delicate Balance

THE SOUTH VIETNAMESE MILITARY RAN the biggest drug trafficking network in South Vietnam. Dick discovered this early in his tour when he arranged to buy five hundred pounds of manicured marijuana from the wife of an important official. "I told her I wanted it delivered to Saigon," he recalled. "She said that would be no problem as she had a South Vietnamese Army captain who regularly ran military convoys from Long Xien to Saigon.

Alas, Dick did not have the authority to investigate the South Vietnamese army; or its air force, which had the marijuana market cornered in IV Corps; or the navy, which after the Cambodian incursion in the spring of 1970 became a primary heroin supplier. That limitation meant that Dick could never smash the narcotics trade in South Vietnam. He did, however, open files on the complicit military men and politicians, and pass them to Ingersoll, Congress, the White House, and the press. Their names would become public knowledge in 1971. Until then, because Kissinger and Nixon needed to hold the North at bay long enough to sell the South down the river, they all enjoyed protection.

Dick did have the authority to clean his own house, and with the help of US Army CID investigator William Lowery, he investigated the South Vietnamese Narcotics Squad. As Dick explained, "Bill came to me and explained that the chief of the Narcotics Squad, Lieutenant Colonel Pham Kim Quy, was a crook." Lowery said that every time the Narcotics Squad arrested a trafficker, they'd shake the guy down.

Dick brought the problem directly to Ambassador Ellsworth Bunker. In response, "Bunker called a meeting at which CIA Station Chief Ted Shackley appeared and explained that there was 'a delicate balance.' What he said, in effect, was that no one was willing to do anything about this allegation."

Shackley had arrived in Saigon after spending two years as station chief in Laos, where he had managed the CIA's secret army of opium-growing hill tribesmen. The FBN had known about this since 1966, when Agent Albert Habib reported that "Mr. [Douglas] Blaufarb [station chief before Shackley] and Mr. Lilley [a confidant of George H.W. Bush] who are very well acquainted with the opium traffic in Laos told me briefly that the opium trade in Laos has been and still is controlled by a group of high Government officials and Army officers. Chinese and Corsicans are also involved but are usually contacts on the buying and selling side."[12]

By never making public its knowledge of CIA drug smuggling, the FBN became complicit in the great conspiracy it had been searching for since its inception. But the CIA jealously protected its drug dealing allies in Southeast Asia and that dangerous fact alone was enough to put Dick at odds with Shackley. But Shackley made the situation worse by getting CIA officers BNDD credentials, and having them tour Vietnam and the Far East gathering intelligence. As Dick said, "Everyone had his rock to hide under, but the CIA kept using our rocks."[13]

Every BNDD badge that was used by a CIA officer prevented Ingersoll from sending an agent to help Dick. In this way Shackley accomplished two things: on the one hand he stayed on top of the narcotics situation, through CIA agents posing as narcotics agents and gathering narcotics intelligence; on the other hand he denied the BNDD the ability to do its job, and uncover CIA drug-related covert actions.

Dick wasn't intimidated, and he told Ambassador Bunker, in Ted Shackley's presence, that South Vietnamese army commanders were using US Army vehicles to move drugs, with the protection of top GVN political officials. Shackley responded angrily, as Dick recalled. "He said that if I didn't stop monkeying around, I'd end up toppling the government."

Dick bided his time and not long after this Colonel Pham Kim Quy, the corrupt chief of the Narcotics Squad, arrested a Vietnamese in possession of a quarter-kilogram of heroin and put the guy in jail. Knowing the colonel's modus operandi, Dick and Lowery followed him. "Lowery was a cracker-jack with a telephoto lens," Dick continues. "It was a boiling hot Saturday morning, and we followed Pham through the back alleys. We saw him go to the defendant's house and have a short conversation with his wife outside. About an hour later, we saw the wife meet Pham at a nearby coffee shop and make a cash payment to him. The next day the prisoner was released and the heroin was returned, for which we could find no entry of this seizure in the police evidence log.

"Meanwhile, Lowery's photos were blown up into eight by ten glossies, and I requested another meeting at the embassy. This time, when faced with irrefutable proof, Bunker and Shackley were willing to act. Pham was relieved of command and reassigned to a training unit, and the entire Narcotics Squad was moved to other duties. A new staff and new agents were hired, and Colonel Ly Ky Hoang was appointed the new commander. Colonel Ly was honest in every respect, and in subsequent years earned a special appointment to the DEA.

"In a couple of months we had an honest, hard hitting squad empowered to set up raids and make arrests throughout the country, armed with a writ of authority from the Saigon court system. If we went into any of the provinces, we could take independent action without having to consult with the province chief or the province police officials. Which was absolutely necessary, because if you went to see them in advance of your action, you would find either an empty house or the drug dealer had disappeared."[14]

Fred Dick could now mount raids and chase Vietnamese and American drug traffickers — as long as he didn't upset the political applecart. But he still needed CIA assistance, and he found it through Tulius Acampora, a renegade army colonel detached to the CIA as an advisor to Saigon's police chief, Tran Si Tan.[15] Dick and Acampora had met in Italy in 1960, while Acampora was advising the Carabinieri and working with Hank Manfredi on the intelligence angle of international narcotics matters. As Tran Si Tan's advisor, Acampora saw all the CIA's narcotics intelligence reports in Saigon. Anything of importance he shared with Dick. He also helped Dick "in the design and repair of electronic equipment [wiretaps and bugs] I was using." In return, Dick helped Acampora and his staff "by relaying any information I received about what was going on in the provinces. I also brought them into contact with anyone who might possess intelligence they were seeking."

Facing the Heroin Problem

IN JUNE 1969, THE US opened an embassy in Phnom Penh, Cambodia and CIA officer John Stein was assigned as chargé d'eaffairs. Stein's job was to prepare the way for a right-wing coup that toppled Prince Sihanouk and paved the way for the US incursion in April 1970. On May 4, 1970, demonstrations against the Cambodian invasion incited trigger-happy National Guardsman to shoot and kill four students at Kent State University in Ohio. In response, students across the country organized a strike that closed hundreds of colleges and universities.

Apart from energizing the anti-war movement, the Cambodian invasion opened a new drug route into South Vietnam and enabled Rear Admiral Chung Tan Cang and the Vietnamese navy to ship narcotics from the Golden Triangle into the Delta. Cang worked closely with General Dang Van Quang, a former commander of the Delta region then serving as President Thieu's national security chief.[16] According to Nguyen Ngoc Huy, a Vietnamese historian and professor at Harvard, General Quang, Admiral Cang, Prime Minister Khiem, Air Force chief Nguyen Cao Ky, and Thieu's military chief of staff, Cao Van Vien, ran the rackets in Vietnam through their wives.[17]

Fred Dick grasped this subtle facet of Vietnamese culture and quickly entered into the game through associations he formed with two Vietnamese women: Thanh, an accountant at the embassy whom he married; and Maggie Ying, a jewelry store owner in Hong Kong. With these alliances, and Tully Acampora's help, Dick became an independent operator.

Being an independent operator enabled Dick to pursue his drug law enforcement mission within the thriving black market system in which it existed — and which many American soldiers, officials and private citizens exploited. The seminal case was the April 1970 arrest of Major Delbert L. Fleener for transporting 850 pounds of opium from Thailand to the Philippines.[18] The Fleener case was especially embarrassing because Fleener often piloted the plane that transported Ambassador Bunker and MACV Commander General William Westmoreland. On the plus side, the Fleener case opened up leads that helped the BNDD break up a group of Filipino couriers moving heroin to New York City for the Santo Trafficante organization. According to Professor Alfred W. McCoy, Trafficante had visited Saigon in 1968 to set up a Mafia narcotics network apart from the usual Corsican suppliers.[19] Based in the Philippines and Hong Kong, the operation supplied, among others, CIA-connected exile Cubans and Corsicans in South America.

The Fleener case also tracked back to seven army sergeants, led by Sergeant Major William O. Wooldridge, working with the Trafficante organization in a scam to rip off military clubs in Vietnam and at R&R (rest and relaxation) spots for US soldiers in the Far East. Stationed at the Pentagon, Wooldridge was the sergeant major of the army and thus "in an ideal position to manipulate personnel transfers and cover up the group's activities."[20]

The Fleener case led to a Congressional investigation of the company Wooldridge managed with the Trafficante organization.[21] But the investigation was half-hearted. As the head of the investigation, Carmen Bellino told Tulius Acampora, "If I were to do my job, I'd have to arrest half the US military army officers and officials in Vietnam."[22]

By 1972, even White House officials were suspected of complicity in the Far East black market trade. Author Dan Moldea discovered that Alexander Haig "wanted to know whether [White House security officer John] Caulfield ... had been to the Far East and carried back any money for Nixon."[23] US army investigators had no proof, but, Moldea adds, they surmised that Trafficante was paying off Nixon with millions of dollars funneled through the Wooldridge military service club operation.

Fred Dick knew all this, but when asked if the American Mafia was involved in drug trafficking in Saigon, he said he found no evidence to support that claim in the dusty South Vietnamese police records he examined.[24] Dick played it smart and avoided investigations that led to American officials and their crime connections. Instead, when Egil Krogh visited Vietnam in the summer of 1970 to gauge the extent of addiction among US soldiers, Dick told him that the only way to stop the drug traffic in Vietnam was at the source, in the CIA's "No-Hunting" ground in the Golden Triangle.[25]

Krogh grasped the political implications: American soldiers in Vietnam got hooked on Golden Triangle heroin, and when they returned to the US, brought their habits with them raising addiction statistics and preventing Nixon from claiming victory in the war on drugs. Krogh was determined to do something about it at the presidential level — something the BNDD could not do. But the CIA and military did not want Nixon to bust the generals and hill tribesmen in Laos who were fighting the crucial flanking war that kept the Communists from conquering South Vietnam. Nor would they allow the BNDD to pursue the corrupt Thai police, military and political leaders who allowed the CIA to use Thailand as a base for its regional operations. This conflict of interest was the main reason the "war on drugs" pitted the Nixon White House against the military and the CIA.

Thailand

FRED DICK IN SAIGON DID not report to regional director William Wanzeck in Bangkok, but directly to John Ingersoll in Washington. Dick's was the only "stand alone" office in the BNDD, largely because the Bangkok regional office was already overworked. An agent stationed in Bangkok at the time, who asked not to be identified, described it as "severely understaffed" with only six agents.[26] Official corruption was the other major problem. As the agent recalled, "A typical Thai police officer might have made $30 a month and if he was offered several thousand dollars to look the other way, he would.

"The main Thai heroin kingpin in Thailand at the time I was there was Poonsiri Chanyasak, who operated unrestrained as he was controlled by and paid off corrupt Thai enforcement officials, the pay-off going all the way up to the Prime Minister. Pramual Vanigbandhu was the police colonel in charge of all narcotic suppression and he was arrested on corruption charges around 1974 but shortly thereafter bought his way out. The only major Thai trafficker that I am aware of in the early seventies who was arrested in the States was Sukit Benjatarupong, Poonsiri's lieutenant, was also under the control of the Thai police. Thai officials knew all the principal violators and exacted significant payoffs from them to let them continue in business. They didn't bother too much to cover this up. We used to see Poonsiri and Sukit outside the main police office in Bangkok waiting to see their police controllers.

"A significant impediment was the absence of conspiracy laws. In the US, we caught many of the major people behind the scenes by charging conspiracy, many of the conspirators never laying their hand on the contraband; but in the Orient absence of conspiracy laws makes it next to impossible to effect apprehension of the financiers, the overseers of the illegal operations, etc. It was well known in Thailand who the financiers and controllers were but they would never take physical possession of the merchandise which was the primary element, at least at that time, in being able to effect arrests. In other words they had to have the narcotics in their possession if a person could be charged with a narcotic offense.

"We had to have the Thai police effect all arrests. In one case a deal was set up with a Chinese gold dealer who, according to the police, was a 'fugitive' but who owned 4 operative gold shops in Bangkok and lived openly in a fashionable neighborhood. I contacted the Thai police to make the arrest but they wanted to know the subject's identity. I told them that our source didn't know who he was but that he was going to deliver several kg of heroin to our undercover Agent. They wanted to know where the deal would go down and I told them that it was a moving operation and we didn't know where the transaction would be made. They agreed to pick me up at the embassy and arrived about 45 minutes later, in the meantime apparently attempting to determine who of their people was making the deal. I directed them to the area and got the signal from our undercover Agent that the deal was ready. I told the police to go arrest the subject and they readily did so. The police captain remained in the car with me and his face had turned pale, saying 'I know that man-he's a major trafficker.' The next day his colonel advised that the subject had been 'interrogated,' had confessed and would now be an informant for him. We heard later that this man sold heroin under police protection, splitting profits with them. He had strayed and was making a deal on his own (which had bad consequences) and reportedly he had to pay off forevermore.

"The official word from the police was that Thailand was not the problem; that the US users were. A case in point involved overdose deaths of students at the International School where in an approximate six-month's period in 1971, five or six students had died from heroin overdoses. They were obtaining the heroin from cab drivers waiting outside the school compound or from a noodle shack located nearby on the Chao Pya River. I asked the Colonel if he was saying that a 16-year-old American kid who bought a vial of pure heroin outside the International School compound from a 45-year-old Thai cab driver for $5 was the guilty party and the taxi driver the innocent person. He said that that was correct, that if the American kid had not induced the cabdriver to sell the heroin, there would have been no violation.

"The State Dept. embassy officials weren't 100% helpful, several times letting us know that we were not to attempt apprehension of parties we considered significant and sometimes we were restricted from entering certain areas, e.g. the Riau Islands area in Indonesia where we felt heroin manufacturing was taking place. The Vietnamese War was going on at that time, so that could have entered into State's reluctance. BNDD/DEA was not welcomed with open arms by some embassy officials. We opened a regional office in Manila in 1972 where we were met with essentially open hostility by State embassy officials. A few years later I was transferred there as the DEA Regional Director and was told by the ambassador that he did not welcome my arrival and that he intended to get the regional office closed, which he subsequently succeeded in doing. He criticized us one time after we had the Constabulary arrest an American dependent smuggling several ounces of heroin into Manila. He calmed down after he was asked if he was officially telling us not to advise proper authorities of Americans violating Filipino law.

"We knew the principal Chinese kingpin (one of his three names was Lim — a Chinese subject could be known by 3 or 4 Chinese names as well as a Thai name) that supplied virtually all of the essential chemical acetic anhydride to heroin lab operators in northern Thailand, southern China, Laos and Burma. But when we attempted to target him we encountered opposition from Embassy officials who had other priorities, and neither he nor Poonsiri were ever apprehended, to my knowledge."

Fighting Customs in Vietnam

THE INTENDED RECIPIENT OF MAJOR Delbert Fleener's opium was a crime organization managed by a Szechuan Chinese member of the Big Five tontine that financed most of the South East Asian drug trade. This tontine was Fred Dick's primary target, but he needed an informant inside in order to make a case that would provide Krogh with the symbolic victory he wanted in Vietnam.[27]

While Fred Dick followed this path, Customs was conducting unilateral narcotics investigations in Southeast Asia. Customs had an established relationship with Colonel Cao Chuong Kong, the Customs chief in Saigon. According to David Ellis, then chief of operations of the Customs Service, Ambrose and Rossides had accompanied Krogh on his 1970 journey to Vietnam, but spent most of their time partying.[28] They sent Ellis back to find out what was really happening, and he discovered that kickbacks from Customs revenue were going all the way up to President Thieu. He also discovered that drugs were being sent back to the US through the army's postal facilities — and in the body bags of dead soldiers.[29] With the help of an army colonel, Ellis identified a specific shipment of body bags and notified Ambrose, who tracked the plane to San Francisco. Ambrose kept the operation secret and according to Ellis, "we shut it down with military consent."[30]

But top Vietnamese officials (including the Customs chief) were immune from prosecution. So Ellis threatened to have the Customs chief killed if he didn't comply.[31] Ellis said he wasn't serious, he was just lighting a fire under the guy. Then he sent three Customs agents on temporary duty to Saigon specifically to investigate narcotics trafficking. Running the operation at Customs headquarters was Wallace Shanley. Fred Dick at the time chaired a joint narcotics sub-committee under deputy ambassador Sam Berger's Irregular Practices Committee. Customs agents engaged in drug investigations were obligated to report to Dick and register their informers with him. Two of the three agents Ellis and Shanley sent from headquarters — William Knierm and Robert Flynn — did not abide by this rule. The third Customs agent, Joseph Kvoriak, complied, said Lawrence Byrne, head of the Customs advisory team in Saigon. "But Knierm was off on his own following conspiracy theories, and Flynn wouldn't even report to me!"[32]

And thus the war with Customs reached Vietnam.

Bob Flynn's narcotic investigations began in the summer of 1970 when he met Egil Krogh in Saigon.[33] According to Flynn, Ambassador Bunker had sided with the BNDD and the CIA against Customs. Flynn had to submit his reports to Dick, and that enabled Dick to claim credit for Customs investigations. This indignity led Flynn to conduct unilateral operations and to reveal to Krogh the CIA's role in the heroin trade in South Vietnam.

Xenophobia

THE MEKONG RIVER ORIGINATES IN China and flows into Laos past the village of Houei Sai near the northern part of the Thai border. Houei Sai, at the heart of the Golden Triangle, was the destination point of a CIA opium caravan that circulated through China.[34] From Houei Sai the Mekong flows east into Laos and south to the Thai border. It scribes the Thai-Laos border until it reaches Pakse in Laos. It is smooth sailing from Houei Sai to Pakse, where the first rapids begin. From Pakse the river plunges into Cambodia, passing through Phnom Penh into South Vietnam and, through a thousand tributaries, into the South China Sea.

The CIA constructed bases in the major Laotian towns along the Mekong, and from these bases it launched commando raids against Communist troops coming down the Ho Chi Minh Trail. The town of Savannahket was particularly important because it was parallel to the de-militarized zone between North and South Vietnam. Several miles northeast of Savannahket was a village named Xeno, population about 3000. CIA-employed Filipinos built a hospital in Xeno, and French nationals owned rubber tree plantations in the area. Laotian royalty, especially drug lord Bao Oum, vacationed in Xeno.[35]

After the Cambodian incursion and the establishment of a South Vietnamese naval presence along the Mekong, Customs agents Knierm and Flynn discovered that the CIA was flying heroin out of Xeno.[36] They conducted their investigation unilaterally, not through Vietnamese Customs, whose sole function, according to Customs agent Joe Kvoriak, was "to assist the smugglers to bring in their contraband without hindrance."[37]

It happened that Flynn had an informer who knew the mistress of the II Corps Commander, a powerful Vietnamese warlord. The mistress said that traffickers in Houei Sai were shipping heroin in logs down the Mekong to Savannahket. From there, trucks drove the logs to Xeno, where the CIA had an airstrip and a base for Cambodian commandos. A Viet Cong brothel owner confirmed the mistress's story. The Communist procurer had videotaped the chief of Vietnamese Customs with a little girl. In return for the tapes, the Customs chief revealed what the CIA was doing at Xeno.[38]

What happened next is a textbook example of how and why spies play a critical role in the war on drugs. Flynn's information was so important that Krogh insisted on meeting the VC informant to confirm it. Flynn arranged the meeting and Krogh was convinced that the man was telling the truth. Krogh gave Flynn and Knierm permission to send their report directly to Wallace Shanley in Washington, avoiding Dick and the CIA. The report, presented to Nixon in September 1970, described how CIA helicopters flew heroin from Xeno to Da Nang, Bien Hoa, and other places in South Vietnam. The CIA denied it, but the White House and certain members of Congress knew it was true.[39] Indeed, Prince Norodom Sihanouk in his 1972 book, *My War With The CIA*, said that Lon Nol, one of the CIA-backed Cambodians who had ousted him, was supplying drugs to the GIs in Vietnam from a training center in Southern Laos. According to Sihanouk, a US Congressional investigation team found Xeno to be "a key link in the chain of distribution of everything from hashish to heroin!"[40]

Dick's Big Investigation

WHILE CUSTOMS WAS HUNTING THE CIA, Fred Dick was focusing on American trafficker Joseph Berger — no known relation to Sam, the embassy's narcotics attaché. Dick's plan was to turn Berger into an informant and use him to smash the Chinese tontine that was behind most narcotics transactions in Vietnam and Southeast Asia.[41]

"I had compiled a dossier on Berger before leaving Washington," Dick recalled. "He'd started out as a bookmaker in Los Angeles, and during the Korean War he went to Seoul, where he opened a combination casino and bordello. All went well until he came into possession of a quantity of radium, which he passed off as uranium, and sold to someone in the Korean government. The end result was that Berger fled to Saigon, where he married a Vietnamese woman, and got into the black market and drug smuggling.

"We knew that Berger brought suitcases full of kilogram bags of Double U-O Globe heroin into Saigon from Bangkok. He paid off cops, then sold the heroin in kilo lots at a sizable mark-up to local dealers and distributors, most of whom were in Cholon. The junk was retailed in its pure state in small, clear plastic screw-top containers to the GIs for about five dollars a hit. This heroin could be smoked, inhaled or injected, and it was [strong] enough to knock you on your ass.

"I wanted very much to use Berger as an intelligence source and informer," Dick continues, "but he evaded me at every turn. I left messages for him all over town. No result. When I called at his villa he would go out through a door in the roof and cross over to the neighboring houses and disappear. This went on for months. Then I got my break.

"Berger was posing as an employee of a civilian contracting firm in Vietnam, and had forged military travel orders that permitted him to fly from country to country on US military aircraft, on a space-available basis. Then in early 1970, an ONI agent found a crate of smoking opium that had been shipped by military air from Thailand to Saigon. The agent thought it was some sort of indigenous medicine, and in an effort to find out, he took a block to a Chinese herbal shop in Cholon. The old man who ran the shop said he didn't know what it was either, but he was willing to buy it for $1500." Dick sighed. "At least the agent wasn't dumb enough to sell it to him.

"I got wind of this episode a few days later, and went to ONI to look at the crate and its contents. Lo and behold, there was Berger's company name, as well as his travel-order number stenciled on the side. Now I had something to use as leverage in dealing with this bird, and after several days of flying around I pieced the story together. Berger had purchased and crated the opium in Thailand, then trucked it to Laos where he went to a US military airfield and, with his fake orders, had the crate stenciled for delivery to a freight holding facility in Saigon. Then he went home to await the free arrival of his crate. Only it didn't come. It got mixed up with a crate of movie film cans intended for the troops in Thailand. Result, the opium went back to Thailand and the film cans went to Saigon.

"After about two weeks this mess was straightened out and the opium crate did arrive in Saigon. But by this time Berger was so alarmed that he wouldn't go near the freight holding facility. He was now in hiding for sure.

"A while later I got a call from an army CID agent, telling me that Berger was having breakfast at the USO club on Nguyen Hue Street. I sent one of my agents to pick him up and take him to the National Police Compound. Later that day I went to the compound, where the drug squad had him in custody.

"Berger was then in his sixties," Dick explained, "but after a year of playing cat-and-mouse with this man, I was so furious I couldn't see straight. I said to him, 'Do you know who I am?' He said, 'Yes, I do.' Then I punched him square in the mouth, walked out, and told the police to lock him up for three days.

"Three days later I went back and found Joe Berger like a pussy-cat. If you could have seen that jail you would understand why — it looked like something out of one of the old French Foreign Legion movies. We could not prosecute him on this opium caper, however, because the crate had been all over the barnyard before it got to Saigon, and I couldn't find any US servicemen at the air base in Laos who could positively identify him as the man who shipped the crate. But Berger did work with me through the years, and he did furnish some very valuable intelligence."

Indeed, two years later, Berger would lead Dick to the ultimate prize: a Chinese syndicate.

The Kuomintang-Burma Connection

FRED DICK QUIETLY VISITED BURMA in 1970. He described it as "something out of a bad dream. I saw abject poverty on the streets of Rangoon. There was a port with abandoned warehouses, long rusted harbor cranes and rail equipment, and flocks of black crows daily circling the port."[42]

According to Dick, the northern Shan and Kachin states were beyond the government's control. The area was lightly forested, with low rolling hills, and heavy poppy cultivation. Kuomintang Generals Le and Twan were there. Posing as an American journalist, Dick visited one of their rest camps in northern Thailand. "It was very well maintained," he said, "and the soldiers were armed with the latest automatic weapons. Through the years the troops married local tribal women, raised families, and settled down to stay. Their base camps housed their families, schools, and cottage industries. The advance camps inside Burma contained their arms, excellent radio equipment, and horses for their caravans, etc.

"The Thais, of course, had an accommodation with the KMT, which was there to defend the northern border from Chinese Communists. In exchange, the KMT made monthly incursions into the Shan and Kachin states to buy "green" opium from the hill-tribe farmers. Before the spring planting they would go in and pay the farmers in advance for their estimated opium production that year. Payment was made in gold or silver coins, with the solid-silver trade dollar favored over all others.

"When the KMT marched," Dick continues, "their caravans consisted of anywhere from one hundred to one hundred fifty well-armed mounted troops, and half again as many horses and pack animals. As they passed through the various villages, en route to the opium fields, they did not rob, rape or pillage, and if they needed food, they paid for it. The KMT never processed the opium, they merely bought it, brought it out, and resold it. You might say they were kind of like the UPS.

"Now this is where the sticky business begins. In Thailand and Laos the crude opium was bought by a number of Chinese syndicates, comprised of gangsters and businessmen who formed a tontine, in which six or eight members contributed a little money and shared in the profits, so if the venture was not successful, no one was wiped out. The Chinese assumed Thai and English names. Chiu Chao Chinese chemists recruited from Hong Kong worked in jungle laboratories in Laos and Thailand, usually for six months, then they returned to Hong Kong. These men consistently turned out a product in the ninety-eight percent purity range. Heroin produced in France was generally ninety-four percent. The syndicate even had its own quality-control systems. Finished heroin, in one-kilogram lots, was packaged in double clear-plastic bags, hermetically sealed, bearing the "Double U-O Globe" logo. The bags had the same Chinese words which, when translated said, 'This product is of the highest quality, it will put wind in your sails.' Between the outer and inner bags was a small white paper bearing a stamped date in reverse order. In this way the lab operators knew which chemist had produced that particular batch in the event there were customer complaints. Pretty cute, huh?"

Dick also knew that the CIA used this Kuomintang opium caravan — which it called Strategic Intelligence Network 118A, because it operated from CIA base 118A in Nam Yu a few miles north of Houei Sai — to spy on Chinese troops. In other words, the KMT operation, which provided the bulk of narcotics in the Far East, was a protected CIA operation. Organized at CIA HQ in 1964, it started in 1965 when CIA officer Bill Young inserted Lahu tribesmen Moody Taw and Isaac Lee into the caravan.[43]

FBN Agent Albert Habib, assigned to Bangkok in 1965, reported that CIA officer Don Wittaker in Vientiane confirmed that opium drums were dropped from planes originating in Laos to boats in the Gulf of Siam.[44] Wittaker identified the Chinese chemist in Houei Sai and fingered the local Yao leaders as the opium suppliers. Wittaker reported all this to his boss, James R. Lilley — a close friend of George H. W. Bush, who, of course, was Nixon's first US ambassador to China. By 1966, when Agent Doug Chandler arrived in Bangkok, the existence of the CIA's 118A opium caravan was known to the FBN. As Chandler recalled, "An interpreter took me to meet a Burmese warlord in Chiang Mai. Speaking perfect English, the warlord said he was a Michigan State graduate and the grandson of the King of Burma. Then he invited me to travel with the caravan that brought opium back from Burma." Chandler pauses. "When I sent the information to the CIA they looked away, and when I told the embassy they flipped out. We had agents in the caravan who knew where the Kuomintang heroin labs were located, but the Kuomintang was a uniformed army equipped with modern weapons, so the Thai government left them alone."[45]

As BNDD agents knew, Thai and Vietnamese officials were buying opium at Houei Sai, as were Corsicans and CIA renegades working for Air America and Continental Air, which had a State Department contract to fly food and supplies to the Yao in Houei Sai. Also involved was Prime Minister Souvanna Phouma's son, Panya, who built a Pepsi-Cola bottling plant in Vientiane, Laos, with US State Department support. Better than "the real thing," the plant served both as a cover for buying the chemical precursors necessary for converting opium into heroin and as a money laundry for Vang Pao's profits.[46]

As Dick concludes, "I will believe until my dying day that there was, and probably still is, an unholy alliance between the CIA, the Kuomintang, and the Thai government. And if any of this is true, the agency is aiding and abetting the opium-smuggling traffic in the Golden Triangle, while at the same time the DEA is trying to combat it."

8

RUDE AWAKENINGS

WHILE MANAGING NEW YORK'S INTERNATIONAL Division, tireless Tony Pohl found time to refine the Franco-American Agreements, which would make it possible to smash the French connection that supplied most of America's heroin. The documented Agreement between the BNDD and the General Directorate of the French National Police consisted of 26 articles outlining rules for cooperation and mutual assistance.[1] Implementing the articles meant, among other things, teaching US agents how the French judicial system worked, and how to execute the "letters rogatory" that empowered agents to investigate French citizens. With the signing of the Accords in February 1971, all that remained was catching the traffickers and bringing them to trial — which posed a new set of legal problems, considering that many of them had never set foot in the United States.

There were other problems. Pohl knew that a single chain of command was essential to getting the job done. But Ingersoll, by agreeing to the "Memo of Understanding" with Ambrose, had "fumbled the ball."[2] Pohl insisted that Nixon's edict trumped the Memo, and gave the BNDD "exclusive authority" to form narcotics enforcement relations with foreign police forces, and he was frustrated to find himself fighting for French connection cases with John Fallon, the Customs boss in New York. A burly Irishman called "Footsie" because of his colossal feet, Fallon's legions were led by inseparable Eddie Coyne and Al Seely, aka "Ass and Pants."

The time-consuming, bureaucratic battles were not just with Customs; they were waged within the BNDD as well. In working on the Agreements, for example, Pohl had to by-pass Francophobe Jack Cusack in Paris and talk directly to the French. Out of spite, Cusack deliberately obstructed Pohl's cases.

Pohl's army of loyal soldiers was headed by the International Division's three group leaders; Charles D. Casey at the Asian group; Gerard F. Carey over Latin America; and Mortimer L. Benjamin covering Europe. The European group was primary and worked with headquarters and overseas agents against the AM-1 French connection. Pohl's top targets were the "controllers."[3] As the indispensable individuals in the overlapping drug smuggling organizations, the controllers knew the suppliers, recruited couriers, supervised delivery to the buyers, and managed financial transactions. More specifically, Pohl sought those controllers, financed largely by the Orsini organization, who brought heroin directly into the country — mainly to Mafiosi in New York and Miami, often through the services of Maurice Castellani. Pohl considered direct shipments into the US a "slap in the face," and Ingersoll supported him in this regard.

Making arrests and cases in America also brought greater political rewards than making arrests and seizures in Europe, so when possible Ingersoll and Pohl arranged controlled deliveries with the French, who agreed with the goal of prosecuting the case in New York, where sentences were more severe.[4] This policy fueled Cusack's resentment of Pohl. To compensate, Cusack focused on Turkey's role as the major source of opium converted into French connection heroin. The Nixon White House had political reasons for supporting this view, and the State Department pressed Jack Cusack's eradication plan. Cusack, however, displayed little tact in his dealings with Turkish officials. As Andy Tartaglino said about him, "He'd been all around the world, but never left New York."[5] Consequently, the Turkish ambassador asked Ingersoll to replace Cusack, and in January 1971, Ingersoll sent John Warner to Turkey to repair relations and change the focus from opium reduction to morphine-base interdiction. To keep Cusack, still the RD in Paris, at arms length, Warner formed a new region based in Ankara. It was outside of Cusack's jurisdiction, as were the countries grouped in his new region — Afghanistan, Pakistan, India, Iran, Turkey and the entire Middle East. A corresponding Near East desk was created at headquarters.[6]

At this time certain Israelis emerged as major traffickers, so Ingersoll sent Dick Salmi to help form narcotic squads in Tel Aviv and Jerusalem.[7] In exchange for Salmi's services, the Mossad provided narcotics intelligence on Syria and Egypt, which had been removed from the BNDD's area of operations after the 1967 Arab Israeli War.

Despite the emphasis on France and Turkey, by 1971 the Nixon White House could no longer deny that the Far East produced a substantial percentage of the narcotics that reached America. According to Clyde McAvoy, First Secretary of the US Embassy in Rangoon, Burma, "In 1971 analysts put the annual total output of illegal opium from [Burma, Thailand and Laos] at 700 tons, more than seven times the production of Turkey."[8] The timing of this change of heart was political and, as we shall see, directly related to Nixon's need to withdraw from Vietnam. Meanwhile, drug law enforcement in the Far East remained elusive and illusory. It was equally hard to make cases on Asians in New York. Initially, Charlie Casey's Asian Group had trouble recruiting Asian informants, because Asians rarely reported crimes to the police, and there were no Asian agents in the group. As a result, Casey's group relied heavily on the US Immigration and Naturalization Service (INS) for sources of information in Chinatown.[9] The group was in touch with BNDD agents in Hong Kong, Bangkok and Singapore; but those agents worked more closely with the San Francisco office, on the assumption that the West Coast Mafia was supplying New York. It was actually the other way around. For these reasons, the Asian group was slow getting started.[10]

Agent Thomas de Triquet, a Vietnam veteran assigned to Casey's Asian group in 1971, said the situation improved after the November 11, 1971 arrest of the Philippine attaché to Laos, Domingo S Canieso, and his Chinese partner from Bangkok at the Lexington Hotel with 15 kilograms of Double U-O Globe heroin.[11] At this point New York replaced San Francisco as the locus of cooperation between BNDD agents in the US and Asia, and undercover police officers from Hong Kong started working with Casey's Asian group.[12]

Di Trinquet described Casey as "a great supervisor," who had been stationed in Bangkok in the mid-1960s and had traveled far and wide across the Far East posing as an Air America employee. Casey's tales of derring-do motivated the group, which "had great sources and worked crazy hours." The group acquired lots of intelligence about the Mafia's involvement with the Chinese. It worked closely with the INS, using the threat of deportation to get informants to work. It uncovered information on corruption within the NYPD's 5th Precinct and Chinese organize crime, and served as a training ground for agents who would eventually serve in posts throughout Southeast Asia.

The Latin American group had no trouble swinging into action and under energetic Gerry Carey would develop over a hundred cases in Latin America.[13] Carey worked with federal prosecutors in both New York's Eastern and Southern District. US Attorney Whitney North Seymour, in the Southern District, played a crucial role by restructuring the judicial system to allow defendants to get immunity for testifying in court.

Working with Carey was Lawrence "Jerry" Strickler, chief of the Latin American desk at headquarters. As Strickler notes, the BNDD was a fragmented organization, with people often operating in isolation.[14] But when leaders emerged, they were followed. And when Pohl and Strickler found each other, the horses finally started galloping in the same direction. In Latin America, for a brief period, this included the horses at Customs, the State Department and the CIA.

George Belk arranged for Pohl and Strickler to meet in New York when it became evident that a gigantic South American system existed, and that new investigative techniques were required to smash it.[15] To this end, Pohl and Strickler agreed to have traffickers outside the US indicted in New York, and trick them into traveling to countries that had extradition treaties with the US. When extradition wasn't possible, the BNDD used an obscure "bounty hunter" law to kidnap traffickers and bring them back to New York. According to Strickler this technique was approved by BNDD legal counsel Candy Cowan, and relied on the CIA and the type of "extraordinary renditions" that became fashionable in Bush's war on terror.[16]

When Ingersoll put his stamp of approval on the "bounty hunter" plan, the thrust of federal drug law enforcement changed forever. Jerry Strickler was a key player, and how he got there is critical to understanding how things evolved.

Operation Eagle

A FORMER BDAC AGENT, JERRY Strickler served in the BNDD's training division until 1969, when he was transferred to criminal investigations. Belk was selecting agents to head the nine systems, and naturally, he preferred FBN agents. But there was a hiring freeze, so Strickler, almost by accident, became one of two BDAC agents in Belk's office. Strickler managed three Mafia sub-systems under the organized crime systems coordinator, Gabriel Dukas, a veteran FBN agent from New York.[17]

"Belk had money," Strickler recalled, "which he made available to each systems manager for buys. That was the key, because we at headquarters had no informers. The edict went out to the regions, 'No more small buys. The first priority is the system.' The regional directors complained, of course, so Ingersoll called them into headquarters and put them all in the same room with Belk and the systems managers. Ingersoll turned to Belk and said, 'Have a solution by time I come back.' Then he left the room."

The regional directors eventually complied, but tensions persisted due to the "Goodfellows" culture, which placed a premium on romantic "rugged individualism" at the expense of mundane management skills. Like Pohl, Strickler wasn't of the Goodfellows culture and by taking a studious approach, and diligently pouring over reports, even those outside his area, he discovered that the Mafia was in cahoots with two Cubans in Miami: Rafael Patino Delgado Pujol, the son of a Cuban vice president under Fulgencio Batista; and Mario Escander, a former Cuban Senator linked to the Trafficante organization. Strickler found that the Cubans were importing cocaine from Peru into South Florida, and were using Colombian pickpockets and shoplifters as couriers out of Chile. More cocaine was being seized in Miami than the rest of country combined, and when Belk realized the importance of what was happening, he reassigned Strickler to the AM-2 Cuban system. Strickler and his new boss James Burke poured over all reports involving Cubans anywhere in the country. They charted relationships and gathered enough evidence to obtain Justice Department authorization to place wiretaps on several suspects, including on Escander in Miami.

Meanwhile, the Chicago office had the opportunity to buy a kilogram of heroin — not cocaine — from a Cuban for $25,000. "We did buy it," Strickler said, "and for the first time we let the money walk." Meaning the BNDD *officially* let a drug trafficker keep the buy money for a chance to get at everyone in the system. Letting money walk was another new investigative technique, something the cash-poor FBN could never afford.

Strickler continues: "Then Agent Dom Petrossi went to the Blue Mirror Bar in New York and made another buy. Some ragged-ass Cuban delivered it. Dom went back and bought two more kilograms, and that's when Operation Eagle began."

"Operation Eagle was not named out of patriotism," Dominick P. Petrossi said with a chuckle.[18] "Belk came up with the name while drinking at the Golden Eagle bar located in the same building as BNDD headquarters on 14th Street. That's the mind of a federal narcotic agent at work," Petrossi laughs. "So they dubbed it Operation Eagle and put it into AM-2."

Petrossi's part of the case began when a Cuban taxi driver walked into his office. The cabbie was a Bay of Pigs veteran and offered, free of charge for "patriotic" reasons, to introduce Petrossi to the biggest Cuban drug dealer in Chicago.

Petrossi has no doubt the informant was a CIA agent.

When he met the Cuban drug dealer in Chicago, Petrossi expected to be offered cocaine. He was offered heroin instead. Belk preferred heroin cases and readily okayed the deal. The courier delivered it and accepted $15,000 from Petrossi. The money walked. "Later we bought stuff in New York," Petrossi notes, referring to the buy at the Blue Mirror Bar, "... to continue the investigation. We bought half a kilo, and let that walk too."

Through his CIA informant, Petrossi eventually met controller Mario Escander in Miami. Escander took Petrossi to an upscale condominium, with a doorman and valets. "We get out and walk into a banquet hall. No one's there," Petrossi recalled. "We sit down in the middle of the room and in walks a sixty-some-odd-year-old man, a real Spanish gentleman. He's wearing a silk tie that costs more than my suit. He's got diamond jewelry. You can tell he goes to the barber daily. My informant says, 'Juan wants to know what you need?'

"Juan" was Juan Cesar Restoy, a member of Operation 40, a group the CIA created to stage terror attacks against economic and political targets in Cuba. Restoy and Petrossi made the deal for heroin and as a result, Restoy was arrested in Dade County in June 1970.[19] Later that month, hundreds of BNDD agents, working around the clock, made coordinated arrests (in Las Vegas, Chicago, New York, Puerto Rico and New Jersey) of approximately 120 drug traffickers, mostly Cubans, and seized huge quantities of cocaine and heroin. Attorney

General John Mitchell held a press conference to announce the Nixon Administration's latest symbolic success in the war on drugs.[20]

The Lessons of Operation Eagle

IN 1970 IN BALTIMORE, THE seizure of a kilogram of marijuana galvanized the entire office. Eagle changed that. Eagle was also significant because it proved that drug traffickers were turning from heroin to cocaine. "The Cubans were the largest per capita users of cocaine," Strickler observed, "and when Castro overthrew Batista, the Cubans who fled to the US brought their habits and trafficking systems with them. And where did they get money to fund their anti-Castro operation? From coke. That's anti-Castro Cubans in South America, Spain, Italy, all working together. And when they needed heroin, they knew where to score through their old Mafia and Corsican connections."[21]

At first the Cubans didn't have a market in US. But as demand for cocaine rose, the Cubans fought the Italians over distribution and created their own market. "That's the first lesson," Strickler said. "Then, while our agents are conducting surveillances, they notice that they're being watched — counter-surveillance is very unusual — and that leads to the realization that the CIA was involved. We asked our Cubans informants how they learned counter-surveillance, and they explained that they're CIA-trained Bay of Pigs veterans. Now we start to understand how they use CIA techniques to manage their couriers and cutouts.

"Unfortunately," Strickler sighed, "Many of the defendants in Eagle (including Escander and Restoy) were released, because Mitchell screwed up the warrants." It may not have been an accident. Dan Moldea explained that, "John Mitchell was personally responsible for numerous aborted prosecutions of underworld figures during his four year term."[22] The cases made off direct "buys" were successfully prosecuted. But two years after the Eagle arrests, Judge William O. Mehrtens "bitterly assailed Mitchell" and "threw out the wiretap evidence against Mario Escander and his buddies on the grounds that the Justice department had not complied with the law in securing court orders for the taps."[23]

Operation Eagle taught the BNDD two other hard lessons; that politicians, through ineptness or other reasons, could wreck its cases; and that the lily-white BNDD needed more Spanish-speaking agents. To fill this need, the BNDD recruited a small group of Mormons (who had gained Spanish language skills while proselytizing in Latin

America) and it deputized a number of Cuban soldiers in the US Army. Many CIA-trained Cubans arrested in Eagle also went to work for the BNDD, most in Miami, where Strickler began working closely with deputy regional director Thomas F. Hurney. As Strickler recalled, "Through Tom Hurney in Miami we began sending Cuban informants throughout South America." As Strickler notes, they got "fantastic intelligence," often in regard to the location of labs.

Alas, many of the Cubans were still working for the CIA.

AM-10: The Chilean System

IN OCTOBER 1970, BELK REASSIGNED Strickler to the foreign office under David Costa. An FBN veteran since 1951, Costa had replaced Hank Manfredi, who died in January 1970. Costa and Strickler ran the desk by themselves, reviewing all overseas and domestic reports pertaining to overseas cases. But reports flowed in haphazardly, and it was left to the desk officers to sift through the paperwork. Many threw up their hands in frustration. However, Strickler spent countless hours checking the files, and eventually found a relationship between a major seizure in Miami, the December 1969 "Wine Jug" case at the McAlpin Hotel in New York, and the April 1970 arrest of Yolando Sarmiento by New York's Special Investigation Unit (SIU).[24] He also began to see subtle divisions of labor: how the Chilean middlemen acquired cocaine from labs operated by Japanese chemists in Bolivia and Peru; how Chileans used Colombian couriers to bring it to the Cubans; how drugs were stored at a military field in Paraguay; and the central role played by Manual Noriega, chief of Intelligence of the Panamanian Defense Forces in Panama.

AM-10 advanced in February 1971 when Andy Tartaglino assigned Frank Monastero and his enforcement policy staff the task of reorganizing and expanding the BNDD's systems. At the same time, Belk promoted Strickler to the position of chief of the Latin American desk. Strickler started managing a new AM-10 system designed to smash the French connection in Latin America. Strickler now reported directly to Belk and, on Top Secret assignments, to Andy Tartaglino as well.

Not hampered by old FBN biases, Strickler formed relations with Customs agents in Miami, Washington, and New York, tracking their seizures through couriers to controllers in South America. He also coordinated his headquarters operations closely with Tony Pohl and Gerry Carey. Having recognized the importance of AM-10, Ingersoll arranged for Strickler to brief deputy Attorney General Richard

Kleindienst, and that, Strickler explained, is "when the vehicle went into high gear. Kleindienst approved the bounty hunter plan without realizing its implications." More AM-10 meetings followed with Customs and the CIA in Miami, in pursuit of leads in Chile developed from the Sarmiento case.

In another new "extra-legal" practice, BNDD Agent George Frangullie, equipped with a false Mexican passport prepared by the CIA, was sent to Chile to get Sarmiento's chemist Francisco Guinart. Frangullie's informant bought five kilograms of cocaine from Guinart and the US Air Force attaché arranged to fly it, and the informant, to Maguire Air Force Base.[25] Strickler got US Attorney Thomas Puccio in New York's Eastern District to agree to allow the informant to sell the cocaine and "let it walk.' Strickler had taken a sample of the cocaine, added an invisible marker and re-sealed the package, which was placed in a locker at Penn Station. Although the surveillance team lost the receiver, an agent had taken pictures of him and when he was arrested later in another case, the film was used as evidence to charge him.[26]

AM-2 was a domestic operation that did not permit Strickler to pursue the people supplying the Cubans. AM-10, however, had no boundaries and once Kleindienst gave his consent, the BNDD expanded the Miami office's operations beyond the Caribbean into South America. The CIA began to provide Strickler with money, documentation, boats, safe houses, and "real time" communications for the slew of agents and informants Strickler and Hurney scattered throughout Latin America.[27]

Strickler and Pohl obtained venues to prosecute the people in New York, where they worked with US Attorney Puccio to indict people outside the United States. With the assistance of the National Security Council and the State Department, the BNDD opened offices throughout Latin America. By the end of the year, the BNDD had permanent posts in every country except for Guyana, Suriname and French Guyana, while scores of BNDD agents embarked on intelligence gathering and enforcement missions. Strickler paid particularly close attention to the abilities of agents sent to Latin America. Those who were good at investigations did undercover work and ran informants; those who were good at liaison work were used to press for changes in extradition laws at the ministerial level.[28]

The BNDD had no investigative authority in any of these countries and Strickler secretly hired a group of Argentine Customs agents to fill the gap. Through the Argentine Customs agents, the BNDD acquired access to an informant net, which, using cut-outs, was expanded throughout South America. The importance of this Argentine network cannot be overstated.

Paraguay

TONY POHL DEVELOPED THE FAMOUS case against Group France leader Auguste Ricord in conjunction with Jerry Strickler and cooperating Customs agents, through US Attorney Puccio in New York. Puccio's team was simultaneously preparing evidence for the Eagle case, and a number of Cuban defendants had become cooperating witnesses. According to Strickler, the Cubans said that vast quantities of narcotics were stored at the military's Hernandez Field outside Asuncion in Paraguay. They said that an air force of mercenary pilots was flying contraband south to Paraguay, and drugs north to Texas, New Orleans and Florida. Customs Agents Ed Coyne and Al Seely had one of these "contrabandista" pilots as an informant and through him learned that Ricord was in Asuncion. Though his organization had splintered, Ricord was still held responsible by Customs for 50 to 75 percent of the heroin entering the US.[29] The figure was fantastically unreal, but making a case on Ricord became urgently important for purely symbolic purposes.

Through informants and police contacts in Argentina, Pohl and Strickler knew that Ricord had fled to Paraguay in 1968, where he was warmly received by President Alfredo Stroessner, a graduate of the US Army's Command and General Staff School and overlord of the rackets in Paraguay. The BNDD agents were also aware of the movement of narcotics from Marseille to Madrid, through Chile and Paraguay, to distributors in Miami via an airline operating out of the Panama Canal Zone. Customs and the BNDD separately investigated this so-called "Condor Network," its satellite rings, and Mafia customers in America (most notably Carlos Marcello), until July 1970, when they grudgingly joined forces in Miami.[30]

Customs Agent Paul Boulad is often given credit for mapping out the Condor Network of contrabandista pilots flying out of protected airstrips in Paraguay and Panama. The Customs Service's answer to Tony Pohl, Boulad was born in Cairo of a French family. He had been the Customs Representative in Paris for two years, where he had met Pohl, and was thought to have acquired his information about the Condor Network from the CIA. Boulad briefed Pohl and, in return, the BNDD provided "informants with a battered secondhand cargo aircraft complete with dummy serial numbers and a false ownership history."[31]

To indict Ricord, Customs and the BNDD needed to link him to a specific heroin shipment; and as if by magic, on October 18, 1970 the FBI received an anonymous letter (one in a series) listing the registration numbers of a plane making a drug flight from Paraguay.[32] The letter indicated that a particular plane had departed Panama and was "loaded." The author of the letter, Eddie Cantrell, was a former CIA mercenary turned contrabandista. After his son died in a plane crash while flying dope into the US, Cantrell became an informant for Gerry Carey and, seeking redemption, gave up his former partner, Cesar Bianchi, the pilot of the plane mentioned above. Bianchi was wanted for murder in Brazil, easily compromised, and thus perfectly suited for setting up Ricord.

On October 19, Customs and the BNDD mounted a joint surveillance of Bianchi's drug shipment to a small airstrip near Miami. Bianchi was arrested two days later, with 42.5 kilograms of heroin.[33] Bianchi cooperated and in a controlled delivery, led Customs and BNDD agents to Felix Becker, a Paraguayan in Miami. Becker in turn informed on Ricord's logistics chief, Enio Varela, and their main customers in New York, Cuban José La Torriente (the Phillip Morris representative in the Caribbean) and Pierre Gahou. Gahou fingered Mafioso Nick Giannattasio as the receiver and Ricord as the owner of the dope. Varela and Bianchi gave corroborating testimony, and Ricord and seven others were indicted in the Eastern District New York. Ricord was arrested on March 25, 1971 and held for extradition.

Arresting Ricord in Paraguay was not an easy thing to do. Paraguay was not a member of Interpol, and an abundance of Paraguayan officials were invested in Ricord's operation. The sinister chief of Paraguay's secret police, Pastor Coronel, spied on BNDD informers and passed the information to traffickers.[34] Corrupt military officers rented their private landing strips and guarded the warehouse at Hernandez Field. General Patricio Colman financed Paraguay's anticommunist counter-insurgency through drug profits, while his CIA counterparts turned a blind eye. Colman was godfather to Ricord's logistics chief, Enio Varela. Paraguay was one of America's staunchest anti-Communist allies and again, as if by magic, Varela escaped from the West Street Detention Center in New York in January 1971.[35]

Despite all these obstacles, BNDD Agent Frank Macolini set up Ricord in a slick operation using the regular police to sidestep secret police chief Pastor Coronel. Within hours, however, one of Stroessner's political advisors called the police and demanded Ricord's immediate release. A judge related to Varela dutifully halted Ricord's extradition. This was quite a disappointment, as Tony Pohl and Paul Boulad were waiting in Asuncion with a US Air Force plane which they intended to use to fly Ricord out of the country. But Ambassador J. Raymond Ylitalo delayed the transfer, rather than be party to an "informal agreement" that might disrupt relations with Paraguay! [36] A diplomatic impasse ensued, and began lengthy proceedings in which Henry Kissinger personally played a pivotal role. [37]

Such were the impediments to federal drug law enforcement when staunch anti-Communist allies were involved. The result — in April 1971, seething BNDD agents watched while Auguste Ricord met at a plush hotel with Armando Gagliani, Jean Claude Kella, and Ange Simonpierri, the man with the French connection in the Far East. [38] Ricord would not be extradited until September 1972.

The Panama Connection

IRONICALLY, THE AM-10 CHILEAN SYSTEM would bring about the end of Ingersoll's vaunted systems approach. As Jerry Strickler explained: "A system is not an organization. It's a collection of organizations. We found you can't really disable a system. Targets at the start are different than the targets at the end. But it did bring focus, spark and innovation, and it knocked out the French connection. The French traffickers were trying to figure out what was going on. And the people we put away weren't just traffickers either; they were guilty of all sorts of crimes."

While it existed, AM-10 sought Europeans in every Latin America country except Guinea. It resulted in some of the BNDD's most spectacular successes, and it prompted the BNDD to re-organize the region into two sections: Joe Arpaio kept Mexico and the Caribbean; and Frank Macolini in Buenos Aires opened a second office that covered every country as far north as Panama, which became the next focal point of BNDD operations. [39]

Information gained from AM-10 also revealed that the Orsini organization relied not only on labs in Marseille, but on Swiss suppliers with mobile labs as well. It exposed the fact that a large percentage of French connection heroin came not from Turkey, but from the

Golden Triangle via Manila and Hong Kong. Henrik Kruger, author of *The Great Heroin Coup*, names "Ng Sik-ho (Limpy Ho) as Ricord's connection and "a major Nationalist Chinese heroin smuggler well connected to the Taiwan regime."[40] AM-10 also raised the issue of the BNDD's extra-judicial proceedings to the diplomatic level; only in the case of Panama the issue was kidnapping, based on the old "bounty-hunter" law, not extradition.

Gerry Carey's informant, pilot Eddie Cantrell, not only informed on Cesar Bianchi in the Ricord case, he told how contrabandistas flew through Panama with the help of Joaquim Him Gonzalez, Panama's chief of air traffic control and deputy inspector general of civil aviation. In these positions, Him was instrumental in assuring the clearance of aircraft used by drug traffickers on their way from South America to the US. Him received a kickback on all narcotics smuggled through Panama, and was closely involved with Ricord and his associates.

Cubans arrested in Operation Eagle confirmed the information, but the actual case against Him began when a pilot walked into the BNDD's Dallas office and told one of the agents that a group of Chilean traffickers, aided by Him, planned to smuggle a quantity of heroin into Brownsville, Texas. Him's American partner in the venture, Robert Louis Robertson III, owned an aircraft company in Dallas. After one of Robertson's pilots was murdered in June 1970 in an airport motel while in possession of 23 pounds of cocaine in his suitcase, the BNDD arranged for its informant in the case to take the murdered pilot's place.[41] The informant, Ronald D. Watkins, introduced Agent Vic Maria to Robertson. Posing as Watkins' Mafia connection, Maria negotiated with Robertson.[42] Their conversation was recorded. Then Watkins set up a sting operation in which Robertson agreed to fly Maria from Texas to Panama City to make a deal with Him. Robertson, Watkins and Maria met Him on December 2, 1970.

Maria's presence in Panama was covert.[43] Neither Noriega's CIA advisor nor the US ambassador was told. Not even Joe Arpaio knew. Strickler and Belk felt that Arpaio would tell the Mexicans and that the Mexicans would alert Him, so they sent a teletype to Arpaio, notifying him of the operation, but they "misdirected" it through Bangkok, so it would arrive ex post facto. And yet, despite all these precautions, Him cautiously retreated to the other room before the transaction with Maria was made.

According to Maria, Him knew that he had met with a BNDD agent. It's unclear if he learned that fact during the transaction or after, but it made no difference. Overcome with greed, he continued to deal anyway and shortly thereafter he sent narcotics to receivers (one Chilean, one Cuban) in Miami. He did not travel to Miami himself, but he was charged with conspiracy for this act, and for having agreed to deliver 100 kilos of coke to Maria.[44]

The case now entered stage two: the kidnapping of Him in the Canal Zone. Andy Tartaglino was the brain behind the daring and imaginative scheme. Him was a baseball fanatic and on February 6, 1971, he was lured into the US Canal Zone at the prospect of playing in a softball game between Panama's civil aviation team and the US Federal Aviation Authority (FAA) team. At that time the Canal Zone was US property and, when he arrived, he was arrested at gunpoint by Joe Grills, a detective with US Canal Zone police, backed up by BNDD Agents Ruben Manzone and Bill Plase. Grills put Him in the US Canal Zone prison.

Although it was a legal arrest, it had the look of a kidnapping, and Andy Tartaglino, suspecting that it might raise an uproar, had timed it to happen while Mitchell and Ingersoll were in France. That was a smart move, because the Him operation created a diplomatic firestorm that rivaled the Intercept debacle. Panamanian President Omar Torrijos threatened to attack the Canal Zone unless Him was released, and the US Ambassador in Panama screamed that the BNDD was making foreign policy without consulting him.

Panic ensued. Strickler and Tartaglino were summoned to a meeting with Army Department Counsel Fred Buzhardt and a State Department counsel. They wanted Him released, but Tartaglino, who was never intimidated by anyone, said that only the US Attorney in New York had the authority to quash the indictment. Deputy AG Kleindienst agreed, as did Secretary of State William Rogers; at which point the US military flew a helicopter into the Canal Zone and took Him to an airport, from which he was flown to Andrews Air Force Base. Strickler was on the plane and recalled that, "Andy started screaming at Him, 'You're responsible for the deaths of innocent children.'"

The uproar was far from over and while Him awaited trial, Ambassador Robert Sayre, whose negotiations with Torrijos over the return of the Panama Canal had stalled as a result of the kidnapping, summoned Strickler and Tartaglino to a meeting in Manual Noriega's office. Noriega was there with his CIA interpreter, Captain Drake. At this meeting Minister Juan Tack expelled BNDD Agents Manzone and Plase from Panama and closed the office. This was a big blow, as the BNDD was running many of its Latin American informants out of the Panama office. The operations continued, but through Agent Plase's wife, who acted as the de-facto agent-in-charge until her husband returned.[45] And kidnapping became standard BNDD operating procedure.

As for Joaquin Him Gonzalez, he was tried in Dallas, convicted and sentenced to five years in prison. However, as Vic Maria recalled, "The two South Americans with Him were acquitted, even though they handed me a [kilo]. The back-up agents in the next room overheard the transaction. But at the trial they said we never received the cocaine.

"Who laid the arm on that?" Maria asks facetiously, referring to the mysterious CIA agent, Captain Drake, who was monitoring the case. "Everyone knew Him and Torrijos and Noriega were in the drug traffic. It was in our files in Panama."[46]

The Mafia in Latin America

THE ITALIAN MAFIA WAS WELL established in Latin America and, naturally, the Italians and the French Corsicans cooperated when there was money to be made. The Mafia even financed the operations of several of Ricord's top lieutenants (including Christian David, Lucien Sarti, Michel Nicoli, and Claude Pastou) through Tomasso Buscetta.[47] The Mafia had been doing so since 1966, shortly after Buscetta was arrested by the INS, but used a fake identity to escape to Brazil. This monumental oversight leads some people to speculate that Buscetta was a CIA informant.

Whatever his affiliations, Buscetta and his associate, Giuseppe Catania, moved about 200 kilograms of heroin a month from Italy and Madrid through Argentina and Mexico directly to Neapolitan Carlo Zippo, one of the biggest distributors in New York. They also supplied the Cotroni organization in Montreal, and Mafiosi in Texas and California. Catania worked with Asaf Y Bala in Mexico and Buscetta used the services of, among others, Italian controller Felice Bonetti.[48]

Buscetta routinely traveled to Montreal and on December 9, 1969, Customs officers intercepted him, with Giuseppe Tramontana of Brooklyn and Anthony Settimo of Queens (American Mafia representatives to the Cotroni family) at the Canadian border.[49] The urbane Italian had four passports in his possession and managed to slip away again, fueling the theory that he was an informant or otherwise had government protection. It is also possible that he was incredibly clever and lucky; in June 1970, he was stopped in Milan with his Italian connection, Gaetano Badalamenti. Using an alias, Buscetta once more got away.[50] The BNDD stayed on the case, however, and soon discovered that Buscetta's son Anthony was living with Rosario Gambino, a nephew of Carlo Gambino. Buscetta also had a document with Carlo Zippo's name on it, and the BNDD began to watch him as well.[51]

The Italian police wanted Buscetta for the murder of seven policemen in 1963, and asked to be notified if he was located. Relations between the American and Italian police services were strained, however, and the BNDD did not reveal that it had Buscetta (or Italian national Zippo) under surveillance. In fact, BNDD agents knew a heroin shipment was coming to Zippo's office in Manhattan, and they watched while Zippo and Buscetta went to a New Jersey motel and met a contact from Mexico in a Mercedes. The three traffickers then drove to a Mafia-owned garage but were not stopped and searched. The BNDD was expecting the heroin to come in religious statues and did not want to blow a chance to make a big seizure by alerting the traffickers.[52]

Zippo vanished altogether in August 1970 after New York State Police arrested Buscetta and his son Benedetto. Charged with illegal entry into the US, Buscetta was detained for a third time by US authorities, held for several months in detention, and then granted bail — even though it was known that he was wanted in Italy for murder and in Colombia for the sale of 14 kilos of heroin. Buscetta surfaced in Mexico, and then Brazil, "where he became owner of a taxi fleet and a restaurant chain, as well as a member of the gang of Corsican Auguste-Joseph Ricord."[53]

It would be two more years before the BNDD finally got him and turned him over to the Italian police. Buscetta, however, was soon released and returned to trafficking. Not until 1983 did he actually land behind bars in the United States.

9

ESPIONAGE INTRIGUES

SPIES AND SMUGGLERS HAVE A lot in common. Both are expert at assuming false identities and crossing borders to deliver contraband to co-conspirators. The Office of Strategic Services (OSS) combined the two trades in the Second World War, when it flew Iranian opium to Kachin guerrillas fighting the Japanese in Burma, as payment for services rendered. As OSS Detachment 101 commander William Peers succinctly stated, "If opium could be useful in achieving victory, the pattern was clear. We would use opium."[1]

Like its forefather the OSS, the CIA uses drug smugglers as assassins, spies, and couriers. The CIA always helped anti-Communist warlord henchmen traffic in narcotics, especially in the Far East, and nowadays it does the same thing in Afghanistan, in the name of anti-terrorism.[2]

Joseph Califano, the individual in the Johnson Administration credited with creating the BNDD, almost certainly knew about the CIA's dirty dealings. In 1963 and 1964, as a special assistant to the Secretary of the Army, he recruited assassins in the CIA's secret war against Cuba. According to author Joseph Trento, Califano and Alexander Haig (Kissinger's deputy at the NSC in 1970), "checked out potential members for the hit teams with older members of the Cuban Brigade."[3] The Cuban Brigade consisted of some 1400 exiles. From it, the CIA recruited assassins whom it sent into Cuba and other foreign countries to murder members of Castro's regime. In exchange, these Cuban agents were allowed to traffic in narcotics.

The interests of its secret army of exile Cuban drug-smuggling assassins, and its secret army under drug trafficker Vang Pao in Laos, were advanced by the fact that the CIA's initials did not appear on the BNDD's organizational chart. But the CIA did play a role in the BNDD's creation and operations. Through its counter-intelligence and security staffs, the CIA deals with every federal law enforcement agency. It has cognizance of all their intelligence operations and cheerfully plays one federal agency against the other to achieve its secret agenda. In one famous case, a CIA station chief told a Customs official that a narcotics delivery was being made. Customs inspector Lynn Pelletier soon "discovered" 97 pounds of heroin in a Volkswagen van on an ocean liner in Port Elizabeth, New Jersey. The owner of the van, Roger Delouette, was busted when he came to claim it. "The press made it look like luck," Myles Ambrose explained, but the CIA had tipped off Customs to create the impression that SDECE employed drug smugglers.[4] In exchange for going along with the charade, Customs made a sensational seizure.

Jerry Strickler concurs. "One thing the CIA did was cut a deal with Customs when Myles was the boss. Customs wanted seizures. They didn't care about the people. So the CIA would give them intelligence that would lead to busts that would negatively impact our cases."

The CIA exploited the BNDD in other ways too. For example, information gained from CIA wiretaps is inadmissible in court. Hence, the CIA had merely to tap the phone of any drug smuggler it wanted to protect. When such subtlety failed, the CIA used blunt instruments. In Vientiane, Laos in 1963, FBN Agent Bowman Taylor busted General Vang Pao with 50 kilograms of morphine base. When the CIA found out, it returned the dope to Vang Pao and kicked Taylor out of the country.[5] Why? Because, in exchange for providing his people as cannon fodder in the CIA's secret war against the communists, the general was allowed to enrich himself by dealing drugs.

During the Nixon Administration, the CIA's involvement in drug trafficking reached new heights; which is why Nixon's war on drugs became a defining issue in his downfall.

Nixon and the CIA-Crime Nexus

NIXON'S POLITICAL DILEMMA REQUIRED THE resolution, through covert action, of opposing policies. He wanted to be perceived as waging a war on drugs; but he also wanted to wage secret wars that required the support of drug smuggling warlords. This gap between his stated and unstated policies was his Achilles heel.

Nixon was also compromised through his friendship with Charles 'Bebe" Rebozo, a Cuban American with ties to Santo Trafficante and Mafioso Al Polizzi in Florida.[6] Rebozo allegedly laundered drug money generated by anti-Castro terrorists; and his brother William and William's son were busted on a narcotics charge in March 1969.[7]

Nixon also maintained ties to organized crime figures. His pardon of James R. "Jimmy" Hoffa in 1971 earned him the votes of the Teamsters Union and garnered its support for his wage/price freeze and war in Vietnam. But every veteran FBN agent knew that some teamsters provided cover for Mafia drug traffickers. Frank Coppola was godfather to Hoffa's foster son and in return, Hoffa protected Coppola's narcotics receivers in Detroit "by assigning them to Teamsters Local 985."[8] Frank Dioguardia, the Mafia Teamster boss busted in the 1965 Nebbia case, provided Trafficante with an office that served as a front for his mob's narcotics activities.[9]

While in prison Hoffa befriended Carmine Galante, the former narcotics boss of the Bonanno family, and an ally of Santo Trafficante. Galante in the early 1950s set up major smuggling routes out of Cuba and Montreal. In testimony before the Senate Rackets Committee in 1958, Jack Cusack linked Carlos Marcello and Santo Trafficante with Jimmy Hoffa — and gunrunning to Cuba.[10]

Having served as President Eisenhower's "action officer" during the planning stages of the CIA's failed Cuban Bay of Pigs invasion, Nixon was certainly aware of Hoffa's activities on behalf of the CIA. Hoffa is said to have been "the original liaison" between the mob and the CIA in its plots to assassinate Fidel Castro, and to have brought numerous Mafiosi into the conspiracy.[11] It was a criminal conspiracy that forever bound the Mafia, the CIA, and Nixon.

Nixon needed to manage the CIA-crime nexus carefully. This was made clear on the "smoking gun" Watergate tape when he derailed an FBI investigation into a CIA activity in Mexico.[12] Nixon felt that activity was connected to the Bay of Pigs debacle, perhaps through Watergate burglar Eugenio Martinez, a CIA employee and vice-president of Rebozo's Keyes Reality firm in Florida. The "smoking gun" may have been that Nixon knew that the CIA had hired Santo Trafficante, the patron saint of drug traffickers, to recruit Cuban exiles to assassinate

Castro. Nixon may also have known that Mafioso Sam Mannarino ran guns to Castro for the CIA with Meyer Lansky's close associate and fellow drug financier, Norman Rothman; and that Mannarino, Rothman and Pepe Cotroni (the Mafia's narcotics connection in Montreal) were partners in the theft of $8.5 million in securities from a Canadian bank, with which they funded their gun running escapade. They were caught redhanded, but acquitted.[13]

Mannarino's protection persisted and in 1970, he was acquitted in New York of taking Teamster kickbacks, thanks to the testimony of Mario Brod, "the local head of the CIA."[14] (Brod, FBN Agent Charlie Siragusa and CIA Counter-Intelligence Chief James Angleton had served together in the OSS in Italy, recruiting Mafiosi to help stamp out communism.) When the US Attorney in the Mannarino case discovered that a Swiss bank laundered money for Lansky and the Teamsters, John Mitchell turned the investigation off. Mitchell also intervened when several Mafia chieftains were charged with a stock swindle in Florida with Lansky's son-in-law. One of their representatives approached Kleindienst in November 1970 and offered him a $100,000 campaign contribution. After mulling it over for a week, Kleindienst reported the bribe. Everyone in the stock swindle case was acquitted, and only the messengers were convicted of attempted bribery.[15]

Nixon's CIA-crime connection was the insurmountable problem for the BNDD. This sad fact of life became manifest during Operation Eagle, when it was discovered that many defendants were disgruntled CIA-employed Cuban terrorists. Feeling betrayed by the CIA, the exile Cubans had taken to blowing up people and places in the US, and had come under investigation by the FBI. Eagle was a convenient way of rounding them up and redirecting their efforts on behalf of the BNDD, under the guidance of the CIA — which is why the case was sparked by a CIA asset, as related by Agent Dom Petrossi in the previous chapter. As we know, the Eagle case was blown by the Nixon administration and many defendants set free.

The practice of subverting CIA/Mafia connected cases became routine. Referring to another case a few years later, author Hank Messick said, "once again the heroin had been confiscated while the pipeline was left undisturbed: Had the wiretap procedure been installed as a safety valve, perhaps, to accommodate the persons capable of developing the cocaine business? It sounded incredible, but privately, a lot of people in official positions began to wonder." Messick added that the

Nixon Administration used, "the same illegal procedures ... in scores of cases against fifteen hundred racketeers of all kinds."[16]

To insure that future BNDD operations would not expose its Mafia contacts like Santo Trafficante, or its anti-Castro terrorist assets, the CIA assigned officer James E. Anderson to the BNDD in the wake of Eagle.[17] A veteran with years of experience running surveillance teams against pro-Castro Communists in Mexico, Anderson was from the clandestine services division, not Angleton's counter-intelligence staff. He and his staff helped Strickler by providing wiretaps, surveillances, false passports for undercover agents, and timely, on-the-spot support from CIA officers in embassies throughout Latin America. Anderson worked personally with Strickler to isolate and interrogate suspects and turned them into informants in safe houses in Florida.

At first, it seemed like just the thing the BNDD needed.

Enter Peter Scrocca

CUBAN TRAFFICKERS ARRESTED IN OPERATION Eagle were turned into informants and made cases for the BNDD in South America and Europe. They had a Chilean connection and when the Socialist Party of Salvador Allende prepared to take power in Santiago after the September 1970 elections, these anti-Castro Cuban drug traffickers, now working for the CIA and BNDD, were used to attack Allende's government. BNDD Agent Peter M. Scrocca played an unsuspecting role in this development.

An FBN agent since 1962, Scrocca specialized in making undercover cases on Mafia hoods in the Bronx, and South Americans on the Lower East Side.[18] But Scrocca had a checkered past and Tartaglino kept him under constant scrutiny.

Tall and lean with thinning blond hair, Scrocca described Tartaglino as suffering from "a Richelieu complex." The antagonism grew in 1970 when Tartaglino tried to get Scrocca to quit the BNDD by reassigning him to Miami. Scrocca's wife was pregnant and he did not want to go. It was a tough decision, but he needed his job, so initially he went without his family. When he arrived in Miami he suffered the additional indignity of being assigned to work undercover. Scrocca had replaced Dennis Dayle as a group supervisor, and it was demeaning that he had to live in a crumby apartment on twenty-two dollars per diem. Miami RD Ben Theisen, however, had a plan in mind. The plan paid fabulous dividends too, but only after Scrocca dodged one of Tartaglino's torpedoes.

Upon arriving in Miami, Scrocca was contacted by Richard Lawrence. A convicted murderer, Lawrence had been an informant for several FBN agents in New York. As Scrocca recalled, he met Lawrence at a motel with Agent William Hudson. Lawrence said he could make a case on a New Jersey trafficker in Miami, and Scrocca agreed to use him. As part of the plan, BNDD technicians wired the motel room where Scrocca was to make the buy. While waiting for the trafficker to arrive, Lawrence suggested that he and Scrocca keep some of the drugs and money for themselves.

Lawrence, of course, was secretly working for Tartaglino. He was wired and was trying to get Scrocca to commit a crime or admit to past sins. Scrocca didn't fall into the trap. But he did make a stupid wisecrack. He said, "This isn't the old days."

Tartaglino seized upon that statement and after the case went down, he grilled Scrocca about what he meant by "the old days." Scrocca talked his way out of the jam, but such were the stressful conditions that he and the other "unresolved" agents were working under. Not only did they have to watch out for dangerous drug traffickers while trying to make cases, they had to beware of their informants and fellow agents.

Oscar Squella Avendano

WHILE A GROUP SUPERVISOR IN New York, Scrocca had made a string of cases on Mafia-connected South Americans. In Miami, he continued this line of investigation, drinking steadily at a bar patronized by anti-Castro Cuban cocaine traffickers. Scrocca posed as a fugitive making connections for his Mafia associates in New York. To back up his cover story, Theisen would arrange for New York agents and informants, posing as Mafiosi, to visit Scrocca at this bar.[19]

After the Operation Eagle arrests, Scrocca started working with a "wild woman" sent from New York. She introduced him to a "gay" Cuban man, who introduced him to a trafficker named Ochoa. Ochoa imported cocaine from Chile and agreed to sell Scrocca 500 pounds. The deal was arranged and Ochoa sent word to Scrocca that half of the shipment was coming in. The Miami office set up surveillance and Scrocca made an undercover purchase of 204 pounds of cocaine on July 17, 1970.[20]

Prior to the buy and bust, Agent Hudson had followed Ochoa and an accomplice to the Miami International Airport. Hudson saw the traffickers in their car near a runway. A short time later another accomplice arrived in a second car and parked near a plane. The pilot helped the Cubans unload several boxes into the trunk of one of the cars. Everyone drove back to Ochoa's pad, where Scrocca made the buy and bust. The pilot, Oscar Squella Avendano, was arrested too.

The owner of a private airline and a member of Salvador Allende's inner circle, Squella was accused in right wing Chilean newspapers of using the money he allegedly made from trafficking cocaine to help fund Allende's campaign. The newspapers also claimed that in return, Allende was going to name Squella as Minister of Transportation. Squella vehemently denied the allegations and after being freed on bail and returning to Chile, he voluntarily returned to the US to stand trial. He pled not guilty, but was convicted and incarcerated. He may have been set up. According to Strickler, an address book was found in Squella's possession when he was arrested. One of the numbers in the book belonged to Chilean diplomat, Orlando Letelier. At the time, Strickler suspected that Orlando was related to cocaine trafficker Oscar Letelier, a defendant in the Yolando Sarmiento case.[21]

The address book was never introduced as evidence, and Squella never mentioned it to his attorney Donald Bierman. But a State Department officer told Strickler that Squella had purchased the address book in Moscow. Whether or not the address book was real or a CIA forgery, Squella was now suspected of being a Soviet agent, and Strickler and the BNDD were not allowed to speak to him after his arrest.

According to Strickler, the CIA in 1972 tried to exchange Squella for the captain of the *Johnny Express*, a "mother ship" used by anti-Castro Cuban terrorists to launch cigarette boat attacks against Cuba. The *Johnny Express* and its crew were seized by the Cubans in December 1971. The owner of the *Johnny Express*, Teofilo Babun, was a close friend of Bebe Rebozo. Manuel Noriega was the middleman in failed negotiations between the CIA, Castro, and Allende.[22]

Squella's attorney, Donald Bierman, was unaware of these machinations. He does, however, believe that Squella was set up by the CIA. ITT (International Telephone and Telegraph) of which Chile's phone service was a subsidiary, was concerned that Allende would nationalize its holdings in Chile. According to Bierman, a high ranking ITT official contacted Squella and asked him to bring several boxes of important documents to the US. Considering that US Customs inspected Squella's plane when it landed and found no drugs, it's likely the CIA repacked the boxes of documents with drugs, and then used its assets in the Chilean media to exploit the scandal to discredit Allende.[23]

Allende was elected anyway, so the CIA launched a "black propaganda" campaign to terrorize the Chilean bourgeoisie and pave the way for a bloody military coup in 1973, in which Allende was assassinated.

The French Connection

THE CIA'S SECRET ARMIES OF drug smuggling Cubans, Laotians and Nationalist Chinese were not the only espionage impediments to federal drug law enforcement in 1970. According to Agent Tom Tripodi, the CIA formed a narcotics smuggling organization shortly after the Second World War through the AFL-CIO's overseas representative, Irving Brown.[24] Tripodi referred to it as "the Brown-Angleton" network because James Angleton, the CIA's counter-intelligence chief, managed it with certain FBN agents and the aforementioned mob attorney-cum-CIA agent Mario Brod.

Angleton, Brod and FBN Agent Charlie Siragusa had served together in Italy in the Second World War. As head of the FBN office in Rome, and as the FBN's liaison to the CIA until his retirement in December 1963, Siragusa worked closely with Angleton, who relied heavily on Siragusa's underworld contacts. CIA officer Vincent Thill, as part of an operation put together by Angleton and William Harvey, asked Siragusa to recruit Mafia and Corsican hit men for the CIA, although Siragusa denied having done so.[25]

Siragusa's disciples in the FBN — including Tripodi, Andy Tartaglino, Hank Manfredi and Paul Knight — were aware of the Brown-Angleton history, which began when Brown, using CIA funds, formed "compatible left" unions in Marseille and hired Italian and Corsican thugs to break a strike by communist longshoremen.[26] The gangsters, including a young Corsican named Maurice Castellani, were rewarded with "free passage" to smuggle drugs without interference.[27] French author Alain Jaubert notes that in Bordeaux in 1952, Corsican gangster Antoine Guerini took part in a "mysterious meeting" with Brown (the American Federation of Labor's representative in Europe), Guerini's chemist Jo Cesari, and two other traffickers.[28] Jaubert reported that Corsican crime lord Guerini soon thereafter brought CIA Agent Brown into contact with the Mafia in Italy.[29]

In the early 1950s the French secret services launched their own drug smuggling operation, in which French Special Forces purchased opium in the Golden Triangle and flew it to Hong Kong and Marseilles via Vietnam.[30] SDECE agents, working with Corsican gangsters like Irving Brown's associate Maurice Castellani, oversaw its conversion into heroin and sale on the black market, as a way of financing the French counterinsurgency in Vietnam. After 1954, when America displaced the French in Indochina, SDECE subsidized Corsican traffickers to maintain this drug distribution system. According to Tripodi, CIA General Edward Lansdale did a study on this development in 1960 and concluded that, "elements of the French government were engaged in the heroin traffic."[31]

The French struck back and in April 1962, Corsican Etienne Tarditi, "a man with connections to SDECE front groups," exposed the Brown-Angleton network.[32] Tarditi did this by telling Andy Tartaglino (then head of the FBN's "conspiracy squad" in New York), that Irving Brown was involved in a case in which Tarditi was arrested while delivering 100 kilograms of heroin to members of the Gambino Mafia family in New York. Tarditi made the provocative statement that he "was involved in intelligence work beneficial to American interests."[33] The CIA quickly shut down Tartaglino's investigation.[34]

In 1965, the Brown-Angleton operation again flashed across the FBN's radar screen. This time FBN Agent Frankie Waters discovered that Brown's Corsican drug smuggling friend Maurice Castellani was bringing cash to Francois Scaglia, one of the traffickers busted in the famous 1962 French Connection case. Brown enjoyed "port privileges" in New York – meaning his bags were not checked by Customs – and when Brown and Castellani flew into New York, they were not required to fill out immigration forms.[35]

Once again the CIA shut down the FBN's investigation of Brown, and once again Castellani escaped to France where, in 1966, he figured in the cover-up of the FBN's involvement in the kidnapping and murder of Mehdi Ben Barka, an exiled Moroccan opposition leader. This disturbing chain of events began when the CIA falsely informed Jack Cusack, then head of the FBN's foreign operations office in Washington, that Barka was trafficking narcotics.[36] Cusack passed the disinformation to Victor Maria, the FBN's resident agent in Paris, and Maria shared it with the Paris narcotics squad. In October 1965, two Paris narcotic agents, at the direction of SDECE Agent Antoine Lopez – a double agent working for the CIA – kidnapped Barka outside the Brasserie Lipp. The cops rendered Barka to Corsican gangsters and SDECE agents, who subsequently took Barka to a remote location where French and Moroccan intelligence agents slowly tortured him to death.[37]

To provide itself with plausible deniability in Barka's kidnapping and murder, the CIA forced drug trafficker Joseph Zurita to deliver a CIA composed article to *L'Express*. The article, published in January 1966, blamed the Barka affair entirely on a Moroccan general. Right after delivering the article, Zurita applied for a US visa. While in New York, under FBN surveillance, Zurita met daily with Maurice Castellani for a week in mid-April 1966.[38]

Castellani, a likely CIA agent, trafficked in narcotics into the 1970s with impunity.

Paris Agent Vic Maria insists that Joseph Attia, the boss of the criminal organization whose members had taken custody of Barka, "was definitely not into drugs. But the CIA said to pursue it, even if he wasn't. That's how they operated. They'd front you, then tell you to fade the heat, which in this case meant that cooperation with the French authorities ended for quite some time after the Barka affair."[39]

Convinced that the CIA had arranged Barka's murder through double agents within SDECE, French President Charles de Gaulle severed relations with the CIA and began courting the Soviets. What he didn't know was that the CIA plot "went beyond certain French intelligence units to" his closest advisors.[40] In this way the Ben Barka affair helped to assure de Gaulle's demise and the ascent of Georges Pompidou, whose policies were more compatible with America's. All this happened thanks to the CIA's successful exploitation of a self-serving faction in the FBN – a faction that would grow within the BNDD and command the DEA into the mid-1980s.

While the CIA used drug traffickers to meddle in France's political affairs, SDECE allowed agents like Michel Victor Mertz to sell narcotics in the US.[41] Most SDECE traffickers were Corsican members of the Service d'Action Civique (SAC) – de Gaulle's non-governmental "political action" goon squad. The aforementioned Jo Attia was a member, as were traffickers Christian David, Ange Simonpierri, Lucien Sarti, Claude Pastou, Michel Nicoli, Paul Mondoloni (a former police chief in Saigon), Dominique Venturi, Marcel Francisci, Andre Condemine, Andre Labay and Roger Delouette.[42]

The Corsican members of SAC had earned a special place in de Gaulle's heart for putting down rebellious French military men in Algeria. But, like the CIA's anti-Castro Cubans, the Corsicans overstepped their bounds and de Gaulle turned on them. By 1966, many had fled to South America to join Ricord's Group France. But they remained "auxiliary agents" and kept their "special three-colored" SAC credentials and performed mercenary duties for SDECE while remaining fugitives from the French police.[43]

Like the CIA's stable of anti-Castro Cubans, the Corsicans were adept at forging documents, communicating in coded messages, conducting counter-surveillance, and utilizing espionage-style smuggling techniques. The average BNDD agents was no match, which is why John Ingersoll, Jerry Strickler, and many other naïve BNDD agents were willing to accept CIA assistance. The CIA took full advantage of the BNDD's innocents, by covertly hiring arms trafficker to smuggle guns to insurgents in Communist countries, while allowing the smugglers to move drugs out – often to America.

Tom Tripodi insisted the CIA traffic was unintentional, the result of unscrupulous assets who exploited their free passage. "Just because they're dealing," he said, "it doesn't necessarily mean they're dealing for their respective secret service."[44]

But as another CIA facetiously noted, "It is nice to have plausible deniability."

The BNDD, SAC, and SDEC

IN NOVEMBER 1970, GEORGES POMPIDOU appointed Alexandre de Marenches chief of SDECE and directed him to purge the organization of Soviet influence. Pompidou also accepted IBM chairman Arthur Watson as the new US Ambassador to France, although IBM was rumored to provide CIA agents with cover. Watson's narcotics coordinator, Thomas Murphy, addressed the drug issue at the diplomatic level, while CIA officer Paul Van Marx guided Jack Cusack on the BNDD's dealings with SDECE.[45] Van Marx was knowledgeable about drug trafficking; he had managed the CIA's Uruguayan desk in 1964, when Uruguayan foreign ministry official Juan Carlos Arizti – part of a diplomatic smuggling ring formed in Tel Aviv in 1951 – was being busted in New York with 60 kilograms of heroin destined for the Gambino family.[46] Van Marx served in Bogotá, Colombia until 1968, when he landed in Paris.

The Franco-American Agreement on drug control signaled a new era of cooperation began between the BNDD and SDECE. Prior to Pompidou, the BNDD had developed an expansive informant net of cooperating individuals (including French policemen) so it could work around SDECE. After the Accords, the BNDD worked with SDECE to move information more quickly, place wiretaps, and convince the French police to make arrests.[47] The Agreement also meant better relations with the police. BNDD undercover operations were allowed in certain situations, with judicial approval, as were controlled deliveries emanating from France. The French police also permitted renditions (the type of made infamous by the CIA during the Bush administration's war on terror), in which traffickers were kidnapped and carried to countries where they could be indicted or tortured and turned into informants.

The French even made cases on de Gaulle's beloved SAC members in France. The round-up began in 1969, when French and BNDD agents developed a case in Marseille on SAC leader Jean Audisio.[48] A few weeks later Audisio's accomplice, the mistress of the SAC chief in Grenoble, was arrested with 50 kilograms of heroin.[49] In February 1970, French and BNDD agents slipped an informer inside the SAC ring. The case culminated in April following the delivery of six kilograms of heroin to New York receivers. The French arrested SAC members Marcel Galvani, Dominique Giordano and Jean Audisio. The receivers revealed the organization's customers in New York.[50]

French spies officially left the drug business in November 1970, when Interior Minister Marcellin publicly confessed that "a large number of narcotic traffickers were recruited from among the members of SAC."[51] But at least one highly placed and well protected SAC member got away. The smuggler was Marcel Francisci, an associate of Lucky Luciano and Meyer Lansky since 1949.[52] An influential member in the Gaullist political party, Francisci's protection extended to legendary traffickers Dominique and Jean Venturi, Paul Mondoloni and Jean Croce. The protection came through de Gaulle's personal attorney, Pierre Lemarchand, former Interior Minister Roger Frey, and Jacques Foccart, the founder (with Mertz's father-in-law, Charles Pasqua) of SAC. Frey's deputies in Corsica were also close to Francisci.[53]

Though the Francisci organization was penetrated by CIA agent Herbert Itkin and exposed in numerous books, Francisci remained untouchable.[54] The moral, of course, is that just as Lansky, Trafficante and Rothman were protected in the US, so too were traffickers protected by political patrons in France...and Turkey and the Middle East.

Byzantium

MUCH OF THE MORPHINE BASE that fueled the SAC organization came from Turkish and Lebanese suppliers. BNDD agents pursuing these suppliers often formed relations with CIA officers in the region. Others, like Paul Knight, who had opened the FBN's office in Beirut, were in fact CIA officers masquerading as federal narcotics agents.

In Turkey, BNDD Agent Richard E. Salmi formed a fast friendship with CIA officer Duane "Dewey" Clarridge. Later chief of the CIA's Counter-Terror Center, Clarridge worked with Salmi tracking the movement of drugs from the Middle East through Turkey to Western Europe, as well as the weapons going back to the Kurds on Iraq border. The Soviets were thought to be involved through the official Bulgarian travel agency, Kintex, as be discussed in Chapter 11.[55]

The guns for drugs trade was at the center of espionage intrigues in the Middle East. The Israelis, of course, were interested in identifying anyone supplying weapons to their Arab enemies. Increasingly isolated and ever more dependent on America, Israel had formed close relations with the FBN. As Agent Bob DeFauw recalls, "Yitzak showed up at my door about two weeks after I arrived, and thereafter visited me about three or four times a year. He was a general in the Mossad and had responsibility for the same geographical areas as I. His people had the book on everything that went on in their backyard, and whatever I needed to know about the Bekka Valley in Lebanon, he got for me. In return, Yitzak liked hearing about what we had on the Lebanese heroin families, the Makkoots and the Maaloufs. He was also interested in gun running: 'Where are the guns coming from?'

"The Israelis helped us move people around, too. They'd fly a guy to Franco's people in Spain where, if there were drug charges pending, we could deal with them. We're talking serious interrogations. So these people became useful informants by virtue of the Israelis moving them to places where they'd face problems."[56]

Congressmen and senators, as well as police and security officials, were involved in drug trafficking throughout the region. In August 1970, for example, a member of the Lebanese Parliament, Niaf Masri, invited a group of American traffickers to his estate in Baalbek. After preliminary negotiations at the St George Hotel in Beirut, Masri's son prepared a landing strip for the Americans. Alas, BNDD and Greek agents arrested the Americans with 648 kilos of hash upon their return to Cyprus. A month later, the Lebanese minister of interior ordered an inquiry into the production of hashish, which led to the "biggest political names in the country," including members of parliament.[57]

In Turkey in mid-1970, Congressman Refet Sezgin, a close associate of trafficker Nuri Bosna, was forced to resign after a narcotic scandal. As reported by BNDD Agent Dick Salmi, Senator Almet Karayigit from Afyon was known to deal in precursors for heroin conversion.[58] Meanwhile, the head of the Turkey's Central Narcotics Bureau in Ankara, Galip Labernas, whom Jack Cusack once described as "not to be trusted," ran Turkey's eradication program.[59] The corruption in Turkey was so bad that Gordon Liddy, at a Heroin Committee meeting, proposed bombing Istanbul![60]

The Strange Case of Manuel Suarez Dominguez

AN INTERNAL DEA/CIA REPORT RELEASED in 1973, Project Pilot III, describes "the strange case of Manuel Suarez" as having "all the earmarks of an intelligence, rather than a heroin trafficking, operation. The source of heroin in that case has never been clarified."[61]

BNDD Agent Wayne T. Valentine managed the Suarez case in San Antonio, Texas. Valentine was a close friend of George Belk, who had hired him into the FBN in Minnesota in 1958. Bill Durkin, another powerful Purple Gang member, was godfather to Valentine's children.[62]

The Suarez case was part of the AM-5 system that included French nationals. On the surface it was a relatively simply case that began in early 1970 when Valentine placed an undercover agent inside the Alfredo Montemayor ring in San Antonio. Montemayor received heroin from Suarez and supplied distributors in San Antonio and Chicago. Valentine's undercover agent bought one kilo from Montemayor's Mafia associate, Salvador Mazatini. The BNDD let that kilo "walk", then arrested Montemayor in May while he was delivering 15 kilos to the undercover agent. Arrested with Montemayor were Manuel Suarez Dominguez and Suarez's girlfriend Yolanda Schmidt. Suarez, it was discovered, was a colonel in Mexican federal police and carried secret service credentials. And that's when the case began its descent into unfathomable espionage intrigues.

In a lengthy statement to BNDD agents, Suarez revealed that he had a French connection in Marseille and another source behind the Iron Curtain.[63] Andy Tartaglino subsequently put Valentine in charge of a team that went to Europe to investigate this East German connection. Valentine's team was accompanied Suarez's girlfriend Yolando, who remembered the location of the apartment building where Suarez had bought his narcotics in Marseille. French officials confirmed that Yolando was correct - but they conducted a separate investigation. And they never revealed what they found. Indeed, several years later through a friend in the French police, Valentine was told that the source was a SDECE general from Algeria.[64]

Valentine's efforts to find the Iron Curtain connection were also frustrated. He learned that the CIA knew about the hotel where Suarez bought narcotics in East Berlin, and that it was a well-known way station for spies. But that's all he ever discovered.

The Suarez Statement

SUAREZ GAVE HIS STATEMENT IN February 1971 in exchange for immunity for Yolando. In it, he said that he had become director of intelligence security for the Petroleum Industries of Mexico (PEMEX) when his political patron, Don Adolfo Ruiz-Cortines was elected president in 1952.[65] Ruiz-Cortines and Suarez had met and formed a close relationship in Veracruz in 1943. In the cushy PEMEX job Suarez formed relations with the important businessmen, spies and crooks in Mexico, including Attorney General Fernando Lopez-Arias and a top federal judicial policeman, Hector Hernandez Tello, both of whom protected Mexican drug lord Jorge Asaf y Bala and his Mafia and Corsican accomplices.[66] In 1959 Lopez-Arias appointed Suarez director of the Mexican Federal Judicial Police; Tello became his deputy in Veracruz where, in 1962, Suarez became director general of public security.

By 1966, Suarez was a millionaire and a degenerate gambler who squandered his fortune at the casinos in Las Vegas. As so often happens in these situations, a mobster at the Flamingo, Arthur Newman, compelled Suarez to enter into a smuggling venture with Emanuel Sperling Gross, a Czechoslovakian jeweler in Gibraltar. Gross smuggled drugs with Raymundo Pena Galan, a former bodyguard for a Mexican president. Gross and Pena hid their drugs in warehouses in Laredo and Brownsville. Pena had a New York buyer, and Gross had a source in Europe.[67]

In February 1968 Suarez met Gross and his supplier Rachmiel Widawski in Antwerp, Belgium. A Polish spy and black marketer, Widawski's narcotics were in East Berlin. Suarez flew there with Widawski and stayed at the Hotel Mitropa. East German Customs did not check their papers. At Widawski's house, "Henry and Elsa" sold Suarez sealed glass jars full of pharmaceutical grade morphine. The jars had the manufacturer's label on them. Suarez smuggled the glass jars through East German immigration without being checked, and, of course, through Customs in Mexico City, where he was a well known and important police official.[68]

Suarez, Gross and Widawski repeated the process in November 1967 and March 1968. On one occasion Suarez met "a Negro man" and on another he met with Joseph Simon Goldenberg, an alleged Communist agent and Turkish national with a French connection. Henry and Elsa provide 37 kilos and 50 kilos of heroin on these two occasions. On another occasion Suarez did a deal with John J. Ford, III, an attorney from San Francisco.

In November 1968, Suarez met with a Frenchman identified as "Mr. Senore" at the Clarridge Hotel on the Champs-Elysees in Paris.[69] The proposed heroin deal with Senore fell through, however, and in January, Suarez bought 100 half-kilogram packages of heroin from Gross and Widawski in East Berlin. Suarez in turn sold the heroin to Pena. Then in March 1969, Suarez bought 25 kilos of factory sealed heroin from Gross and Widawski at the Hotel Royal in Nice. The heroin was provided by a Frenchman, but Pena's customer in San Antonio, a Cuban named Jose, claimed it was bad and sent it back. Deep in debt and desperately needing a new customer, Suarez in January 1970 approached Montemayor, who had once been a chauffeur for the mayor of Mexico City. The introduction was made by the chief of the Mexican Judicial Police. Montemayor agreed to buy 50 kilograms of heroin.[70]

Suarez had a friend smuggle ten of the 50 kilos of factory sealed heroin to Montemayor in Laredo. In April he met Pena in Paris and bought 40 kilos of the same factory sealed heroin from Mr. Senore. Mr. Senore (in fact, Jean-Jacques Bunel-Gourdy) was in his fifties, spoke Spanish and French, and was accompanied by a hard to forget, four foot-ten-inch tall Italian. In May, Montemayor requested more heroin and while making that delivery Suarez was arrested at the Saint Anthony Hotel in San Antonio.[71]

All in all, Gross, Widawski and Goldenberg delivered 350 kilos of heroin to Suarez in East Berlin and Nice.[72] Suarez shipped much of the narcotics through a funeral parlor under a contract with the American Embassy. The caskets and cadavers of US citizens who had died in Mexico were packed with heroin. Suarez's accomplice in San Antonio, Luis Ortega Gomez, sold the dope to distributors in New York.[73]

Suarez was incarcerated at the Federal Correctional Institution at La Tuna, Texas, where he committed suicide in August 1971, precluding the successful prosecution of Widawski and Gross, who were suspected of being Mossad agents working with a corrupt Stasi general. Widawski retired in Lebanon. A Congressional investigation determined in 1973 that "elements of the East German Secret Police" were involved.[74]

The case studies presented in this chapter are only a hint of what is possible in the twilight zone where political espionage and international narcotic trafficking converge.

10

THE FIRST INFESTATIONS

DAVID R. WISER SERVED FOR two-and-a-half years on the CIA's Far East Asian desk before joining the FBN in April 1968. He was the last agent hired before it was reorganized within the BNDD. Joseph "Nickel Bag Joe" Arpaio hired him. Arpaio asked two questions during the interview. Was it true that Wiser had a degree in sociology? Wiser replied in the affirmative and Arpaio recoiled in horror. Then he asked, "Can you type?"[1]

Wiser could type and despite the stigma of sociology, was hired and assigned to the Washington, DC field office. A year later, in September 1969, Wiser was working at his desk when an elderly man walked up and introduced himself. The elderly man had been one of the first Afro-Americans on the DC police force in the mid-1940s. Segregation was the norm and the black cop had the misfortune of winning an alley fight with a few white men. It was unfortunate because the whites lodged a police brutality complaint against him. It was their word against his and he surely would have lost in court if it weren't for the fact that a "street person" witnessed the fight and testified on his behalf.

The old cop and the street person stayed in touch, even though the street person, Robert D. Williams, went into the heroin business in Washington, Philadelphia, and New York with (among others) Mafiosi

Joe Valachi, Joey Paradiso (murdered October 23, 1966, allegedly by an FBN agent) and Joey's brother Willie, an FBN informant.[2] Standing six-two and weighing two hundred and fifty pounds, Williams also had the distinction of either 1) having driven Frankie Waters to a meeting with Charlie McDonnell at La Guardia airport, or 2) having met Waters in the men's room afterwards by accident. As recounted in *Chapter 1*, Andy Tartaglino had wired McDonnell and was hoping Charlie Mac would get Frankie Black to incriminate himself. That didn't happen.

After the confrontation between Waters and McDonnell, Williams became concerned for his safety. Someone was shaking him down — he didn't tell the old cop whom — but he did say that Waters had met with some Italians from New York's Lower East Side on a boat on Long Island Sound to discuss whether or not Charlie Mac ought to be killed. According to Tom Tripodi the Italians were Frank and Joseph Malizia, intended recipients of French connection heroin in the Nebbia case who were under investigation by Frankie Waters.[3] The Malizias were at odds about what to do; one wanted to kill him, the other didn't. Waters cast the deciding vote in favor of Charlie Mac. He saved his life.

Wiser wrote up the old cop's statement and sent a copy to William J. Olivanti, the agent-in-charge of the Washington, DC field office. In early October, Olivanti instructed Wiser to set up a meeting at a safe place — Wiser selected a motel on New York Avenue — so that some people from headquarters could meet privately with Charlie McDonnell to discuss what Williams had said. On the day of the meeting Phil Smith and Inspector Robert Goe came to the Washington office. Smith was the BNDD's liaison to the Justice Department's drug task force in Washington and had managed the BNDD's first successful Title III wiretap case on Lawrence "Slippery" Jackson, a major Afro-American violator, and his Mafia associates Harry Tantillo and Carmine Palladino.

As the BNDD's expert on organized crime in the nation's capital, Smith had a legitimate investigative reason to meet with McDonnell — although he denied the meeting ever took place.[4] Inspector Robert Goe was at the meeting because someone had shown Williams a copy of his FBN file. The file had been obtained from the FBI, and only someone from the FBN or FBI could have acquired it. Wiser, however, had no reason to be there and was surprised when the senior agents invited him to join them. "They had Charlie Mac with them and we all go to the motel," Wiser recalled. "Right away Charlie starts turning back the clock. He made allegations of corruption about high-ranking people who were still around." Williams mentioned six people, including Gaffney, Durkin and Belk. Wiser wouldn't mention the other three names. "It was a very tense atmosphere," he continues. Then Smith and Goe left and that was the last Wiser heard about it — for two years.[5]

Chief inspector Pat Fuller and John Ingersoll also wanted to forget McDonnell's allegations about "high-ranking people who were still around." Gaffney was Ingersoll's special assistant on Mexico and the BNDD's liaison to the Defense Department. Belk was revered and in charge of criminal investigations. Bill Durkin ran the premier New York region. These three men were ranking members of the Purple Gang fraternity of FBN agents and, as recounted in Chapter 3, Andy Tartaglino in June 1969 had asked Inspector Goe to prepare a report on the Purple Gang conspiracy theory. And yet, despite the history, shortly after Smith and Goe met with McDonnell, chief inspector Pat Fuller and William J. Ryan at the Justice Department's narcotics and dangerous drugs unit dismissed the Purple Gang conspiracy theory as incredible.[6]

The issue would resurface six years later with a vengeance. In the meantime it simmered.

Dennis Hart's Gun

CHARLIE MCDONNELL CLAIMED THAT HE, Bill Durkin and FBN Agent John Dolce had, in 1956 in New York, shaken down a drug trafficker for $16,000, and had divvied up the money.[7] Andy Tartaglino knew about the allegation, as well as allegations made by Customs Agent David Ellis about Bill Durkin's activities in Mexico in 1964.[8] Ellis believed his allegations against Durkin and another agent in Mexico prompted the IRS to begin an investigation in 1965 of all agents in the FBN. The IRS investigation led to Tartaglino's purge of 1967-1968.[9] As of March 1969, Tartaglino was actively investigating Bill Durkin.[10]

Tartaglino's concerns about Durkin were further aroused in October 1969, concurrent with McDonnell's allegations, when informant Bobby Clemons was found under the Verrazano Bridge, with four bullets in his head.[11] Clemons, an informer for BNDD Agent Dennis Hart, was investigating two retired African-American soldiers turned drug smugglers. The former soldiers, Herman Jackson and

Leslie Atkinson, owned a bar in Bangkok and hired African-American enlisted men to smuggle heroin in their duffle bags from Bangkok and Saigon to military bases in the US.

In February 1969, informant Clemons had taken Agent Hart to an apartment in Queens, where Hart had arrested Atkinson's sister and brother-in-law for possession of 22 pounds of heroin. In August, as the case was being prepared for trial, Hart visited Atkinson in Goldsboro, North Carolina. Goldsboro is near four major military bases where Atkinson received and sold heroin. At this meeting, Atkinson agreed to pay Hart a $50,000 bribe. Two months later, Clemons, the only witness against Atkinson's in-laws, was murdered.[12]

Hart testified against Atkinson and Jackson at their trial, but his testimony was useless without corroboration from Clemons. The case was dismissed and the Atkinson-Jackson drug smuggling ring flourished. In December 1969, Hart resigned from the FBN and joined the Bureau of Alcohol, Tobacco and Firearms in Illinois. Bill Durkin got involved a few weeks later, when NYPD homicide detectives discovered that Clemons had been Hart's informant. They suspected Hart of murdering Clemons and asked Durkin to produce Hart's gun, so they could match it with the bullets.[13] When Durkin refused, Tartaglino's suspicions grew.

In December, Hart went to Goldsboro to collect the balance of his bribe from Atkinson. With him was his former partner, Richard Patch, who had resigned from the BNDD in May 1969. Patch had served with the FBN in Greensboro, North Carolina in the 1950s, had connections to officers at Fort Bragg, and had worked as a contract agent for the CIA.[14] BNDD inspectors arrested Hart and Patch in Goldsboro, and on February 27, 1970, the case made the front page of the *New York Times*. (The charges against Hart and erstwhile CIA agent Patch were dismissed after two mistrials.)[15] A follow-up article in the *Times* dated March 3, 1970, indicated that, despite Tartaglino's purge, the murder rate of federal narcotics informers was rising.[16]

This was bad news for John Ingersoll. Coupled with Detective Frank Serpico's revelations of corruption within the NYPD's narcotics unit, and statistics about rising drug addiction, the rash of informant murders prompted Mayor John Lindsay to form a five-member panel, the famous Knapp Commission, to investigate police corruption.[17] And Ingersoll resorted to an extraordinary measure that forever compromised the integrity of federal drug law enforcement.

Enter the CIA

JOHN INGERSOLL HAD LITTLE DESIRE to pursue agents accused of past wrongdoing by Charlie McDonnell. Andy Tartaglino, although motivated, was swamped with enforcement matters. That left the matter in the hands of chief inspector Pat Fuller, who was not about to spark an integrity investigation that would undermine his friend and patron saint.[18] Indeed, on January 23, 1970, Fuller wrote to Ingersoll saying that further investigation would not clarify the truth of McDonnell's allegation against Durkin.[19] On January 26, 1970, Inspector Paul Creamer wrote a memo saying, "Mr. Ingersoll indicated [the Durkin] investigation should be considered closed."[20]

Ingersoll's closing of the Durkin investigation was part of a pattern. In late 1968, Inspector Robert Goe had found enough evidence to warrant a full-scale investigation of the Purple Gang, but that never happened. And chief inspector Pat Fuller had let Tartaglino's 35 unresolved cases go stale, presumably at Ingersoll's insistence. Ingersoll obviously felt that he could not win the war on drugs while investigating the people he relied upon to wage it. But in April 1970 Mayor John Lindsay launched his investigation of the NYPD. The BNDD worked closely with the NYPD's narcotics squad and Special Investigations Unit (SIU), and any investigation of those outfits was bound to lead to the BNDD. Thus, according to the Rockefeller Commission Report of 1975, Ingersoll in 1970 suddenly became "vitally" concerned that some of his employees had been corrupted by drug traffickers.[21] Lacking the means to expunge these corrupt agents, the report said, he asked the Director of Central Intelligence, Richard Helms for help building a "counter-intelligence" capacity. The request was "apparently" supported by John Mitchell.

Ingersoll, of course, did have the means. He had merely to ask the FBI, which alone among federal agencies has an "internal security" mandate. What Ingersoll lacked was the will. He knew that several top BNND officials named by Charlie McDonnell, including Bill Durkin and George Belk, worked closely with the CIA. An FBI investigation into the BNDD would have opened a closet full of CIA skeletons, and neither Helms nor Ingersoll had any love for the FBI. Mitchell went along for the purely political purpose of avoiding a scandal that would impede Nixon's war on drugs.

The result was a super-secret program called Operation Twofold, which ostensibly involved the hiring of CIA officers into the BNDD to spy on top BNDD officials. As Fuller recalled, "We recruited the CIA officers for BNDD through a proprietary company. A corporation engaged in law enforcement hired three CIA officers posing as private businessmen to do the contact and interview work."[22]

The principle recruiter was Jerry Soul, assisted by CIA officers John F. Murnane and Chick Barquin. Then a personnel officer at CIA headquarters, Soul had managed Cuban exiles during the Bay of Pigs invasion, and later directed the CIA's exile-Cuban mercenary army and air force in the Congo. Soul worked closely with two recurring characters in this book, infamous CIA officers Theodore Shackley and Thomas Clines.[23]

The CIA agents interviewed for Operation Twofold were, typically, paramilitary officers whose careers had stalled due to the reduction of CIA forces in Vietnam and Laos. Those hired were put through the BNDD training course and assigned by Fuller to spy on a particular regional director and his trusted subordinates. No records were kept and, of the twenty-odd participants in Operation Twofold, some have not been identified. All were supposed to be sent overseas (Fred Dick was a primary target) but only a few actually were.[24]

Twofold remains a mystery because, as the Rockefeller Commission reported in 1975, it "violated the 1947 Act which prohibits the CIA's participation in law enforcement activities."[25]

No one was ever officially revealed or prosecuted.

Operation Twofold was also the first step in the CIA's infiltration and subordination of federal drug law enforcement.

Twofold Case Studies

TWOFOLD WAS AIMED AT THE BNDD's top managers. One target was Joseph J. Baca, the assistant RD in Los Angeles. The cousin of a top Mexican cop, Baca in July 1969 was charged by the New Mexico State Police with trafficking in drugs and stolen property.[26] He was accused of arranging burglaries and holdups, and allegedly sold heroin to a drug smuggler. But the local investigations were closed without any adverse action against Baca, so Charles "Chuck" Gutensohn was asked to investigate.

Chuck Gutensohn, a typical Twofold torpedo, had served with the Special Forces in South Vietnam.[27] He left the army in 1964, earned a college degree, and in 1968 joined the CIA. For the next two years, Gutensohn served in Pakse, Laos, one of the major drug transit points between the Golden Triangle and Saigon. Upon returning to the US,

Gutensohn was given the choice of being the CIA's liaison to the BNDD in Laos or joining Twofold. Gutensohn's brother Joel, also a Vietnam veteran, had joined the program six months earlier in Chicago, so Chuck joined too.

"After meeting with Jerry Soul," Gutensohn recalled, "I met Fuller at a hotel near Tyson's Corner. He said that when we communicated, I was to be known as Leo Adams for Los Angeles. He was to be Walter DeCarlo, for Washington, DC."

Fuller recruited Gutensohn and the other CIA officers because they did not have to be trained in the "tradecraft skills" required for the job. But Gutensohn's cover was blown before he got to Los Angeles. As he recalled, "Someone at headquarters was talking and everyone knew. About a month after I arrived, one of the agents said to me, "I hear that Pat Fuller signed your credentials."

A similar situation occurred in Miami, where Fuller's targets were RD Ben Theisen and Group Supervisor Pete Scrocca. Terry Burke, who would cap his career as the DEA's acting administrator in 1990, was one of the Twofold agents assigned to investigate Theisen and Scrocca.[28]

Burke's background is fascinating. He had met Tartaglino while serving as a Marine guard at the Rome embassy in 1957 and Tartaglino attended his wedding in Rome in 1959. Burke left the Marines with the goal of joining the FBN but ended up in the CIA instead. He served as a paramilitary officer in Laos from 1963-1965, working for legendary CIA officer Tony Poshepny at the 118A base near Ban Houei Sai — the epicenter of the Golden Triangle's opium and heroin trade. Burke received the CIA's highest award, the Intelligence Star, for gallantry in combat in Laos. He served his next tour in the Philippines and in 1969 was assigned to a dead-end job at CIA headquarters. Knowing his career had stalled, Burke contacted his friend from Italy, former FBN Agent Fred Cornetta. Then serving as the Customs agent in charge at Dulles airport, Cornetta persuaded Burke to join the BNDD.

Burke applied and in December 1970, Tartaglino hired him and sent him to Miami, where he was assigned to Pete Scrocca's group. According to Burke, Scrocca's face "turned white" when he found out that Tartaglino had hired him. But instead of spying on his new colleagues, Burke set about proving that he was tough and smart enough to work "undercover cases on bad guys with shotguns in motel rooms." Burke never sent any negative reports to Fuller, and Theisen and Scrocca eventually accepted him.[29]

Gutensohn and Burke's experiences were not unusual, and Two-fold never resulted in a single dismissal. The astonishing reason for this derives from the second of the "twofold" purposes of the operation, to be discussed in a subsequent chapter.

Bigger Problems

INGERSOLL'S STRATEGY FOR STEMMING CORRUPTION did not rely solely on Fuller's office of inspections, or the handful of CIA officers in his Twofold program. Ingersoll wanted to prevent corruption by eliminating the incentive to accept bribes. He felt the way to do this was by turning to highly paid informers to do the bulk of dangerous undercover work. To this end, Ingersoll in May 1970 obtained a $500,000 supplemental appropriations from Congress for informant payments. When told that some informants might receive $50,000 for a case, House Appropriations Chairman John J. Rooney was amazed and confounded.[30] He noted that the BNDD already spent an average of $18,000 per arrest, including kids busted with a couple of ounces of pot, and expressed profound dismay that the price was about to go up, while the number of arrests was going down.

BNDD agents would continue to work undercover on big domestic cases, like Operations Flanker and Eagle, and on promising small cases as well, but to a lesser and lesser extent. Old FBN agents like Durkin found it troubling that young agents were spending all their time on paperwork and going home at five o'clock. The rookies didn't know how to prowl the back alleys and bars after midnight, when the drug world came alive. The new breed needed experience on the street, so they could learn how to recognize and turn junkies into informants. But that meant getting your hands dirty, and Ingersoll wanted his agents clean.

Ingersoll's other problem was convincing his White House bosses that the systems approach was viable overseas. And that meant relying on the controlled delivery, which afforded corrupt agents and informants the opportunity to make vastly more money than ever before — which is why the CIA initially intended to send its Twofold shooflies overseas. One example suffices. When Agent Jack D. Compton arrived in Mexico in July 1970, he found that the BNDD "had a habit of running dope into the United States, past Customs."[31] Compton said that Jerry Strickler "flew it out of South America," and that [the dope] "went on the street." Compton was told that Strickler and RD Joe Arpaio were trying to "enhance the credibility of the undercover agent." But, he noted, there were never any arrests.

Compton added that, "it was known and encouraged" that agents go into Mexico and "smuggle the stuff back." It was done different ways and "known from the very top." But his complaints fell on deaf ears, because Ingersoll was in "very solid" with John Mitchell. "I sat in on some of the meetings where this was discussed: that they had nothing to worry about. This came out of Ingersoll's mouth," Compton said.[32]

Mounting controlled deliveries without notifying Customs, and allowing the dope "to walk," was symptomatic of the desperation of the BNDD's senior managers, as was their growing reliance on the CIA.

The Godfrey Report

BY EARLY 1970, CONGRESSMAN ROONEY and the White House were becoming impatient with the BNDD's failure to stop international drug trafficking. Blame was placed on its poor intelligence capabilities, and Ingersoll's response was predictable: he contacted DCI Richard Helms, who arranged for his recently retired chief of continuing intelligence, E. Drexel Godfrey, to lend Ingersoll a hand.[33]

In May 1970, Ingersoll formed an Intelligence Task Force under Godfrey to review BNDD operations and recommend the type of intelligence needed to improve them.[34] John Warner guided Godfrey during his inspection of BNDD headquarters and its regional offices. In October, Godfrey submitted a report recommending that: 1) BNDD create regional intelligence units to support the regional directors with tactical intelligence; 2) create an office of strategic intelligence reporting directly to Ingersoll for the purpose of responding to long-term goals; and 3) dismantle the "rigid" systems approach. Citing the AM-10 Chilean system, Godfrey said the systems approach was not conducive to discovering new narcotics networks.[35]

However, Ingersoll, Tartaglino and Belk were wedded to the systems approach, so Godfrey's third recommendation was summarily shelved. In a response to Warner about Godfrey's report, Tartaglino turned the tables and cited the AM-10 Chilean group as proof that the BNDD was not as Godfrey said, "locked in" to the nine major systems.[36] Tartaglino characterized Godfrey's assertion that Customs had discovered the Chilean network in 1968 as "questionable." He said investigative efforts in South America were being made "before this" and that the BNDD's effort "was made on considerably more intelligence input than the arrest of two couriers of a particular ethnic group."

With so many senior BNDD officials in an uproar, Ingersoll formed a Task Force to study the issue. The Task Force, composed of four senior staff officers, said in a December 1970 report that regional intelligence units (RIUs) and an office of strategic intelligence (SIO) were needed, as Godfrey suggested.[37] As a function of the well-developed enforcement division, the RIUs were easier to implement than an entirely new intelligence office, and in January 1971, all the regional directors were instructed to set up an RIU and assign an agent to head it.[38] The RD was to make sure the RIU knew everything about the region's operations in regard to assigned systems. He was to furnish the RIU with investigative reports, as well as access to all informant debriefings and criminal intelligence. The RIU would analyze all of this and report to the headquarters bosses in charge of criminal and compliance investigations. The RIU was also to be "the focal point of exchange of information" between BNDD task forces and DOJ strike forces in the region.

Many regional directors viewed the RIUs as an infringement on their sovereignty. Some went along grudgingly; others set up an RIU and then ignored it. Former CIA officers were often assigned to RIUs, prompting regular agents to view the units as repositories for secret Twofold inspectors. Women agents were often placed in RIUs, thus being assigned to one was something of an insult, except in New York where the RIU thrived as an integral part of Tony Pohl's International Division. The New York RIU soon consisted of 15 members from the various enforcement groups. Intelligence it gathered led to gambling halls in Chinatown and contributed to the realization that Southeast Asian traffickers were feeding the Mafia.

The Office of Strategic Intelligence (SIO) was also a fine idea, it just took longer to establish than the RIUs. Whereas the RIUs, under the control of regional directors, would remain in the enforcement division for the purpose of serving both criminal and compliance investigations, the SIO was a new center of power at headquarters. That terrified the enforcement bosses. Belk in particular wanted to know how strategic intelligence would complement tactical and operational intelligence. In plain terms: how would knowing the amount of opium grown in Pakistan help a BNDD agent know what apartment door to kick down in Albuquerque? Other officials, like William T. Ewell, a special assistant in the Office of Administration, doubted that other agencies would supply usable intelligence. Ewell in his report said, "In my experience, the CIA has always been the worst."[39]

But the SIO was not conceived as an enforcement tool. As John Warner explained, it was designed to help Ingersoll and other senior managers formulate plans and strategies "in the political sphere." According to John Warner, "Ingersoll felt he needed a clearer international perspective. The Heroin Committee was asking about production of opium worldwide, but our intelligence office consisted of two guys reading *High Times* magazine. There was a need for a strategic view on the production and transportation of heroin from Southeast Asia to the US, and we needed to understand the political climate in Thailand in order to address the production of illicit opium there. We needed to know what kind of protection the Thai police were affording traffickers. We were looking for an intelligence office that could deal with those sorts of issues, on the ground, overseas."

As Ingersoll's most trusted lieutenant, John Warner became the SIO's acting director and set about recruiting a deputy and desk officers for Latin America, the Near East and Europe, and the Far East. To enhance Warner's stature, Ingersoll arranged for Warner to sit on the US Intelligence Board, ostensibly to obtain intelligence from the CIA, though in reality the CIA took more than it gave. In order to exchange information with the CIA, the SIO would have to adopt the CIA's idiom and security procedures. The CIA assigned Officer Stanton Mintz to establish the SIO's own file room and computer system. The SIO would also have CIA analysts and a CIA statistician.[40]

Under Warner, the SIO would report directly to Ingersoll while the operational intelligence function at headquarters remained in the office of enforcement.[41] With the creation of the SIO, the Drug Control and Laboratory Operations Divisions also developed separate intelligence units and information systems. Lest intelligence become fragmented, a BNDD intelligence board was created with John Warner as its chairman. Through the SIO, headquarters would henceforth reach into field operations via the RIUs. To this end the SIO would establish a training program for analysts, often former CIA officers, not gun-toting BNDD agents, to staff the RIUs. In this way the CIA's influence would eventually alter the attitude of everyone in the BNDD. The specter of an intelligence unit packed with CIA agents wielding that much influence is another reason the SIO was slow getting off the ground.

False Starts

THE SIO WAS TO BE the BNDD's point of contact with the CIA and the intelligence community, and the job of writing up its enabling documents fell to former CIA agents Tom Tripodi (Tartaglino's man at the SIO) and Adrian Swain.

Swain's presence was indicative of the BNDD's focus on Southeast Asian affairs. A former FBI agent, Swain had spent four years as a contract officer with the CIA, first in South Vietnam, then for two years in opium-drenched Pakse, Laos. Through political contacts in the Justice Department, Swain was introduced to Warner's deputy, John Parker, who arranged his transfer to the BNDD in February 1971, while the SIO was being organized. Swain was surprised to discover that the BNDD office building was "in the midst of the District's pornography and neon-lit discotheque area."[42]

Swain was well-connected, and through his CIA contacts obtained maps of drug smuggling routes in Southeast Asia. In April 1971 he accompanied Ingersoll to Vietnam with the State Department's narcotics liaison officer, Harvey Wellman. They conferred with BNDD agents in Japan and Hong Kong, and in Saigon they met with Ambassador Bunker and President Thieu. Fred Dick briefed Ingersoll, as did CIA station chief Ted Shackley. Shackley "briefed Ingersoll on the personalities, politics, background, strengths, and weaknesses of a half-dozen South Vietnamese officers and civilian chiefs with whom Ingersoll was scheduled to meet."[43]

Next they went to Bangkok, then Chiang Mai, "the gateway to narcotics production," where RD William Wanzeck explained that the biggest dealer was warlord Chang Chi-Fu (aka Khun Sa) in Burma. Wanzeck explained that the Thai government had no control over his or anyone else's smuggling ventures. As if to hammer home Wanzeck's point, Thai officials announced Ingersoll's presence in Chiang Mai.[44] In Burma, Swain and Ingersoll met General Ne Win and his intelligence chief and obtained their permission to place CIA officer Terry Baldwin in Rangoon as the BNDD's narcotics liaison officer. Baldwin would join the DEA in 1973.[45]

Upon his return to Washington, Swain and Tom Tripodi drafted a memo recommending the expansion of the SIO. They said the systems approach was failing due to a lack of adequate and timely intelligence. They were also frustrated by the fact that BNDD agents could not make arrests overseas, and that the CIA had access to people capable of providing narcotics intelligence, but these people "… were involved in narcotics trafficking and the CIA did not want to identify them."[46] The CIA, for example, had an agent inside Khun Sa's pack mule caravan, but the BNDD only got sanitized reports about it.[47]

Tripodi and Swain recommended that a "special operations or strategic operations staff" function as the BNDD's own CIA, "using a backdoor approach to gather intelligence in support of operations." Those operations would rely on "longer range, deep penetration, clandestine assets, who remain undercover, do not appear during the course of any trial and are recruited and directed by the Special Operations agents on a covert basis."[48]

This was exactly what Belk and the other enforcement chiefs feared. Then on June 17, 1971, President Nixon gave a speech in which he declared that drug addiction was higher than imagined and had assumed the dimensions of a national emergency.[49] He described the drug traffic as "public enemy number one" and declared "a total offensive." Congress responded with the necessary funding for the SIO — and the type of operations Tripodi and Swain suggested.

"I'd sat on the [SIO] implementation committee for months with Tartaglino and Bill Coon," John Warner recalled, "but we couldn't get any resources. Then Nixon declared the war on drugs a matter of national security and CIA sends people and resources."[50]

The SIO was officially formed under Warner in July 1971. His assignment to this critical post reflected Ingersoll's desire to have a loyal subject managing political intelligence operations and liaison with the CIA. Warner replaced foreign intelligence chief John Parker (a former BDAC agent) on the Heroin Committee, and Parker became Warner's deputy, working closely with Jim Ludlum at the CIA. Warner, as noted, was assigned several officers from the CIA, along with several BNDD agents and State Department security officer Cyril "Bud" Frank. The first three CIA officers reported to Warner in September. They were George Oakey, Walter Mackem and John Bacon. SIO was divided into geographic sections: Oakey covered Europe and the Middle East; Mackem got the Far East; and Bacon had Latin America. Former BDAC Agent Richard Bly was brought on by John Parker to run the SIO's domestic intelligence unit. Bly's duties consisted largely of surveying hospitals and acquiring statistics on addicts.[51]

Tartaglino wanted some control over SIO and arranged for his trusted friend Tom Tripodi to be assigned as its chief of operations. Tripodi had spent six years working for the Special Operations Branch of the CIA's Security Research Services, where his duties were linked to the CIA's illegal domestic program, "Operation Chaos." His job included the penetration and surveillance of peace groups, and setting up private investigation firms to conduct illegal black bag jobs. Ironically, E. Howard Hunt inherited Tripodi's CIA Special Operations unit, which included some of the Watergate burglars.[52]

As SIO's operations chief, Tripodi liaised with the CIA, "on matters of mutual interest and the covert collection of narcotics intelligence outside of routine BNDD channels."[53] Tripodi was one of the Twofold Program's creators and had brought several CIA officers into it. He also enlisted CIA officers into the SIO to conduct specific operations. In one instance he asked CIA officer Rich Kobakoff to go to Turkey to blow up labs.[54] Then studying Arabic for an assignment in the Middle East, Kobakoff decided it was not possible to carry out the task and turned the job down. After the BNDD offered him a promotion, Kobakoff joined the SIO in April 1972 as a desk officer.

Tripodi also concocted an "extra-legal plan," in the process turning the SIO from a benign gatherer of strategic intelligence into a cover organization for mounting unconventional warfare operations.[55] Tripodi's Medusa Plan included, among other options: recruiting a Brazilian Army major to blow up contrabandista planes while they were refueling at clandestine strips; sending SIO agents to the Golden Triangle to place transmitters in heroin labs (located by CIA agents), and then call in Air Force bombers to blow them up; and for SIO agents to ambush drug traffickers and take their drugs and money! To obtain White House funding for these escapades, Ingersoll, Tripodi and Warner took the plan to Mitchell, who covered his ears and said, "I don't want to hear it. All I want is for you to just show me X's on the map." They eventually received White House funding and Justice Department approval for Medusa, but as Tripodi ruefully notes, the people at enforcement "eviscerated" his plan.[56]

It Takes a Thief

ALSO JOINING SIO WAS LEGENDARY CIA officer Lucien Conein. Books could be written about "Black Luigi" Conein, aka "Three-Fingered Lou."

A natural-born adventurer, Conein was born in America and joined the OSS at the start of World War II. According to one romantic legend, he parachuted behind enemy lines in France to form underground resistance cells composed of Corsicans to fight the Nazis. Some of Conein's Corsicans were gangsters, and the grateful "milieu" inducted Conein as an honorary member into their secret brotherhood, the Amicale Corse.

Richard "Dick" Bly worked with Conein and tells how he got his nickname, "Three-Fingered Lou." While behind enemy lines, Conein went to a bar for a few drinks with a pretty French girl. While he was inside, Nazis sympathizers cut the fan belt in his jeep. "Lou was juiced up with this woman," Bly explained "and she turned the engine over while he was poking around inside. Voila: 'Three-Fingered Lou'."

After the liberation of France, Conein served in Vietnam with the OSS. At the end of the war, he married a Vietnamese woman. He officially joined the CIA in 1954 and returned to South Vietnam to help General Edward Lansdale organize anti-communist forces in North Vietnam and displace the French in the South. Conein was a renowned master of "dirty tricks," such as staging fake funerals and filling the coffins with weapons for later use by the anti-communists.[57] He left Vietnam in 1958 and spent the next few years in the opium rich outlands of Iran as a military advisor to the Shah's Special Forces.[58] In 1962 he returned to Vietnam as a "floating emissary," reporting directly to the White House while secretly coaching the cabal of generals that murdered President Diem in November 1963. After the coup d'etat, Conein remained in South Vietnam until 1968, when, due to his drunken antics, the Far East Asian Division's chief, William Colby, fired him. Conein opened private (some say "pharmaceutical") businesses in Israel and South Vietnam, but without success.[59]

Watergate burglar E. Howard Hunt had served with Conein in the OSS in the Far East. Right after Hunt was hired by the White House to mount dirty tricks against its political enemies, he suggested to Egil Krogh that they hire Conein. Krogh conferred with Charles Colson and they hired Conein in July 1971. Conein's tasks were: 1) to help Hunt frame President Kennedy for the November 1963 assassination of South Vietnamese President Diem; 2) discredit Daniel Ellsberg, who had worked closely with Conein in Vietnam, for leaking the *Pentagon Papers*, and; 3) serve as an expert on Corsican drug traffickers in Southeast Asia.[60]

The White House needed a cover job for Conein, and Ingersoll complied. As SIO Director John Warner recalled, "Ingersoll said 'Krogh is sending Conein here, get him a job.'" Warner assigned Conein as a consultant to Walter Mackem, the Far East desk officer. CIA officer John Bacon was sitting beside Conein one fine day when Howard Hunt called. Bacon had worked for Hunt in Uruguay, and as

Bacon recalled, "Conein turned and said, "That goddamned Howard Hunt wants me to help him write letters about Kennedy!"[61] And on December 22, 1971, Conein did appear on an NBC documentary to discuss the contents of a cable forged by Hunt, implicating JFK in the Diem assassination.

According to Warner, the SIO was slow getting off the ground in part due to Krogh's meddling. Another problem was that Tartaglino had "no vision" and assigned Tom Tripodi as chief of operations. Tripodi's Medusa Plan obviously backfired and prompted more prudent BNDD officials to impede the SIO's growth.[62] Others say the problem was that Warner was a blowhard and not an intelligence expert. Bureaucratically he was no match for Tartaglino, Belk or Phil Smith. Those wily veterans had their own CIA connections and, according to Warner, they were only concerned with putting people in jail.

Belk, however, recognized the SIO's permanence and promise and in September 1971, when he became Assistant to the Director for International Affairs, he started leveling intelligence requirements on it.[63] At the same time Belk viewed the SIO as competition. Belk's close friend Phil Smith had been appointed head of the Office of Special Projects, and Belk started using Special Projects as a parallel intelligence organization. Through his own CIA connections, Belk, for example, obtained cameras for Special Project's nascent air wing. The CIA in turn used Special Projects for its own purposes. As Belk developed White House connections, his power grew even greater.

Another reason the SIO was slow getting off the ground, according to Jim Ludlum, was the CIA's reluctance to share intelligence.[64] But after Nixon's June 1971 declaration that the drug war was a national emergency, and the appointment of William Colby as the CIA's executive director, the CIA began helping BNDD agents in the field. The CIA provided false documents, helped make travel arrangements, and facilitated communications. The Agency also began to train suborned BNDD agents, most stationed overseas, in covert operations. Indeed, as George Corcoran, the Customs attaché in Paris reported to Myles Ambrose on June 18, 1971, Jack Cusack was outraged that the Paris regional office would henceforth be reporting to John Warner at SIO, and no longer to the Enforcement Division. As Corcoran noted, "this move will also encompass changing BNDD's approach overseas from primarily operational to one of greater emphasis on intelligence gathering."[65]

At this point, safes and steel doors were installed at BNDD head-quarters to protect CIA information, and witting agents were com-pelled to undergo background checks and acquire CIA security clearances — which meant swearing an oath to the CIA. Resentment grew as the CIA began mounting drug shipments into the US, apart from the BNDD, in order to identify recipients. "Individual stations allowed this," John Warner explained.

Federal narcotics agents had always helped the CIA, to the extent of providing safe houses for CIA drug testing and blackmail schemes, as well as recruiting Mafia and Corsican gangsters for CIA dirty work.[66] But the old timers drew the line at allowing drugs into the country. In 1950, for example, FBN Agent Charlie Siragusa refused when Tom Karamessines, then the CIA's station chief in Athens, suggested they mount a controlled delivery into America. Siragusa explained that, "The FBN could never knowingly allow two pounds of heroin to be delivered into the United States and be pushed to Mafia customers in the New York City area, even if in the long run we could seize a big-ger haul."[67]

But the rules changed under Ingersoll's reign. As Agent Bob DeFauw explained, "Our best informants were arms merchants, often quite wealthy and very influential. Some were bankers dealing in gold and diamonds too. They had tremendous political clout, and this is why narcotic agents were so valuable to the CIA: our sources were often their principal means of evaluating and corroborating informa-tion." It was a perfect match. "Like the CIA," DeFauw continues, "narcotic agents mount covert operations. We pose as members of the narcotics trade. The big difference is that we were in these for-eign countries legally. We were accepted by police agencies through-out the world, and through our police and intelligence sources, we could check out just about anyone or anything. Not only that, we were operational. So the CIA jumped in our stirrups." Meaning, as Fred Dick indicated earlier, that CIA agents posed as narcotics agents — or Customs agents, or big city narcotics detectives.[68]

The overarching problem of the CIA's infiltration of the BNDD was the potential for offensive counter-intelligence style "operations within operations." The influx of a politically indoctrinated CIA and military officers also made it easier for the White House to reach into the BNDD for illegal domestic spy operations. The CIA's infiltration of the BNDD, through Twofold and the SIO, also served its interests at a turning point in its history. FBI Director Hoover had severed relations with the Agency and the CIA found the BNDD a convenient place to enhance its domestic spying programs. It is no coincidence (as we shall see in the next chapter) that the infiltration began in earnest in June 1971, after the *New York Times* started publishing the *Pentagon Papers*.

11

ANGELS AND ARCHANGELS

ON MAY 27, 1971 THE House Foreign Affairs Committee issued a report titled "The World Heroin Problem." Referred to as the Murphy-Steele Report, it was the product of a three-week "special study mission" conducted in April 1971 by Congressmen Morgan F. Murphy (DIL) and Robert H. Steele (R-CT).[1] The report, notably, found fault with every aspect of White House foreign drug interdiction policy. In particular, it exposed the enormity of the illicit drug traffic emanating from the Golden Triangle, and drew a direct connection between the failure to honestly confront the issue of troop addiction and Nixon's failure to resolve the Vietnam War. The report stated that if efforts to stop the flow of illegal heroin into South Vietnam failed, "the only effective solution [to troop addiction in Vietnam] is withdrawal of all troops from the area."[2]

The Murphy-Steele Report had the intended effect. By June, Defense Secretary Melvin Laird had expressed his unhappiness with the South Vietnamese and on June 6,1971, the *New York Times* reported that the drug problem had accelerated the US troop withdrawal.[3]

Robert Steele was the impetus behind the Report. An intelligent, engaging man, Steele had served in the CIA from 1963 until 1965.[4] But there is no evidence that he was acting on behalf of the CIA when he co-wrote "The World Heroin Problem." By his own account, Steele did not learn that the South Vietnamese were supplying drugs to US troops until he was elected to Congress in 1970. That knowledge did, however, infuriate him. A member of the Foreign Affairs Committee, Steele convinced the chairman to let him mount a mission to study the problem. The Democrats in charge of the committee saw that they could score political points by bashing Nixon with more bad news about Vietnam, and so they agreed — as long as Steele operated under the guidance of Democratic Congressman Morgan Murphy. Murphy and Steele were accompanied by CIA officer Fred Flott and Dr. John J. Brady, Jr, a public health consultant.

Steele insists he had no hidden agenda. He simply wanted to know how drugs got from Turkey through Marseille to the US, and what could be done to stop drugs from reaching US soldiers in Vietnam. He never anticipated "the raw nerve" his report would touch.[5]

Steele's team, on the other hand, was briefed by BNDD agents in the US before it departed, as well as in every country it visited, and the BNDD had a very good idea of what would be revealed.[6] In France, BNDD agents told Steele that four men ran the drug business in Marseille: Dominic Venturi, Marcel Francisci, Antoine Guerini and Joseph Orsini.[7] Steele made sure to include their names in the report as a way of pressuring the French to mount serious operations in Marseille, where Venturi's contracting firm was renovating the town hall.[8] (Dominic, through his brother Jean, had been supplying Canadian and American traffickers since 1950.[9]) Steele also emphasized the importance of locating labs in and around Marseille.[10] Privately French officials scoffed, and explained that if Marseille were put out of business, labs would simply pop up elsewhere.

What the French said was true. In June 1971 the US gave $35 million to Turkey's military government to compensate opium farmers and entice them to reduce opium cultivation.[11] With this action, heroin conversion labs immediately started popping up along the Iranian border.[12] Iran had harsh penalties for traffickers, but members of the oligarchy owned vast opium plantations, so the Iranian government subsidized its Establishment opium lords by providing free heroin for 50,000 registered addicts.[13] This double standard encouraged trafficking by the protected few: in 1972, the Shah's sister was accused of smuggling heroin into France, and one of the Shah's aides was charged with smuggling opium into Geneva.[14]

A similar situation existed in Thailand, where CIA Station Chief Louis Lapham told Steele that Kuomintang drug-trafficking warlords were out of reach in Burma, and that top Thai officials were involved in trafficking.[15] What Lapham neglected to say was that the slippery CIA protected the KMT generals in Burma and complicit Thai officials because they, like the Shah of Iran, were fighting Communists.

Clearly, there were angels and archangels in the war on drugs. The angels were the protected traffickers; the archangels their benefactors behind the scenes. Steele recognized the overarching fact that powerful Americans were protecting drug-dealing Vietnamese officials, while America's drug-addicted, demoralized fighting machine was breaking down. His response was to hold a press conference and tell how he ventured into the streets of Saigon and bought a vial of heroin from a six-year-old girl.[16] Steele offered the vial as evidence, and gained fame as the first official to tell the American public the truth. John Ingersoll could have had that distinction. Instead, having joined forces with the CIA, he was relegated to the sidelines. "I watched Ingersoll age, day by day," Steele said sympathetically. "He would call me on the plane. But we shined a spotlight on the problem. We created a crescendo of support."

The Murphy-Steele Report forced the military to start treating drug-addicted soldiers in South Vietnam and elsewhere around the world. He also recommended "That substantial new funds be made available to the BNDD," and more money was quickly forthcoming.[17] But Steele's success earned him powerful right-wing enemies, for crippling "the war effort."[18] Seeking redemption, he agreed to say in his final report 1) that the survey team had exaggerated the percentage of addicted troops in Vietnam; 2) that around 875 African-American deserters in Saigon, with police protection, were the biggest problem; and 3) that China was a source country.[19] No top Vietnamese generals or politicians were ever tried and convicted of drug smuggling. Their names, however, were widely published — which made it easier to sell those fallen angels down the river.[20]

Indeed, the Murphy-Steele Report proved a blessing in disguise for Nixon. A few weeks before the report was issued, the Chinese suggested normalizing relations with the US. Nixon and Kissinger seized the opportunity and by July, Kissinger was playing "the China card" as a way of transforming America's ignominious defeat in Vietnam into a diplomatic success of historical proportions. The China-card gambit had the added advantage of dovetailing neatly with the policy of Vietnamization — of gradually withdrawing US forces and turning the war over to the hapless South Vietnamese. Indeed, once the initial shock was over, the White House happily used the Murphy-Steele Report to stigmatize its Vietnamese allies as corrupt drug-smuggling warlords.

The Mysterious White House Meeting

THE MURPHY-STEELE REPORT ARRIVED LIKE a suicide bomber at the White House and forced the Nixon administration to re-think its position. Indeed, on May 27, 1971, the day the report was issued, Ehrlichman and Krogh met in the Oval Office with Nixon, Kissinger and a parade of experts to discuss new actions in the war on drugs.[21] Donald H. Rumsfeld, back from a survey of military bases in Europe, pressed for a $110 million supplemental appropriation; half for enforcement, and half to establish an office to address the problems of demand. This recommendation formed the basis of the White House's new strategy for fighting the war on drugs.[22] Contrary to whatever fantasies the BNDD may have entertained while helping Steele, this new White House strategy took the matter of foreign enforcement out of Ingersoll's hands and kicked it into the realm of the NSC, State Department, and CIA.

On the demand side, Dr. Jerome H. Jaffe, a Chicago psychiatrist, was selected to head the Special Action Office for Drug Abuse Prevention (SAODAP) in the Department of Health, Education and Welfare.[23] Jaffe's program set up methadone rehabilitation centers for addicts, most of whom had been processed through the criminal justice system. SAODAP stressed prevention through urinalysis, education and research. Jaffe formed the National Institute of Drug Abuse and promoted a methadone maintenance program for addicts. A marijuana commission would be formed in 1972 to study the liberal notion of decriminalizing marijuana, and legislation resulting in the 1972 Drug Abuse and Treatment Act was initiated to address the problem of demand.

The May 27, 1971 Oval Office meeting featured an appearance by Henry Kissinger. Few if any historians have delved into Kissinger's narcotics policy, but that auspicious day he presented a $120 million proposal drafted by NSC staffer Arthur T. Downey.[24] This money was, very likely, the source of a huge covert action anti-drug program with a nefarious domestic spying aspect, for immediately following Kissinger's presentation, the meeting turned to the issue of plugging leaks by Nixon's enemies.[25] Columnist Jack Anderson and DCI Richard

Helms topped the list. IRS audits and Justice Department wiretaps by Internal Security chief Robert Mardian were initiated against the usual suspects. The words "political enemies" were emphasized. To address the problem, it was decided that Lt. General Vernon A. Walters would become Helms' deputy at the CIA. Next to Walter's name was the word "conspiracy," implying that his job was to find out who in the CIA was conspiring against Nixon. Actions considered against Anderson would be more extreme.[26]

This direct connection between drug policy and internal security raises the question of how the millions of dollars Kissinger proposed for drug law enforcement was used. According to Edward J. Epstein, Nixon approved a chunk for "clandestine activities" aimed at "destroying or immobilizing the highest level of drug traffickers."[27] Epstein cites Krogh as saying the fund would be used for "underworld contacts and disruptive tactics," like the kind presented in Tripodi's Medusa Plan.

Epstein also claims that Ingersoll presented a memo (perhaps the Medusa Plan) to Krogh, which went under Ehrlichman's signature to Nixon on May 27 with a plan for "clandestine law enforcement." The program was to be funded "along the lines of the CIA" so that only a few Congressmen would know.[28] The minutes of the meeting indicate that $50 million was to go to Ingersoll, who claims the money never went to him and was possibly some sort of "slush fund."[29]

Jeffrey Donfeld, a member of Krogh's staff whom Epstein credits with composing the memo on clandestine law enforcement, allegedly said that assassination was "a very definite part of the plan."[30] According to Epstein, Gordon Liddy, then a drug policy advisor at the Domestic Council, convinced Krogh that assassination of top drug traffickers was the answer to all their problems.[31] Assassination may also have been viewed as the answer to some of Nixon's political problems, for within two months, Howard Hunt and Liddy were contemplating killing Jack Anderson (by rubbing LSD obtained from the CIA on his car's steering wheel) for (among other things) leaking information about drug lord Moises Torrijos, brother of the president of Panama.

According to Epstein, the CIA reported "that there were only a handful of kingpin traffickers in Latin America, who could be eliminated very swiftly."[32] At this point, Epstein adds, Howard Hunt "approached the Cuban exile leader Manuel Artime [and] asked him about the possibility of forming a team of Cuban-exile hit men to

assassinate Latin American traffickers still operating outside the baili-
wick of United States law."[33]

Although assassinations probably were employed, killing drug traffickers did nothing to disrupt the Latin American connection. According to Agent Tony Pohl, the South Americans did not want to rely on
French traffickers. They wanted to build and manage their own heroin
labs. However, they failed to do so, as the raw material remained under
French control. "So they diversified a little bit in pot," Pohl explained,
"but very quickly they switched to cocaine for which they had the raw
material, the knowledge, the territory and the "infrastructure." They
had learned how to keep control of their operations from the Mafia
and the French controllers. The rest of the story is public knowledge,
but when this was first projected by Special Operations, people were
skeptical about the South Americans (Latinos) being able to make that
happen."[34]

The murderous Cocaine Wars of the 1970s and 80s would make
everyone believers.

The Cabinet Committee for International Narcotics Control

PERHAPS THE MOST SIGNIFICANT DEVELOPMENT stemming from the
May 27, 1971 meeting was the decision to give the State Department
a lead role in foreign operations. To this end the White House named
Nelson Gross, chairman of the Republican Party in New Jersey, as an
assistant secretary of state and told him, "to lead a worldwide attack
on drugs."[35] In September, Krogh's Heroin Committee was reorganized as the Cabinet Committee for International Narcotics Control
(CCINC) under the chairmanship of Secretary of State William Rogers. Its mandate was to "set policies which relate international considerations to domestic considerations." In practical terms, that meant
making drugs scarcer, more expensive, and more dangerous to buy.

The formation of CCINC elevated the management of international drug operations to the cabinet level. Krogh was its executive
secretary, Geoffrey Sheppard its chief of staff, and a young army lieutenant, Walter Minnick, its staff director. Assigned on Labor Day to
Room 16 in the Executive Office Building, where the Plumbers were
assembling, Minnick was a Harvard grad with no drug enforcement
experience. What he had was determination and a fierce loyalty to
Krogh and his conservative views.[36]

"CCINC membership existed at two levels," Minnick explained.
"The top level consisted of cabinet appointees who participated to

varying degrees." Kissinger and Defense Secretary Laird had little interest. DCI Richard Helms and William Rogers took a greater interest, as did the Departments of Agriculture (which was involved with crop substitution and eradication programs), Treasury and Justice. CCINC member George H.W. Bush, Nixon's ambassador to the UN, tried to persuade foreign governments to join the war on drugs.[37]

"Treasury and Justice each sent a representative," Minnick continues, "and were represented twice, in so far as Ingersoll attended from the BNDD, and Ambrose from Customs." All in all, CCINC had 24 departments and agencies represented on it. "There were only three or four choreographed meetings when Cabinet level members attended," Minnick explained, "and these were for ratifying programs worked up at the task force level. The second tier, composed of staff aides, is where the action took place."

As chair of the coordinating committee, Minnick passed along Krogh's instructions, oversaw international programs, and got involved in overseas operations. At Minnick's urging, CCINC had the US embassy in each source country assign a Narcotics Control Officer (NCO) to create an action plan. By mid-1973, some sixty countries had been selected for Narcotics Control Action Plans.[38] NCOs generally came from State, the CIA, the military, or the BNDD. Nelson Gross chaired the Working Group and managed the NCO program. The NSA helped with phone taps, and by placing undercover agents in telegraph companies overseas.

Gross's Working Group featured five regional sub-committees. "We had a plan for every country, managed out of the sub-committee for that region," Minnick explained. CIA officer Richard Welch and BNDD Agent Jerry Strickler were prominent on the South American committee. Gordon Liddy worked with CIA officer Tom Lawlor and BNDD Agent Howard Safir on Southeast Asia affairs. India, Turkey, Pakistan and Iran were primary in the Middle East. Germany, Holland and France were the focus in Europe. The Working Group had an enforcement sub-committee chaired by George Belk (who'd been in the business 23 years — Minnick for 23 days) and an intelligence sub-committee chaired by CIA officer Jim Ludlum. Army counterintelligence officer Werner Michel represented the military's interests on the intelligence sub-committee. The military's interests were substantial, in so far as the CCINC staff was detailed to the Pentagon to reduce White House costs.[39]

AID controlled CCINC's initial $42.5 million budget. But AID didn't want to pay for helicopters for drug operations in Southeast Asia, on the assumption that Asian governments would use them to suppress their political opposition. So Krogh and Minnick worked with the OMB to pass CCINC finances to Minnick. By 1975, the budget amounted to $875 million.[40]

CCINC's priorities were shutting down the French connection and the flow of drugs from the Golden Triangle to US servicemen in Vietnam. It tried to do this by convincing ambassadors and CIA station chiefs to pressure host governments to comply with US policy, often as part of trade agreements. In Panama, the return of the Canal was used as leverage. Some ambassadors, like Daniel Moynihan in India, were eager to provide people and resources. It was harder in Laos, where Ambassador William H. Sullivan wouldn't let Gross in the country![41]

Gross had more success with Counsel Clyde McAvoy in Burma. Through CIA officer Terry Baldwin and his informant net, McAvoy knew where the poppy fields and heroin factories were located, and provided intelligence on CIA-supported KMT generals involved in the drug trade.[42] But, according to Minnick, the CIA "would never" tell where it was conducting its anti-drug operations. So CCINC tried to pressure the CIA. "Krogh was just back from Vietnam with Ehrlichman and was energized," Minnick explained. "Our view was to get CIA involved in Laos, Cambodia, Burma and Thailand." Jim Ludlum was the key player, for he could reach into stations and bring people over to Minnick's side. The problem, according to Minnick, was that the CIA had a conflict of interest. It had to reconcile winning the Vietnam War and winning the war on drugs. The higher priority was winning in Vietnam, so it reorganized its narcotics unit under a new chief.

To this end, CIA officers Jim Ludlum, Jim Anderson and Tom Lawlor composed a two-page charter transferring responsibility from Angleton's office of counter-intelligence to Deputy Director Tom Karamessines and the CIA's Department of Plans. As Ludlum explained, at this point "narcotics became an agency-wide effort ... with the DDP in the forefront." Ludlum became "the requirements man" with the job of getting CIA intelligence analysts to work with CCINC and the SIO.[43] But the CIA continued to play a double game and, according to Minnick, the military "carried the ball until the creation of the DEA [in July 1973]."

CCINC and the BNDD

JOHN INGERSOLL DESCRIBED THE CCINC as a "powerful negative force" that diminished the BNDD. SIO Director John Warner claims it turned Krogh from a BNDD supporter into "a megalomaniac who decided to wage the war on drugs on his own."[44]

Krogh was already angry with Ingersoll for over-estimating the number of addicts. According to Epstein, Krogh resolved the problem, "by ordering that all press statements and public speeches on narcotics be coordinated and cleared by his office."[45] Krogh named NBC correspondent Richard Harkness as his press coordinator for matters concerning drug abuse.[46] He also began to push Ingersoll to abandon the systems approach and make more street level arrests. But Ingersoll continued to enjoy Mitchell's support, and his systems approach remained - for the moment.

Mitchell, however, was slated to head Nixon's 1972 re-election campaign, so Ingersoll started looking for a new patron. He found one in William Colby, who returned to CIA headquarters from South Vietnam in the fall of 1971 as its executive director. The introduction was made by Dr. Richard Blum, a liberal, social scientist friend of Ingersoll's from their days together in "the Cell."[47] Blum, who had been serving on the BNDD's scientific advisory board, introduced Ingersoll to Colby, thus initiating one of the BNDD's most significant relationships. Besieged by Krogh's endless demands, Ingersoll turned to Blum and Colby for ideas.

Helms had helped Ingersoll in a number of ways; by providing agents for the Twofold shoofly program, the SIO, and the liaison unit to Strickler in Latin America. But Helms, unlike Colby, had no use for the BNDD. Nixon had ordered Helms to lend a hand. Colby, however, saw the war on dugs as a growth industry and a place to put excess officers from the Far East Division. He needed Ingersoll, and courted his affections. Under Colby, CIA and BNDD statistics on opium production were squared up and the agencies enjoyed closer cooperation.

Helms saw CIA involvement in drug law enforcement as a liability, and Krogh and the White House Plumbers would prove him right.

Al McCoy's Big Adventure

BY LEAKING THE *PENTAGON PAPERS*, Daniel Ellsberg caused Richard Nixon some restless nights. The president lay awake thinking of nothing but revenge — which is one reason the White House hired Lou

Conein and hid him in the BNDD's Office of Strategic Intelligence..
As mentioned in the previous chapter, one of Conein's jobs was to
help discredit Ellsberg.

Conein had met Ellsberg in 1965 in Vietnam. Then a pro-war
"hawk," Ellsberg on behalf of the Department of Defense monitored several experimental CIA "revolutionary development" programs managed by CIA General Edward Lansdale. Conein was one
of Lansdale's advisors, and in that capacity introduced Ellsberg to the
exciting world of paramilitary operations. Ellsberg and Conein went
on counter-terror "snatch and snuff" operations together, drank and
womanized together, and bonded as only comrades in arms can. Their
swashbuckling adventures were the stuff of legend. On one memora-
ble occasion, Conein, by his account, prevented an opium-addicted
Corsican drug smuggler, Michel Seguin, from murdering Ellsberg,
who was romancing Seguin's beautiful fiancée Germaine.[48]

According to Professor Alfred W. McCoy, Conein at the time was
also negotiating a "truce" with Corsican drug traffickers in Saigon.[49]
The truce allowed the Corsicans to continue smuggling drugs, in
exchange for spying for the CIA. Michel Seguin was one of these protected Corsicans, who were connected to various Chinese gangsters,
Laotian officials and, allegedly, General Nguyen Cao Ky's drug ring
in South Vietnam.

If McCoy is right, this truce between the CIA and the drug-
trafficking Corsicans in Saigon advanced the interests of the Far East
facet of the French connection. Conein, however, denied that his
meeting with the Corsicans concerned drugs; its sole purpose, he said,
was "ameliorating a tense situation engendered by Daniel Ellsberg's
peccadilloes with the mistress of a Corsican."[50] Ellsberg admitted that
Seguin put a gun to his head and warned him to stay away from Germaine, but denied that Conein intervened on his behalf. Ellsberg also
denied that General Lansdale and Conein were involved with Corsican drug smugglers.[51]

It's impossible to prove which of these conflicting stories is true.
What's provable is that, in the fall of 1970, inspired by beat poet
Allen Ginsberg, Yale graduate student Al McCoy decided to write a
book about drug trafficking. He did his preliminary research and in
March 1971 traveled to Paris to meet SDECE officer General Mau-
rice Belleux. Belleux had been involved in "Operation X," in which
French Special Forces moved opium from Laos to Saigon for sale on
the open market as a way of financing the French counter-insurgency

in Vietnam. When Belleux told McCoy that the CIA had inherited the Operation X network, McCoy decided to go to Southeast Asia to check it out.[52]

In May 1971, former CIA officer Tom Tripodi, then organizing the SIO at the BNDD, was assigned to help McCoy. They dispute the extent of this help: Tripodi said it was a lot; McCoy says it was minimal.[53] The point is that the BNDD did help McCoy, and he does cite interviews with BNDD agents in his book. This help must be viewed in the context of the BNDD's conflicted relationship with the CIA, and the need to advance its self-interests.

Before heading overseas in the summer of 1971, McCoy also interviewed CIA officers Ed Lansdale and Lou Conein, who "told stories about drug trafficking in Saigon by the French, the Corsicans, and the intimates of President Ngo Dinh Diem."[54] They must have done this to advance the interests of the CIA, and when McCoy landed in Saigon he was given access to a US Army CID report that indeed served the CIA's interests. The report indicated that General Ngu Dzu, a candidate in the up-coming presidential election, was trafficking heroin with Chinese racketeers and Vietnamese generals.[55] A few months earlier Congressman Steele had accused General Dzu, a nationalist opposed to President Thieu and the CIA, of being one of the chief heroin traffickers in South Vietnam.

When Fred Dick made the same charges about the South Vietnamese military a year earlier, he was accused of trying to topple the government. But by the summer of 1971, the truth was tumbling out, albeit in a carefully guarded way. Indeed, leads given to McCoy led him to conclude that General Nguyen Cao Ky, and Ky's follower Colonel Phan Phung Tien, commander of the 5th Air Transport Wing, were at the center of one of South Vietnam's major drug smuggling operations.[56] Ky had long been on the CIA's payroll, and almost certainly was involved in drug trafficking. But by 1968 he had fallen into disfavor with the Agency.[57] McCoy reported police officials as saying that Tien was "close to some of the most powerful Corsican underworld figures," and was "a central figure in Vietnam's narcotics traffic."[58]

McCoy was certainly being used by the BNDD and the CIA, and both organizations were pleased as long as he constrained himself to fingering Vietnamese on the CIA's hit list. But when McCoy tracked the CIA connection back to its source in Laos, the CIA took exception. As McCoy discovered, the CIA would stop supplying rice to

Lao chieftains when they stopped providing their young men to fight the communists. That's when the CIA took a few warning shots at McCoy.[59] The BNDD, on the other hand, was pleased with McCoy's discoveries, and perhaps coincidentally, was allowed to open an office in Laos that fall.

As noted in Chapter 7, BNDD agents in November 1971 arrested Domingo S. Canieso, attaché at the Philippine Embassy in Laos, with 20 kilos of heroin in a New York hotel. This is curious, as McCoy had just visited the Philippines, where he met Norma "Silky" Sullivan, an associate of the infamous Sergeant Wooldridge (see Chapter 6) and numerous Mafia and Corsicans drug traffickers. Silky referred McCoy to a Hungarian, Lars "Da" Bugatti, living in Paris. With this particular tip the circle was closed, for the BNDD had in September identified Bugatti as a trafficker with ties to the Corsicans. The BNDD knew about Bugatti from a letter written by French drug trafficker Jean Marie Le Rouzic, and sent to a Sûreté police officer in Nice on May 15, 1971.[60] Le Rouzic's letter described the same Corsican network McCoy outlined in his book, with some very important additions. One short day after meeting Norma, McCoy landed in Paris and confronted Bugatti. Bugatti denied the allegations and threatened McCoy.[61] McCoy wrapped up his investigation and published his book in 1972. But much of the CIA's Corsican connection in Southeast Asia remained to be uncovered.

Le Rouzic's Revelations

LE ROUZIC'S LETTER TO THE Sûreté police officer is worth an appendix. In it he explained that Bugatti, "a former Nazi officer" and "occasional Vientiane resident," was employed by the Americans. He said that Bugatti arranged shipments for large quantities of drugs belonging to Camille Perez and Ralph Smok (Ange Simonpierri) with the help of American pilots and mercenaries in Vientiane and Bangkok.[62]

Among his many other revelations, Le Rouzic said that Henri Flamant of the Laos Air Charter Society handled most shipments from Laos to Marseille. Flamant worked with Pierre Segui and Nguyen Van Thoai, the former Vietnamese attaché in Vientiane, and later its information officer in Bangkok, as part of the Bugatti team. By 1973, Segui and many of the Corsicans mentioned in Le Rouzic's report were working for the BNDD. Le Rouzic noted that Roger Zoile, the manager of the Laos Air Charter Society was, like Bugatti, an American agent who arranged transportation of narcotics by US pilots at Udorn airbase, a CIA facility in Thailand, to Hong Kong. Zoile was named by McCoy, but not as an American agent. Zoile and Segui were connected to General Ky's operation in Pakse, Laos, the site of a major CIA base.[63]

Le Rouzic mentioned Mr. Danis, an employee of the Royal Air Lao Company who arranged transportation of opium to the Gulf of Siam, where it was dropped near waiting boats. This group had the approbation of a Thai minister working for CIA General Vang Pao's Xieng Khnong Air Transport Society in Long Tieng. Le Rouzic cited Vang Pao's relationship with Mr Gorce, an American co-pilot for the CIC station in Saigon. Yvon Flairat, formerly of Aigle-Azure Society in the Far East, who dropped opium in Ban Me Thuot, Vietnam, was part of this operation.

Le Rouzic suggested that the "present ambassador of Laos in France" be put on the BNDD blacklist. On April 26, 1971, the ambassador, Prince Sopsaisana from the same "Plain de Jars" area of Laos as Vang Pao, was arrested in Paris carrying 60 kilos of heroin, which according to the BNDD had been manufactured at Vang Pao's factory at the CIA outpost in Long Tieng. McCoy, unaware that Operation X Corsicans were passing from the CIA to the BNDD, suggested that the ambassador was set up.[64] He apparently didn't know that it was Corsican informants who did the dirty deed.

Le Rouzic also told how a team of Frenchmen under CIA-asset Michel Theodas smuggled heroin from Laos to Saigon, Hong Kong and France. The heroin was provided by Heng Tung, a CIA-protected Chinese national in Vientiane, and smuggled in the luggage of Prime Minister Souvana Phuoma, a "neutralist" connected to the Chinese. He also explained how a Chinese trafficker from Shanghai supplied Air America and Continental Air customers in Vientiane, and how a Chinese chemist enjoyed the protection of the President of the Lao National Assembly, while "working closely with the Americans" and "members of the Chinese Communist network."[65]

The above revelations point clearly to a CIA counter-intelligence operation that used, with the help of the BNDD, Corsican drug smuggling networks to identify Soviet and Communist Chinese agents. This final revelation of Le Rouzic's shows that the CIA and BNDD reached a *modus vivendi*, in which the archangel CIA maintained control of its Corsican informants and traffickers, while sharing them with the BNDD, and in this way controlled, who was targeted.

As noted, McCoy finished his manuscript in the spring of 1972. It was presented to the CIA for prior review, but published without changes. While embarrassing to the CIA, it did not name or lead to the indictment of any CIA officers.

The Mafia

INGERSOLL FELT THE CCINC DIMINISHED the BNDD's stature; but it was he, personally, not the agents who felt that way. Prior to Nixon declaring the war on drugs a "national emergency," BNDD agents were at the bottom of the diplomatic corps. With the CCINC, everything changed. Once the CIA started sharing informants and State started sending narcotics reporting officers to coordinate the war on drugs, the BNDD became successful and glamorous. "We got press coverage, space in embassies, and helicopters," one agent recalled. "Even the NSA cooperated by intercepting calls."

According to Jerry Strickler, "This was the time when we just grabbed them." During this period, he added, the BNDD engaged in "wet work [assassination] ... things better left unsaid."[66]

After Nixon directed each embassy to create a strategy, Strickler started working with Foreign Service Officer George Lister. Lister helped to the extent that he would by-pass Kissinger's NSC and ambassadors and go directly to foreign officials to set up major traffickers. In one case engineered by Lister, BNDD Agent Bert Moreno persuaded his cousin, the deputy attorney general in Mexico, to set up Italian Mafia trafficker Giuseppe Catania in Mexico. Lister sent a cable to the American embassy in Mexico saying Catania was as important as Auguste Ricord, and that it should assist the BNDD. Krogh at the White House situation room saw Lister's cable. Krogh called the CIA, and the CIA called Strickler and asked if Catania was really that important.

He was, and he was more accessible in Mexico than Italy, where Mafia angels were flourishing while the BNDD was obsessed with the French connection. Sicily was virtually off-limits. Gaetano Badalamenti was among the primary Italian targets, often supplying the heroin that Tom Buscetta provided, through Catania, to Mafiosi in Montreal and New York including Guido Penosi and the Salerno brothers of the Eboli organization. Other major Italian traffickers included Luigi Greco, Genco Russo, Salvatore Riina, and Stefano Bontade.[67]

The Mafia itself had heroin and hashish sources in the Middle East, of whom legendary Omar Makkouk was the most enduring.

Heading up BNDD investigations in the Middle East was Agent Alan McClain in Beirut, the region's money-laundering center. According to McClain, the breakthrough came when the BNDD, working with the general investigations section of Lebanon's Judiciary Police, intercepted a courier moving from the Middle East through Aruba to Miami. The courier revealed seven interrelated networks, and named "Omar" in Damascus as the brain behind the operation.[68]

The ring also had transportation routes through Canada and Mexico. The Canadian connection surfaced in May 1971 with a seizure at Dorval airport and the arrest of a Syrian cop. Many more arrests ensued and in November 1971, the BNDD tracked the ring to a group of Lebanese priests in Pittsburgh. From there the investigation expanded to Houston, Albuquerque and El Paso (where attorney Lee Chagra was implicated) to the Salernos in New York and Caesar's Palace in Las Vegas, and finally to Luigi Greco in Italy. Called Operation Sandstorm, the investigation led to the expansion of BNDD efforts into Mexico, Central America and North and Central Africa.[69]

The Politics of Turkey

IN JANUARY 1971, ANKARA BECAME regional headquarters for the BNDD's Middle Eastern operations. Two months later the Turkish military toppled the elected government. The Counter-Guerrilla Center in Istanbul, composed of an ultra-nationalist terrorist militia advised by CIA officers Henry Schardt and Duane "Dewey" Clarridge, provoked the coup by warning of an imaginary Leftist insurrection and instigating a series of murders and bombings of government buildings. After the military took power, this militia, guided by the CIA and Turkish security forces, started murdering suspected subversives, Leftists, and trade union leaders thought to be under Soviet influence.[70]

In June, Agent Frank Briggs became the BNDD regional director in Ankara. That same month the multi-million dollar AID package kicked in and Ingersoll sent six agents on temporary assignment duty (TDY) to Turkey to help verify that the Turks were not growing opium.[71] Partnered with Turkish police officers, they were supposed to travel on busses to opium growing areas to do surveys and engage in enforcement activities. But most sat in the American embassy and twiddled their thumbs while the ultra-nationalists battled Leftists on the blazing streets. The portion of the AID package earmarked for enforcement came in the form of materiel, not money. Dick Salmi, the agent-in-charge in Istanbul, said "It was ridiculous. "We got guns but no bullets; cars but no gas; flashlights but no batteries; cameras but no film."

The BNDD's real enforcement success came as a result of the friendship, forged in 1968, between Salmi and the aforementioned Dewey Clarridge, CIA liaison to the Counter-Guerilla Center with its terrorist Gray Wolves unit. As Salmi notes, he and Clarridge established personal trust. "When I asked for a flash roll [money]," he recalled, "Dewey would give it."[72]

In 1971, CIA headquarters directed Clarridge to officially join the war on drugs. "With Dewey it was informal," Salmi adds. "He didn't know what to say in his reports, so I told him." Salmi provided information on major crime families, trends, and analysis. In exchange, Clarridge gave Salmi a list of airstrips, shipping companies, and political figures the CIA knew to be involved in drug trafficking. Clarridge was interested in how arms traffickers were smuggling guns to the ever- rebellious Kurds in Western Turkey. Salmi knew that the gun runners worked with Turkish, Iranian, Syrian and Jordanian traffickers, and he knew which Israelis (ever instigating trouble in Muslim nations) were facilitating shipments from Iran to selected Kurdish insurgents. Using the information gathered and provided by Salmi, Clarridge shined at Langley.

In Istanbul, Clarridge and Salmi discovered some startling information about Bulgaria. Through a defector, Clarridge learned that the Bulgarian Secret Service, at the behest of the KGB, was facilitating the gun and drug smuggling activities of Turkish crime families through a Bulgarian tourist agency named Kintex.[73] Salmi obtained further information about complicit Bulgarian spies from his Interpol contacts. Clarridge helped Salmi investigate and together they were able to chart the flow of Turkish drugs west, through Bulgaria to France Germany, Italy, and east into Afghanistan and Iran. Nothing, however, came of their efforts to implicate the Bulgarians. The archangels in Washington had other priorities and, in November 1971, Customs and BNDD officials traveled to Sofia and began to instruct Bulgarian customs officials in American drug interdiction techniques.[74] The Kintex scandal was swept under the carpet as part of the arrangement.

Salmi and Clarridge continued to make progress and mounted a joint CIA/BNDD/military effort against wealthy Turkish financiers who owned hotels, import-export companies, factories, and transportation lines. Called Operation Bruit, it resulted in a case on Mehmet

Kulecki, an arms exporter to the Kurds who sold morphine base in Germany.[75] Alas, Kulecki was able to buy off the courts, the major witnesses, and the police. "It was out of anybody's control," Clarridge said.

To get CIA officers involved operationally, Clarridge did mount unilateral operations against labs in Istanbul. "We also did some unilateral interdiction," he acknowledges. But "Narcotics was more complex than terrorism, because state and local agencies were involved."[76] This meant the CIA officers had to organize their official police assets. It also led to bureaucratic in-fighting with the BNDD, which the freewheeling CIA officers found objectionable.

Personal relationships were critical. Eventually Clarridge was transferred to Ankara and began working with Frank Briggs. The BNDD had substantial on-going operations and Clarridge was told to support them, which he did primarily by providing analysts. But Clarridge wasn't interested anymore, and he did not click with Briggs like he did with Salmi. "There was confusion on [Briggs'] part over as to who would get credit," he explained. The CIA avoids the limelight, so this was an alien concept to him. According to Clarridge, the BNDD had "a cut-throat mentality" and was constantly in competition for informants. "Briggs was afraid we'd try to co-opt them — take over his operations and take credit." The CIA case officers didn't want to work narcotics and, apart from Salmi, the BNDD agents didn't want them in it. "It was a tough time in the early days," Clarridge concludes. "We had to get exempted by the legal system, because the CIA can't testify in court. This is why they closed down a CIA wiretap in Mexico, because the information gathered was not actionable against so many US citizens."

Due to the enmity between Briggs and Clarridge, the CIA and BNDD soon went their separate ways in Turkey. The BNDD and the White House also parted ways, as Krogh started questioning Ingersoll's loyalty. According to Agent Bob DeFauw, Cusack was feeding Ingersoll "bull.... on production in Turkey," and Ingersoll made the mistake of passing the cooked statistics to Krogh. Cusack claimed that ten percent was being diverted, "when it was more like fifty." There were also far more narcotics coming from Mexico and Southeast Asia than the BNDD was reporting. Suddenly there was a realization that the 30 million dollars given to Turkey (which would start growing poppies again in 1974) had been flushed down the toilet — and that did not endear Ingersoll to Krogh or anyone else in government.

12

THE POLITICS OF ENFORCEMENT

SO MUCH OF HISTORY IS coincidence. To wit: in 1969, after completing a four-year tour in Southeast Asia, Al Habib returned to Washington headquarters to await reassignment. He was in the office building elevator when someone asked him, "Are you Habib?"[1]

That someone was Jack Cusack, the recently appointed regional director in Paris. Cusack knew Habib by reputation and told him in the elevator that he wanted him to replace Bob DeFauw in Marseilles. Cusack felt DeFauw was too close to the French cops and he wanted Habib to identify the cops who were crooked, incompetent, or impediments. And that's why Al Habib landed in Marseilles in July 1969, and in return for the plum assignment, helped Cusack squeeze the French and Agent Tony Pohl.

Habib investigated the French cops first. "Out of twenty-five guys on the force in Marseilles, "Habib asserts, "ten were not trustworthy." He also set about making narcotic cases, one of which fell into his lap from the sky. One morning Habib's secretary said there was an American who wanted to talk to him. It was November 1970. The man had holes in his socks and was wearing a T-shirt. He wore no jacket. In his mid-thirties, he introduced himself as the son of an American Foreign Service officer. Habib dubbed him "Rudy" (after the reindeer) in honor of his big red nose.

Rudy told Habib he could make a case on one of Pohl's primary targets, Joe Orsini. When Habib asked how, Rudy said he'd been in the Atlanta penitentiary with Orsini. They were "friends," and Rudy met with him that day at his brother's brasserie. Habib and another agent watched the meeting and saw Orsini kiss Rudy when they met. Orsini even gave Rudy money to buy new cloths.[2]

Given the possibilities, Habib hired Rudy as an undercover agent and instructed him not to come back to the office. Rudy called a few days later to say that Orsini was sending him to Detroit, New York, San Francisco and other major US cities to meet contacts and arrange huge heroin deliveries. Habib dutifully wrote a report and sent it to his patron Jack Cusack in Paris. Cusack instructed Habib not to tell the French that Rudy was working for the BNDD. Alas, a copy of Habib's report found its way from BNDD headquarters to Tony Pohl in New York.[3]

Agent Morty Benjamin, head of the European branch of Tony Pohl's International Division, did a little checking and reported that Joe Orsini was in Corsica at the time Habib saw him with Rudy in Marseille.[4] Based on other reports, Pohl doubted Rudy's reliability. Having already launched an expensive undercover operation against Orsini, (featuring undercover Agent Joe Quarequio posing as a crooked pharmaceutical company executive willing to transport drugs on his yacht), Pohl, as instructed by regional director Bill Durkin, took control of Rudy. When Habib next saw him in Marseille, Rudy said he was working for Pohl and was not allowed to talk to him.[5]

According to Habib, Pohl, abiding by the Franco-American Agreements, told the French police about Rudy, and crooked French cops immediately informed Orsini. The case died, Rudy fled France, and *then* Orsini fled to Corsica. Habib blamed Pohl — Pohl blamed Habib. In either case, tensions between Pohl and Cusack reached new heights.

Tony Pohl's Big Adventures

TONY POHL WAS SMACK DAB in the middle of the palace politics that were ripping apart American drug enforcement. The seminal event occurred on April 5, 1971 when a Customs port inspector, acting on a CIA tip, "discovered" 97 pounds of heroin in a VW van coming off an ocean liner in New Jersey.[6] The defendant in the case, Roger Delouette, spun a tall tale that France's Defense Minister Michel Debre would liken to a "confused novel."[7]

Customs legitimately claimed the case and Agent Paul Boulad inter-rogated Delouette with Daniel Hartwig, a French policeman assigned to the New York consulate. During the questioning, Delouette said the mastermind of his smuggling venture was a senior SDECE offi-cial using the *nom de guerre* Colonel Paul Fournier.[8] Delouette said that he was delivering the heroin to a SDECE agent at the French consulate in New York. He implied that Fournier intended to use the profits to fund a political spy ring in America.[9] According to Cusack, who spent a considerable amount of time spying on his French coun-terparts, Hartwig at once called Michel Nocquet, chief commissioner of the Police Judiciare in Paris, and Nocquet immediately tipped off Fournier.[10]

Was it conceivable that SDECE officials were peddling heroin in America? Herbert J. Stern, the youthful US Attorney prosecuting the case in New Jersey, believed so, as did Customs and a few Franco-phobic BNDD agents, including Cusack in Paris. Cusack believed Delouette because he felt that Delouette had acted in a manner incon-sistent with that of a professional drug smuggler.[11]

The French believed that Delouette had tricked the actual con-troller in the case, Robert Marchiani, into believing that he, Delou-ette, had diplomatic privileges. The French agreed with Cusack that Delouette was an amateur, which is why he packed the van in a hap-hazard way that became apparent to the Customs port inspector.[12] They argued that Fournier had fired Delouette from SDECE; that he was financially strapped; and that he was trying to "gray-mail" his way out of trouble by implicating Fournier.[13] They said that if there were a SDECE connection, it was possibly through Delouette's Corsican cousin, who had been fired from SDECE for misconduct and had narcotic connections.[14]

The French invoked the Franco-American Agreements, which gave them the right to question Delouette. But Stern ignored the agree-ment and demanded that SDECE Officer Fournier be extradited to Newark.[15] France, which does not extradite its nationals, refused, just as President George W. Bush refused in 2007 to turn over to a Ger-man prosecutor 13 members of a CIA "abduction" team that kid-napped an innocent Lebanese national in Germany.[16] A stalemate in the Fournier case ensued and was milked for months by American Francophobes for political purposes.

While Ambrose, Cusack and Stern were willing to build a case against Fournier on Delouette's dubious word alone, Tony Pohl was instructed to begin a routine criminal investigation of the case. He had seen in Delouette's notebook the names "Salles" and "Fenwick."[17] If it were Jean-Claude Salles, as Cusack insisted, then Salles was simply one of Delouette's business associates. Alexander Salles, however, was a big league drug trafficker whom Pohl had been chasing since 1970. Joe Quarequio, the undercover agent Pohl inserted into the Salles/Signoli organization, had recorded his conversations in New York with Salles and Joseph Signoli.[18] Both were later indicted along with Louis Cirillo, their recipient in the US.

The name Fenwick raised a red flag as well.[19] Elizabeth Fenwick was the mistress of Andre Labay, a drug trafficking SDECE agent. Labay, since April 1970, had been delivering heroin to the United States for Salles and Signoli.[20] According to George C. Corcoran, the Customs attaché in France, Labay was under investigation by the Paris Police narcotics squad. Tony Pohl, said Corcoran, had asked the French police about a possible connection between Delouette and Labay, but neither Pohl nor the French had included Cusack in this line of inquiry. And when Cusack found out, he went haywire.[21] In a three-part interview in late August 1971 with the right-wing French newspaper *Le Meridional-La France*, Cusack said that "8 to 12 clandestine laboratories" operated in Marseille in "tranquility."[22] He declared that French policemen, spies, and politicians were complicit.

The French were not amused, and demanded that Cusack provide the names of the guilty persons. Sûreté chief Jean Dours reminded the *New York Times* that Cusack had made similar charges in the past, which "have proven totally unfounded." Dours quoted from a letter Cusack wrote saying, "I do not possess any document or any specific information on these dealers and their political protectors."[23]

Cusack smugly replied that the names of the guilty parties were published in the Murphy-Steele Report. He mentioned, among others, Marcel Francisci. Francisci promptly sued the *Times* and within days, the French were insisting that Cusack be recalled. Ingersoll (up to his ears in the diplomatic row caused by the Him "kidnapping" scandal in Panama) transferred Cusack to Belk's newly formed office of international operations. In an attempt to control the damage, Tartaglino authorized SIO operations Chief Tom Tripodi to tell a popular French newspaper that Cusack was a "high-spirited Irishman" and had been disciplined for his remarks.[24]

Some of this was play-acting, for in the arcane world of international drug trafficking things are rarely what they seem. Some say Cusack was simply following instructions from Krogh, as part of a campaign to pressure the French while marginalizing Ingersoll. Pohl reported a comment made to him by Raymond Marcellin, the French Minister of Interior, that the Delouette affair was "an American mirage" and that prosecutor Stern, as a Jew acting on behalf of the Israeli lobby, wanted to embarrass the French for having sold Mirage jets to Saudi Arabia.[25]

There was also the possibility, as *Newsweek* suggested on November 29, 1971, that the CIA "masterminded" the whole affair in retaliation for the French having kicked the US Ambassador out of Malagasy, and as a way of blackening Fournier's reputation.[26] Or perhaps the CIA had tipped off Customs and set up Delouette in an attempt to preempt Al McCoy's imminent publication of Belleux's allegation that the CIA controlled Corsican drug smugglers in Southeast Asia. Delouette had worked with Colonel Roger Trinquier, commander of the French Special Forces involved in SDECE's opium smuggling ring, Operation X, and with Renaud Desclers, a Corsican arrested in South Vietnam in 1959 for smuggling 300 kilograms of opium. He was not an amateur, as the French claimed, and perhaps Fournier (a Service d'Action Civique (SAC) member, like Delouette) was part of a rogue operation organizing heroin shipments to New York.[27]

Nevertheless, in November, while the movie *The French Connection* premiered in New York City, a grand jury directed by Stern passed down indictments for Delouette and Fournier. And the epic battle between Customs and Tony Pohl intensified.

The Jaguar Case

WHILE THE DELOUETTE CASE SIMMERED, Customs and the BNDD clashed over four other French connection cases — all of which Agent Pohl unraveled.

The Jaguar case began in July 1971 when a "walk-in" informant told BNDD officials in Paris that controller Donald Maenhout had recruited him to smuggle 100 kilograms of heroin to the US.[28] The French narcotics unit was informed and immediately recognized the *modus operandi* of the Etienne Mosca gang. Surveillance was established and BNDD and French police officers watched while Maenhout gave the informant money to buy a Jaguar. The informant arranged to ship the Jaguar on the Queen Elizabeth II to Bayonne, New Jersey. Pohl notified Customs, and both agencies presented an operational plan to the Justice Department.[29] Pohl's action plan — which he supervised and which involved 50 BNDD agents and 25 Customs agents — was accepted, with the provision that the heroin not leave the BNDD's sight. BNDD Agent Nick Panella, a Cusack ally, was assigned to accompany the Jaguar on the ship and keep watch.

Everything went according to Pohl's plan ... almost. The Cuban buyer, Luis Gomez Ortega, and the receiver, Jean Orsini, were arrested when they went to retrieve the Jaguar. Mosca and his accomplices were arrested in France.[30] More leads were developed, and the case led to the indictment of an additional 36 traffickers. Pohl considered it one of his greatest successes, in part because the Jaguar Case revealed the duplicity of the Customs Service, which secretly deviated from the plan.

To wit: On the day the Jaguar was dismantled at the garage, BNDD Agent Gerry Carey saw Customs Agent Paul Boulad rapping on the front left fender.[31] Boulad said he had a hunch that heroin might be hidden there. Carey reminded Boulad that Pohl's plan called for the entire shipment to be stored in the car's console. However, when Carey removed the panel, he found packages similar to those being removed from the console. The bags were initialed PB-BI and JT (9-15-71). Boulad admitted that "PB" were his initials, but denied putting them on the bag.[32]

The awful truth soon unfolded. While Panella was looking away, Customs agents had removed two kilos of heroin from the Jaguar while it was aboard the QE II. Boulad had reportedly done this at the request of Coyne and Seely as a "safety measure."[33] The Customs agents wanted to be able to prove in court that there was indeed heroin in the car, in case the surveillance failed and the car was delivered to some unknown recipient.[34] Senior BNDD agents aligned with Cusack and Panella were involved in the plot, and one senior agent tried to prevent Carey from removing the panel. The complicit senior agent, Jerry Jensen, "left with tail between legs."[35]

Two days later came the Berdin case, paving the way for the Labay and Cirillo cases.

Labay, Berdin, and Priess

THE FALL OF 1971 WAS the pivotal moment in the BNDD's history. Issues related to the French connection, corruption, and bureaucratic conflicts converged and prompted Andy Tartaglino to transfer New York regional director Bill Durkin to headquarters. Tartaglino replaced Durkin with Daniel P. Casey.

An FBN agent since 1951, Casey had worked continually in San Francisco until 1965, when Fred Dick was named district supervisor and Casey was transferred to Atlanta as district supervisor. In 1967 he attended the National War College and in 1968, with the formation of the BNDD, he was named RD in Los Angeles. An expert on the Far East, Casey was said to be "a shrewd street agent with a gift for making an informant feel a part of the team."[36]

Casey said that he was brought to New York specifically to combat Myles Ambrose, with whom Bill Durkin was loosely aligned.[37] Casey described New York as "the varsity." The main target was the Mafia and there was a "tremendous case load." Based on the Narcotics Intelligence Network unit he created in Los Angeles, Casey formed the Cooperative Narcotics Intelligence Committee in New York, which underscored the new emphasis on intelligence and brought together NYPD, Customs, and the Joint Task Force.[38] The Cooperative Narcotics Intelligence Committee's main ingredient was a "source register" that prevented informants from playing one agency against another. The information in its data base was sent to the SIO and, when relevant, was shared with other federal agencies including the CIA.[39]

Casey's deputies in the battle against the Mafia were former BDAC agent Jerry Jensen (the Cusack ally who tried to cover for Customs in the Jaguar case) and Frank Monastero, who served as Tartaglino's eyes and ears in the New York office. The problem was that Tony Pohl ran his headline-grabbing investigations "out of school," meaning apart from the Purple Gang. To prove his loyalty to the Gang, and to reduce personal conflicts in New York, Casey disbanded the very successful International Division and turned its functions over to his third deputy, Wayne Valentine.[40]

John Ingersoll, however, valued Pohl's expertise and personally directed Casey to assign Pohl to another very important job. John Mitchell and Interior Minister Raymond Marcellin had signed the Franco-American Accords on February 26, 1971.[41] During the ceremonies, the French had informed Ingersoll of a large drug ring that was smuggling heroin to the US. They specifically named Richard Berdin, Andre Labay and a few other traffickers. Casey gave Pohl a tiny "special operations division" and told him to focus solely on the Berdin-Labay operation and its buyers. Ironically, this assignment placed Pohl at the forefront of the BNDD's next battle with Customs.

Richard Berdin was a dashing but undisciplined "controller" working for Alexander Salles and Joseph Signoli since the spring of 1970.[42] Salles and Signoli shipped heroin directly to Mafia "sleeper" Louis

Cirillo in luxury cars supplied by Andre Labay. What Berdin didn't know was that Labay, a suave, conceited, middle-aged conman had been watched by the BNDD and French CNO since September 1970.[43]

Briefly, Berdin felt he was being short-changed by Signoli and was deathly afraid of murderous Louis Cirillo. When 102 kilograms of heroin went missing from a shipment in November 1970, and the French crime bosses sent enforcer Maurice Castellani to investigate the disappearance, Berdin asked to be replaced as the group's receiver.[44] He suggested the organization hire in his place Roger Preiss, a thirty-something check forger with no narcotics experience.[45] Berdin then went to work as a controller for the Picpus Gang, and on its behalf agreed to deliver a car loaded with 84 kilos of heroin to a white-haired Frenchman in New York.[46] In August 1970 Berdin returned to the Salles-Signoli organization, but kept his Picpus contacts, and in July 1971 he asked Preiss to work with Labay on a new Picpus deal, while he pursued yet another deal on his own.[47]

On September 20, 1971, the French police watched Berdin board a flight to Montreal. They kept their US counterparts informed, and BNDD and Customs agents watched while Berdin met with Michel Mastantuono, a Frenchman in charge of transportation across the Canadian border.[48] Mastantuono gave Berdin the keys to a Ford Galaxie packed with heroin and destined not for Louis Cirillo, but for other Italian customers in New York. Berdin flew into JFK, where a Customs agent actually drove the cab that took him to his hotel.

On September 21, a Customs inspector searched the Ford Galaxie as it came off a ship at a New York City pier. The inspector tried rolling down a window, but failed. Upon closer inspection he found a half-kilogram package of heroin (part of an 82.5 kilogram load) stuffed in the door panel that was stopping the window. While BNDD agents watched in amazement, a team of Customs agents quickly arrested the Galaxie's owner, Giuseppe Giacomazzo. Giacomazzo agreed to cooperate with Customs agents and at their direction drove the car to a shopping center for a scheduled rendezvous.[49]

To move the narrative along, it's necessary to skip over a lot of details. Berdin went to Giacomazzo's house in Queens ostensibly to help retrieve the car; but instead, he announced that he and Mastantuono knew the car was being watched and thus were dropping out of the deal.[50] Giacomazzo's boss, pizza parlor owner Frank Rappa, was unfazed and stupidly decided to retrieve the car anyway. Rappa and

Giacomazzo drove in separate cars to a rest area on the Long Island Expressway, where the exchange was to be made. On September 21, 1971, Customs agents, to the horror of BNDD agents, arrested Rappa.[51]

Customs agents knew that the BNDD had been following Berdin for months in an operation designed to identify his American customer and his connection in France. But the Customs agents were angry over the Jaguar and Delouette cases, so they arrested Berdin when he returned to his hotel to collect his belongings. This preemptive act was juvenile at best. As one BNDD official recalled, "We gave our word to the French that we wouldn't arrest him, and Customs is a part of this government and was bound by it whether it wants to admit it or not."[52]

Making matters worse for the BNDD, Berdin agreed to work for Customs. He did this to protect his girlfriend, whom the Customs agents were threatening to arrest.[53]

Unaware of developments in New York, Andre Labay and Roger Preiss were preparing to deliver a load of heroin to New York for the Picpus gang. The French police and BNDD in Paris had been investigating Labay through an informant since September 1970. They knew through the informant that Labay had met with a Russian financier on September 28, 1971 and had compartments built into a Bentley at a garage used by French traffickers.[54] Then, on October 5, Labay (who was being watched by the French police) went to the BNDD office in Paris and offered to betray Preiss and his other accomplices. All he asked for in exchange was the $200,000 he would have made from the delivery of the Bentley. With their fingers crossed behind their backs, the Paris BNDD agents agreed, but on condition that they inspect the car. On October 6, Labay drove the car straight into a trap and the French police busted him with 106 kilos of heroin. Shortly afterwards the Picpus gang members were arrested too.[55]

Unaware that Labay and Picpus gang members had been arrested in France, Roger Preiss traveled to New York and called Berdin. They agreed to meet at the Waldorf Astoria to sell Labay's heroin to Cirillo. On October 7, BNDD agents arrested Preiss (moments before Customs agents tried to arrest him) and took him to their office. Tony Pohl began a slow and careful interrogation, during which Preiss revealed that Signoli was scheduled to deliver a large quantity of heroin to the hitherto unknown American customer, whom he identified from photographs as Louis Cirillo.[56]

Pohl instantly saw the opportunity to nail Cirillo through Preiss. It would not be easy, however, as Customs was mounting its own operation against "the customer" through mercurial Roger Berdin.

Special Tactical Unit #1

AS NOTED EARLIER, DAN CASEY had Tony Pohl form a special "tactical unit" to focus on the Louis Cirillo sub-system. Pohl's Tactical Unit #1 started out with five agents (Ross Riley, Jeffrey I. Scharlatt, Francis M. Gill, Robin E. Cushing, and Michael J. Waniewski) and one secretary, Connie Belluardo. Despite its modest origins, it grew and made some of the BNDD's biggest cases ever.[57] The Cirillo case was the first.

As a teenager in the 1940s, fledgling predator Louis Cirillo had held-up at gunpoint and robbed a high-ranking member of the Genovese family in the Bronx. For having committed this unforgiveable indiscretion he could never become a made member of the Mafia. But his moneymaking talents were appreciated and the Mafia bosses were glad to have him do their bidding. In return for his services, the Mafia bosses financed his drug operation and provided him with protection. Cirillo bragged that he also enjoyed protection from BNDD agents in Miami and cops in New York.[58] Although the FBN had known of his connection to Santo Trafficante since 1959, and though by 1970 he was responsible for roughly twenty percent of the heroin consumed in America, no federal agent ever penetrated his organization. Cirillo was indicted on a narcotics charge in 1967, but the case was dropped when the main witness, a beautiful prostitute and model named Erica Bunne, disappeared.[59] An informant in the case claimed that Cirillo had killed Bunne and buried her body. The informant also claimed that Cirillo paid $5000 to two FBN agents for information on Bunne's security detail.[60]

Using a bagel bakery as a cover, Cirillo viciously went about his burgeoning business. At its peak, his operation relied on a fleet of small pleasure craft and fishing boats to smuggle heroin from Europe to the Caribbean and on to Florida. He paid around one million dollars each month for the heroin he bought, and made fantastic profits.

Preiss knew little about Cirillo's operation, but he did provide Pohl with the location of a garage in New Jersey where the French connection heroin he had imported had been transferred. Preiss also stated that Signoli had given Cirillo a Piaget watch "to maintain customer satisfaction."[61] BNDD laboratory chemists found traces of heroin in the garage and, when Miami agents arrested Cirillo in October, he was wearing the Piaget watch. These pieces of evidence would contribute to his conviction. Pohl's special tactical unit also provided the French police with all the evidence and information, and soon after Cirillo's arrest, the French police arrested Signoli, Salles, and 21 other traffickers.[62]

The arrest of Cirillo and his French connections eclipsed all previous BNDD successes. But before Cirillo was placed permanently behind bars, Pohl first had to jump through a few more flaming political hoops.

Delouette Part IV

DEFENDANT RICHARD BERDIN TOLD HIS Customs handlers that a courier working for "Dominic" had been arrested in the VW Camper case. As Pohl informed the French, this was an unmistakable reference to courier Roger Delouette. The question was, "Who is Dominic?"

Soon thereafter, CNO Chief François Le Mouel arrived in New York with a Letter Rogatory from the French courts requesting that Berdin be questioned. Pohl was sworn in as a "commissioner" to execute the letter rogatory, with Le Mouel as his technical assistant. They immediately presented Berdin with a photo of Delouette's controller, and Berdin identified him as Dominic Mariani.[63]

This development destroyed the theory, held so closely by US Attorney Herbert Stern, Customs Commissioner Myles Ambrose, Jack Cusack and others, that Delouette's controller was a SDECE official. Unable to acknowledge the error of their ways, the propagandists joined in a pitiful effort to prevent Pohl from moving the case out of the political realm into the field of criminal conspiracy. The first move in the effort to hijack the case occurred in November, when Stern indicted SDECE officer Fournier. The next move occurred a few days later when Customs Agent Al Seely prevented Pohl from interviewing Berdin's girlfriend, Nancy Grigor. Grigor had met with Maurice Castellani, Andre Labay, and Joseph Signoli, and she was considered to be a crucial witness, whose life was in danger.[64] Last but not least, Purple Gang members Wayne Valentine and Jerry Jensen, ignoring the stipulations of the Franco-American Accords, sent BNDD evidence to Stern in Newark.[65]

Frustrated by these attempts to sabotage the case, Ingersoll and Andy Tartaglino accompanied Pohl to Washington to brief Attorney General Mitchell about the criminal nature of the case. Mitchell began the December 6 meeting by stating his belief that the French were "in the process of double-crossing U. S. Justice."[66] Agent Pohl presented his evidence and calmly explained the difference between Delouette's espionage relationship with SDECE, and his criminal work for Dominic Mariani in the Signoli-Salles case. Mitchell saw the light; he abandoned his political prejudices and honorably instructed everyone involved to keep the letter rogatory sealed, so the criminal conspiracy case could be made against some three-dozen major traffickers in France.

Stern and Ambrose, however, felt they could defy Mitchell, who was leaving to run Nixon's re-election campaign, and once again they tried to impede Pohl. Although Pohl had subpoenaed Berdin's girlfriend, Nancy Grigor, she was intimidated by Customs agents and refused to speak to Pohl.[67] Then Ambrose's political ally, Assistant US Attorney Arthur J. Viviani, determined that Customs agents, not Pohl, should handle Grigor's case, as a way of preventing her testimony from reaching the French before Stern could score the necessary political points.[68]

The BNDD objected to these machinations and Mitchell, frustrated by the infighting, sent the Grigor dispute to his deputy, Harlington Wood, for disposition. At a meeting with Wood, held four days prior to Nixon's December 14 meeting with French President Pompidou, Pohl produced documents showing that Berdin and Preiss had both identified Dominic Mariani as the controller behind the Delouette case. Then Pohl convinced Wood that Customs and Stern were playing politics with Grigor's life — that the Mafia had a contract on her.[69] As Pohl had explained specifically in an earlier memo to Casey, "It should be noted that through the notorious Maurice Castellani, the French gang has a direct link to some very dangerous criminal elements of the New York waterfront."[70]

Wood played it by the book and informed Stern and Ambrose that the case rightfully belonged to the BNDD through the Franco-American Agreements. He decided that Grigor was a federal witness, not a Customs witness. As a result, Pohl finally obtained her statement, a copy of which he sent to the French as stipulated by the Agreements.[71]

In France in mid-December, Ingersoll tried to put the SDECE matter to rest by saying the "cold war" with French narcotics agents existed only in the rhetoric of politicians. Despite Delouette's accusations, he said SDECE was not "officially involved" in the drug traffic. However, he did add rather devilishly that there could have been a

private initiative, and "Marseille remains the crossroads of the narcotics traffic."[72] Meanwhile, two other developments confirmed the
criminal nature of the Delouette case. On February 19, 1972, Dominic Mariani confirmed that Delouette had been working with Richard Berdin.[73] And in the spring of 1973, Claude Pastou revealed that
Christian David had asked him to go to New York in 1971 to pick
up a load of heroin. To facilitate the transaction, David introduced
Pastou to François Orsini. Orsini told Pastou that Roger Delouette
was delivering 50 kilograms of heroin in a VW camper. Pastou was to
take possession of the camper after meeting with the intended recipient, Carlo Zippo. Delouette, according to Pastou, told Pastou not to
worry; that he had an alibi. We now know that his alibi was posing as
a SDECE employee.[74]

Louis Cirillo's Demise

ON NOVEMBER 19, 1971, THE judge in the Cirillo case reduced Ciril
lo's bail at the behest of Assistant US Attorney Arthur Viviani.[75] The
cold-blooded murderer hit the streets. Aghast at Viviani's "unstable
emotional reaction," Pohl retrieved all BNDD evidence and documents from Viviani's office.[76] It was time to regroup. By then Pohl's
Special Operations Division consisted of 24 agents. They were operating around the clock, keeping track of Cirillo's every move. At one
point Agent Jeff Scharlatt received a tip that Cirillo planned to kill
every witness who was going to testify against him, as well as BNDD
Agent John LePore, who was in charge of preventing Cirillio's escape
while he was out on bail.[77] Cirillo had actually purchased photos of
the witnesses and LePore from corrupt cops, and he planned to blow
up the Coast Guard building on Staten Island, where cooperating
defendant Roger Preiss was being "secretly" held.[78]

Given these developments, Pohl had Cirillo taken back into custody and convened a meeting at his office on 90 Church Street. Pohl
sat at the head of a long table. The group supervisors working on the
case were seated along each side. Agent LePore sat directly across
from Cirillo. "I understand you are trying to get my men killed," Pohl
said in his most intimidating, thickly accented baritone voice. "I'm
asking them what we should do with you."[79] Everyone had a pad and
pencil and, on that prearranged cue, broke his pencil in half. Cirillo
staggered to his feet and said, "Oh, no! I have to go to bathroom,"
where he threw up. As Pohl observed, they didn't have to torture or
kill him to end the threats.

Pohl then went to the FBI for assistance in pinning the murder and bomb plots on Cirillo, only to learn that Cirillo's designated hit man, Joe Bux, was an FBI employee![80] Pohl was informed that the FBI was relying on Bux as an informant in a hijacking case and would not allow the BNDD to arrest him or use him as an informant. Pohl did not think the FBI was acting in the interests of justice, so he had Agent Scharlatt bring Bux to his office, where he offered the nervous hit-man more money than Cirillo, plus a new identity, if he would inform on his boss. Bux accepted Pohl's offer and subsequently testified to a grand jury that Cirillo was planning to kill Preiss by hiring a Puerto Rican to blow up the Coast Guard building where he was being held. Cirillo was indicted on the attempted murder charges, as well as the drug conspiracy charge. He was tried, convicted and sentenced to 25 years in prison. To the chagrin of Customs agents, the primary evidence in the drug case was the 106 kilos seized from Labay and the Picpus gang in France.

Mafia drug trafficking, naturally, did not abate with Cirillo's demise. The Mafia bosses simply anointed qualified successors and the heroin business proceeded apace. There were, however, repercussions in the underworld. Tom Eboli, the financially strapped head of the Genovese family, had been Cirillo's partner in his last transaction. Carlo Gambino had fronted Eboli a large portion of the $4 million used to purchase the French connection heroin. Unfortunately for Eboli, the money — along with $1,078,100 that Cirillo had buried in his backyard, and which the BNDD seized — was irretrievably lost. When Gambino asked Eboli for his money back, Eboli was unable to comply.[81] On the morning of July 16, 1972, Eboli was shot five times. No one was ever arrested for the murder.

The new breed of African American heroin traffickers also thrived without Cirillo. The BNDD was particularly interested in Frank Matthews, whose descent into a life of crime began in the 1950s when Louis Cirillo hired him to run numbers in Harlem. Around 1967 Matthews obtained his own French connection and started his own heroin business, using his numbers runners to distribute the drugs. Matthews prospered and eventually opened a heroin packaging plant in Brooklyn, with two-dozen employees. He hired policemen for protection and laundered his profits in Las Vegas.[82]

In June 1972, a BNDD wiretap on Matthews led to the arrest of his associate Miguel Garcia in Caracas, Venezuela, with heroin acquired from Frenchman Andre Condemine.[83] Various Puerto Ricans and anti-Castro Cubans working off the inter-island freighter *The William Express* were also involved. Notably, nine anti-Castro CIA assets indicted as couriers in the Matthews enterprise were set free when Judge Joe Eaton suppressed evidence in the case, leading author Hank Messick to speculate that "If someone had wanted the heroin seized but the pipeline left undamaged for possible future use, then that someone had succeeded."[84] Matthews was arrested in early 1973 but fled in July with $20 million. He was still operating in 1975.

Other prominent Afro-American traffickers were Nicky Barnes, who had a connection to Mafioso Joey Gallo and dealt mostly in Manhattan; Frank Lucas, glorified in the black exploitation movie *American Gangster*; and Elvin Lee Bynum in Brooklyn.

Pohl's interest in the Cirillo case ended on April 19, 1972, when Dan Casey sent him to meet with White House representatives regarding allegations that he "stole" the Preiss, Cirillo and Jaguar cases from Customs.[85] Pohl told the White House officials that the underlying problem was that Custom's jurisdiction placed it in the middle of BNDD overseas and domestic drug trafficking investigations. The White House people saw his point and dismissed the frivolous Customs allegations. Having re-established the BNDD's preeminence and his own prominence as the grand master of narcotics investigations, Agent Pohl began his last great case, clashing directly with Ambrose while smashing the largest heroin trafficking ring in New York.

13

SHOCK TREATMENT

As 1971 CAME TO A close, Myles Ambrose's star was rising and John Ingersoll's was setting. Customs had seized an amazing 1,309 pounds of heroin in 1971.[1] Yes, the BNDD was finally making the big conspiracy cases it had promised. But it was making fewer arrests, while the number of addicts was rising. There were even ugly rumors that the BNDD was claiming credit for narcotics seized by foreign police, and exaggerating its domestic successes by reporting the street value of seizures even if the narcotics were seized in bulk.

Ever the opportunist, Ambrose did what he could to hasten Ingersoll's fall from grace. He constantly reminded Egil Krogh (and anyone else who would listen) that while the BNDD was busy abroad, the situation at home was so bad that "black mothers" were organizing vigilante gangs and killing drug peddlers on their blocks in order to protect their kids.[2] He complained that the BNDD computer system did not include new drug pushers, who were popping up every day. He even claimed that the BNDD's major buy program was actually fueling the growth of the addict population.[3]

The timing was right for Myles to make his big move. Customs in 1971 had seized over a thousand pounds of heroin in a series of headline-grabbing busts. The Vietnam War was winding down and the war on drugs was the government's new growth industry. Ingersoll's patron, John Mitchell, was resigning to manage Nixon's re-election campaign. All that remained was for Ambrose to yell: "The cities are burning!" Which he did, at the top of his lungs.

People were listening. They asked, "What can we do?"

What was needed, Ambrose said, was "shock treatment."[4]

When the White House demanded action, Ambrose was ready with a proposal (drafted by Gordon Liddy, the White House resident expert on the virtues of shock troops) for a new organization devoted entirely to knocking drug pushers off the streets. This new organization would provide the White House with a rationale for reorganizing federal drug law enforcement in a way that would, in an election year, garner the numbers needed to show symbolic success in the war on drugs. It would also increase the stature of Myles Ambrose, who was destined to head it.

Called the Office of Drug Abuse Law Enforcement (ODALE), this new federal agency was to achieve the goals Ambrose and Liddy set forth based on its "extra legal" powers to kick down doors and conduct warrantless searches without probable cause.[5] ODALE needed these extralegal powers, Ambrose and Liddy explained, in order to assist local police in the war on drugs. It was also tacitly understood that an apparatus with extra-legal powers could help plug leaks and beef up the White House's private political action forces in anticipation of the 1972 election. Thus, in January 1972, Nixon established ODALE by executive order, without Congressional review.[6] Ambrose resigned as Customs Commissioner to become ODALE's director, as well as assistant attorney general and special advisor to the president on drug law enforcement. Ambrose was now Ingersoll's boss, and Ingersoll was asked to resign. He refused.

ODALE

ODALE WAS THE "TASK FORCE" concept on a national scale, combining more than a dozen federal agencies with state and locals forces.[7] The federal forces numbered about 2500 and included people from BNDD, Customs, ATF, IRS, CIA, Public Safety and the various military investigative services. For every federal agent there were ten local law enforcement officers. The cooperating entities all came under the direction of special prosecutors in key cities. The prosecutors used "secret grand juries" to indict street-level pushers "selling dope in bars, not in Amsterdam," as Ambrose put it.[8] The top prosecutor was Henry E. Petersen, chief of the criminal division at the Justice Department.

ODALE covered ten regions, with offices in, among other places, New York, Houston, Denver, Washington DC, Miami, Chicago and Los Angeles. It had less success in big cities than in suburbs and small cities, but it did better in big cities like St. Louis where the prosecutors did not already have professional narcotics units at their disposal.

Ambrose selected John R. Bartels, Jr. as his deputy. In June 1973, Bartels would become the first chief administrator of the DEA, and thus deserves an introduction.

The son of a federal judge, John Bartels had served as an assistant US attorney in New York's Southern District, prosecuting drug cases.[9] He had worked with FBN agents, and he knew what federal drug law enforcement was all about. Bartels had also headed the Justice Department's Strike Force in Newark, New Jersey, and afterwards had then served as a special counsel to an FBI unit investigating waste and fraud in New York City. A Democrat, Bartels quit the Strike Force when he realized that Governor Rockefeller was using his unit to sabotage Mayor John Lindsay. At this point, Henry Petersen asked Bartels to run ODALE in Newark. Ambrose interviewed Bartels for the ODALE job in Washington and, though political rivals, they bonded on a personal level.

John Bartels described Ambrose as "a rough-and-ready street guy." Ingersoll, in his opinion, was "pompous" and "looked down on Myles." But Ingersoll didn't promote his agency, while Ambrose did, and for that reason, "Ambrose cleaned Ingersoll's clock."

According to Bartels, ODALE had two major goals. The first was to coordinate investigators with prosecutors, who would decide whether to take the case to a federal or state court. The other goal was to see "if the soufflé holds." If it did, the next step was to come up with a permanent organization based on the ODALE model. The soufflé held, and resulted in the formation of the DEA in July 1973.

Customs and Ingersoll

AMBROSE DID NOT INFORM INGERSOLL of the creation of ODALE until New Year's Day, 1972, shortly before he asked him to resign. In the days that followed, Ingersoll got most of his information about ODALE from John Mitchell's successor as attorney general, Richard Kleindienst.[10]

Ingersoll described ODALE as "devastating," primarily because he was obligated to assign several hundred BNDD agents to it. Not only was his work force diminished, but BNDD agents were suddenly uncertain if they would continue pursing their BNDD cases or ODALE's.

Most agents saw ODALE as a new bureaucratic foe, but a few senior agents, like Jack Cusack (whose standing with Ingersoll had plummeted after his outburst against the French), willingly joined its management team. Cusack became ODALE's assistant chief of operations under Richard Callahan. In this position Cusack worked closely with Ambrose, with whom he shared an affinity; both were Fordham graduates and had known each other since the early 1950s.

Other BNDD agents paid a heavy price. Tony Pohl, for one, had trumped Ambrose in the Delouette, Jaguar and Cirillo cases. Ambrose and his clique of like-minded BNDD, Customs and ODALE agents were looking for revenge, so they spread the rumor that Pohl was a SDECE agent "in place" for Emil Benhamou.[11] This ridiculous charge stuck in some paranoid circles, although Pohl, after a thorough CIA background check, obtained upgraded classified security clearances.[12]

Characteristically, Ambrose's exit from Customs was not without controversy. Under his leadership, Customs was modernized and grew in manpower. But his successor, Vernon D. Acree, was not a career Customs agent. "Iron Mike" Acree had been chief of IRS Inspections and his main qualification for the job was his allegiance to the Republican Party.[13] Many Customs agents had hoped to see Dave Ellis appointed commissioner, and when he was not, resentment among Customs agents towards Ambrose began to swell. Only Ingersoll was happy with the disruptive regime change at Customs.

The White House attempted to placate Customs by restoring its overseas function and allowing it to send 17 agents overseas to focus specifically on gathering narcotics intelligence. Former FBN Agent George C. Corcoran, who had joined Customs in 1955 and totally adopted its values, was sent to Paris to do whatever he could to subvert Paul Knight, the BNDD's new regional director in Paris.[14] A memo Corcoran sent to Acree on July 10, 1972 sums up the situation. Corcoran said, "Customs for sometime has had intelligence in the Richard and Sauveur investigations not known to BNDD. And except for my contacts with the CIA, this information would not be known to me."[15]

Knight in Paris

PAUL KNIGHT KNEW EXACTLY WHAT he was doing. Before he left Kabul for Paris, the US ambassador in Afghanistan had warned him that he was stepping into a political hornets' nest.[16] Knight knew it would be the toughest challenge of his career, which was no small thing. Apart from a year at headquarters in 1968 and 1969, Knight had worked continuously overseas since 1952, and since 1960 as a CIA officer under FBN and BNDD cover. He was accustomed to chatting with attaches in embassies. He knew people at Interpol. And he knew most of the top traffickers, informers, and policemen in Europe and the Middle East, in his own words, "as people." Urbane, articulate, and multi-lingual, Paul Knight was the polar opposite of the abrasive man he replaced, Jack Cusack. Indeed, upon taking control of the Paris office (the most complex and expensive region next to New York) in January 1972, Knight quickly formed a rapport with CNO chief François Le Mouel, and together they oversaw the demise of the French connection.

Early in Knight's tour, White House counsel John Dean arrived in Paris to say how important it was to close down the labs in Marseille. It is unclear why Dean was involved in international drug operations, but he told Knight that the White House would provide all the necessary money and support. As Knight told Dean, it wasn't quite so simple. The French were going through an intense political power struggle. Algerians, Basques, OAS paratroopers and de Gaulle's SAC political action committee were opposing Pompidou. Even policemen in Marseille were part of the intrigues. Some were being bribed, some were motivated by politics; in either case, profits from clandestine heroin labs were used in this domestic French political squabble. The idea, Knight told Dean, was to motivate the French and then stand back and watch. "We were asking for French political involvement," Knight explained, "and they were asking, 'What's the quid pro quo?'"

Marseille was the flashpoint and that's where Interior Minister Roger Fry aimed Knight's counterpart, François Le Mouel. Against the wishes of Marseille's Socialist Mayor, Le Mouel put together a team of narcotics agents composed of his own men from the Paris Brigade of Criminal Intelligence and Intervention.[17] Formed in 1964 to disrupt an armed robbery gang in Paris, Le Mouel's Brigade (known as "the traction squad" for its daredevil car chases in Citroen "Traction Avants") had narcotics experience; specifically, in 1965 it had discovered that Lyon Gang members were smuggling heroin on Air France flights to New York. Le Mouel's Brigade identified their contacts in New York, Spain, Uruguay, and Montreal, and initiated leads into parallel rings managed by Domingo Orsini and Jack Grosby.[18]

What the Brigade had uncovered, without the aid of the Americans, was an entirely new French narcotics network. Le Mouel's initiative also represented a new determination on the part of certain French officials to combat narcotics trafficking in France.

After Pompidou's election as president, François Le Mouel would assume national responsibility for narcotics investigations and, between 1972 and 1975, with the help of Paul Knight, smashed the criminal element of the French connection. According to Knight, Le Mouel went after the old Gaullists and "let the chips fall where they may." Le Mouel's unilateral operation uncovered seven heroin labs and was the deciding factor in smashing the French connection.[19]

Le Mouel's men in Marseille operated as part of a Franco-American Task Force and made spectacular cases like the Caprice de Temps bust that netted 500 kilograms of heroin in July 1972.[20] The BNDD provided intelligence and technical support to the Task Force, but, Knight said, "The French did ninety-nine percent of the work. They could have done it without us. Our big contribution was information out of Middle East, where we had more informers." The French in turn watched French nationals who had been indicted in the United States, and set up arrests for BNDD agents.

Disrupting the French connection was a good approach to fighting the war on drugs, Knight reminisces, but was inherently futile. "Vietnam had ended Mafia control and allowed independents to take over supply," he said. "DC was no longer supplied out of New York. The Bolivians went through the Mexicans and by-passed the Colombian cartels. From then on we were fighting an army of ants."

Knight's work in Paris would end on a successful note in 1975, when he joined American Express as its security chief in Europe. (Stationed in London and Moscow, he was well situated to continue his clandestine CIA activities.) According to Knight, the Hong Kong Chinese would, around 1975, step in to fill the gap left by the demise of the French Connection.

To control the demand side of the equation, the White House created the Drug Abuse Council in 1972, with Ford Foundation financing and Congressional support. In existence until 1978, the Council's purpose was to study ways to reduce demand. Its original operating unit was a task force consisting of Ingersoll, Acree, as well as representatives from the NSC, CIA and departments of Justice, Defense, Treasury and State. Krogh and the White House also created a National Commission on Marijuana and Drug Abuse, with BNDD deputy counsel Michael Sonnenreich as its executive director. In a sign of things to come, the Commission stunned the Nixon administration by advocating the decriminalization of marijuana. To the anguish of all, BNDD deputy director John Finlator supported the commission's findings, and then retired in 1972.

Curbing demand had its merits, but fighting the war on drugs on the supply side was where the glory was, and that's where the politicians and bureaucrats focused their attention.

G-Dep and the New Emphasis on Intelligence

AFTER THE SPECTACULAR CIRILLO CASE, Ingersoll was forced to admit that the systems program had failed. Cirillo, the biggest wholesale distributor in New York, was a mere subsystem. Ambrose had also convinced everyone that "the barbarians were at the gates" and that the only way to win the war on drugs was to fight them one by one.

The systems approach was indeed deficient, primarily because trafficking organizations were fluid, with traffickers moving from one organization to another. The solution was the creation of the Geographical Drug Enforcement Program.[21] G-DEP has remained the principal means of prioritizing investigative efforts up to the present day. Instituted in July 1972, G-DEP identified the nature of the drug being investigated (heroin, pot, upper, downer), and the geographic area and agencies involved in the investigation. The importance of the trafficker factored into the equation and high-ranking individuals were targeted rather than groups. Using criteria established in the Controlled Substances Act of 1970, traffickers were identified as Class I, II, III, or IV "violators," depending on the type and quantity of drug they dealt. Desk officers at headquarters were re-assigned from systems to geographic areas and types of drugs. Conspiracy and forfeiture laws were fine-tuned as well.

The BNDD was restructured from top to bottom along G-Dep lines, so agents could better connect with officers in other agencies, in particular the State Department. Under the system approach, a country attaché had to work with two BNDD officers — the agent in-country and the desk officer at headquarters. This created problems, because the desk officer held the purse strings, while the field agent knew the particulars of the case. G-DEP theoretically overcame that problem.

Cost effectiveness also played a big part in the switch to G-DEP. The General Accounting Office had studied the systems approach to see how much money was spent on any trafficker. It found there was no way to make this determination, and attributed this deficiency to the need for better intelligence. As a result, SIO Chief John Warner no longer reported to Ingersoll, but to his Deputy Director for Operations Andy Tartaglino.[22] And one of the first things Tartaglino did was task John Warner to redirect the SIO in support of the BNDD's domestic war on organized crime.

Warner did this with the assistance of his deputy, John Parker, a soft-spoken maverick from Mississippi. Their new priority was to bring strategic, operational and tactical intelligence closer together.[23] Advising Ingersoll on policy was still a function, but the SIO began to support enforcement in more practical ways as well: by doing background checks, debriefing informants, and providing technical support to all other BNDD branches and regional intelligence staffs.[24] The SIO produced weekly situation reports and summaries for the attorney general. It did special studies (often with CIA consultants), translations, tradecraft training, and maintained the intelligence database.

SIO had already begun a series of special studies to support enforcement. By early 1972, Jerry Strickler had so much information pouring into his Latin America desk that he couldn't keep up with it, so he asked John Bacon at SIO for help. Bacon went to John Parker, who enlisted CIA officer Jim Ludlum. Bacon, Ludlum and Strickler then went to Egil Krogh and asked for more CIA analysts to help organize all the extant material on the French connection.[25] Krogh agreed and arranged for the CIA to send two analysts, one of whom liaised with the CIA's Western Hemisphere desk. Tartaglino provided the two BNDD agents to help get the job done.

The result was Project Pilot, begun in May 1972 under John Bacon. Having labored for 15 years in Latin America for the CIA, Bacon had fully adopted the "intelligence" mindset. However, his SIO bosses, Richard Bly and Bob Goe, were from a different mold. Goe, a former Baltimore cop and BNDD inspector, "didn't understand" according to Bacon.[26] Goe believed strategic intelligence was solely for the management of the organization, not for making cases. Bly, according to Bacon, felt Project Pilot was too expensive and that Bacon wanted "the whole army." Bly wanted Bacon to use his CIA analysts as research assistants, and have them solicit requests for assistance from the RIUs and even local sheriffs.

Bacon found this demeaning. But he and his team forged ahead. At first their job was to provide Strickler with day-to-day support by

finding helpful information in BNDD and CIA files, and by coordinating with BNDD agents and policemen in New York and Miami,
and with Customs Agent Vincent Egan. They also conducted a comprehensive review — "the systematic and blind capturing of all drug
related information" — which they collated and compared.[27] In the
process they found similarities in cases, such as telephone numbers.
The BNDD/DEA agents and their CIA counterparts assigned to Project Pilot read over 100 files and in 1973 compiled a book in three
parts, with one volume on the French Corsican role in South American traffic.

Before it was compiled in bound volumes, Pilot intelligence was
delivered orally by Bacon to Strickler. This intelligence consisted of
some hard facts that were helpful to agents. These facts dealt primarily
in case histories and personalities and gave a picture of how individual
traffickers worked. The 1973 Project Pilot book began with the 1950
Joe Orsini case, outlined the French/Canadian/Mexican Group, and
fanned out into every other facet of the French connection. In the
process, according to Bacon, his team discovered that the people who
had prepared the nine "systems" didn't know what was in the files.
Each region also kept separate records. Bacon and his team put all of
it together, first on 3x5 cards and later on computer.

According to Bacon, the purpose was to build conspiracy cases that
went as high up the chain of command as possible. The problems were
resistance from George Belk and other BNDD enforcement gurus,
and finding competent prosecutors. Bacon felt Pilot was "a Maserati
on blocks. The technicians tested it and it worked fine, but they never
put it on the road. It was never applied."

Ingersoll did, however, value the role of intelligence in federal drug
law enforcement. Thus as part of the G-Dep reorganization he turned
both the SIO and Belk's Office of International Affairs over to Andy
Tartaglino as Chief of Operations.[28] With that move, intelligence took
another small step toward achieving parity with enforcement, and
became the integral facet of overseas operations.

Enter Seymour Bolten

ANOTHER MAJOR CHANGE IN 1972 was the reorganization of the CIA's
drug unit. Early that year, at the direction of Richard Helms, Jim
Ludlum (assisted by his CIA colleagues Jim Anderson and Tom Lawlor) wrote a two-page charter transferring the CIA's drug unit from
Angleton's counter-intelligence unit.[29] Ludlum wanted the office

directly under Helms (as the CIA's representative to CCINC) but it wound up under CIA operations chief Tom Karamessines. Karamessines in turn created a narcotics operations unit and in June placed the unit under Seymour Bolten, a veteran CIA officer fresh from a year-long seminar at the State Department for senior diplomats and executive branch officers.[30]

Known as a wheeler dealer and an extrovert, Bolten from 1968-71 had been chief of a "functional staff" responsible for intelligence activities dealing with Soviet and Eastern European affairs. He had served as special assistant for operations from 1962-65, dealing largely in Latin America where he had been chief of several staffs and a liaison to the Kennedy White House on Cuban affairs.[31] Bolten had worked closely with Ted Shackley, whom he knew from his days as Willie Brandt's case officer in Germany, 1956-60.[32] As author Burton Hersh observed, "The Socialists in Germany would eventually become a prime CIA asset, a matchless conduit for money and information."[33]

Bolten's manipulation of Brandt is highly ironic, for Bolten, a Jew and native New Yorker, was an avid backer of Israel's rabidly right-wing Zionist Likud party. Captured in Poland in World War II, his religious affiliations apparently went unnoticed while he was held in a German POW camp. When released, Bolten was hired onto General Lucius D. Clay's staff within its Civil Administration Division, which was responsible for restoring Germany's political system. Bolten then joined the CIA as a member of its powerful Jewish clique.

As a native New Yorker and arch-conservative, Bolten was politically aligned with Myles Ambrose. Some say he was an intellectual with a broad view. Others say he was patronizing, de-stabilizing, and paranoid. He claimed he became interested in the drug problem while serving as a jury foreman in a case involving a pot pusher.[34]

Bolten's title at CIA was Special Assistant for the Coordination of Narcotics. His unit did not have fully-integrated staff officers working undercover to penetrate drug organizations, but it did direct CIA division and station chiefs in unilateral operations using mercenaries and paramilitary agents. In 1973, Bolten moved Dewey Clarridge from Turkey to Iran to oversee narcotics matters. But, as Clarridge explained, "It was hard for Seymour to keep the lines clean. He was a staff officer with no money and no troops; a coordinator for Helms over area divisions who provided resources and people."[35]

Bolten also replaced Jim Anderson, the CIA's liaison to Jerry Strickler, with Drake Reid. Strickler developed a close relationship with

Reid and his female analyst. "They would call on CIA stations to help BNDD agents in the field," Strickler recalled.[36] The CIA installed a special phone that scrambled calls to Strickler's office, and Strickler spent much of every day consulting with the CIA. This was helpful, and Bolten's shop helped in other ways; for example, by forging identification for undercover agents. But Bolten had a dark side too. Strickler doesn't mince words. "Bolten screwed us," he said, "and so did Shackley."

Bolten further encroached on BNDD turf by "re-tooling" CIA agents and slipping them into the BNDD and DEA.[37] Several went to Lou Conein, whom Bolten knew from Germany. Jack Cusack, whose work for the CIA dated back to 1951, worked closely with Bolten, as did several regional directors overseas. Within his office Bolten also set up a computer system modeled on the CIA's Phoenix "assassination" Program in Vietnam, for identifying and neutralizing drug traffickers. In this way, "archangel" Bolten raised drug enforcement to a new level of sophisticated brutality.

Andy Tartaglino referred to Seymour Bolten as "the chief spook" and said that Bolten hand carried everything directly to the intelligence office in the BNDD (and later the DEA) without consulting with him.[38] But, he added, with Bolten "it was a one-way street" and everything went directly to him from the BNDD (and later the DEA).

SIO chief John Warner often traveled with Bolten and his deputy Stanley Archenhold.[39] An Army Counter Intelligence Corps officer in the Second World War, Archenhold had served as a CIA officer in Mexico for five years before becoming a training officer at Camp Peary, the CIA's training facility near Williamsburg, Virginia. He was Bolten's liaison to Henry Kissinger and the National Security Council. Archenhold also worked with Bob Goe at SIO compiling a Source Register debriefing guide.[40]

Walter Minnick recalled that Bolten cooperated more closely than Jim Ludlum, whom he replaced as chair of the CCINC's intelligence subcommittee. Ludlum, by Minnick's account, was more protective of his parent agency and kept CIA operations apart. "While he was there, we didn't know what CIA was up to," Minnick said. Bolten, however, bent the rules and introduced Minnick to CIA agents operating under deep cover in drug production areas. He would bring someone into Minnick's office and say, "We're going to send this guy undercover to Peru; it would help his motivation if someone at the national level shook his hand and wished him good luck."[41] According to Minnick,

Bolten and Shackley were a team that included "rogue" CIA officers Ed Wilson and Frank Terpil, as well as Lawrence Sternfeld, who had served continually in Latin America since 1954.

Bolten served as an advisor to DCI George H. W. Bush in 1976, and his son Josh would follow in his father's footsteps, serving President George W. Bush as Policy Director of the Bush-Cheney presidential campaign; Bush's Deputy Chief of Staff for Policy, and as an architect of the war on terror and the propaganda campaign that preceded the invasion and occupation of Iraq; and finally as Bush's chief of staff. Josh eventually became the target of a Congressional subpoena for suppressing information. On February 14, 2008, the full House of Representatives voted to cite Josh Bolten for contempt, for not providing documents relating to his role in the dismissal of US Attorneys for political purposes.

National Narcotics Intelligence
IN AN ATTEMPT TO GIVE his White House minions more control over the targeting of individual drug traffickers, President Nixon created by executive order the Office of National Narcotics Intelligence (ONNI) on July 27, 1972.[42] Walter Minnick said the idea came out of the CCINC Working Group. There were two reasons: first, because there was no way of coordinating international intelligence on traffickers, and second, because the BNDD wasn't getting the job done. Ingersoll, according to Minnick, was causing the problem by not being "pro-active."[43] The BNDD, for example, had information from the Colombian police department but was not sharing it, or its informants, with Customs, the CIA, or the CCINC. So the Working Group decided to create ONNI as a central repository for all drug intelligence.

Former FBI executive William C. Sullivan was named ONNI director on August 9, 1972. As chief of domestic intelligence, Sullivan had managed the FBI's notorious COINTELPRO (Counter Intelligence Program), which specialized in blackmail, break-ins, and all manner of illegal activities directed against Civil Rights groups. He was famous for his hatred of Martin Luther King and his "extra-legal" attempts to discredit him. Sullivan once sent King a blackmail tape urging him to commit suicide.[44]

Sullivan was the kind of guy the Nixon White House admired. He was resentful and ambitious and after 30 years of subservience, he longed to replace J. Edgar Hoover. In 1971 he betrayed his boss; Sullivan told Justice Department Internal Security chief Robert Mardian that Hoover was using secret "official and confidential" documents to blackmail Nixon into keeping him (Hoover) in office. Mardian told Ehrlichman, and soon thereafter, Ehrlichman told Sullivan that Henry Kissinger's deputy, Colonel Alexander Haig, wanted him to hand over the incriminating records. Sullivan complied and Mardian put the documents in a safe in his office. Hoover got wind of what Sullivan had done, and sent a team of agents into the office to retrieve the wiretap transcripts. Hoover sealed Sullivan's office and in October 1971 fired his unfaithful deputy.[45]

Sullivan went to work as an insurance investigator in Connecticut. But just like the Mafia needed Louis Cirillo, Nixon and Ehrlichman needed Sullivan, and when Hoover went to his reward in May 1972, they brought Sullivan back into the fold. Walter Minnick described Sullivan as "burned out, tired, worthless," but White House officials nevertheless asked him to manage their anti-drug operations as chief of ONNI.

On September 28, Sullivan outlined the new organization to the Congressional subcommittee on government agencies chaired by John J. Rooney.[46] Sullivan said ONNI would have ninety employees and a $2.5 million budget funded by the Law Enforcement Assistance Administration. It would oversee liaison and information exchange with other agencies, and provide all-source, timely and responsive intelligence support to the Attorney General.[47] Sullivan described his job as working with presidential advisor Myles Ambrose to develop and maintain a national narcotics intelligence system that would 1) restrict the flow of narcotics from abroad by assigning analysts to overseas offices, 2) strengthen domestic enforcement activities in all areas, and 3) initiate programs for prevention, treatment, education and rehabilitation.[48]

ONNI could, theoretically, demand information from any federal, state or local agency, domestic and foreign, and share it with anyone it wished, including prosecutors and the United Nations. It shared informants with the FBI, sent personnel overseas, engaged in law enforcement activities, reviewed US narcotics intelligence, and recommended improvements in collection, analysis and security. It had nearly half a million dollars worth of computers and a "24-hour Watch Center" operated by DIA, NSA, State, Treasury, Justice, and CIA officials. Sullivan could also call upon academics and consultants from outside government to respond instantly to requests and developments of significance.[49]

Sullivan's deputy was NSC official Russell Asch. Twenty-four liaison officers assigned to almost every agency in the government (including Jim Ludlum as liaison to the CIA) made up the bulk of his staff. ONNI was a spooky outfit. When this author filed a Freedom of Information Act request for ONNI records, the Department of Justice claimed to be unable to locate any.[50] They may have been purged for a good reason. According to author Edward J. Epstein, CIA officers assigned to ONNI worked "on a plan for disrupting the cocaine market in the United States 'by poisoning it with methedrene [*sic*]' a domestically manufactured stimulant that could be made to resemble cocaine in color and taste. The bogus cocaine, according to this plan, would cause violent reactions in the cocaine users (if they survived) and thereby turn them against the cocaine dealers."[51] Epstein said the plan was rejected and records of its existence destroyed.

Despite all its potential energy, ONNI (like Seymour Bolten) had no overt operating units or investigators and was, essentially, as Director William Sullivan referred to it, a "clearinghouse." It did not receive funding until December 1972, and in its short and unproductive lifespan, ONNI acquired and used only a fraction of the information that was potentially available to it.

ONNI was just another aspect of Ambrose's "shock treatment" and, like ODALE, came as a total surprise to Ingersoll and the BNDD. Ingersoll assigned John Parker as his liaison to ONNI, and sent John Warner to meet with Sullivan to discuss their official relationship. Warner recalled that the meeting occurred on a hot summer day and Sullivan's office was not yet air-conditioned. Sullivan "was very upbeat," Warner explained. "But that was because he needed us, because he didn't have files of his own."[52]

By Andy Tartaglino's account, Ehrlichman and Krogh initially tried to plant ONNI at the White House, but Ingersoll and Kleindienst raised so much hell, it ended up in the attorney general's office, where Robert Mardian held it hostage in his bid to take over the Justice Department. Tartaglino said that ONNI was staffed with analysts from Mardian's Internal Security Division as well as "CIA refugees" from Vietnam. "After Hoover turned down the Huston Plan," Tartaglino said, "Bob Mardian started trying to take over the FBI. Then after Hoover dies in May, Nixon sets up ONNI with Mardian's help, and Sullivan gets it. Kleindienst announced its formation at a staff meeting, and that's how we heard about it. Apart from Jim Ludlum, it was a collection depot for CIA's unusable people — chauffeurs classified as intelligence analysts — most of who had been kicked out of the CIA."[53]

By the time ONNI got off the ground, Myles Ambrose was planning to include it in his new creation, the DEA. As part of this new development, CIA deputy Director Vernon Walters assigned Colonel Tulius Acampora to the Pentagon to work on military aspects of the drug problem with CCINC liaison Werner Michel. Acampora and Michel recommended to Walters that the CIA and military get out of the drug business. But Nixon and the White House wanted everyone involved. According to Acampora, it was the "operation by committee" concept, made fashionable by the CIA's Phoenix Program in Vietnam and adopted by Seymour Bolten and Myles Ambrose being applied to drug law enforcement. But the more everyone pooled resources, Acampora explained, the more the BNDD's mission was diluted. Many of its overseas operations were turned over to CIA's Special Operations Division under Evan Parker, a former director of the Phoenix Program and close friend of William Colby. The military stayed involved too and assigned people who, like the CIA officers involved, hid behind plausible denial.[54]

Echoing Acampora was Thomas Fox, the Defense Intelligence Agency liaison at ONNI. Fox agrees that the military was not anxious to get involved.[55] It did not want to share its precious resources (like exotic sensing devices for patrolling the Ho Chi Minh Trails) to patrol the Mexican border in search of drugs. The military also felt its participation might be illegal under the Posse Comitatus Act. This feeling was based on a disturbing incident that occurred in Eureka, California in October 1972, when ODALE borrowed military helicopters to stage a drug raid. According to one eye witness, it looked like an assault on a Viet Cong village.[56] As 24 year old Dirk Dickenson hopped off his back porch and ran for the woods, BNDD Agent Lloyd Clifton leaped out of the chopper and shot him in the back. The "million-dollar meth lab" the ODALE agents were looking for was nowhere to be found. After that, the military was pretty much relegated to helping overseas, where the Posse Comitatus Act did not apply.

The BNDD actively contributed to the "operations by committee" modus operandi. In August 1972, Regional Director Dan Casey in New York formed a Cooperative Narcotics Intelligence Committee, based on a similar committee he had formed in Los Angeles.[57] The Cooperative Narcotics Intelligence included representatives from

BNDD, Customs, ODALE, the NYPD's Intelligence Division, and the New York Joint Task Force. While visiting Andy Maloney, the ODALE chief in New York, Myles Ambrose was given a personal briefing about the Committee by the NYPD. This was somewhat frightening to Ingersoll, as the Committee's computer was to be linked to the Data Systems Division computer at BNDD headquarters. The idea that Ambrose might use the Committee's computer to sneak a peek at BNDD case information was, however, viewed as a concession worth making, for, as Casey explained, "the concept of a mutual repository system is founded on trust, sincerity, and good will."[58]

There was another problem: the Cooperative Narcotics Intelligence Committee was ostensibly limited to domestic intelligence. But IBM, which sold and installed the Committee's computer, was also servicing the CIA, and the CIA was a covert member of the Committee. This meant the CIA could access domestic intelligence and identify and steal BNDD, ODALE, Customs or NYPD informants. Casey's solution was for each member to create a "repository index" (or "source register") to prevent informants from playing one agency against the other, and to prevent members from investigating the same cases.[59] But the Committee's Executive Council that oversaw the index system had no way of knowing if its members were hacking into the BNDD computer or sharing files with outsiders.

In presenting his proposal to Ingersoll, Casey noted that the idea had worked well in the area of foreign intelligence, and that "we are participating in such a program with our foreign sources of information."[60] That system, managed by the CIA, was known as the International Narcotics Information System.[61] The CIA managed the INIS because the director of Central Intelligence has "cognizance" over all US foreign intelligence entities, and if Customs or the BNDD mounted intelligence operations overseas, the CIA had the legislative mandate to screen informants to keep foreign agents from penetrating their operations and using them against the US.[62]

Casey's connections to the CIA dated back to his salads days in San Francisco as an administrative assistant to George White, the CIA's operating agent in the MKULTRA Program. Knowing this, it's hard to believe that Casey would be so naïve as to think that the CIA would not use the source register to spy on the BNDD's domestic investigations, through informants operating overseas and within the US. In any event, such "collateral" operations eventually became "integral." Along with the Watergate scandal, Ambrose's unfettered ambition, and Ingersoll's weak leadership, the new emphasis on sharing intelligence and conducting joint operations would exacerbate the BNDD's ongoing bureaucratic and personal rivalries, and hasten its loss of integrity and identity.

As the French connection began to wind down, developments in Vietnam and the Far East would have a greater and equally negative impact as well.

14

CHASING THE DRAGON

Agent Tony Pohl, commenting on the situation in Southeast Asia during the Vietnam War (and the US intervention in Afghanistan after 2001), said "Anything is possible in a war zone, except law enforcement."

Amen.

Fred Dick knew this as well as anyone. Somewhat cynical in world affairs, he purchased the beautiful, engraved, silver inlaid ivory pipe that once belonged to President Diem's opium addicted brother, Nhu.[1] According to Al McCoy in *The Politics of Heroin*, Lucien Conein told him that Nhu in 1958 "established two pipelines from the Laotian poppy fields to South Vietnam. The major pipeline was a small charter airline, Air Laos Commerciale, managed by Indochina's most flamboyant Corsican gangster, Bonaventure "Rock" Francisci." Nhu "supplemented these shipments by dispatching intelligence agents to Laos with orders to send back raw opium on the Vietnamese air force transports that shuttled back and forth carrying agents and supplies."[2]

After McCoy's book was published, Conein wrote to Harper & Row President Winthrop Knowlton, denying, among other things McCoy attributed to him, "That Nhu was a secret partner in a Corsican charter airline so that he could finance his secret police."[3] But in promoting the Diem regime as the model of Christian propriety, successive US governments overlooked this obvious fact. They also buried the fact that the South Vietnamese assassins of Diem and Nhu (who were advised by Conein) inherited Nhu's drug network. All such plausible denials are part of the on-going psychological warfare that shapes the perceptions of the gullible American public.

Likewise, the vices of its puppet rulers around the world serve the US government well, and after the Murphy-Steele Report was issued, the White House declared the war on drugs a "national emergency" and used drug smuggling as a way of vilifying the same people it had supported. As noted in Chapter 10, most were named in a series of articles for the *New York Times* in the spring and summer of 1971. Air Force General Ky was tied to a heroin lab near Vientiane operating under the protection of Laotian General Ouane Ratikone, and the *Times* quoted the Vietnamese Customs director as saying planes of the South Vietnamese Air Force were "the principle carriers of dope into South Vietnam."[4] Ky's controller allegedly worked with Corsican gangsters in Vietnam and Laos, presumably the same ones employed by Nhu.

President Thieu's political foes, such as Ky, were not the only ones implicated. Thieu was said to use drug money to finance his campaigns while his national security chief, General Dang Van Quang, was reportedly one of the biggest pushers, along with Admiral Chung Tan Cang, whose naval officers moved dope through rivers in Cambodia.[5] Quang and Cang, naturally, were also in charge of anti-narcotic efforts in South Vietnam, working with CIA Station Chief Ted Shackley's deputy Ron Landreth.[6]

Prime Minister Tran Thien Khiem was another CIA connected politician who made a fortune in narcotics.[7] CIA officer William Colby was Khiem's case officer from 1969 until his return to Langley in the fall of 1971 as the CIA's executive director.[8] Colby, as chief of station in Saigon and chief of the Far East Division throughout the 1960s, had first knowledge of the drug trafficking activities of Vietnamese officials. He certainly had a hand in protecting them and reportedly helped set up banks for their drug money, and helped fly their dope around on CIA proprietary airlines. Colby's outlook toward his Vietnamese counterparts, if not the CIA, changed upon his return to Washington and his enlistment in Nixon's war on drugs.

Helms had already sent CIA officers Richard Long and Frederick W. Flott to investigate Air America, but Helms and Colby saw to it that no CIA officers were indicted as co-conspirators, abducted, and rendered back to the US for trial. On the contrary, Helms, although he had decided to "break their rice bowls," had already begun a concerted propaganda campaign to cover up the CIA's past sins.[9] Ever willing to help, the *New York Times* reported that CIA agents had identified 21 opium refineries in Laos, Burma, and Thailand.[10] The labs, it said, were producing 700 tons annually, half the world's production. Air America choppers, it said, attacked a heroin refinery in Laos. All of which was true.

But evidence continued to surface that the CIA coordinated a facet of the Southeast Asian drug trade, and used drug money to finance the Kuomintang and Thai, Laotian and South Vietnamese officials. Much of the detail came from Jean Marie Le Rouzic's letter to the Sûreté in May 1971. Rouzic's revelations about the Corsican-CIA connection are outlined earlier in Chapter 10, and concern the Royal Air Lao team out of Pakse; the Vietnamese military men at Xeno working with Thai generals and Laotian officers; and the aforementioned Air Laos Commerciale first out of Pakse, then through Cambodia into Saigon. One Corsican organization under Henri Flamant and Roger Zoile worked with Nationalist Chinese, and the prime minister's son in Laos. Another was connected to the wife of the Justice Minister through a woman who owned a jewelry store. A third Corsican organization (Le Rouzic's) sent dope to Nice using diplomatic luggage and military planes.[11]

By November 1971, with the arrest at JFK Airport of the Filipino attaché to Laos, Domingo S. Canieso, with 34 pounds of heroin, it became clear that the Golden Triangle had replaced Turkey as the main source of the problem. The Murphy-Steele Report had emphasized this fact, and by 1972 the BNDD was doing a Project Pilot-type study on the problem. Authored by CIA officer Tom Becker and BNDD Agent Paul Brown, the report described how Chinese chemists made highly refined heroin for Rattikone and his Chinese partner.

The CIA knew, but did nothing. As Fred Dick noted: "The Agency was amassing far more drug intelligence than they were ever passing to me. Their position was more strategic than tactical and they were governed by ever changing political considerations, whereas BNDD and later DEA were cast in more of a tactical role. This situation tends to create a divergence I do not believe will ever be overcome in the international arena."[12]

Dick realized the CIA was protecting its drug-dealing clients in South Vietnam. He wouldn't fight a battle he couldn't win, so he used informant Joe Berger to make a case on a major Chinese trafficker.

He took what he could get from the CIA, including access to CIA polygraph experts who coaxed confessions from drug dealers, helped investigate Vietnamese employees of Air America, and tested potential informants for the BNDD.[13] But most of what Dick got from the CIA came unofficially through his friend Colonel Tulius Acampora and Acampora's protégé, William Logay.[14]

Acampora refers to Logay as "the original Mississippi Riverboat gambler."[15] A former college football player and Oakland cop, Logay took a contract with the CIA from 1965 until 1968 as a security officer at the Saigon embassy.[16] He did well and returned to Vietnam in 1971 to work as a Special Branch police advisor under CIA employee Acampora in Saigon. Acampora advised Tran Si Tan, the Special Branch policeman in charge of Saigon, and also sat on the CIA's narcotics intelligence committee. Logay worked as a bagman for the special police in several of Saigon's precincts, and, at Acampora's direction, shared sanitized CIA narcotics intelligence reports with Dick. Logay sent the raw reports to station chief Tom Polgar's narcotics deputy Vince Lockhart. A former station chief in Argentina, Uruguay and Peru, Polgar arrived in Saigon in the summer of 1971. Polgar was more involved in drug interdiction than Shackley and actually had CIA agents recruit informants and make buys.[17]

Through Tully Acampora, Fred Dick and Bill Logay soon became friends. Logay knew things Dick wanted to know, and even told him a little — although, referring to his CIA secrecy oath, he insists he "never broke [his] mandate." Logay also explained that intelligence collection is driven by money, and that those with money get friends, and thus intelligence.[18] The fact that the CIA had far more money for informants than the BNDD was the harsh reality that confronted Fred Dick; he had some funds, but a miniscule amount compared to the Agency's bulging black bag. Dick had the status of an army general, Logay of a captain, and yet Logay, through Acampora, had a $10,000 monthly revolving account to wine and dine and recruit assets. Dick relied on persuasion, mano a mano, but that approach could only get him so far in a world where money mattered most.

Fred Dick and Bill Logay were friends, but Dick did not have a friendly relationship with Steve Greene, the BNDD agent assigned to help him in late 1971. Greene was no stranger to the wicked ways of the world; he had served as a Marine in Vietnam in 1966-1967, and unlike Dick and Logay, he viewed the scene from that violent perspective. The clean-cut image of the modern DEA official, Greene would became acting administrator of the DEA in 1991. In Saigon in 1972 he enjoyed closer relations with the CIA security staff than his boss Fred Dick. He had better political connections too: Greene's father was a deputy commissioner at the INS and knew Andy Tartaglino personally. For all these reasons, Dick suspected that Greene was a shoofly and kept him at arm's length.[19]

Greene had joined the BNDD in September 1968, serving in Baltimore until early 1971, when he did a three-month TDY tour in Turkey. In the fall of 1971, after his father pulled strings, he was assigned to Vietnam, where he wanted to be. Fred Dick was there with one other agent, Joe Daly, who had been assigned to the BNDD from the US Army CID. As a three-person "stand alone" office reporting directly to headquarters, Saigon was unique within the BNDD.

As Greene recalled, "Fred was in a free-for-all environment in which he thrived." He knew which South Vietnamese officials were off-limits, so he went after the Chinese tontine "like a New York agent making the Mafia." According to Greene, Dick knew it would take careful planning, and had Joe Berger arrested and made him go to work for him. Dick did not step on any important Vietnamese or CIA toes, but Berger had to deal dope to make cases, and he was, inevitably, busted in June 1972 in possession of 400 pounds of opium from Bangkok. It was a very big case, involving Wan Pen Phen ("the Phantom"), who moved tons of opium through Thailand and Laos to a hotel owner in Saigon.[20] Phen was fair game, as were his Vietnamese civilian connections.

There was no way, however, that Fred Dick could conceal his old-school methodology, or his extra-curricular activities, and Greene quickly learned that Dick was using the BNDD's postal account to send ceramics and gold to his business partner Maggie Ying, a jewelry store owner in Hong Kong.[21] Greene became a potential witness against Dick, and felt he might be tainted by Dick's wheeling and dealing. But Fred Dick didn't care. He never introduced Berger to Greene, and was rounding up big league outlaws for Ingersoll and Krogh. Apart from Andy Tartaglino, the bosses apparently had no problem with him making a buck on the side. On the contrary, in 1972 they promoted Dick to regional director in Bangkok. At this point the Far East was sub-divided into two regions; one under Dick in Bangkok, the other under Mike Picini in Manila. Agent Bill Cunningham took charge in Saigon, with Steve Greene and several newly arrived BNDD agents as his assistants.

Laos

THE BNDD OPENED ITS FIRST office in Vientiane, Laos, in the fall of 1971, when that nation's first sweeping anti-narcotics laws were enacted. Manufacturing and trafficking in heroin was already a crime and the government formed a Special Narcotics Enforcement unit advised by US Public Safety official Major McBee and several of his colleagues.[22] The Special Narcotics Enforcement unit, however, was not allowed into the military regions where the CIA's secret army under General Vang Pao operated. Like Fred Dick and the BNDD agents under his command, the Lao narcotics unit could only go after apolitical or politically incorrect individuals.

Charlie Vopat was one of the first two permanent BNDD agents in Laos, arriving in Vientiane in May 1972.[23] Already there was Anthony Morelli, a dark-haired agent, fluent in French, with a lovely French wife and two kids. Morelli's parents had lived in the Far East and he was familiar with the culture. Morelli enjoyed good relations with the Laotian Groupe Speciale d'Investigation (GSI), a narcotics enforcement unit which primarily gathered intelligence and went after Corsican pilots and their Chinese accomplices. Fred Dick was the boss in Bangkok and came unannounced every two months. According to Vopat, Dick was effective and acquired good Chinese informants; Vopat recruited them with help from his Vietnamese wife, who got along with Dick's wife Thanh. A warehouse in Vientiane was known to be the staging area for heroin produced at a nearby lab owned by Laotian General Ouane Rattikone. BNDD agents believed this warehouse was protected by Public Safety officials working for the CIA, whose only concern was fighting communists.

Public Safety had several narcotics officers in Laos, including Gordon Young in Houei Sai, Peter Hurst in Pakse, and Fred Dick's nemesis Major McBee in Vientiane. McBee's priority was organizing the Narcotics Unit, then leaving it alone. "We had a committee composed of Customs, military, BNDD, and Public Safety people," he said. "If the case was outside Vientiane, it passed through the committee." Public Safety had no planes and was dependent on Air America, which fueled the rumors that all Public Safety officers in Laos were CIA.[24]

McBee said he conducted training and did investigations, and that he spoke daily with Tony Morelli, who did not object to his involvement. McBee would pass information to Morelli if a buy could be made. The BNDD and Public Safety advisors mounted joint checkpoint operations, but each relied on his Laotian police counterparts to do the work, and as in Thailand and Vietnam, corruption was a huge obstacle. McBee explained that he "had to be diplomatic" because the director of the anti-narcotics unit was involved in drug smuggling. McBee tried to get him replaced, but that was impossible, as the director kicked money up to his bosses. "The one lab that was seized," McBee adds with a fatalistic sigh, "wasn't even active."

Customs in Laos

MYLES AMBROSE HAD TO FIND a way to get rid of Dave Ellis, the rightful heir to the Customs throne, and the leader of the forces opposed to Ambrose in Customs. Ambrose knew that Ellis was an action oriented combat veteran of the Pacific Theatre in the Second World War, and that he had been the Customs Service's liaison to the CIA for many years; so Ambrose gave Ellis several top-secret special assignments in the Far East. In his self-published autobiography, Ellis claims Treasury Secretary John Connelly, along with White House officials John Ehrlichman, Egil Krogh, Walt Minnick, and Jeffrey Donfeld, also sent him on secret missions.[25]

Ellis relished these jobs. His first special assignments were in Vietnam, resolving a problem with narcotics being shipped through the military postal service and morgue, and another problem with corrupt Customs officials. Krogh was impressed with the results, and Ellis' next assignment was a special job for Customs and the White House in Laos and Thailand.[26] With CIA assistance, he explored the area in Laos along the Chinese border and found out where opium caravans were entering. He then went to Bangkok and, as part of a Customs agreement to train Thai officials, explained to the Thai Minister of Finance that opium caravans were coming into Houei Sai, and that narcotics were also coming into Thailand from the Northeast, in the vicinity of Udorn.

According to Ellis, he and the Finance Minister, Thongtanag Thongtam, traveled to Chiang Rai to inspect Thai Customs operations. While visiting the consulate, the US Counsel told Ellis there were two people upstairs who wished to speak to him about his investigation. The first was an Army major on loan to CIA. The major, dressed in a Lao field uniform, was working with Vang Pao's troops on the Plaines Des Jarres. "The officer was so weary he cried," Ellis said. The major said that Ellis' investigation was going to put Vang Pao out of business. The CIA was trying to win the war and needed his troops. The major told Ellis to back off.[27]

Ellis went across the hall to another room. A man inside the room asked if Ellis remembered him. His name was Jim and he said that Ellis had hired him in Houston for a specialized CIA program spying on exile-Cuban terrorists in Miami. Afterwards Jim had gone to work for the CIA. Jim said the five provinces in eastern Thailand belonged to the Thai army by day, the communists by night. People in the drug business were furnishing weapons to the insurgents, but the CIA had the matter in hand. Jim said he had two choppers and 25 men. They tracked communist drug traffickers and assassination squads in Laos, Thailand and Vietnam, and killed them. He described himself and his crew as "the trackers."[28]

CIA officer Jim then explained to Ellis how Kuomintang opium caravans in Burma traveled into China and returned to Thailand with opium. Jim said that the traffickers had the assistance of the Chinese Communists planning to take over the Northeast part of Thailand and were assisted by the BNDD and corrupt Thai officials. The Thai Finance Minister gave Ellis permission to target the officials involved, but the operation never got off the ground, and the US government decided to purchase the opium crop instead.[29]

Ellis regrouped and in September 1971, while organizing a joint Laotian-US Customs assistance program, identified a saw mill owned by Laotian General Ouane as the site of a heroin lab. Ellis arranged to have the Chinese chemists killed and the lab blown up.[30]

Ellis also did his best to convince the White House that Fred Dick was "salting diplomats."[31] Worse, he felt that Dick and the BNDD had doctored the CIA maps that Ingersoll presented to the White House staff in 1971.[32] The maps showed that China was not involved in the drug trade, and gave Nixon and Kissinger the opening they needed to court China, against the wishes of the military establishment. Ellis claims his investigations proved the Chinese were involved.

This claim is supported by Dr. Joseph D. Douglas in his book, *Red Cocaine: The Drugging of America and The West*.[33] Douglas claims the CIA map showed the Golden Triangle source in China, but "a new version of the map emerged from the White House." The tip of the triangle had been moved from China into Laos. He adds that a CIA analyst detailed to the BNDD's Office of Strategic Intelligence. wrote a report about the involvement of Communist China's intelligence service in narcotics trafficking. The report traced the history and listed names, dates, and places. But it was suppressed. "The cover-up of Communist China's drugs and narcotics trafficking appears to have started in the early 1960s," Douglas said. "It took on greatly increased scope during the Nixon Administration, and it appears to be continuing today." Douglas adds that the Department of Defense used reconnaissance planes to help identify poppy fields in Burma and Laos, but Kissinger stopped them to "avoid threatening *détente* with China."[34]

Conceding the point, CCINC staff director Walter Minnick said, "From our perspective we didn't care about China being Red; Taiwan was not going to win the mainland back." Minnick, however, denies sending Ellis on any secret missions.[35]

According to Ellis, a higher authority, John Ehrlichman, did instruct the CIA to help him disrupt this Chinese Communist operation, but covertly, in order to avoid a "drug flap with China" as well as alienating Republicans wedded to Taiwan.[36] Kissinger had just returned from his first visit to China, and a former Thai diplomat and member of one of the most respected Thai families was one of the key figures in the opium, morphine base and heroin operations in that country and throughout Southeast Asia. This Thai was an archangel, so Ellis and the CIA were limited to targeting native tribes who were competing with and fighting Vang Pao's CIA army on behalf of the communists.[37]

The communists in Burma, Thailand and Laos allegedly harvested and sold opium to support their insurgencies. They moved their product through known entry points from China, as did the Kuomintang caravan that operated with Thai police and military support.[38] Erstwhile CIA officer William Young, in a 1972 report to US Customs, claimed that the police commander in northern Thailand used US vehicles and aircraft to transport opium. He was fired, but only "because he wasn't paying his superiors enough of the take."[39]

According to Ellis, the complicit Thais were all part of the same family, but "one side was making love to Chinese, just to hedge their bets in case the US lost the war." American officials, including the BNDD, were walking on tip-toes, as it had taken the State Department until mid-1971 to convince the Thais to allow the BNDD to open an office in Chiang Mai. So Ellis was given the job of eliminating the Communist Chinese native Thai accomplices "without a trace."[40]

By his account, Ellis mounted this secret operation with money from William Boleyn at OMB and with CIA paramilitary officer Anthony Poshepny, aka Tony Poe. A Marine veteran who had served with the CIA in the Philippines, Indonesia and Tibet, Poe was the balding, robust model for Marlon Brando's Colonel Kurtz in *Apocalypse Now!*

He also served as a father figure to the junior CIA officers he commanded in the savage jungles of Laos, including Terry Burke, the future acting chief of the Drug Enforcement Administration. Beginning in 1965, Poe managed the CIA's 118A Strategic Intelligence Network out of the Nam Yu base just north of Houei Sai.[41]

In an interview with the author, Poe said he "hated" Vang Pao because the greedy general was selling guns to the communists. But Poe was a company man; he held his tongue and made sure that the CIA's share of opium was delivered from Nam Yu to the old French airfield at Houei Sai. It was then packed in oil drums, loaded on CIA C-47s, flown by Taiwanese mercenaries to the Gulf of Siam, then dropped into the sea and picked up by accomplices in sampans waiting at specified coordinates. The people on the sampans ferried the drugs to Hong Kong, where the opium was cooked into heroin by Kuomintang chemists and then sold to Mafiosi. As described by Poe and Bill Young, this was the CIA's private channel to its long-standing Mafia partners in Hong Kong.[42]

Poe was, in Ellis' border patrol lexicon, "a man you could ride the river with."[43] Poe and Ellis went to one of Vang Pao's bases in north central Laos near the border of China and North Vietnam, where they obtained Hmong native recruits to target the communist-aligned tribes moving opium. Ellis returned to the US and enlisted eight CIA supplied Green Berets at a hotel in Arlington, Virginia. He briefed them for a week with a senior Customs inspector. Ellis obtained Boston Whaler boats from the CIA through the Agency for International Development, and sent the Special Forces soldiers back to Laos undercover as customs inspectors. When they ascertained a delivery was to be made, the soldiers contacted Poe and his tribesmen. Together they had a "corrective influence on those tribes which used horses to transport" opium from China into Laos.[44]

Ellis' operation with mad Tony Poe, famous for decapitating his enemies, was a token gesture at best. But it was indicative of the extreme measures that defined the government's war on drugs. These measures were supported by the usual disinformation and in April 1972, General Lewis W. Walt, USMC (retired) told the US Senate Internal Security Subcommittee that he had found "no indication that the CIA is in any way conveying or in any way taking part in or supporting or condoning drug traffic in Southeast Asia."[45]

Those same Hearings would acknowledge the "establishment of CIA responsibility for narcotic intelligence coordination."[46]

Operations in Thailand

IN THAILAND, BNDD AND CUSTOMS agents concentrated on criminal cases involving Americans, especially the Atkinson-Jackson ring, in which smugglers stuffed heroin inside the chest cavities of soldiers, and flew the cadavers to US military bases inside flag-draped caskets.[47] Accomplices at the bases withdrew the heroin and re-stitched the bodies. As the reader may recall, BNDD Agents Richard Patch and Dennis Hart were accused in 1970 of protecting the Atkinson-Jackson operation, but were acquitted after two mistrials.

Jackson and Atkinson operated out of Bangkok, with protection from a Thai legislator on their payroll. They were not immune in the US, however, and the big break in the case came when Air Force investigators warned Customs in December 1971 that a shipment of heroin was flying into Dover Air Force Base in Delaware. The shipment was tied to Jackson and his main courier Andrew Price, who were arrested in January 1972. Jackson was convicted, but his partners Leslie Atkinson and Thomas E. Southerland, although indicted in Baltimore in December 1972, continued to operate until 1975.[48]

The Atkinson-Jackson source likewise continued to operate out of northern Thailand. Cross-border spy operations into China, managed out of the CIA's 118A base a few miles north of Houei Sai, Laos, ostensibly stopped sometime prior to August 1972, probably on orders from Nixon and Kissinger.[49] However, the US Army's 500th Military Intelligence Group (which did not contribute to the central narcotics source registry) continued to run agents into China; the CIA kept "stay behind agents" in place in the opium caravans, which continued to move; the Kuomintang still manned their base on the Chinese border through which the caravan passed; and the Shan turned to the Communist Chinese for aide.[50] These developments directly impacted Agent Jim Pettit, who had opened the BNDD's office in Chiang Mai in late 1971. Forbidden from making cases on Thais and the Kuomintang, Pettit's primary target was the Yao tribal leader in Houei Sai, who sold raw opium to various customers, including Americans like Leslie Atkinson, and CIA employees of Continental Airlines, which had a State Department contract to fly food and supplies to the Yao.[51]

Pettit organized five Special Narcotics Organization (SNO) mobile paramilitary strike teams composed largely of members of the CIA, advised by Thai Border Patrol Police (BPP). SNO teams began operations in March 1972, but the BPP did not cooperate unless ordered by their national commander, and the only time he gave the okay was when

Pettit went after the hill tribes.[52] It was a tragic situation. The hill tribes were a factor in the opium trade but suffered far more than the Shan, Kuomintang and Thai officials who ran the business. Due to BNDD successes, many were forced to turn to the communists for help, and thus became part of the insurgency the US was hell-bent on fighting.[53]

Pettit did identify complicit Thai officials, and BNDD headquarters revealed their identities to White House officials; in an interview with the author, CCINC staff director Walter Minnick specifically named General Kriangsak Chamanand, who would become prime minister in 1977.[54] But there were many more, and, as had occurred in Vietnam the year before, their names were leaked to the press. Word quickly spread and in a February 1972 column in the *Washington Post*, Jack Anderson referred to a letter from Congressman Lester Wolff complaining that Thai officials were dealing narcotics. But that particular leak had little effect, for Thailand was not at war and its leaders were not planning to flee their country (like the Vietnamese) to America. The Thais were, on the contrary, well aware that they were the bulwark of US national security interests in South East Asia, and they simply laughed at the Americans and told them to chase after Chen Shi-fu (aka Khun Sa), the Shan warlord whose private army of some 2,000 men had sparked the 1967 Opium War. It was common knowledge that Khun Sa moved only about ten percent of the region's opium, while the CIA's Kuomintang moved about seventy. More to the point, the Thais were now running cross-border intelligence operations for the CIA through the Kuomintang caravans and the Border Patrol Police, and for that reason were immune.

BNDD Agent Jim Pettit was unhappy with the situation, and the CIA base chief in Chiang Mai, Robert Brewer, was unhappy with Jim Pettit.[55] Brewer had ten agents and one pilot, focused not on narcotics interdiction, but on counter-insurgency. Indeed, to fight the counter-insurgency, he had to support the Thais, who protected the prime drug movers. The communists were making gains in the region, which was the pretext for the military coup in Thailand that made Thanom Kittikachorn prime minister and virtual dictator in November 1971. The insurgency was spilling over into Burma where dissident tribes, incited by the communists, were trading opium for guns. So Brewer asked his CIA masters to make everyone (except the Chinese brokers and chemists) happy, by buying the 1972 opium crop.[56]

The BNDD had worked hard to open an office in Chiang Mai and, in return, Ingersoll was authorized to pay Thai officials one million dollars to buy 20 tons of opium from Kuomintang warlords Li Wen-huan and Tuan Hsi-wen on the Burma border in April 1972.[57] The opium was ostensibly burned, though half was reportedly replaced with dung and resold by Thai officials. As Fred Dick recalled, "Just before I got to Bangkok there was a deal hatched involving the agency and BNDD with the KMT in northern Thailand. They had ceremonial mass opium burning in northern Thailand. I don't know who came up with the money, but I do know the agency wrote the words and music for this opera. When I got to Bangkok it was all very hush-hush so I ignored it and went on to other things in the region."[58]

Dick arrived in Bangkok in summer 1972. Agent John Doyle was his deputy and Adrian Swain headed the region's intelligence unit with CIA officer Tom Becker, yet another protégé of Tully Acampora in Vietnam. Dick sent Agent Harry Fullett to Vientiane to replace Tony Morelli. Wise to the wicked ways of the world, Dick took the Zen "middle path." About his relationship with the CIA, Dick said, "The agency had a station in Chiang Mai and they were working with the Thai Border Patrol. I do not know what they were doing. We did exchange intelligence and their files were open to us, as ours were to them. We never worked jointly in field operations."[59]

Whereas Pettit had reported negatively about Brewer's activities, Dick formed a rapport with him and the station chief in Bangkok, Lou Lapham. To make a fresh start, he had Pettit shipped back to the US "for more language training." Pettit never returned.

Burma the Bountiful

CIA OFFICERS JIM LUDLUM, JOSEPH E. Lazarsky and Clyde McAvoy wrote "the scenario" in Burma.[60] To insure that the military's interests in Southeast Asia were not compromised, Deputy Director of Central Intelligence General Robert Cushman attended the CCINC meetings where Lazarsky, Ludlum and McAvoy presented their plan of attack.[61] An OSS veteran and commander of the Kachin Raiders in Burma in the Second World War, Lazarsky served in Burma again with the CIA from 1955-1958. In Vietnam in 1970-1972, he was Ted Shackley's operations chief and in this capacity he monitored Air America's activities with the station's special assistant for narcotics, Richard Sampson.[62] CIA officer Clyde McAvoy, the first secretary at the American embassy in Rangoon, had roamed the Far East for fifteen years.

Tribesmen in northern Burma moved opium to Tachilek on the Thai border in the Shan State. According to McAvoy, Tachilek had the largest refinery of premium "China White" heroin in the world.[63] It was well guarded by Khakweyei irregulars. The problem was how to enlist General Ne Win, Chairman of Burma's Revolutionary Council, in Nixon's war on drugs. Ne Win had no love for Americans and had, at one time, defeated a CIA-supported Kuomintang force. He had publicly displayed two CIA agents killed in the action and kicked the US military advisory group out of Burma.[64]

In September 1971, through CIA officer Bob Six of Continental Airlines, senior advisor to the State Department on International Narcotics Matters (INM) Nelson Gross purchased an audience with Ne Win.[65] Gross presented the Ludlum-Lazarsky-McAvoy plan, which made Lo Hsing Han (the Phantom's rival) the fall guy. A Chinese national, Han's 1500 man Khakweyei army was equipped with American M16s diverted from the Lao army. The Khakweyei had faithfully served Ne Win by fighting communist insurgents, and he knew that the Chinese would make gains in the Shan State in their absence. But he approved the plan anyway. In a matter of weeks his six-foot-three intelligence chief, Colonel Tin Oo, infiltrated agents into Tachilek, where they found eight heroin production plants. They also discovered that Burmese army officers were involved, along with several of Tin's intelligence officers and the local Thai BPP commander. Ne Win had regular army troops destroy the factories, arrest the corrupt officers, and disband the Khakweyei.[66]

Khun Sa's Shan national Army and the Thai-based Kuomintang picked up the slack, and Khun Sa would become an enduring target of the DEA for the next 20 years. About the Kuomintang, Fred Dick said: "We all know they never got out of the opium traffic. They probably would have been better off to give the money to the Salvation Army."[67]

Dick visited Rangoon in mid-1972 and set up a SNO paramilitary strike team program. He then sent his star informant, Joe Berger, to trap Lo Hsing Han. Based in Rangoon and Singapore, Han was busted in 1973. That year the BNDD also penetrated a huge network that supplied most of the China White heroin in America. Arrested in the case were San Franciscan Wong Shin Kong, and his numerous Chinese and America accomplices.[68] The BNDD also made the Thai Trawler case in April 1973. Thai smugglers moved tons of opium and marijuana on trawlers from southern Thailand to Hong Kong through the South China Sea. With the help of the South Vietnamese Navy, two trawlers were intercepted and two tons of opium seized. US Defense Attaché Richard Armitage, according to BNDD Agent Thomas de Trinquet, "put the Vietnamese Navy at our disposal and got us down to the Vietnamese Navy base to interrogate prisoners and inventory the catch."[69]

It was a major victory and reduced the amount of China White heroin on the American market in 1973. Thus, despite his flaws, Fred Dick had done his job.

Fred Dick's Problems

CONGRESS APPROPRIATED $56 MILLION FOR the BNDD in 1972, and George Belk and Ron Metcalf traveled to Thailand to see how Fred Dick was spending his portion. Metcalf handled a variety of jobs at Special Projects, including technical aides like body bugs, printing false identification for agents, fugitive recovery, and liaison with Public Safety. When Belk and Metcalf visited Chiang Mai, Jim Pettit complained to them that the Kuomintang ran CIA listening posts in all the major opium areas. The posts intercepted walkie-talkie caravan talk, which meant the CIA got the information "in real time," while Pettit had to wait a week for the NSA to pass the information through BNDD headquarters. Meanwhile, the CIA would hit the caravan and make the seizure. Pettit also complained that the CIA subverted the BNDD in other ways as well. In one case they printed fake orders on BNDD stationary. The Thai border police arrested the impostor with explosives and a BNDD note of passage.

Metcalf described Pettit as "brilliant" and said he made the famous trawler case. According to Metcalf, Pettit told the Thais he was "losing face," so they introduced him to a Chinese trawler captain. The captain planted the bugs, monitored by the US Air Force, which guided the South Vietnamese Navy.

But Fred Dick not only took the credit for the trawler case, he broke his promise to send Pettit to language school. So Pettit started a smear campaign back at headquarters. Pettit accused Dick of using front money to purchase ceramics, gems and gold, then smuggling them to Maggie Ying in Hong Kong through the military postal service. Soon after that, Maggie Ying was stopped by Customs with a load of jewelry. She politely told Customs to talk to Fred. Seymour Bolten was already unhappy with Dick's free-wheeling attitude, and believed that Fred had salted the Filipino diplomat busted in November 1971. Feeling self-righteous, Bolten made the mistake of having Dick searched upon his arrival in Hong Kong. Bolten was present, and though Fred was laden with pricey objects of art, he calmly told Bolten to fuck off.[70]

According to Tully Acampora, "Fred left himself open. He loved jewelry and art, and went into business with Maggie. Andy [Tartaglino] wanted to do an inspection and he called me up in Saigon. So I told Andy the truth — that Fred was too naive to be a crook. But Andy went out anyway, and eventually pulled Fred back to Miami."

Indeed, corruption was by no means a phenomenon peculiar to the Far East, and by 1972, Tartaglino was well into his next purge in New York.

15

NEW YORK, NEW YORK

THE CORRUPTION ISSUE IN NEW York came to a head in October 1972, when a woman reported being raped by a police detective.[1] During a routine search of the detective's house, investigators found narcotics that had been taken from the NYPD's Property Clerk's warehouse. A scrupulous check of the Property Clerk's stockpile in November revealed that 57 pounds of heroin from the 1962 French Connection case had been replaced by flour and cornstarch.[2] The search intensified and approximately 261 pounds of heroin and 137 pounds of cocaine were found to have been stolen.[3] It was the biggest police drug rip-off in history.

Much of the missing narcotics had been signed out by someone using Special Investigative Unit (SIU) Detective Joseph Nunziata's badge number, and forging his name as *Nuzziato*.[4] The thief obviously hated Nunziata enough to frame him. According to the Property Clerk's records, the first batch of French Connection heroin was signed out on March 21, 1969, while Nunziata was part of an SIU team investigating Vincent Papa, a drug trafficker allied to the Mafia's Gambino and Tramunti families.[5] Papa bought most of his heroin in 50-to-100 kilogram consignments from Louis Cirillo, and managed a major distribution network based in Harlem.[6]

As inspectors pieced together what happened, they discovered that the SIU had in January 1969 wiretapped Papa's home and a "social club" that he frequented.[7] However, the senior member of Nunziata's SIU team, Frank King, shut the case down on March 9, 1969.[8] In late 1969 Nunziata began to track Vincent Papa again and by 1970 his reports were being sent to the BNDD; and on March 20, 1970 Agents Mike Powers and Jim Beachell reported seeing Papa and another man driving a car with license plates traced to the NYPD. Beachell identified the person with Papa as Frank King. Powers was uncertain, however, so he was taken to a bar where King liked to drink. Powers surreptitiously identified King as the person he too had seen with Papa.[9]

Based on the testimony of Mike Powers and several former SIU detectives, US Attorney Tom Puccio in 1973 would charge Frank King with selling Papa incriminating wiretaps from the March 1969 surveillance.[10] King was acquitted of the charge in 1974, but suspicions persisted that Papa had SIU protection.

Indeed, suspicions of rampant SIU corruption existed long before the November 1972 discovery that the French Connection heroin had gone missing. There were around 70 men (and a few women) detectives in the SIU at any one time, and of them it was said: "They were poor in their twenties, rich in their thirties, and in jail in their forties."[11] Sporting an obligatory Rolex watch, three-quarter length black leather jacket, and soft Italian shoes, an SIU agent was known as a "prince" of the city, because he could get away with anything.

BNDD Deputy Director for Operations Andy Tartaglino was well aware of the SIU's extra-curricular activities. After his 1968 purge of crooked FBN agents, Tartaglino's inspectors in New York, Tom Taylor and Ike Wurms, compiled the so-called "Can of Wurms" report on corruption in the SIU and NYPD narcotics unit.[12] The report, however, sat on the top NYPD inspector's desk gathering dust until February 12, 1970, when narcotics detective Frank Serpico did a sensational exposé in the *New York Times*. Serpico's allegations of rampant corruption in the NYPD lit a fire under New York's wizened crime reporters, and on March 3 the *Times* revealed that nearly 100 informants had been murdered in the previous 15 years in *federal* cases alone.[13]

In response to Serpico's allegations, Mayor John Lindsay concluded that police corruption was eroding drug law enforcement in New

York City, and formed the famous Knapp Commission to investigate the NYPD.[14] The Knapp Commission, however, focused solely on cops, not the corrupt judicial system within which they existed. As the investigation proceeded, the Knapp Commission's chief prosecutor, Nicholas Scoppetta, realized the problem transcended the police and was systemic to New York. With the backing of US Attorney Whitney N. Seymour Jr. and NYPD Commissioner Patrick Murphy, Scoppetta sought help from the Justice Department. Knowing the Knapp Commission was under funded and overwhelmed with the complexity of the task before it, Criminal Division Chief Henry E. Petersen asked Andy Tartaglino for help. Tartaglino agreed, but on condition that he would have "total control" of the Special Corruption Unit he would form to conduct the sweeping investigation.[15]

If the reader will recall, Charlie McDonnell had alleged that Frankie Waters had absconded with a portion of the 1962 French Connection seizure and sold it off a piece at a time.[16] Tartaglino suspected that Waters' SIU partners Eddie Egan and Sonny Grosso were involved, but he had no proof. As one assistant US attorney observed, "Egan and Grosso often held onto their narcotics seizures for several months and then vouchered the narcotics in a Property Clerk office in a different borough, which made it impossible to track down the narcotics."[17] Secretly, Tartaglino savored the opportunity to finally nail Waters, Egan and Grosso.

In mid-1971, John Ingersoll agreed to fund the sweeping New York corruption investigation from the BNDD's operations budget, and Tartaglino recruited Tom Tripodi and Tom Taylor as his top assistants in the Special Corruption Unit.[18] At the time Taylor was an assistant RD in charge of an enforcement division in New York. Taylor worked closely on the corruption investigation with IRS Inspector George Carros and John Guido, head of the NYPD's office of Internal Affairs. Under the supervision of assistant US attorney Rudolf "Rudy" Giuliani, the future mayor of New York, Taylor, Carros and Guido would eventually manage a team of 150 men and women, including BNDD and IRS agents, as well as New York City and state police inspectors.

Enter Bob Leuci

TARTAGLINO'S PLAN, MADE IN CONSULTATION with US Attorney Seymour, Special Prosecutor Scoppetta, and Commissioner Murphy, was to turn one SIU detective into an informant and use him to make cases on his colleagues. IRS Inspector Carros and Scoppetta suggested Robert Leuci as the best candidate for the job. An SIU detective since 1967, Bob Leuci had all the right qualifications. He was easily squeezed, as the Wurms Report was replete with allegations about him, including one that he and his partner Frank Mandato had hijacked narcotics from South American couriers.[19] In his autobiography *All The Centurions*, Leuci acknowledges that one of his cousins was a made member of the Mafia, and he describes Joe Nunziata as his mentor.[20] It was also privately alleged that Leuci had sent a Mafia emissary to warn Frankie Waters about Charlie McDonnell.[21]

Bob "Baby Face" Leuci and Frankie "Black" Waters did know each other, but not as friends. After Leuci opened a case on Bonanno family member Alphonse Indelicato, a police sergeant from Brooklyn brought Waters out of retirement as a consultant on the case. In a menacing tone of voice in Leuci's kitchen, Waters said that Leuci's informant in the case, Richard Lawrence (whom Tartaglino had sent to Florida in 1970 to make an integrity case on Agent Pete Scrocca), was lying. Waters insisted that Indelicato was not a trafficker and allegedly hinted he might shoot Lawrence. To protect his informant, Leuci promised to close out the case.[22]

Leuci did not explain why Waters was protecting Indelicato, but one is left with the feeling that the Mafia drug trafficker was either an informant for the BNDD, or a protected trafficker. Leuci also revealed that Waters and SIU Detective Sonny Grosso hated each other. The feud started years earlier when author Robin Moore gave Grosso and Eddie Egan credit for making the French Connection case.[23] Everyone who had worked on the case knew that Waters played a bigger role, but Moore bonded with Egan and Grosso and, at Grosso's urging, had the disreputable Waters character killed off in the movie. Waters sued Moore over the insult and won a small settlement.[24] Adding to the intrigue, Joe Nunziata (who had a walk-on role in *The French Connection* movie) told Leuci about the feud between Waters and Grosso.

Caught in the emotional storm swirling around him, and feeling remorseful, Leuci agreed to become an informer, on condition that he not inform on his partners. Tartaglino agreed and started putting his pieces in place. One of the first things he did was negotiate an "operational exchange" with the CIA, in which the Agency obtained BNDD and NYPD credentials for its agents. In exchange Tartaglino acquired a CIA safe house on Sutton Place.[25] The Sutton Place pad became his base of operations. CIA agents, some with NYPD or BNDD credentials, monitored Tartaglino's corruption investigation to make sure it did not expose CIA sex-and-drugs blackmail schemes directed against diplomats at the UN, or CIA informants inside the NYPD and drug trafficking underworld. The fact that CIA officers used the NYPD credentials as cover was exposed in the 1975 Rockefeller Commission Report; in 1960, nine CIA officers posed as New York detectives while Fidel Castro was in town.[26] CIA officers routinely trained and recruited members of several big city "Red Squads."[27] Through the NYPD's Red Squad, the Bureau of Special Services and Investigations (BOSSI), the CIA ran all manner of covert operations, many as part of Operation Chaos.

The Reorganization

TARTAGLINO FELT THERE WAS A "direct parallel between rising heroin traffic and the lack of an effort to fight corruption," and that "New York City was the hub of it all."[28] He felt that many of the major suppliers, receivers, and distributors were protected. For example, Elvin Lee Bynum's connection tracked through Mafioso James Altamura to Pino Catania in Mexico and Frank Dasti in Montreal.[29] BNDD agents Clarence Cook and John O'Brien had arrested Bynum in late 1968 in a hallway in Brooklyn, after his Italian source had delivered five kilograms of heroin. Bynum became an informant for the BNDD, revealing and helping to set up his customers and Mafia sources. Even while he awaited trial, Bynum continued dealing, and the telephone in the apartment out of which he dealt was wiretapped so the BNDD could continue making cases. Bynum was tried and convicted in 1972.[30]

The problem began when someone told Tom Taylor that O'Brien was leaking information from wiretaps he and his crew had on Bynum.[31] John O'Brien was one of the most productive and respected agents in New York, but was unloved by Tartaglino. According to O'Brien, Tartaglino had come to New York, summoned all the agents to a meeting, and accused everyone of corruption. O'Brien alone stood up and demanded proof, thus putting himself squarely in Tartaglino's gun sights.[32]

Initially, Tartaglino sent Inspector John Thompson to investigate RD Bill Durkin and all the New York Agents. Thompson reviewed the files at headquarters, and then went up to New York and talked to the suspect agents and their informants. He found no evidence that anyone was corrupt. Obviously, this was not the result Tartaglino wanted. As Thompson said facetiously, "There was a period when the higher-ups realized we weren't making cases in New York, so there had to be corruption."[33]

Tartaglino definitely believed the agents were corrupt. He also believed they had out-smarted Thompson and, in mid-1971, as he began his corruption probe, he arranged for Durkin's transfer to headquarters. Tartaglino also arranged for Bynum to confront one of the suspect agents while secretly wearing a wire. The agent was so angry at Tartaglino, and felt so betrayed by Bill Durkin, who did nothing to defend him, that he quit the BNDD — as Tartaglino hoped and intended.[34]

Around Christmastime, 1971, Tartaglino met Bob Leuci at a Brooklyn Heights apartment. He found him credible, accepted his terms of service, and began using him as his key informant in an investigation into corruption among judges, bail bondsmen, the grand jury system, current and former federal agents and SIU detectives. Tartaglino's main target was Frank R. Klein, a public defense attorney who, on behalf of his clients, paid Norman Archer, the head of the grand jury system, to have cases dismissed.[35] The arresting SIU detectives got a piece of the action.

Tartaglino sent Inspector John Thompson back to New York to help manage the Leuci operation with Taylor and Carros. This time Thompson reported to Tom Tripodi (Tartaglino's liaison to the CIA) and Frank Monastero, whom Tartaglino had transferred to New York as an assistant RD. To augment Leuci, Tartaglino brought in BNDD agents and special employees from other states and overseas. One of the more exotic agents operating out of the safe house on Sutton Place was Santo Allesandro "Sandy" Bario. An Italian national and former Carabinieri officer, Bario was a dashing, 36-year-old undercover agent with a CIA connection. He had recently completed assignments for the IRS in Boston, the Senate Commerce Committee, the BNDD in New Orleans (where he penetrated the Carlos Marcello organization) and the BNDD in Paris, where he penetrated Jo Attia's organization.[36]

As part of Tartaglino's plan to entrap Klein and Archer, Leuci leaked information to a corrupt police sergeant, Pete Perraza, on the DA's narcotics squad. They thought the information would go to dirty SIU detectives, but it went instead to Joe Nunziata, who had recently been reassigned to the Joint Task Force. With this development, a new investigative thread began to unravel, one that was laden with intrigues, as Nunziata worshipped Sonny Grosso (one of Tartaglino's prime targets) and was friendly with Bob Leuci (Tartaglino's main informant).

With Tom Taylor acting as Bario's case agent, Tartaglino sent Bario, posing as a hit man, into a situation where Sergeant Perraza, who believed the cover story, had no choice but to arrest him. Bario paid a bribe to Perraza, a portion of which went to the assistant DA in charge of the grand jury. The Bario case would become the centerpiece of Tartaglino's investigation of the grand jury system.

In another instance Tartaglino's close friend from the early 1950s, veteran Agent Mike Picini, posing as Mafioso "Tony Bianca from Philly," flew to Detroit and then into La Guardia with a handgun in his pocket. Having been informed by Leuci of Picini's schedule, Sergeant Perraza and two SIU detectives stopped him and searched him. As Tartaglino intended, they found the gun and ten thousand dollars in (unknown to them) marked bills. They arrested Picini. Short and plump and puffing casually on his ever-present cigar, Picini explained that he was merely the middleman between Mideast heroin labs and European syndicates, through Milan. All he wanted was to move stuff through the airport. Was that too much to ask? Perhaps he could fix things? Perraza grasped the situation and made an offer. Picini accepted, was released on his own recognizance, and moved into a Stanhope Hotel to wait while Perraza jumped into the trap.[37]

Case Studies

OTHER BNDD AGENTS WERE ALSO slipping into New York to make cases on corrupt cops. Agent Ted Hunter arrived from California in May 1972 and was assigned to the Joint Task Force.[38] A police science graduate of San Jose State, Hunter served for several years in IRS inspections. He joined the BDAC and worked undercover as a love child in San Francisco's Haight Ashbury. In 1970 he was transferred to Los Angeles where he worked for Dan Casey as a group supervisor. He describes Casey as "a classy guy, fair." Hunter describes Andy Tartaglino as "heavy-handed" and New York as having "none of the glamour of Hollywood. In New York," he said, "you're not dealing with the beautiful people. There are no flower children, no rock and rollers getting drugs in Jamaica."

In a traumatic experience that left him shaken for years, Hunter was arrested with a shotgun on the front seat of his car. He was lucky he wasn't shot dead while being arrested. Sandy Bario paid his bail and put him into the criminal justice system, including a short stay in a grungy New York City jail called "the Tombs." Hunter's name stayed in the FBI's computer system for years. "It was sheer folly," he said, "why people decided to create a crime!"

Agent Bill Hansen was recruited from the BNDD's Phoenix office.[39] As a cover for his anti-corruption work, he was listed as a criminal in the Phoenix police department files, replete with a false arrest record saying he was the hitman nephew of big-time drug dealer. Fluent in Spanish, and of Mexican descent on his mother's side of the family, Hansen had grown up in a bario called El Hoyo ("the hole"). He had been in seven shootings and had killed four men. And yet, he said, "I was still not prepared for the job in New York." His job was to get arrested and go to jail in New York. The bosses told him not to tell his wife and to prepare for a long stay. "Not even the other BNDD agents knew we were there."

The inspectors in charge of the undercover agents included Chuck Sherman, Bob Goe, and Johnny Thompson. They formed the agents into four-man cells, with the "deep cover agent," like Hansen, as the principal. The other agents, including some women, were for back-up. Hansen's cell included, for a brief period, Sandy Bario, whom he described as "aloof, an elitist, but a gentleman. Strictly Italian, but he had the best credentials and the most money."

Hansen, because he spoke Spanish, worked in Spanish Harlem on the Angelet crime family of New York and Puerto Rico. He had a handgun with the number filed off. The Gallo and Gambino Mafia families were at war and importing hit men; in one famous instance, Joey Colombo was shot by an African-American who was immediately shot and killed, CIA-style, by an anonymous gunman in the crowd. "I go into the bar," Hansen said breathlessly. "The informant cuts me into crooked cops. One cop puts a revolver to my head." The back-up team and informant watched while the bad cops worked Hansen over, and then took him to the Tombs. "There were sixty of us in the holding cell," he said; "mostly Hispanics and Blacks, and one other white guy beaten to a pulp and stripped naked."

The person who was supposed to pay Hansen's bond was delayed and Hansen spent a second night in jail before being brought to a crooked public defender. The attorney had enough influence with the judge to get Hansen's case sent to a particular court. Meanwhile, the NYPD's CIA-trained Bureau of Special Investigations and Intelligence was investigating Hansen as a hitman! They stopped him on the courthouse steps and asked, "Who are you? We hear you're here to make a hit. You can tell us, or we can tell the mob." As Hansen explained: "The part of the mob that's paying off the police thinks I'm there to hit one of theirs; the Gallos think I'm there to hit them, the Gambinos think I'm there to hit them ... cause neither one of them hired me. So I started to get concerned. They know where I'm staying. I'm sleeping with a .45 in one hand and a .38 in the other.

"In the beginning it was loose," Hansen continues, "but after awhile you see the futility. Leuci ends up a hero, Scoppetta's headlining, all the crooked cops are in with the mob, and I'm getting twenty-five dollars per diem. I ended up paying eight hundred out of my own pocket." Hansen shakes his head. "New York has its own culture. The cops are born into it. If you're gonna indict the cops, you gotta indict the vibrance, the culture of New York." He shrugs. "They asked me to go back again, to work on a BNDD agent, but I refused."

The Tangled Web

DAVID WISER, INTRODUCED IN CHAPTER 9, was present in 1969 when a black cop in Washington set in motion a series of events revolving around former FBN agent Charlie McDonnell and his heroin-dealing informant, Bob Williams. In mid-1971, while in the preliminary stage of his New York corruption investigation, Tartaglino summoned Wiser, a former CIA officer, into his office.[40] "Andy had a way," Wiser recalled, "of making you feel important. His beautiful secretary, Jean Philpot, would invite you into his office and Andy would sit you down on the sofa. If it were spring, there'd be a bowl of cherries on the coffee table. It was all first class, and by the time he was done charming you, you were willing to do anything for him."

In this instance, the job was to use Bob Williams to nail Frankie Waters. As Wiser recalled, "Rudy Giuliani had issued a subpoena for Bob, so I went looking for him in New York. We knew through phone bills that he had a girl friend, Barbara Jacquette, the former wife of jazz musician Illinois Jacquette. Barbara lived on the West Side in a gorgeous brownstone. I went to her and she was a real lady. She didn't know where Bob was, but she knew that his daughter from another marriage had married a prominent physician. I went to see the daughter, and she agreed to ask her father to call me.

"I went back to DC and Bob calls me from New York. We arrange to meet at Union Station. I'm there with my partner. We pick Bob up and drive down Pennsylvania Avenue. I show him my ID and say I have a subpoena for his arrest. Well, old Bob is a smooth guy, but he's also emotional. And he gets very upset in the car and tries to jump out the door. Apparently from what Barbara and his daughter said, he thought I was FBI. He never would have come if he'd known I was narcotics. So I told him to forget about the subpoena and he calmed down. He agreed to cooperate."

Then in his early sixties, Williams explained how he'd progressed from running numbers, to pulling off armed robberies, to buying dope from Joe Valachi, to being an FBN informant. The FBN agents had tape recorded him doing a drug transaction. They let him listen to the tape and said they would sell it to him, if he agreed to work for them. Williams said that Frankie Waters was one of the agents that recruited him. "Williams is careful to point out that Waters' partner is more dangerous than Frankie is," Wiser said. "It's the partner he's afraid of!"

Williams told Wiser that Frankie Waters had saved Charlie Mac's life at a meeting on a boat with Italians in Long Island Sound. The Italians had heard that Charlie Mac had flipped and they wanted Waters to kill him. Waters said he would rather go to prison than kill Charlie Mac, even if Charlie Mac had betrayed him.

Williams bought narcotics from these anonymous Italians, and Tartaglino wanted Wiser to find out who they were. But Williams wouldn't tell. "I spent days with him," Wiser said, "sitting under the George Washington Bridge, looking across the River at Fort Lee. He'd smile and say in his Mississippi accent, 'Mr. Wiser, a lot of them Italian boys is over there.' But he wouldn't say who they were."

Frustrated with Wiser's lack of success, Tartaglino came to New York to try to turn Williams himself. Tartaglino talked to Williams for half an hour and was, according to Wiser, "persuasive. But when he was done, Williams drops to his knees. There were tears coming down his cheeks. He's got a handkerchief in his hand, and he says, 'You might as well take out your gun and kill me now, Mr. Tartaglino. You might as well kill me now.' Later, Andy took me out to dinner, and over dinner he said, 'You're right. He's not going to testify."

So Tartaglino turned to Clarence Cook in his effort to get Waters. As Cook recalled, "I was in Washington and he wanted to make a case on Waters. Bob Leuci comes down and starts asking me questions. But I didn't know enough about Waters to discuss the subject."[41]

Leuci said he slipped Cook a matchbook saying, "I'm wired." Accepting the matchbook (and not turning it in for a week) was, in

Tartaglino's opinion, evidence that Cook was crooked. Cook was in line for a promotion, and Tartaglino sat on it for the next five years.[42]

Frustrated, Tartaglino turned Williams over to Agent Lee Volmer for safekeeping until he could amass enough evidence to bring Waters to trial. With that part of his investigation on hold, Tartaglino put Wiser and Charlie Vopat inside Johnny Thompson's group. It was their turn to cover Bob Leuci.

"I followed Leuci's footsteps in Greenwich Village one night," Wiser recalled, "and watched while he met Mickey Coco — that's Murad Nursessian, a hit man who'd been a paratrooper in World War II. On behalf of the criminals and criminal cops, Mickey's there to make determination if Leuci is to live. Leuci's wired. He's gonna catch Mickey in the act. Well, Taylor and Carros hated Leuci, because of an informant homicide. But Leuci was the bravest man I've ever seen. I was on foot so I couldn't follow him, but he got in Coco's station wagon in a sleet storm, and drove off into the night."

Dandolo

AGENT MIKE PICINI, POSING AS Tony Bianca from Philly, told greedy Ser geant Perraza that he worked for a major dope dealer from Milan. Perraza thought it might be profitable to deal directly with Bianca's boss, and thus was susceptible to being fooled. To play the role of the dope dealer from Milan, Tartaglino recruited special employee Carlo Dandolo, a short stocky conman of mixed nationality who owned cafes in Marseille, Turkey, Syria and Beirut. Tartaglino had met Dandolo in 1956 in Rome, while Dandolo was making cases for Charlie Siragusa in Europe and the Middle East. Tartaglino established Dandolo at the Americana Hotel and Dandolo contacted Perraza. To everyone's surprise, instead of sending SIU agents, Perraza sent Joe Nunziata. In January 1972, Nunziata and his partner Sal D'Ambrosia took Dandolo's passport and heroin, and dragged him down to the federal courthouse. By coincidence, Tony Pohl was in court that day and saw Dandolo, whom he'd worked with overseas. Knowing his cover was blown, Dandolo immediately went to Tom Taylor and said he wanted out of the game. Taylor sent Dandolo to Washington where Tartaglino calmed his fears and gave him access to the CIA safe house on Sutton Place for security. Dandolo regained his confidence and, though he was aimed at the assistant DA and the judge, began to set up Joe Nunziata. Tartaglino, naturally, thought he could use Nunziata to nail Grosso and Waters.

Nunziata and Dandolo met at a restaurant in February to discuss business. Dandolo told Nunziata he had 200 kilos of heroin coming in, but that he had to return to Italy to make the arrangements. Nunziata was suspicious. He followed Dandolo back to the Americana and on March 10, had his partner D'Ambrosia install a wiretap. Soon thereafter Dandolo gave Nunziata a $4,000 bribe, which Nunziata accepted and split with D'Ambrosia. Dandolo vanished and Nunziata wrote a fake contact report.[43]

At the time, the head of the narcotics unit in the Southern District, Andy Maloney, was transferring to ODALE. His colleagues were throwing him a farewell dinner at a nice restaurant. Tom Taylor and George Carros were invited and in the middle of dinner, they saw D'Ambrosia and Nunziata leave in a hurry.[44]

Dave Wiser, Santo Bario, Carlo Dandolo and Charlie Vopat were in Dandolo's hotel room, which D'Ambrosia had bugged, playing gin rummy. As Wiser recalled, "The phone starts acting funny. It's half ringing, but no one's there when we pick it up. So me and Charlie head to the basement to find the junction box. We look around and see wires going to a sound-activated recorder, the kind the NYPD use. There are two exits, one to the parking garage and one out the front door. I head for the door and Charlie heads for the garage, where he sees a guy wearing a tool belt like a telephone repairman. Charlie lost him, so I call Taylor and Carros at Maloney's farewell party. But they had already followed D'Ambrosia and Nunziata into the basement. They'd called the cops and arrested D'Ambrosia and Joe Nunziata - who'd been an extra in the movie *The French Connection*, which is playing all over New York at the time. He's the guy in the camel's hair coat."

That night, Andy Tartaglino flew to New York in an effort to flip Nunziata. At a meeting on March 15, Tartaglino confronted Nunziata with the $4,000 bribe and wiretap. Tartaglino called him a whore and a thief in the presence of Taylor, Wiser, Vopat and other law enforcement officials. By recent standards, in which waterboarding was considered de rigueur by the Bush Administration, it was not a harsh interrogation. Tartaglino's tactics were psychological, designed to break Nunziata and induce him to inform on Frankie Waters and Sonny Grosso. Based on hearsay evidence gathered by his Special Corruption Unit, Tartaglino believed Waters was on a murder rampage, killing off old informants and hoods. He had sent an army of agents to try to trap Waters, but they all failed. Charlie Vopat, for example, met

Waters at a restaurant in New Jersey. "I asked the bartender where I could find him. Waters came over, shook my hand, and wouldn't let go."[45]

As Vopat recalled, Tartaglino wanted Sonny Grosso too. During the interrogation on March 15, "Tartaglino told Nunziata to get Grosso on the phone. He wanted Nunziata to set up a get-together with Egan. It was all about the French Connection case."

Tartaglino believed that Egan, Grosso and Waters stole 17 kilograms of heroin in the French Connection case and that Waters was selling portions of it. Egan's ex-wife reportedly told Tartaglino that Egan had suggested to Robin Moore, author of *The French Connection*, that Moore ought to include a chapter in his book about some wicked cops stealing the heroin from the Property Clerk's office.[46] The conversation allegedly occurred in 1967, before the heroin started to go missing. By Moore's account, the suggestion was made by Nunziata, not Egan.[47]

Nunziata was a patsy from the beginning, but he remained naively and stubbornly true to his hero, Sonny Grosso. As one of the agents present recalled, "Nunziata was on his knees, sobbing, saying, 'Anyone but Sonny. Not Sonny!'"

Tartaglino calmly told Nunziata he could rat out Grosso, go to jail, or kill himself. "You been through this," he reportedly said. "You've given other guys the choice. Now it's your turn."[48]

The next day, Joe Nunziata supposedly shot himself in the heart while his partner was inside a store making a phone call. He was double-parked, sitting in a squad car in the middle of the day in Brooklyn. There was no suicide note. The forensic evidence was inconclusive. Nunziata was left- handed, and his clothes went missing from the evidence room. Cynics found it hard to believe that he gave his life for Sonny Grosso. Rumors began to spread that Nunziata had damming evidence on Grosso, Waters, Leuci and active duty federal agents. Some felt that he'd been murdered.

Dave Wiser got nervous and left New York, as did Ted Hunter. After receiving Waters' death grip, Charlie Vopat retreated to the safety and security of Laos. Bill Hansen happily went home to the border wars in Arizona. As Hansen recalled, "Nunziata had committed suicide and now they're gonna send me in to make a buy off Frankie Waters. He's working at a bar in Germantown. I told them they're crazy. I'm gonna hustle Frankie Waters? Next they're gonna send me on Pete Scrocca. 'He's worse than Waters,' they say. I told them to fuck off. Later, in Miami, I told Scrocca. All he could do was laugh."

With Nunziata's mysterious death, Bob Leuci fell into a depression and told his partner that he was working for Tartaglino. He told Tartaglino that he'd had enough stress for one lifetime, and he refused to cooperate anymore. And with Leuci's exit from the Corruption Unit, people started scrambling. Prosecutor Nick Scoppetta quickly held a press conference and claimed credit for all the cases made to date. Scoppetta's grab for glory sent the remaining bad guys running for cover, so US Attorney Whitney Seymour called up Tom Taylor and told him to "Gear up."[49] Taylor and a contingent of BNDD agents hit Norman Archer's house and found marked bills that had been handed by Sandy Bario to Sergeant Perraza. In early 1973 Archer went on trial. He was convicted in a controversial case that called into question Tartaglino's motivations and tactics.

Dénouement

A LOT OF PEOPLE ON BOTH sides of the law were mad at Bob Leuci. According to Johnny Thompson, "Leuci turned us around and blew the thing. It could have gone further, to judges."[50]

Tom Taylor was feeling deflated too. Leuci was scheduled to testify in the case of Edmund Rosnor, an attorney representing Leroy "Nicky" Barnes (aka Mr. Untouchable), a major heroin distributor in Manhattan and an associate of Mafioso Joe Gallo. Rosnor allegedly paid a bribe to get secret grand jury testimony that got Barnes off a narcotics charge. Taylor told prosecutor Rudy Giuliani that Leuci was an unreliable witness, and asked for a chance to prove it. Giuliani agreed. Taylor summoned Leuci to his office, read him his Miranda rights, and told him that US Attorney Tom Puccio was going to indict him in Eastern District. It was a bluff to make him confess to a myriad of crimes. Instead, Leuci went back to Giuliani and admitted a few indiscretions. Taylor bitterly claims that Giuliani allowed Leuci to "present himself as saint" and "perjure himself" in the Rosnor case, so he could be used to make cases on other cops.[51] As an interesting aside, Alan Dershowitz defended Rosnor. As the main defense witness, Dershowitz called none other than convicted murderer, drug dealer, and FBN, BNDD and SIU informant Richard Lawrence.

In Robert Daley's book about Bob Leuci, *The Prince of the City*, Taylor and Tartaglino are presented as villains. Daley described Tartaglino as being obsessed with corruption. "When he found it he would crush it, and the people involved in it, too, according them no sympathy, no understanding, and no quarter."[52]

Tartaglino characterizes Daley's book as "fiction." He said that NYPD Commissioner Pat Murphy wanted the BNDD to hire Leuci as a Special Employee. Tartaglino promised to do it, but Leuci wanted to be a full-fledged BNDD agent.[53]

"Leuci wanted to be a Serpico," Tom Taylor said. "But he wasn't a Serpico. Leuci was dirty, so he didn't deserve the same treatment."

Leuci, who later became a novelist and college professor, is kinder in his appraisal. Tartaglino was "exuberant," he said, and "had an esoteric smile without mirth."

For his part, John Ingersoll was glad to write the whole sordid story off as history. And as history tells us, dozens of SIU detectives were indicted. The unit was disbanded, but stealing money and junk from dope dealers remains a habitual and unbecoming lifestyle for dishonest American law enforcement officers.

Papa's End Game

IN 1972, THE CIA WAS protecting drug traffickers, informants and law enforcement officials on its payroll. It had an entire division devoted to domestic operations, as well as a branch for domestic contacts. Both were centered in New York City. Its Office of Security trained and worked closely with detectives in New York's Bureau of Special Services and Intelligence and other "Red Squads" in major cities around the country. The CIA's illegal Operation Chaos was in full swing, spying on and "neutralizing" anti-war activists. Much of this would become public knowledge in 1972, after several CIA officers and agents were found to have participated in the Watergate burglary and other illegal domestic White House operations. The White House, notably, coordinated its domestic operations through an Intelligence Evaluation Committee in John Dean's office. Former BOSSI detective Jack Caulfield was Dean's liaison to the CIA.

The CIA's role in the Prince of the City scandal is, as one might expect, hazy. There is a rumor that policeman Albert Carone, a precinct conditions man, had CIA and Mafia contacts and was tied to Bob Leuci's partner Frank Mandato.[54] The heroin seized in the French Connection case was kept in the Property Clerk's office as evidence to be used against two French fugitives in the case. Like Maurice Castellani, those fugitives were never arrested. If, like Castellani, one of those Frenchmen was working for the CIA, it would have been to the Agency's advantage to have the heroin vanish, along with any chance of a trial.

After writing his famous book *The Green Berets*, which glorified US Army Special Forces units making incursions for the CIA into Laos and Cambodia, Robin Moore wrote the novel *The Country Team*. Written in 1966 and set in a country resembling Thailand, the novel features rubber plantation owner Mike Forrester. The CIA asks Forrester to buy up the local poppy crop before the Communists can get to it and sell it to the American Mafia. The CIA tells Forrester that it will sell the opium crop to American pharmaceutical companies, and that he can have half of the profits to keep his machine "oiled."[55] His machine consists of mercenaries who will identify and then kill the Chinese Communists and their cronies.

Forrester then arranges to buy the harvest from a tribal chief who resembles the real one in Houei Sai, Laos. He brings along a CIA-supplied press to squeeze the opium into bricks, and when the deal is consummated, the Communists, as anticipated, descend on his plantation and into the CIA's trap. Waiting for them is a Phoenix Program-style assassination team managed by a CIA officer named Scott working undercover for the US Information Service. When Scott meets Forrester, he produces a deck of cards. Each card is black "with a hideous white eye in the center." As Scott explained, the US Information Service printed twenty thousand such cards in South Vietnam. "When we discovered who the Communist agents in a city or village were, we assassinated them and put this eye on the body," Scott explained. Scott then deploys his Phoenix team on Forrester's plantation, to ambush the Communist drug dealers.[56]

Moore obviously had a deep understanding of world heroin trafficking and the CIA's role in it long before he wrote *The French Connection*. Presented as heroes in *The French Connection*, Egan and Grosso are characterized as "sloppy and stupid" if not downright disreputable, in Moore's 1977 mea culpa book *Mafia Wife*.[57] Considering the history, this change of heart makes sense only from the CIA point of view.

Several agents with CIA links were in Tom Taylor's special unit, including William Mockler, Harold Campbell, and Michael Powers. An erstwhile member of the Phoenix Program in Vietnam, Powers said that Jim Hunt, the agent-in-charge of the Newark, New Jersey office, interviewed him for the BNDD.[58] When Hunt asked him what the Phoenix Program was, Powers said the job was to capture insurgents whose names appeared on a blacklist. "What did you do when you couldn't capture a guy?" Hunt inquired. "We killed him," Powers replied. Hunt liked the answer and hired tough guy Mike Powers on the spot.

Tom Tripodi offers another explanation as to how Powers joined the BNDD. Tripodi claims he hired Powers as part of the Medusa Plan, with the intention that Powers would find heroin labs in Southeast Asia and place transponders in them so they could be bombed by the CIA.[59] Tripodi said that Powers went into Fuller's shoofly program, but Powers denies that. Some agents suggest that Powers, like Joey DiGennaro, was spun off into the CIA's secret anti-narcotics unit. Considering his Phoenix background, this seems plausible. Powers also denies being in Tom Taylor's special anti-corruption unit in New York, although Taylor says he was.[60]

What is known is that Powers was assigned to the "Italian Squad" in New York. One day he was in the office, alone, when the phone rang. A gravelly voice said three guys were selling dope outside the social club in Queens frequented by drug trafficker Vincent Papa. Powers started watching Papa and his associates and, one night, by himself, tailed Papa to a meeting with four men. He saw them pass something — money or dope — but did not believe he had probable cause to make an arrest. Considering that this was around the same time Joe Nunziata and Frank King were wiretapping Papa, and allegedly taking money from him, it's possible that Powers stumbled on an exchange of tapes for money between Papa and the SIU detectives.

Not making the arrest could be construed as a rookie mistake. If Powers had arrested Papa, as any veteran agent would have done, the chain of events that lead to Joe Nunziata's death might have been prevented. In any event, Carlo Dandolo, the CIA-connected special employee Tartaglino hired to catch Sergeant Perraza, made a narcotics deal with Papa in late 1972. Dandolo's deal provided BNDD agents with cause to arrest Papa in January 1973. When he was arrested, Papa had $967,000 in cash in his suitcase. Papa was tried and convicted and sent to federal prison.

The theft of the French Connection heroin has never been solved. It is theorized that the NYPD Property Clerk let detectives on Papa's payroll take the heroin, and that the Property Clerk or some SIU detective with a personal grudge against Nunziata signed the vouchers with the name Nunziata. Frank King was charged with the theft, but acquitted, even though, shortly after Nunziata's death, King resigned from the NYPD and went to work as a bodyguard for Papa's sons.[61] Frank King was eventually convicted on tax evasion charges.

In July 1977, while incarcerated in the Federal Penitentiary in Atlanta, Vincent Papa was stabbed to death by three black inmates. Perhaps their employer felt that Papa had information on federal government involvement in Nunziata's death?

There were certainly plenty of people in the White House with dirty little secrets to hide.

16

CAPITOL CAPERS

THE SCANDAL THAT SANK RICHARD Nixon began June 17, 1972, when
Detective Carl Shoffler arrested former CIA security officer James
McCord and four accomplices inside Democratic National Committee headquarters at the Watergate Hotel in Washington, DC. McCord
was a paid security coordinator for Nixon's re-election committee.[1]
The others were Frank A. Fiorini (aka "Sturgis" after a character in
one of Howard Hunt's novels), Bernard Barker, Eugenio Martinez
and Virgilio Gonzalez.[2] Barker, Martinez and Gonzalez were anti-
Castro Cuban veterans of the CIA's Bay of Pigs. Martinez was still on
the CIA's payroll.[3]

The five had snuck into the Watergate to fix a faulty phone tap
they had planted during a previous break-in, and they planned to steal
documents. Monitoring their progress by walkie-talkie from a look-
out post across the street was former FBI Agent Alex Baldwin, under
the direction of former CIA officer E. Howard Hunt and former FBI
Agent G. Gordon Liddy.[4] Hunt had provided Sturgis and McCord
with false identification prepared by the CIA. He had also recruited
Barker, Martinez and Gonzalez for the job. Martinez, still on the CIA
payroll, was vice-president of Bebe Rebozo's real estate firm in Florida.

Upon learning of the arrests, Nixon immediately authorized a
cover-up. He was especially worried that Hunt might reveal dirty little

secrets. On the famous "smoking gun" tape, the paranoid president was heard to say, "Of course, this Hunt, that will uncover a lot of things. You open that scab ... that it is going to open the whole Bay of Pigs thing up again."[5]

No one knows what Nixon implied by the "Bay of Pigs thing." His chief of staff Bob Haldeman said Nixon "was actually referring to the Kennedy assassination."[6] That is a provocative statement, but for the purposes of this book, I will take Nixon literally — that the CIA's Bay of Pigs fiasco caused Nixon concern. As noted in Chapter 8, Nixon had served as President Eisenhower's "action officer" in 1960 during the planning stages of the failed invasion. In this position, he was certainly aware that Jimmy Hoffa was said to have been "the original liaison" between the mob and the CIA in its plots to assassinate Fidel Castro, and that Hoffa brought numerous Mafiosi into the conspiracy.[7] Nixon probably knew that Mafioso Sam Mannarino ran guns to Castro for the CIA with Meyer Lansky's close associate, drug smuggler Norman Rothman. Nixon certainly knew that the CIA had hired Santo Trafficante, the patron saint of drug traffickers, to recruit Cuban exiles to assassinate Castro.[8] The use of a drug smuggling Mafiosi to assassinate Castro is probably the Bay of Pigs "thing" Nixon feared the press would discover through Hunt and the Watergate Cubans.

This uneasy criminal conspiracy, with all its espionage intrigues, forever bound Nixon to the CIA, its army of mercenary anti-Castro Cubans, and organized crime. Thus, when Nixon decided to buy the silence of the Watergate defendants, he turned first to the CIA. As Helms' deputy General Vernon Walters testified to Congress, John Dean asked him on June 27, 1972 if the CIA could provide bail and continue paying the salaries of the Watergate burglars. Walters refused.[9] Backed into a corner, Nixon turned to the faithful "mob." "After the Watergate burglars began blackmailing the White House," author Dan Moldea writes, "the mob came through in January 1973 with a million dollars in hush money."[10]

The need to conceal the illegal activities of this unholy trinity also explained why Nixon, through Haldeman, asked Helms to stop an FBI investigation of the finance chairman of Nixon's re-election committee in Texas. The finance chairman had laundered money through a Mexican bank account belonging to Watergate burglar Bernard Barker, and Liddy was using the money to fund his covert political actions (including the Watergate break-in) against the Democrats. After Haldeman raised the specter of the Bay of Pigs, Helms had Vernon Walters tell

Acting Director Patrick Gray that the FBI's investigation would compromise CIA assets and channels for handling money.[11] Gray called off the investigation, thus contributing to the cover-up.

Myles Ambrose told this author that public knowledge of this CIA operation in Mexico could have saved Nixon. He would not say what the CIA operation was, but he felt that Nixon had no reason to worry about it. This raises the question: what ongoing CIA operation in Mexico could have been so important that Nixon risked his presidency to protect it?

A connection to the Kennedy assassination is a possibility. The money the Watergate burglars carried at the time of their arrest was part of an $89,000 donation from four Texas businessmen that had been laundered through Barker's account in a Mexican bank.[12] The FBI was investigating the deposits into Barker's account until Helms and Nixon intervened; then, according to author Peter Dale Scott, the FBI "called off a proposed interview in Mexico City with CIA officer George Munro, the CIA official in charge of the electronic intercept program which allegedly overheard Lee Harvey Oswald [while Oswald was in Mexico shortly before the Kennedy assassination]."[13]

More likely, Nixon and Helms felt they had to protect drug-smuggling Mexican officials on the CIA's payroll. CIA station chief in Mexico Winston M. Scott (1956-69) alone had recruited twelve agents in the upper echelons of the Mexican government, including Presidents Gustavo Diaz Ordez and Luis Echeverria, and Dirección Federal de Seguridad (DSF) chief, Fernando Gutiérrez Barrios.[14] Other CIA officers had certainly recruited other Mexican officials. We know from the Suarez case that many officials were involved in drug smuggling, and Ambrose spoke of corruption among Mexican officials as the main impediment to drug interdiction.

It is this author's opinion that Nixon and the CIA were concerned the FBI would discover that drug money was being laundered through Barker's bank account for Liddy's dirty tricks, and that a CIA-protected drug ring in Mexico used it to fund covert operations like the Bay of Pigs.[15]

Having protected drug smuggling officials in Mexico since its inception, the CIA helped with the cover-up. Walters did ask Gray to stop the investigation, and Gray complied. But privately Nixon may have suspected that the CIA had deliberately bungled the Watergate break-in as a way of destroying him; Helms was a Democrat, and there was a rumor that Hunt was working for him.[16] On June 26, 1972,

Dean asked Walters if the CIA may have been involved in the break-in without his knowledge.[17] Haldeman believed the CIA blew the break-in: that burglar Eugenio Martinez told his CIA case officer about the pending operation; that the case officer told Helms; and that Helms had someone notify Detective Carl Shoffler ahead of time.[18] Others believe Shoffler's involvement was coincidental and that McCord was more likely the CIA agent provocateur.[19]

Perhaps Haldeman and Nixon would have fingered Hunt as the double agent if they had known that Hunt had blown the Bay of Pigs operation; when Russian agents reportedly stole his briefcase in Mexico City, which contained the CIA's operational plans, a few days before the invasion.[20] The Russians reportedly passed the plans to Castro's Cubans, who were able to prepare for the invasion. According to this source, CIA Counter-Intelligence Chief James Angleton knew of Hunt's blunder (if it was a blunder) but did not tell the CIA officer in charge of the Bay of Pigs operation. If this is true, then Hunt intentionally sabotaged the Bay of Pigs plans for Angleton, for some obscure reason. Hunt, by nature, was capable of such duplicity. In one of his novels he revealed his secret self, saying, "It is in the political agent's interest to betray all the parties who use him and to work for them all at the same time, so that he may move freely and penetrate everywhere."[21]

Assuming the worst, Nixon sacked Helms in February 1973 and replaced him with James Schlesinger, whose mandate was to rattle the Agency into compliance with his wishes. The turmoil Schlesinger generated would hurt the CIA's reputation, but not its operational capabilities, for the Agency was, by then, an entity outside presidential control. The CIA made this clear in July 1973 when former CIA officer Alex Butterfield (whom Haldeman felt might be a CIA plant) revealed the existence of a tape recording system in the Oval Office.[22] Butterfield, notably, had been the director of a CIA-funded Cuban resettlement program that included Joseph Califano and Alexander Haig, and which served as a cover to recruit anti-Castro Cuban assassins. Butterfield's revelation led to the discovery of the "smoking gun tape" and precipitated Nixon's resignation.

Whether or not the Watergate break-in was facilitated by a secret CIA faction opposed to Nixon's Soviet and Chinese policies, it did expose Nixon's consummate hypocrisy — his reliance on denial and dirty tricks while espousing "law and order." Americans identify with the president, and discovering that Nixon was a depraved character was a blow to the national psyche. The Watergate and Vietnam syndromes festered unresolved until, under George W. Bush, America relinquished any pretense of Constitutional behavior, and with the invasion of Iraq in 2003, embraced its dark side.

Apart from all this philosophizing, Watergate did impact the BNDD, so there is a need to examine more closely the federal drug law enforcement angles.

Cubans in the Closet

CHARLES COLSON BROUGHT HUNT INTO the White House in July 1971 from Robert R. Mullen and Company, a "brass plate," which provided CIA agents with cover around the world; Haldeman said that no one at the White House had any idea of this until years later.[23] The owner of the firm, Robert Bennett (later a Mormon Senator from Utah) worked for the CIA and was the Washington representative of Howard Hughes. Bennett took over the Hughes contract from Larry O'Brien, the Democratic National Chairman and target of the Watergate break-in. Bennet, while working for the CIA, suggested that Colson hire Hunt.[24] It is thought that Colson sent Hunt to find out if O'Brien had, in his desk, evidence of an illegal $100,000 cash campaign contribution from Hughes, made through Nixon's "wedge" Bebe Rebozo.

Meanwhile, the 1972 presidential election approached, and Haldeman approved a one million dollar budget for Operation Gemstone, a covert political action project managed by Gordon Liddy. Haldeman liked the Gemstone idea so much he sought to use the BNDD as cover for Gemstone employees, many of whom were Cuban exiles recruited by Hunt or his agents. We know this for a fact, through BNDD Agent Ralph Frias.

Ralph Frias had been an effective FBN undercover agent in Europe with Andy Tartaglino in the 1950s. Frias quit in 1959 and labored in other fields until 1972, when, seeking a trustworthy Spanish-speaking ally, Tartaglino offered him a job. According to Frias, Tartaglino was having trouble with Haldeman and Ehrlichman. Tartaglino referred to them as "Nazis" and said they were putting political agents inside the BNDD and other "agencies all over town."[25] Tartaglino wanted Frias to screen these people out. Frias went to work as a senior staff aide for International Affairs chief George Belk. When Haldeman sent over three Cubans, Frias interviewed them and realized they were "plants." They were not hired.

But other CIA-connected Cubans already worked for the BNDD, many as informers after Operation Eagle. How many were using their CIA "get out of jail free" privileges to pull off black bag jobs? Ehrlichman said one of the Cubans told him that he had "performed over two-hundred break-ins" for the CIA.[26] The Chilean Embassy was burglarized four times between 1971 and May 1972.[27] Why? Was it related to the CIA's plans to overthrow the Allende government, or because Chilean Ambassador Orlando Letelier was related to cocaine trafficker Oscar Letelier, a defendant in the Yolando Sarmiento case? Remember, Liddy was a White House liaison to CCINC; and Hunt admitted that in November 1971 he was working "in Room 16 on a narcotics intelligence proposal."[28]

According to Jerry Strickler, the CIA tried to exchange Oscar Squella, the Chilean defendant in a bizarre BNDD case in Miami, for the captain of the *Johnny Express*, a "mother ship" used by anti-Castro Cuban terrorists to launch attacks against Cuba. The owner of the *Johnny Express*, Teofilo Babun, was a close friend of Bebe Rebozo. Manuel Noriega was the middleman in the negotiations. And after Allende was assassinated and his government overthrown, Chilean traffickers were captured and returned to New York to testify against corrupt SIU detectives.[29] With all the double dealing going on, any connection between covert narcotics and political actions was possible.

Assassination Mambo

EDWARD J. EPSTEIN ATTRIBUTES A secret CIA drug-trafficker assassination program to Howard Hunt, and claims that Hunt asked his counterpart from the Bay of Pigs invasion, Manuel Artime in Miami, to assemble "hit teams" of anti-Castro Cubans for jobs in Latin America.[30] In the 1960s Hunt had used CIA money to finance Artime's exile government in Nicaragua. During his Nicaraguan sojourn, Artime and his merry band of terrorists launched raids on Cuba using torpedo boats equipped with 57 mm guns and recoilless rifles. But in one fatal case of poor spelling, they hit the Sierra Aranzazu instead of the Sierra Maestre. The ship's captain was killed and the US government had to pay one million dollars in damages.[31] Not long after the Sierra Maestre flap, Artime's camp on Somoza's ranch in Costa Rica was identified as a transit point for Colombian cocaine.[32] In his exit interview for the CIA, Jake Esterline, who managed the Bay of Pigs operation, said about Artime that he "probably made, in addition to stealing money from us, probably made a lot of money in the drug traffic in the last few years, among other things."[33]

Artime subsequently went to work as Somoza's business agent in Miami, and his lieutenants — Rafael "Chi Chi" Quintero, Felix Rodriguez, and Ricardo Chavez - were sent to the Congo to fight rebels receiving assistance from the legendary Argentine revolutionary, Ernesto "Che" Guevara, and some one hundred Cuban advisers.[34]

In 1972, Watergate burglar Bernard Barker (the former chief of Fulgencio Batista's secret police), on behalf of Hunt and Artime, reportedly assembled a secret army of some 120 Cubans as part of Liddy's Gemstone Program. Barker said his team was designed "to hit the Mafia using the tactics of the Mafia."[35] Apart from assassinations, Gemstone agents conducted break-ins, wiretappings, sabotage, kidnapping, muggings, and prostitution for political blackmail. Author Len Colodny says the CIA, John Dean, and Lucien Conein participated in Gemstone.[36] BNDD Agent Richard Bly worked with Conein. According to Bly, Conein "would do anything" for Liddy.[37] Author George Crile claimed (as Tartaglino complained to Frias) that Conein hired three agents and assigned them to commit assassinations.[38]

Hunt is on record saying that Panamanian President Omar Torrijos was "going to be wasted" if he didn't cooperate.[39] It is unclear if this cooperation was related to Nixon's war on drugs or some other matter, but Artime is on record as saying that Hunt asked him to join in disrupting the Panama narcotics traffic.[40] *Newsweek* on June 18, 1973 cited John Dean as saying that Hunt had his hit team in Mexico. The mission, designed by minor White house officials to kill Panamanian President Omar Torrijos, was aborted.

Hunt definitely had first-hand knowledge about the Torrijos family's drug trafficking activities. It was far from a secret. Indeed, on July 8, 1971, the son of Panama's ambassador to Taiwan, Rafael Richard Gonzalez, was stopped by a Customs port inspector at JFK Airport. A search of his four suitcases revealed 156 pounds of heroin.[41]

Richard broke down under questioning and admitted to making five similar drug smuggling trips. He also implicated Moises Torrijos, brother of Panamanian President Omar Torrijos.[42] Richard's bodyguard was a Panamanian secret agent, and his controller, uncle Guillermo Gonzalez, was Moises Torrijos' bodyguard. Moises had personally met Gonzalez at Tocumen airport in Panama and carried the heroin-packed suitcases through Panamanian Customs. Gonzalez was tied to anti-Castro Cubans, Israeli traffickers, the Mafia, and

Meyer Lansky, who worked with Panama's ambassador to Great Britain laundering Mafia drug money through the Panamanian branch of a Swiss bank. Lansky was introduced to the ambassador by Tibor Rosenbaum, a Mossad agent and owner of the drug money-laundering bank, BCI.[43] Moises sold ambassadorships to people willing to smuggle dope from source countries. Panamanian Transportation minister Juan Tack assisted by issuing diplomatic passports to non-diplomats.

Customs secretly indicted Moises Torrijos in the June 1971 Rafael Richards case.[44] But other forces were at work and according to Jerry Strickler, the CIA station chief in Panama, Lawrence Sternfeld personally put the kibosh on the cases against Moises Torrijos and Noriega.

According to journalist Jonathan Marshall, "Four days after the arrests at Watergate, Ingersoll visited Panama to warn Torrijos ... that 'narcotics enforcement is in your government's best interest.'"[45] The indictment against Moises was never executed, but its mere existence served as leverage to keep Omar cooperating politically — as did the threat of assassination. All was well with the world: the CIA continued to use the AID International Police Academy in Panama to train and recruit policemen and military officers - like Torrijos and Noriega — to fight Communism in return for free passage. Western Division Chief Ted Shackley not only allowed Noriega to profit from drugs, he provided him with a slush fund a well.[46] In return, Noriega reported directly to his CIA case officers on Torrijos, Castro and, most importantly, the Soviets.

Hunt acknowledged that he was working on "a narcotics intelligence proposal" while co-located with the Plumbers in the Executive Office Building. Not only did Hunt recruit Lou Conein for covert political actions related to drug law enforcement, he recruited Frank Sturgis, an occasional employee of the Trafficante organization. After his arrest at the Watergate, Sturgis said he had joined Hunt in an investigation of the drug traffic from Mexico, Paraguay and Panama, and that the focus was Ricord's Group France.[47] This indicates the existence of a clandestine anti-drug unit, managed by the CIA and operating parallel to the BNDD. As we shall see, French traffickers took a beating in South America in 1972, when Cuban trafficker Alberto Sicilia Falcon inherited, with CIA sanction, their network of official protectors.

Sturgis said Hunt was involved in assassinations, and Hunt admitted doing a "national security" job in Panama shortly after January 7, 1972, when he got a Mexican tourism card. Sturgis had the card when arrested at the Watergate.[48]

Cross Purposes

MANUAL NORIEGA WAS INDICTED IN Eastern District in New York in 1972, when the Coast Guard seized a Panamanian ship, the Sea Witch, in Miami harbor. A vast quantity of marijuana was found aboard and the captain said he had to pay a fee to Noriega in order to leave Panamanian waters. But the case evaporated when Omar Torrijos, John Ingersoll and the US Ambassador to Panama set up a drug task force between the Panamanian National Guard and the BNDD. Much to the chagrin of marijuana aficionados around the world, the task force eradicated plantations of Panama Red pot grown on Las Perlas Islands. This successful operation restored relations and enabled the BNDD to reopen its office in the wake of the Him kidnapping flap.[49]

But the White House drug unit wanted Noriega out of its hair and, in an apparent attempt to circumvent the CIA, Krogh gave Ingersoll the job. Ingersoll in January 1972 asked John Warner in the Office of Strategic Intelligence to present options on how to get the job done. Warner handed the task to CIA officer John Bacon, then working under Lou Conein.[50] Bacon's first option paper suggested, among other non-lethal ideas, leaking Noriega's drug trafficking activities to the press. Ingersoll took Bacon's paper to the White House, but Krogh rejected it as too mild. Bacon went back to the drawing board and added three more drastic options: 1) to plant pot on Noriega and have him arrested in the US; 2) to link him to a coup plot against Omar; and 3) his "total and complete immobilization."[51]

Krogh was thrilled with the idea of bloody murder, and perhaps sent Hunt, replete with a tourist card visa good for three months, to Mexico with his Cuban hit team to kill Noriega along with Torrijos.[52] In any event, the CIA caught wind of the plan and vetoed it. Panama was ruled off-limits, but the anti-drug faction kept plugging away and on March 14, 1972, columnist Jack Anderson mentioned Omar Torrijos in relation to drug trafficking. Leaking information to the press was one of Bacon's options — the one Ingersoll and the CIA obviously chose. Both were witting and closely monitored Omar's reaction.[53] Henry Kissinger, however, was incensed when he found out, and ordered a faction within the CIA's DDI to set a trap to find out who the leaker was at the BNDD.[54]

By the time Watergate exploded, many BNDD officials were angry at being used for cross-purposes by the White House and CIA. Strickler complained that the CIA shared intelligence with the White House but not the BNDD. "They would get our documents, steal our informants, and send over faulty intelligence reports. They were not just spinning wheels. They were causing damage."[55]

These cumulative intrigues, ranging from Mafia involvement in CIA assassination plots against Castro, to the Watergate break-in, to assassination plots against Torrijos, Noriega, and hundreds of other individuals, would set the BNDD and DEA on a one-way journey into a dark realm of political corruption.

The French Connection to Vesco

AUTHOR JIM HOUGAN OFFERS TWO novel ideas as to what Watergate was all about. In *Spooks*, he suggests that the Watergate break-in was conducted to find out what the DNC knew about the Nixon drug connection.[56] This theory fits in neatly with the notion that the CIA arranged the theft of the French Connection heroin. It even has overlapping characters.

Hougan's source, William Spector, a former army intelligence officer, claimed his unfaithful wife Patricia stuffed hundreds of toy animals full of heroin and smuggled them into the US for Paul Louis Weiller, a French industrialist and former chief executive officer at Air France. According to Hougan, "One of the purposes of the Watergate burglary was to learn what, if anything, the Democrats intended to do about Paul Louis Weiller's connection to Richard Nixon and Spector's charges of narcotic smuggling."[57]

Spector allegedly took his claims to Bud Krogh, but Krogh recoiled in horror. So Spector went to Agents Stephen McClintic and Jacques Kiere at the BNDD. The agents "found unconscionable lapses in the intelligence-gathering of their subordinates. DEA officials in New York seemed never to have questioned Spector's wife or, in fact, anyone involved."[58] French officials had informed the BNDD about Patricia's nefarious activities, but reports from the French were lost or ignored. The DEA officials blamed the FBI, whom they said had found the issue unworthy of investigation. The FBI said it had no information on Spector's charges, and had never investigated them.[59]

Frustrated, Spector finally took his charges to DNC chairman O'Brien and his aide, Spencer Oliver.[60] Learning of this indiscretion, Krogh sent the plumbers to bug Oliver's phone to find out what the Democrats knew about Nixon's alleged connection with Weiller, who was known within some BNDD inner circle as "the" French connection. However, apart from allegedly receiving a hefty campaign contribution from Weiller, it's unclear if Nixon even knew the man. They reportedly lunched together in the company of Bebe Rebozo and several Middle Eastern power brokers; one of whom, Adnan Khashoggi, later popped up in the Iran-Contra scandal.

While Spector's claims seem fantastic, they do dovetail with other Watergate and international narcotic matters. For example, Patricia Spector was linked to Palestinian entrepreneur Yousef Beidas. Among his many holdings, Beidas owned Intra Bank and the Casino du Liban in Beirut. The casino was managed by Marcel Francisci, whom the *New York Times* in 1971 labeled "One of the richest and most influential members in the Union Corse." Francisci sued the *Times* for libel and several FBN agents testified at the trial, which was remarkable for its lack of coverage in the US press, and for the testimony of CIA agent Herbert Itkin, who had penetrated the Francisci/Mafia drug smuggling operation.[61]

According to Hougan, Patricia also knew drug traffickers Christian David, a mainstay of Ricord's Group France, and Louis Marcel Boucan, captain of the yacht, Caprice du Temps, which was seized in March 1972 with 935 pounds of heroin bound for Louis Cirillo. More importantly, she knew Conrad Bouchard, a heroin trafficker linked to the Cotroni family in Canada. The RCMP had arrested Bouchard in January 1972. The BNDD's office in Mexico played a role in the case, which led to Mafia families in New York. The intriguing aspects of the Bouchard case are: 1) that he was an associate of Marius Martin and Jean Jehan, fugitives in the 1962 French Connection case, and thus a factor in the 1972 corruption case involving the theft of the French Connection heroin that was unfolding in New York City; and 2) his case involved Robert L. Vesco, who had attempted to gain control of Intra Bank after Beidas was murdered. Weiller, a likely French agent, is thought by DEA Agent McClintic to have deliberately bankrupted Intra Bank, which allegedly laundered Francisci's drug money.[62]

Robert Vesco is famous for having made an illegal campaign contribution to Nixon, and for being indicted along with John Mitchell. Both were found not guilty, however, after the government decided not to kidnap Vesco and render him back from Costa Rica to testify. Instead, US Attorney Whitney North Seymour "chose one of Vesco's own former attorneys to press for the fugitive's extradition from the Bahamas."[63] Vesco was "represented in the proceedings by one of Weiller's attorneys."[64]

At the time of the Watergate break-in, Vesco "employed a large contingent of Cuban exiles in his Costa Rican sanctuary."[65] He had also been named in the Bouchard smuggling conspiracy, and was under investigation by BNDD agents in France and Switzerland. At the same time, in June 1972, concurrent with Watergate, BNDD Agent Jack Kelly, the assistant regional director in Los Angeles, sent Agents Sergio Borquez and Robert P. Saunders to Vesco's house in New Jersey. Their job was to find bugging devices planted by SEC investigators. At that moment, Vesco was meeting with Lansky-connected Mafiosi in an attempt to buy Paradise Island with money he had looted from an investment scam, but the deal was quashed in November 1972 when the SEC brought its case against Vesco.[66]

One can only wonder: was Kelly acting on his own, or if he had authorization from Ingersoll, perhaps at the request of John Mitchell? Mitchell did call SEC Chairman William Casey in December 1971 about the SEC's investigation of Vesco, but at Mitchell's trial Casey denied fixing the case.[67] A notorious fabricator, Casey (head of the CIA under Ronald Reagan) was closely connected to Paul Helliwell. Casey's colleague from the OSS, and a finance officer during the Bay of Pigs, Helliwell, based in Florida, set up CIA banks in the Caribbean, and was tied to Santo Trafficante and other organized crime syndicates. As author Jonathan Kwitney notes: "the one CIA career officer definitely known to have planned narcotic smuggling as an instrument of American foreign policy was Paul Helliwell."[68]

Helliwell was not the only CIA officer who planned narcotics smuggling as an instrument of American foreign policy, and it was only natural, as BNDD management formed tighter bonds with a particular faction within the CIA — and as agents became aware of the Borquez-Saunders escapade and the failed SEC investigation of Vesco — that people would suspect that top BNDD, CIA and Nixon administration officials were engaged in drug smuggling operations for personal profit. Government officials were, at a minimum, granting Vesco sanctuary in Costa Rica for partisan political purposes. The Vesco affair, in all its manifestations, was certainly the start of a trend that would further subvert federal drug law enforcement.

Jim Hougan's second theory about Watergate also has a criminal cover-up twist. In *Secret Agenda* he writes:

"In early June 1974, White House Chief of Staff Alexander Haig had ordered the Army's Criminal Investigation Command (CIC) to make a study of the President's alleged ties to organized crime and also to the smuggling of gold bullion to Vietnam. The results of that investigation, carried out by the CIC's Russell Bintliff at the direction of Colonel Henry Tufts, were submitted to Haig in late July 1974.

Whether Haig confronted Nixon with the CIC report, or whether Haig informed Nixon's successor, Gerald Ford, of the report and its contents, is unknown. Bintliff himself is convinced that both events occurred, and that the President's resignation followed as a consequence of his investigative findings. But Bintliff cannot prove that, and since Haig refuses to discuss the issue, the matter remains in doubt. Still, Ford's pardon of Nixon, enacted in the absence of any criminal charges, remains a disconcerting anomaly in American history. Indeed, it seems almost a contradiction in terms. For how does one forgive and forget what has not been committed or what remains unknown?"[69]

Sex and Dean

JOHN INGERSOLL TOLD ME THAT someone at the White House asked him to help with the Watergate cover-up. He would not say if it was his erstwhile patron, John Mitchell, or someone else. If it was someone else, it may well have been his friend John Dean.

According to author Len Colodny, Dean engineered the Watergate burglary to protect his wife-to-be, Maureen Biner, from a sex scandal.[70] Dean's big concern, according to Colodny, was Henry Rothblatt, the lawyer for the Watergate burglars. Rothblatt was probing into the sex life of DNC members, including the people whose phones were bugged. The alleged sex scandal tied into an FBI case against Phillip Bailley, a conman who cruised Capitol Hill bars, got pretty young women drunk, took photos of them in compromising poses, and then blackmailed them into prostitution. By Colodny's account, when Bailley was arrested in June, Earl Silbert, the US Attorney for the District of Colombia, called Dean and said the case had the potential to embarrass Nixon.

Allegedly, DOJ attorneys also had evidence that Jack Caulfield and White House lawyer Jonathan C. Rose had used the mob call-girl ring for which Bailley procured. Rose's father was a big Nixon contributor and in 1969, Rose served as Nixon's personal aide. In 1972 he headed a task force for the Domestic Council which did a study on drugs. In this capacity Rose worked closely with Jerry Strickler, preparing BNDD cases for prosecution. Rose's wife, Susan Porter Rose, would become chief of staff to First Lady Barbara Bush.

While reading through Bailley's address books, which the FBI had seized, Dean allegedly saw a reference to "Clout," which author

Colodny believes was a code name for Maureen Biner. It's not clear how Dean knew Clout was Maureen, but she certainly did have clout. Twice married and divorced by 1972, gorgeous "Mo" had been an airline stewardess in Dallas. In 1969 she moved to Washington and became good friends with Heidi Rikan and BNDD attorney Candy Cowan. Rikan, aka Cathy Dieter, was a stripper, madam, and girlfriend of Joe Nesline, the Mafia godfather of our nation's capital, a Lansky associate, and the force behind a prostitution ring that threatened to embarrass numerous Washington officials.

Maureen befriended Candy Cowan while both worked for BNDD counsel Michael Sonnenreich. Maureen became Sonnenreich's executive assistant on the Marijuana Commission. In 1972 she returned to the BNDD as a secretary for training division chief Perry Rivkind and his international branch chief, Robert Stutman. She married John Dean in October 1972.

Colodny insists that Dean had people break into Hunt's safe to get two envelopes with sensitive material. One envelope contained Hunt's forged cables about JFK. Colodny says the other had salacious information about Maureen.

Dean denies he ever saw the name Biner or Clout in Bailley's notebook. He says Colodny is a vehicle of right-wing Republican propaganda.[71] But there is circumstantial evidence linking Dean to a prostitution ring and prior knowledge of the Watergate break-in on June 17, 1972. In his autobiography, BNDD Agent Robert Stutman revealed that Andy Tartaglino had charged Stutman with providing prostitutes to Dean. Stutman does not say how Tartaglino came by this information, but Tartaglino obviously believed it. Stutman says it is untrue. Very strange, until one realizes that Stutman worked for the CIA until 1965, when the FBN hired him as a propagandist to link pot puffers to the anti-war movement.

For no apparent reason, other than his friendship with John and Maureen Dean, Stutman became chief of the BNDD's international training division in December 1971. Dean and Stutman were together in San Francisco on June 18, 1972 when Fred Fielding called Dean about the Watergate break-in.[72] They were returning from a lecture Dean had given to the Philippine narcotics bureau on the day of the break-in. The trip was organized by Maureen. Dean says it was all very innocent: that Perry Rivkind had invited him and that Haldeman had given permission. Colodny suggests that Maureen persuaded Rivkind to extend the invitation. He sees the hastily organized trip as a sign that Dean knew the break-in was coming and wanted to be out of town when the crap hit the fan.

"No," said Dean: "I agreed to make the June 1972 trip and speech because I had never been to the Philippines, the occasions seemed important, and in those days my body thought nothing of a quick trip half-way around the world in just a few days."[73] Dean also denies that Krogh consulted him about the legality of kidnapping drug traffickers. He had no knowledge about Hunt's plot to assassinate Omar Torrijos, or that Hunt's team was in Mexico before the mission was aborted.

In the absence of any smoking gun, one must take Dean at his word. But prior to his Ellsberg-like tilt to the Left, he was a hard-line right winger who once wrote a memo titled "How can we use the political machinery to screw our enemies." This was vintage Krogh, who boasted that "Anyone who opposes us, we'll destroy. As a matter of fact, anyone who doesn't support us, we'll destroy."[74]

Using political machinery to screw one's enemies remains as American as apple pie and motherhood.

Krogh was sentenced to prison in January 1974 for two to six years for authorizing Liddy and Hunt to burglarize Dan Ellsberg's psychiatrist's office. Dean never did a day, in return for testifying against his former colleagues.

What's important in all this Watergate speculation is the recurring fact that Nixon's "Merry Pranksters" had at their disposal the DC police, the military, and all the various resources of the federal government, including the BNDD. They had the will to use these forces for partisan political purposes. To help suppress a May Day 1971 antiwar demonstration in Washington, the White House borrowed 200 BNDD agents from around the country and infiltrated them into the crowd, ostensibly for drug law enforcement purposes but, in reality, to suppress political dissent.[75] Future Republican Administrations would be more subtle in their manipulation of the DEA.

While the Nixon White House geared up for an all-out assault on its political opponents, Congress attempted to energize and focus the BNDD by enacting "No-Knock" legislation that empowered drug law enforcement agencies to conduct warrantless searches. It also passed the Controlled Substances Act, which created a classification system for dangerous drugs. The result of this convergence of ideological extremism and federal legislation was the permanent politicization of drug law enforcement. Nixon's use of federal narcotics agents as a secret police force, and his loosening of laws guaranteeing the Fourth

Amendment to empower ODALE, would eventually earn federal narcotic agents a reputation as an American Gestapo.

These external developments coincided with a greater emphasis on intelligence within the BNDD. By late 1972, the BNDD's intelligence experts were being called upon to brief US and foreign officials, to respond to Congressional inquiries, and provide the intelligence community with "specialized intelligence and operational security services as required."[76] That last function meant that the BNDD's growing intelligence office could be used for partisan political purposes outside its legislative mandate. In the Watergate "dirty tricks" environment, when BNDD agents were sweeping Robert Vesco's house for SEC bugs and protecting him in Costa Rica, that spelled big trouble for our republic.

17

COVERT INTELLIGENCE

IN THE WATERGATE SUMMER OF 1972, Egil Krogh and his Merry Pranksters were dreaming up new ways to merge the war on drugs with the political war against "campus bums" and Democrats. One of their more bizarre plots wed the BNDD and CIA in a program called BUNCIN — the Bureau of Narcotics Covert Intelligence Network. This time the Defense Department joined in the fun.

BUNCIN's stated purpose was to gather long-range strategic intelligence, covertly, for the purpose of "neutralizing" traffickers.[1] Neutralize was a word that had become fashionable after the CIA introduced it into the intelligence community through its nefarious Phoenix Program in Vietnam. Neutralize meant to assassinate, kidnap and/or indefinitely detain targeted individuals. BUNCIN included psychological warfare tactics such as "provocations, inducement to desertion, creating confusion and apprehension."[2] BUNCIN psywar operations, in theory, would reduce the ability of drug traffickers to recruit new members by "introducing the certainty of apprehension and detention regardless of their country of residence."[3]

These tactics had been standard fare for FBN agents since the 1920s. The FBN had been in existence long before the CIA, and the CIA learned many of the tricks of its trade from the FBN. Garland Williams, the FBN's Regional Director in New York City in the late 1930s, helped establish OSS training schools in Maryland and Virginia. Williams was also the OSS's chief of sabotage training and, along with other FBN agents, trained OSS officers in undercover work, as well as how to elude the security services of enemy nations.[4] Some BUNCIN "intelligence activities" were directed against "senior foreign government officials" and were to be "blamed on other government agencies, or even on the intelligence services of other nations."[5] Even the BUNCIN tactic of targeting foreign officials and blaming foreign secret services for the havoc wrought by BUNCIN assets was nothing new, as demonstrated in the Delouette Case discussed in Chapter 11. What was new about BUNCIN was that its assets were working for the CIA as well as the BNDD, and that the principal agents would report on "civic and political groups in addition to monitoring the activities of other assets in the net."[6]

In September 1972, at the instigation of the White House, DCI Richard Helms and John Ingersoll met together at the Hays-Adams Hotel to seal the deal.[7] Helms (already knee-deep in the Watergate cover-up) said the CIA had prepared files on several drug traffickers in Miami, the Florida Keys, and the Caribbean. He said the CIA would provide Ingersoll with CIA assets, most of whom were anti-Castro Cubans, to pursue known traffickers, as well as to develop information on hitherto unknown targets of opportunity.[8] The CIA would provide operational, technical, and financial support. Being a "cloak and dagger" buff, Ingersoll agreed. He put Andy Tartaglino in charge. Tartaglino had the witting support of a few senior administrative officials, as well as Miami RD Ben Theisen, Bill Durkin at Criminal Investigations, Phil Smith at Special Projects, John Warner at Strategic Intelligence, and George Belk at Foreign Operations.

CIA officers Robert Medell and William Logay were selected to run BUNCIN in the field.[9] Known by his BNDD colleagues as "the Cuban Ghost," Medell was born in Cuba in 1940. The CIA hired him for the Bay of Pigs invasion and afterwards re-hired him to recruit soldiers of fortune (some of whom were drug smugglers) from Spain, Belgium, Argentina and elsewhere, to fight Congolese forces led by Cubans backed by the Soviets and Chinese. The CIA won the Congo War and Medell's contract was renewed in 1966 under the Chilean Task Force. Next he was assigned to Panama as a principal agent for CIA officer Lawrence Sternfeld, the chief of station and Manuel Noriega's case officer. Sternfeld was a case officer to many Cuban exiles, some of whom were BUNCIN agents including a vice president at

Continental Bank. He was also close to the Israelis and, according to Medell, gave them privileged information.

In June 1972, CIA personnel officer George "Jerry" Sohl introduced Medell to Tom Tripodi. Sohl had been Medell's case officer during the Congo War and knew many of the CIA's assets in the exile Cuban community. Tripodi, a former chief of CIA Security's Special Operations Branch in Miami, knew the milieu too; he had even employed some of the Cubans bagged in the Watergate affair.[10] Tripodi arranged for Tartaglino and Ingersoll to interview Medell at a motel in Arlington, far from the rumor mill at headquarters. They hired him and sent him to Inspections chief Pat Fuller. Medell worked for three months on the administrative side of Fuller's "Twofold" shoofly program.

When BUNCIN surfaced in September, Medell was assigned to it. He brought to the job Spanish language skills and experience as a recruiter of drug smugglers in far away places like Africa, Bogota and Geneva. He and Bill Logay developed the BUNCIN operational plan based on the standard CIA principle of developing intelligence with strategic and tactical value on a long-term basis. Medell, the covert agent, was to have no contact with Logay, the overt agent. Adding another layer to Medell's cover, only the most senior Miami agents were to know that Logay had a safe house near the airport, and that he and Medell were recruiting anti-Castro Cuban traffickers to report on civic and political groups (the sort of intelligence that was bound to please Nixon), as well as corrupt BNDD agents.

Medell and Logay submitted their plan in November. Tartaglino approved it and BUNCIN was activated in December. Tartaglino had direct operational control, although Lou Conein was deeply involved through a parallel but separate chain of command.[11]

While in army intelligence in the early 1960s, BUNCIN's administrative officer, Rich Kobakoff, had served in Morocco and the Mideast in a military unit commanded by Conein. The unit was under CIA control and included Colonel Joseph Lagattuta, who bounced back and forth between the CIA and the army throughout his career. Lagattuta, like Kobakoff, wound up working for Conein in the DEA. After working with Conein, Kobakoff joined the CIA, where he remained for several years. In April 1972, as part of a reduction in force that dove-tailed with the end of the Vietnam War, he was assigned to the BNDD's Office of Strategic Intelligence. CIA officers Jerry Sohl and Chip Barquin made the arrangement. Within the SIU

Kobakoff handled the Middle East, except Turkey, which was covered by CIA officer George Oakey.[12]

Kobakoff resigned from the CIA in October 1972, shortly after the G-Dep reorganization. At this point he became the intelligence desk officer for SIU domestic east operations. He was, concurrently, Conein's administrative aide for BUNCIN finances, logistical and technical support. Kobakoff began his BUNCIN assignment by obtaining, from Tartaglino's safe, a handful of classified reports which had not gone into the BNDD's investigative files. These top-secret files referenced the CIA agents, almost all of whom were exile Cubans, who were to become BUNCIN assets. Kobakoff and Clarence Cook, a desk officer at headquarters, then flew to Miami to meet Medell and Logay.

BUNCIN Begins

WHEN MEDELL ARRIVED ON THE scene, Conein was already running operations through an older Cuban man with assets in the targeted areas. The man occupied an office adjacent to chief inspector Pat Fuller. He was married to a rich woman in Maryland who owned race horses. Unfortunately, he had Democratic Party friends in Miami, and Krogh doubted his loyalty; so BUNCIN informant Ricardo "Monkey" Morales introduced the older Cuban man to a pretty young girl. In the finest CIA sexual blackmail tradition, Morales acquired photographs of them naked and snorting cocaine. The photos were passed around, the man had a disabling heart attack, and Medell stepped in to replace him.[13]

Pat Fuller, whose Office of Inspections provided communications equipment to the BUNCIN agents, said quite bluntly that BUNCIN had two agendas.[14] As with Operation Twofold, there was a box within a box. One agenda "was told" and had a narcotics mission. The other was secret and had a partisan political agenda. Instructions for the secret facet of BUNCIN emanated from Egil Krogh, and were passed through Conein and Hunt to Gordon Liddy and the Gemstone team, led by Bernard Barker and staffed by exile Cuban terrorists.[15]

Another source claims this chain of command included Hunt's asset Manuel Artime and Rolando Cubelas Secades, an exile Cuban asset of CIA officer Nestor Sanchez. In 1972, having returned from a tour in Colombia, Sanchez managed the Cuban Group at CIA headquarters. Said to be Medell's rabbi, Sanchez's Cuban operation had a unilateral CIA agenda which, under cover of BUNCIN, targeted terrorists and gun runners selling boats and helicopters to Fidel Castro.[16]

Krogh reportedly ran his political operation under cover of BUNCIN until his January 1973 appointment as Secretary of Transportation. Krogh did this directly with Lou Conein, apart from Tartaglino or anyone else in the BNDD. Under cover of BUNCIN, Conein, Hunt, Sanchez, and their Cuban assets allegedly assassinated and kidnapped people in Colombia and Mexico for the CIA. To whom Krogh passed his mantle is unknown, but BUNCIN's White House sponsors sent BUNCIN assets to gather dirt on Democratic Party politicians in Key West; and, among other non-drug law enforcement matters, foiled an assassination attempt on Henry Kissinger.[17]

Medell's primary job was recruiting principal agents to run agent nets and anti-drug smuggling operations not only in Miami, but "throughout the Caribbean and South America."[18] In doing this he posed as Robert Martin and formed Robert Martin Enterprises, a "national" consulting firm near Miami International Airport, were Logay kept the safe house. Both Medell and Logay ventured into Latin America on BUNCIN assignments. Medell set up a nominee account in the Miami Bank and started running agents in March 1973. He briefed Ingersoll that month on his recruitment of assets in Miami, the Caribbean and New York, and about his plans to penetrate the Cuban side of Santo Trafficante's organization based in Tampa. At this point SIU analysts began to research files by BUNCIN assets related to the Trafficante organization.[19]

Medell and Logay folded their agent contact reports into National Intelligence Requirement reports. The NIRs were hand carried from Logay's safe house to Homestead Air Force Base and flown to Andrews Air Force Base. From there they were delivered to headquarters via the Defense Department's classified courier service and handed to Tartaglino. Tartaglino reviewed the NIRs and distributed them to Durkin, Belk, Smith, and Warner; they in turn compiled investigative files and a Narcotics Intelligence Requirement List. The Defense Department was in charge of emergency planning and provided BUNCIN agents with special communications equipment. The CIA supplied forged foreign IDs that allowed BUNCIN assets to work for foreign governments or intelligence services.[20]

As noted, BUNCIN assets targeted the Cuban side of the Trafficante family (his daughter had married a Cuban) and its drug and gambling operations. Medell hired several notorious Cubans to carry out this task. The assets knew Medell was CIA. They all had worked for the CIA before, and they believed they were working for the CIA again. And many were.[21]

Medell's Principal Agent was Bay of Pigs veteran Guillermo Tabraue, whom the CIA paid a whopping $1400 a week. While receiving this princely sum, Tabraue was participating in the "Alvarez-Cruz" multi-million dollar drug smuggling ring.[22] A compatriot of Howard Hunt's friend, Manuel Artime, Tabraue ran his operation out of a jewelry store in Miami, reporting on Cuban civic and political groups with connections to Santo Trafficante and his partner, Meyer Lansky. Through Tabraue's sub-agents in the construction, drug and gambling rackets, Medell developed counter-intelligence information on how Manuel Noriega's security forces were investigating CIA agents in Panama and Colombia.[23]

Another important BUNCIN agent was CIA contract officer Grayston Lynch in Key West. A tough World War II veteran of Omaha Beach, Lynch joined the Special Forces in 1955 and the CIA in 1960.[24] He was one of two Anglos to hit the beach during the Bay of Pigs invasion and thus was trusted by the exile Cubans. He had also served with Conein "all over" the world. On behalf of the CIA, Lynch was already running agents from Miami into Latin America when Conein hired him into BUNCIN. Lynch's main job was to identify "suppliers at the other end," largely through contrabandista pilots. An experienced sailor, he also penetrated an exile Cuban smuggling ring belonging to Francisco Chanes Rodriguez (of Iran-Contra infamy), owner of the CIA front companies Ocean Hunter and Mr. Shrimp. Chanes' fishermen had contact with Cuba's fishing fleet and exchanged all sorts of information and items. Another BUNCIN asset, Sixto "Tito" Mesa in Key Biscayne, was one of the most powerful drug smugglers in the anti-Castro community. (Mesa was also connected to Rafael "Chi Chi" Quintero and Thomas Clines, also of Iran-Contra *and* Edwin Wilson infamy). According to Lynch, Tito offered him $80,000 to hire Cuban mercenaries for President Anastasio Somoza in Nicaragua. Such was the double-dealing underworld in which the BUNCIN agents navigated.

Medell hired many agents from Manuel Artime's organization, which operated throughout the Caribbean, Latin America, and Mexico. Among them were the Villaverde brothers (who helped set up the terrorist organization CORU in Mexico), Felix Rodriquez, Chi Chi Quintero, and Ricardo Chavez.[25] Howard Hunt had been Artime's case officer for years, and Artime's milieu had worked for Ted Shackley when he ran the CIA's Miami station in the mid-1960s. In 1973, as chief of the Western Hemisphere Division, Shackley appointed his trusted friend, Tom Clines, as chief of operations in the Caribbean.[26] Clines had worked for Shackley in Miami and Laos, and knew every Cuban of importance in the exile community, including, as noted, Tito Mesa. BUNCIN assets worked closely with Clines.

Carlos Hernandez Rumbault was another infamous BUNCIN agent. A member, like Tabraue, of the Alvarez-Cruz drug smuggling network, Rumbault in 1969 inexplicably did a u-turn on the main drag in Mobile, Alabama. He pulled into a gas station, parked beside a police cruiser, got out of the car and surrendered, saying, "You got me."[27] He had hundreds of pounds of marijuana in his car. Rumbault was prosecuted, but had not been sentenced when he volunteered to work for the BNDD during Operation Eagle. Tabraue generously posted his bail, and Rumbault went to work for the BNDD. As a reward for making several cases, he was sent to Costa Rica where he became second in command of its federal narcotics unit. Rumbault worked closely with BNDD agent Arthur Sedillo making heroin and cocaine cases.[28]

Shortly after Rumbault's arrival in Costa Rica, fugitives Robert Vesco and Santo Trafficante popped up in the country. Both were friends of Costa Rican President José Figueres, and Rumbault was soon spying on them for Lucien Conein. Criminals in Costa Rica had their own private armies, and Rumbault's tactics were brutal. Jerry Strickler said that Rumbault formed a vigilante squad with President Figueres' son and an assistant attorney general, and that together they wiped out rival narcotics gangs. Rumbault liked to use a machine gun.

The State Department wasn't happy about that, but bigger trouble was brewing. As Strickler recalled, "Costa Rica's president had an American wife and she had directed her son to become supportive of the BNDD." The BNDD wanted fugitive Segundo Coronel de Torop, and the president's son agreed to bring him back. The president's son, accompanied by the head of the Costa Rican narcotic unit and Rumbault, flew Coronel to Miami. Alas, Coronel was wanted on a Customs indictment and Al Seely was waiting at the airport. As Coronel stepped off the plane, BNDD Agent Pete Scrocca put a handcuff on one wrist and Seely cuffed the other. Strickler had to call US Attorney Tom Puccio in New York to get Seely to back off.

The shock waves from this confrontation alerted an Alabama prosecutor to the fact that Rumbault was working for the BNDD and had been in the States. He immediately summoned Rumbault back for sentencing. But like every Cuban CIA agent in BUNCIN, Rumbault had a "get out of jail free card." Complicating the matter, Guillermo Tabraue wanted back the $20,000 he had posted for Rumbault's bond, and was threatening to kill him unless he got it. Strickler asked Belk to pay Tabraue in order to protect Rumbault. Belk objected, noting that Tabraue had purchased the services of several corrupt BNDD agents and cops in the Miami area. Strickler pressed the issue and Belk eventually relented. Federal officials convinced the governor of Alabama to make the prosecutor stop the extradition proceedings in the interests of national security. They also got the State Department to pull in its horns.[29]

The Mississippi Riverboat Gambler

ACCORDING TO RICH KOBAKOFF, BUNCIN was an experiment in how to finesse the law. The end product was intelligence, not seizures or arrests. But it was underfunded, kept getting handed around, and no one had the time to properly manage it. Kobakoff might have added that BUNCIN was also subverted by a personality conflict between diminutive Latino Bob Medell, nick-named "El Anano" (the Evil Dwarf), by his detractors, and big blustery Anglo Bill Logay, a former college football player and Oakland cop whom Tully Acampora described as "the original Mississippi riverboat gambler."

Medell felt that institutional racism fueled his personnel problems with Logay, and ruined BUNCIN and his career. CIA case officers appreciated Medell's talents and were only concerned about results; the "tough cop" attitude, exemplified by Logay and Phil Smith, put conformity first. Medell said that BNDD managers were not respectful of peoples' rights and behaved like an American Gestapo. As an example he points to Howie Safir, whom he described as Phil Smith's "enforcer." Assigned to Special Projects, Safir, according to Medell, was "ruthless, callous, the worst; a man who would plant five pounds on someone just to get them to go to work."[30]

When Logay appeared on the scene, Medell was already working with Conein, Bud Frank (who did Conein's "legwork") and Kobakoff. Logay had been CIA Station Chief Ted Shackley's bodyguard for a year in Vietnam, and in 1970 returned to Saigon to work under Tully Acampora as a CIA special police liaison in Precinct 5.[31]

Acampora understood that Logay should have been a conman or perhaps a cop, but not a CIA agent. So he made Logay his drug coordinator and introduced him to Fred Dick. Logay and Dick clicked and in June 1971, Dick suggested to Logay that he join the BNDD. Acampora agreed that it was a good idea and recommended Logay to Andy Tartaglino. Tartaglino despised Fred Dick and would not have accepted Logay on Dick's word alone. But Acampora was a dear friend of Tartaglino's mentor, Charlie Siragusa, and had worked closely with Hank Manfredi (whom Tartaglino greatly admired) for years in Rome on collateral CIA/FBN operations.

Based on Acampora's recommendation, Tartaglino sent the required paperwork to Saigon, where in January 1972 Logay was hired into the BNDD. Upon arriving in the States, he completed the mandatory twelve week basic training course. Tartaglino assigned him to Miami where he quickly struck up a friendship with Fred Dick's old partner from St. Louis, Regional Director Ben Theisen. Within a week Logay was tossing down shots with Theisen and Agents Pete Scrocca, Bill Hudson and Harry Hyman. Theisen assigned Logay to the regional intelligence unit under Edward Heath, and Logay started working undercover cases in Jamaica, Aruba, and the Bahamas.

In October 1972, Tartaglino summoned Logay to Washington and introduced him to Ingersoll. By Logay's account, Ingersoll asked him to help establish a CIA-type operation directed at Cubans in South Florida. The goal was to get strategic intelligence, as well as to offset an OMB report that was highly critical of the BNDD's intelligence capabilities. Bob Medell was to be the covert agent, Logay the overt agent, and only Theisen was to know what he was doing. Logay agreed. After the meeting, Tartaglino told Logay that Pat Fuller wanted to see him. Logay went to Fuller's office, and Fuller asked him to spy on Theisen, Scrocca, Hudson and Hyman.

Logay was confounded and amazed. He had already bonded with Theisen, who was famous for consuming a fifth of Johnny Walker Red and a wholesome quart of milk as a chaser every evening. Logay retreated to Tartaglino's office and said he'd be glad to do the BUNCIN job, but refused to be a spy. Tartaglino agreed and let Logay off the hook.

In a dramatic coincidence, Theisen was on the same flight that took Logay back to Miami. When Logay told him what Fuller had proposed, Theisen wept at the realization that people at headquarters were secretly plotting against him. Theisen immediately told his deputy Tom Hurney about Fuller's dastardly shoofly program, and about BUNCIN. Hurney's reaction was typical of the majority of BNDD agents: he could not understand why BUNCIN was needed or why BUNCIN agents were allowed to keep unregistered informants. "If you become corrupt in methodology," he said, "you become part of the problem."[32]

Or, as Logay openly observed, "We all committed felonies."

Bill Logay was assigned full time to the BUNCIN "overt" office on 36th Street. He reported to Tartaglino. Through Tartaglino's staff coordinator Robin Cushing, some of his reports were sent to Jerry Strickler at the Latin American desk in enforcement. Medell dealt directly with Conein, and that caused communication problems with and for Logay. As Rich Kobakoff explained, Medell knew nothing about the BNDD and Logay was vulgar and disparaging when telling him what to do, so "Medell got disenchanted."

Medell was sensitive about cultural issues, Logay was politically incorrect, and they clashed. Defending his actions, Logay claims that Medell was a shoofly for Fuller and not qualified to run agent nets. It also hurt that Medell was Conein's golden boy, and that Rumbault passed Medell hot tips on Robert Vesco in Costa Rica. Worse, Medell did not follow Logay's orders or introduce him to important BUNCIN assets like Rumbault and Monkey Morales. Medell's excuse was that the Cubans didn't trust Logay. This forced Logay to report what Medell said, without being able to verify it. However, Logay eventually forged a relationship with Guillermo Tabraue, with whom he had lunch once a month. Tabraue always trying to do him little favors and Logay, having been tutored by Fred Dick, had a hard time resisting. On one occasion Tabraue presented expensive diamond earrings for Logay's wife, Loretta, a CIA officer. Logay brought them home and Loretta tried them on, but Logay gave them back. He told Tabraue, "I can't afford them."

But, by then, the damage had been done.

Special Projects

APART FROM BUNCIN, THE OFFICE of Special Projects under Phil Smith was involved in a wide range of covert activities. It provided support to Fuller's "Twofold" shoofly program and to Tartaglino's special corruption unit in New York. Special Projects was even dragged into the French connection through Nixon's White House and Thomas Watson, the US Ambassador to France. Watson's science advisor, Dr. Edgar Piret, envisioned a machine that could spot clandestine labs by detecting in the atmosphere the chemical precursors used in processing morphine base into heroin.[33] Krogh liked the idea and sent John Dean to Paris to tell Paul Knight and Francois Le Mouel to support it. When Le Mouel expressed his reluctance to re-assign agents from standard investigations to an experimental project, Dr Piret gave him a stern lecture on American "know-how" and the critical importance of the heroin "sniffer." Le Mouel acquiesced with the admonition that "it better work."[34]

Agent Howie Safir at Special Projects managed the sniffer project, which was contracted to a Stanford scientist. After being field tested in California, the sniffer was sent to France and driven around the streets of Paris and Marseille concealed inside a Volkswagen van. One can picture Peter Sellers as Chief Inspector Clouseau behind the wheel. Even dour Le Mouel laughed.

The sniffer found no heroin labs, just a lot of cleaning stores that used the same chemical precursors. As Paul Knight wryly noted about such whimsical misadventures, which the BNDD was trying with ever increasing frequency: "If it's worth doing at all, it's worth overdoing,"

Special Projects had more success developing the BNDD's air wing, starting with one Cessna acquired by Agent Marion Joseph. Money was the problem, but Customs used planes along the border, so the BNDD's Congressional backers came through, and by 1973 the BNDD had around 40 pilots operating some two dozen fixed-wing aircraft and a few helicopters in several major American cities.[35] Most were used for domestic surveillance along the Mexican border.

Perhaps the most controversial special project began in August 1972, when the sheriff of Las Vegas obtained information about a mob-operated drug ring at the Frontier Hotel. Nixon campaign contributor Howard Hughes owned the Frontier, which gave the case high priority.[36] The Frontier, alas, was protected by the private security company Intertel (International Intelligence, Inc), and through Intertel's involvement in the case, potential conflicts of interest arose which further inflamed tensions between Andy Tartaglino, Phil Smith and the Purple Gang.

Intertel was formed in 1968 by several former federal law officers, including US Attorney Robert Peloquin. Tartaglino's problem was that Special Projects chief Phil Smith had formed a friendship with Peloquin while they were serving together in 1966 on the Buffalo Strike Force.[37]

In February 1973, Smith assigned his "enforcer" Howie Safir to manage the case, dubbed Operation Silver Dollar. Safir elected to send undercover ace Santo Bario, posing as a high roller, into the mob drug ring operating inside the Frontier. Smith wanted Bario to gamble using BNDD funds, but Chief Counsel Don Miller said it was illegal. Showing what some would call "initiative and ingenuity," Smith asked Peloquin to front the money. Peloquin agreed and arranged for Bario to get $20,000 from the Summa Corporation, a subsidiary of the Hughes Corporation. Perhaps to curry favor with the White House, Ingersoll approved it. Bario went to work, and eventually six mobsters were arrested and convicted.[38]

But Bario's luck at the tables was not as good as his undercover skills, and he lost $17,000 of Summa Corporation money. When Peloquin asked for the return of the front money, Smith used Special Projects funds — and Andy Tartaglino took exception.[39]

Tartaglino had objected to Silver Dollar for two reasons. His mistrust of Peloquin was the first. In 1968, while deputy director of security for the National Football League, Peloquin had passed proprietary information to Commissioner Pete Rozelle about a federal probe into gambling by pro football players.[40] The IRS found interference in the issuance of a subpoena, which was later withdrawn, to Washington Redskins football player Vincent Promuto. Tartaglino was also aware of a July 1972 BNDD report linking Intertel to the Meyer Lansky branch of organized crime.

Intertel provided security for the Paradise Island casino complex (which Robert Vesco was trying to buy in November 1972) in the Bahamas. Paradise Island was owned by Resorts International. The Lansky mob, including associates of Santo Trafficante, had invested in Resorts International, which was a stockholder in Intertel. In January 1966, while still employed by the Justice Department, Peloquin wrote a report citing Resorts as "ripe" for a Lansky skim.[41]

As Tartaglino knew, Peloquin in 1969 had offered Smith a job with Intertel. Smith had gone to Nassau on a vacation to check it out. A transfer Smith didn't want was rescinded, so he stayed with BNDD, but Tartaglino felt that Smith was "feathering a nest for himself down the road."[42] He did not like Smith, and the feeling was mutual. The anger between them would eventually erupt with catastrophic consequences for the fledgling DEA.

Strategic Intelligence

THE OFFICE OF INTELLIGENCE WAS also involved in covert activities apart from BUNCIN. SIO Chief John Warner recognized intelligence

as the new wave and did everything possible to promote his bureaucratic fiefdom. Perhaps its strongest selling point was that the SIO
served as the BNDD's point of contact with the CIA. Warner's intelligence chief Richard Bly handled that liaison function, as well as liaison
to the ONNI. Warner was liaison to the Foreign Intelligence Subcommittee of the CCINC.[43]

The SIO covered a lot of ground. It prepared the BNDD's annual
high profile report to the United Nations. It conducted studies on
politics and corruption in Spain, Thailand, Lebanon, Africa, the
Persian Gulf, Mexico and Afghanistan. Its analysts debriefed a Chinese chemist in Hong Kong and a Chinese courier caught in New
York City. Ongoing projects included Pilot and a separate Corsican
study; work with a German Task Force; a damage assessment of the
Anderson-Torrijos leak; a review of Operation Sandstorm; a Mexican Border Study; a Colombia Corruption Study; a Hong Kong Corruption Study; a top secret intelligence-gathering operation in the
Far East using Chinese nationalists; and a CIA-style disinformation
program designed to destabilize drug trafficking groups by having
articles printed about their members in foreign newspapers. SIO was
also responsible for expanding the NADIS and DAWN data bases.[44]
Warner regularly briefed the White House on SIO operations.[45]

Dr. Richard Blum conducted one of SIO's most secret endeavors
in 1972 and 1973. A liberal Democrat, Blum had met John Ingersoll
in "The Cell," which, by Blum's account, was trying to put "a new
face on law enforcement" by combining public health and criminology.[46] Blum was a psychologist in residence at San Quentin Prison
at the time. He had just done a study on LSD, through which he
met Sid Gottlieb, the man in charge of the CIA's MKULTRA "mind
control" program. Blum also knew William Colby and when Colby
returned from Vietnam to Washington in 1971, Blum — then serving on the BNDD's scientific advisory board — introduced him to
Ingersoll. Blum claims that he, Ingersoll and Colby conceived of SIO
and selected Warner to head it. They also jointly conceived of the first
money-laundering investigations in Mexico.

As Andy Tartaglino recalled, "Ingersoll's social scientist friend set
up a clandestine unit in Mexico, and Bob Goe went ahead with it."[47]

Blum described the mission in Mexico as an effort to learn why
some drug smuggling rings were protected and others were not. He
studied at a Federal Judicial Police station in northern Mexico, where
the federal agents managed the traffic through their station. In one

instance they seized a caravan of fourteen trucks filled with pot; they killed the drivers and stored the pot in their warehouse until they were able to sell it. Out of courtesy, they asked Blum if he wanted a share of the profits. Blum refused, but he is careful to explain that it was not a bribe. It was simply business as usual.

Quartered in the American Embassy, Blum worked with the Mexican Attorney General setting up and training a clandestine unit to track drug money. "To have competent intelligence," Blum asserts, "you need to know more than what the local newspaperman knows, or what you learn at a dinner party." In Mexico, patterns of corruption were defined primarily by family and location. "It was hard to find the mules, but easy to find the bosses. However, once you learn who the bosses are," Blum adds, "You can't do anything about it. Mexico did not have an addiction problem. Peasants used opium for teething their kids, that's all. Plus which management was involved in the traffic." As Blum concluded, "If the desire is to interdict, there is no efficient way."

Blum was in favor of closing down overseas enforcement operations, while maintaining intelligence. This view, and Blum's conviction that the Customs approach had the highest yield and lowest cost, was unpopular at headquarters, as was his discovery of corruption within the US Customs Service. According to Blum, Customs agents had a deal with "second-level retailers" moving ten to fifty thousand dollar lots. Through informants, the Customs agents let the traffickers know when new US customers appeared on the scene. In return the seller would report short term people — people who were in business for one score. Customs agents would arrest them at the border. The seller would get half the money from the sale, plus some of the seized heroin. Customs would get credit for the bust and half the net profits.

Blum reported his findings to headquarters, and Inspections Chief Pat Fuller sent a small team to the border to investigate. The inspectors found more trouble than they were looking for. Texas mercenaries were trading arms for drugs, as part of a CIA counter-intelligence operation in Mexico that was monitoring rebel groups and their interactions with Russian and North Korean agents. Things started getting tense. Fuller said to Blum, "Did you know there's a [murder] contract out on you?"[48]

BNDD agents thought Blum was a shoofly and one agent, known as the Fat Mexican Assassin, was gunning for him in Mexico. CIA officer Rich Kobakoff at SIO took it upon himself to report Blum's findings to "a friend at CIA, a young case officer, now a high official."[49] Kobakoff told his CIA friend that "a renegade group with BNDD was perpetrating a wrong-headed operation" and suggested they "cut it off at the pass." The CIA passed along the names of the people in Blum's clandestine unit to its contacts in Mexico. These protected drug traffickers put an end to it. Within a week, Kobakoff was transferred to Conein's outfit and assigned to BUNCIN.

Blum wrote a novel based on his experiences, titled *The Mexican Assassin*.

Says Blum: "We spend one billion annually in California imprisoning non-violent drug offenders. They don't come out rehabilitated. You can't control criminal behavior. You can't use drug laws to establish social goals. It costs too much money. The idea is to adapt drug law enforcement to reality."

True believer John Warner took a narrower view. According to him, opposition from enforcement was the thing that kept his intelligence program from achieving the prominence it deserved. People like Durkin, Belk, Pohl and Strickler were "only concerned with putting people in jail. In Warner's world, they were also jealous of SIU's relations with the CIA. "This is the thing Drexel Godfrey tried to avoid by creating an office of strategic intelligence," Warner sighed. "He saw the potential for conflict."[50]

That conflict, and all the others, would only get worse.

18

THE PARALLEL MECHANISM

BY THE FALL OF 1972, Tony Pohl had been transferred from New York's International Division to a special tactical unit that, after dispensing with Louis Cirillo, mounted a huge conspiracy case on seven related Mafia drug trafficking rings. The chief of the International Division's South American group, Gerry Carey, was working with Jerry Strickler at headquarters, and Paul Knight had replaced Jack Cusack as regional director in Paris. Finally, the right personalities were in place to truly smash the French connection: at its source in Latin America, and at the receiving end in the United States.

The impetus came from Carey and Strickler in October 1972, when they proposed a "Special South American Task Force" (Operation Springboard) to corral the French and Italian traffickers moving heroin from Europe through South America to the US.[1] Their idea was to fuse an element of Carey's Latin American group with an element from John O'Neill's European group. Building on the foundation that Pohl had put in place — using New York as a venue point where foreigners could be extradited — they concentrated on five ongoing cases that involved the Andre Condemine organization in France. The first step was to gather and refine intelligence to initiate a huge conspiracy case against the targets worldwide. As Carey explained, they didn't need seizures or "dope on the table" to include someone in the conspiracy: the trafficker just had to commit an overt act in furtherance of the crime.[2]

Springboard was approved at headquarters and funded through Special Projects. A special team, including two Customs agents and two NYPD detectives, was assembled and given its own space inside the office of US Attorney Tom Puccio. Every relevant defendant the BNDD and Customs had in custody was debriefed. According to Carey, "Puccio didn't refuse anything" and eventually they obtained 19 indictments on 108 people; by June 1973, 51 defendants were incarcerated in the US and abroad.[3]

"Springboard proved you could get them and their bosses," Jerry Strickler said. "But we had to be creative." The kidnapping of Joaquim Him Gonzalez, Panama's chief of air traffic control, in February 1971 was a good example; the pressure applied to extradite Auguste Ricord from Paraguay was another. In the Ricord case, assistant secretary of state Nelson Gross went to Paraguay and, citing the Foreign Assistance Act, threatened to suspend US credits to Paraguay for beet sugar unless Ricord was extradited. Ricord was extradited the next month, and tried and convicted in the US.

Many members of Ricord's Group France would tumble in late 1972 and 1973 thanks to such innovative thinking. One of them, Lucien Sarti, had been trafficking in South America since 1966. He supplied Louis Cirillo and Carlo Zippo in New York, Ricord's logistics chief Enio Varela in Paraguay and the Torrijos organization behind the Rafael Richard case in Panama. Based in Mexico City and wanted for the murder of a Belgian policeman, Sarti obtained Mafia heroin from Italy through Pino Catania.[4]

Sarti's downfall began in November 1971, when French couriers made an important delivery to his Uruguayan partner (and Customs informant) Housep Caramian in Lima, Peru.[5] Sarti was tracked to Brazil where, in January 1972, the police arrested him and his partner Jean Paul Angeletti. Sarti paid a hefty $60,000 bribe and fled. A few days later, however, the Bolivian police arrested him in La Paz. This time the cost of freedom was $200,000! Sarti paid the price and once again got away.[6]

BNDD agents were hot on his heels, and although they arrived in La Paz too late to capture him, they did find calls he had made to Mexico. Caramian, meanwhile, came in from the cold and was flown to New York on a US Air Force C-130. He provided the information that resulted in the case that initiated Springboard: the August 30,

1972 seizure in Buenos Aires of 46 kilograms of heroin belonging
to the Francois Rossi group, and the arrest of controllers Francois
Chiappe, Michel Russo and more than two-dozen other traffickers.[7]
Caramian also gave the information that enabled the BNDD to locate
Sarti in Mexico. Customs Agent Tom Cash at Interpol persuaded the
international police organization to cover Sarti's extradition fees. Tom
Puccio issued an indictment, and Jerry Strickler got George Lister at
the State Department to prepare provisional arrest warrants.

Caramian, meanwhile, revealed that a delegation of French traffickers was traveling to Mexico for a summit meeting to discuss how to
refinance Sarti, who had paid out $260,000 in bribes. While waiting
for the traffickers to arrive, BNDD Agent Bob Moreno in Mexico City
called Strickler at headquarters to say that BNDD and Mexican agents
had Sarti under surveillance. Sarti was a slippery character, so Moreno
asked if Strickler could obtain technical support from the CIA. Subsequently, at Strickler's request, Drake Reid arranged for the CIA's
highest level surveillance team in Mexico to assist. But clumsy Joe
Arpaio, the BNDD's regional director in Mexico City, invited Mexican officials to the briefing for the CIA surveillance team. Aghast that
Arpaio blew the cover of so many of its top-secret agents, the CIA
refused to assist.[8]

It was time for drastic action. BNDD agents watched while Sarti,
his mistress and her daughter parked their car outside his residence.
What happened next is in dispute. Some say Sarti started running as
the agents moved in for the arrest. Others say the agents were waiting
in ambush. Either way, Sarti was shot and killed on April 27, 1972,
without having returned fire.[9]

According to Strickler, informant Housep Caramian was key to the
Sarti case, as well as to Operation Springboard and the dismantling
of the Francois Rossi drug ring which cut across the entire French
connection in South America. Caramian also precipitated the arrest of
Francisco Toscanino, who had introduced Sarti to heroin trafficking
in 1966.[10]

An Italian national, Toscanino surfaced in Latin America in 1968.
He supplied Carmine Troianiello and Carlo Zippo in New York, and
was kidnapped in Montevideo, Uruguay in January 1973.[11] Not
yet officially arrested, he was taken to Brazil and tortured for 17
days before being taken to New York, where he was tried for sending two shoemakers to France to obtain heroin. "Uruguay does not
extradite shoemakers," Jerry Strickler explained "so we tricked them

into coming to US as character witnesses." Apart from promising the naïve shoemakers that they were not "defendants," the BNDD agents enticed them with first class tickets and a promise of a good time under the bright lights of New York City. "They were arrested when they landed, cooperated, and we indicted more people in France."[12]

Toscanino's torture was not admitted during his trial, nor was his statement that the Brazilians had acted as agents of the US. One reporter, citing testimony in the case, says: "Toscanino was tricked by Uruguayan officials, acting under the instructions of DEA [*sic*] agents, into leaving his Montevideo home. He was knocked unconscious, gagged and bound, and bundled onto the back seat of a car. He was then taken to the Brazilian border where he was met by Brazilian officials, again under DEA [*sic*] instructions, who took him into their physical custody. Denied any food or water, Mr. Toscanino was brought to the capital, Brasilia, where he was incessantly tortured and interrogated for seventeen days. A DEA [*sic*] agent was present throughout and, with the full knowledge of the United States prosecuting attorney, participated in the interrogation. The only form of nourishment administered to Mr. Toscanino was given intravenously and was barely sufficient to sustain life. He was deprived of sleep for days at a time. When incapable of standing after being forced to walk up and down a hallway for eight hours at a time, he was kicked and beaten. When refusing to answer questions, his fingers were pinched with metal pliers, alcohol was flushed into his eyes and nose, and other fluids were forced up his anal passage. DEA agents themselves attached electrodes to Mr. Toscanino's earlobes, toes, and genitals. (United States v. Toscanino)"[13]

Jerry Strickler denied the BNDD took part in the barbaric proceedings described above. But what happened to Toscanino was hardly exceptional.

Case Studies in Brutal Ingenuity

AFTER SARTI WAS ASSASSINATED IN April, Italian Tomasso Buscetta went into hiding in Sao Paulo, Brazil. The BNDD had been looking for him ever since he and Carlo Zippo had slipped away after meeting in New Jersey with a Mexican in a Mercedes Benz. As Jerry Strickler recalled, "Buscetta and Zippo did get heroin. The Mexican car was loaded and we did identify the driver. Louis Freeh from the FBI worked with informant Giuseppe Catania."

Strickler and the BNDD had apprehended Catania, again thanks to Agent Bob Moreno, whose cousin, the deputy attorney general in Mexico, had Catania arrested on a trumped-up charge. Catania was told he'd been arrested at the request of the Italian government and was being deported to Italy. But he was arrested again when his plane touched down in Houston. He was taken to New York, and during interrogation revealed the name of the man who drove the Mercedes. The driver, through his attorney, agreed to come to New York and testify in return for immunity. He admitted driving the car to Zippo, and based on his testimony Puccio indicted Buscetta in Brazil, Frank Cotroni in Canada, and several others.[14]

Strickler, meanwhile, was informed that Buscetta, Michel Nicoli, Claude Pastou and Christian David had been arrested in Brazil. Buscetta was wanted in Italy for murder and the US Ambassador in Brazil persuaded the police to lure him to Uruguay, which, unlike Brazil, had an extradition treaty with Italy.[15] Buscetta was arrested in November 1972, while Italian officials were meeting with Strickler in Washington. Strickler explained that the BNDD had Buscetta and offered to exchange him for a major Italian trafficker the BNDD wanted. The deal was made and the Brazilians sent Buscetta to Italy where he began serving a ridiculously short three-year sentence for murder.

As noted in Chapter 11, Christian David in 1971 had asked trafficker Claude Pastou to go to New York to pick up heroin. To facilitate the transaction, David introduced Pastou to Francois Orsini, who explained that Roger Delouette was delivering 50 kilograms of heroin in a VW camper. Pastou was to take possession of the camper after meeting with Carlo Zippo, the recipient. Delouette told Pastou not to worry; that he had an alibi.[16] With Pastou's confession another nail was driven into the mythological Delouette "SDECE" case propagated by the CIA. But the issue was not laid to rest, for David had SDECE connections too.

The controller behind the Delouette deal, Christian David, was a fascinating character. He was wanted in France for the murder of a detective investigating the kidnapping of Moroccan exile leader Mehdi Ben Barka in Paris in 1965.[17] David fled to Ricord's Group France in Brazil where, in exchange for his mercenary services, he obtained the protection of CIA asset Sergio Fleury, commander of the Brazilian state security force's narcotics and death squads in Sao Paolo.[18] When David was arrested, his safety deposit box contained a silenced pistol and a Uruguayan diplomatic passport with his photo.[19]

Like Toscanino, David was allegedly tortured by Fleury's unit into making a confession, in the presence of BNDD and/or CIA agents.[20] More important, is what David told Tony Pohl and Customs Agent Paul Boulad in US Attorney Tom Puccio's office on 28 November 1972. In exchange for his freedom, David offered to inform on everyone he had met over the last seven years, excluding his Mafia customers in the US. He offered to penetrate Maurice Castellani's elusive Trois Canards Gang in Corsica, as well as the Gegene le Manchot gang in Marseille. (Castellani and the three ducks were not Springboard targets because they did not operate in South America.) Then to everyone's amazement, David said he had hired himself out as a professional hit man in Uruguay, Brazil, Argentina, and other countries in South America. He said that when he was arrested in Brazil, he was on his way to kill Communist agents in Chile.[21]

Pohl rejected as preposterous David's offer; then wrote a scathing letter in which he said: "It is hoped that the treatment of DAVID, NICOLI and to a lesser degree PASTOU, by the 'Brazilian Police' is of some concern to the United States Authorities. However heinous the crimes of DAVID et al, and however important the need for this Government to obtain custody of narcotics violators 'hiding' in Brazil, the 'special method' employed by the Brazilian Authorities cannot be condoned. It should be noted (see attached translation of an article having appeared in the French Magazine *Paris Match* dated October 7, 1972) [in Pohl's original]that these methods are already attracting world-wide attention. That certainly some official United States voice will be raised on the subject so that the BNDD Creed does not become a meaningless document [i.e. I believe in the dignity of man, etc.].[22]

"In addition one should not discount the fact that incidents of this type tend to come back on the international scene, to haunt the perpetrators as well as those who appear to profit by these methods and therefore fail to oppose their use."[23]

Pohl's prediction that torture would come back to haunt the perpetrators was sadly prescient, in view of the blow American stature has taken as a result of George W Bush's widespread use of torture and other human rights abuses in his savage "War on Terror."

Pohl was not a lone voice condemning torture as an investigative technique. CIA officer John Bacon, in an interview with the author, expanded on the subject of using extra-legal methods in the war on drugs. "In law enforcement," he said, "the person accused of a crime has the right to face his accuser." The government must "expose its source or not make the accusation. A law enforcement officer simply cannot violate the law and intelligence officers do not have a license to commit crimes."[24]

Alas, Pohl and Bacon's noble position has become passé. Ironically, the descent into the moral maelstrom began not with Bush's war on terror, but, as we have seen, with the war on drugs.

Waiving the Rules

"THE RULES OF THE GAME were changing," Jerry Strickler explained. "We weren't interested in getting drugs, we wanted bodies. And not everyone was indicted on conspiracy to traffic, either; it could be auto theft, fraud, murder ... whatever. So now the traffickers were worried about the FBI too. Behind the scenes, the NSA helped with phone taps and agents in telegraph companies overseas. Our liaison to the NSA, Ed Drynan, brought raw stuff to me regularly."[25]

By mid-1972 the BNDD was using unconventional methods such as kidnapping suspects and covering their heads with hoods so they wouldn't be able to identify their American captors. Many abuses suffered by narcotics suspects were engendered by the BNDD's partner in crime, the CIA, which in 1972 acquired Ted Shackley as chief of its Western Hemisphere Division. Shackley was not happy that Latin America was the focus of BNDD operations and that, as part of Nixon's war on drugs, CIA headquarters had saddled him with a requirement to gather drug intelligence. At the Mexico City meeting in 1972, he stressed to Strickler that the CIA mission was non-drug related. Then he asked Strickler to brief the new CIA officers on what the BNDD was doing.[26]

Strickler earnestly gave his lecture and afterwards thanked Shackley for the opportunity. In a sign of how strained relations were going to be, Shackley dismissed the meeting as merely a vehicle to orient his people. He then told Strickler to hand over all BNDD files, informant lists, and cable traffic relating to Latin America. The one positive thing Shackley did was to have Drake Reid install a secure phone and scrambler in Strickler's office. Thereafter, Reid and Strickler talked every day. They set up an efficient system in which Reid provided surveillance teams and flash rolls from his narcotics unit staff officers in the various embassies.[27]

Shackley heaped indignities on Strickler, but the BNDD needed the CIA's help, so he swallowed his pride. To help restore relations with the CIA in Mexico, where Arpaio had blown the cover of the CIA's top surveillance team, Strickler and Belk sent an undercover agent to Mexico without Arpaio's knowledge. They "misdirected" a cable through Bangkok, so Arpaio, who told the Mexicans everything, would become aware of the operation only after it was over.[28]

But Shackley was not the type to forgive and forget, and under his direction, with the full support of Seymour Bolten, the CIA started to separate itself from BNDD in Latin America. According to Strickler, "Bad things happened." There were instances when, without telling the BNDD, station chiefs allowed drug shipments to go through to identify a recipient. In other instances the CIA was secretly working with BNDD targets.[29] There was mounting evidence, for example, that the CIA was underwriting Alberto Sicilia Falcon in Mexico.[30] An exile Cuban, Falcon had taken over the official contacts that once belonged to Ricord's Group France, including CIA assets in the Mexican Federal Police.[31] Falcon was working with another exile Cuban, José Egozi-Bezar in Las Vegas, the Colombo family, and various independent American traffickers.

CIA officers were using BNDD credentials as cover. Others recruited BNDD assets without telling their bosses. Walk-in informants at embassies were directed to CIA officers, not to the resident BNDD agent. In one case the Argentine police arrested a trafficker and called Frank Macolini. They said, "We have an individual working for your federal government." The individual, a Venezuelan national, had been recruited by the CIA at the Public Safety School in Panama. He thought he was working as a courier for the BNDD in Colombia, carrying drugs to England and Canada as part of a controlled delivery.[32]

There were lots of cases like this, Strickler said, and Seymour Bolten's people were responsible. Strickler knew who they were and wanted to indict them. But that never happened. In fact, the CIA got deeper than ever into the drug business.

Novo Yardly

REMEMBER THE "SECRET FUND" THAT would absolve the BNDD from ac countability for "destroying or immobilizing the highest level of drug traffickers?"[33] Ingersoll admitted its existence, but denied it was for assassinations. He said it was for a three-year program to buy informants abroad.

Epstein cited Krogh as saying that Ingersoll was not trusted to disburse the funds, but that they were used to pay for assassinations in

Southeast Asia.[34] The US Ambassador in Vietnam in 1973, Graham Martin, told Nelson Gross that the only way to rid the Golden Triangle of opium lords was through assassination.[35] A Thai narcotics officer, recruited by the CIA, played a double game and told opium lords they were on the hit list. Dave Ellis's experiences, recounted in Chapter 13, confirm all this.

There is overwhelming evidence that assassinations were conducted not just in Southeast Asia, but in South America and Europe as well. In September 1972, BNDD officials in Marseilles reportedly broached the idea of assassination teams to J. Thomas Ungerleider, MD, of the National Commission for Marijuana and Drug Abuse, saying 150 "key assassinations" could do the job.[36] Doctor Ungerleider said he thought it might be "beer talk."[37] But as the BNDD's chief inspector Pat Fuller told me, "There was another operation even I didn't know about. Why don't you find out who set that one up, and why?"

I did find out about this operation. Quite by accident, while interviewing a DEA agent in Miami, I was introduced to Joseph C. DiGennaro, a member of the CIA's secret facet of Operation Twofold, its unilateral drug operations unit. The purpose of the CIA's unilateral drug unit was to identify drug-dealers worldwide, and selectively kidnap and/or kill them.

As DiGennaro explained, his entry into the program began when an eminent surgeon, a family friend who knew Jim Ludlum, suggested that he apply for a job with the BNDD.[38] Then working as a stockbroker in New York, DiGennaro in August 1971 met Fuller at a Howard Johnson's near the Watergate complex. Fuller told him that if he took the Twofold job, he would be given the code name Novo Yardly. The code name was based on DiGennaro's posting in New York, and a play on the name of the famous American spy, Herbert Yardly. DiGennaro's job was to spy on Dan Casey.

DiGennaro took the job and was sent to a CIA security officer to obtain the required clearances. That's when he was told that he and several other recruits were being "spun-off" from Fuller's inspection program into the CIA's "operational" program. He was told that he had been selected because he had a black belt in Karate and the uncanny ability to remember lists and faces. The background check took 14 months, during which time DiGennaro received intensive combat and trade-craft training. In October 1972 he was sent to BNDD regional headquarters in New York and assigned to Joe Quarequio's group as a cover. His paychecks came from official BNDD funds, though the program was funded by the CIA through the Department of Interior's Bureau of Mines. The program had been authorized by the "appropriate" Congressional committee.[39]

DiGennaro's special group was managed by the CIA's Special Operations Division (then under Evan Parker, first director of the CIA's Phoenix Program) in conjunction with the military, which provided assets within foreign military services to keep ex-filtration routes — air corridors and roads — open. The military also cleared air space when captured suspects were brought into the US. DiGennaro spent most of his time on operations in South America, but was in Lebanon and other places too. Within the CIA's special narcotics group, which numbered about 40 men, were experts in printing, forgery, maritime operations, and telecommunications. The operatives knew one another by first name only. DiGennaro, however, was aware that other BNDD agents, including Joseph Salm and Paul Seema, were in the program. Tom Tripodi said that Agents Mike Powers and Mike Campbell were in it as well.[40]

No one else in the BNDD knew about the program. When the call came, DiGennaro would check with Fuller and then take sick time or annual leave to go on missions. There were lots of missions. As his group leader Joe Quarequio told me, as a subtle way of confirmation: "Joey was never in the office."[41]

The job was tracking down, kidnapping, and if they resisted, killing drug dealers. The violence was the result of the "limited window of opportunity" (usually two to three days) needed to get the job done, coupled with the need for plausible deniability. There was minimal contact with the US Embassy. DiGennaro had "a Guardian Angel" who "assembled intelligence, developed routines, and contacted informants." But the host country and its uniformed services were rarely aware of his presence, and there was little coordination with the local BNDD outpost.[42]

The operations usually lasted seven to 14 days and were extremely dangerous. As DiGennaro recalled, "There was a case in Colombia. There was seventy-two to ninety-six hours to get it done. I was flown to Colombia where I contacted my Guardian Angel. He had paid someone off and that someone had led him to a cocaine lab. The operators of the lab had been surveilled and followed to their hideout. In order to capture them, we had to work with a local military unit, which we contacted by two-way radio. In this particular instance, someone intercepted the call, and the next thing we know there's a woman on the radio alerting the suspects. She was an agent of the traffickers inside the local military unit. We hear her screaming at the soldiers. Then she's shot. We didn't know who she was calling," he continues, "so we had to leapfrog by helicopter and military truck to where we thought the subjects were. That time we happened to be right. We got the violators back to the United States. They were incapacitated by drugs and handcuffed in various men's rooms in Chicago and Miami."[43]

As Gerry Carey recalled, "We'd get a call that there was 'a present' waiting for us on the corner of 116th St. and Sixth Avenue. We'd go there and find some guy, who'd been indicted in the Eastern District of New York, handcuffed to a telephone pole. We'd take him to a safe house for questioning and, if possible, turn him into an informer. Sometimes we'd have him in custody for months. But what did he know?"[44]

If you're a Colombian or a Corsican drug dealer in Argentina, and a few guys with police credentials arrest you, how do you know it's a CIA operation?

Expendable operative DiGennaro did not see the apparatus that was supporting him. He never knew much about the people they were snatching and snuffing either; only that people were prosecuted and defendants screamed. As a result, the program, covered by Fuller's shoofly program, was perfectly suited for counter-intelligence style "operations within operations." Indeed, DiGennaro's last operation in 1977 involved the recovery of a satellite that had fallen into a drug dealer's hands. By then DiGennaro had all the tradecraft skills; he learned who owned the satellite, he negotiated in good faith for it, and bought it back on the black market. Such was the extent of the "parallel mechanism" the CIA had with the BNDD; a mechanism the CIA used for its own purposes.[45]

Lest there be any doubt, John Ingersoll confirmed the existence of this secret facet of Operation Twofold. He said the CIA agents in it weren't operational in the US and that's why he did not think it was illegal, even the shoofly aspect. He said the program didn't have a single purpose; that the idea was to put people in deep cover in the US to develop intelligence on drug trafficking, particularly from South America. It was closely held and even the regional directors weren't aware. He got approval from Mitchell and probably told Kleindienst and Elliot Richardson. He passed it on to John Bartels, first head of the DEA.[46]

Ingersoll said one purpose was investigating corruption; to find material evidence of wrongdoing. He had legal advice from either BNDD counsel Don Miller or Michael Sonnenreich. He picked Fuller to be the contact to the group because Fuller had the time and flexibility. But, Ingersoll added, Tartaglino and Belk were primary in the operational unit, as was Jerry Strickler. Ingersoll concluded by saying he was surprised that no one from the Rockefeller Commission ever asked him about it.

The Parallel Mechanism

TO MANAGE INTERNATIONAL DRUG LAW enforcement, the CIA needed to control targeting, so it could eliminate the competitors of its protected traffickers. To properly target, it needed cold professionals not dedicated to the president or any agency fighting some ludicrous War on Drugs. Veteran CIA officer Seymour Bolten was such a man.

Bolten's role was different from Ludlum's, reflecting the CIA's new interest in drugs and the advantages it saw in circumventing the BNDD. Close to William Colby and Ted Shackley, Bolten did not believe in reciprocity; only the interests of the CIA. To this end he set up a parallel mechanism, based on a register of international drug traffickers and a communications intercept crew that monitored calls from traffickers in the US to their accomplices around the world — the CIA always being careful to erase its own assets off the list, just as it erases its client terrorists off its master list in the War on Terror.[47]

Joey DiGennaro's special group was Bolten's operations element. For intelligence, Bolten relied on a network of "re-tooled" CIA officers infiltrated within the BNND and other government agencies, and senior CIA officers working in major stations.[48] Nick Natsios (a former station chief in Vietnam) in Tehran, and Paul Von Marks in Paris, were the key players in Europe and the Middle East.

Not everyone in government was happy about the arrangement. In late 1972, Colonel Tulius Acampora was reassigned from Saigon to the Pentagon to study the military's role in the war on drugs. He worked closely with Werner Michel. They asked the question, "Is there a legitimate reason for the military to engage in narcotics intelligence?" Nixon's minions had "pooled resources" and enlisted the CIA. The military also assigned people and, like the CIA, hid behind plausible denial. "Initially it was operation by committee," Acampora explained, "then it was ... integral. Miles Ambrose wanted to take charge and was looking around, trying to figure out how."[49]

Factions within the CIA were divided about how to proceed. The CIA was facing court actions over its agents and informers, and the Deputy Director for Plans, William Wells, was concerned. Wells asked Acampora to document how the CIA could extract itself. Acampora wrote a paper recommending that the CIA pass responsibility back to the BNDD, back to law enforcement. But another faction, headed by Colby, Bolten and Shackley had already decided to take the BNDD's informants and use them for their own purposes. They prevailed and to this end, Bolten set up a CIA computer system for drug intelligence and informants modeled on the Phoenix "assassination" Program computer program.

Acampora emphasizes the CIA undermined the BNDD's integrity by preempting it. Several top BNDD officials, including Tony Pohl and Fred Dick, resisted and were hurt by it, and by the political action system Egil Krogh and Myles Ambrose put in place to cover it. Other BNDD officials, like Jack Cusack, played along.

As Paul Knight complained, "Activity became the measure of success; striving was more important than accomplishing. Narcotics law enforcement became an industry based on motion for the sake of motion, generating heat rather than light."[50]

As a prequel to the war on terror, a greater emphasis on violence accompanied the CIA's use of drug law enforcement as a pretext to expand the American empire. And yet, despite the CIA's participation, and the BNDD's success against the French connection in South America, the "army of ants" (as Knight described the emerging horde of drug traffickers) kept concocting new and improved smuggling methods: small amounts of heroin and cocaine were hidden inside table tops, peg legs, even human stomachs; bulk shipments arrived by the boatload and were unloaded by frogmen.

As Strickler noted, "Springboard proved you could get them and their bosses." But only if you knew who they were and how they were smuggling. Truth be told, no one really knew, and the army of ants was winning.

19

MYLES TO GO

BY LATE 1972, MYLES AMBROSE had reached the pinnacle of his government career. As head of ODALE and advisor to the president, he outranked his arch rival John Ingersoll. To a large extent he determined federal drug enforcement policy. But he was frustrated. The bureaucrats at ODALE, Customs and the BNDD kept fighting, nothing was coming out of ONNI, and Seymour Bolten and the CIA were off on a tangent. There was an urgent need to galvanize the forces. So Ambrose decided to create a super agency which, under his direction, would manage all aspects of the war on drugs.[1]

That super agency, the Drug Enforcement Administration (DEA), would materialize in July 1973. But fate would prevent Ambrose from fulfilling his vision and becoming the DEA's first chief.

Fate appeared in the person of Alder B. "Barry" Seal. In the spring of 1972, Seal was on leave from his job as a pilot for TWA.[2] It is also said that Seal, as a pilot for TWA, was flying cargo planes overseas, perhaps as a cover for ferrying weapons into Vietnam for the CIA. With Seal, it's hard to tell what really happened. His own stories fluctuate. Thus his service in the mid-1980s as an informant for Vice President George Bush's South Florida drug task force, his involvement in the Iran-Contra scandal, and his murder in 1986 (which shall be discussed in a later chapter) are shrouded in mystery.[3]

What is known is that on July 1, 1972, Seal was arrested in New Orleans for violating the Mutual Security Act. Eight other individuals were arrested in Louisiana and Texas. Among them were likely CIA informant Francisco Flores, mobster Murray M. Kessler, connected to the Gambino family in Brooklyn, and Richmond C. Harper, "a millionaire banker and meat-packing plant owner from Eagle Pass, Texas."[4] Seal claimed that Flores brought the deal to Harper, who contacted Kessler, whose mob associates recruited Seal to fly a plane packed with tons of C-4 explosives from the Shreveport Regional Airport in Louisiana into Mexico.[5] Seal believed that Flores represented a group of Cuban exiles in Mexico who wanted to blow up anything or anyone connected to Fidel Castro.[6] However, in a statement made after his trial in 1974, Seal changed his story and said the operation was designed to ingratiate the CIA with Fidel Castro.[7]

It's unclear if anyone in Mexico was actually waiting to receive the explosives. BNDD agents say the entire operation was a sting.[8] The situation is made murkier by the fact that Herman K. Beebe, an associate of Nixon's ambassador to the United Nations, George H.W. Bush, owned the warehouse where the explosives were stored.[9] That fact fuels the conspiracy theory that Barry Seal was a CIA agent.

The arms deal, as noted, was a sting operation put in motion by undercover Customs Agent Caesar Diosdado on behalf of BNDD Agent Art Sedillo in Mexico City and the Brooklyn Task Force.[10] There is, however, the possibility that Flores, who disappeared before the trial, was a CIA asset facilitating anti-Castro terror activities in Mexico.[11] It is also likely that the FBI was investigating the Mexican facet of the Seal-Kessler-Harper-Flores operation. If all that is true — and given the fact that the arrest of Seal, Harper, Kessler and Flores occurred a mere two weeks after the Watergate arrests — it is possible that Nixon had the FBI call off the Seal investigation in Mexico because it might blow a CIA operation and open up "the Bay of Pigs thing" due to the involvement of militant Cuban exiles. As Ambrose lamented, public knowledge of this CIA operation facilitated by Flores, to supply of arms to Cuban exiles, could have saved Nixon.

Perhaps it could have saved Ambrose's career, as well.

The case against Seal, Harper, Kessler and Flores et al began in May 1972, when BNDD Agent Arthur Sedillo summoned Customs Agent Caesar Diosdado Nunez to Mexico City.[12] Sedillo told Diosdado that Murray Kessler in Brooklyn had weapons he wanted to trade for heroin, and that Harper was looking for a heroin connection on Kessler's behalf. Although Sedillo did not explain how he knew this, Diosdado was the perfect choice for the role of undercover agent in the case. Born in Laredo, Texas, he had worked for Customs since 1957 and (under Customs cover) for the CIA since 1961.[13] The CIA had used Diosdado exclusively to spy on the Cuban exile community, another fact that throws gasoline on the CIA conspiracy fire — especially if Flores was a double agent working for Fidel Castro.

Posing as a trafficker out of Mexico, Diosdado met with Harper in Eagle Pass. Harper believed the "heroin-for-money for anti-Castro Cubans" cover story and sent Diosdado to Kessler in New Jersey. Diosdado, however, delivered defective heroin and, naturally, the deal fell through. (If the BNDD had arranged for Diosdado to deliver real heroin, the deal would have ended there.) Despite the fact that the heroin was defective, all (from Kessler's point of view) was not lost. Using one million dollars in front money provided by the Brooklyn Organized Crime Strike Force — which was making a related drug case on Mafioso Felippo Casamento — Diosdado offered to buy 13,500 pounds of explosives from Kessler. Happier to have cold hard cash than heroin, the greedy mobster readily agreed.[14] The deal went forward and everyone was arrested after the explosives were packed in Seal's plane in Shreveport.[15]

According to BNDD agents, the explosives-for-drugs deal was a sting operation that evolved from the Brooklyn Organized Crime Strike Force case on Casamento.[16] On behalf of his godfather Carlo Gambino, Casamento had, coincidentally, given Tomasso Buscetta his first job in America as a pizza maker in 1963.[17] Buscetta branched out and eventually become Casamento's source in Canada and Mexico. But after Lucien Sarti's murder in April 1972, Buscetta went underground, forcing Casamento to find a new supplier — which explained why Kessler, as an associate of the Gambino family, was willing to trade guns for heroin. The Brooklyn Organized Crime Strike Force, through a well placed informant inside Kessler's operation, knew that Kessler could be persuaded to sell explosives to Diosdado for cash instead of heroin. In this way the sting operation grew to encompass Seal, Harper and Flores in Mexico. Imaginative federal agents simply put the bait in front of the crooks and let them hook themselves.

The Task Force sting had nothing to do with Myles Ambrose. His problem was his association with banker-rancher Richmond Harper, a truly despicable man who in 1958 was charged with shipping dog food to Mexico for human consumption. Harper owned thousands of acres in Texas, and his brother Tito owned thousands more across the border in Mexico. Customs agents in Texas knew the area was an entry point for narcotics destined for drug dealers in Chicago. They also knew that Harper's ranch was perfectly placed to be a staging point for smugglers and that Harper was as crooked as a corkscrew. Although rich, he routinely smuggled "merchandise" from Hong Kong through Houston "in bond" to his ranch. All this was known because one Customs agent's son was having an affair with Harper's daughter, Dixie. But Harper was close to the governor of Texas, White House officials, Congressmen, and Dave Ellis at Customs headquarters. Harper spread his wealth around and the Texas agents looked away from his wheeling and dealing — until they found a personal reason (Myles Ambrose) to lower the boom.[18]

William Hughes was the Customs agent in charge in San Antonio. "Sometime prior to Christmas 1972," he recalled, "Harry Smith, the head of all the Customs agents, called me and said 'the Messiah' was coming down with his kids to visit Harper for Christmas vacation." Hughes told Smith that Harper was "bad news" and asked him "to dissuade" Ambrose.[19] But "the Messiah" either ignored or never received the warnings. In any event, Ambrose felt no need for concern, for he was secure in the knowledge that artists, poets and priests were also attending Harper's shindig. Ambrose felt that Harper's ranch, among such a respectable crowd, would be the perfect place to reconcile with a wayward son.[20]

Alas, it wasn't until the day after Ambrose arrived at Harper's ranch that Diosdado told Hughes that Harper was about to be indicted in the drugs-for-explosives case. To the amusement of the Ellis men, it was too late to warn Ambrose. Straight-faced, they stood back and watched as the press began to question the ethics of the relationship between Ambrose, then jockeying to become head of the nascent DEA, and dastardly Richmond Harper — who reportedly became a heroin addict and died under mysterious circumstances in Mexico City.[21]

The trial of Harper and friends was delayed until the summer of 1974, after Nixon's resignation. Two witnesses (including defendant Flores) were unavailable and the court dismissed the government's case. Former assistant US Attorney Richard Gregorie, who in 1984 used Seal as an informant, said the case was dismissed because of "government misconduct."[22] Barry Seal went free, entered a life of crime and "began working full-time for the CIA, traveling back and forth from the United States to Latin America."[23] The only victim in the whole sordid affair was Myles Ambrose, whose visit with Harper would compel him to resign from government service on May 22, 1973. He did not go gentle into that good night.

Stinging Myles

WILLIAM HUGHES, A CUSTOMS AGENT since 1960, described Ambrose as "Jimmy Walker re-incarnated."[24] He acknowledges that Ambrose did a lot of good things for Customs. He didn't dislike Ambrose per se, and he denies having foreknowledge about the Harper indictment. And Hughes did warn Smith to warn Ambrose not to go to Harper's party.

However, a few ranking officials in Customs did know about the pending indictment. Dave Ellis was a likely candidate. Not only that, he had hired Diosdado into Customs in 1957, and had eased him into the CIA in 1961 when he set up a special CIA unit to spy on exile anti-Castro Cuban terrorists in Florida.[25] Ellis was destined to be Customs Commissioner until Ambrose stepped in; and when Ambrose chose Mike Acree as his successor, Ellis was furious. He had an axe to grind, but he had retired from the Customs Service in May 1972, and would probably not have known.

The real culprits can be found in the Customs Service Association. These officials felt betrayed by Ambrose, who was preparing to transfer over 500 Customs agents into the DEA. These Customs agents couldn't stop Ambrose from pushing for the merger, but they could prevent him from heading it. Likewise, members of the INS union were gunning for Ambrose for arranging the transfer of several hundred Border Patrol agents into the DEA. The Border Patrol concerns itself with "proof of national origin," not drugs, and the INS did not want its mission undermined by the loss of so many men.

The INS union flexed its muscles, and a week after Ambrose resigned, two members of Congress introduced an amendment to Reorganization #2 (the legislation that created the DEA) to keep Border Patrol agents from being moved to the DEA.[26] The AFL-CIO, however, belonged to Nixon and the Republican Party, and readily signed away rights of the Customs agents destined to be transferred to the DEA. To most of them, being forced into the DEA was a criminal act. As one agent explained, "With the stroke of the pen I went from working for 15 years in Customs into the DEA." The agent believes

Customs got the short end of the stick, and that ever since it has been struggling "to get something back."[27]

Ambrose believes the INS union leaked the fact of his visit with Harper to the press, and that disgruntled Customs agents stabbed him in the back by talking to reporters.[28] In revenge, he is said to have compiled a hit list of BNDD and Customs agents he blamed. Bill Hughes was high on the list. As Hughes recalled, "Mike Acree called me on the Sunday after the DEA was created and said, 'you've been selected as deputy in Laredo.'"[29]

It was a deep demotion, the kind many Ambrose enemies would feel.

The Collinsville Massacre

DESPITE THE HARPER SCANDAL, AMBROSE by 1973 had won his bureaucratic war with Ingersoll. ODALE was in full swing and he, not Ingersoll, was creating the DEA. Ambrose was loyal to Nixon and beloved at the White House. Ingersoll, on the other hand, having rejected White House pleas for help in covering up the Watergate break-in, was told in February 1973 by Attorney General Kleindienst that his services were no longer required.[30]

Ingersoll was hurt that the White House rejected him. He wanted to head the DEA, but his bad feelings subsided and he has no regrets.[31] Indeed, in hindsight, Ingersoll could see that the federal drug law enforcement apparatus was spinning out of control, and he was glad to avoid responsibility as a series of disasters began to cast federal drug agents in a bad light. It may even have been something of a consolation to know that Ambrose, as the front man, took the full brunt of the backlash.

The first disaster occurred in Collinsville, Illinois, in April 1973, when an ODALE task force, led by BNDD Agent Kenneth Bloemker, raided the homes of two innocent families.[32] Without having obtained search warrants, the ODALE agents crashed into the homes of Herbert Giglotto and Donald Askew. The agents were described as being dressed like members of the Charlie Manson cult. They were waving hand-guns and automatic weapons, yelling at the top of their lungs. One agent put a gun to Giglotto's head. Another paraded his wife around in her underwear. They threatened to kill the couple unless they revealed where the non-existent dope was hidden.[33]

For ODALE it was lawless business as usual. While Bloemker's team terrorized the Giglottos, another team terrorized the innocent

Askews across town. That same week, in Evansville, Indiana, an ODALE goon squad snatched John Meiners from his house and held him for three days before acknowledging his innocence. In all three cases the ODALE agents were charged with conspiring to violate the constitutional rights of the innocent families. They were suspended with pay, tried, and acquitted.[34]

Bloemker claims the Giglotto incident was blown out of proportion. He admits they "hit the wrong houses," but notes they were cleared of criminal conduct. He feels they were sold out. He says there is a Watergate tape with Liddy saying words to the effect of: "We'll just sell [the ODALE agents] out to get us out from under this." Bloemker also notes that ODALE was making lots of arrests without warrants, and that even if they had the time to get a warrant, they weren't required to do so. All they needed was probable cause and "intent to arrest." The day of the "Collinsville Massacre," the magistrate wasn't around and the ODALE lawyer said, "Go ahead." So Bloemker raced over to the four-unit town house where the Giglottos lived. Unfortunately, there were no letters on the doors. Not wanting to waste time, they picked an apartment (the wrong one) at random. In the case of the Askews, a cop called in the address, but the ODALE secretary copied it down incorrectly.[35]

The amazing thing is that Bloemker believes he made an honest mistake, which sums up the Fearless Fosdick mindset of ODALE agents. This mindset, in the opinion of many, undermined the victim's Fourth Amendment rights. The raids traumatized and stigmatized the victims for life. Their neighbors couldn't believe that federal agents could make such a stupid mistake. The victimized families were ostracized for years by their incredulous neighbors.[36]

Terrified, traumatized, stigmatized and ostracized are the operative words. The twisted minds behind ODALE made federal drug policy to subvert the civil rights of the American public. In this sense, the war on drugs was the model for the war on terror, with its repressive Patriot Act and secret military orders. Even if wrong, government agents are not held accountable. Agent Lloyd Clifton, who shot and killed an innocent man during a BNDD raid as described in Chapter 12, got away with murder. This is how the war on drugs became the template for George W. Bush's "war on terror," especially overseas, where government agents went on a rampage of far more lethal proportions.

Reorganization Plan #2

CCINC STAFF DIRECTOR WALTER MINNICK recalled, "Between the 1972 elections and the new administration, Domestic Council Chief John Ehrlichman wanted to reorganize the executive branch. He wanted to cut staff, departments and agencies. Roy Ashe at OMB managed a commission on the subject, and one of his recommendations was cutting drug law enforcement out of the Domestic Council. The recommendations were accepted and as part of the resulting Executive Order, the drug coordinating office was assigned to OMB." Krogh's position as executive director of CCINC was given to a State Department official under State's control.[37]

In early 1973, Ambrose proposed that the White House combine Customs drug agents, ONNI, ODALE and BNDD into a new organization. The White House Office of Management and Budget (OMB) and Ehrlichman agreed, and the overall plan became the basis for Reorganization Plan #2. "Krogh became an official at the Department of Transportation," Minnick said, "and Fred Mallek, the head of White House personnel, ended up as Ashe's deputy. Fred asked me to take over from Krogh and I became an assistant deputy director of OMB reporting to Mallek. My job was to reorganize drug law enforcement under OMB. My staff organized the new organization like Krogh organized his. Lee Gladden from the Pentagon handled international narcotic matters. A lieutenant colonel near retirement, Dick Williams, had domestic law enforcement. Tom Peters had management. Richard Harkness was a part-time consultant.

"BNDD and Customs were proud and parochial with overlapping jurisdictions," Minnick continues. "They were extremely competitive and it was obvious to the White House that we would have to referee. A re-organization seemed logical, but the problem was, unless we gave the job to Customs, we would still have the borders to guard. So we decided to take everything except the border and give it to the BNDD."

Minnick's next problem was convincing the powerful department secretaries to go along. He wanted to do it in-between administrations, but Congress and Nixon were fighting over Watergate, and even though the White House had the power to propose legislation, it had to be passed by a certain deadline. In addition, the Democratic controlled Congress limited Nixon to a straight up and down vote with no opportunity for amendments. "Our proposal was sent to the

Government Operations Committees in the House and Senate," Minnick recalled, "and they gave us until late spring to come up with a plan."

It was a frustrating process, and Minnick quit and was replaced by Tom Peters, who wrote the bestseller *In Search of Excellence*, and became a famous business consultant. After the FBI declined to become involved, two plans for reorganization were submitted; one by Ambrose and the White House staff, the other by Ingersoll and the BNDD. The Pentagon and CIA reviewed the proposals and a compromise was reached. The big decision, made by Roy Ashe, was that someone other than Ambrose should head the new agency. The Harper affair and the BNDD's negative feelings about Ambrose were the main considerations.[38]

"The last hurdle was to convince Congress," Minnick said, "which was very hard. The AFL-CIO got involved over the labor issue. We had proposed to transfer 600 INS Border Patrol agents into Customs, as compensation for Customs losing the 600 narcotic agents we were going to put in the DEA. No one thought it would be a problem, but the Border Patrol was represented by the American Federation of Government Employees, while Customs was an independent affiliate of the AFL-CIO."

Minnick lost on the issue of the Border Patrol agents. The legislation couldn't be amended, and the Nixon-mob-controlled AFL-CIO sold out the 600 Customs agents.

As Seymour Bolten surmised, all this maneuvering was part of Watergate damage control. Federal drug law enforcement was more effective under the White House and the move to State "sure wouldn't have happened during a normal time."[39]

Tony Pohl Strikes Again

MYLES AMBROSE WAS SERIOUSLY DAMAGED by the Harper affair. Collinsville didn't help, and Watergate was the coup de grace. Haldeman, Ehrlichman, Dean and Kleindienst resigned en masse on April 30, 1973. In May, Attorney General Elliot Richardson appointed Archibald Cox as a special prosecutor to investigate Nixon. In July, at the same moment the DEA was being formed, CIA officer Alex Butterfield revealed that secret tapes had been made of Nixon's incriminating conversations in the White House. Customs agents, ironically, had done some of the taping. Nixon's new chief of staff, Alexander Haig, shut down the system and grabbed the tapes. Cox issued a subpoena for them, and chaos ensued as Nixon fired one attorney general after another. The Justice Department fractured along political fault lines. Law enforcement agencies like the DEA and the IRS were drawn into the fray and were fully expected to support Nixon. The historical stench has yet to clear.

What really hurt Ambrose, however, were the BNDD's successes. For while Myles was chasing political power, the Grand Master of federal drug law enforcement, Tony Pohl, was crafting the BNDD's last great case against Mafia boss Carmine Tramunti and five related drug rings under Herbie Sperling, John Capra, Louis Inglese, Genardo Zanfardino and Joseph Cappuccilli. Also ensnared were their Montreal and French connections. The case began in December 1971 with an SIU wiretap on Stephen Della Cava. The SIU shared its information with the BNDD and the Joint Task Force. All three joined forces and in January 1972, they launched Operation Undercover.[40]

Pohl, naturally, had to fight Ambrose for control. By October 1972, Ambrose wanted his ODALE chief in New York to take over the operation and make the busts, to help the Republicans win the upcoming elections. As an enticement, Ambrose offered Pohl a promotion and a job at ODALE. When Pohl refused to hand over his files and tapes, Ambrose summoned him to Washington for a tongue lashing. Pohl still refused to fold and Ambrose backed off only after US Attorney Whitney Seymour went to Attorney General Kleindienst and got permission to personally prosecute the case. Seymour then put Pohl in charge.[41]

In December 1972, to further the investigation, Pohl was asked to create Special Tactical Unit Two and to relocate his command center in the BNDD's new office building on West 57th Street. Initially the unit consisted of 25 BNDD agents, 15 NYPD detectives, six ODALE agents and assorted support staff. Ultimately it totaled 200 individuals, including state policemen, Customs and IRS agents, and lawyers from the District Attorney offices. The operational plan was Pohl's most intricate ever. Under his direction, Special Tactical Unit Two members tracked Della Cava to his boss, John Capra, and Capra to a club in East Harlem where Mafia mastermind Genardo Zanfardino managed distribution nets nationwide. In February 1973, Special Tactical Unit Two agents made three buys from a Zanfardino employee. Those buys led to one of Herbie Sperling's couriers, who quickly revealed Sperling's French connection.

Before the other American traffickers started running for cover, Pohl orchestrated a massive round-up called Operation Window. After a federal grand jury had handed down 86 indictments for drug dealers in New York, New Jersey, Connecticut, Washington DC, and Detroit, Pohl gathered all 200 agents at the command center. He divided everyone into teams, with target folders, shotguns, and bullet-proof vests. At midnight everyone moved out to the bars, nightclubs and homes where the arrests were to be made. Simultaneous raids were conducted over the weekend of May 22-24, and all but three of the targeted hoods were arrested. The NYPD was given credit in the newspapers, to protect the identity of federal agents.[42]

No one was more surprised than Ambrose, who had not even been notified that the arrests were going to be made. Fixated on Watergate, the public never understood that this last great BNDD operation temporarily shut down the Mafia's major drug distribution network in America. Even the Corsicans were afraid of the Mafia, but Pohl and the BNDD had taken them on and won. It was the triumphant end of the French connection in America. But it was the BNDD's swan song too.

Count Ingersoll Out

INGERSOLL WAS MR. CLEAN, BUT his demise was down-and-dirty. The trigger was Ingersoll's affair with his secretary, which had been known since 1969, when the French saw them tip-toeing between hotel rooms in Paris during the Franco-Americans Accords.[43] After that, one agent cynically observed, Tartaglino kept sending Ingersoll on overseas trips so Tartaglino could run the show. Ingersoll gladly went so he could be alone with Sheila. Shocked at his behavior, some old friends like Pat Fuller and John Warner moved away.[44]

John Mitchell told Ingersoll to do the right thing and get divorced. But Ingersoll's passions prevailed. "He was summoned to the White House to give a briefing," Fred Dick recalled, "but the message never got to him. Of course, if he hadn't been stuck to the bed sheets in a motel outside town, they might have gotten to him in time. As it was, he was an hour late and the White House locked him out."[45]

According to two other agents, Ingersoll was preparing a press release about BNDD successes in South America. He was scheduled to deliver it on a Monday morning and sent it for review to Richard Harkness, the Domestic Council's public relations man. Harkness wanted to make a few changes and tried to contact Ingersoll. When he couldn't reach Ingersoll, he gave it to Krogh who sent it to Nelson Gross in Paris. Gross edited it and released it over the weekend. By Monday it was old news, but Ingersoll was forced to deliver it again.[46]

Having his own secrets to hide, Ingersoll endured these indignities. But when he publicly announced his resignation on June 30, 1973, he finally let go. The headline in the New York Times read: "Drug Unit Chief Resigns, Assailing Ex-Nixon Aides." Ingersoll resigned, "Charging that the inter-agency rivalry, confusion and intervention by the White House had blunted the efforts of the Nixon Administration in drug control." He slammed ODALE as having fostered "a disruptive rivalry" and said that Haldeman and Ehrlichman "squeezed him out of government." He couldn't exercise personnel choice selections, he said, and their interference "got into implementation of policy and how you should go about doing your job." Ingersoll said his resistance to their meddling was one reason for his demise. His anger over the disruptive rivalry fostered by Ambrose and ODALE was another. He referred specifically to the Collinsville Massacre.[47]

Ingersoll's resignation went into effect on August 1, 1973. That same day Attorney General Eliot Richardson named John Bartels as head of the DEA. Taking the job was the biggest mistake Bartels made in his entire life.

20

THE DEA

CREATED IN JULY 1973 WHILE the Watergate crisis had everyone in Washington running for cover, the Drug Enforcement Administration included approximately 1400 BNDD agents, 550 disgruntled Customs agents, and a smattering of people from ONNI, ODALE and the CIA. The DEA was very much the invention of Myles Ambrose and he thought he would head it; but fell victim to scandal. Ingersoll wanted the job too, but he was never in the running, and instead took a job at IBM.[1]

The DEA's first chief administrator was John Bartels, but he wasn't the first choice. The White House's first choice was Illinois Governor Richard B. Oglivie; then US Attorney Paul Curran; and then the commissioner of the INS, Marine General Leonard Chapman.[2] But Ambrose rejected them all in favor of his friend. As Walter Minnick recalled, "Finally John Bartels comes up. Bartels had been Ambrose's deputy at ODALE and had been helpful, but not a protagonist, in formulating Reorganization Plan #2. Bartels saw the logic of what we were doing. He had been in the drug wars and he had the credentials."[3]

Bartels had the credentials, but he lacked the wisdom and the strength. Dozens of jaded BNDD agents in top pay grades had been thrust upon him, and he knew that many of them perceived him as a creation of their arch enemy Ambrose. He especially feared Andy

Tartaglino. He felt that Tartaglino wanted to run the organization from behind the scenes, as he had with Ingersoll.[4] And Tartaglino had to some extent shaped the DEA in his image; while second in command at the BNDD, he had promoted his protégés, people like Frank Monastero and Dave Westrate, to important administrative posts. That sort of screwing with the system did not seem fair to Bartels or Ambrose. They were the fair-haired boys of the ruling political elite, and screwing with the system was their prerogative, not Tartaglino's.

Having taken that attitude, Bartels made the fateful decision to embrace anyone who supported Ambrose and opposed Tartaglino. To that end Bartels and Ambrose appointed Bill Durkin head of enforcement and Jack Cusack as chief of international operations.[5] In consultation with Durkin and Cusack, and cronies at ODALE, Bartels and Ambrose then put Customs agents in charge of the Big Three Regions: Los Angeles, New York, and Miami.

Putting Customs agents in these premier enforcement positions enraged many of the senior BNDD agents who dominated DEA headquarters. Adding to their fury was the "hit list" Ambrose compiled of his personal enemies. According to a group supervisor in New York, "Some of us were on the destroy list because we'd fought Ambrose and won. So he replaced us with Customs and ODALE people ... and now there's turmoil again."

Tartaglino said it wasn't exactly a "hit list;" it was a series of teletypes from Ambrose to Bartels that mistakenly came across his desk. The first said, "Get rid of Andy."[6] More followed, around two dozen altogether, about specific individuals. Dan Casey and Tony Pohl were right behind Tartaglino. Casey was a GS-17 and New York's regional director, but he had defied Ambrose in Operation Window. So Ambrose moved him to headquarters as chief of domestic enforcement and put loyal Customs Agent John Fallon, a GS-15 with far less experience, in charge of New York. Pohl was remaindered to a cubbyhole in DC under Casey to develop the DEA's conspiracy unit.

Many BNDD agents were shuffled around, often from places they had been for years, often for no discernible reason. Some felt Ambrose was exacting revenge, or sending them into administrative limbo because he felt they were a threat to the Customs-ODALE-ex-patriot BNDD clique that was usurping power at the DEA. Knowing that Ambrose was pulling the strings did nothing to improve their opinion of Bartels either. As Agent John Evans explained, they felt Bartels was inept, made rash decisions, and played favorites. They smiled to his face, but among themselves they said the ship was adrift, its captain missing.[7] Waiting for an opportunity to strike, the Wolf Pack circled his campfire.

Bartels caught the vibes and asked his old friend Bruce Jensen (a BNDD agent who had been assigned to the Joint Task Force and ODALE in New York) to serve as his executive assistant. Jensen arrived in Washington around Thanksgiving 1973. As he recalled, Bartels immediately complained that he was "up to my ass in alligators."[8]

"It was a crazy time," Jensen sighed. "We used to say, 'If you see the attorney general, get his name.' Because of Watergate, Bartels got no support from people who put him there. He had no one below him either, no deputy to help."

Bartels wanted Jensen to provide him with "the BNDD agent's perspective." Jensen replied that the DEA was an unpopular mix. The Customs guys were angry because they had been torn from a heritage that went back to the formation of the federal government. The BNDD people were asking, "Where can I go?"

Bartels' solution was to send Jensen and a small group of ODALE and Customs agents out on a cross-country juggernaut designed to sell the DEA concept. In reality, that meant BNDD agents tolerating Customs agents and ODALE lawyers in leadership roles. It was an impossibly big pill to swallow.

Another poor decision Bartels made was naming his ODALE crony, Vince Promuto, as deputy chief of Public Affairs under John Enright. According to Enright, "Bartels comes in with Bill Durkin to head the transition team. We get our assignments. I get PR and Congress, and start working with Bartels' assistant, Vince Promuto. Well, Vince can see Bartels, but I can't."[9]

Compounding the problem was the rumor that Promuto's uncle owned a Mafia-connected garbage business. Bartels knew this, as did everyone else, but Promuto was a former Washington Redskins football player and Bartels was star-struck. Bartels and Bill Durkin (a college football player) routinely socialized with Promuto at Fran O'Brien's sports bar in Washington. It was unprofessional behavior and Enright clashed with Durkin over the issue. But Durkin sided with Bartels and Promuto, which led Enright to express the general feeling that Durkin had "sold us out."[10]

As Purple Gang veteran John Evans explained, "People start calling me about Promuto. They're saying, 'He's line mob' with 'blood ties.' According to Evans there were rumors that Promuto was taking

Bartels on junkets to Vegas and Hollywood, and that "Vince was using his mob connections to get Bartels laid."[11]

Other agents say Bartels' fatal mistake was naming Customs Agent George Brosan as acting chief of inspections. But the real reason for his undoing was his mistreatment of Andy Tartaglino. Bartels needed to accommodate Tartaglino, not alienate him. When the DEA was being formed, Tartaglino told Bartels that he wanted to be appointed chief of enforcement. Bartels, however, gave the job to Tartaglino's rival, Bill Durkin. And that was his prerogative. So Tartaglino accepted the job of acting deputy administrator, but on condition that he would become a chief inspector in the career service. The deputy administrator was an appointed position that served at the pleasure of Bartels. Knowing he was atop Ambrose's "hit list," Tartaglino did not want to be in position to be fired. Bartels agreed, and then cut Tartaglino out of any role in DEA operations. Tartaglino rightfully considered that a "slap in the face."[12]

Bartels acted out of fear and arrogance. He believed that Tartaglino kept secret "open" files on people like Bill Durkin, leaving them "vulnerable to extortion."[13] He believed Tartaglino used the files to control agents and even BNDD Director John Ingersoll, the way former FBI Director Hoover had used open investigations to blackmail Congressmen. So Bartels shunned Tartaglino, but he couldn't make him disappear. According to Bartels, Tartaglino was "the chess piece nailed to the board."[14]

Tartaglino saw the situation in broader terms. He knew that the Purple Gang wanted both him and Bartels out of the way, and it fueled the war between them. Tartaglino said he had "never seen anyone used like Bartels."[15] Meanwhile, acting chief inspector George Brosan kept coming into Tartaglino's office for guidance. Brosan, a former Customs agent, had come across the thirty-five unresolved integrity cases while perusing the inspection files. He had never seen anything like it in his career as a professional inspector and had no idea how to proceed. Tartaglino helpfully suggested that he focus on Bill Durkin.[16]

Formulating Policy

WHILE THE INTERNECINE WAR BREWED, Bartels turned to policy matters. One major change he made was the placement of more agents overseas. On the surface this development was a natural outgrowth of the mandate Congress gave to FBN Commissioner Harry Anslinger, way back in 1930, to "go to the source" to solve America's craving for illegal drugs.[17] The deeper reason transcends drug law enforcement;

expanding the DEA's overseas agent force was an essential component of the inescapable expansion of the American empire, at a time when the Vietnam War had resulted in the reduction of US military and CIA paramilitary forces in the Far East. Bartels also presided over the inclusion within the DEA's training program of more foreign military officers and policemen. This was done in the belief that their gratitude and cooperation would enhance overseas operations. This policy too served the nation's security interests in so far as Congress was about to abolish the Office of Public Safety due to a "torture" scandal.[18] Congress needed to find another means to finance the CIA's covert recruitment of foreign officials, and the DEA's training program was, as we shall see, a convenient vehicle.

The most important thing Bartels did was expanding the office of intelligence and placing it under George Belk. Bartels understood the need for better intelligence and had contributed to Reorganization #2 by chairing an intelligence committee that included Tom Peters at OMB, William Sullivan at ONNI, senior Customs officials, as well as Andy Tartaglino, George Belk (chair of the DEA's Foreign Intelligence Subcommittee), and John Warner (chair of the DEA's Domestic Intelligence Subcommittee).[19] Bartels' Intelligence Committee broke intelligence down into strategic, operational and tactical needs and functions.[20] For the first time these terms were defined: strategic intelligence as "the knowledge required by the administrator to allocate resources, to develop strategy, and to establish policy;" operational intelligence "lends itself to the development of conspiracy cases" and enables "the operational commander to plan action;" tactical intelligence was "the information collected by the narcotics investigator for the purpose of making a case."[21] Half of the DEA's Special Projects allocation was dedicated to intelligence, which boasted foreign and domestic sub-divisions, its own Special Projects unit within the Intelligence Group/Operations (IGO) under Lou Conein, and an independent computer system under Stanton Mintz.

Within the office of intelligence, Belk's friend Phil Smith ran the domestic division and Warner became chief of foreign intelligence. Jim Ludlum, then Tom Fox, served as chief of strategic intelligence. The intelligence division was allotted 202 positions, 109 at headquarters, the rest in the regional intelligence units. Sixty people entered from ONNI, many of whom were CIA.[22]

The State Department continued to play a guiding role in overseas operations, and the CCINC selected 60 countries for Narcotic

Country Action Plans.[23] In January 1974 Bartels and his senior staff briefed Ambassador Sheldon Vance, the Assistant Secretary of State for International Narcotics Matters (INM), on the intelligence office and its activities. Present was the CIA's Deputy Director of Operations. By February 1974 all regional directors had been briefed on how to set up intelligence nets and recruit assets, and were instructed in CIA "tradecraft" skills, such as how to use agents to insulate the US government from its dabbling in drug trafficking.[24]

Regional Directors and enforcement managers at headquarters began coordinating intelligence operations with other agencies. For example, the Interagency Drug Intelligence Group — Mexico, with a working group of full-time representatives attached to and located at the DEA Office of Intelligence, was formed with the CIA, State INM, OMB, Customs, DIA and NSA to create clandestine agent networks in Mexico.[25] A parallel structure was established at the American Embassy in Mexico City to monitor the net.

Some DEA intelligence networks were quite imaginative. "Merlin," run by Conein's Intelligence Group/Operations (IGO), consisted of missionaries in opium growing areas. The clergy gathered drug intelligence for the DEA and political intelligence for the CIA. That particular operation was expanded into Colombia and Bolivia.[26]

George Belk was the force behind the emergence of intelligence operations and was considered a visionary. His mission was clearly defined by statute in USC 3011 28 USC 509-510, Section 103. The mission was "The development and maintenance of a National Narcotics Intelligence System in cooperation with federal, State and local officials, and the provision of narcotics intelligence to any Federal, State or local officials that the Administrator determines has a legitimate official need to have access to such intelligence."[27] But the functions of intelligence in drug law enforcement had yet to be resolved, and points of contention quickly arose. One was the formation in late 1973 under Lou Conein of a Special Operations Staff and Clandestine Intelligence Field units (based on the DEACON I model) reporting through a separate system, apart from enforcement, to Belk.[28] Also known as the IGO, the Special Operations and Field Support Staff administered Special Field Investigations Projects at home and abroad. Another point of contention was the DEA's intelligence data base, which was accessible to the CIA.

William Colby was the main player at CIA. As his beloved Agency looked for new rocks to hide under, Colby saw the political points he could score, and the money he could acquire from Congress, by getting more deeply involved in drug enforcement. By July 1973, when Colby became DCI, the CIA had already dipped its fingers in many of the BNDD's overseas and intelligence functions. Some CIA drug intelligence collection was done apart from the BNDD for its own purposes, but the Agency also engaged in paramilitary operations like the program Joey DiGennaro was in. All in all, the DEA was a ripe plum waiting to be plucked.

Mexico

THE DEA WAS TURNING ITS attention away from the French connection toward South America and the Far East. This change was already in the works when on October 20, 1973, under orders from President Nixon, Solicitor General Robert Bork fired special prosecutor Archibald Cox and forced the resignation of Elliot Richardson. The "Saturday Night Massacre" occurred while Richardson was chairing the CCINC. He was actively involved in CCINC affairs and was preparing to host Mexico's attorney general to formulate a plan to curb the production of Mexican brown heroin. He never made it to the Monday meeting.

"This was traumatic," CCINC staff director Walter Minnick said of Richardson's dismissal. Making matters worse, Myles Ambrose had replaced hapless Joe Arpaio in Mexico City with Customs Agent Tom Dean. This was retaliation, pure and simple, for Arpaio refusing to allow the Customs attaché in Mexico access to the judicial police, thus reducing the long-established Customs role in Mexico. Installing Dean was meant to assuage the soreheads at Customs. But they were inconsolable, for with the creation of the DEA, Customs was stripped of its drug intelligence gathering and investigative authority, and was prohibited from everything but routine search and seizure. Some Customs agents made it their job to cause problems, and tensions between Customs and DEA agents soared along the border. One of Brosan's first jobs as chief inspector was investigating shootouts between them![29]

Disgruntled Customs agents kept the DEA from getting off the ground at a time when Mexican narcotics were pouring over the border. International Enforcement chief Jack Cusack tried to overcome the problem by getting additional funding for the Mexican police. To this end he arranged for Congressman Charlie Rangel to observe, from a CIA helicopter, a dozen teenage Mexican soldiers whacking poppies with sticks. "This is eradication?" Rangel asked. "Jesus, they're hitting flowers with sticks!"[30]

Mexican officials were, as always diverting technical aide into their pockets, and Rangel tried to get the State Department to squeeze Mexican President Luis Echeverria to eliminate corruption. To assuage the gringos, Echeverria fired the chief of police in a northern province. But the police chief wasn't corrupt. As he explained to Jerry Strickler, "I shipped the rake-off money to Mexico City, like I was supposed to!"

Corruption inside Mexico and competition with Customs would only worsen.

Chile

AGENT GEORGE FRANGULLIE OPENED THE BNDD's office in Santiago in May 1973 with Agent Charlie Cecil. It was the first office opened in a Marxist country and put the DEA in the midst of yet another CIA coup d'etat.[31] President Salvador Allende had nationalized Chile's copper mines and Nixon, Kissinger and the CIA ousted him in a military coup led by General Augusto Pinochet. Many of the Chilean officers involved in the coup had been trained by the US and were glad to do its bidding in return for power and wealth. Ted Shackley ran the covert operation with Tom Clines as head of the Chilean Task Force at Langley headquarters.[32]

The coup climaxed on September 11, 1973 with Allende's murder. Pinochet declared marshal law and suddenly the DEA agents needed a pass to travel around. Through the CIA, Jerry Strickler got one for Special Agent in Charge (SAC) George Frangullie. CIA officers also got the Chilean military to round up 21 drug traffickers and confine them in National Stadium, which was used as a concentration camp for some 40,000 Allende supporters, many of whom were tortured and killed.[33]

Under Pinochet's emergency laws, the DEA did not need arrest warrants. As Strickler recalled, "We made contact with the new government and when they rounded up Allende's supporters and put them in the stadium, we were given clearance to get our people. Our fugitives were roped off from the political prisoners, some of whom were Chileans, some not."

As part of Springboard, which dispensed with the niceties of extradition, Strickler and Cusack leased a Chilean plane to fly 16 of the traffickers to New York. They got five more out on Braniff. Agent Mickey Tobin from New York was in charge. When the traffickers disembarked, they still had hoods on their heads. Strickler recalled that on the second flight, captives were hurt by the agents. "These people started talking," Strickler adds, "and their information lead to more indictments." It also meant more corruption charges, as the traffickers revealed which NYPD people took their drugs and money. This facet of the Chilean operation dovetailed with the Prince of the City affair.

Around this time, relations with the DEA and CIA started to sour. Strickler was working with Drake Reid's special unit to get around the State Department. It was fun at first, but soon Strickler realized that the CIA was playing a double game that adversely affected his cases. It started when Shackley demanded a list of all DEA informants overseas for the CIA's drug data base. The situation got worse when Belk, who saw the CIA as his benefactor, complied. It didn't adversely affect DEA intelligence but it affected enforcement, and that's how the battle between the divisions began.

The crux of the problem was that the CIA was recruiting drug smugglers like Alberto Sicilia Falcon in Mexico as political assets. In one case Strickler was chasing a Chilean colonel whom the CIA had blackmailed into becoming an informant by using DEA reports. After the colonel tried to shoot Charlie Cecil, the CIA protected him. That angered everyone in the DEA and Bill Durkin gave Strickler permission to defy the CIA. DEA agents went to Chile and kidnapped the colonel, who, under harsh questioning, threatened to reveal CIA shenanigans unless he was released.[34]

The situation boiled over and Seymour Bolten replaced the Latin American counterpart office under Drake Reid with new people. Cooperation ceased and bad things happened. A DEA informant in Colombia asked to see the narcotics attaché. But the person he met and shared his information with was a CIA agent, equipped with DEA credentials. In another instance the police in Costa Rica complained that their narcotics squad was asked to do things by someone with DEA credentials. What he asked them to do adversely affected DEA cases on Robert Vesco and Santo Trafficante. In Argentina, Agent Frank Macolini discovered that an undercover CIA agent was arranging drug shipments with his CIA case officer.[35]

Finally the Canadian police called Strickler. A Venezuelan police officer they had arrested claimed he had been recruited by an American doctor at the International Police Academy in Panama. The doctor introduced the Venezuelan to a CIA officer at the Colombian

Embassy. On behalf of the CIA officer, the Venezuelan cop became a courier for a trafficking group moving drugs from Venezuela to Colombia.

Weary of busted cases, Strickler obtained a photo of the CIA case officer and threatened to expose the CIA's misdeeds. "The relationship between the CIA and DEA was not as it was originally intended," he argues. "The CIA does not belong in any type of law enforcement intelligence activity, unless it can result in a conviction, which it rarely does. They should only be supportive, totally."

Unfortunately, Bolten, who had worldwide responsibilities and reported directly to Colby, prevailed. Colby called Bartels. First Cusack (who had recruited assets for the CIA since the early 1950s and was firmly in its thrall) divided the Latin American Division in half, to dilute Strickler's authority. But when he continued to complain, Bartels removed him from operations altogether and reassigned him to a management group to review the relationship between intelligence and enforcement. Bartels, too, was clearly in the CIA's camp, and neither he nor Colby would tolerate troublemakers.[36]

Colby and Bolten were also protecting the CIA's assets in Southeast Asia, who by 1973 were smuggling narcotics from the Golden Triangle to Australia, Latin America and Mexico. Many of the transactions were handled by the newly formed Nugan Hand Bank, based in Australia and composed largely of CIA officers and retired American generals from the Vietnam debacle.[37] But there were no DEA agents in Australia, and when Latin American agents seized the refined heroin, they couldn't trace it. In addition, the CIA was protecting the smugglers.[38]

As Strickler recalled, "We negotiated with a guy for a delivery to be made in Mexico. He was a relative of the principal's wife. The Mexicans cooperated, but the guy disappeared." Strickler knew where he was hiding and naively asked the CIA to help track him down. However, as soon as he asked, he started getting "far out intelligence." Next, his new CIA counterpart asked to meet for lunch: Bolten was there with Shackley. They explained that their source and the DEA informant were the same person. They asked for Strickler's cooperation and he agreed. "Just give us back our source," he said. They did, but only after sending him to another DEA office in a third country. Before Strickler could meet and debrief the guy, he perished in a plane crash.

Strickler was then transferred to a headquarters planning committee tasked to better coordinate the offices of enforcement and intelligence.

There he saw the contaminating effect the CIA had on the DEA. "There was no cooperation because Belk wanted to be operational and went his own way," Strickler said. "We had an informant net in Argentina and Belk and Conein sent Bud Frank down to take it over. It was a real professional operation throughout the entire Southern Tier. It was so good the CIA asked them to do work for them." And the money was better, so they did.

May the Circle Be Unbroken

WHEN CIA ASSETS ARE BUSTED, the Justice Department is there to help. The premier case occurred in July 1973, when CIA agent Puttaporn Khramkhruan was arrested and charged with smuggling 59 pounds of opium. The case began in 1972, when Puttaporn sold opium to several young Americans through "Peace Corps volunteer" Bruce Hoeft in Chiang Mai. Hoeft and the Americans packaged the opium in film canisters. An initial 40-pound shipment went through without any problems, but the second 59-pound package was spotted by Customs agents and the receiver was arrested when he came to pick it up. When they examined it, the agents found that Puttaporn had foolishly wrapped the opium in a magazine that had his name and address on it.[39] A Customs agent sent to Chiang Mai to investigate Puttaporn was snubbed by the CIA in Chiang Mai, but learned that Puttaporn was in the US as part of a business seminar sponsored by the Agency for International Development; AID had loaned him $1600 for airfare.[40] When questioned by Customs agents in the US, Puttaporn named Hoeft and the American he was conspiring with. Puttaporn was arrested and incarcerated in the Cook County jail.

A 31-year-old Burmese national, Puttaporn worked for DEVCON, a component of Taylor Associates, a CIA proprietary company started as a community development counseling service by retired Marine Corps Colonel Joseph Zachary Taylor. DEVCON sponsored the Hilltribe Research Center in Chiang Mai. The CIA engages in "civic action" programs like Hilltribe Research Center as a way of maintaining contact with agents and recruiting informants. As a cover, the Research Center bought and marketed the handicrafts of indigenous Burmese, Thai and Lao. It also employed Thai teachers, agronomists, animal husbandry-men and engineers, as cut-outs to debrief the tribal people on insurgents and drug traffickers. CIA agent Puttaporn and Hoeft worked at the Hilltribe Research Center in Chiang Mai.

Through a contract with the AID, Taylor's CIA contract employees, working under DEVCON cover, armed and trained the Thai Border Patrol Police (BPP), a paramilitary force of approximately 10,000 airborne rangers developed by the CIA in the early 1950s and charged with "internal security." The Thais used the BPP to locate and destroy insurgents in Thailand — and to guard the King's opium fields, protect official drug smuggling networks and lead raids on competitors. The CIA used the BPP as a cover to recruit agents to spy on the Chinese and Russians in countries bordering Thailand.[41]

Puttaporn was also an officer in Kuomintang General Li Mi's army. He told DEA Agent John Bax that he guarded Li Mi's 8th Army opium-mule caravans out of Burma, and that his CIA case officer was the US consul in Chiang Mai, James Montgomery.[42] In August 1971, Nixon had ostensibly ordered the CIA to cease its cross-border operations.[43] But, as Puttaporn revealed, the operations never stopped, nor did the CIA's involvement in drug trafficking. When George Belk and Ron Metcalf visited Chiang Mai, DEA Agent Jim Pettit complained that CIA listening posts in Burma picked up opium caravan "walkie-talkie" chatter. The intercepts enabled the CIA-advised Border Police to hit the caravans and take the drugs before the DEA could make the seizure.[44]

Fred Dick explained how the line was drawn between the CIA and DEA. "During the time I was in Thailand," he said, "we were supporting and funding a Thai police unit, part of the SNO Program at Chiang Mai. The agency had a station in the same town and they were working with the Thai Border Patrol. I do not know what they were doing. We did exchange intelligence and their files were open to us, as ours were to them. We never worked jointly in field operations."[45]

Unlike the DEA, Colby was looking at the big picture, meaning Nixon's overture to China, which included negotiations over the status of Taiwan. Many right-wing generals and CIA officers considered Taiwan a strategic military base against Communist China. They were opposed to rapprochement with China and would gladly have mounted covert operations using opium caravans to detect Chinese troop movements, despite any presidential directives to the contrary. It is also possible that Puttaporn was involved in the intrigues between the CIA, Kuomintang in Burma and Taiwan, and the Chinese. Nixon took a personal interest in his case, especially after Puttaporn told DEA agents that he had led more than a dozen commando raids into China and was debriefed by the CIA about those raids.[46] Puttaporn threatened to reveal that fact in court, as well as the fact that he had smuggled the opium at the request of the CIA. His lawyer was planning on calling Hoeft and Taylor, CIA station chief Louis Lapham in Bangkok, and Pat Landry, its base chief in Udorn, Thailand as witnesses. His defense team was also preparing to subpoena incriminating documents.

The CIA's reaction was predictable. It refused to provide the documents and witnesses, and directed the assistant US attorney in Chicago to dismiss the case in April 1974. (And on July 24, 1974, two short weeks before his resignation, Nixon appointed Joseph Z. Taylor as Assistant Inspector General of Foreign Assistance.) CIA Director William Colby told a Congressional Committee, "We requested the Justice Department not to try him for this reason. They agreed."[47] CIA lawyers also told Senator Charles Percy (R-IL) that Puttaporn was hired in 1972 to report on narcotics trafficking in northern Thailand, that's all, and that his crime was a controlled delivery committed to counter narcotic trafficking. Percy said with a sigh, "CIA agents are untouchable — however serious their crime or however much harm is done to society."[48]

As Fred Dick explained, "The agency folks are masters at going behind the scenes in the US court system and convincing the judiciary an open exposure of this sort would jeopardize national security. To my knowledge they have never failed with this ploy."

Other DEA agents also knew the CIA was lying, and they told Senator Percy that Puttaporn had been employed by the CIA in Thailand since 1969 and "was a member of a multi-million dollar opium ring."[49] They also told Percy that Puttaporn's close friend, Victor Tin-Sein, "had been killed while living in the United States by unnamed parties for his involvement in and knowledge of Puttaporn's smuggling ring."[50]

The murder likely involved a case Agent Joe Lagattuta was working on. A member of Conein's special unit, Lagattuta was sent to Amsterdam where he hired a Chinese "asset." The asset was not an informant, as he was part of a CIA operation "for Conein and a significant figure who must remain nameless." One might assume the significant figure was Colby. "We were very successful," Lagattuta continues, "not just in heroin seized but the planning and execution of the sting leading to arrests and destruction of several significant trafficking rings."[51]

Unfortunately, Lagattuta's asset — perhaps Victor Tin-Sein — was sent to San Francisco where he was "badly managed by the DEA and murdered." Lagattuta was convinced the asset "was assassinated as opposed to being murdered."

DEVCON

WEST POINT GRADUATE RAY COFFEY fought with the US Army 101st Airborne Division in Korea and with the US Army Special Forces in South Vietnam starting in 1961. He then served as a CIA agent in Thailand (concurrently with Joseph Taylor) from 1966 till 1974.[52] Taylor had a contract to train the Border Patrol Police (BPP) and Coffey was his chief trainer, working undercover for Taylor Associates as its DEVCON representative.[53] The BPP consisted of approximately 10,000 Thai Army airborne rangers, headquartered in Bangkok but scattered around the country in 32-man platoons. Formed in the 1950s by the CIA as a paramilitary police force, the BPP was viewed with suspicion by the regular army due to its preferential treatment and "internal security" mission — protecting the interests of the royal family, which included opium plantations. In the 1970s, it was still advised by the Bangkok CIA station.[54] Taylor worked at that strategic level with senior Thai police and political officials planning intelligence operations against Chinese agents in Malaysia and Russian agents in North Vietnam.[55]

Coffey and his six Green Beret assistants helped the BPP to improve its intelligence collection, counter-insurgency and border control capabilities in northern Thailand. Ray Coffey's specialty was conducting psychological warfare "hearts and minds" operations in remote areas. Establishing medical field services and other types of "civil operations" is a standard way for CIA paramilitary forces to maintain contact with local people who are then recruited as informants and agents. To this end, through DEVCON, Coffey and his assistants created the Hilltribe Research Center that employed Puttaporn, where opium growing natives brought and marketed their handicrafts, and were recruited and sent back into the field to gather intelligence.[56]

In 1972, DEVCON-advised BPP operations in northern Thailand were redirected toward narcotics interdiction and intelligence collection at the urging of Washington; to the despair of BNDD, which knew this would allow the CIA to penetrate their operations and run unilateral operations using agents like Puttaporn. The BPP was already taking heavy casualties, and Coffey was not happy about the reassignment either; he recalled sitting on a mountain side in 1973 and watching a battalion of KMT soldiers with 200 mules moving a huge opium shipment. "I had 30 men to stop a battalion," Coffey recalled, "so I said, 'Forget it.'"

According to Coffey the Thai Air Force also moved drugs: "ten tons of opium on barges at a time in Chiang Mai." In the early 1980s, when author James Mills was in Chiang Mai writing about DEA operations, the BPP was considered "totally corrupt and responsible for the transportation of narcotics."[57]

Coffey steered clear of the BNDD but worked closely with Public Safety officers like Gordon Young. A CIA officer since 1954, serving originally as a BPP advisor, Gordon Young, brother of Bill Young, was assigned to Houei Sai, Laos in 1972. He described the anti-narcotics effort between 1972 and 1974 as "a messy, uncoordinated affair" with "each outfit (CIA, USAID, State, military and Customs) all pulling in different directions — each looking jealously for the rewards!" As a result, "we did not seize huge quantities, but we did drive them underground."[58]

Like Coffey (who claims to have fired Young for falsifying reports, although Gordon claims it was his brother Bill who was fired), Gordon was not under the illusion that he could overcome official corruption, fueled by the CIA, and stem the flow of drugs. "No one was there to be heroes," he said. "It was like dealing with Mafia chiefs." He recalled a trip he took up the Bong River on the Burma border to meet a BPP captain in the jungle. The captain was sitting beside a huge pile of heroin, morphine and opium. Gordon asked if he would surrender it. "'You may have it,' the captain said, 'but by time you get through....'"

The Return of Robert Vesco

As JERRY STRICKLER NOTED, THE police in Costa Rica complained that their people were asked to do "things" by someone with phony DEA credentials. That action negated a possible DEA prosecution of Robert Vesco and Santo Trafficante.

Who would want to do that?

Consider that Nixon's friend, John Mitchell, was indicted with Vesco in May 1973. In October 1973, while prosecutors were preparing the case against Vesco and Mitchell, Customs informant Frank Peroff told investigators that Vesco had offered to finance a narcotics smuggling venture with him and Conrad Bouchard. A heroin supplier loosely tied to a Watergate conspiracy theory involving Paul Louis Weiller (see Chapter 15), Bouchard was an associate of Marius Martin and Jean Jehan, the fugitives whose prosecution in New York was sabotaged by the theft of the heroin seized in the 1962 French Connection case. The timing seems eerily preordained; after 20 years in Buenos Aires, Bouchard returned to Marseille in 1963 and then relocated to Montreal. Bouchard was linked to Mafiosi in Italy, and his customers were major Mafiosi in New York and Detroit.

A BNDD case in France led to Frank Dasti in Canada and Mafioso Paul Oddo in New York.[59] Bouchard was arrested in this case in 1972, but released on bond. A year later Peroff, then working for both the DEA and Customs, met Bouchard in the Bahamas. Bouchard knew where major French clandestine labs were located and the BNDD hired Peroff to find out where they were. Customs, meanwhile, offered Peroff a whopping $250,000 reward to set up Bouchard, who was negotiating a transaction with Mafioso John Fecarotta in Detroit.[60]

Everything got scrambled together when the DEA was formed and Peroff's control agent went to work for former BNDD agent John O'Neill. In the midst of the constant squabbling and misunderstandings, Bouchard in July 1973 called Peroff and asserted that Vesco would front $300,000 for a heroin buy. Peroff recorded the conversation on tape. But Peroff's case agent, John O'Neill, felt that Bouchard was lying about Vesco and that Bouchard merely wanted an excuse to use Peroff's Lear jet to flee.[61]

More confusion ensued and in September, Peroff gave the tapes to Queens County prosecutors. When the federal prosecutors found out, they subpoenaed Peroff and his tapes. This did not bode well for Peroff. US Attorney Paul Curran had, for some unexplained reason, asked Vesco's lawyer, Cecil Wallace-Whitfield, to extradite Vesco from Costa Rica to New York to appear at the Mitchell-Stans trial. Obviously, that never happened. Curran's assistants on the Peroff case were John Wing — who prosecuted the politically charged, Watergate-related Mitchell-Stans case — and Arthur Viviani.[62]

An ally of Myles Ambrose, Viviani seemed to have a political agenda as well; if the reader will recall, it was Viviani who had refused to allow Tony Pohl access to Richard Berdin's girlfriend, as a way of preventing her information from reaching the French before US Attorney Herbert Stern could score the necessary political points in the Delouette-SDECE case. Viviani also convinced the judge in the Cirillo case to reduce Cirillo's bail, allowing the murderer to hit the streets.

Viviani put Peroff's tapes in a safe, declaring there was no possibility of resurrecting the Vesco lead.[63] DEA agents then leaked Peroff's name to the press as the person who had ratted out Bouchard. Fearing for his life, Peroff ran to the Permanent Subcommittee on Investigations. While his allegations were never proven, they were investigated in early 1975. In its staff study on the Peroff case, the Subcommittee stated: "Policing the drug traffic in the United Sates is a serious matter. This responsibility today belongs to the DEA. By their performance in the Peroff matter, by their lame inquiry with Customs into Peroff's allegations, by their inconsistent testimony before the subcommittee, by their fierce determination to defend obvious incompetence by their own personnel, DEA officials have shown themselves to be deserving of responsible criticism."[64]

How the Subcommittee came to the conclusion that DEA officials deserved responsible criticism is the subject of the next several chapters. Yes, the Republican-controlled Justice Department protected Vesco, but that's politics as usual. What is truly disturbing is that DEA agents were complicit. Agent Bruce Van Matre was assigned to Costa Rica in 1974. His kids went to school with Vesco's kids.[65] A hundred DEA agents could have grabbed Vesco, like they kidnapped hundreds of other traffickers. Why not?

The obvious conclusion is that the DEA had become a tool of the Republican Party and, through the CIA, the Establishment's national security apparatus. Indeed, by 1974, the Vesco investigation was safely in the hands of CIA officer Lou Conein and his asset Carlos Hernandez Rumbault, bodyguard of Vesco's patron, Costa Rican President José Figueres. Conein's special operations group is the subject of the next chapter.

21

THE DIRTY DOZEN

THE DEA'S ARCHITECTS SAW A greater need for intelligence and gave responsibility for meeting this need to George Belk. His job was to gather intelligence to help enforcement officers identify, among other things, the major sources of narcotics, and the biggest traffickers and their weaknesses. It was a good idea, but of the DEA people under Belk's command, few were intelligence experts capable of performing the analytical tasks required of them; which is why Belk gladly welcomed CIA officers onto his staff. It was easy too; many spooks were already in the Office of Strategic Intelligence, and dozens more dribbled into the DEA through ONNI. When more were needed, Colby was happy to oblige. Belk, along with Phillip Smith, the DEA's Acting Deputy Assistant Administrator for Intelligence, also inherited control of Tartaglino's BUNCIN Project, which was renamed DEACON I (DEA Clandestine Operations Network) in July 1973.[1]

The DEACON I program was expanded to include a secretary and Customs agent, both paid from mobile task funds, and other DEACONs were developed through "specially funded intelligence operations."[2] The CIA was still involved and Smith noted that reimbursement for the DEACON I covert agent (Bob Medell) "is being made in backchannel fashion to CIA under payments to other agencies and is not counted as a position against us."[3] CIA funding for the covert agent was later withdrawn.[4] The chain of command passed from Tartaglino to Smith, and Bartels urged that the covert agent, under Smith's direction, "travel to Caracas or Bogota to develop a network of agents."[5]

Bartels pressed for more "covert intelligence" programs and on January 4, 1974 "established a priority on foreign clandestine narcotics collection."[6] Through the first half of 1974, he issued a flurry of memoranda regarding every aspect of intelligence operations. But George Belk wasn't all that excited about gathering intelligence. Looking through keyholes wasn't quite as cool as kicking down doors, guns blazing. Belk longed to be making cases and to that end he proposed a special operations group in intelligence (DEA-SOG), formally known as the Special Operations and Field Support Staff.[7] Bartels approved it in March 1974, and Belk assigned the unit to mischievous Lou Conein.[8] As chief of the Intelligence Group/Operations (IGO), Conein administered the DEASOG, Special Field Intelligence Program (SFIP) and National Intelligence Officers (NIO) programs.[9] The chain of command, however, was "unclear" and while "the overt agent in Miami continued to report directly to Belk and Smith," Conein coordinated with anyone he wanted to, including CIA agents.[10] Conein kept his operations compartmented even within the intelligence division through a separate chain of command. The IGO even had its own safe house for DEASOG agents located outside DEA headquarters in downtown Washington, DC.

Directly through William Colby and his assistant Jack A. Mathews at CIA headquarters, Bartels, Belk and Conein hired a "dirty dozen" of CIA officers as NIOs to staff DEASOG.[11] They NIOs did not buy narcotics or appear in court. Instead they used standard CIA operating procedures to recruit assets and set up networks for the long-range clandestine and secure collection of intelligence. Some NIOs worked with regional intelligence units in support of enforcement operations, but covert NIOs reported solely to Conein.[12]

The first CIA recruits were Elias P. Chavez and Nicholas Zapata.[14] Both had paramilitary experience in Laos near the CIA's drug-drenched commando base at Xeno. Colby's assistant, Jack Mathews (famous for recruiting American smoke jumpers into the CIA to support and train mercenary commando units) had been Chavez's case officer at the CIA's Long Thien base, where General Vang Pao ran his secret drug-smuggling army.

Next came a group of eight CIA officers. Wesley Dyckman was a Chinese linguist with service in Vietnam. He was assigned to San Francisco. Louis J. Davis, a veteran of Vietnam and Laos, was assigned to Chicago. Christopher Thompson from the Phoenix Program went to San Antonio. Hugh E. Murray from Pakse, Laos (the major drug shipment center into Vietnam) and Bolivia (where he participated in the capture of Che Guevara) was assigned to Tucson. Thomas D. McPhaul, who had worked with Conein in Vietnam and against the Red Brigades in Italy, was sent to Dallas. Thomas L. Briggs, a veteran of Laos and close associate of Ted Shackley, went to Mexico. Vernon J. Goertz, another Shackley associate and veteran of Laos who served in Chile during the Allende coup, went to Venezuela. And David A. Scherman, a Conein cohort and former manager of the CIA's brutal interrogation center in Da Nang, was sent to sunny San Diego.[15]

Gary Mattocks, who ran CIA counter-terror teams in South Vietnam, and Robert Simon, a CIA interrogator masquerading as an Air Force colonel, were the eleventh and twelfth members. The thirteenth member, Terry Baldwin, had managed CIA air operations in Chiang Mai. Joe Lagattuta worked for Conein too, as did several other CIA agents who were not formally part of the "dirty dozen" infiltration. DEASOG was as far-flung as it was far-fetched.[16]

Clandestine Operations Networks

Lou Conein's job was to direct the dirty dozen in long range penetrations in classic CIA-style operations. His first step was to develop five new DEACONs and assign NIOs to them. DEACON II agents debriefed ethnic informants with unusual languages and translated documents; DEACON III was located in Mexico; DEACON IV replaced DEACON III and was directed against Pedro Aviles Perez, certain businessmen, as well as Mexico's drug smuggling security forces and air force; DEACON V "was never really implemented" and DEACON VI, as of 1976, remained "a regional probe."[17] Of the 36 field projects funded by Conein's IGO through 1976, 20 were classified as "intelligence collection probes." Eleven of those 20 accomplished their mission, but only four (LAZO, NORD, MELON and TAMERLANE) were said to have "warranted funding."[18]

In Operation Mooncake, the IGO's most successful case, Conein's staff worked with foreign and domestic regions, several US embassies, Special Projects and the SIO.[19] Named for a Chinese pastry, Mooncake was a "long-range, high-level penetration of the Hip Sing Tong."[20] It began when a DEACON asset stumbled onto a Hip Sing Tong plan to join with the On Leong Tong to ship 165 pounds of heroin from Thailand through various Far East ports to customers in major American cities. Mooncake continued for years and converged with national security affairs; as a result, the DEACON asset was transferred to the CIA, which handled that aspect of the case. The narcotics aspect led to Hip Sing Tong official John Liu in Dallas, among other Chinese traffickers scattered around the US and the world, and to the On Leong Ghost Shadows. Several Ghost Shadow ships were sunk and much heroin was seized, forcing the groups to lay low for awhile — though by the mid-1990s they were back in full swing.[21]

Less successful was DEACON I, which included Bob Medell and Bill Logay and their disruptive personality conflict. BNDD employee Cecelia Plicet quit her job to join the dysfunctional team as its deniable secretary. Michael Brom — a CIA officer according to some agents, a Customs officer according to others — was assigned to conduct file research, prepare reports, and handle liaison with Conein's headquarters assistant, Rich Kobakoff. Brom would eventually replace Logay as the overt agent. Robert Simon (a CIA employee undercover of the US Air Force from 1958 until June 14, 1974, when he entered the DEA) was assigned to debrief potential assets and coordinate the Interagency Narcotics Intelligence System (INIS) task force in Miami.[22]

DEACON I inherited BUNCIN's intelligence networks and exile Cuban CIA assets, including known terrorists from the infamous anti-Castro Brigade 2506.[23] Medell's assets continued to spy on Cuban cocaine traffickers, their Latin American sources, African-American receivers in the Miami area, and Mafia heroin traffickers connected to Santo Trafficante.[24] Their reliability was often in doubt, however, as they often worked for traffickers, as well as the CIA, DEA and FBI. For example, Medell's asset Roberto "Monkey" Morales worked for Customs, the CIA, FBI, DEA, anti-Castro Cuban terrorist Orlando Bosch, as well as drug smuggler Alvarez-Cruz. Due to his importance to so many government agencies, Morales allegedly got away with murder.[25]

DEASOG heightened tensions between the CIA and DEA. Santo Trafficante was a prime target, so Andy Tartaglino introduced Medell to Sal Caneba, a DEA informant and retired Mafioso who had been in business with Trafficante in the 1950s and '60s. Caneba *in one day* identified the head of the Cuban side of the Trafficante family and its organizational structure.[26] But the CIA refused to allow the DEA to pursue its criminal investigation, because it had employed Trafficante in its assassination attempts against Fidel Castro. The Torrijos clan in Panama was another sore spot, as was Robert Vesco, whom DEACON I assets spied on in Costa Rica.

DEACON assets often had purely CIA assignments, such as "violations of neutrality laws, extremist groups and terrorism, and information of a political nature."[27] They also performed an "internal security" function.[28] Most troublesome, however, was the personality conflict between Medell and Logay. Indeed, Logay made an accusation that exile-Cuban DEACON I assets had actually penetrated the DEA through Medell, on behalf of Trafficante.[29]

DEACON I secretary Cecelia Plicet concurred. Plicet joined the BNDD in Hartford, Connecticut in 1968. In 1972 she transferred to Miami and when the DEA was created, Logay asked her to be his secretary at the safe house. Looking for action, she took a chance and resigned from the BNDD to work undercover. Phil Smith and Lou Conein guaranteed that her job would be waiting when the program was done. It wasn't. Plicet asserts that Medell and Conein worked for "the other side" and wanted the DEA to fail. She said there was more than one safe house and that Tabraue was the highest paid but not the most significant asset. She said that Conein and Medell were using Tabraue to circumvent the DEA; that Medell had unauthorized meetings with Tabraue and that Tabraue played a double game.[30]

These accusations, true or false, prompted Conein to send a Special Agent from his office to Miami in May 1974.[31] The agent did not acknowledge evidence of a penetration, as alleged, nor were any assets compromised; but he did report that Medell and Bill Logay were known to the Miami Region office, as was the location of their safe house. As Miami Agent Terry Burke put it, "All you had to do was follow the trail of beer cans that led to Logay's secret office."

Shortly after the inspection of the DEACON I office, Bill Logay was relieved of his DEACON duties and given a job with inspections. It was decided that the Miami regional office was not equipped to manage "a sophisticated intelligence program such as DEACON."[32] The big problem was the DEA's inability to control protected CIA agents. To wit, Medell's principal agent, CIA agent Guillermo Tabraue, was financing loads of cocaine and using DEACON I assets to smuggle them into the country. DEA agents in the Miami office knew about it, and some local law enforcement officials were allegedly accepting bribes. And yet Tabraue continued to wheel and deal with impunity. When he was finally brought to trial, the CIA intervened on his behalf.[33]

Gary Mattocks and DEACON I

DEACON I HAD A STATED agenda, and an unstated agenda known only to the CIA and Lou Conein. Ever the merry prankster, Conein fooled his DEA colleagues by pretending to be an "average Joe," even a clown, and not the super-spook he was. He was friendly with agents, carpooled and drank with them. But he was a friend to them like he was friendly with the generals who assassinated South Vietnam's President Diem. In other words, Conein fooled DEA agents, including Belk, into covering his CIA schemes. Helping Conein were his "Dirty Dozen" NIOs.

Conein's problems began in November 1974, after Grayson Lynch's cover was blown in the Key West operation, and Bob Medell was blamed and moved to other IGO functions. Medell was bitter, and fixed his fall from grace on the institutional racism that wracked the DEA. He considered DEA agents to be an abusive and prejudiced group. He refers to Belk as "a racist from the South" while Phil Smith had "the football mentality."[34]

Gary Mattocks has a different perspective. After completing the CIA's Spanish language training course, he arrived in Miami in July 1974 as Medell's replacement during Conein's reorganization of DEACON I.[35] In Mattocks' opinion it was a case officer's dream.[36] He had a car, an office, a promotion, and hazardous duty pay. He was not, however, an 1811 gun-carrying DEA agent, because if an "1811" witnesses a crime and doesn't report it, by law he becomes part of the conspiracy. Insofar as DEACON agents were enmeshed in drug conspiracies, Mattocks became a 311 analyst.

Mattocks hailed from North Carolina, where he had been a college football coach. As a CIA officer in Vietnam he ran counter-terror teams and befriended Saigon station chief Ted Shackley. According to Mattocks, Shackley helped Colby set up DEASOG and brought in "his" people, including Mattocks, Tom Briggs and Vernon Goertz.[37] Shackley, notably, was chief of the CIA's Miami station when Trafficante and other Mafia hoods were hired to kill Castro. He knew where all the CIA's Mafia skeletons were buried. When Shackley became chief of the Western Hemisphere Division he put his close friend, Thomas Clines, in charge of Caribbean operations. Clines had worked for Shackley in Miami and together they had formed intimate relations with most of the anti-Castro Cuban terrorist/drug traffickers on the DEASOG payroll. Clines later worked in the Cuban Group as deputy to Medell's rabbi, Nestor Sanchez. Dirty-dozen member Vernon Goertz worked for Clines in Caracas while under DEACON cover.[38] All these CIA officers, and more, were part of Conein's parallel mechanism that used DEASOG as a cover.

Mattocks, under an alias, on behalf of DEACON I, set up the Cuban Businessman's Club, which was designed to improve relations between Cuban and American businessmen. It was a very clever and convenient cover. He also managed a CIA-connected Ford franchise in South Miami. Under these cover jobs he employed Watergate burglars Rolando Martinez and Bernard Barker. He also hired Cuban CIA officer Felix Rodriguez, with whom he had worked in Vietnam.[39] A Bay of Pigs veteran, Felix Rodriguez and his comrades Ricardo Chavez and Rafael "Chi Chi" Quintero (former employees of Manuel Artime) would become enmeshed in the Ed Wilson and Iran-Contra scandals with Ted Shackley and Tom Clines. It is suggested that Wilson, Shackley and Clines and their crazed exile Cuban henchmen carried forward the CIA-Mafia-Cuban assassination squad developed to kill Castro, and used it for both private and professional purposes.[40]

Mattocks replaced Medell as DEACON I's covert agent, and Medell introduced him to unscrupulous drug smuggler Guillermo Tabraue. Mattocks and Tabraue thereafter worked side by side developing "targets of opportunity" for the DEA, FBI, IRS, Customs and CIA. Under the July reorganization reporting was improved, and higher level traffickers were targeted.[41] All was going according to Conein's plan until Bob Simon, the professional interrogator who managed the Miami facet of the CIA's drug data base, the Interagency Narcotics Intelligence System, was found to be monitoring "a foreign terrorist organization" involved in drug trafficking. In a lawsuit against the Office of Personnel Management brought by CIA agents who joined the DEA, Simon stated that he had "to endure the tragic ordeal of burying a young daughter, brutally murdered by narcotic dealers in vengeance for his success."[42]

The murder of Simon's daughter by exile Cuban drug trafficker/terrorists sent shock waves through the DEA. As Mattocks explained, "It got bad when the Brigaders found out Simon was after them."[43] But there were no recriminations. None of the murderers were hunted down and arrested. Instead, Conein sent a directive to Michael Brom, the Agent-In-Charge of DEACON I, prohibiting DEACON I assets from reporting on domestic political affairs or terrorist activities.[44]

Meanwhile, Conein was having PR problems with DEACON III.

DEACON III: February -August 1974

ELI CHAVEZ MUSTERED OUT OF the 82nd Airborne and joined the CIA in 1967. He was sent to Laos in 1971, as a paramilitary officer working undercover as an operations officer with Air America. He served in Pakse, Savannahket, and Long Thien, and received the CIA's Intelligence Star for Valor, its highest honor, from William Colby on February 8, 1974. Another thing he did in Laos was destroy opium fields; on another occasion in Pakse he seized heroin aboard a Cambodian aircraft.[45]

DEA officers Ralph Frias and Robert Goe recruited Chavez and Nick Zapata (who had also trained and led special commando units in Laos) at CIA headquarters in 1973. Colby was directly involved. Unlike Mattocks, Chavez entered the DEA as a regular 1811 agent. He was introduced to Conein and, with Zapata, was assigned to DEACON III, which was aimed at smuggler Pedro Aviles Perez in Mexico, godfather of the next generation of Mexican smugglers. DEACON III was considered a top priority and prior to its implementation, DEA agents briefed the CIA about it. "The concept received CIA's endorsement with the proviso that DEA would be required to place all approved assets into the source registry and that unilateral operations would be coordinated with the CIA under NSCIDD-5, as revised September 15, 1958, and other applicable directives."[46] Among those briefed were: Assistant Secretary of State for Narcotic Matters Sheldon Vance, the CIA's Deputy Director of Operations, and numerous CIA division and station chiefs.

DEACON III was a big deal and the CIA played an integral role. Chavez was told that a White House Task Force under Howard Hunt had started the Aviles Perez case, and that Conein was involved on behalf of the CIA. The CIA part of the Task Force provided Chavez with photographs of the Aviles Perez compound in Mexico, from whence the trafficker shipped truckloads of marijuana to the US.[47]

CIA officer Barry Carew was also assigned to DEACON III. Carew had served under Andy Tartaglino's old friend, Tully Acampora, as an advisor to the special police in Saigon. In early 1973, Acampora and Tartaglino arranged for Carew to join the BNDD. Carew initially worked for Pete Scrocca in Miami, making small buys and busts, and hating every minute of it. When the DEA was created, Carew, who spoke Spanish and had served in South America before his transfer to Vietnam, was detailed to headquarters as an interpreter in the police training program. Belk was looking for DEASOG recruits and, after meeting with Robert Goe and John Warner, Carew was sent to work for Conein as his Latin American desk officer.[48]

DEACON III began in January 1974, when Chavez and Carew met "Rosa," an informant inside the Aviles Perez organization. In a day they trained Rosa how to collect information, use a camera, take undercover notes, and determine what information was useful. They coordinated their activities with Belk's staff aide on Mexico, Ralph Frias.

In February, Chavez met Goe and presented a plan (which also targeted the Leonsio Pina organization) and received operational funds. Chavez and Zapata traveled undercover to Mexico City as representatives of the North American Alarm and Fire Systems Company. They met in Mazatlan with Carew, who stayed at a nice hotel and played tennis every day, while Chavez and Zapata fumed in a "flea-bag motel." Finally, Rosa arranged for Chavez, posing as a buyer, to meet Perez. DEA chief John Bartels did not want to irritate his enforcement managers with a surprise bust of major proportions, so he instructed Carew, Chavez and Zapata to brief the DEA's regional office in Mexico City. The DEACON III agents met Robert Iman and Ed Heath at the Embassy. They had photographs and maps of Pina's house, and the names of his buyers in the US. But they caught the DEA agents off guard. As Carew recalled, "We go into Ed Heath's office and he says, "What are you doing here?"

Carew quickly found himself caught in the tug-of-war between the DEA's enforcement and intelligence divisions. According to Carew, Belk was powerful and wanted DEACON III to work, but Iman and the enforcement agents did not. They also suspected that Carew, Chavez and Zapata were part of a new CIA "shoofly" program. Then the unexpected happened. Intelligence analyst Joan Banister was at the meeting, and when the subject of "neutralizing" Perez and Pina came up, she took this to mean assassination. (Perez was killed in 1978). Not versed in the code of silence protocols of the good-old-boy network, she reported her suspicions to headquarters. To sabotage Belk, Conein and their CIA cohorts, enforcement officers at DEA headquarters gleefully leaked the report to Jack Anderson, who reported the story, raising the specter that the DEA was providing cover for a CIA assassination unit.[49]

When Carew complained, Heath rewarded him with a bad fitness report. It was "an uphill fight," Carew said wearily. The DEA didn't like former CIA officers and eventually Internal Affairs broke into Conein's safe house and bugged it. "Andy [Tartaglino] was on the way out," Carew explained, "and it didn't help to have been preceded by Logay. The DEA's leadership and management were inept and couldn't cope with [the CIA] problem."

There was also a racist angle to the demise of DEACON III: Conein treated Carew better than Chavez and Zapata, and called them "pepper-bellies" when they complained.[50] But African American, Hispanic, and female agents were no longer submitting to such insults, and several class action law suits were looming on the horizon.

The DEACON That Never Was

LOU DAVIS JOINED THE CIA in 1961 and served largely in Laos and Viet nam as a paramilitary officer. He had more than a few encounters with the drug trade. As he recalled, "In Laos we'd have evening meetings; the new kid would always say, 'I found a block of some gooey, sticky, black stuff in a poncho. What should I do with it?'"[51]

Like the other "Dirty Dozen" former CIA officers, Davis had experience in drug interdiction. One of his agents in Vientiane frequented the Corsican-owned bars and restaurants and learned that a French military officer was shipping heroin to Paris. Actually a SDECE officer, he was in Laos undercover as an instructor to the Lao Air Force. Davis notified Adrian Swain, then running the RIU for Fred Dick in Bangkok. Davis knew Swain, when Swain worked for the CIA in Pakse. When the plane with the Frenchman's heroin touched down in Bangkok on its way to Paris, the Thais, using a bomb scare as a pretext, searched the plane for the dope. None was found and the French colonel was allowed to flee, most likely, it was believed, because the operation had been blown by the Thai police.

As Conein explained to Davis when Davis joined the DEA, Nixon realized that most illegal drugs came from outside the country. So he pulled together all the agencies with arrest authority to address the problem, but they spent their time fighting each other, rather than the drug traffickers. Having no place else to go, Nixon went to Colby (who had managed the CIA's Phoenix "assassination" Program in Vietnam) and Colby sent Conein to the BNDD for "one last fling."

Conein set up DEASOG to do Phoenix-style jobs overseas: the type where a paramilitary soldier breaks into a house, takes a trafficker's drugs, and slits his throat. In other words, the people running the war on drugs were going to use CIA methods. For example, they were going to "neutralize" (a Phoenix term) the police chief in Acapulco if he was the local drug boss. When they couldn't neutralize the boss, they'd bomb his labs or use psychological warfare to make him look like he was a DEA informant, so his own people would kill him. The DEASOG people "would be breaking the law," Davis observed, "but they didn't have arrest powers overseas anyway."

As part of this plan, Conein's recruits were to go to different countries under diplomatic cover and target people the police couldn't get — the prime minister's son or other protected people who were ring leaders. International Intelligence Division Chief John Warner proposed placing NIOs in Caracas, Quito, Lima, Santiago, Mexico City and Bogotá.[52] Conein in a February 1975 memorandum noted there were eight NIOs and three in training; six had been deployed, including one in Michigan, three in Miami, one in El Paso, and one in Hong Kong. The remainder were to go to Chiang Mai, Bangkok, Santiago, Bogotá, La Paz, Quito, Islamabad, Paris, Frankfurt, Brussels and San Ysidro. Conein envisioned 19 foreign and 6 domestic NIOs for 1976, and 50 operating worldwide by 1977.[53]

But the "Dirty Dozen" tactics created too much controversy and the DEA lawyers ultimately said "Stop!" The war between Bartels and Tartaglino was commencing, and Belk was getting nervous. To lower his profile, he instructed Conein to use the Dirty Dozen in some more subtle fashion. "Belk tried to be tough," Davis notes. "He came in, sat us down, and said, 'You're not going to put us out of business.' He was afraid that our loyalty was to Conein, which it was."

According to Davis, crafty Lou Conein publicly gave pep talks, but privately he mistrusted DEA agents. He could not see the incentive in making a career out of drug law enforcement. If they won the war, Conein quipped, they would put themselves (as Belk feared) out of business.

When Davis arrived in Washington he was assigned to headquarters with Bob Medell. The dirty-dozen occupied the tenth floor of the LaSalle Building, eight blocks from DEA headquarters. Having known Conein in Vietnam, Davis was trusted with a key. For the first few months he and Medell trained Latino agents in New York and sent them into Mexico and Argentina.

The NIOs were all supposed to be sent overseas, many to Pakistan, but few went anywhere after the DEACON III Mexican "assassination" flap.[54] Davis was destined for Belgium but was sent to the three-man Chicago RIU. He described the RIU as a place to dump the sick, the lame and the lazy; not a place for casemakers. Davis arrived with $96,000 and an operational plan aimed at Jamie Herrera in Durango. According to Davis, "Herrera was the whipping boy for Chicago DEA; he kept 200 agents occupied." Herrera had a real estate business and Davis's plan was to hire a retired hispanic Special Forces soldier to rent a bar that Herrera owned. The Green Beret would then buy a bus and use it to run dope from Herrera's bar into Durango. The bus would stop in Amarillo at a motel the DEA secretly rented. DEA agents would monitor the rooms and recruit couriers who would then penetrate Herrera's organization. Davis planed to recoup the DEA's front money by seizing Herrera's property.

But the plan was rejected and Davis was isolated and ignored for the ten years he was in Chicago. One reason was that everyone thought he was an undercover inspector. Davis described Chicago as "completely disorganized." There was no cooperation between intelligence and enforcement and the agents competed fiercely among themselves. They would even steal cases from one another. Agents drove 30 miles to work in bumper-to-bumper traffic and, after fighting each other for cars, were sent right back out. They drank all the time. A guy who bragged about spending $5,500 on drinks for big shots was made deputy regional director.

"Chicago was a bottomless pit of corruption," he said. "The big dealers lived in the suburbs. The local cops knew and could have mounted operations with the DEA, but instead they learned how to kick in doors and grab as many small fry as possible to run up the numbers without putting themselves out of business. This way drones who couldn't write a clear sentence catapulted into leadership jobs."

The Assassination Stigma

WES DYCKMAN JOINED THE CIA in 1962 and served in Vietnam 1964-1966 as a liaison to the police special branch. He worked closely with Lou Conein, who arranged for his job with the DEA in May 1974. Dyckman started out by running errands for Conein. A retired CIA Technical Services guy had a printing shop near the PGA hall of fame at Pinehurst Country Club. He fashioned phony driver's licenses and

IDs for the dirty-dozen in cahoots with the DMV in New York and Virginia. Dyckman worked out of the safe house on 14th Street.[55]

As soon as the DEASOG group was assembled, Dyckman recalled, Jack Anderson blew the DEACON III operation in Mexico. Anderson said a DEA unit was formed to commit assassinations of major drug dealers. Anderson, according to Dyckman, claimed the CIA was using the DEA for cover. And, according to Dyckman, there was a period when "we were piggybacking slots." But there was no merit to the assassination claims, although every one of the dirty dozen was under scrutiny by Internal Affairs "for the rest of his career."

According to inspector Luke Benson, the focus was Nick Zapata, aka "the Fat Mexican Assassin." A polygraph exam of Zapata led to Dealey Plaza.[56]

Conein was another Benson target. Described as a hard drinker, Conein became a caricature of himself. Colby had nearly fired him from the CIA for getting drunk and dropping something off the roof of a hotel in Saigon. Some say it was flowerpots; others say it was a North Vietnamese agent. His antics continued after his transfer to the DEA, where he rented the safe house in the LaSalle Building from John Muldoon. A CIA officer who had served with Conein in Vietnam, Muldoon operated a private investigation firm as a CIA front. He was at the time, "a representative of the CIA."[57] Muldoon's company occupied the floor above the DEASOG safe house, which concerned DEA inspectors.

Strange things happened at the safe house. The very public scandals began in May 1974, when Muldoon introduced Conein to Michael Morrisey, an attorney and salesman for B. R. Fox Laboratories, a company he had formed with Bernie Spindel, a convicted wireman who had worked for Jimmy Hoffa. Morrisey was licensed to sell CIA bugging equipment and had obtained a security clearance through his former employer, the Halliburton Company. Morrisey met Muldoon through work he did for Halliburton at CIA interrogation centers in Vietnam.[58] Muldoon had managed the construction of the CIA's provincial interrogation centers in Vietnam.[59] Morrisey, for his part, had developed the Astro line of surveillance equipment and explosive devices sold by Fox, and in May 1974, through Muldoon, he made a pitch to Conein at the LaSalle safe house. Conein reportedly passed on the bombs, but did buy $4,760 worth of "sanitized" surveillance equipment for his DEASOG team.[60]

Another denizen of the LaSalle safe house was Mitchell Werbell. One of Conein's comrades from the OSS, Werbell had been a security consultant to Rafael Trujillo and Fulgencio Batista. He had participated in the Bay of Pigs and socialized with Watergate burglar Frank Sturgis and other DEACON assets. His claim to fame, however, was developing the Ingram M-10 silenced submachine pistol preferred by Latin American death squads and drug traffickers, including Sicilia Falcon. Werbell was a deniable asset used by Conein for parallel CIA operations. He certainly had the right connections.

In 1973, Werbell tried to sell Robert Vesco 2,000 Ingram M-10s.[61] Tom Richardson, the LA stockbroker who had hired the BNDD agents to sweep Vesco's house in New Jersey, had helped Vesco establish a factory in Costa Rica for manufacturing Werbell's guns. Meanwhile, DEASOG was targeting Cubans and organized crime figures in Costa Rica and New Jersey, and Vesco (a native of New Jersey) was living in Costa Rica surrounded by Cuban exiles. According to author Henrik Kruger, the CIA had forced Vesco into the guns and narcotics business in 1971, while he was in prison in Switzerland for defrauding shareholders in his company Overseas Investors Services. While in prison, Vesco met Fernand Legros, an associate of Yousef Beidas, Andre Labay and Christian David. Legros and Vesco were "reunited" in the Bahamas in 1973.[62]

Meanwhile, erstwhile CIA asset and DEACON target Santo Trafficante arrived in Costa Rica in January 1974 and, like Vesco, enjoyed safe haven thanks to CIA asset President Figueres whose son Marti — famous for forming a death squad with DEACON asset Carlos Rumbault — bought automatic weapons from Werbell. Marti was Vesco's business partner and pal. All of the above positioned Werbell to spy for Conein and enjoy a get out of jail free card, which he needed. Apart from smuggling marijuana, Werbell and Walter Mackem in April 1974 trained mercenaries for an invasion (later called off) of the island of Abaco in the Bahamas. Their plan was to convert the island into another Paradise Island. Initially on the Far East desk at the SIO, CIA officer Walter Joseph Mackem (another friend of Conein's from Vietnam) was fired from the DEA after it was discovered that he had taken classified material to Conein's safe house and given it to Muldoon.[63]

John Warner posed the obvious question about Mackem and Werbell: "How did these guys get in?" The answer is quite simple. George Belk covered for Conein in exchange for the chance to make cases. That egomaniacal impulse hurt the DEA. As Paul Knight explained, "intelligence gathering people as a function are okay; but as an operating unit it's a bad idea. When Belk started his CIA collaboration, those people were assigned to "the awkward squad" [the Dirty Dozen]. They led him astray. Conein was one of them. Conein had a parallel operation and was trying to dismantle the Corsicans using Lagattuta."[64]

Knight was bemused by their ineptitude. Others were angered. John Bacon fought DEASOG as "harmful and futile. Intelligence collection and law enforcement are antithetical," he insists. "Only a rare person can do it" because legally "an agent is bound so tightly that he can't operate and is tempted to breech, or bend, or ignore the law. It opens the door to corruption."[65]

Operation Croupier

IN APRIL 1974, WHILE MITCH Werbell and Walter Mackem were planning to conquer Abaco Island, their patron, Luigi Conein, was sending undercover ace Santo Bario to the Bahamas to identify croupiers suspected of drug smuggling at the Paradise Island casino. Conein worked on "Operation Croupier" with Phil Smith, the project's mastermind. As we know, Smith's friend Robert Peloquin was part owner of Intertel, the company that provided security to the Paradise Island casino. Peloquin had offered Smith a job with Intertel. Former Customs agent Fenalin Richards, another part owner of Intertel, made the same offer to George Belk.[66]

Peloquin feared that Paradise Island croupiers were involved in drug smuggling; and as a favor for their friend, Smith and Belk decided the DEA should investigate. Bario traveled to Nassau in mid-August 1974 posing as a high-roller, as he had done during Operation Silver Dollar at Howard Hughes' Frontier Hotel in Las Vegas. Conein's trusted agent Bob Medell carried messages from Conein to Bario. According to Medell, at one point Bario told him that Smith was playing a double game. Conein in turn warned Medell to beware of what he said to Smith, on the assumption it might get back to Vesco.[67] Conein, it seems, had learned through DEACON assets that Vesco was planning to use his profits from a drug deal he was financing for Conrad Bouchard to buy the Paradise Island gambling complex from Resorts International.

A Smith-Vesco connection was never proven. But, as happened in Silver Dollar, Bario lost all his front money gambling at the Paradise Island tables. For some unknown reason, Conein asked Bario to rewrite his final report and omit any mention of Intertel or gambling losses. When Bario refused, Conein rewrote the report himself, using his own (or someone else's) money to cover Bario's losses.[68]

For not playing along with Smith and Conein, Bario was transferred to Mexico. In 1978 he was arrested for trafficking in narcotics and, while incarcerated in a Texas jail, slipped into a coma and died. Some people felt it was no accident. Indeed, something untoward was going on behind the scenes and in 1975, Croupier, Silver Dollar and DEASOG would become the subject of Congressional inquiries.

Meanwhile, in July 1974, the House Judiciary Committee took the momentous step of recommending that Nixon be impeached and removed from office, primarily for misusing the CIA for political purposes. Nixon had done exactly that, and in August 1974 he resigned. His replacement, Gerald Ford, reconfirmed the CIA's narcotic intelligence collection arrangement with DEA.

With the DEA on the verge of a nervous breakdown, Belk and Mark Moore in October 1974 wrote a memorandum declaring that: "The intelligence techniques used by the Central Intelligence Agency preclude the use of this type of intelligence in criminal proceedings. There are at least two major prosecutions pending which may have to be aborted because of the possible disclosure of CIA involvement."[69] But the CIA continued to have its way.

22

THE SERPENT IN MY GARDEN

IT WAS INEVITABLE THAT JOHN Bartels and Acting Chief Inspector George Brosan would clash. Devoutly religious, Brosan was dedicated to the cause of truth and justice. His father had been a cop on the beat in Queens, his mother a maid at the same police station. Following in their humble footsteps, Brosan joined the NYPD and served in Harlem. In 1962 he switched to Customs, first as an inspector and later as an agent in the Joint Task Force in New York. There he came to know the freewheeling FBN agents who were cozy with fun-loving John Bartels. He knew what they were capable of, and on Andy Tartaglino's advice, he went after them.[1]

Brosan, all on his own, initially got on Bartels' bad side by pursuing two Watergate related investigations. The first concerned Silver Dollar, in which the BNDD, through Intertel, did an investigation at Howard Hughes' Frontier Hotel. If the reader will recall, some people thought the Watergate break-in was staged to see if the Democrats knew about any illegal campaign contributions Hughes may have made to Nixon. Brosan's second investigation was also Watergate related and involved a probe of the BNDD agents who swept Robert Vesco's house while he was being investigated by the SEC for making an illegal contribution to the Nixon campaign.[2]

In addition, Brosan also upset Bartels by preparing a case against Frankie Waters. The case was based on Charlie McDonnell's allegation that Waters had sold him a pound of pilfered French Connection case heroin. Bartels was afraid that Waters would flip and point prosecutors at former FBN agents in senior DEA positions. But again, at Tartaglino's urging, Brosan pressed ahead. He studied the thirty-five unresolved cases that Fuller and Ingersoll had buried, including allegations against (among others) Bill Durkin, George Belk, and Phil Smith.[3]

The Tartaglino-Brosan alliance unnerved Bartels, and when they petitioned him for seven more inspectors, he refused, fearing they would use the extra forces to pursue Tartaglino's old enemies.[4] Forced to make do with only nine inspectors at headquarters, Brosan put Inspector Tom Cash on the explosive William Durkin case.[5] Durkin had been accused of covering up agent abuses in New York in 1961; of being corrupted by the Nagelbergs — the infamous husband-wife drug trafficking duo; and of taking money from a drug trafficker and falsifying an informant payment receipt in 1956.[6] Inspector Cash, a former Customs agent with no love for the old FBN "Purple Gang," found corroborating information in at least one instance.[7]

In early September 1974, Brosan told Bartels about his integrity investigations, and the battle royal began.[8] DEA agents started choosing up sides, with the virtuous few feeling it was a matter of following proper procedure, and the silent majority feeling that Brosan had gone too far. Then Bartels sank himself.

The Promuto Affair

IN JANUARY 1974, DETECTIVE CARL Shoffler of the Washington, DC Intelligence Squad followed arms trafficker William Westerlund to an alley near Fran O'Brien's nightclub. Shoffler watched from the shadows while Westerlund displayed an array of suits to a group of men. Famous for having arrested the Watergate burglars, Shoffler approached the men while they were trying on the suits. One of them, to Shoffler's surprise, flashed DEA credentials and asked, "What's the problem, officer?" Shoffler said it seemed strange that grown men were trying on suits from the trunk of a car at night. (He might have added that it was strange for a DEA officer to be consorting with a known felon.) Then he took a close look at the DEA officer's credentials. The man was Bartels' deputy public relations officer, Vincent L. Promuto.[9]

A former Washington Redskins football player and ODALE prosecutor in New Jersey, Promuto had gotten his ODALE job at the request of Redskins owner Edward Bennett Williams (who at one time represented Robert Vesco and, at another, hired Intertel to investigate Watergate) through influential Myles Ambrose.[10]

Vince Promuto was no stranger to Carl Shoffler. He had first appeared on Shoffler's radar screen in 1969, when it was alleged that Promuto had relations with an associate of Joe Nesline, the Mafia boss in DC.[11] Shoffler checked around and found that Promuto's uncle owned a waste disposal company in New York and was connected to Mafioso Tony Salerno. Promuto's name also popped up during investigations of illegal gambling.[12]

Shoffler bided his time, while Promuto's luck ran out. Three things happened. The first occurred in May 1974, when an informant told Shoffler that Promuto had tipped off the owner of Fran O'Brien's nightclub that a cab driver named Smitty was an informant for the DEA.[13] Then in July, by cruel coincidence, Brosan and Cash saw Promuto and Bartels at Dulles Airport with a prostitute later identified as Diane De Vito. Employed at the Alibi Room in Las Vegas, De Vito had been arrested in 1973 for possession of marijuana in San Diego. The third and most damning incident occurred on August 9, 1974, when an informant told Shoffler that Promuto was consorting with a drug dealer from Laredo at Fran O'Brien's nightclub, where Bartels, Durkin and Promuto often drank after work.[14]

Shoffler dutifully called the DEA's Washington office and relayed this information to Agent John F. Arntz, who immediately called Dennis Dayle, the acting agent in charge. A Purple Gang member of the 33rd Degree, Dayle first called the regional director in Baltimore, Irving Swank, and then his old friend from Chicago, Bill Durkin. Although none of the agents put any of Shoffler's charges in writing — in violation of the inspection's manual — word got around, and Bartels and the Purple Gang began to plot their separate courses of action.[15]

Fate lent them a helping hand, for Andy Tartaglino was out of town investigating the August 5, 1974 collapse of the DEA headquarters building in Miami. A two-story building with a parking garage on top, the building collapsed due to inferior materials used when it was built, prior to the Second World War. Seven people were killed and many injured. Bill Logay and Dave Westrate played central roles in the rescue operation. That terrible tragedy eclipsed all other DEA business for days. To some, it was an omen of the ruination to come.

After two weeks, having received no feedback from the DEA, Shof-fler sent his "Promuto Report" to Assistant US Attorney Donald E. Campbell. Meanwhile, Promuto blithely went about his business and on August 25, attended a mob wedding at Mama Bellosi's in DC. Joe Nesline was there.[16] Back from Miami, Tartaglino sent another in a series of memos to Bartels requesting more inspectors and resources for Brosan.[17] Inspectors were falling behind and could not perform all their tasks, he said, adding that "the reputation of the entire agency was at stake."[18]

Bartels gave him two secretaries ... and Tartaglino did a slow burn.

Three weeks after Shoffler notified DEA Agent Arntz, William Durkin reported the Promuto allegations to Acting Chief Inspector Brosan.[19] As Durkin and his Purple Gang cronies knew, Bartels, Pro-muto and Jack Cusack had recently left for Europe and would not return until September 16. Brosan sensed he was being blindsided, but he didn't realize how many shocks were yet to come. He had no idea, for example, that Bartels had hired Dr. Mark Moore to form a management study group that had, among other tasks, the job of evaluating the Office of Inspections. Moore would get access to all of Brosan's files and keep Bartels informed of Brosan's progress on his integrity investigations.[20]

On September 10, after he finally obtained Detective Shoffler's report listing the Promuto allegations, Brosan consulted Tartaglino. It was the first time they had seen the allegations and, naturally, they wondered why it had taken 21 days for the allegations to reach Bro-san. The scales began to fall from their eyes when Brosan asked Assis-tant US Attorney Campbell why *he*, Campbell, had not informed him. In response, Campbell said that he had told his boss, US Attorney Earl Silbert, and that Silbert had said that the Promuto matter should be brought directly to Bartels, not to Brosan.[21] Earl Silbert, notably, was a Republican Party political hack famous for shielding Egil Krogh from the Watergate grand jury. It was Silbert who had called John Dean and said the Bailley prostitution case had the potential to embar-rass Nixon. Silbert had also received the same Intramural scholarship to Harvard that Bartels had received. Silbert liked Bartels so much that he decided not to tell Brosan about Shoffler's report.[22] Instead, Silbert suggested that Bartels tell Vince Promuto to stay out of Fran O'Brien's bar.[23]

But Bartels had other ideas. Rather than discipline Promuto, Bar-tels instructed Associate Chief Counsel Robert Richardson to contact

Geoffrey Sheppard at the Ford White House and recommend that Promuto be promoted to deputy administrator of the DEA, replacing the acting deputy administrator ... Andy Tartaglino.[24]

Brosan and Tartaglino knew that Promuto was not living up to the minimum standards of the "Employee Integrity" section of the inspection manual.[25] But with Campbell and Silbert's actions, they realized that a conspiracy was brewing at the Justice Department. Thus, while Bartels was in Europe, Brosan exercised his judgment and assigned Tom Cash the job of investigating Shoffler's allegations about Promuto. Meanwhile, Tartaglino confronted Bill Durkin. Why, Tartaglino asked him, didn't you tell *me* about the allegations? Durkin coolly replied that he had relayed them to Counsel Richardson and Bartels' executive assistant, Bruce Jensen. He said that if they felt Tartaglino should have known, they would have told him. Durkin added that there was no evidence that Promuto was guilty of anything. Then he turned and walked away ... and Tartaglino's slow burn started to sizzle.[26]

By the time Bartels returned from Europe, Cash had finished his investigation of the Promuto allegations. On September 17, Brosan confronted Bartels with the unhappy results. Brosan said that Promuto, as deputy chief of Public Affairs, was briefed on big cases before the arrests were made. Then he said there was an allegation that Promuto was leaking classified information to known criminals; and that Promuto had been seen with Diane De Vito, who was listed in DEA files as an associate of Gerald LeCompte, a dealer shipping cocaine from Laredo to DC. Brosan said there were three things Bartels could do: let Promuto resign, fire him, or do nothing.[27] The choice was easy and even DEA Counsel Richardson asked Bartels to persuade Promuto to resign.[28]

Bartels refused. Instead, he asked Special Assistant Thomas E. Durkin in Newark (no relation to Bill Durkin) to come to Washington to personally handle the Promuto case. His executive assistant, Bruce Jensen, advised him not to do it. As Jensen recalled, "I told him, 'This can cost you your job.'"[29]

Instead it cost Jensen his job. Looking for a more pliant assistant, Bartels replaced Jensen with Dan Casey. And Tom Durkin proceeded to work his magic.

Tom Durkin

TOM DURKIN WAS A LAWYER in New Jersey whom Ingersoll had made a "Special Adviser" on drug conspiracy cases. This was a shameless pretext, as Durkin had no law enforcement experience. In reality, Durkin provided legal services for Bill Durkin, Dan Casey, Jerry Jensen, and other agents purchasing homes upon their transfer to New York.[30] With Ingersoll's blessings, Durkin also arranged luncheons for foreign officials on behalf of his client, Joseph Kahn, owner of Sea Train International, a freight forwarding company. When Spain's Minister of Interior came to New York with the head of the Spanish Narcotics Police, Attorney General Kleindienst approved the use of BNDD funds to entertain him at the Wall Street Club. How the Spaniards reciprocated is not known.[31]

Bartels retained Tom Durkin in more sinister capacities. In one instance, Bartels asked Durkin to torpedo a Congressional investigation into the Vesco sweep scandal.[32] To take the heat off the agents involved, Durkin cleverly suggested that Bartels ask the US Attorney in Los Angeles to convene a federal grand jury on the sweeps. The compliant Republican US Attorney complied, and issued federal subpoenas to the agents who did the sweeps. This perfectly legal act sabotaged the subcommittee's investigation by providing "use" immunity to the agents! [33]

Tom Durkin may also have had a personal reason for sinking the Vesco sweep investigation. He and Vesco were from the same town in New Jersey and, according to Tartaglino, had a "bad connection." For all these reasons, Tartaglino felt the same way about Tom Durkin as he did about Promuto: they were given access to highly classified information without having had background checks, and may have been mishandling that information.[34]

The Xerox Incident

AT A SEPTEMBER 17, 1974 meeting, Bartels expressed his anger at Brosan and Richardson for suggesting that Promuto be fired. Bartels felt that Promuto should have an opportunity to explain himself. Brosan, at the 17 September meeting, gave Bartels a four page report alleging, among other things, that Promuto falsified travel vouchers to cover up his trysts with Diane De Vito.[35] Executive secretary Elsbeth Kerr made a copy of Brosan's report. The machine she used was located near three offices belonging to Bartels, Promuto and Brosan. Kerr may have accidentally left a copy in the machine, or else someone took a copy from the safe. However it happened, the report reached Tom Durkin prior to his conversation with Vince Promuto.[36]

To insulate himself, Bartels placed deputy assistant administrator for enforcement John Lund (a former Customs inspector) and Counsel Robert Richardson in the chain of command between himself and Brosan. Richardson and Lund became, in effect, Brosan's bosses.[37] Bartels then instructed Tom Durkin to interview Promuto at a nearby Ramada Inn about Brosan's report, which Durkin did on September 24 or 25, 1974. Immediately thereafter, Durkin informed Bartels that Promuto was guilty of no criminal actions and that the sex charges against him were based on a false premise: Promuto said it was Candy Kruse, not Diane De Vito, whom Promuto and Bartels were seen with at Dulles airport in July.[38]

Unfortunately for Bartels, Associate Chief Counsel Richardson had seen Bartels with De Vito in San Francisco earlier in the year — which meant that Bartels could be tied to De Vito, even if Cash and Brosan had seen him with Kruse at Dulles airport.[39] Aware that Bartels was grasping at straws, Richardson advised that the inspections staff question Promuto under oath. Bartels rejected the idea and, to establish his authority once and for all, declared that the Promuto investigation was being handled incorrectly. On the advice of former Customs inspector John Lund and "Special Advisor" Tom Durkin, Bartels directed Richardson to have Brosan 1) submit written questions for Promuto to take home over the weekend and answer on Monday; and 2) submit a written report by October 2.[40]

Richardson delivered the orders to Brosan verbally. Brosan argued that the orders were irregular and premature. Secretly, his feelings were even stronger: he and Tartaglino felt that Bartels was covering up Promuto's misdeeds in violation of a federal law that prohibits obstruction of justice.[41] What if new suspicions arose, Brosan asked Richardson? Too bad, he was told. Bartels did not want new avenues of investigation to be opened up.[42]

This was not surprising, considering that Bartels had something to hide and was obstructing the Promuto investigation to protect himself as well as his friend.

On October 1, Bartels summoned George Brosan to his office to brief Mark Moore, Dan Casey, John Lund, Robert Richardson and Andy Tartaglino on the Promuto investigation. At this meeting, Brosan and Tartaglino strongly objected to the tactic of submitting written questions to Promuto.[43] Tartaglino said that Promuto should never have been notified of the investigation and that if proper procedures had been followed, DEA inspectors would have tailed Promuto

and watched him to see what they could uncover.[44] Knowing Tartaglino was right, Lund and Richardson asked to be removed from the
investigation over the issue.[45]

With his executive staff (minus Moore) in revolt, Bartels, at the
October 1 meeting, asked who among them had originated the idea
of providing Promuto with a written questionnaire.[46] When neither
Richardson nor Lund reminded him that it was his decision, Bartels
passed authority for the investigation back to Brosan. He instructed
Brosan and Tartaglino to question Promuto, but with the proviso that
they not open up any new lines of inquiry. In preparation they asked
Casey for a copy of Promuto's responses to Tom Durkin's questions,
but Casey never complied.[47]

Richardson, by this time, had already passed Brosan's questionnaire to Promuto. Promuto was not placed under oath and, having
seen the questionnaire beforehand, he knew how to skirt the trick
questions. In one glaring example, he simply did not say if he had
been with prostitute Diane De Vito in Salt Lake, Las Vegas, and San
Francisco.[48] Promuto then gave his answers to Lund, who gave them
to Bartels. From Bartels' perspective, the questionnaire provided him
with a handy exit strategy in case Tartaglino and Brosan opened the
dreaded new avenue of investigation.[49]

The Cover-Up

PRESSURED BY BARTELS TO CLOSE the investigation quickly, Tartaglino and Brosan grilled Promuto on October 8 about the trips he
took with Bartels and their encounters with Diane De Vito. They
asked Promuto about his association with shady characters at Fran
O'Brien's, including cocaine trafficker Gerald LeCompte. Promuto's
replies led Tartaglino and Brosan to conclude that he and Bartels were
engaged in a cover-up.[50] They sent their conclusions to the Civil Service Commission for a final decision, and were devastated when, on 6
November 1974, Civil Service Officer Harry Gastley ruled that Promuto should be admonished, but not fired.[51]

Feeling vindicated, Bartels asked Mark Moore to write a memo
closing the Promuto investigation. Moore wisely demurred, saying
he was too busy, so Bartels gave the unenviable job to Tartaglino.
Adding insult to injury, he told Tartaglino to fire Brosan. Tartaglino
agreed to write the memo but refused to fire his friend. In the letter he
facetiously asked if Tom Durkin was Promuto's lawyer or the DEA's.
He also asked why Bartels would not turn Durkin's report over to

Brosan.[52] Bartels responded at a 13 November meeting with Brosan by bragging that he had known about Diane De Vito all along, and that he was present when Promuto met with gamblers and felons at Fran O'Brien's. Then he told Brosan that his services as acting chief inspector were no longer required.[53]

When Brosan reported this to Andy Tartaglino, Tartaglino reached the end of his rope. That evening he complained to Glen E. Pommerening, the assistant attorney general for administration at the Department of Justice, that Bartels was interfering in the Promuto case.[54] Pommerening told Tartaglino to write a memorandum listing his complaints, which Tartaglino did the following day. Tartaglino's memo ended up on the desk of Deputy Attorney General Laurence H. Silberman, a rabid Republican who promptly handed the "Request for Investigation" memo to Henry Petersen, Chief of the Criminal Division, with instructions to launch an investigation. Petersen was a loyal Republican, and the man Nixon had chosen to replace Archibald Cox as the Watergate special prosecutor after the Saturday Night Massacre. For the sake of appearances, Petersen instructed Associate Deputy Attorney General Michael Spector to call Bartels and read him his rights.[55]

On 21 November 1974, upon arriving at New York's Kennedy Airport from Jamaica, Bartels was informed by a DEA agent that Petersen was trying to reach him. Bartels called Petersen and was told by Spector that he was the target of an investigation. "I was given my rights," Bartels recalled, by a deputy assistant attorney general who said, 'Tartaglino says you're corrupt.'"[56]

Although a blow for Bartels, Spector's call was hardly a surprise. Indeed, behind the scenes, Henry Petersen had called Bartels a week earlier, right after Tartaglino's "Request for Investigation" memo had arrived at the Justice Department. During this conversation, Petersen had assured his close friend, John Bartels, that he would not investigate Tartaglino's charges. In fact, Petersen recused the entire criminal division from the case, and instead told Silberman to get the FBI to do the investigation.[57]

Enter the FBI

A FORTY-YEAR OLD "NEO-CON" BEFORE the term existed, Laurence Silberman would endear himself forever to the ultra-conservatives on December 31, 1974, when he and CIA director William Colby discussed how best to diffuse legal questions raised by the exposure of the

CIA's "family jewels" in the *New York Times*. Silberman also showed his knack for dissembling on behalf of the right wing by defending Bartels and attacking Tartaglino during the Jackson Hearings in 1975, as chronicled in the next chapter. Silberman eventually became an advisor to candidate Ronald Reagan and, in 1980, while President Carter was desperately trying to negotiate the release of American hostages in Tehran, Silberman took part in a meeting between Reagan campaign advisors and Iranian government officials. At that meeting Silberman rejected the Iranian offer of a settlement.[58] For playing his part in the "October Surprise" that delayed the release of the 52 hostages until after Reagan's inauguration, Silberman was made a federal judge. Later he served President George W. Bush as part of the cabal that directed the propaganda campaign that led to the war in Iraq. He was rewarded with a seat on the Foreign Intelligence Surveillance Court of Review, a body that hears appeals in matters of intelligence gathering. On June 11, 2008, George W Bush awarded Silberman the Presidential Medal of Freedom, the highest civilian honor granted by the government of the United States.

Described as acerbic and arrogant, Silberman in early December 1974 deputized FBI agents Bill D. Williams and Edward D. Hegarty and told them to conduct an administrative inquiry into Andy Tartaglino's allegations about John Bartels.[59] It was the first time a Justice Department official had used FBI agents as private investigators. Insofar as the FBI agents turned the inquiry upside down and used it to investigate Tartaglino, it was a purely political decision meant to protect Republican appointees Bartels and US Attorney Earl Silbert, who had sat on Detective Shoffler's original report, and with whom Bartels consulted regularly during Silberman's inquiry.[60] Obviously, the tide had turned. The FBI agents were not interested in Promuto, only in Tartaglino's motives for accusing Bartels of impeding the Promuto investigation, and in mistakes made by Tartaglino and Brosan at the Office of Inspections.[61] The FBI agents interviewed Tartaglino, Brosan, Bartels, Richardson, Pat Fuller and Tom Durkin. But only Tartaglino and Brosan were required to submit a written report.[62]

Tartaglino had been fighting the FBI all his professional life and was not intimidated. On the contrary, he used his December 11, memorandum to the FBI as an opportunity to expand his charges to include the murder of informants in New York by federal agents![63] In connection with those crimes, he cited unresolved cases against high-ranking DEA agents like Bill Durkin. Faced with such explosive material, the

FBI agents quickly completed their review. They didn't read Detective Shoffler's report and, as implied in Silberman's charge, they found that Bartels and Promuto had committed no criminal violations and no obstruction of justice. Their only conclusion was that the DEA's Office of Inspections was in shambles.[64]

Silberman's use of the FBI to exonerate Bartels and Promuto, and blame Tartaglino and Brosan for the DEA's problems, gave Bartels all the encouragement he needed. Routine mail to Tartaglino ceased and on December 20, a teletype was sent to all DEA offices announcing that Tartaglino and Brosan had been relieved of their duties. Bartels' executive assistant Dan Casey told Tartaglino that he had been reassigned to a task force at the Law Enforcement Assistance Administration. Brosan was told to write a training manual in a barren room with a grey metal desk, a straight-backed chair, trash pail and telephone in the basement of the DEA building.[65]

Not everyone at Justice was a fanatical Republican, and some disgruntled person sent a letter to Senator Henry M. Jackson (D-WA), chairman of the Permanent Subcommittee on Investigations under the Committee on Government Operations. The letter recited Tartaglino's allegations to Petersen. Smelling political blood, Jackson would soon convene hearings into the allegations.

In a vast understatement, Tartaglino said it was "unfortunate" that his letter to Jackson was leaked. "What was the motivation," he asked. "Was it to achieve justice? In the process, it hurt a lot of people ... a lot of young people."[66]

As Brosan recalled, "This began even more investigations, and the death threats."[67]

Once Jackson became involved, Bartels went ballistic. He kept thinking about all the time and energy that had been wasted on the Promuto investigation. Fifteen inspectors had worked on the case; they had checked financial records, credit ratings, telephone calls, travel vouchers, bank accounts, and mortgages. Three subpoenas had been issued. And now there were going to be Congressional Hearings! To Bartels, it seemed like Tartaglino wanted to destroy the DEA. So he and Silberman, who characterized Tartaglino as "vicious," intensified their attacks.[68] On January 16, Silberman issued a press release claiming Tartaglino's allegations were without foundation.[69] Silberman then arranged for Tartaglino's reassignment to a DEA task force.[70]

There was more to come. In a January 16, 1975 column in The *Washington Post* titled "Internecine War at DEA Command," Jack

Anderson said that Bartels' underlings were using integrity investigations to blackmail one another. Cases were kept open as a management tool to keep officials in line for excessive drinking and loose
morals. Anderson knew all the dirty details, because Bartels, with Silberman's permission, had allowed one of Anderson's aides to review a
copy of the Promuto investigation file in Casey's office! A *Washington
Star* article published the same day got into allegations against specific
individuals.[71]

Indeed, bringing the battle to the light of day, in the press and at
the Jackson Committee, nearly destroyed the DEA.

The Return of Burke and Logay

IN JANUARY 1975, SENATOR JACKSON started his investigation of the
DEA. His chief investigator, Philip R. Manuel, was a 20-year agent
with the army's super secret 902nd military intelligence group.[72]
Manuel and his assistant, William Gallinaro, interviewed everyone
involved in the conflict in preparation for hearings that began in June
1975. George Brosan alone was "interrogated" by Manuel some two-
dozen times on Capitol Hill.[73]

Bartels geared up for the Hearings by choosing to replace Brosan
with Phillip R. Smith, "as my personal representative."[74] Bartels claims
not to have known Smith, or that Smith was Tartaglino's arch enemy.
He said he forgot why "his advisors" picked Smith to head inspections. According to Tartaglino, they picked Smith not just to remove
the cloud that hung over Purple Gang veterans like Durkin and Belk,
but to destroy both Bartels and Tartaglino. Smith's first move in this
direction was to take Brosan loyalist Tom Cash off the Promuto investigation, and in February 1975 he reassigned it to apprentice torpedoes Terry Burke and William Logay, under the guidance of veteran
Inspector Edward Stamm. He gave them six weeks to complete the
investigation.

Smith called this author while undergoing treatment for lung can-
cer. He would not answer questions about anything other than his
investigation of Promuto. Smith has several children in law enforcement, including at least one in the DEA, and wanted to set the record
straight on their behalf. Smith said unknown people came to him.
They had been approached by agents in Tartaglino's camp and told to
"play ball' or "the problem wouldn't go away."[75]

Smith refused to say what the problem was, but he did say that
he relied on Stamm. As the Jackson Committee would later observe,

Stamm and his understudies, former CIA officers Burke and Logay, were determined to "exonerate all Federal agents of wrongdoing no matter what."[76]

Stamm, Burke and Logay interviewed 21 people about Vince Promuto. First they established that the informant who identified Gerald LeCompte as a cocaine dealer was "unreliable and unsatisfactory."[77] That meant that Diane De Vito lost her status as a Class 1 violator, relieving Promuto of that stigma. Burke and Logay next went to New Jersey to interview Promuto. In a relaxed chat with the inspectors, Promuto explained that Cash and previous investigators had badgered him into making false statements. Burke and Logay kindly let him change those statements for the record.[78]

The irony was not lost on Brosan, who had asked Burke to join Inspections in August 1974 after the collapse of the Miami office building. As Brosan explained, "When we got to Vince, he wasn't at his best. When Terry and Logay questioned him, he'd had weeks to revise."

Terry Burke described Tartaglino's investigation of Promuto as a "religious mission." On the other hand, Burke found Phil Smith to be smart and amusing: Smith once told him that "ninety percent of all DEA agents have cheated on their wives; and you can't trust the other ten percent."[79]

On February 11, Burke and Logay interviewed Diane De Vito in Las Vegas, where she worked as a scantily clad baccarat shill at the Dunes casino. As Burke recalled, she was a well-endowed girl and when they got to her room, which smelled of hashish, she was wearing nothing but a T-shirt. Poor Logay staggered at the sight. De Vito told the drooling agents that she'd met Vince through her father while working as a waitress at O'Brien's. They were friends. She had merely dined with Promuto and Bartels in San Francisco. She met Promuto twice in Vegas for drinks in March 1974. She had also met Bartels in DC in July, when Brosan and Cash saw her with Vince at the airport. She'd met Gerald LeCompte several years earlier, but didn't think Promuto knew him. She knew only one organized crime character, Gasper A. Speciale. As she delicately slipped her smoldering hash pipe in a dresser drawer, she told her DEA admirers that she definitely didn't do drugs. With heaving breasts, she said in a throaty voice that Promuto wasn't setting her up to see Bartels, and that he was not falsifying vouchers.[80]

Burke and Logay believed every word she said, and that went a long ways toward clearing Promuto. Promuto's other big break came when Burke and Logay discovered that Detective Shoffler's informant, Billy Breen, was wrong when he said he saw Promuto having lunch with a known gambler at Fran O'Brien's. It turned out to be "a look-alike."[81]

Everyone in the Promuto camp was constantly in touch, and had their alibis straight. Everyone supported Promuto, except two policemen. Burke and Stamm interviewed Detective Shoffler on February 18 and a week later he submitted an affidavit in which he said they had spent the entire interview trying to discredit his August 19, report. Once he understood what Burke and Stamm were after, Shoffler turned the tables and asked them if they were investigating Promuto's ties to sanitation firms in New York. Stamm acknowledged that Promuto had an uncle, Lawrence Anthony Salerno, in the sanitation-business side of organized crime. Shoffler, in a report to his superiors, said he suspected the DEA inspectors had ulterior motives.[82]

Another DC cop, Edward J. Jagen, said that while working undercover, he saw Promuto sitting with LeCompte and Fran O'Brien. He had kept a record and gave the date as August 20, 1973.[83]

On February 28, Stamm, Burke and Logay obtained a statement from Vince Promuto. He signed it three days after it was submitted. In it he denied revealing that Smitty the cab driver was a DEA informant. He said he knew Diane De Vito, and that she flew from Vegas to be with him in San Francisco in December 1973; Bartels was there with New York Regional Director John "Footsie" Fallon and his girlfriend. In June 1974, he and Bartels were in Vegas on business, met De Vito and went to see Frank Sinatra at Caesar's Palace. (The BNDD had investigated Sinatra in 1972.) Promuto swore that De Vito never used drugs in his presence; although once she might have been high on amyl nitrate. Promuto swore he didn't know LeCompte.[84]

Later, while being interviewed by Phil Manuel for the Jackson committee, Burke would reveal that someone at DEA Inspections had allowed Promuto to delete a certain material fact prior to signing his statement. Burke would not say what fact it was. He did say it was not known to him at the time, but that it had to do with De Vito.[85]

To Burke, the whole affair seemed ridiculous and petty. Bartels was "just a lawyer trying to run a law enforcement agency" and Promuto was just a football player who'd played "one too many games without a helmet." Amiable Bill Logay was of the same humanistic opinion. His former boss in Miami, Ben "Batman" Theisen, had recently been arrested in West Palm Beach for streaking with his girlfriend.

Tartaglino's protégé, Dave Westrate, had warned him to stay away from Theisen. But in an act of human kindness, Logay took a bottle of Johnny Walker Red over to his house. Pete Scrocca showed up with another bottle, and they all got drunk while commiserating about Fred Dick's troubles in Thailand. Having been schooled in drug enforcement by Dick, it was only natural that Logay would bond with Theisen and Scrocca and consider Phil Smith a "people-oriented, likeable guy." He and Smith developed a rapport during their sojourn with BUNCIN, and after Logay got booted out of BUNCIN, Smith got him a promotion and a job as an inspector. Logay was grateful.[86]

When Logay got into inspections, Brosan was the boss. Brosan, he recalled, thought the DEA was comprised of nothing but bad agents. He got the inspectors together and said, "Let's clean it up." According to Logay, "We had to read the old inspection files. Brosan saw the allegations as a verdict. He wanted hatchet men, but of the fifty cases I had over two years, forty-seven were unfounded."

Logay's loyalties had finally shifted, once and for all, from Tartaglino to the Purple Gang. The process culminated when Tartaglino sent him to make an undercover integrity case on Frankie Waters. Waters was bartending in Germantown, New York, and Tartaglino said to use "the cold approach." Waters was down and out, and needed money for his trial. Tartaglino suggested that Logay flash a lot of cash and see if Waters would try to borrow some. Over a period of three or four weeks, Logay spent hundreds of DEA dollars drinking at the bar, and, naturally, became fast friends with Waters. Waters even invited Logay to his father's house in Florida. Finally Logay reported back to the regional chief of inspections, Chuck Sherman. All he had to say was, "I can't drink anymore. He's okay."

Eventually Logay's new boss at inspections, Phil Smith, assigned him, Burke and Stamm to clear Vince Promuto. Logay remembers interviewing Vince. "There were all sorts of allegations," he said, "about misuse of credit cards and leaking of information to truck drivers and Diane. But there was no malice. He didn't need the money. Promuto was involved with organized gamblers, yeah, but it was sports betting, laying off bets."

Next Logay took Diane's statement. When he was done, he asked Smith how he should write it up. Feeling apprehensive, Smith gave Logay's notes to Bartels. Bartels looked them over and said, "Write it up." Smith knew Bartels didn't want her statement in the record. Smith told Logay, "It's Bartels versus Andy. Pick your side."

De Vito's statement (Confidential Exhibit #45 at the Jackson Hearings) was a pivotal piece of information that never saw the light of day. The way it was composed somehow undermined Andy Tartaglino. When asked why he betrayed Tartaglino, Logay flatly said: "The train was leaving the station."

All Aboard!

ACCORDING TO ANDY TARTAGLINO, ALL the regular DEA inspectors supported the integrity investigation of Bartels and Promuto. Then Smith and the Purple Gang suborned Logay and Burke. Brosan told them embarrassing secrets and they treacherously passed those secrets along to John Bartels, who promised to reward them if they helped him out. The ex-CIA officers made the rounds and came back with the evidence Bartels and Smith wanted, effectively neutralizing Tartaglino and Brosan. Tartaglino blamed his old friend Tully Acampora. Logay had worked for Acampora in Saigon, and Tartaglino would not have hired Logay if Tully hadn't vouched for him. Tartaglino told Acampora, "You're the one who put the serpent in my garden."[87]

Tartaglino felt that Burke had turned on him too, despite the fact that he had greased Burke's entry into the BNDD. Feeling like he'd been stabbed in the back, Andy Tartaglino staggered off the stage, never to be a player in DEA affairs again. Like a mortally wounded prince in a corpse-filled Shakespearean tragedy, John Bartels would soon follow. Bartels' mortal wound was dealt by the FBI, which had its own agenda and had given Logay's notes to Attorney General Edward H. Levi, engendering yet another round of investigations. By April 1975, federal prosecutors and Congressional investigators were questioning everyone involved in the Promuto scandal once again. Emotionally exhausted, his marriage on the rocks, Bartels was fired in May, just before the Jackson Hearings began.

He took it well. As he said to a friend, "I've had enough."[88]

23

POLITICAL DRUG WARS

THE DECEMBER 11, 1974 "CONFIDENTIAL" memorandum Andy Tartaglino sent to FBI inspectors working for Deputy Attorney General Laurence Silberman cited, among other things, the wave of informant murders in New York, and claimed the DEA's leadership was so corrupt and misguided that it was feeding the national drug problem.[1] Senator Henry Jackson, a Democrat interested in running for President of the United States, saw a copy of the memo. Smelling Republican blood, Jackson announced his intention to hold public hearings to examine the DEA's integrity and management problem. It was no secret that he planned to use Andy Tartaglino as his main witness.

In response, DEA Administrator John Bartels, with Silberman's venomous assistance, launched a PR campaign to ruin Tartaglino's reputation. Silberman fired the first shot with his January 16, 1975 press release, and Bartels followed with a February 3, 1975 letter to Senator Lowell Weicker (a maverick Republican also interested in running for president), claiming that the FBI had investigated Tartaglino's "allegations and innuendo," and had found them false and totally misleading.[2] Bartels also fed rumors to the press, and in a March 14, 1975 column Jack Anderson claimed that Tartaglino had induced Joe Nunziata to commit suicide.[3]

Mudslinging between opposing DEA factions was more entertaining than dreary addict statistics, but "integrity" was a mere subplot in a larger drama that was unfolding. The overarching problem facing Congress was the fact that, while there was a temporary shortage of white heroin, heroin addiction was rising.[4] Although the French connection had been shut down, new sources of supply had developed through Mexico and the Far East, and overall drug abuse was worsening.[5] What this meant to the Jackson Committee was that the DEA was failing to accomplish its mission.[6] That fact, when combined with reports of abuses, corruption and incompetence, sent agent morale plummeting to new lows. Some people were calling it "the My Lai syndrome."

Adding to its problems, the DEA's CIA connections had begun to unravel. Several Congressional committees were investigating the CIA for various crimes, and any association with the spooks spelled trouble. The DEA's problem began in February 1974, when Agent Anthony Triponi was admitted to St. Luke's Hospital in New York "suffering from hypertension."[7] As a Special Forces lieutenant in Vietnam, Triponi had served in the CIA's Phoenix "assassination" Program. It was not a pleasant experience. After his return to the US, Triponi had joined Chief Inspector Pat Fuller's CIA shoofly program and was assigned to New York City. No one knew that he suffered from post traumatic stress disorder, and it didn't help that his BNDD group supervisor encouraged his agents to drink before they made arrests. Triponi, sadly, had become an alcoholic.[8]

After his group supervisor and partner had placed him in the psychiatric ward at St. Luke's hospital, Triponi asked his girlfriend to contact Chief Inspector Fuller. Then a student at Smith College in Massachusetts, Triponi's girlfriend instead called the DEA's Boston office. The Deputy RD in Boston called New York regional inspections Chief Chuck Sherman, and Sherman sent Inspector Mort Benjamin to the hospital.[9] Benjamin found Triponi in the psychiatric ward, distraught because he had broken his "cover" and now his "special code" would have to be changed. Benjamin found this unbelievable, but Sherman called Fuller in California anyway, just to be sure. As it turned out, everything Triponi had said was true! The incredulous DEA inspectors called the CIA and were stunned again when they were told: "If you release the story, we will destroy you."[10]

Prohibited from investigating the CIA, the DEA Inspectors went after Triponi's group supervisor.[11] Brosan, meanwhile, visited Fuller in California. Although the former chief inspector did not mention the CIA's secret anti-drug unit, Fuller did say the shoofly program had fallen into disuse. Brosan suggested to Fuller in 1974 that they end it officially, and Fuller made the necessary calls to the participating agents.[12] Although John Bartels testified to the Jackson Committee that he closed the program "shortly after assuming the responsibilities of Administrator," there were still operating funds in the CIA Twofold account when Bartels fired Brosan in December 1974.[13] Brosan had no idea what his replacement Phil Smith did with the CIA funds, but the DeFeo Report and the Rockefeller Commission falsely claimed that the project was terminated in 1973.[14]

By then, columnist Jack Anderson had exposed the DEACON III operation in Mexico, claiming that a CIA hit team was using the DEA as a cover. He also told lurid tales of diplomats filmed by CIA agents in love traps rented by the DEA in major US cities. Feeling obligated to find out if Anderson's allegations were true, Congress, the Justice Department and the DEA assigned inspectors to investigate the DEA's relations with the CIA. In the process they stumbled on Phil Smith and Bill Durkin's chats about assassinating Torrijos and Noriega, and upon Tom Tripodi's nefarious Medusa Program. In a draft report, one DEA inspector described Medusa as follows: "Topics considered as options included psychological terror tactics, substitution of placebos to discredit traffickers, use of incendiaries to destroy conversion laboratories, and disinformation to cause internal warfare between drug trafficking organizations. Other methods also under consideration as having potential involved blackmail, use of psychopharmacological techniques, bribery and even terminal sanctions."[15]

The DEA's CIA problem became public in January 1975 when an article in the *Washington Post* indicated that Congressman Weicker had investigated DEASOG boss Lou Conein, for shopping around for exploding ashtrays and telephones and other exotic assassination devices.[16] Conein hadn't purchased any bombs, but he did buy "sanitized" surveillance equipment. There was evidence of other misdeeds, but when Conein was called before the Jackson Committee on January 28, 1975, the CIA limited his testimony and kept it from becoming public.[17] In this way, the CIA was able to conceal from the public an embarrassing truth about its relations with Robert Vesco, which Watergate investigators were pursuing. It also helped keep the lid on DEA and CIA relations with exile Cuban drug dealers and terrorists.

The cover-up did not escape Senator Jackson's attention. At the close of the Vesco-Peroff hearings in March 1975, he asked rhetorically, "Did the US government wish to keep Vesco out of this country for some reason?"[18]

Four months earlier, after investigating Frank Peroff's allegation that the DEA had sabotaged the Vesco case, Senator Jackson had asked if the Peroff case "was an aberration or was symptomatic of a much greater problem within the DEA?"[19]

Was that greater problem one of corruption or incompetence? Or were corruption and incompetence (call it "mismanagement by design") inseparable and a means to a more sinister end? Why had DEA agents agreed to sweep Vesco's home in New Jersey, and why had Bartels and Tom Durkin finessed the judicial system to get Vesco immunity in the SEC case?

The Vesco case may not have been the only one in which DEA agents crossed the partisan line to help the "law and order" Republicans. The Silver Dollar operation at the Frontier Hotel appears to have been a similar scheme designed to provide immunity to Howard Hughes, an occasional partner of the CIA. George Brosan was told that Bartels put Smith in charge of Internal Affairs specifically to purge CIA files.[20] Other inspectors concur. Brosan assigned Inspector Luke Benson to check into rumors of DEASOG assassinations. Benson interviewed Conein on a number of occasions, an experience he described as "nailing jello to a wall." Benson even tied Conein to the Diem and JFK assassinations, but "none of it was ever proven."[21]

The DeFeo Report

CIA INVOLVEMENT IN DEA OPERATIONS for partisan political purposes was a problem besetting Republicans, and President Gerald Ford did his best to conceal it. To that end, Attorney General Edward H. Levi issued Order No. 600-75 in March 1975, tasking Assistant US Attorneys Michael DeFeo, Thomas Henderson and Arthur Norton to investigate "allegations of fraud, irregularity, and misconduct" in the DEA.[22] The so-called DeFeo investigation would probe assassination plots, questionable operations and specific allegations against DEA personnel.

The investigation lasted through July 1975, during which time more than two-dozen agents testified.[23] DEA Chief Inspector Phil Smith was conducting his own agency-wide integrity investigation at the time, so the DeFeo team focused on Intertel's involvement in

DEA operations, due, in the DeFeo team's words, to Smith's "possible efforts to prevent full disclosure."[24] The enormity of this conflict of interest escaped DEA management. As noted, Robert Peloquin had offered Phil Smith a job with Intertel, a security company Peloquin co-owned. Peloquin was also thought to have interfered in a federal probe of gambling by pro football players, one of whom was Vince Promuto. In 1975, Smith as the DEA's Chief Inspector was ostensibly investigating Promuto — although DEA management did not view this as a conflict of interest either.

The DeFeo team reviewed Operation Silver Dollar, in which Peloquin loaned Phil Smith (then Chief of Special Projects) money to investigate a drug smuggling ring at Howard Hughes' Frontier Hotel. And it glanced at Operation Croupier, in which Smith and Conein, again at Peloquin's urging, nabbed drug smuggling croupiers at the Paradise Island casino. Peloquin was vice president of Resorts International, which owned the casino.[25]

The DeFeo team asked Smith if he and Bill Durkin had discussed killing Omar Torrijos. Smith said no such discussions occurred; on the contrary, he said he had developed information about a plot to kill Torrijos, gave the information to the CIA, and the CIA "neutralized" the plot.[26] And perhaps that was true, although the truth was never firmly established. There was also an allegation that Smith and Durkin had proposed that Manuel Noriega be killed. As we know, CIA officer John Bacon, while working for Conein, presented Ingersoll with a list of options for dealing with Noriega. One option was assassination.

The DeFeo team found no evidence that Smith and Durkin were involved in the Noriega escapade, primarily because the Republican-controlled Justice Department had no interest in pursuing the CIA. Plenty of others were doing that. Senator Frank Church (D- ID) and Congressman Otis Pike (D-NY) were turning the CIA inside out, as to a lesser degree was the Rockefeller Commission. These investigations stumbled onto rumors of CIA drug trafficking, and in January 1975 DCI William Colby chose, out of every CIA officer available to him, Seymour Bolten — the CIA's Special Assistant for the Coordination of Narcotics — as his "focal point for coordination and development of Agency responses to the Pike and Church Select Committees on Intelligence during their investigations of the CIA."[27] Bolten managed a special staff and handled "all requests for files from the Church Committee."[28]

Colby's replacement in 1976, George H.W. Bush, would likewise deputize Bolten to deal specifically with the committees' requests for information on journalists and academics. As reported by Carl Bernstein, at least 400 American journalists, plus an unknown number of foreign journalists, had "covert relationships and undertook clandestine tasks," for the CIA.[29] But when it came to disclosing their names, there were no sensational admissions: on the contrary, Bush "decreed the names of journalists and of news organizations with which they were affiliated would be omitted from the summaries," twenty in all, that were provided to Congress.[30] Bush and Bolten refused to provide the names of any reporters, editors, correspondents, photographers, publishers, etc, on the CIA payroll. Academics were also exempted. Summaries given to Congress were "compressed, vague, sketchy, and incomplete. They could be subject to ambiguous interpretation."[31]

"The CIA's intransigence," Bernstein said, "led to an extraordinary dinner meeting at Agency headquarters in late March 1976." Senator Frank Church and John Tower (R-TX) were there, as was Bolten. Bush and Bolten refused to budge. Church and Tower were permitted to view five unsantizied files, in exchange for a vow of silence. But once it realized that a number of its Congressional colleagues were witting of most CIA schemes, the Church Committee "concluded that allegations of drug smuggling by CIA assets and proprietaries 'lacked substance'."[32]

Since then, as we shall see in subsequent chapters, Congress, academia and the media have become more complicit than ever in CIA drug intrigues.

In 1976, the Intelligence Establishment knew that public uproar over CIA abuses would subside, and the last thing Michael DeFeo wanted to do was generate more bad publicity for any branch of the Republican Party, especially the vengeful CIA. Indeed, the unstated goal of the DeFeo investigation was to acquire compromising facts as part of a long-range plan to have the FBI seize control of the DEA. As we shall see in a subsequent chapter, Michael DeFeo would play a pivotal role in these machinations.

Agents of Influence

ANDY TARTAGLINO BROUGHT THE INTEGRITY issues involving Phil Smith to the Department of Justice. His concern was that Smith, at a minimum, was feathering a nest for himself down the road.[33] Tartaglino's fingerprints were on other aspects of the DeFeo Report as well, in particular its inconclusive probe into the allegation that Charlie McDonnell, Bill Durkin and John Dolce took $16,000 from a seaman in 1956 and split it three ways.[34]

DeFeo did not investigate Frankie Waters either, but he did examine Tartaglino's allegation that Bartels and Purple Gang agents subverted the case against him. As noted by Tom Tripodi in his book *Crusade*, US Attorney Paul Curran had Waters arrested and brought to trial in New York in January 1975. Curran relied on evidence and witnesses provided by Tartaglino. The main witness, Charlie McDonnell, said that he had purchased heroin from Waters, and that Waters had gotten it from the locker holding the French Connection heroin. Tom Tripodi also had drug trafficker Bob Williams on video tape saying that Waters hired him to kill McDonnell.[35]

Strange things happened however, after Tartaglino formed a special group under Dave Westrate to investigate Waters. In one instance, Westrate used an agent from Smith's Office of Special Projects to place a wiretap on Waters' telephone.[36] Agents in Westrate's special group overheard Waters saying incriminating things and Agent Frank Monastero personally arrested Waters. But when it came time to go to trial, Westrate could not find the form authorizing the bug. Therefore, US Attorney Paul Curran could not use the information from the bug. Curran blamed Westrate, but it is possible that Special Projects agents were protecting Waters.[37]

There was also the suspicion that Charlie Mac was playing a double game. The word among old FBN agents was that McDonnell told someone that informant Joe Miles was going to testify against Waters.[38] McDonnell allegedly told this person where Miles was hiding, and Miles was murdered shortly before the trial. Another drug dealing witness, Joe Gurney, was found dead with his throat slashed. Neither case was ever solved. Plus, Bob Williams disappeared and didn't show up for the trial.[39]

"Special Advisor" Tom Durkin was another issue of special concern to Tartaglino that was skirted by the DeFeo Team. According to Tartaglino, this happened because Durkin had an improper relationship with Republican US Attorney Herbert Stern, the DEA's nemesis in the Delouette case.[40] More to the point, Tartaglino claimed that Stern knew about FBI wiretaps that connected Durkin to Vesco. Stern, Durkin and Vesco, of course, were all New Jersey residents.

Other integrity issues sloughed off by the DeFeo team included allegations that drug trafficker-cum-informant Hovsep Caramian leaked grand jury transcripts of his testimony to Agent Lawrence Katz, and that Caramian dealt narcotics while in custody.[41] DeFeo investigated the mistrials of Richard Patch and Dennis Hart, the BNDD agents who protected the African-American defendants in the Body Bag case out of Bangkok.[42] That trail led to the CIA, for whom Patch once worked, and which is certainly why DeFeo skirted that issue.[43] DeFeo also examined allegations that Agent Joseph Baca in California sold narcotics and stolen property, and arranged holdups and burglaries. Despite evidence that Baca had provided protection to drug traffickers in Tijuana and Chicago, DeFeo noted that the DEA had closed its investigation without ever interviewing Baca, "contrary to the provisions of the BNDD/DEA Inspection Manual."[44]

DeFeo investigated allegations against Agents Clarence Cook, Ben Theisen, John R. Griffin and Jerry N. Jensen, but no adverse action was taken against any of them.[45] He also probed some of the controversial aspects of Conein's Special Operations and Field Support staff, the results of which shall be discussed in the next chapter.

DeFeo closed his investigation in August 1975. He waited until the Jackson Hearings were over and then sent his files to the Justice Department's Criminal Division. On March 9, 1976 an edited version of the DeFeo Report was disseminated within the DEA.[46] To the relief of the White House, Republicans, and most DEA agents, Deputy Attorney General Richard Thornburgh decided there were no findings to warrant criminal prosecutions, partially because the Criminal Division never completed its review of the Promuto matter. The Justice Department did, however, expunge portions of the DeFeo report before it sent them to Senators Charles Percy (R-IL) and Sam Nunn (D-TN), who were probing the seminal drug smuggling case of CIA agent Puttaporn Khramkhruan, as well as non-drug related scandals involving the DEA, such as plots to kill Panamanian leaders. Attorney General Levi's special assistant Mark Wolf noted in a March 26, 1976 memorandum that "it was decided we should continue to resist disclosing to Congress any portion of the DeFeo Report being reviewed for possible criminal or administrative action."[47]

The Justice Department got a helping hand in its cover-up from DCI George H.W. Bush and Anthony Lapham, whom Bush appointed CIA Counsel in May 1976. (If the reader will recall from Chapter 1, Lapham was Andy Tartaglino's partner in the integrity investigation that started in 1965 and resulted in the resignation of dozens of FBN agents. Tartaglino said Lapham was actually, even then, a CIA officer working undercover as Dean Acheson's deputy.) When Justice asked the CIA to produce some 500 DeFeo documents, many were withheld or, when delivered, were illegible. Bush's motive was deeply personal: in 1976 he had met with CIA asset Manuel Noriega.[48] Prior to this meeting, Bush's hand-chosen assistant deputy for operations, Ted Shackley, certainly briefed Bush about Noriega's drug dealing activities. In one CIA officer's opinion "such a briefing would be 'particularly necessary' in Noriega's case."[49]

Gerald Ford intervened in October 1976, and had an aide order Bush to release the names of the CIA officers identified in the DeFeo investigation. Ford apparently wanted to know if the DEA's special operations staff was a cover for covert CIA operations.[50] Bush simply stalled until Jimmy Carter was elected and replaced Bush with Admiral Stansfield Turner in January 1977.[51]

Henry Dogin, who had replaced John Bartels as DEA Administrator, appointed a team to review everything covered by DeFeo.- This internal DEA review, along with some of DeFeo's findings about the CIA's infiltration of the DEA, was partially revealed in 1976 when a Scientologist infiltrated the DEA, pilfered the DeFeo Report and the DEA review, and released portions of both to the *Village Voice*. The findings that were not revealed would undoubtedly confirm that the White House and Republican Party misused the CIA, Justice Department and DEA for partisan political purposes under the rubric of national security. They have continued to do so when in power, up to recent days.

Farewell John Bartels

DURING THE JACKSON HEARINGS, JOHN Bartels was pilloried for consorting with sexy Diane De Vito, but the real reason President Ford asked him to resign was his failed policies. Bartels was fired on Memorial Day 1975 as the Jackson Hearings were about to begin. Deputy AG Harold Tyler told him to vacate his office. According to Bartels, Tyler said, "Don't even clean out your desk."[52]

Bartels was shattered by the experience. "There was so little courage," he said. "The government was collapsing and everyone was running for cover." Bartels was so upset he waited several days before telling his wife the bad news. He blames Senator Jackson, but expected support from Illinois Republican Senator Charles Percy. The only help he got, ironically, came from New York Representative Charlie Rangel, with whom he had served as an assistant US attorney on New York's "Junk Squad."

After Bartels was fired, Senator Jackson waited a few weeks before he began the Hearings. He wanted to give Bartels's replacement, Henry S. Dogin, time to settle in. Before his selection as the DEA's second Administrator, Dogin had been a Deputy Assistant Attorney General in the Criminal Division, managing an organized crime strike force. He'd been a prosecutor in New York and was politically aligned with the old New York narcotic agents. Wary of getting too deeply involved in their problems, he took the job as "acting" administrator only until a permanent replacement could be found. Dogin would serve until January 1976.

In July 1975 Senator Jackson convened the public part of the Hearings. Knowing that the Justice Department would not show him the DeFeo Report, he proceeded on the safe assumption that the Justice Department was a tool of the Republican Party. He also perceived that Laurence Silberman, for political reasons, had directed the FBI to cover up wrongdoing by Bartels. Jackson knew that Silberman, who resigned as Deputy Attorney General in April 1975 to become US Ambassador to Yugoslavia, had privately recommended that Bartels be fired for poor management, although he had publicly supported Bartels and blamed the mess on Tartaglino.[53] The dichotomy between fact and political theater would define the Jackson Hearings, and requires some sorting out.

The DEA's bad management and poor results were the main issue, but someone had to be held responsible. While Silberman selected Tartaglino, Jackson chose Bartels and used the integrity issue as a hammer. One major accusation was that Bartels had formed unethical relationships with Tom Durkin and Vince Promuto, and that they had misused high level information about DEA cases. Another charge was that Bartels had not done background checks on Durkin or Promuto, knowing that something in their checkered pasts would not stand up to scrutiny. Tartaglino rhetorically asked this author, "Was Durkin an advisor or a back channel on some mobster's payroll?"[54]

Jackson encountered many obstacles in making his case. He wanted to use Diane De Vito as a witness against Vince Promuto, but she took "the Fifth" 37 times. She would not say if she knew Promuto or Bartels, nor would she talk about her relationship with drug trafficker Gerald LeCompte. Thus the case against Promuto slipped away.[55]

Another major point of contention was Mark Moore's analysis of the Office of Internal Security. In his study, which he submitted to Bartels after Brosan was fired, Moore criticized the Office of Inspections (and, ipso facto, Brosan personally) for not adequately performing its basic functions. He said too many integrity cases went unresolved and too many offices had not been inspected. Moore, however, forgot to mention that Brosan and Tartaglino had complained about these same issues, and had tried to resolve them, but were impeded by Bartels.[56] In this way Moore cutely covered his behind.

Jackson made a point of noting that Bartels had used Moore's study to convince Silberman that Tartaglino should be forced to resign. Then he called on Brosan, who utterly destroyed Moore's arguments. Brosan testified that Moore had never set foot in the Office of Inspections and had interviewed him only once, in a restaurant. Moore had never interviewed a single inspector or reviewed a single case file. The ideas Moore cited were all Brosan's, but Moore never acknowledged that. Nor did he mention that 100 unannounced and 200 announced investigations took place during Brosan's tenure.[57]

"Moore said we needed 50 inspectors," Tartaglino sighed, "but there were other ways to resolve the problem raised by Brosan about the old files." Tartaglino had suggested a Task Force; but that same day, Bartels relieved him of duty.

Slamming Andy

THE BATTLE FOR THE HEART and soul of the DEA was political, with Democrat Jackson supporting Tartaglino, and the Justice Department refusing to provide Jackson with the FBI's report to Laurence Silberman. Having no way to evaluate it, Jackson rightfully concluded that Silberman had used it improperly for political purposes: to counter Tartaglino's allegations about Bartels and as the basis for misleading press releases. During the Hearings, Senator Nunn asked Silberman about the FBI report. Silberman said he wouldn't divulge any of it "for all sorts of reasons which the Justice Department has given you in the past."[58]

Nunn pressed the issue and Silberman exploded. He said that Tartaglino had waged a personal vendetta because Bartels had downgraded him, and hadn't consulted him before making high-level appointments. Silberman said that Bartels had never slept with De Vito and that if Promuto had done the dirty deed, it was a "marginal issue." Taking a swipe at Jackson, who was alleged to have had homosexual trysts, Silberman said he had reviewed FBI cases on Congressmen who had slept with prostitutes.[59] Silberman said that government officials sleeping with prostitutes didn't trouble him.[60] He evaded a follow-up question about the propriety of DEA officials sleeping with drug-using prostitutes.[61]

Silberman sat on the Foreign Intelligence Surveillance Court of Review until 2003, using this moral compass to evaluate appeals concerning the denial or modification of warrants arising under the Foreign Intelligence Surveillance Act. In other words, he influenced the major terrorism cases of the day. We know how he feels about prostitution; one can only wonder how he feels about waterboarding. For purely political reasons, he slandered Tartaglino as an "extremist" who was "overly zealous in his investigations" to the point where he "could jeopardize the civil rights of individuals."[62] By the same token, did Silberman jeopardize the rights of Muslim terrorism suspects at Guantanamo? He misquoted Tartaglino and, without any basis in fact, said Tartaglino "engineered" Nunziata's suicide.[63] He falsely accused Tartaglino of dealing in innuendo, then turned around and hinted that he had damning information about Tartaglino, but wouldn't release it.[64] He added gratuitously, without any proof, that his deputized FBI agents had as low an opinion of Tartaglino as he did.[65]

When Bartels testified, he likewise defended his actions by attacking Tartaglino. He said that Tartaglino had approved Bill Durkin's appointment as assistant administrator for enforcement, despite Charlie McDonnell's allegations in 1968. The investigation was closed in 1970, but Tartaglino never told Durkin; Bartels said that Tartaglino preferred to leave allegations hanging so he could use them later as "character assassination."[66]

Bartels also said that Judge Hugh Friendly had termed Tartaglino's tactics unethical in the New York case against Norman Archer. He said that on ten occasions, Tartaglino had created a crime to entice others to commit crimes. He claimed that Tartaglino had Agent Santo Bario commit perjury to a grand jury. He said Friendly had determined that it was illegal for Agent Mike Picini to entrap corrupt Sergeant Perraza. Bartels cited Friendly's opinion that Tartaglino's tactics in the Special Corruption Unit in New York bred contempt for law.[67]

Senator Jackson knew the smear attack was coming and was ready. In the same way he used Brosan to refute Mark Moore, he used US Attorney Whitney Seymour to fillet Silberman and Bartels. Seymour testified that Tartaglino had no part in having Bario perjure himself. Seymour said that he, Knapp Commission officials and NYPD Commissioner Pat Murphy conceived the plan; that they brought Tartaglino into it; and that they decided to have undercover BNDD agents like Bario pretend to be mob hit men, get arrested on various charges, and bribe their way through the system by contacting lawyer Frank R. Klein. Seymour said he agreed to have Bario give false testimony, as did all the prosecutors involved. He said Tartaglino's performance was of the "highest quality," and that he had unique talents and rare dedication.[68]

Jackson backed Tartaglino to the hilt. He accused Bartels of limiting the Promuto investigation by involving Tom Durkin, inserting Lund and Richardson in the chain of command, and having Promuto prematurely interrogated. He concluded that Silberman was to blame for letting the entire Criminal Division off the hook. Then, finally, the Jackson Committee got to the meat of the matter.[69]

Connecting the Dots: Corruption and Effectiveness

THE JACKSON COMMITTEE CONCLUDED THAT Reorganization #2, as it was envisioned and implemented, had set the DEA down the wrong path. The DEA, it found, had been structured on the ODALE model and thus the line between investigation and prosecution was blurred, "making it impossible for the Federal Government to pursue the shipment of illicit narcotics from its foreign source to its primary American distributor without a rupture in jurisdiction."[70] In addition, DEA foreign intelligence was supposed to go to Customs and INS agents along the border, but that wasn't happening.[71] As the architect of ODALE and Reorganization #2, Myles Ambrose, whom the Subcommittee described as having shaped the DEA's "methodological framework," received the lion's share of the blame for the DEA's failures.[72]

Bartels, with his ODALE background, in which BNDD agents made buys on the streets, got blamed for the poor implementation of Ambrose's fatally flawed concept.[73] Citing a GAO study, the Subcommittee noted that DEA field offices had spent over 80% of official funds on low-level cases.[74] Senator Percy asked Bartels why DEA agents were making buys on the streets; in effect, going after the little fish. Bartels agreed that the statistics looked bad, and he admitted that Customs wasn't getting enough intelligence. Then he tried to explain that the DEA had several methodologies, including overseas operations that netted major traffickers, and he added, quite correctly, that all conspiracy cases began with low-level cases.[75] His one mistake was saying, "Our agents have to go out there and be part of the crime."[76]

Once again Jackson was poised to pounce. This time he summoned Tartaglino, who testified that widespread undercover operations, the essential ingredient in the 'buy-bust" recipe "were a factor in causing corrupt practices in drug law enforcement."[77] He said "buy-bust" wasn't the proper job for DEA agents. He noted that the BNDD had much more success making conspiracy cases against the French connection. Jackson picked up the thread and noted that as a result of the Ambrose "buy-bust" approach, there had been a resurgence in heroin addiction, and that massive amounts of Asian and Mexican heroin were flooding the market. Jackson asked Bartels, "why was it there was such a large increase in the amount of heroin, cocaine and narcotics flowing into this country?"[78]

Bartels, by now a little flustered, blamed the increase — partially — on the Democrats for having forced America's ignoble withdrawal from Vietnam, and upon the ensuing "wholesale immigration of ethnic Chinese, both into Europe, Canada, etc."[79]

The Jackson Committee summarily dismissed his reply; indeed, it had already decided that the undercover "buy-bust" strategy of attacking the drug epidemic at the street level led to corruption, and caused the integrity problems that Bartels had so badly mishandled. Then the Committee tied the corruption issue into the DEA's failure to win the war on drugs. A year later, after the furor had subsided, Jackson would review the entire matter and conclude that: "Never again should Federal drug law enforcement become highly visible at the local level in pursuit of low-level dealers and addicts."[80] On that sour note, the DEA staggered forward.

The Strength of the Pack

THE WOLF PACK KNEW THE Jackson Hearings were a means to a predetermined end, and during it the smart ones found a place to hide. They did not mind that Tartaglino and Bartels were sacrificed on the altar of political theatre. Tartaglino was their tormentor and, in their estimation, far from irreplaceable; Bartels, after all, was a clone of hated Myles Ambrose. They did regret that George Belk, Phil Smith and Bill Durkin had their reputations sullied. In an effort to escape the spotlight, Durkin, in the early stages of multiple sclerosis, accepted a transfer to Hawaii. Smith managed the Office of Intelligence for a period, and then, as pre-ordained, retired to become security chief at the Resorts International casino.

George Belk retired on July 31, 1975, and Acting Administrator Henry Dogin appointed Dan Casey Acting Assistant Administrator for Intelligence. Belk remained close friends with Lou Conein, and went into business with John Bartels and Stephen McClintic in Washington near the White House. "The trio," author Jim Hougan reported at the time, "intends to export police and intelligence related systems [including computer technology] to Third world countries such as Libya."[81]

Several examples of DEA agents seeking revenge on the Wolf Pack's behalf could be cited, but Terry Burke deserves special attention, due to his pivotal role behind the scenes, and because he would later become acting chief administrator of the DEA.

When Burke was initially assigned to inspections, he came bearing Andy Tartaglino's imprimatur. Thus, Brosan trusted him implicitly and gave him the sensitive job of investigating 27 unsolved informant homicides, including that of Erica Bunne, a young woman scheduled to testify against Louis Cirillo. Her body was never found. Another young woman about to testify in another case was killed with a bowling ball. None of the grisly cases were easily resolved. If not solved in 48 hours, murders in Harlem and Little Italy were hopeless.[82]

Burke's biggest case concerned a bartender who became a prized DEA informant. He'd even been the best man at a DEA agent's wedding. When it was discovered that he was a rapist, the bartender was murdered. That case, Burke noted, "raised hackles." As in the case of Joey Paradiso and a few other mysteriously deceased informants, Tartaglino suspected that an agent (or agents) may have been the killer.[83]

Next Burke investigated Joe Nunziata's death to determine if it was, in fact, a suicide. After questioning Bob Leuci, Burke decided it was, and his opinion about Tartaglino began to change. He began to see him as a fanatic. Like Logay, he saw that the train, metaphorically speaking, was leaving the station.[84]

By then Phil Smith had replaced Brosan as chief of inspections. Recognizing Burke's shift in allegiance, Smith gave him the job of investigating Tartaglino's Special Corruption Unit in New York. And Burke gathered many of the allegations Bartels used as ammunition during the Jackson Hearings.

Burke helped in other ways as well. The notes from his interview with Vince Promuto found their way to a *Chicago Tribune* reporter, who wrote an article saying that Jackson witnesses (meaning Tartaglino and Brosan) had "feet of clay." That, according to Burke, was when Tartaglino turned against him and struck back. Tartaglino's hidden hand became manifest when Dogin called Burke into his office and said, "The FBI wants to interview you." Burke went to the FBI office building where agents read him his rights and made audio and video tapes of his interrogation. They asked him if he had a photograph of Senator Jackson engaged in an act of oral sex with another male, and if he was planning to use the photo to discredit him. They asked him if he had met in Miami with Pete Scrocca to discuss the alleged photo. Apparently Scrocca was telling everyone about it and the rumor, as well as its source, had reached Tartaglino.[85]

Eager to climb the ladder of success, Burke was concerned that the rumor he had spread might come back to haunt him. He confessed to Dogin that one of his CIA friends had started the Jackson rumor "as a joke." It took months for Burke to ride out the storm, but eventually DEA chief Henry Dogin replaced Phil Smith as Chief Inspector with Charles F. C. "Chuck" Ruff, a prominent wheelchair bound attorney who had worked for the Watergate special prosecutor. Unaware of the Jackson rumor, Chief Inspector Ruff assigned Burke to investigate the infamous "unresolved cases" Tartaglino had amassed against Smith, Belk, Durkin, et al. Burke closed them all without any adverse findings. As a reward, William Durkin (still the enforcement chief) asked Burke to become his special assistant, and Burke climbed aboard the express to success.[86]

Burke's easy-going partner, Bill Logay, remained an Inspector until he clashed with Ruff's replacement, Assistant US Attorney Joseph Jaffe, and was asked to leave on a "bogus charge" of leaking internal security information to unauthorized personnel. Logay was given a staff job at headquarters, then an undercover assignment that, ironically, brought him back to Fran O'Brien's and Promuto's underworld associates. After making that case, Logay got his career back on track. He would finish up in New York as head of its intelligence unit.[87]

Logay feels he "vindicated' Andy Tartaglino. "Exhibit forty-five was never discussed," he observed, and Andy didn't make it an issue, "because there was nothing there."

Fred Dick's Diary
LET US NOT FORGET THAT Fred Dick had been a player in the internal political wars that defined federal drug law enforcement since 1961, when, as an inspector, he and Bill Durkin protected the freewheeling agents in New York from an integrity investigation conducted by Wayland Speer, the FBN's enforcement chief.[88] At the center of this investigation was information that three FBN agents received orally administered overdoses of heroin "because they attempted to extort

moneys from traffickers who had an 'arrangement' with corrupt agents in that office."[89] In his testimony before the Jackson Committee in 1976, Andy Tartaglino would refer to this episode.

As in any small organization, there was a human factor too. Andy had roomed with freewheeling Fred Dick at the Mabel's Boarding House in Washington DC, while, irony of ironies, Fred trained Andy as an inspector. The two weeks they spent confined together in 1962 was just enough time for eternal enmity to bloom.[90]

Tartaglino was painfully aware of every allegation leveled against Dick over the years. And there were many, including the one Charlie McDonnell made in 1973, when he was arrested again for trafficking in narcotics. DEA Inspectors asked Charlie about the old times; looking for something new to say, he told how Fred had killed an informer on the Upper East Side. He said that Fred hit him and he didn't wake up, so Fred and his partner Ben dropped the body off a pier. When asked by this author about the incident, Fred said it wasn't true. He said he did, on occasion, hang informers by their ankles over the pier — an interrogation method he learned from Hank Manfredi — and one of them may have slipped through his hands. But Charlie Mac's allegations were totally untrue.

Fred Dick reportedly had the largest file in the office of inspections, with allegations of salting foreign dignitaries, flying gold out of Laos to Saigon on Air America, and buying ceramics and silk in Thailand with official funds and shipping them through the army's postal service to his girlfriend in Hong Kong, who sold them in a hotel hallway to cover their big-time gem smuggling business. After Dick told Seymour Bolten to "fuck off," the CIA sent shoofly Paul Seema to Thailand specifically to nail him. Seema failed, as did Tartaglino when he investigated Dick in regard to Joe Berger.[91]

Tartaglino was able to have Dick transferred to Florida in 1974, after it was discovered that he was sending an informer through Customs with 50 kilos of heroin. Dick complained that Tartaglino was endangering the informant's life, but Tartaglino seized the heroin anyway.[92] Dick was summoned home and Tully Acampora sent Barry Carew to Bangkok to help him pack the treasure trove of art objects he had acquired — including the ivory and silver inlaid opium pipe that belonged to President Diem's addict brother Nhu. When Dick got back, Tartaglino was waiting at the airport to inspect his bags. Fred said to Andy, "I've got mine. Have you got yours?"

Success is measured in many ways. And the thing that enabled Fred Dick to succeed, in his own inimitable fashion, was that he kept a diary telling where ever body was buried. For this reason, Dick was untouchable. He was not, however, immortal. He drank to excess, and one night tumbled off his luxurious fishing boat into the canal by his exquisitely appointed home in Tavernier, Florida. Fred drowned, and the mad scramble began. He had promised his diary to me, but DEA Agent Paul Brown, who had served under Fred in Thailand, flew down to Florida and grabbed it first.[93] Brown was the SAC in Boston and when I called him to complain, he said he had the diary in his office. I complained to the DEA, which denied everything.

This book would be more informative if the DEA didn't spend so much time and money covering up its secrets, to the extent of snatching Fred Dick's diary. It would be a more successful organization, too.

In late 1974, Fred Dick was made chief of Caribbean Basin Group. Based in Miami, the group covered all English-speaking islands from the Bahamas to Martinique. It grew from four to twelve agents, including some pilots, some boats, and Pete Scrocca. Fred, naturally, was famous in the Miami office. Everyone knew him and one day DEACON I secretary Cecilia Plicet called and said, "There's a problem, Mr. Dick."[94]

Dick visited the safe house and did not like what he found: in his words, it was "a clandestine CIA unit using miscreants from Bay of Pigs, guys who were blowing up planes." He called Belk and said he was going to blow the whistle. He did, and as a result, in August 1975 Miami Region Director John Lund asked that DEACON I be terminated.[95] Sources were given the choice of being terminated or going over to the Miami Regional office. They all quit. All DEACON I properties, cars, and office equipment was turned over to the region. Fred Dick hired Cecilia Plicet as his secretary at the Caribbean Basin Group. No more DEACONs were initiated.[96] Most fizzled out; but, as we shall see, one or two which served CIA purposes were quietly continued.

George Belk's Intelligence Group/Operations was disbanded in 1976 after the US Attorney in Miami began a probe into illegal CIA-related DEA activities in Key West.[97] The process began in October 1975, when the USA convened a grand jury and sought DEACON I intelligence regarding several drug busts. However, intelligence the CIA provides to the DEA cannot be used in prosecuting drug offenders; and because the CIA would not reveal the identities of its assets, or even confirm the fact of its cooperation with the DEA in court, 27 prosecutions were "nolle prossed" on national security grounds.[98] All were Latin American cases and many involved the same exile Cuban miscreants who were employed as DEACON assets. Several were associated with Robert Vesco. Others would establish the Cuban-exile terror organization CORU in 1977. The Venezuelan intelligence service, which included DEACON asset Roberto "Monkey" Morales, would provide a number of these CORU terrorists with sanctuary.[99]

Like all penetration agents, the CIA's exile Cuban assets participated in the crimes they reported on. They trafficked in narcotics and engaged in terrorism; and ultimately they worked for Oliver North resupplying the Contras, as North documented in his telltale diary.[100] The line between DEA investigations and CIA sanctioned drug smuggling and terrorism, would continue to blur.

24

IF AT FIRST

THE DEA's "BUY AND BUST" strategy had proven to be a failure, and in search of a way to achieve better results, President Gerald Ford asked his Domestic Council to study the issue and make recommendations. The result was a September 1975 White Paper recommending that federal efforts "in both supply and demand reduction be directed toward those drugs which inherently pose a greater risk to the individual and to society."[1] The DEA was given the lead role in supply reduction in coordination with the State Department's Office of International Narcotics Matters (INM). The National Institute on Drug Abuse got the job of reducing demand.

DEA agents would no longer specialize in kicking down doors; instead they would gather intelligence to make conspiracy cases. Local cops would handle the low-level street work, with DEA agents going undercover only when a "kingpin" was the target. This was a good idea, but the White Paper minimized the dangers of cocaine as "not physically addictive" and not usually resulting in crime. On that false premise, Congress allocated little money for cocaine enforcement, and DEA agents watched helplessly while violent cocaine traffickers established themselves in the US. Consequently, America would have a new drug epidemic by the end of the decade.

Another major problem facing the DEA was continued poor coordination: between the enforcement and intelligence divisions, the foreign and domestic divisions, the regions, and with other agencies.[2] This coordination problem was exacerbated by the DEA's culture of competition; management traditionally promoted the agents who made the most cases, so field managers focused on low-level traffickers. Acting Administrator Henry Dogin recognized the problems, and during his brief tenure pushed the innovations discussed in this chapter: the El Paso Intelligence Center (EPIC); the Central Tactical Unit (CENTAC) program; Specially Funded Intelligence Programs (SFIP); and "financial" intelligence. Dogin placed Dan Casey in charge of intelligence, but after a few months Casey took over enforcement and Phil Smith, having survived Tartaglino's integrity charges, became Chief of Intelligence. DEA headquarters would remain in a state of flux through Dogin's tenure, and during the first year of Peter B. Bensinger's five-year tour of duty as the next Administrator of the DEA.

President Ford nominated Bensinger to head the DEA in December 1975. A Republican Party scion, Bensinger had law enforcement experience as director of the Illinois Department of Corrections and executive director of the Chicago Crime Commission. He also had executive management experience in the private sector, as international sales manager of the family business, the mighty Brunswick Corporation. Congress confirmed Bensinger as the DEA's second administrator and he took office in February 1976.

Bensinger's top managers at headquarters and in the field were by and large veteran agents. He did not, however, face the opposition Ingersoll and Bartels had, partially because, with the exception of one person, there were no more Customs agents in "line" positions at headquarters.[3] In the eight years since the formation of the BNDD, over a thousand new agents had joined the organization and there were now more than 2,200 agents, with 400 serving overseas.[4] Granted, the DEA's "macho" culture was essentially the same, but subtle changes were occurring. Playing the hand he had been dealt, Bensinger kept Jerry Jensen his deputy. A former BDAC agent aligned with the Purple Gang, Jensen had been one of Tartaglino's prime targets and a contentious subject of the 1975 Jackson Hearings.[5] Bensinger also kept Dan Casey at enforcement and Phil Smith at intelligence. These were signs that all was forgiven, and Bensinger began to push the programs that temporarily got the DEA back on its feet.

Some of these programs began as early as 1973; so please forgive the initial backtracking in this chapter.

The CENTAC Program

HIGH ATOP MYLES AMBROSE'S "HIT list," Tony Pohl, although upgraded, was transferred to a cubbyhole in Washington upon the creation of the DEA.[6] Pohl was assigned as Dan Casey's special assistant with the job of formulating the policies, procedures and programs of the DEA's nascent conspiracy unit.[7] Extrapolating on his Special Tactical Units in New York (which former Customs Agent John "Footsie" Fallon dissolved in July 1973 after being named regional director), Pohl initiated what was arguably the most effective DEA enforcement program ever, the Central Tactical Unit (CENTAC) program.

In a March 1974 briefing, Pohl explained that a CENTAC was a task force that made a series of "far-flung, complex conspiracy investigations."[8] Through a CENTAC, Pohl explained, various enforcement entities and headquarters components were brought under a "unified tactical command" with "unity of effort toward a common goal."[9]

John Bartels loved the idea, as did the OMB, and five CENTACs were set in motion. CENTAC 1 targeted a Lebanese narcotics ring in Pittsburgh that operated through transit points in Canada, Belize and Aruba and served as a supply source for Elvin Lee Bynum in New York, as well as distributors in Miami, Nashville, Boston, El Paso and Las Vegas.[10] CENTAC 2 was aimed at Frank Matthews and his national and international connections. CENTAC 3 focused on ethnic Chinese in the Far East, Canada and the US.[11] Staffed by seven agents under Doug Chandler, CENTAC 4 targeted amphetamine labs in Mexico and outlets in Southern California.[12] CENTAC 5 went after amphetamine traffickers in Canada. All five CENTACs rounded up scores of violators.[13]

Peter Bensinger, according to an agent assigned to the program, also loved CENTAC because it was "political and allowed him to become a player on the international scene." But the region directors hated CENTAC because it had no field agents of its own. It had a cadre of six agents, each of whom, like desk officers, handled one or two CENTACs. A region would start a case, but if it grew beyond the region's geographical boundaries and budget, headquarters could arbitrarily turn it into a CENTAC. The regional director would lose control and have to detach agents, often his best, to the CENTAC. The RDs were more concerned about making local cases, rather than helping headquarters make one big conspiracy case, because the administrative managers evaluated them on the basis of production; i.e. seizures, and arrests. The RDs were so uncooperative that Pohl, after two years, threw up his hands and fled to IBM at the invitation of its security chief, John Ingersoll.[14]

According to Pohl's replacement, Martin Pera, "The DEA CENTAC effort was reduced to a shambles as a result of continued pressure to decentralize it."[15]

An FBN agent since 1948, Pera had supervised Pohl in New York in 1960 and again in 1962, when Pera ran the Rome office and supervised Pohl in Marseille.[16] Allied with Andy Tartaglino against the corrupt agents in New York City, Pera quit the FBN in 1963 out of frustration with its "buy-bust" approach. He joined Naval Investigations, and in 1971 he entered Customs as chief of scientific and technical support. He entered the DEA with the merger in 1973 and in October 1975 became chief of Domestic Investigations, overseeing the CENTAC program.[17]

In August 1976 Pera testified to the Permanent Subcommittee on Investigations about the nuts and bolts of making conspiracy cases. The big obstacle, he said, was "The politicization of drug law enforcement by the Office of the Chief Executive."[18] He specifically blamed the Domestic Council and OMB under Nixon and Ford. He said there was a "vacuum of professional leadership in the various levels of DEA" and that "this vacuum has been filled by opportunists ....concerned with "image-enhancing, short-term, high visibility operations or studies." He said that the last thing they desired was "a candid evaluation."[19]

Pera's entire testimony is worthy of citation, but two short sentences from Senator Nunn are sufficient to sum up its impact: "We asked Mr. Bensinger about your particular position. He testified that that position had been abolished."[20] Exit Pera.

In one of the great ironies in DEA history, Deputy Administrator Jerry Jensen selected Dennis Dayle as CENTAC's next manager. One of Tartaglino's most ardent foes, Dayle had played a pivotal role in the Promuto affair by not putting his notes in writing, thus allowing the Wolf Pack time to organize its counter-offensive. Dayle was also one of Tartaglino's infamous "unresolved" cases. Dayle jokes that he was the only DEA agent to get demoted three times and still retire as a super grade.[21] But Dayle was a competent conspiracy case-maker and slid effortlessly into the CENTAC saddle. Being a "publicity nut" didn't hurt either, according to his former boss John Evans, who served as enforcement chief while Dayle was running CENTAC. "We'd make a case and I'd tell Dennis not to talk," Evans sighed, "but he'd talk anyway."[22]

Dayle's intriguing CENTACs are written about exhaustively in *The Underground Empire* by James Mills, so there's no point in reviewing them here. Suffice it to say they were significant, and Dayle overcame tremendous obstacles starting them up. To his credit, he expanded and refined CENTAC into a powerhouse that mapped the DEA's major enforcement effort through the early 1980s. But, as Dayle said with dismay, "The major targets of my investigations almost invariably turned out to be working for the CIA."[23]

Dayle privately longed to mount a super-CENTAC that brought together all the CENTACs and focused on the archangels. Considering that straight arrow John Evans called the CIA, "the biggest drug trafficker in the world," it's easy to understand why that super CEN-TAC never materialized.

A CENTAC Case Study

CENTAC 12 ENCOMPASSED MOST OF the political espionage elements discussed in this book. The focus was Cuban exile Alberto Sicilia Falcon, whose rise and fall is chronicled in *The Underground Empire*.[24] Falcon's criminal career began in 1965 in Miami, where he befriended José Egozi-Bejar, an exile Jewish-Cuban millionaire.[25] A CIA-trained intelligence officer in the Bay of Pigs invasion, Egozi was connected to the Cuban exile crime community and Mafiosi in Las Vegas. By 1970, Falcon was living in Tijuana and importing hash oil from Morocco. He invited Egozi to join him. Egozi declined, but did introduce Falcon into the dark world of Swiss bank accounts and tax evasion.

Falcon had plenty of drug money to launder. While BNDD agents in Operation Springboard were rounding up remnants of the French connection in South America, Falcon was acquiring the Mexican officials who had protected them. Through these officials and his exile Cuban contacts, Falcon met cocaine suppliers in Colombia, Peru and Bolivia. By 1972, he was shipping marijuana, heroin and cocaine to American distributors Roger Fry and Carlos Kyriakides. He was also in the arms trade. With Egozi's help, Falcon "assisted the CIA by supplying weapons for an intended Portuguese coup d'etat."[26] Lou Conein's asset Mitch Werbell and American arms trafficker James

Morgan, also linked to the CIA, sold sophisticated weaponry to Falcon.[27] Indeed, with Falcon, the war on drugs entered both a more violent and sophisticated stage, with drug traffickers armed with automatic weapons, as well as being linked to CIA counter-revolutionary activities in Mexico and Latin America.[28]

Falcon admitted working for the CIA, "to set up a network exchanging Mexican heroin and marijuana for weapons."[29] The guns were sent to guerrillas in hopes that besieged governments in Latin America would petition for US military aide. As recounted in *Underground Empire*, Peter Bensinger thought Falcon was a double agent for the Soviets, while several DEA agents thought he was a CIA informant reporting on Mexican revolutionaries in exchange for free passage. The CIA's motive, naturally, was to destabilize the Mexican government, so US corporations could more easily manipulate Mexico's competitive oil industry.

The DEA in 1973 initiated a case on Falcon and his American distributor Carlos Kyriakides. The DEA put an informant inside their operation and in late June 1975, Falcon was arrested and imprisoned. The case evolved into CENTAC 12. Designed to investigate Falcon's connections, it became the subject of Congressional hearings in 1977.[30] Most significantly, CENTAC 12 would uncover information implicating Mexican President Luis Echeverria and his successor José Lopéz Portillo in the drug business, as well as numerous Mexican police, intelligence and military officers. Along with rumors that DEA agents were on Falcon's payroll, the case would fuel the DEA's obsession with Mexico.[31]

CENTAC 12

DEA CASE AGENTS WORKING ON Falcon were assigned to CENTAC 12. Leading the charge was former CIA officer Pat Gregory, an alleged member of Chief Inspector Pat Fuller's infamous CIA Twofold program.[32] Assisted by DEA agents in California, and equipped with CIA charts showing organizational relationships, Gregory uncovered Falcon's official contacts. Gregory's closest ally in Mexico was Florentino Ventura-Gutierrez, commander of a special group that worked on national security cases. Gregory said Ventura was "the cruelest human being that I personally know," and that "I admire the man."[33]

Through Ventura, Gregory interrogated Egozi in Santa Marta prison shortly before Egozi committed suicide. Gregory was also nearby when Ventura's men tortured Falcon into spewing information linking him to President Echeverría and his inner circle. Though Gregory hotly pursued these powerful officials, Ventura's superior officer, CIA asset Miguel Nassar Haro, intervened to protect them.[34] One DEA agent speculated that when Falcon became too powerful, the CIA sent Gregory in to destroy him.[35] In this case it appears that when Gregory got too close to upsetting the political applecart, the CIA turned the tables and used a Mexican asset to sabotage the DEA — a phenomenon that would reoccur at an alarming rate over the ensuing thirty years.

The CENTAC 12 investigation badly embarrassed Mexican officials, and Echeverria's successor, José Lopéz Portillo announced in 1977 that the presence of the American government would be sharply reduced in Mexico.[36] Observers attributed his anti-Americanism to a sharp devaluation of the peso and a dispute with the US over natural gas prices. The drug business was certainly not the prime motive, but DEA agents saw this policy shift as a means for Mexican officials to acquire a piece of the burgeoning drug trade. And Manuel Ibarra Herrera, whom Portillo appointed head of the Mexican Federal Judicial Police, not only turned a blind eye toward drug lords who contributed to Portillo, he was later accused of conspiring to kidnap and murder a DEA agent.[37] Thus the DEA would walk a thin line in Mexico for the next ten years, trying to make cases that would not anger the Mexican officials it relied upon, or the amoral CIA officers working with Mexico's equally corrupt security forces.

> *"It's not the drugs that do the most harm, it's the money."*
> — Alberto Sicilia Falcon

The Falcon case was the first in which financial intelligence was applied within the DEA. The impetus, according to DEA Agent Rich Kobakoff, came from CENTAC 12 case agent Pat Gregory, who went to Falcon's Mexican banker and asked, "Who is your correspondent?" Gregory took the information to his bosses and asked them to find out what Falcon did with his money. As Kobakoff explained, "All banks that conduct business internationally have correspondent relations to adapt to the exchange rate. But there was no international authority regulating exchange. The FDIC regulated some banks, Treasury and the Federal Reserve some others."[38]

At the same time Gregory was asking questions, IRS official Robert Stankey at the Treasury Department's Office of Law Enforcement approached DEA officials in September 1975 and said there was a fortune in drug money fueling the underground economy. The FBI was looking at bank fraud and embezzlement, the IRS at tax evasion, and Customs was following money US citizens saved by not declaring merchandise they purchased overseas. But the largest percentage of underground money, Stankey told Kobakoff, was generated by drug trafficking; so he went to the DEA knowing all the other agencies would have to follow drug cases the DEA initiated.

Phil Smith, having replaced Dan Casey as Acting Assistant Administrator for Intelligence, told Kobakoff to start exploiting the financial aspects of the Falcon case. Strategic Intelligence chief Tom Fox saw the potential and detailed Kobakoff to work with Stankey as part of a Specially Funded Intelligence Program called Operation Goldfinger. By examining wire transfers, Kobakoff and Stankey learned how Falcon's money had been transferred to Switzerland. Using a letter rogatory from a US court, they asked a Swiss court to order Falcon's Swiss bank to release certain records. Swiss officials went into the bank and got the necessary correspondent statements, which Kobakoff took to Detroit for the trial of Falcon's major American distributor, Robert Fry, in July 1976. Fry pled guilty.[39]

As Kobakoff and Stankey learned what other laws were applicable, financial intelligence became one of the DEA's premier investigative tools. But first Bensinger had to sign on to the new innovative idea.

The Bensinger Briefing

AFTER THE SUCCESSFUL FRY PROSECUTION, Smith instructed Kobakoff to brief Bensinger. Kobakoff began by explaining that IRS economists estimated that the underground economy was fueled by billions of dollars in drug money. Much of the money left the US and bolstered foreign economies, some of which were considered hostile. Having established financial intelligence as a matter of national security, Kobakoff got down to the nuts and bolts. First he presented financial intelligence as a function of strategic intelligence. He gave four examples. 1) The Jamaican economy was more reliant on pot than on tourism. 2) Colombia's biggest export was cocaine. 3) Haiti was unstable because its generals were making too much money taking bribes from drug traffickers to restore an elected government. 4) Many inner city economies in the US were based on drugs, which was a serious public health issue.

Then Kobakoff compared the strategic, operational and tactical "financial intelligence" aspects of a case in which an informant told DEA agents that a Peruvian freighter in Baltimore harbor had cocaine aboard. Strategically, Kobakoff asked, was this the start of a trend? If the Peruvians were trafficking, what impact did cultivating, producing, transporting and distributing drugs have on the Peruvian economy? Operationally, two financial intelligence questions were: which trafficking organizations were profiting, and how should the DEA deal with them? If this was the Lima cartel (whose advisor was the head of the Perez Lima Bank) how was the money washed? A typical tactical intelligence question was: can we seize the traffickers' boat and other assets through civil forfeiture laws absent a criminal conviction, if they plead guilty to a minimum sentence?

For Bensinger it was love at first sight, and the financial intelligence program took a giant leap forward. According to Kobakoff, the DEA chief said: "This is the future. This is where we're going to hurt them. Now we can pay for ourselves." Then he told the DEA officials at the meeting to "Push it."

Dr. Peter Bourne, who ran the Office of Drug Abuse Policy for the Carter White House, was also pushing financial intelligence on the recommendation of his intelligence advisor, erstwhile CIA officer Seymour Bolten. On Bourne's behalf, Bolten in early 1977 did a study on intelligence which, he claimed, resulted in the creation of the National Narcotics Intelligence Consumers Committee in 1978.[40] Modeled on the CCINC, the NNICC was chaired by the DEA's Assistant Administrator for Intelligence and included representatives from several government agencies. The purpose was to coordinate the collection, analysis, dissemination and evaluation of drug-related intelligence, both foreign and domestic, and to publish annually a National Intelligence Estimate on the Supply of Drugs to the US Illicit Market from Foreign and Domestic Sources.

The NNICC, like the CCINC, put White House staff members in the position of making drug policy, a dangerous situation Martin Pera had warned Congress about only a year earlier. But DEA officials did not object, for Bolten saw financial information on drug traffickers as their principal vulnerability; and based on Bolten's recommendations, the Carter White House allotted more money to the DEA for financial intelligence.

In the beginning, however, it was a one-man show with Bensinger reaching around everyone to task Kobakoff directly. After the

Bensinger briefing, Kobakoff was assigned two female analysts and started working with Justice Department attorneys and IRS Agent Vincent Gambino. In 1977, Bensinger's new intelligence chief, W. Gordon Fink, assigned Kobakoff a Special Agent as a deputy. In March 1978 Bensinger reorganized the Office of Intelligence to include an operational intelligence division and an intelligence systems division. A Financial Intelligence Section was, at the time, established in the Office of Plans and Evaluation.[41] Along with federal laws stipulating the forfeiture of narcotics proceeds, financial intelligence by the early 1980s was in high gear and revenue from seizures enabled the DEA to return its allocation to the general fund; it was even allowed to spend some of the surplus on new equipment.[42] Financial intelligence is now a highly sought after job and is taught at Quantico by DEA instructors.

EPIC

BY 1975 IT WAS WELL known that drug smuggling across the Mexican border was increasing and, in response, the El Paso Intelligence Center (EPIC) was created to stem the flow. Many people claim credit for the idea, but EPIC was officially proposed in 1974 in a Justice Department report to the OMB titled *A Secure Border: An Analysis of Issues Affecting the U.S. Department of Justice.*[43] Based at Fort Bliss and initially called BRAIN (Border Regional Area Intelligence Network), EPIC was billed as an all-purpose service center specific to the Southwest border.

DEA Agent Jacques Kiere initially ran EPIC when it went operational in October 1974.[44] But Kiere was transferred to Mexico after irritating local lawmakers by talking to the press about illegal air strips in Texas.[45] Art Fluhr, the assistant RD in Dallas, took over in September 1976.[46] Though a native New Yorker, Fluhr had been in the area for eight years and knew most senior federal law enforcement officials. Fluhr remembers that his transfer to EPIC occurred during the Conein assassination and bomb crisis. Headquarters wanted to transfer Conein to Texas as a way of getting him out of town, but the old spy had enough clout (and nerve) to ride out the storm.

Fluhr proved perfect for the EPIC job: he was a good money manager and got along well with the Customs and INS officials assigned as his deputies. He managed EPIC until 1982 when he retired and became chief of security at El Paso Gas. According to Fluhr, the CIA was "behind the whole thing" and wanted EPIC as a forward base for gathering covert intelligence inside Mexico. Fluhr had to get CIA clearance to run EPIC, and many CIA people were assigned to the facility. The National Security Agency and Army CID had people there too, and a regular army colonel was in charge of security.

There was "no control" and people "were writing reports from newspaper articles" when Fluhr arrived. To overcome this deficiency, he installed EPIC's computer with the assistance of Stanton Mintz, a former CIA officer in charge of the Intelligence Systems Division at DEA headquarters. The FAA set up a global communications system at EPIC, and Fluhr had military radios installed in DEA cars as far away as Peru. When an agent saw a suspicious aircraft he would call EPIC, relay the plane's tail number, and if no flight plan was found, EPIC would notify "people" in Panama who would intercept the plane and seize the dope. DEA agents could also place a transponder on a suspect ship and, using an "old Air Force satellite," EPIC could locate it anywhere at sea and then call upon the Coast Guard to seize it. Using this same system, Fluhr tracked migrating whales for government oceanographers.

"We got good intelligence," Fluhr said, "but the first question was, what do you do with it? The answer was 'Spread it around,' and we shared ours with the CIA, which had just formed its counter-terror center [in 1977 under Howard Bane]." Fluhr also signed agreements with all 50 states giving them access to EPIC.

Fluhr's other question was: "If EPIC was so great, why not set up places like it elsewhere, too?"[47]

Intelligence in Limbo

THE PROCESS OF REORGANIZING THE office of intelligence began in December 1974, with the Analysis of the Headquarters Intelligence and Enforcement Structure study conducted by Jerry Strickler, Tom Hurney and Mark Moore. Submitted in May 1975, the 75-page study singled out the lack of a "unified information system" and a "clearly enunciated program for the professional development of analytical personnel," as the main problems.[48] It emphasized the need for strategic intelligence and better foreign collection. In so far as Narcotic Country Action Plans were the basis for foreign operations, it suggested that headquarters find ways of improving relations with the State Department.

The study claimed the overall problem was DEA's strategy of decentralization. If the Office of Intelligence had more money and more control, intelligence could be more supportive of enforcement, and more people would know more about what was going on; not only overseas, but between the cracks: in regions and on the streets of New York and California. The study recommended a review of every report and telex, and the deployment of analysts (often women) to area desks at headquarters, to bring operational intelligence closer to enforcement section chiefs and suppression desks. It suggested that the DEA have one "Mr. Enforcement" instead of three chiefs — for enforcement, domestic investigations and foreign investigations. It wanted a heavier reliance on strategic intelligence for better coordination with State, the CIA and other agencies.

Almost all of these recommendations were accepted. One point of contention was the IGO function (the NIO Program), which the study described as having "more potential for harm than for good."[49]

The obvious failure was DEACON I, which ostensibly developed intelligence on organized crime figures in Costa Rica, Ohio, and New Jersey; political figures trafficking in Key West; terrorists involved in gun running in Miami; information on the sale of boats and possibly helicopters to Fidel Castro's government, and major Cuban smugglers. However, as a report stated, "25 assets were used to produce large amounts of worthwhile, substantiated intelligence."[50]

With the exception of one case made in April 1974, DEACON intelligence went nowhere. Plus, Conein's "Dirty Dozen" had an unpleasant CIA odor: the State Department was reluctant to provide them with cover, and foreign governments did not want them slithering around. So in October 1975, the Justice Department established a DEA Guidelines Committee to establish new rules for the covert collection of narcotics intelligence.[51] As a result, Gary Mattocks was returned to the CIA; five NIOs continued to function, three overseas and two at home; and the rest, including Robert Medell, were put in RIUs or assigned to headquarters as analysts monitoring SFIPs.[52]

Lou Conein, the Acting Chief of Special Operations and Field Support (IGO), argued for the need to maintain long-range collection on high level targets, as the best way to get away from low-level cases. On October 8, in a position paper presented to John Warner, the chief of the international intelligence division, Conein pressed for more intelligence collectors with better tradecraft skills overseas.[53] He even tried scare tactics, saying, "If DEA is unable to continue covert operations, the responsibility for the operations should be turned over to the US

Customs Service and the CIA."[54] Conein also raised the specter of the FBI taking over DEA's domestic intelligence functions.[55]

The internal debate continued until February 1976, when Jerry Strickler and Tom Hurney at the Office of Planning and Evaluation proposed a thorough reorganization of the Office of Intelligence. As they envisioned it, the new office of intelligence would provide "more actionable operational intelligence to the Office of Enforcement and [be] more responsive in terms of providing strategic intelligence to DEA management and other concerned agencies."[56] To this end they suggested filling the Deputy Assistant Administrator for Intelligence position, which had been available since the inception of the DEA. They also suggested increasing the international intelligence staff from 6 to 15 and the strategic intelligence staff from 13 to 24.

Conein expressed his frustration in March 1976 in a memorandum to Dan Casey's special assistant, Jesse M. Gallegos, noting that "financial" investigators had recommended that the DEA cease covert operations, while "the operational entity" (the CIA, perhaps?) wanted them to continue.[57] Conein pointed out that "All of the sensitive items were discussed with [Acting Chief Inspector] Mr. Joseph Jaffe and the Staff of the Office of Internal Security (DEA) and insisted, "in the interest of justice and fair play," that "every effort should be made to resolve ... unresolved allegations or implications of impropriety" directed against IGO personnel.[58] But that wasn't about to happen. The Purple Gang wasn't about to rescue Lou Conein and the awkward squad of former CIA spooks.

Totally disgusted, Conein gave a lengthy interview which appeared in the June 1976 *Washington Post*.[59] The article did not please Conein's bosses. He was transferred to Strategic Intelligence and his covert operations staff was abolished. But protected CIA-connected drug operations continue apace. In one noteworthy case, Conein's friend and DEACON asset, Mitch Werbell, went on trial in Miami in August 1976 on charges of plotting to smuggle "500,000 pounds of marijuana a month from Colombia to the United States."[60] But luckily for Werbell, his co-defendant in the case, Ken Burnstine, an arms dealer connected to the Cleveland mob, perished in a suspicious plane crash in June 1976, thus precluding a successful prosecution.

International Operations

CHANGE WAS SLOW IN COMING to the DEA, and when it did, it was in small ways. In September, John Warner divided the international intelligence division into desks for the Far East, Europe, Near East, Mexico and South America.[61] Louis Bachrach replaced him shortly thereafter and Warner became the RD in Paris. But overseas, where the CIA had a free hand, DEA guns continued to blaze and the bombs continued to explode until the Mansfield Amendment to the International Security Assistance and Arms Control Act of 1976, when Congress stepped in and curtailed the DEA's extralegal activities abroad. Presaging the "extraordinary renditions" of George W. Bush's "war on terror," the DEA had abducted or arranged for the abduction of as many of 150 suspected traffickers, not all of whom were guilty. For that reason, and due to the involvement of DEA agents in gun fights with traffickers in Mexico and Thailand, Senator Michael Mansfield (D-MT) introduced an amendment that prohibited agents from making arrests or conducting unilateral actions without the consent of the host government. They could work undercover but not unilaterally. They could not torture, kidnap, or kill. No more blazing submachine guns and exploding telephones — at least not until the Reagan Administration.[62]

The CIA, of course, was exempt and continued to mount covert drug operations, even though some were harmful to the DEA. Others were duplicative of DEA's efforts, but all tainted potential prosecutions, and caused confusion and suspicion among counterpart police agencies. None were useable in court because of security classifications. Because the CIA provided narcotics intelligence acquired by electronic surveillance overseas, several DEA investigations and prosecutions had to be terminated.[63] This was no accident: the DEA's "gentleman's agreement with CIA to ask for dismissals rather than expose sensitive sources or techniques" was a policy that went back to FBN days.[64] As noted in the previous chapter, 27 DEA prosecutions were "nolle prossed" on national security grounds, due to the participation of CIA assets.[65]

Meanwhile, Congresswoman Bella Abzug at the House Subcommittee on Government Information and Individual Rights was investigating the Puttaporn Khramkhruan case discussed in Chapter 19. She submitted questions to DCI George H.W. Bush. As advised by Seymour Bolten, Bush explained in writing that the cover-up was legal under a 1954 agreement between the CIA and the Justice Department, giving the CIA the right to block prosecution or keep its crimes secret in the name of national security.[67] In its report, the Abzug Committee stated: "It was ironic that the CIA should be given responsibility of narcotic intelligence, particularly since they are supporting the prime movers."[68]

The CIA was causing so many problems that in early 1977, outgoing Assistant Administrator for Enforcement Dan Casey sent a three-page, single-spaced memorandum to Bensinger expressing his concern "over the role presently being played by the CIA relative to the gathering of operational intelligence abroad."[69] Signing off on the memo were six enforcement division chiefs. "All were unanimous in their belief that present CIA programs were likely to cause serious future problems for DEA, both foreign and domestic." Unilateral CIA programs in foreign countries were a "potential source of conflict and embarrassment and which may have a negative impact on the overall US narcotic reduction effort." Casey referenced specific incidents, citing CIA electronic surveillance and the fact that the CIA "will not respond positively to any discovery motion." Casey foresaw more busted cases and complained that "Many of the subjects who appear in these CIA-promoted or controlled surveillances regularly travel to the United States in furtherance of their trafficking activities." The "de facto immunity" from prosecution enabled the CIA assets to "operate much more openly and effectively."

Casey was especially upset that the CIA demanded that DEA provide telephone numbers for its operations. "This practice is most disturbing because, in effect, it puts DEA in the position of determining which violators will be granted a de facto immunity." Considering the seriousness of the problem, he recommended that "all DEA support for CIA electronic surveillance be suspended at once." He asked Bensinger to insist that the CIA adhere to guidelines set by the Domestic Council and stick to gathering strategic intelligence. He advised that DEA personnel not request CIA support "which might tend to prejudice the domestic prosecution of any drug trafficker."[70]

A February 11, 1977 memo from Strickler to Casey's replacement, Wayne Valentine, harshly criticized Bensinger's Acting Assistant Administrator for Intelligence, Gordon Fink, for failing to address the problems caused by the CIA. Fink had sent a memorandum to Bensinger's Deputy Administrator, Donald E. Miller, listing "a number of supply reduction gains alleged to have been achieved as a result of CIA efforts." Referring to Casey's memo, Strickler said it was "unanimous" among enforcement chiefs, that "Of greater evaluative significance is the supply reduction losses incurred by DEA as a result of

CIA operational drug intelligence activities." Below is a sampling of the list Strickler and his colleagues compiled.[71]

1) A DEA fugitive was apprehended abroad. Ministerial level officials in the country offered to deport the fugitive to the US for prosecution, but before the offer could be accepted, the CIA notified DEA that the fugitive had been the subject of a CIA electronic surveillance which would result in the dismissal of charges.

2) A key heroin trafficker was indicted after 20 years of case development, but he was the principal in a unilateral CIA electronic surveillance. The trafficker was immunized from prosecution, along with all the traffickers he had met.

3) One of 20 top level international drug traffickers became a cooperating informant for the DEA and testified against his co-conspirators. However, his lawyer filed for discovery. When the CIA revealed that it had coordinated an electronic surveillance against the defendant, charges were dropped against all 20 traffickers.

4) A case against a foreign-based head of a multi-national drug trafficking organization, with over 50 members, including the head of a major domestic distribution network, collapsed due to a CIA intelligence collection effort. As Strickler noted, "The violator, one of the most significant traffickers known to DEA, continues to operate."

The following examples, cited by Strickler, had nothing to do with electronic surveillance, but illustrated other impediments the CIA threw in the path of the DEA.

5) A policeman in a foreign country facilitated the movement of drugs to the US. The DEA gathered enough evidence to indict him, but (like so many worldwide) he was a CIA informant and his protection extended to "virtually all major violators" in that country.

6) The CIA provided a trafficker with false documentation so he could travel to the US for debriefing. Arrested in a third country, he honestly claimed to be working for "American drug law enforcement." As Strickler noted, "At the loss of its own prestige and good will, the DEA did not identify the CIA's role in this matter."

7) In a major investigation, the CIA used DEA confidential information "as blackmail material to induce recruitment of the DEA target." Not only did the recruitment fail, it compromised the DEA investigation.

8) A major DEA target was recruited by the CIA. The CIA then used confidential DEA information to protect him. "When the facts

became known, it was clear that commitments made by CIA precluded successful prosecution of the criminal."

Alas, Bensinger and certain members of his senior staff suffered the CIA at the expense of the DEA's integrity. Bensinger ignored Casey and his division chiefs.

The Office of Intelligence 1977-1980

ANY NUMBER OF AMBITIOUS DEA agents would gladly have accepted the position, but Bensinger on January 9, 1977 named NSA official W. Gordon Fink as Assistant Administrator for Intelligence.[72] Fink was responsible for the domestic and foreign regional intelligence units (abolished a couple of years later) as well as the office of intelligence at headquarters. Under Fink, the Deputy AAI position was finally filled, first by Frank Monastero (with Jim Ludlum as his special assistant) and later by Dave Westrate.

As an outsider, Fink was not a wildly popular boss within the DEA, but Phil Smith helped him get off to a good start. As pre-ordained, Smith then retired and became security chief at the Resorts International casino. Having none of Tartaglino's prejudices in this regard, Fink "took advantage of Smith and others who retired in similar positions with the start of gambling in Atlantic City." He did not want the Mafia to get a foothold in either place, as they had in Las Vegas, which they were using for their money laundering.

Fink guided DEA intelligence into the New World, first by restructuring the office based on how drugs were produced, imported, and sold in the US He knocked heads together and made sure that headquarters desk officers worked closely with their assigned field offices. He also set up a group to support the Office of Compliance, which worked on diversion of legally produced drugs. Under Fink, EPIC became "a showplace" that responded to "over 65% of those who queried." Stepping out of DEA tradition, in which undermining Customs was a holy mission, Fink "made a lot of trips to the field to insure that our DEA field-intelligence activities were coordinated with headquarters and that the field Customs installations were receiving intelligence support.

"I also set up a Board of Directors for managing EPIC," Fink continues, noting that "Senator Weicker used to really challenge me during testimony ... to insure that I was not combining data from the participating agencies data bases. DEA's was the most sensitive DB since it had active case investigations." Under Fink, an expert in information technology, agents developed the DEA's own software and a new position was established to manage that responsibility. Fink's cadre of programmers developed modules for both analysts and agents to use at headquarters as well as in the field.

As suggested by the Strickler study, the role of regional intelligence units expanded, and intelligence analysts finally started receiving promotions. Fink also "started several training courses including one that was for both field DEA agents and analysts in intelligence collection that assisted in the establishment of special field intelligence programs." By then, the SFIPs had passed from Conein's disgraced IGO to the Operations Division. Highly prized, the SFIPs were a good way for regional directors to obtain manpower, material and money for operations that got too big for them to handle. According to Fink, each SFIP was reviewed at headquarters and lawyers at Main Justice "to insure that they would withstand court challenges when implemented and went to trial. We funded a large number of very creative, successful field intelligence/enforcement programs - all of them survived numerous court challenges including at least one that went to the Supreme Court!"

The SFIP program included elements that worked on special projects, like organized crime or motorcycle gangs, as well as providing support to CENTAC programs. "Full time analysts were detailed to the CENTACs but also worked closely with their 'home' Office of Intelligence Section to insure that we were tracking the 'splinter' groups outside of the CENTAC targeting."

As part of the March 1978 reorganization, the international intelligence division was eliminated and its chief, Lou Bachrach, became Chief of Operational Intelligence with responsibility for the geographic drug-source sections, as well as for the SFIP program. According to Fink, the new "emphasis was to work from the source to the domestic trafficking structure. At the same time I reorganized my office, I worked with the field including the large (over 500 people) Unified Intelligence Division in New York to insure healthy, constant interchange. We reorganized the UID along the ethnic trafficker lines (blacks, several Hispanic elements, Chinese, Organized Crime, etc.). I was challenged in an administrative court action with setting up this structure — the black agents objected to the Black unit. After I told the judge that our emphasis was to understand how the Italian heroin sources that imported heroin got to the mostly black organizations (Nicky Barnes, etc.) that sold to sources who trafficked on the streets he accepted my rationale which ended the court challenge!"

Fink knew Seymour Bolten and hotly contests Bolten's claim to have created the National Narcotics Intelligence Consumers Committee (NNICC). "I created it and served as the Chairman," Fink said, adding that he "used the NNICC to formulate and coordinate" the National Narcotics Intelligence Estimate, which he also started. Produced by the Strategic Intelligence Division, the Estimate was an annual product that Fink coordinated with the Intelligence Community and "which became a very useful product especially with the Congress and media. It contained specific estimates of how much money was spent in the US on specific illicit and diverted legal narcotics. It also proved to be instrumental in getting the Congress to 'direct' the IRS to form joint investigative Grand Juries with DEA something both the Administrator and I had been unable to accomplish. It helped provide the basis for initiation of DEA's financial investigations which became very successful using the civil asset forfeiture/seizure authority contained in the RICO statute."

According to Fink, "the toughest coordination point was State Department, not the Agency as many might have guessed. State did not want to see the magnitude of our consumption problem documented." After a while, however, State saw the value of the annual estimate, which helped them get additional funding for their overseas activities. Fink sees that development as "their turning point."

Fink's principal contact with the Agency was Eloise Page. A legend in the CIA, she began her spy career as OSS Director William Donovan's secretary; by 1976, she was the CIA's highest-ranking female officer. Fink "had working relationships with both the Strategic Intelligence reps in [CIA's Directorate of Intelligence] as well as relationships with [its Directorate of Operations] field operations. I did negotiate new field relationships for DEA operations which were documented in a classified document signed by the [CIA] Director and the Administrator."

The Strategic Intelligence Division continued to guide policy makers, but operational intelligence programs subsided due to concerns about CIA assassins. (Fink placed Conein in strategic intelligence and told him to stop talking to reporters.) The Strategic Intelligence Division started working on financial intelligence and was responsible for the heroin signature program. "The Operations Division worked with the signature program in requesting domestic street-buy programs from our field offices assisting in the targeting of specific organizations that we suspected were importing from "new" foreign sources - e.g. the emergence of Southwest Asian heroin."

Meaning Afghanistan. Before we get there, however, we must first return to Mexico and Thailand.

25

GOING UNDERGROUND

WHEN PRESIDENT JIMMY CARTER TOOK office in January 1977, he retained Peter Bensinger as DEA Administrator but brought to the White House a new team of drug policy advisors. Carter's outlook on drug law enforcement helped fracture the DEA along ideological lines and enabled the CIA to expand its unilateral drug operations, despite the opposition to CIA operations expressed by DEA agents in early 1977.

Carter was not entirely to blame for the troubles that ensued. A White Paper authored by the Ford Administration had understated the dangers of cocaine, and by 1977 cocaine had become a status symbol associated with celebrities. Health risks were said to be minimal if the drug was moderately used; according to one Harvard doctor, that meant "two or three times a week."[1] Carter's Special Assistant for Health Issues, Dr. Peter Bourne, described cocaine as "probably the most benign of illicit drugs currently in widespread use. At least as strong a case could be made for legalizing it as for legalizing marijuana."[2] Although Carter was against legalizing marijuana, he did not view it as a serious threat.[3] However, under Carter, drug supply reduction expenditures declined and marijuana and cocaine use increased. This trend would not be reversed until Ronald Reagan took office.[4]

On national security policy, Carter again followed a liberal trend set by Congress and the Ford Administration. In 1974, Congress abolished the Office of Public Safety, which was accused of teaching torture techniques to foreign policemen and military officers. Also closed was the Border Patrol Academy in Los Fresnos, Texas, where CIA officers "trained students in making criminal terrorist devices and in assassination methods."[5] At a four-week course at "the Bomb School," students were trained "not in bomb disposal but in bomb making."[6]

President Ford outlawed assassinations, although, of course, they continued unabated through proxies.[7] In 1976 under DCI George H.W. Bush, official right-wing terrorism took root and flourished in Latin America through the CIA-supported "Operation Condor" network of foreign intelligence services, which pooled resources to identify and neutralize threats to wealthy landowners, industrialists, and fascist regimes.[8] The threats invariably came from labor leaders and poor people trying to organize for better living conditions. Meanwhile, CIA personnel from abandoned outposts in Southeast Asia poured into Latin America to support the repressive Condor apparatus. With them came the usual exile Cuban miscreants. While Bush was DCI, exile Cuban terrorists Luis Posada and Orlando Bosch, both connected to the CIA, blew up a Cuban passenger plane in Venezuela in October 1976, killing 73 people.[9] They were connected to the murder of Cuban diplomats in Argentina, and through the Chilean secret service, they were also involved in the September 1976 assassination of Chilean diplomat Orlando Letelier in Washington, D.C.[10]

Seeking to stem CIA abuses, Carter replaced Bush with Admiral Stansfield Turner, who in October 1977 cut some 800 positions from the clandestine service.[11] Turner also scrapped Air America, the CIA's private air force known to FBN agents as "Air Opium." Holding their hatred close to their black hearts, CIA officers still on the payroll burrowed deep within the labyrinth at Langley headquarters. To ensure Carter's defeat in 1980, they and their ideological supporters in the media, academia, private enterprise and government sabotaged Carter's liberal "Human Rights" policies. To compensate for the reduction in CIA forces, the Army created Delta Force and the Navy organized SEAL Team Six. "At the same time," author Michael McClintock asserts, "Israel and Argentina stepped in to fill overt advisory and materiel requirements that could not be met by the United

States." As McClintock notes, "Neither arrangement could have gone forward without a green light from Washington."[12]

As we shall see, Carter's lax drug policies inadvertently aided this silent coup.

Panama

CARTER'S HUMAN RIGHTS POLICY HAD little effect and, according to McClintock, abuses actually peaked "in Argentina and Nicaragua, and reached new and unprecedented levels (to be exceeded only in the Reagan years) in Guatemala and El Salvador."[13]

Carter's "see no evil" policy also extended to Panama, where, in September 1977, he and President Omar Torrijos signed the Panama Canal Treaty, which provided for the return of the canal to Panama in December, 1999. The treaty needed Senate approval, however, and was fervently opposed by conservatives concerned that the Soviets might seize control of the canal. The effort to block ratification was led by Senator Robert Dole (R-KS).[14]

To assuage moderate Republicans, Carter and Torrijos in October 1977 agreed that the US could use military force to keep the canal open, but that the US would not use military force to interfere in Panamanian affairs. This side deal was sufficient to garner the votes needed for ratification. But conservatives quickly seized upon Panama's central role in international drug trafficking, and at Dole's insistence the Senate Intelligence Committee began hearings in February 1978 into allegations that General Torrijos and members of his family had engaged in narcotics trafficking to the US.

Crucial to proving this point were DEA documents, and according to a series of articles published in the *New York Times*, 45 files on allegations about the Torrijos family were provided by the DEA.[15] Named in the allegations were Manuel Noriega and Omar, Hugo and Moises Torrijos. The DEA documents included the embarrassing fact that the Nixon Administration used the 1972 indictment against Moises to pressure Omar into cooperating with the BNDD, and that it had refused to pursue a case against Noriega, rather than risk losing the CIA's International Police Academy in Panama and Noriega's espionage services. In December 1972, Ingersoll had assigned Agent Leland Riggs the job of arresting Moises, should he set foot in the Canal Zone, but the CIA or State Department tipped off Moises and he avoided the trap.[16]

Oblivious to these skeletons in the Republican Party's overstuffed closet, Dole and other treaty opponents publicly stated their belief that drug dealing by the Torrijos family proved that Panama could not be trusted to honor its commitments.[17] Treaty advocates, however, said there was no proof among the DEA documents. Senator Robert C. Byrd (D-WV), the majority leader, said there was "no evidence that would stand up in a United States court," against Torrijos.[18] Thus the Treaty was ratified in September 1978.

The reason for the lack of proof, according to Jerry Strickler, is that documents were purged from the DEA's files. According to Strickler, Attorney General Griffin Bell asked DEA to gather up every report and intelligence file on Panama for review by the Justice Department. Bensinger says it happened on his initiative, and that Bell "made no effort to minimize the information about Panama." Peter Bensinger's executive assistant William Lenck supervised John Bacon in the effort to identify and collate all reports and intelligence files on Panama. It was not a carefully managed operation. According to Bacon, "Back in 1978, anyone could have access to central files at DEA. You didn't have to sign or justify anything. Agents could go in and look at their own files, and if they wanted to, they could even take them out."[19]

Bacon filled 13 boxes with all original case files having anything to do with drug trafficking in Panama. The files contained "the names of thousands of people involved in drug traffic." Bacon described the documents as "hard forensic evidence about Torrijos and official protection — an ongoing mass of corruption." Bacon separated classified from unclassified documents, then sealed the boxes and prepared a transmittal slip for Lenck to sign. Lenck signed for the documents and that was the last Bacon saw of them. "Lenck said he took them to the Senate," Bacon recalled, "but as far as I know, the boxes never came back."

Lenck Responds

As WILLIAM LENCK RECALLED, CONGRESS wanted to see DEA information regarding Panama. Congress asked Attorney General Griffin Bell, Bell asked Bensinger, Bensinger asked Lenck, and people starting gathering files. When they were done, Lenck put "13 or 14 boxes" in the trunk of his Chrysler. It was Friday evening, so he drove home with the intention of bringing them to Congress on Monday morning.[20]

Later that night Bensinger called Lenck. Bensinger told him to return the documents to DEA headquarters because they contained CIA information that had to be deleted before it could be presented to Congress. Lenck took the files to the DEA's Washington field office for safekeeping, and on Monday returned them to DEA headquarters. Three to four weeks passed while someone sifted through them and cleaned out the CIA material. Only after the documents had been sanitized did Lenck take them to the Senate Intelligence Committee. He presented them one box at a time to Dole, and Dole personally signed 13 or 14 transmittal slips indicating that he received them. Then they came back to the DEA. "That's the way it happened," Lenck said.

But no one at DEA signed a transmittal slip indicating they were returned.

"This type of action was unprecedented and a sham," Strickler contends. "Actual procedure would, at most, have called for providing Justice with a copy of the reports that were relevant. But in this case, every [original] file on Panama and the Panamanians was removed from DEA and carted away never again to surface. I was familiar with most of the material and, in fact, wrote some. They would have been very damaging to those who endorsed the treaty.

"As far as the purging of the DEA files," Strickler continues, "this was not known throughout DEA, and only people like Bacon were aware of its full impact. Years later, when Noriega was on trial and his defense stressed that he had received letters of commendation from DEA and that DEA had no prior negative information, I called DEA and told them about the purge. So the DEA checked and said the index cards were present, but the reports and files were not. The index cards serve as a "road map" for locating the data, but the data itself was gone. The data," Strickler emphasizes, "was very specific and in the Sea Witch case, there was enough evidence to indict Noriega."

In response to my Freedom of Information Act request for documents about the Sea Witch case, the DEA said there were no responsive records. This supports Strickler's claim of a purge. But the question remains: who stole the damaging documents? Dole did not respond to a September 13, 1999 letter asking him if he had proof that he returned the documents to the DEA. Thus, the paper trail ends with him.

Going Under Ground

THIS CHAPTER EXPLORES THE NOTION that during the Carter Administration, a faction within the national security establishment managed a secret foreign policy apparatus. At times their objectives dovetailed with Carter's. When their objectives differed, they launched covert actions behind his back. The field operators were often CIA officers who had retired or resigned before Turner's reduction in force, along with those who were fired. These secret agents obtained employment in legitimate America businesses, foreign intelligence services, and in various arms, oil, shipping, computer consulting and other kinds of proprietary companies established by deep cover intelligence officers.

Edwin P. Wilson, the epitome of a deep cover CIA officer, factors into the "off-the-shelf" operations that provided cover for CIA drug trafficking activities. After resigning from the CIA in 1971, Wilson joined the Office of Naval Intelligence's Task Force 157. A perfect "deniable" deep cover agent, he had set up a number of CIA proprietary shipping companies which the Navy adopted and used to spy on Soviet activity in foreign ports.[21] After the Navy fired him in April 1976, Wilson maintained ownership of his companies. According to one of his employees, Wilson's case officer in these ventures was CIA officer Tom Clines, reporting to Ted Shackley.[22] When faced with termination by DCI Stansfield Turner for associating with Wilson, Clines, confirming the above, said "he had been assigned during the Bush years" with "penetrating the Wilson gang."[23]

Shackley admitted socializing with Wilson to DCI Turner. For this and other reasons Turner reassigned Shackley in late 1977 from his powerful post as associate deputy director for operations to lesser duties.[24] Shackley and Clines soon retired from the CIA and, with a $500,000 loan from Wilson, they and Major General Richard Secord formed EATSCO, which had a contract from the Pentagon to ship US arms to Egypt.[25]

Soon thereafter, on November 4, 1979, fundamentalist Muslims overthrew the government of Iran, commandeering the American Embassy in Tehran and holding its employees hostage. This crisis allowed Ronald Reagan to defeat Carter in the 1980 presidential election. How that happened is often ascribed to an "October Surprise," in which Reagan's campaign manager William J. Casey and vice presidential candidate George Bush allegedly made a secret agreement with Iranian officials in October 1980.[26] In exchange for holding the hostages through the election, then releasing them, Bush and Casey agreed to sell weapons to Iran, despite an embargo. Iran had been invaded by Iraq and agreed to the deal. The hostages were released the day Reagan took office. Reagan then repudiated Carter's Human

Rights crusade and declared a war against terrorism. US Government sanctioned arms and drug smuggling became integral components of Reagan's national security policy, and ideological DEA agents would facilitate the process. Two examples follow; one in Thailand, the other in Mexico; both were major areas of concern singled out for DEA Action Plans and expanded intelligence operations in 1974.[27]

Thailand

As a DEA agent explained in Chapter 6, the DEA in Thailand was stymied by official corruption. The heroin kingpin in 1971 was controlled by corrupt Thai enforcement officials, "the pay-off going all the way up to the Prime Minister." The police colonel in charge of all narcotic suppression was arrested on corruption charges but bought his way out. As the DEA agent said, "Thai officials knew all the principal violators and exacted significant payoffs from them to let them continue in business."[28]

DEA agents used trickery to make cases, keeping the Thai police in the dark until they were ready to pounce. Thai officials did not find this amusing; they were a major ally in the war in Southeast Asia and complained to their counterparts in the CIA and State Department. As a result, the DEA was prevented from making cases on certain significant traffickers and restricted from entering certain areas. [30]

Under John Bartels in 1974, the DEA began to expand foreign regional intelligence units and clandestine operations.[31] The CIA's hidden hand in this development was apparent in DEA directives filled with CIA jargon instructing "case officers" how to recruit "principal agents," conduct background checks, and provide secure communications.[32] Thailand, where the heroin trade was booming, was of special concern and in April 1974, Deputy Regional Director John R Doyle in Bangkok sent a memo to all personnel in Region 16 with instructions on how to set up intelligence nets.[33] Targets now included drug organization front companies, arms traffickers, political or intelligence organizations selling drugs to promote political activity, and militant political groups selling drugs to finance terrorists. The DEA's "direct intelligence collection activity may or may not be carried out with the knowledge of the local police services," one directive emphasized.[34]

By the time Dan Addario replaced Fred Dick as regional director in Bangkok in 1975, the DEA was routinely conducting "unilateral" actions as a way of circumventing Thai officials.[35] A veteran agent who had joined the FBN in New York in 1959, Addario (whose first partner and teacher was the infamous Frankie Waters), brought a new team of eager agents with him to Thailand. Under Addario the DEA got tough, attacking opium caravans and bombing labs in Burma with CIA assistance.[36]

Meanwhile, as Vietnam, Laos and Cambodia fell to the communists, the DEA started hiring old French smugglers in Bangkok. As Agent Thomas de Triquet notes, there was an intelligence vacuum in Laos, "and we wanted to know what was going on. We ran sources who reported on the involvement in drug trafficking of [official Laotians] and others. We would meet with sources in Udorn and Nong Khai [Thailand] as they came out of Laos."[37]

DEA agents gathered lots of intelligence which led to the opening of district offices in Udorn, Thailand and Vientiane, Laos. New regional intelligence units were set up in Chiang Mai, Thailand and Hong Kong as well. The DEA spent $400,000 on covert intelligence collection in 1976 alone.[38] And yet, despite its new emphasis on gathering intelligence, the DEA seemed unaware that Australia had become a major transit point for narcotics heading to the US. This is strange, for in 1965, FBN Commissioner Henry Giordano had sent his foreign operations chief, Jack Cusack, to Australia to investigate reports that the Calabrian Mafia was smuggling drugs into Australia.[39] Giordano would have sent Cusack only if reports indicated that Australia was a transit point of narcotics to America.

Curiously, at the same time Cusack trailed the Mafia into Australia, the CIA reportedly recruited Australian Special Branch Detective John Wesley Egan as a drug courier.[40] In 1966 Egan started making drug runs from Hong Kong to Sydney to New York. He recruited others, often police officers, and used the shotgun approach, sending three or four couriers at a time with a supervisor on board the flight. When arrested in New York in 1967, Egan said "working or ex- members" of the CIA were instrumental in the trade, because they could move their couriers through Customs.[41]

This, of course, was the same CIA methodology Jerry Strickler complained about in Chapter 17, when he cited the Venezuelan official who had been recruited by the CIA at the Public Safety School in Panama. The Venezuelan thought he was working as a courier for the BNDD in Colombia, carrying drugs to England and Canada as part of a controlled delivery.[42]

There is another curious thing. While Cusack was in Australia in 1965-1966, Agent John Evans covered foreign operations. "And that," Evans said, "is when I got to see what the CIA was doing. I saw a report on the Kuomintang saying they were the biggest drug dealers in the world, and that the CIA was underwriting them. Air America was transporting tons of Kuomintang opium.[43]

"Other things came to my attention," Evans adds, "that proved that the CIA contributed to drug use in [America]. We were in constant conflict with the CIA because it was hiding its budget in ours, and because CIA people were smuggling drugs into the US. But Cusack allowed [the CIA] to do it, and we [meaning the FBN] weren't allowed to tell [Congress, for example]. And that fostered corruption in the [FBN]."

The CIA evidently fostered corruption in the Australian Bureau of Narcotics as well, in the person of John Wesley Egan, whom the FBN arrested in New York in 1967. Egan escaped while out on bail by dressing up as a woman at a bridal party. In 1967, FBN Agents Mort Benjamin and John Enright went to Australia to get him back. But US drug enforcement interest in Australia apparently ended after that, despite the fact that by 1967, Australia was a "rest and recreation" playground for American soldiers on leave from Vietnam, with their insatiable demand for easy access to drugs and sex.

Nugan Hand

THE DEA'S COMPLICITY IN THE Iran-Contra scandal will be discussed in Chapter 27. The Nugan Hand scandal is less well known but involves many of the same players, including Ed Wilson, Ted Shackley, Tom Clines, and their Cuban assets Ricardo Chavez and Rafael Quintero. An Australian Task Force report on Nugan Hand's drug activities noted that the history of the people named above "is relevant to a proper understanding of the activities of the Nugan Hand group and the people associated with that group."[44]

The history of Nugan Hand begins in Laos in 1966, while William Colby was chief of the CIA's Far East Asian Division. Ted Shackley was its station chief in Vientiane, Laos, with Tom Clines as his deputy. Concurrently, US Air Force Major Richard Secord was in charge of CIA air operations in Laos from the CIA's base at Udorn, Thailand.[45] Michael Hand, co-founder with Frank Nugan of the Nugan Hand Bank, was there in 1966 too. After serving with distinction with the US Army Special Forces in Vietnam, Hand signed on with the CIA in Laos, training and supplying members of General Vang Pao's secret army of drug smuggling CIA mercenaries.[46] According to one witness before the Australian Joint Task Force investigating Nugan Hand's drug trafficking activities, Frank Nugan too "was a trusted part of the Agency."[47] A member of William Colby's staff in Vietnam in the early 1970s identified Nugan as a finance officer for the CIA.[48]

Shackley and Secord were directly involved in the "Opium War" of June 1967, when Burmese warlord Khun Sa decided to sell 16 tons of opium in Houei Sai.[49] Construing this as a challenge to their monopoly over supply, three Kuomintang generals in Burma mobilized their forces and marched into Laos to intercept him. Shackley in Vientiane informed Pat Landry, chief of the CIA base in Udorn, and Landry ordered Secord to send a squadron of T-28 planes to the rescue.[50] The battle ended with Khun Sa and the KMT in retreat and the CIA in control of the opium trade, as it was conducted by Vang Pao and numerous Laotian political and military officials.

Secord told the author, "We were never dealing opium in Laos. And if we were, it was policy."[51] Which was Secord's way of saying the CIA got its marching orders from the White House and Congress.

A highly decorated veteran of the US Army Special Forces, Michael Hand moved to Australia in 1967 with Kermit "Buddy" King, an Air America pilot he had befriended in Laos.[52] Hand and Nugan ostensibly sold real estate to US servicemen, but in 1973 King's housemaid made allegations to the Australian Bureau of Narcotics that King was "flying heroin into Australia for Hand."[53] That same year King, an obvious liability, fell to his death from the tenth floor of a Sydney apartment building, and Michael Hand and Frank Nugan formed Nugan Hand Limited. The bank provided "a bridge between larger legitimate banks and a shadow universe of organized crime, illegal money laundering, and intelligence operations."[54] Nugan Hand opened offices in Panama, New York, Delaware, Washington and San Francisco.[55]

Rumble Down Under

ONE OF THE LAST THINGS Nixon did before he resigned in disgrace was order a review of US-Australian relations. The reason: Prime Minister Graham Whitlam had accused the CIA of funding Australian conservative parties since 1967, and threatened to close a super-secret CIA spy base in Australia.[56] In 1974, DCI William Colby transferred Ted Shackley from the Western Hemisphere Division to the Far East Asia Division, which covered Australia. The day before Whitlam was tossed out of office, Shackley sent a cable to his Australian counterpart threatening to break relations because Whitlam was a security threat.[57]

In 1975, while the CIA was subverting Whitlam, Michael Hand was selling arms to Rhodesians and Angolans with the help of "deep cover" agent Ed Wilson.[58] Wilson's relationship with Hand continued after Navy Secretary Robert Inman fired Wilson from Task Force 157 in April 1976, a month after Wilson arranged for Hand to get a banking license in the Cayman Islands.[59] In August 1976 Hand and Nugan incorporated the Nugan Hand Bank, offering their clients confidential banking service with coded names and transfers. US Navy Rear Admiral Earl Yates was the Bank's first president. Other bank officers included US Army Generals Leroy Manor, Edwin Black, and Earle Cocke, all of whom had intelligence connections in the Far East.[60]

Hand returned to Australia in 1976, announced his intentions to open offices in Thailand, and began to deal with former Australian policeman turned heroin trafficker Murray Riley. San Francisco Mafioso Jimmy Fratianno and crime figure Danny Stein were among Riley's financiers.[61] Shortly after Hand's return to Australia, Riley shipped five loads of heroin from Thailand to Australia, with the Nugan Hand Bank moving the "buy" money from Sydney to Hong Kong. Riley moved two more shipments in 1977.[62]

Former CIA officer Michael Hand in 1977 opened an office in Chiang Mai, Thailand specifically to facilitate Riley's drug smuggling activities. In May of 1977, the Australian Narcotics Bureau opened a file on Hand and Nugan.[63] According to Australian investigator Clive Small, the Joint Task Force identified Nugan Hand as a money launderer for at least 26 drug networks and syndicates. "In all cases the drugs (heroin and marijuana) were imported from Thailand."[64] And yet, despite the fact that Riley's heroin reached major American crime figures, DEA officers in Thailand claimed not to know of CIA or Nugan Hand involvement.[65] Due to a lack of US cooperation, the Australian investigation was closed in March 1978. One informant claimed the case was closed after $150,000 in bribes was paid.[66]

According to author Jonathan Kwitny, the CIA, if not the DEA, was aware of Nugan Hand's presence in Thailand; the station chief in Bangkok, David Arnold, told Kwitny that Nugan Hand people had approached him and other US officials, played on their patriotism, and tried to get them to invest.[67]

Former CIA Bangkok station chief Robert Jantzen was also aware of allegations about Nugan Hand's drug activities. In February 1978, the US Embassy's Economics and Commercial Affairs counselor in Bangkok, on Jantzen's behalf, wrote a letter to the Australian Bureau of Narcotics asking if they had Nugan Hand under investigation.[68] When Nugan found out about Jantzen's inquiry, he complained to Harvey Bates, the chief of the Australian Bureau of Narcotics. Harvey's deputy then "sent off a secret memo which had the effect of stopping the Nugan Hand investigation."[69]

No corruption investigation was ever conducted.

Nugan Hand and the Enterprise

BY 1979, SHACKLEY, CLINES, AND Secord betrayed Ed Wilson, who had gotten out of control and become a liability after selling several tons of C4 explosives to Quadafi in Libya.[70] The trio then entered into relations with Maurice "Bernie" Houghton, an officer with the Nugan Hand Bank. Secord had known Houghton since 1972 and introduced him to Clines in 1979.[71] Shackley and Hand likewise held several meetings in Washington in 1979.[72] Hand also met with Lou Conein's old asset, Mitch Werbell that year.[73]

One intelligence officer interviewed by Kwitny said Houghton, an ex-patriot Texan who moved to Australia to capitalize on the American GI tourism trade, was involved in Operation 404, in which CIA agents worked with US Air Force officers training Laotian pilots.[74] Apparently Houghton and Hand had met in Laos and a father-son relationship blossomed between them. Houghton may have been Hand's case officer, for it was Houghton who helped established Hand in Australia.[75]

By 1979 Houghton was the Nugan Hand representative in Saudi Arabia, and Shackley and Clines were dealing with him in hopes of moving into that lucrative market through their oil drilling supply company, API, which Ricardo Chavez was managing in Mexico.[76] Houghton set up accounts for companies owned by Clines in Venezuela, El Salvador, Honduras and Panama, while Shackley lurked in the background as a "consultant."[77]

The link between these veteran US spooks and Nugan Hand surfaced in January 1980, when Frank Nugan was found dead of a gunshot wound in his Mercedes Benz. A rifle was found clutched in his hands and his death was ruled a suicide. That same day, Houghton dropped off a briefcase full of bank documents at Wilson's office in Geneva; and two days later Hand began destroying many of the bank's documents at its main office in Sydney.[78] In June 1980, after Houghton obtained a false passport for him, Michael Hand vanished, never to be pursued by any American law enforcement officials, even the DEA. Houghton relocated to Mexico with the help of Tom Clines.[79]

The scandal and rumors of CIA involvement gained momentum when it was revealed that William Colby's business card had been found in Nugan's wallet.[80] As a former director of the CIA, Colby didn't work for just anyone, and considering that Nugan Hand defrauded its investors of some 25 million dollars, people wondered why he had accepted Nugan as a client.[81] Officially, Colby was helping former CIA agent Michael Hand resettle some 3,000 Laotian refugees to a defunct US naval base in the Turks and Caicos Islands. The Joint Task Force, however, deduced a hidden "sinister" motive for the resettlement plan: the base, replete with docks and an airstrip was "a natural transit point for illicit drug shipments" to the US.[82]

One must ask why the DEA did not pick up the trail in 1980; three years after the Australians investigated Nugan Hand in Thailand. Australian investigators made "a routine request through normal channels" to the DEA for assistance; but again, "no replies were received."[83] Any DEA official could have read the November 1982 Joint Task Force report, which noted that Nugan Hand was well established in drug activity. But that never led to an investigation either.

After several honest Australian narcotic agents swore under oath that a deputy prime minister had interfered in their investigation, the Nugan Hand probe was revived under Justice Donald Stewart in 1983, the same year Oliver North and Richard Secord launched their covert Iran-Contra operation. But the Stewart Commission concluded that the bank did not act as a front for CIA operations by laundering drug money. It reached this conclusion based on "assurances given by the US Vice President, Mr. G. Bush."[84]

The Cover-up

CIA OFFICERS SUBORN DEA AGENTS for numerous purposes. From 1952 until 1955, Paul Knight spent half his time in Europe working for the CIA, mostly on matters of East- West trade.[85] In October 1960, the CIA recruited Jack Cusack to recruit safecrackers in Spain.[86] That same year, CIA officer Hal Fiedler recruited FBN Agent Sal Vizzini in Turkey, as a way of improving his position with the police.[87] It happens all the time. The more DEA agents there are overseas, the more it happens. It appears to have happened in Thailand, too, where the CIA station was aware of Nugan Hand's activities.

What did the DEA know about Nugan Hand, and when did it know it? Author Kwitny claimed "the DEA receptionist answered Nugan Hand's phone and took messages when the bank's representatives were out."[88] Another source told him that DEA agents played cards after work with Neil Evans, Nugan Hand's representative in Chiang Mai. One Nugan Hand depositor told Kwitny that "even the American DEA came in and talked to me about Evans."[89]

Neil Evans correctly identified the DEA agents he dealt with in Chiang Mai. But when Kwitny asked to interview them, the DEA declined to disclose their whereabouts.[90] This author had better luck finding them, but also came up empty-handed. When asked if Nugan Hand was located next door, agent Mike Powers, who was stationed in Chiang Mai in 1977 and knew Michael Hand from their time together in the CIA, said "not to my knowledge." Dan Addario, the DEA boss in Bangkok, used the same phrase: "not to my knowledge."[91]

"Not to my knowledge" is not as strong a denial as "No." There's a "maybe" in there somewhere that makes one wonder. Especially when one considers that the secret CIA anti-narcotics "Twofold" unit Joey DiGennaro worked in was still operating at the time. According to one agent, Powers was part of it.

Charles Wilson, the DEA agent in charge in Chiang Mai in 1977 said Nugan Hand was not there, though he did play cards after work with some Rhodesians — which is odd insofar as Ed Wilson supplied weapons to Michael Hand for sale in Rhodesia.[92]

The biggest bombshell Evans dropped was the allegation that Hand collected drug money from major Thai traffickers. (One should recall that CCINC staff director Walter Minnick specifically named General Kriangsak Chamanand, prime minister after an October 1977 coup, as the major drug trafficker in 1972.) Evans identified Police Major General Sanga Kittakachorn as the most significant Nugan Hand drug trafficking depositor in 1977.[93] Younger brother of Thanon Kittakachorn (prime minister and military dictator from November 1971 until October 1973), Sanga had been police minister until his brother sent him into honorable exile (as special envoy to the United Nations) in 1971.[94] Evans and the Nugan Hand people in Bangkok arranged a $500,000 loan for Sanga through the Thai Military Bank upon his return in 1976.[95] Sanga told Kwitny that "the CIA and Thai General Staff worked "very closely with each other."[96] This is a reference to the fact that Thailand was a bigger R&R boondoggle than Australia and that Thai military officials profited hugely from the booming drugs and sex trade. Thai military officials also profited by forming the private construction firms that built the huge US military bases around the country.[97]

An investigation by the Australian federal drug police liaison officer in Thailand into Suraporn Thongyet, another Nugan Hand drug money depositor, was obstructed by Major General Pisakdi, the official in charge of police foreign affairs and Interpol.[98] Yet no DEA agent interviewed by this author admitted they had claimed ever to have even heard of Pisakdi.

Last but not least, William and Gordon Young told Kwitny that Nugan Hand was involved in agriculture, which was a polite way of saying opium.[99] The Youngs were known to all DEA agents in Chiang Mai. It is inconceivable they would know about Nugan Hand and the DEA wouldn't ... or that the Australians did not tell them Hand was responsible with Riley for the establishment of the Thai offices, for the purpose of securing drug money.[100]

The only question is: why the cover-up? The obvious answer is that, having been suborned by the CIA, the DEA had to protect the CIA's Nugan Hand operation, and its official Thai drug trafficking clients, in order to protect itself. In turn the CIA needed to protect the Shackley-Clines-Wilson enterprise, which the Australians had tied to Nugan Hand. As the Australians reported, Hand was in contact with Clines while Clines was still with the CIA.[101]

The Shackley-Clines-Wilson (and later Secord) enterprise was, in this author's opinion, designed to effect foreign policy goals the Carter Administration was not pursuing. Carter, for example, had no stake in resettling general Vang Pao's followers. But Colby, Hand, and Shackley did. And apparently they were raising money the old-fashioned way — through drug smuggling — while the DEA turned a blind eye.

Mexico

IN 1974 THE DEA DEVELOPED action plans for Thailand and Mexico as the centerpiece of its foreign operations policy. The Mexican plan was designed to identify trafficking networks, to locate and neutralize poppy fields and heroin labs, and to identify the political/economic support system of major traffickers.[102]

The American poppy field location facet was known as Trizo. Launched in 1975, Trizo involved the aerial spraying of poppy fields. The State Department provided helicopters and pilots and the CIA provided fixed wing airplanes equipped with cameras and opium sensory systems. Howie Safir at Special Projects was the first Trizo case agent and contracting officer with Evergreen Aviation, a CIA-connected air service.[103] In late 1976 control of Trizo passed to the Mexican desk in the enforcement division. Agent Bruce Van Matre assumed control, working with technicians from the NSA. "They eradicated a lot of poppies," Van Matre notes, but asks, "Did we get into right areas?" The aircraft couldn't cover much ground and DEA pilots "located as many fields by eye" as they did with electronic devices. Better information "should have been available," but "it took one or two days to get information back after the CIA scanned it."[104]

Why would the CIA scan it? To protect its unilateral operations and assets, of course.

Operation Condor, the Mexican facet of Trizo, had DEA-advised units on the ground in Mexico and targeted specific traffickers.[105] Others say it was a conduit the CIA used to funnel money, weapons and other support to repressive Latin American governments.[106] Not surprisingly, long-range intelligence support for Condor/Trizo initially came from a DEACON managed by a former CIA officer, Hugh Murray.[107]

Hugh Murray joined the US Army Special Forces in 1955 and the CIA in 1960.[108] He served in Vietnam with Lou Conein in the early 1960s. He helped capture Che Guevara in Bolivia in 1967. After a two-year tour in Laos in the early 1970s, Murray returned to CIA headquarters and wandered the halls until 1974, when Conein hired him into the DEA, promising career advancement. Alas, that never happened. As bearded, overweight, disheveled Murray rues, "The old FBN guys didn't trust us."

Conein assigned Murray to Tucson, Arizona where in 1976 he set up a private investigation firm, using his office as a safe house to meet informants. Some informants, by his account, were Mexicans, others "bad Americans working the edge." His principal agent, Juan Gonzales, was a former Mexican Federal Police officer residing in the US as chief of an exile political party. All informants used by the DEA overseas were vetted and approved by the CIA, which likely funded Gonzalez and his exile party. Former CIA officer Murray gave Gonzalez narcotics requirements, which Gonzalez passed to sub-agents. The sub-agents acquired license plates and phone numbers of traffickers, and the times of delivery; but they were not allowed to buy drugs. Murray's DEACON was a long-range intelligence program designed to build up dossiers and conspiracy cases on drug dealers, not to arrest them. Despite his own and Gonzalez' likely ties to the CIA, Murray said their sub-agents gathered no political intelligence.

Murray's most controversial agent, Genaro Celaya, begs to differ. Celaya had been working for federal narcotics agents since 1971 when Murray hired him in 1976, and sent him to work in Mexico. Celaya found sellers, and Murray got clearance for them to cross the border. Murray's role was to pose as a buyer, pump the sellers for information, and pass it to other DEA agents. One DEA officer, however, "claimed that other agents in Tucson 'may or may not know what [Murray] is, or what he does, but he sure as hell is not DEA.'"[109]

Murray's relationship with Celaya became controversial after Celaya shot and killed an Arizona state narcotics agent in 1979. During his murder trial, Celaya claimed that Murray trained him extensively in espionage tradecraft skills; for example, how to provide Murray with plausible deniability by communicating with him without making personal contact.[110] During his trial, Celaya said he spied for Murray on President Portillo's inner circle, including Jorge Diaz Serrano, director of Mexico's national oil company, PEMEX.[111]

At the time, Ricardo Chavez was working for Tom Clines' company API, selling oil drilling equipment to PEMEX. The API account was set up by Michael Hand's mentor, Bernie Houghton, who surfaced in Mexico in 1980. This strange coincidence occurred shortly after the assassination of Judge John Wood in San Antonio, and shortly before the Reagan Administration's decision to put a select group of FBI agents and executives in charge of the DEA. It also occurred at the same time that Celaya blew Murray's cover and exposed a broader CIA operation in Mexico — one that seemed to use the gathering of drug intelligence as a cover.

The CIA has cognizance over all DEA intelligence. It also has plausible deniability, and would not allow Murray to testify at Celaya's trial. When questioned by reporters, Murray denied everything. In an interview with investigating officials, he said he was merely an enforcement agent heading a border drug operation called Operation Prueda.[112] In an interview with this writer, however, Murray acknowledges working with "Fred," the CIA officer in charge of Sonora Province across the border from Arizona. CIA spooks like Fred work in every Mexican province, spying on and recruiting Mexican political officials, labor leaders, and businessmen — in short, anyone with influence, including opium growers and traffickers. Suborning these "nationals" and getting them to spy on and subvert their own government is how the CIA keeps Mexico's northern provinces battling the central government, thus destabilizing the country and, as in Iraq after the American invasion and occupation, making it easier to exploit.

Fred was a political espionage agent but occasionally obtained narcotics information, which he passed to Murray, along with knowledgeable assets. DEA officers like Murray were not supposed to recruit agents in Mexico without telling the Mexicans, or the DEA region office in Mexico City. But through Celaya, Murray recruited two ranchers as unilateral assets. One, Congressman Herberto Salazar Montoya, said a DEA agent offered him unlimited campaign funds; the other, Salomon Faz, knew Murray was an agent, but denied meeting him.[113]

Was Celaya a desperate criminal fabricating a story; or were he and Murray playing a double game, using Condor drug investigations as a cover, on behalf of some super-covert CIA operation unbeknownst to the Carter Administration?

Why Spy?

MEXICAN PRESIDENT PORTILLO'S ANTI-AMERICAN SENTIMENTS grew in 1977, when Carter's Energy Secretary, James Schlesinger, vetoed a natural gas agreement between Mexico and six US companies. The situation was precarious, and in 1978 Murray allegedly told Celaya to work with Faz and Salazar to influence Portillo to stabilize oil prices and peg them to OPEC guidelines.[114] Salazar, when contacted by reporters, recalled a meeting between himself, Celaya and Portillo in 1978.[115] It may have been coincidence, but in November 1978 Portillo vowed not to undersell OPEC. Then in February 1979, almost immediately after the overthrow of the Shah in Iran, he reversed his position and said the US was no longer a favored customer. In May 1979 gas prices in the US soared; gas lines and the hostage crisis in Tehran turned public opinion against Jimmy Carter and Reagan and Bush began their ascent.

Was this development another Republican Party dirty trick?

According to Celaya, a CIA officer with a name sounding like Lawrence Sternfeld recruited him at this time specifically to spy on PEMEX director Diaz Serrano.[116] Celaya also spied on people running guns into Mexico and drugs back to the US, and money launderers in Las Vegas. He worked for George H.W. Bush's first employer, Dresser Industries and took Dresser executives to Mexico City to meet political and oil industry officials, including Portillo.[117]

On November 30, 1979, Celaya was scheduled to fly to Mexico for a big oil deal. Instead he shot and killed Arizona Public Safety Officer John C. Walker. In his defense, Celaya claimed Murray had hired Walker to kill him. Murray said that was ridiculous. However, it is alleged that Tom Clines tried to bribe Diaz Serrano (a known CIA asset) through Ricardo Chavez. Adding to the intrigue, Celaya claimed to have met with Clines through El Paso attorney Lee Chagra, the object of a major DEA investigation. If what Celaya said is true, Murray's DEA operation, and the CIA political-economic context in which it unfolded, projects into the Nugan Hand Bank and Iran-Contra scandals.

Before we reach the Iran-Contra years, we must first revisit the DEA's nagging problems with corruption.

26

GEORGE WHITE'S GHOST

THERE WERE TWO INSPECTORS DURING FBN days: one for the East Coast, one for the West. They could barely keep up with the Wolf Pack. The office of inspections while the BNDD existed had ten field inspectors. Inspections were announced and conducted by a team led by a senior inspector. They took one to three weeks to complete and were not well received by the old FBN agents, who preferred to do things their way. As erstwhile Inspector Ted Hunter explained, inspections were a management tool to get people to follow the party line and weed out ineptness in "a brutally realistic way."[1]

In 1972, Chief Inspector Pat Fuller, Andy Tartaglino and John Ingersoll set up the "Two Fold" shoofly program with the CIA, but that was just an elaborate cover for covert operations.

When the DEA was formed, George Brosan tried to modernize the Office of Inspection and Internal Security by bringing in junior agents as inspectors.[2] Under his watch there were, at first, only nine inspectors at headquarters.[3] His program enabled agents like Steve Greene and Terry Burke to advance, but, according to Inspector Ted Hunter, it was ineffective. Brosan also enlisted veteran Customs Inspectors and people from the Office of Naval Investigations who had a real impact. Brosan, however, got swept away in the war between Tartaglino and Bartels. His replacement, Phil Smith, was a fox guarding the hen house.

The scandals that plagued the Bartels Administration prompted Congress to turn the DEA inside out. Henry Dogin's first acting chief of Internal Security, Charles Ruff, served for only three and a half months.[4] Dogin's second acting chief, Joseph Jaffe, a prosecutor out of the southern district of New York, was driven to end corruption, but, according to Ted Hunter, "went too fast and hard." Jaffe left the DEA shortly after Dogin. Under Bensinger's acting chief, Johnny Thompson, the Office of Internal Security grew to 50 agents. But not until July 1976, when Bensinger appointed John Evans as permanent chief inspector did the Office of Internal Security "work through the pain and trauma of the Jackson Hearings and begin to develop a professional staff."[5]

A veteran of the FBN's Detroit office, birthplace of the Purple Gang, Evans was well versed in enforcement efforts against Mafia heroin bosses and their connections worldwide. Having worked for Tartaglino during the 1968 FBN corruption purge in New York, and as a BNDD regional director in Atlanta and Chicago, he also had experience managing inspections. The first case he managed as Bensinger's chief inspector was against Fred Dick, who was charged with misuse of a government car, and retired.[6]

Evans brought inspections "up to compliment" in the field offices and at headquarters. He developed a rules and procedures manual and reintroduced surprise inspections. Evans eliminated the junior agent training program and used only Group Supervisors as Inspectors. Their mandate was to inspect every foreign and domestic facility once a year. They were also sent on special assignments to inspect particular programs or incidents, such as the accidental death by gunshot of CIA shoofly Billy Lightfoot, and the unsolved murder of Agent Mike Powers' wife in Bangkok in 1980. The one problem Evans could not correct was that the DEA was not its own master; the State Department and CIA had control overseas; while the Justice Department and FBI had considerable influence domestically.[7]

In 1976 the Senate Permanent Subcommittee on Investigations reviewed the history of FBN abuses, the failure of the "buy-bust" approach, and the Promuto affair. For the average DEA agent it seemed like change, disruption and experimentation were never-ending. They were all driven by case production and constantly justifying their existence by how much powder they put on the table. And there was always the crisis du jour.

Customs Again

IN 1975, AT THE REQUEST of Charles Ruff, Inspector Morty Benjamin got the job of re-reviewing the Internal Security files closed by Phil Smith and Terry Burke.[8] Through June 1975, he and Agent George Fester flew around the country and read 1153 files. In July they recommended that the infamous 35 "unresolved" cases be re-opened, many of which concerned former FBN agents from New York. There were 55 allegations, including sale of drugs by an informant at the direction of an agent, transfer of drugs to an informant by an agent, planting evidence, leaking information, mishandling evidence, taking bribes, selling counterfeit money, and loss of badge. Featured among the 35 were George Belk, Bill Durkin, Jerry Jensen, Dennis Dayle, Pete Scrocca, and Joe Baca, the assistant RD in New Orleans. The Baca case drew special attention, as it showed conspiracy. There were indications that Baca's cousin, the police chief in Hermosillo, was connected to drug lord Pedro Aviles Perez, the target of DEACON III.[9] The Baca case had been reviewed by the DeFeo team, and was a factor in the Reagan Administration's directing the FBI to take over the DEA's senior management.

Bensinger's acting chief of Internal Security, John Thompson, reopened the Baca case after Customs agents accused Baca and the Monterey Park Ski Club (the West Coast equivalent of the Detroit Purple Gang) of protecting drug traffickers connected to Sicilia Falcon in Tijuana. Thompson assigned Inspector William Coonce to investigate Larry Katz, the region intelligence unit supervisor in Los Angeles, and the other members of the Monterey Park Ski Club. Customs reportedly had a tape of an incriminating phone call between Baca and Falcon. Customs agents also claimed that Baca was seen with Falcon, and that one of Baca's DEA cohorts was running drug money through El Paso.[10]

Everything in DEA history is derivative and, according to William Coonce, the Baca and Katz integrity cases tracked back to Charlie McDonnell. Larry Katz was one of the New York FBN agents Tartaglino had investigated in 1968 as a result of McDonnell's allegations. Katz was transferred to San Diego where he bonded with kindred spirit Baca, who was managing the case against the Tijuana traffickers supplying heroin to McDonnell's informant and partner in crime, Joe Miles. During an interview with Tartaglino, Coonce discovered that Tartaglino had investigated Baca on these matters in 1969 and 1973, but did not pursue the case because the evidence against Baca had come from Customs.

Nothing was ever proven in the Baca integrity case, but a slew of startling new allegations arose — including one that DEA agents were robbing drug trafficker Jimmy Chagra in El Paso.[11] Agent Ted Hunter said that particular allegation was untrue; that the robberies were committed by two informants pretending to be agents. The informants had phony DEA credentials, badges, guns, and handcuffs. They placed drug traffickers under arrest, brought them to a motel for interrogation, demanded payoffs and kept the drugs, which they sold.[12]

All sorts of similar allegations simmered, as did the ancient FBN feud with Customs. The problem flared up in El Paso when a DEA agent was caught with cocaine and hired attorney Lee Chagra to defend him. The agent told Chagra that he and his informant had robbed local drug dealers and sold the dope to Mexicans. He told of traffickers trading weapons for drugs, agents tipping off informants, and the occasional murder in Mexico. The case was taken before Federal Judge John Wood and prosecuted by US Attorney John E. Clark.[13]

El Paso is a tight community aligned with the Texas Rangers, Customs agents and INS Border Rats who rode the Rio Grande in the brave days of old. Federal narcotics agents were never welcomed in Texas, especially after 1954, when FBN Agent George White tried to make an integrity case on Alvin Scharff, a beloved and legendary Customs agent in Houston.[14] Customs agents never forgot that indignity, and after their narcotic expert colleagues were forced to join the DEA, anger among the remaining Customs agents grew. By 1975, Customs reports about DEA abuses were pouring into El Paso Magistrate Jamie Boyd. Most were complaints about agents kicking in doors without a search warrant, and lying under oath. Boyd often found the reports to be true.[15]

As tensions between Customs and the DEA grew, Boyd aligned with Jack Compton, a former BNDD Group Supervisor in Mexico who had witnessed and reported several cases of abuse and corruption, but to no avail. In 1972 Compton quit the BNDD in disgust and joined Customs. Rather than join the DEA during the merger of 1973, he took a job as Director of the Customs Patrol Office in El Paso, where he fought tooth and nail with local DEA agents.

In August 1975, Boyd presented affidavits from Compton and four other federal agents to US Attorney Clark. In separate interviews with Clark in Judge John Wood's quarters, the five men spoke extensively about DEA corruption in Mexico and the US Southwest, citing specific DEA agents and their alleged improprieties. What they said was explosive.[16]

DEA agents uniformly dismiss Compton as bitter. They say he and the other Customs agents were lying when they said that DEA agents were kidnapping, torturing, shooting people and stealing their drugs. But Boyd (a Democrat tied to Senator Lloyd Bentsen) sided with Compton and Customs, and when Jimmy Carter named Boyd US Attorney in the Western District of Texas in May 1977, the fur started to fly. The precipitating event was Boyd's discovery that El Paso DEA Group Supervisor John H. Phillips was secretly recording conversations he (Phillips) had with Boyd's assistant US Attorney, James W. Kerr.[17] Kerr was pursing a drug case against Lee and Jimmy Chagra, who had allegedly bought the loyalty of a number of law enforcement officials in El Paso. Indeed, Boyd believed that Kerr's prosecution plans were being leaked to Lee Chagra's drug dealing clients.[18] As a way of retaliating against Boyd in the Phillips case, El Paso DEA Agent-in-Charge George Frangullie complained to the FBI about alleged misconduct by Kerr. Boyd was so enraged that he sent the statements made by Compton and his four colleagues to Attorney General Benjamin Civiletti.[19]

The dramatic consequences of this epic battle, which helped pave the way for the FBI takeover of the DEA, will be discussed at length in the next chapter. For now it's back to George White and the ongoing criminal conspiracy called the CIA.

George White's Ghost

CORRUPTION BECOMES AN UNSOLVABLE ISSUE within the DEA when CIA officers suborn agents and get them to do their dirty work. Some idealistic agents think they are serving God and country by secretly working for the CIA; others see it in more practical terms, as career advancement. All fall into the abyss. That is why DEA inspectors often have deep insights into covert intelligence operations.

The public got its first peek into the CIA's corrupting influence on federal drug enforcement agents in 1975 when the Rockefeller Commission reported that the CIA, through its MKULTRA program, had tested LSD on unwitting persons, and that one had died as a result.[20] That person was identified as CIA officer Frank Olson.[21] Senator Church picked up the trail in 1976, as did Senator Edward M. Kennedy's Committee on Human Resources in 1977.[22]

Eventually author John Marks, through a Freedom of Information Act Request, obtained documents revealing that the CIA had tested a whole range of powerful drugs on unwitting persons; used electronic and photographic equipment to record their behavior at FBN safe houses; suborned several FBN agents; and that FBN Agent George White had a contract with the CIA to manage the program.[23]

One MKULTRA subproject involved keeping seven criminals high on LSD for 77 days straight.[24] Another used poisonous mushrooms; another used instruments that administered drugs through the skin without detection, as part of an "Executive Action" assassination program.[25] Perhaps most disturbing of all, one CIA document, dated February 10, 1954, described using hypnosis to create unsuspecting assassins.[26]

It was bad enough that the CIA was conducting Nuremburg-style experiments on unwitting US citizens (the Nazis had tested mescaline on POWs in World War II), perhaps with the idea of creating programmed assassins (what author John Marks referred to as "the search for the Manchurian Candidate"), but the Agency had the willing cooperation of numerous universities, hospitals, prisons and drug companies. The CIA's macabre goals were to stockpile "severely incapacitating and lethal materials," develop "gadgets for the dissemination of these materials" and "a capability to manipulate human behavior in a predictable manner through the use of drugs," as well as "to identify new drug developments in Europe and Asia and to obtain information and samples."[27]

Senator Kennedy launched his sensational *Hearings into Human Drug Testing by the CIA* in August 1977. On the eve of the hearings, DCI Stansfield Turner sent a letter to Peter Bensinger "notifying him that the Bureau of Narcotics had been involved with the MKULTRA Program."[28] DCI Richard Helms had ordered the destruction of most MKULTRA documents in 1973, but those that survived fueled the long-standing rumor that the CIA had set up "love traps" in FBN safe houses and video-taped drugged politicians engaging with prostitutes.[29] What was proven was that from 1952 until 1966, CIA and FBN agents had given approximately 50 unwitting US citizens LSD and other dangerous drugs. The hearings featured guest appearances by top DEA and CIA officials, and further damaged the DEA's poor public image.

The hearings focused on CIA officer Dr. Sidney Gottlieb, head of the MKULTRA Program.[30] At the Hearings, Gottlieb admitted hiring FBN Agent George White in 1952 after reading about White's marijuana experiments for the OSS on Mafia hoods in World War II.[31] (Ironically, FBN Commissioner Harry Anslinger called pot the "killer weed" and had his agents pursue its users relentlessly.) While the government's federal narcotics agency feigned moral superiority, its secret service, the Office of Strategic Services (OSS) wanted to know if "chemical materials could be used to elicit or validate information obtained from drug informants."[32] With money from Gottlieb, White in 1952 rented an apartment in Greenwich Village. With the assistance of a few trusted FBN agents, friends and informers, he started dosing people with LSD. Andy Tartaglino was there. He visited White's safe house and saw everything. But for some unexplained reason, Tartaglino was not called before the Kennedy Committee.[33]

White's inside knowledge of the Mafia's committee on assassinations and its murder techniques — such as hiring foreign hitmen, and setting up dupes to take the fall — also made him uniquely qualified for the MKULTRA job, as we shall see. White claimed to have a "pipeline" to the "inner circle" of four Mafia bosses (in New York, Los Angeles, Kansas City, and Chicago) "who passed on murder requests from the underworld and occasionally commissioned a Mafia enforcement ring to do the killing."[34]

Gottlieb was no shrinking violet either, and in November 1954 he dosed a fellow CIA officer, Frank Olson, with LSD. Olson had a bad trip and over the Thanksgiving holiday was sent to New York for treatment. While there he allegedly committed suicide by jumping from his hotel window. After that incident, as White recorded in his diary, the New York safe house was closed and in 1955 he was transferred to San Francisco where he set up three more MKULTRA pads.[35] Helping him were Ike Feldman, Dan Casey, and various FBN and CIA agents. White and his minions hired prostitutes to lure johns to the MKULTRA pads where the victims were dosed with LSD and studied by CIA officers.[36] None of the other San Francisco agents were called before the committee either.

Gottlieb returned from a three-year sojourn in India in 1975 to testify before the Church Committee, after which William Colby arranged for his employment as the DEA's assistant director for science. John Bartels met Gottlieb twice. According to Bartels, Gottlieb had a "nice gentle appearance" and was assigned to benign scientific projects that sought to trace the source of illicit drugs through chemical investigation.[37]

After receiving immunity from criminal prosecution in exchange for his testimony, Gottlieb told the Kennedy Committee that he had stopped the MKULTRA experiments in 1966 when he realized how difficult it was to predictably manipulate the behavior of humans on LSD. Kennedy asked why, if the Soviets (as Gottlieb insisted) were still using LSD, Gottlieb changed his opinion about using the drug.

"We know everything now," Gottlieb said.

Eventually Senator Schweiker asked the overarching question: If "the Executive Action concept, political assassination, was not in any way involved in motivational training studies under any of these categories in MKULTRA?"[38] Gottlieb professed not to know the answer to that. The CIA's murder expert, George White, had died in 1975 and was unavailable for comment. Kennedy, who may have privately wondered if Lee Harvey Oswald had been an MKULTRA assassin working for the CIA, summoned two FBN agents to try to find out what exactly happened in the safe houses and why.

Siragusa, Belk, and MKULTRA

CHARLIE SIRAGUSA AND GEORGE BELK were the only FBN agents called before the Kennedy Committee. Siragusa was summoned because he had set up a CIA safe house in New York City in 1960 with the help of his protégé, Andy Tartaglino, and an FBN electronics expert.[39] The safe house consisted of two adjoining apartments; CIA technicians installed a two-way mirror between them so they could make video tapes. They wired and bugged both places for sound. Siragusa, by his admission, helped the CIA on the understanding "that we were to use this apartment for our own purposes ... to interview informants, to debrief informants, to work undercover operations. Then whenever the CIA wished to use the apartment itself, they would notify us to stay away from the apartment. Dr. [Raymond] Treichler was my contact man. He also furnished me with money."[40]

Kennedy asked Siragusa: "Did you ever have any idea of what was going on in the safe houses?"

"One of my first guesses was perhaps it was being used to uncover defectors in their own organization," Siragusa replied.[41] He claimed he never knew it was being used for drug testing. For more information on that subject, Siragusa suggested that Kennedy ask George Gaffney, the FBN's District Supervisor in New York City at the time. But Robert Kennedy had been Gaffney's political patron, so Ted Kennedy instead focused on Gaffney's arch-rival in the FBN, who happened to be Charlie Siragusa. Kennedy asked Siragusa if he'd set up a safe house in Chicago. Siragusa said that upon retiring from the FBN in November 1963, he had taken a job in Chicago as Executive Director of the Illinois Crime Commission. While there he socialized with his former CIA contact, Ray Treichler, who had retired from the CIA and taken a position with a chemical manufacturing company. Siragusa did not "recall" anyone suggesting he set up a CIA safe house in Chicago.[42]

Kennedy then quoted from a document about MKULTRA Subproject 132: "This project is conducted by Mr. Cal Salerno. Mr. Salerno, a public relations consultant, has recently moved his offices from New York City to Chicago, Illinois. Mr. Salerno holds a top secret agency clearance and is completely witting of the aims and goals of the project. He possesses unique facilities and personal abilities which have made him invaluable in this kind of operation."

Siragusa, who used the alias Cal Salerno throughout his career, said: "There has been some poetic license taken with the truth. I only just learned the name of Cal Salerno was adopted by others that succeeded me."[43]

Kennedy, in disbelief, said, "But in the CIA files they have memoranda that you were completely witting, knowledgeable about these programs, the aims and goals...."

Siragusa: "That is not so. That is entirely inaccurate. It is untrue."[44]

Kennedy's next witness, George Belk, did little to dispel the cloud of deceit and deception Siragusa had created. Belk explained that he had succeeded Gaffney as New York's District Supervisor in April 1963. At the time, FBN Commissioner Henry Giordano "alluded to the fact that the agency, that is the FBN, had an apartment they were responsible for in New York. It was a national security endeavor in collaboration with the CIA, and that he would wish me to continue the project."[45] Belk said he had no knowledge of what the CIA was doing there. He had never heard of MKULTRA.

Kennedy countered: "We have documents, memoranda from the agency itself that have references to your involvement, not dissimilar to the kind of characterization of Mr. Siragusa's involvement. But I understand from what you said here that you would deny that categorically, is that correct?"

Belk: "I would do stronger than that. It is a lie."[46]

Perhaps. Art Fluhr was Belk's administrative assistant in New York from 1963-1967 and according to him, Belk had a CIA contract and a checking account for rent and maintenance of the safe house. Fluhr said the CIA used Belk's account as a slush fund for foreign officials on its payroll. "Sometimes we were told to baby-sit people for the CIA while they were in town," Fluhr said. "One time it was a group of Burmese generals. They came to New York for a couple of days and when they weren't at the UN, they used the money in Belk's account to go on a shopping spree. They went down to the electronics shops on Canal Street and filled suitcases full of stuff."[47]

The Burmese generals had been ushered through Customs without inspection. If they wished, they could have brought heroin into America in those suitcases.

Fluhr frowns. "One day Belk comes up to me and said, 'It's the strangest thing: some days the account's got a million dollars in it, the next day it's empty and I can't pay the rent!'"

A million dollars could buy a lot of heroin.

Flashbacks

IT IS SIGNIFICANT THAT SENATOR Edward Long (D-MS) stumbled on the FBNCIA "love traps" in 1966 while investigating illegal FBI wiretaps. Long asked Treasury Under-Secretary Joseph Barr for an explanation, and Barr summoned Gottlieb and Andy Tartaglino's boss at Main Treasury, CIA Officer Tony Lapham. Gottlieb told Barr that the CIA had shared in the FBN's "intelligence take" and had obtained information "which was of obvious interest to us in connection with our own investigative work."[48]

Gottlieb's explanation satisfied Barr, although it raised questions about the nature of the CIA's "investigative work." Subsequently, Lapham ordered Tartaglino to shut down the New York MKULTRA pad.[49] As Fluhr recalled, "We gave the furniture to the Salvation Army and took the drapes off the windows and put them up in our office." Tartaglino subsequently opened a more luxurious CIA safe house on Sutton Place.

Senator Kennedy also tried to uncover Ike Feldman's role as George White's MKULTRA assistant in San Francisco and as custodian of a second CIA safe house in New York, which Feldman set up after his transfer there in 1962.[50] And yet, despite a string of serious misdeeds, Feldman — like Tartaglino, Casey and Gaffney — was never called before the Kennedy Committee.[51] Nor was Feldman ever prosecuted for lying to the INS about his involvement with "the Fraulein," an East German prostitute whom he used to spy on politicians.[52] According to Howie Safir, Feldman even got away with robbing two Chinese diplomats who were trafficking in opium.[53]

"Feldman agreed to talk to me," Inspector Morty Benjamin recalled, "because we're both Jewish. We met at La Guardia three times. But he never said anything more than, 'You gotta get permission from the Company,' or, 'Have your boss talk to my boss.'"[54]

While all this was unfolding, CENTAC 10 in California was targeting an LSD ring that featured the son of a famous Russian spy, a source in Czechoslovakia, connections in Cuba, and a lab run by Dennis Kelly, who claimed to have worked for the CIA as part of its MKPURPLE program.[55] According to one CENTAC 10 agent, Kelly was linked to three persons, real or imagined, alleged to have been involved in political assassinations: George White; Johnny Roselli (a Mafioso employed by Ted Shackley in a CIA plot to kill Castro, who was himself murdered in the summer of 1976);[56] and the mysterious "woman in the polka dot dress" seen at the assassination of Robert Kennedy.[57]

By the DEA case agent's account, Bensinger shut down CENTAC 10 after it led to a secret CIA facility at Fort McClellan, Georgia. Likewise, all portions of George White's diary dealing with 1963 (the year John Kennedy was killed) were destroyed before the CENTAC 10 agent could read them. As the agent wryly observed, "It was not your average drug trafficking operation."

The Victims Task Force

Dick Salmi joined DEA Internal Security in 1976. By then, Salmi had completed a tour in Tehran as narcotics attaché. He operated in Iran in a purely advisory role, but did assist US Army CID Warrant Officer Gene Wheaton in the December 1972 seizure of 12.7 metric tons of opium on its way by tanker truck from Afghanistan to Iran. It was a record bust that presaged the emergence of Afghanistan as a new major source of opium and heroin. The information that led to the bust came from CIA Officer Nick Natsios.[58] The Shah of Iran was avidly anti-Soviet and the CIA wasn't about to hurt him, but, according to Salmi, it arranged the bust to let the Shah know that it knew that members of his family were involved in the movement of narcotics from Pakistan and Afghanistan through Iran to Europe.

For cooperating with the CIA, Salmi received a glowing report from US Ambassador Richard Helms. The report helped advance Salmi's career. Salmi served in Special Projects until 1976, and then entered inspections as a way of climbing into the ranks of DEA management. To facilitate the process, Chief Inspector John Evans sent Salmi to the DEA's new High Potential Executive Development Program. Salmi spent three years in Internal Security, in part reviewing and cleaning up lingering allegations from the Tartaglino era.[59]

The DEA's next Chief Inspector, Joseph Krueger, assigned Salmi to lead an investigation into the FBN's involvement in MKULTRA. Salmi ran the investigation from July 1978 until April 1979. From January until July 1979 Salmi also worked on the so-called "Victims Task Force" with CIA Officer Frank Laubinger, under the direction of senior CIA Officer Robert Wiltse.[60] While investigating MKULTRA, Salmi discovered that George White, while the FBN's district supervisor in Chicago in 1945, had developed Jack Ruby as an informant. In an interview with the author, Salmi claimed that he found evidence indicating that George White had used Ruby to kill Oswald. Salmi said that he was told by his CIA bosses not to tell Senator Kennedy. Salmi also found out that President Kennedy had used the New York safe house to compromise his political enemies; which is why, according to Salmi, Senator Ted Kennedy agreed with DCI Stansfield Turner to limit the final Victims Task Force report.[61]

Salmi's investigation uncovered the identities of several MKULTRA victims. Working separately on an internal DEA investigation of MKULTRA were Inspectors Steve Greene, Glennon Cooper and Keith Shostrom. Greene reportedly reviewed the aforementioned CENTAC 10 as part of his role in the DEA's review of MKULTRA.[62]

Greene, like Terry Burke, would serve as an acting administrator of the DEA. He figures significantly in the final chapters of this book. Notably, his rise in the DEA was facilitated by solid CIA connections he formed in Saigon as country attaché, 1974-75. Greene played a major role in the evacuation of important people from Vietnam. Upon his return to Washington he served as a staff assistant on the Asia desk at International Operations, working closely with Jack Cusack and learning from him, in his words, "the history."[63]

Greene's stint in Internal Security contributed to his historical understanding as well as his ascent in the DEA. As he recalled, "The DEA had imploded and inspections was in turmoil." Greene was appalled at how Tartaglino and Brosan had handled the Vince Promuto affair. However, unlike Terry Burke, Greene was not aligned with the Purple Gang of old FBN agents. Under acting chief inspector Johnny Thompson, he got the job of re-reviewing the Promuto

investigation and determined that Logay "got the wrong woman."
He also reported that Promuto was double billing. Greene also interviewed Dennis Dayle and Clarence Cook — a daunting experience
for any young inspector. He recalled sitting in front of Dayle, who
"looked menacing" and refused to answer.[64]

"We didn't clean up the sinners," Greene sighed, noting that
his former boss Fred Dick had the largest file, two-thirds of which
involved misdeeds that occurred before he went to Asia. Regarding
MKULTRA, Greene, Shostrom and Cooper found that the DEA was
no longer involved in CIA safe house activity. They absolved Belk and
Siragusa of responsibility for people harmed by CIA drug tests, and
did not try to interview Feldman.[65]

Like the Church and Kennedy Committee Hearings and the Rockefeller Commission Reports, the DEA review was superficial at best,
and left unanswered the question: how many FBN, BNDD and DEA
agents and inspectors had contracts with the CIA?

More Trouble in Texas

IN HIS MAY 31 1978 letter to Benjamin R. Civiletti, US Attorney
Jamie Boyd complained that DEA agents in El Paso tape-recorded
their conversations with his assistant John Kerr. Boyd alleged that
DEA agents also entered buildings without search warrants, held people captive until warrants were obtained, tried to mislead the judiciary
by filing false complaints under oath, and gave false information to
obtain excessive bonds. Boyd wanted some agents fired.

Civiletti contacted Bensinger, who sent John Evans, now chief of
enforcement, to El Paso to calm Boyd down. According to Evans,
Boyd was "in bed with Customs people and trusted no one else."
Trying to defuse the situation, Evans agreed that wire-taping Kerr was
wrong, but insisted that Boyd had overreacted. Evans said that the
wire-tappers simply "didn't want to be misquoted."[66]

Boyd was not mollified by Evans, and his war with the DEA proceeded apace. Ultimately it would intertwine with the DEA's investigation of Jimmy Chagra and the May 1979 murder of Judge John
Wood, and it would directly contribute to the Reagan Administration's decision to have the FBI take over the upper echelons of DEA
management. Boyd's battle with the DEA was a complicated and
messy situation, but there was one incident in particular, according to
Boyd, that connected the Chagra investigation and the assassination
of Judge John Wood. This incident stood out from all the others, and

had both a Purple Gang and CIA connection. It was the mysterious death of ace undercover agent Santo Bario.[67]

After he refused to falsify his vouchers for Lou Conein and Phil Smith in Operation Croupier, Santo Bario was transferred to Mexico in March 1975. Bario was there in February 1976, when Jacques Kiere arrived as the region's deputy director. DEACONs and CENTACs aimed at uncovering the Mexican connection were chugging along, but the DEA's Mexico City office was mounting its own operation to find out how heroin moved from Mexico through Texas to Chicago and other cities in the United States. It was not easy, as many Mexican law enforcement officials were avidly anti-American and informants were unreliable.

In 1977, Bario was working with informant Alfredo Campos, a corrupt attorney who knew many cocaine sources.[68] Alas, Campos worked for the CIA too, reporting political information. Kiere had served in France for many years, and while there he recruited as an informant a former French connection trafficker, Claude Picault. Kiere and Picault had both worked closely with the CIA ever since. Kiere ostensibly assigned Picault to Bario as an assistant, but Picault's actual job was to entrap Bario.

There is speculation that Bario had stumbled, through Campos, on information embarrassing to the CIA, and given his refusal to cooperate with Phil Smith and Lou Conein in covering up abuses in Operation Croupier, he needed to be terminated. Bario had also complained that the Mexican Judicial Police were torturing people, and Kiere (a member of the Purple Gang) was worried that Bario might go public. Bario's informant Campos was in Bolivia, spying on cocaine sources with CIA connections when, in order to "help" Bario, Kiere put Picault in contact with the buyers in Chicago. And Bario suddenly found himself at the mercy of two CIA informants, a boss with CIA connections and a Purple Gang grudge against him.

The affair began in February 1978, when Picault carried cocaine across the border on a practice run designed to establish his bona fides with the Chicago receivers. On the next delivery in April, Picault carried a little extra cocaine across the border. He told Bario he needed to make a little money on the side, as is often the case with DEA informants; but Picault was actually working in concert with DEA inspectors. The set-up culminated in September when Bario, at the insistence of Picault, traveled to Chicago to meet with trafficker Alain Chaillou. Picault was "wired" and when Bario met Picault at the airport, DEA inspectors recorded Bario accepting a $4,000 cash bribe from Picault. In October, Bario was arrested in San Antonio while meeting with Picault. At his attorney's request, he was incarcerated in the Bexar County Jail.

US Attorney Jamie Boyd filed the indictment against Bario. From the law's point of view, it was an open-and-shut case. Bario had gone over to the dark side; he had taken money and let his snitch import drugs. In his defense, Bario claimed that he was merely safe-keeping the money for Picault, but no one believed that. He also claimed the CIA set him up as payback for defying Conein.

Beyond all that was the looming possibility that, at a public trial, Bario would expose the fact that the CIA used the DEA as a front for CIA operations in Mexico and the Bahamas; and that the CIA, with DEA complicity, routinely engineered controlled deliveries of narcotics from its "clients" in Bolivia and Colombia, through its clients in Mexico, into Texas (where various politicians got a hefty cut), on to Chicago and other parts of the country.

Boyd didn't believe any of that. His assistant Fred Rodriguez did, however, and predicted that Bario would not "live to go to trial." Trusting Rodriguez's judgment, Boyd requested reasonable bond, which the Judge refused. Trapped in the basement "hospital" section of the Bexar jail, and fearful of Texas and CIA justice — MKULTRA style — Bario begged to be moved to New Orleans. A week before he was to be transferred, he fell into a coma after eating a peanut butter sandwich. His wife was told that he was taken to the Santa Rosa intensive care unit suffering from strychnine poisoning. The cause of death was listed as strangulation due to a dry mouth caused by the combination of the peanut butter sandwich and the Elavil he was taking to relieve his depression.

One week after Bario died, Lee Chagra was killed and the plot to assassinate Judge Wood went into full swing. And the DEA started to disintegrate.

Santo Bario was in a coma until April 1979, when he died. Inspectors Joe Krueger and Robert Baker did an investigation. This author asked for a copy of that report. In a January 3, 1994 response from Robert A. Rogers, Chief, Freedom of Information Section, DEA, this author was told, "All documentation on Santo Bario has been destroyed."

27

ENTER THE FBI

THE CHAIN OF EVENTS THAT led to the FBI take-over of the DEA's top management positions began on June 20, 1973, when BNDD agents arrested flashy El Paso criminal defense attorney Lee Chagra on what author Gary Cartwright called "trumped-up" charges.[1] Implicated in a vast conspiracy drug case that began in 1968, Chagra was a crude cocaine and gambling addict who lost hundreds of thousands of dollars during wild binges in Las Vegas.[2] But smoking pot and snorting coke were in vogue at the time and, within the El Paso underworld, Chagra had become a local hero by defending drug offenders. His first major clients were Texan Jack Stricklin, Tom Pitts from Tennessee, and various members of the Columbus, New Mexico drug smuggling "Air Force."[3] Mostly ex-military pilots, the Columbus Air Force would land on a dry lake bed in Chihuahua and buy marijuana under the watchful eyes and outreached palms of the Mexican federales.[4]

Indicted in Nashville in the 1973 conspiracy case, Lee Chagra and his 40 co-conspirators "walked" in March 1975 after a Tennessee judge ruled that the indictment was "fatally flawed."[5] By former BNDD Agent Jack Compton's account, the defects were attributable to DEA case agent Frank Guzman, a Spanish-speaking FBN agent exiled from New York to Mexico following Andy Tartaglino's corruption purge in 1968. Guzman bounced from Mexico to New Orleans and finally to Nashville, where he helped develop a BNDD case on Lee Chagra and about 40 others nationwide. The case depended on tape recordings made of an informant in Texas talking to Lee Chagra. But when the case went to trial, the tapes could not be found and Guzman's reports were so poorly written that the charges were dismissed against Chagra and his associates. At this point, Guzman, who had reportedly borrowed money from Chagra's attorney, quietly departed the DEA.[6]

By then Lee Chagra's younger brother Jimmy had abandoned the carpet business for drug smuggling. A "high-roller" like Lee, Jimmy Chagra had connections in Mexico and Colombia, as well as with Mafiosi who sold him protection and laundered buckets of dirty drug money he gambled away in Las Vegas.[7] In 1975, Jimmy Chagra joined forces with chopper pilot Pete Krutschweski, aka Pete Blake. With the consent of the Patriarca Mafia family, Jimmy Chagra, Pete Blake and Jack Stricklin traveled to Colombia and bought tons of marijuana and shipped it on a tramp steamer to Foley's Cove in Massachusetts.[8] According to Detective Carl Shoffler (who had arrested the Watergate burglars and reported Vincent Promuto's indiscretions to the DEA), the Patriarca family's drug smuggling operation into Massachusetts tracked back to Meyer Lansky and the Mossad, and may have had CIA sanction.[9]

The CIA's interest in the Chagras may have evolved from the allegation that Chagra's Syrian contacts had terrorist partners in a Middle East arms-for-heroin operation in Mexico.[10] If so, the CIA would have attempted to penetrate it.

DEA Agent Chris Thompson, a former CIA officer assigned to Lou Conein's DEASOG unit, managed DEACON IV in El Paso. Thompson, through an informant he used in DEACON IV (targeted against Pedro Aviles Perez), assisted the DEA's El Paso office in its investigation of Jimmy Chagra.[11] The FBI was involved as well and kept track of Chagra's interactions with the Patriarca family in Rhode Island and Massachusetts, and with Chicago Mafioso Tony Spilotro in Chicago and Las Vegas.[13] The DEA had no specific CENTAC on Chagra, but other CENTACs dove-tailed with the case, and dozens of federal agents of every stripe in the US and abroad were tangentially involved.[14]

Lee and Jimmy Chagra enjoyed the attention that came from hanging with such a fast and furious crowd. Then in 1973 Jamie Boyd made Lee spend a night in jail, after which the Chagras declared war on DEA agents. Jimmy Chagra accused them of stealing his dope and Lee, while defending drug dealers in court, constantly accused DEA agents of corruption — the same things Compton outlined in his affidavit.[15] Events, however, spun out of their control and the Chagras soon found themselves at the center of a violent storm.

The Blackfriars Massacre

RAYMOND PATRIARCA WAS A MEMBER of the Mafia's Commission, which made important decisions that affected the Mafia worldwide. He may also have had a CIA connection. According to the testimony of Patriarca's former underboss Vincent Teresa, Patriarca accepted $4 million from the CIA in 1960 to kill Fidel Castro.[16] The DEA certainly knew of Teresa's allegation, which was made in 1978 while the Chagra case was climaxing.

In 1978, Patriarca's underboss, Salvatore "Mike" Caruana, kept the family's drug smugglers in line through kidnapping and murder.[17] The focus of a CENTAC, Caruana also managed the family's drug-money laundering operations in the Bahamas and, with Anthony Russo, sold stolen bonds to third world nations. Incidentally, one of Russo's clients, an Iranian named Farhad Azima, had CIA connections and used his Mafia loan to form Global International Airways.[18] Global obtained a contract with EATSCO, the company formed by CIA entrepreneurs Tom Clines, Richard Secord and Ted Shackley. Azima's brother owned Race Aviation, which figured prominently in the Iran-Contra scandal.[19]

As has been firmly established, the DEA shies away from the CIA-Mafia connection. It does, however, make non-CIA related cases when it can, and in November 1976 DEA agents arrested Jimmy Chagra's pilot Jerry Wilson.[20] By early 1978, Jimmy's senior partner in Florida, Henry Wallace, had been busted too.[21] Based on information supplied by Wallace and Wilson, as well as evidence assembled from the 1973 case, Boyd and his assistant James Kerr prepared to indict Jimmy.[22]

As Raymond Patriarca was aware, the CIA cannot always protect its Mafia henchmen from criminal prosecution. Patriarca was under intense FBI scrutiny and did not want Chagra's private war with the DEA to affect his relations with other major Mafiosi, specifically Tony Spilotro and Joe Bonanno, who were being drawn into the Chagra mess.[23] Thus, in the summer of 1978, he summoned Jimmy Chagra to Boston to confer with Sal Caruana, Pete Blake, and Vincent Solomente, a soldier in the Patriarca family who imported marijuana from Thailand through Oregon to Maine.[24] Blake and Solomente co-owned the Blackfriars Pub, and Blake was about to be indicted as a "kingpin."[25] That impending crisis didn't please Patriarca either and on June 28, 1978, Solomente and four associates were slaughtered by shotgun blasts in the tiny basement office at the Blackfriars Pub.[26] The Blackfriars massacre occurred while Jimmy Chagra's stepdaughter was vacationing at Caruana's house. In August, Lee and Jimmy met with Jimmy's Mafia appointed lawyers in Boston, ostensibly to sue the DEA, but more likely to negotiate the safe return of Jimmy's stepdaughter to El Paso.[27]

Jimmy and Lee Chagra's luck began to run out in October 1978, after Jamie Boyd summoned Sal Caruana before a grand jury.[28] People began stalking Lee.[29] Then in late November, someone sprayed Assistant US Attorney James Kerr's car with bullets from the back of a van while Kerr was stuck at a traffic light in San Antonio.[30] Kerr survived with minor injuries, but the attempt on his life prompted a new FBI investigation, which put more heat on the Mafia. Finally, on December 23, 1978, Lee Chagra was shot to death in his office by two armed robbers.[31] The robbers confessed and claimed it was a burglary gone bad, but skeptics believe the robbery was a cover for the assassination of Lee Chagra, and that Patriarca was using deniable hit men, a standard Mafia operating procedure adopted by the CIA. The gun was a .22, the bullet a hollow point, both signs of a professional hit.[33] And Sal Caruana, notably, was in El Paso shortly after the murder took place, tying up loose ends.[34]

The next blow occurred on February 26, 1979, when Boyd indicted Jimmy Chagra on drug trafficking charges.[35] Ironically, Chagra retained the services of Las Vegas lawyer Oscar Goodman, who had represented Santo Bario and Bradley Bryant, a member of a huge marijuana smuggling network connected to Chagra.[36] Jimmy was released on bond in March 1979.[37] He soon thereafter traveled to Las Vegas. While there he bumped into Peter Kay, a member of the Dixie Mafia whom Lee Chagra had defended on murder charges. With Kay was contract killer Charlie Harrelson.[38]

Natural Born Killer

LADIES MAN, RACONTEUR AND NATURAL born killer Charles V. "Charlie" Harrelson got out of Leavenworth Penitentiary in 1978, where he'd been caged for two years after serving several years in various jails and state prisons on a murder charge. Charlie was ready and raring to go.[39] He moved to Dallas and hooked up with Peter Kay, his childhood friend from Huntsville, Texas.[40] Kay was a member of the Dixie Mafia, a confederation of ex-cons known for violence across the Gulf Coast. They engaged in high-profit burglaries and contract killings, illegal gambling, pornography and drugs, in league with Mafia bosses in Dallas. Kay was also closely connected to the Banditos motorcycle gang.[41]

While in Dallas in late April and early May 1979, Kay set up a card game between Jimmy Chagra and Charlie Harrelson, who had put his hours in prison to good use perfecting card tricks.[42] During this period they also planned the murder of federal Judge John Wood, the presiding judge in Chagra's pending drug case.

Why? Jimmy's motive may have been revenge, for he certainly could not prevent a jury from convicting him by killing Judge Wood. Or, he could have been doing the bidding of the hardened criminals to whom he owed his life. Charlie's motive was purely financial. According to some observers, Jimmy Chagra, Charlie Harrelson and Jo Ann Starr were pawns in a larger plot managed by Pete Kay on behalf of organized crime. In any event, Jimmy and Charlie agreed, and Charlie's wife Jo Ann Starr (Kay's former lover) purchased the rifle allegedly used to kill Judge Wood.[43]

The murder plot was already in motion when a grand jury returned an indictment on May 22, 1979 charging Jimmy with masterminding an extensive drug trafficking empire in Texas and Florida.[44] Wood scheduled the trial for May 29 in San Antonio.[45] That morning, as Wood walked to his car, which was parked in front of his condo, he was shot in the back with a high powered rifle.

Three years later at Harrelson's murder trial, cab driver Wesley Coddington would claim that he had picked up Charlie at the airport on May 28 and driven him to the townhouse complex where Wood lived.[46] Another witness, Chrys Lambros, a 28-year old attorney, recalled bumping into Harrelson in the condo parking lot less than an hour before the shooting that left Judge Wood dead on the sidewalk.[47] Their testimony, along with that of Hampton Robinson IIII and a few other witnesses, would lead to Harrelson's conviction in 1982.

The peculiar thing is that three days after the assassination, Robinson called FBI Agent Robert Wyatt. An independently wealthy heroin addict and occasional criminal, Robinson socialized with Dixie mobsters Pete Kay and Charlie Harrelson. However, he had developed a grudge against Charlie after Charlie seduced his girlfriend. Seeking revenge, he told FBI Agent Wyatt that Charlie had bragged about having just done "a job" and was coming to stay with him. Wyatt inferred that the job was killing Judge Wood, at which point Wyatt opened the FBI's investigation of Charlie Harrelson.[48]

Dozens of FBI agents had descended on Texas in the wake of the Wood murder, but their focus was the Banditos motorcycle gang, which had been implicated in the November 1978 attempt on James Kerr. Only a few FBI agents followed leads connected to Harrelson and to that end, in June 1979, FBI agents interviewed Jack Strauss in Las Vegas.[49] The FBI knew that Strauss had been in Rockport, Texas with "Little Larry" Culbreath in January 1979. Judge Wood had a cabin in Rockport, and Culbreath and Strauss had "cased" the area — which raised the possibility that Culbreath and Strauss were involved in the murder conspiracy before Harrelson got involved. On June 12, FBI agents interviewed Culbreath.[50] The FBI, notably, did not share this information with US Attorney Jamie Boyd.[51]

In July 1979, a Fort Worth policeman told the FBI that one of his informants said Culbreath had been paid $1,000,000 to kill Wood.[52] The FBI knew that Culbreath had introduced Harrelson to San Antonio attorney Alan Brown in regard to an arms deal involving Mexican desperado Roberto Riojas. Through Riojas, the FBI even had a photo of Riojas meeting with Culbreath and several other hard-core criminals prior to the Wood assassination.[53] The FBI shared none of this information with Boyd.

Also in July 1979, Peter Bensinger replaced veteran agent John Evans as enforcement chief and sent him to Dallas as the DEA's regional director, specifically to preside over a task force investigating Jimmy Chagra's drug connections.[54] The task force featured Agent Terry Baldwin, a former CIA officer in Burma and Thailand, and included Santo Bario's former boss, Jacques Kiere in Mexico. Evans asked agents around the country to help the task force; but, according to Evans, its job was not the Wood murder investigation; it was drug smuggling, and Billy Breen was the task force's main informant.[55] Breen, had been Detective Carl Shoffler's informant at Fran O'Brien's bar, where Vince Promuto drank beer with a drug dealer from Texas. Promuto and Breen were friends. Indeed, Breen had many mob-connected friends and in the late 1970s, on behalf of the FBI and DEA, infiltrated the gang that distributed Jimmy Chagra's pot in Florida. Breen helped put a lot of people in jail, although none were from Texas.[56]

Although the DEA task force investigating Chagra was not charged with gathering intelligence on the Wood assassination, DEA Intelligence Chief Gordon Fink claims that the DEA had penetrated the Banditos motorcycle gang and had identified Charlie Harrelson as the killer within 36 hours of the crime.[57] That information never reached US Attorney Boyd either, which means the DEA, like the FBI, was also withholding information from him — perhaps as payback for his charges of DEA corruption. In any event, on August 15, 1979, Jimmy Chagra was convicted on drug trafficking charges. He was released on bond and fled before he could be sentenced.[58]

Boyd's Stalled Investigation

US ATTORNEY JAMIE BOYD ALWAYS suspected Charlie Harrelson of having murdered Judge Wood, and in August 1979 he told the FBI its theory that the Banditos were responsible was "crazy." This was not tactful and the FBI complained to the Justice Department about Boyd, while continuing to interview suspects without telling him.[59]

The tensions between Boyd, the DEA, and the Justice Department intensified in September, when Roberto Riojas (who had given the FBI a photo of his meeting with Larry Culbreath) offered the grand jury probing the Wood murder information on a drug deal connected to the assassination. Customs Agent Jack Compton heard about the offer through an informant and Boyd decided to check it out. In what proved to be an untimely coincidence, FBI Director William Webster had, at that exact moment, decided to travel to San Antonio to personally meet with Boyd and resolve their differences.[60] Alas, when Webster arrived, Boyd was in El Paso meeting with Compton's informant and missed meeting with Webster. That unintentional slight further heightened the tension between the FBI and Boyd.

The situation would deteriorate further when Compton and Boyd started visiting Riojas in El Paso. Riojas did not reveal that he was meeting simultaneously with the FBI, but he did show Boyd and Compton the group photo of him with Culbreath — at which point, given his mistrust of the FBI and DEA, Boyd formed his own special investigative unit under Compton. Boyd asked the DEA to contribute two agents and Evans assigned Hank Washington, who in 1978 had replaced George Frangullie as the Agent-in-Charge in El Paso, and former CIA officer and DEACON IV case agent Chris Thompson.[61]

Compton, meanwhile, learned what the FBI already knew: that Culbreath had told Riojas a hit was coming down; that Culbreath was in Rockport when Judge Wood was there in January 1979; and that a Culbreath associate was given $500,000 to open a restaurant in Las Vegas four days before Wood was killed.[62]

Finally, in late November 1979, Riojas offered to tell Boyd all in exchange for freedom. Boyd approached Attorney General Benjamin Civiletti with the idea of making a deal with Riojas. Civiletti accommodated Boyd, and on December 4, Boyd and his team met in Washington with a group of Justice Department officials headed by Criminal Division chief Philip B. Heymann.[63] Unfortunately, Heymann sympathized with the FBI; he dismissed the idea of making a deal with Riojas and accused Boyd of being afraid to prosecute the Banditos. As DEA Agent Hank Washington put it, "They threw us out."[64]

It would take another six months before Boyd finally learned of Riojas' true relationship with the FBI. That hurt, but what upset him even more was that the FBI did not tell him Riojas was providing it with information that was inconsistent with the case they wanted Boyd to press against the Banditos. According to Boyd, the FBI knowingly held back information and failed to disclose operative facts, which could have caused people to be indicted who were not involved in the crime.[65]

From December 1979 into February 1980, Boyd fought Heymann over the FBI's duplicity —, and the Justice Department's complicity —, in the Bureau's flawed murder investigation of Judge Wood.[66] Boyd kept repeating that Customs and the DEA were both interested in Riojas' information about drug routes from Mexico to Chicago. He was relentless and finally, as a way of frustrating Boyd, Heymann put Riojas in the Witness Protection Program. Although Heymann agreed to allow Boyd's investigators to interview Riojas, the prison warden on February 6, 1980 refused Compton access.[67] Furious, Boyd sent a "bombshell" memo to Civiletti asking for an injunction to allow him access to Riojas. He said it was the only way to break the FBI's logjam in the case.[68]

Drew Day, the Justice Department's Chief Deputy for Civil Rights, subsequently gave Boyd access to Riojas, but on condition he withhold the order for the injunction. Boyd complied, and on February 21, 1980 he submitted his "Position of the United States Attorney General for the Western District of Texas on Negotiations for Information in Kerr/Wood cases."[69] The Justice Department threw up more obstacles, and it was not until June 1980, as the presidential election neared, that Boyd was finally allowed to debrief Riojas.[70]

Insiders say there was a sinister reason behind the Justice Department and FBI's obstruction of Boyd's investigation. They say that prominent Texas law-makers, including a Republican Senator with CIA connections, had profited from the Mexico to Chicago drug route since it was established in 1947 — the same year George White's informant Jack Ruby moved from Chicago to Dallas at the behest of organized crime. In 1956, the FBI had identified Ruby as a central figure in a Mafia drug operation between Texas, Mexico, and New York.[71]

Through its organized crime informants, and a wiretap on Carlos Marcello, the FBI certainly kept track of this politically charged drug network, of which Chagra had become an integral part.[72] But the FBI decided not to investigate organized crime's role in the Wood assassination, or in drug trafficking in Texas. Why? Could it be that, as in the case of Santo Trafficante, the US Government did not want to expose the CIA-Mafia connection; or was it because, as Detective Carl Shoffler explained, the mob doesn't kill judges unless they are corrupt. During the Promuto investigation, Shoffler had reported on DEA corruption; and as this author embarked upon a private investigation of the drug intelligence angle of the Wood assassination, Shoffler warned him that he would find evidence of government involvement in both aspects, but would never be able to prove it. As Shoffler added, the stalled investigation of the Wood assassination had the effect of turning the focus away from Chagra's drug dealing enterprise, with its CIA connections. Shoffler referred this writer to Raul J. Diaz, a former Metro Dade County narcotics police officer turned private investigator, whose firm had an office in Washington and was said to have represented drug traffickers. Diaz, notably, was involved with Gary Mattocks in DEACON I.[73]

According to Jamie Boyd, the FBI obsession with the Banditos resulted only in thousands of wasted agent hours. He told this author that in order to tell the true story, he would have to contradict what the FBI said in court. Exposing the FBI's lies might possibly let someone off the hook — and that was something Boyd did not want to do.

According to Jack Compton, the substance of Boyd's injunction gets to the crux of the matter. But by order of Judge Williams Sessions, later Director of the FBI under Ronald Reagan, the injunction is sealed forever.

Closing in on Charlie

MEANWHILE, VENGEFUL HAMPTON ROBINSON HAD provided FBI Agent Wyatt with the serial number of one of Harrelson's guns, which Wyatt passed along to ATF Agent Mike Taylor. In February 1980, Taylor arrested Charlie in Houston.[74] Knowing he would inevitably be returned to the awful Huntsville prison for violating his parole, Charlie posted bail, fled to El Paso, and assumed an alias.[75] That same month DEA agents caught fugitive Jimmy Chagra in Las Vegas. With Chagra's incarceration, the FBI's investigation of the Wood assassination would finally start to focus on Charlie Harrelson. For purposes of protecting the CIA-Mafia crime nexus, it could not, however, follow the same track Jamie Boyd was pursuing.

Although frustrated by Criminal Division Chief Philip B. Heymann, Boyd finally got Riojas to make a Proffer. Presented to Heymann on February 29, 1980, it claimed that the original plan to kill Wood was discussed at a meeting between Anglo and Hispanic gangsters in Alan Brown's law office in early December 1978.[76] Little Larry Culbreath was present, and Boyd suspected Culbreath of being involved.[77] Boyd also believed it was worth accommodating Riojas in order to discover how the Chagras distributed their drugs inside the US. The distribution network involved the Mexico-Texas-Chicago connection Santo Bario was working on when he was arrested, as well as other independent networks around the country. Naturally, Heymann stalled.

Things started happening fast. Pete Kay was jailed for refusing to talk to the Wood grand jury. Harrelson, by then, had begun to believe that Kay and Culbreath had set him up. Knowing this, Kay turned on Charlie and started talking to the FBI. Charlie, meanwhile, was arrested in Van Horn in September after a ten hour stand-off with Texas lawmen. High on cocaine and LSD, Charlie was pointing his gun at his head and holding himself hostage, while babbling incoherently and confessing to various crimes, including the assassination of JFK. He had seven ounces of coke in his possession and was quickly locked away, never to experience freedom again.[78]

Boyd had always felt that Harrelson killed Judge Wood. The only reason he hadn't indicted him was because too many people had seen Charlie in Dallas on the day of the murder. Then a witness identified Charlie in a line-up in Houston around Thanksgiving 1980, and that sealed Charlie's fate.[79]

DeFeo Again

JAMIE BOYD HAD RAISED SO much hell that FBI Operations Chief Francis "Bud" Mullen and his assistant Jack Lawn flew to San Antonio in February 1980, to personally manage the Wood murder investigation. The media and FBI Director Webster were "hot" for results, as Lawn explained, and his job was to get FBI focused. This should have been easy, as the case was broken within days, when Robinson called FBI Agent Wyatt and said that Harrelson had just done a job. But Wyatt was one of only a handful of the FBI agents on Harrelson; all the rest were obsessing on the Banditos. Lawn changed that.[80]

Lawn had been a Marine, was a certified tough guy, and got along well with the DEA's Wolf Pack. He was smart too, and immediately reduced the number of FBI agents in San Antonio and gave those who remained specific tasks: like checking out each of Judge Wood's sworn enemies. Everything pointed at Jimmy Chagra, so Lawn had his intelligence analysts review Jimmy's personal phone log as a way of reducing the number of suspects. They inevitably settled on Harrelson, and Lawn came up with a clever plan to gather the material evidence needed to convict him and Chagra.

Jimmy Chagra had been convicted on drug charges and was incarcerated at Fort Leavenworth in Kansas. Lawn knew Walt Witchard, the FBI agent assigned to the federal prison, and asked Witchard to recruit an inmate with "high visibility" to spy on Chagra. Within a week, Witchard had settled on Jerry Ray James, a bank robber with the Dixie Mafia. James had not committed any heinous crimes, so the FBI offered to help him get parole in 18 months if he could get Jimmy to incriminate himself and Harrelson in the Wood assassination.[81]

James was placed in Jimmy Chagra's cell, and soon Jimmy started bragging that he had hired Harrelson to kill Wood. That confession gave the Justice Department probable cause to wiretap Jimmy's telephone calls. The original affidavit, notably, went through Michael DeFeo in October 1980. There were problems, however, because the wiretaps recorded conversations between Jimmy and his brother Joey, who served as his attorney, as well as with his wife Liz. To overcome the hurdle of attorney-client and husband-wife privilege, Lawn suggested that DeFeo screen the information. DeFeo agreed and organized two teams to review the tapes: a "Dirty Team" listened and screened out everything personal or legal, and then turned the tapes over to a "Clean Team" which looked for admissions of criminal activity. Every 30 days DeFeo obtained a new Title Three permit from the Kansas City Judge, until enough evidence was obtained to bring murder charges against clueless Charlie Harrelson.[82]

Things got worse for Charlie in April 1981, when the rifle he allegedly used to kill Wood was located. By that time Jo Ann Harrelson had been convicted in Dallas of buying the rifle. That October, Charlie stood trial in Houston and in December he pled guilty to gun and drug charges. He was sentenced to 40 years in the Huntsville prison, which makes Guantanamo look like Club Med. Then in April 1982, a federal grand jury in San Antonio indicted him, his wife Jo Ann, and Jimmy, Liz and Joe Chagra for the murder of Judge Wood. The trial began in September 1982. His defense was that he and Chagra did conspire to commit a crime, for which he received a payoff, but that the crime had to do with narcotics, not murder.[83] The jury did not believe him and Charlie was convicted of killing Wood. It was not a terrible blow, however, as it meant he would spend the rest of his life in a federal penitentiary, instead of the hellhole at Huntsville.

The Harrelson murder trial preceded the Chagra murder trial, and after Charlie was convicted, Jimmy asked for change of venue. The government agreed and he was tried in Florida, where, remarkably, he was found not guilty. He did, however, face a lifetime behind bars on his previous drug convictions. For his part, Jamie Boyd was the first federal prosecutor removed from office after Ronald Reagan and George Bush won the 1980 presidential election. The FBI's job was done, and Jack Lawn was transferred back to Washington as Bud Mullen's deputy administrator at the DEA.

Enter the FBI

FBI AGENT BUD MULLEN WAS appointed acting administrator of DEA in July 1981, three months before Harrelson went on trial for murdering Judge Wood. Jack Lawn became Mullen's deputy and acknowledges that if he had not been assigned to San Antonio, and if the Wood case had not been solved, he would not have been assigned to DEA.[84] But, as Mullen explained, it wasn't just the Wood assassination that prompted the Reagan Administration to have the FBI take over the management of the DEA.[85]

According to Mullen, FBI Director Clarence Kelly wanted to take over the DEA in 1974 and formed a commission to study the idea. Fearing the pristine FBI would be overwhelmed by corruption, the commission rejected the idea. However, as a tentative first step toward eventually subsuming the DEA, Kelly created a narcotics liaison agent in each FBI office. The FBI and DEA started working in task forces, while behind the scenes, lawmakers and bureaucrats made plans for their long term assimilation. During the Carter Administration, when the DEA lacked adequate resources, Peter Bensinger even thought of asking the FBI for help. But, Mullen explained, "He was too politically aligned with liberal Democrats to ask."[86]

The idea of a merger continued to gain momentum, and the process culminated when Reagan was elected and made Rudy Giuliani an associate attorney general. Giuliani had served as chief of the US Attorney's "junk unit" in New York City and worked with Andy Tartaglino during his controversial corruption probe. Giuliani knew that the drug business was a growth industry with plenty of political potential. According to Mullen, the idea of imposing the FBI on the DEA was Giuliani's idea, and Giuliani proposed it during the Reagan transition.

A 20-year FBI veteran with vast law enforcement experience across the board, Mullen was a friend of Giuliani's drug advisor, former FBNBNDD-DEA Agent Howie Safir. More importantly, Mullen was a loyal Republican; so Giuliani recommended him for the job as Acting DEA Administrator.[87]

The "precipitating event" for the merger, Mullen explained, was the murder of Judge Wood. It was the "premier FBI investigation" at the time, and, after putting Jack Lawn in charge, Mullen coordinated the investigation in Washington with DEA Operations Chief Marion Hambrick. By then, Giuliani wanted Mullen to take over the DEA.

To this end, Giuliani went to Attorney General William French Smith, who approached Reagan and his chief of staff, Edwin Meese. They signed onto the idea, as did FBI Director Webster. Mullen was appointed in July 1981 and brought on eight people as his management team, including Jack Lawn as his deputy.

According to Mullen, the DEA's most pressing problem was administration, which was a kind way of saying the corruption scandals (documented in this book) had basically ruined the organization's reputation. Mullen put Marion Ramey in charge of administration and Ramey set up an Internal Affairs office and started investigating more than two-dozen DEA agents for serious crimes. Mullen cites the Jeffrey Scharlatt case in Florida as an example. A former member of Tony Pohl's Tactical Unit in New York, Scharlatt went "sideways" in Miami. Mullen and Webster were present for his arrest and saw several million dollars in cash on his bed.

Scharlatt wasn't the only bad apple; a number of DEA agents were living lifestyles they couldn't afford, driving around in fancy cars and wearing Rolex watches. But, Mullen said, the DEA was not taking internal investigations seriously. The inspectors had been trained to be deceitful, were arrogant, and tried to cover up. To show that no one was exempt, Mullen even disciplined Jerry Jensen for having over-billed the DEA for moving expenses, when he was transferred from his post as Regional Director in Los Angeles to Washington, as the assistant administrator for training.[88]

Next, Mullen closed the six DEA regional offices and gave responsibility for integrity investigations to the local agent in charge of existing field offices. Each Special Agent in Charge now had to find a group supervisor who could disengage from his duties and handle internal affairs. When sensitive issues surfaced that required extra resources, Mullen would call upon inspectors from the Justice Department's Office of Professional Responsibility (OPR), which had been established in 1975 after Watergate.[89]

Mullen's appointment as Acting DEA Administrator was not well received. A rumor had preceded his appointment that he had a "hit list" (like Myles Ambrose had in 1973) and intended to fire 148 agents. By Mullen's account, Peter Bensinger believed the rumor and tried to thwart the merger by destroying documents and soliciting negative comments from foreign nations. Iran threatened to cut off liaison if the FBI got involved in narcotics, on the assumption that FBI agents (taking a page from the CIA playbook) would pose as DEA agents and spy on their government.

Mullen responded by firing the top officials Bensinger "could not control." He "hit them hard." One of the first to go was intelligence chief Gordon Fink. Claiming that Fink "had lost touch," Mullen transferred him to the Office of Congressional and Public Affairs. Fink claims that "Mullen was not a supporter of intelligence, which led to its major de-emphasis" and resulted in many of DEA's top analysts leaving for other jobs.[90]

As noted, Mullen closed the six regional offices, which in his opinion "were a way of delaying decisions." He then remodeled the DEA on the FBI's "centralized system." He reorganized headquarters from geographical desks to drug-specific desks and established procedures where all agents-in-charge met their FBI counterparts for annual meetings. The FBI had four times as many employees in its 59 field divisions as the DEA had in its 18 Divisions. Everywhere the DEA was out-numbered.

On the positive side, DEA funding was increased and EPIC and the financial intelligence program were upgraded. To every DEA agent's relief, Mullen stopped short of insisting that they share their confidential informants with the FBI. But he did have FBI agents do background checks on all DEA agents.[91] It is said that the Customs agents laughed loudly over this particular move.

Mullen felt there was an urgent need for "tight" management and, to this end, he decided that agents would no longer be automatically placed in administrative jobs. Instead he created a career development program in which agents had to take classes and pass an exam to get management credentials. Taking advantage of each organization's expertise, DEA personnel were sent to FBI field offices to train FBI agents who hadn't conducted drug investigations before, and FBI agents were assigned to train DEA agents in the intricacies of Title III wiretaps. Mullen's stated goal was to streamline and polish up the DEA so it could become a component of the FBI. His instructions came from Attorney General Smith through FBI Director Webster, both of whom had politics as their number one priority.[92]

Covert operations were a major concern too, and in February 1982, Attorney General Smith exempted the CIA from reporting to other federal agencies on its drug smuggling assets.[93]

After these sudden and radical changes, Mullen looked around and saw tremendous apprehension. The DEA didn't want the FBI. There was "reluctant acceptance" at best. On the other hand, FBI agents felt demeaned by being around rough-and-tumble DEA agents. One FBI agent, when assigned to the DEA, told Mullen, "I didn't want to tell my neighbors what I do." So Mullen made Congressional and public affairs a top priority, and abolished the requirement to do undercover work — though qualified agents did occasionally perform in that capacity. To change their poor self-image, Mullen insisted that DEA agents refer to themselves as "federal agents." He made the topless bar in the lobby off-limits. The Freedom of Information Act office had a backlog of several thousand requests, so he put an FBI agent in charge to clean it up. And, to please the Reagan White House, Mullen launched political action programs like the Sports Drug Awareness Program, in which high school coaches encouraged students to "just say no."[94]

When Mullen became Acting Administrator of the DEA, a group of black agents had recently won a class action discrimination suit, based on a statistical analysis of the inequality in promotions. The verdict was handed down in February 1982 and compensated 200 black agents for past discrimination. As part of the settlement, one black agent was to be promoted for every two whites until blacks comprised ten percent of management.[95] To show his support, Mullen put a black agent in charge of the career development program — a move he described as "window dressing."

Indeed, racial discrimination remains the DEA's unspoken policy, and after a select group of veteran black agents led by Carl Jackson got promoted, they faced the inevitable backlash from white agents.[96] The judge who decided the so-called Seager-Davis discrimination case created a committee to oversee his Stipulation, and white agents were forced to participate. Hard feelings festered. White agents believed they had all the same problems as black agents, whether as managers, supervisors, or street agents.[97] Feeling they were victims of reverse discrimination, a number of bitter white agents in senior positions used their clout to nit-pick the black agents who had benefitted from the Seager-Davis case, forcing many to quit in frustration. Many of the surviving black agents complain that the post-FBI generation of black DEA agents, who enjoy big salaries, equal status with white agents, and no requirement to do dangerous undercover work, have become complacent.

Speaking of the advancements made during the by-gone Civil Rights era, Agent Clarence Cook said, "There was esprit de corps back then. But young people today don't know the history. They got comfortable and most of the gains were lost. There is a built-in hostility and you can't stop it."[98]

As we shall see in the next chapter, a concerted effort at political indoctrination has banded together DEA agents of all ethnicities and genders for their mutual benefit. This development started before 9/11, with the FBI take-over and the rapport Mullen forged with the CIA; a rapport based on Attorney General Smith having exempted the CIA from reporting on its drug-smuggling assets. According to Mullen, the DEA was always fighting CIA. DEA agents involved in international affairs would even "burn CIA informants" to make cases. To improve relations with the CIA and appease the Reagan White House, Mullen made FBI Agent John McKernan his special assistant for investigations and McKernan immediately abolished Dennis Dayle's CENTAC program. Mullen notes that the regions didn't cooperate with CENTAC anyway. "If you have central control," he said, "you don't have regional discord." McKernan replaced the CENTAC program with "special enforcement operations" and a new focus on RICO cases, and left William Casey and the cowboy CIA to control the overseas action.[99]

Requiem for a Wolf Pack

THE FBI IS A DOMESTIC law enforcement agency, and international operations were not Mullen's top priority. By his own account, he did not expand the overseas agent force. Instead he systematized operations in little ways, like buying overseas offices more furniture and limiting overseas tours to five years. This policy certainly reflected the Reagan White House's desire that the DEA not become a stumbling block in the slew of covert CIA operations it had in store.

Mullen did not question his White House marching orders. He simply notes that the CIA under Casey was never "fully forthcoming … never fully came on board … always felt their mission was primary … and didn't trust the DEA."

Indeed, according to DEA Agent Michael Levine, the June 1980 "cocaine coup" in Bolivia "was part of a worldwide plot by the CIA to throw the election to Reagan."[100] An Argentine front company in Miami laundered drug money that financed the coup, in which drug lord Roberto Suarez joined with Bolivian military officers to seize power in the name of anti-Communism. Bolivia was a sign of things to come, and in 1981 Reagan would authorize the Argentines to finance the CIA's Contra mercenary army in Nicaragua. The use of drug-trafficking profits to partially fund the counter-insurgency would become a centerpiece of the ensuing Iran-Contra scandal.

DEA Administrator Bud Mullen worked closely with CIA Deputy Director John McMahon, former head of the Agency's clandestine and intelligence services. They had a good personal relationship and when the CIA-backed Thai military bombed a village with DEA agents in it, Mullen did not make a fuss. When the CIA wanted DEA helicopters to fly over Jamaica, Mullen approved it. Mullen also reversed Bensinger's policy of not handing out DEA credentials to CIA officers, thus allowing them access in and out of Eastern Europe, especially Poland. When a New York Congressman and a former Special Forces colonel sent agents into Laos looking for MIAs, Mullen gave them DEA credentials. He blindly approved whatever Reagan wanted, and under his direction the DEA became a mere adjunct of the CIA.[101]

According to John Evans, to appease Reagan Mullen, even claimed that Manuel Noriega wasn't into drugs; although "there was a thick file sitting right in front of him." When Evans complained, Mullen said it was a State Department problem.[102] Reagan, according to Evans, deliberately shut down the DEA overseas operations, even closing the office in Honduras to pave the way for CIA-supported drug smugglers. Reagan's point man in this venture was Vice-President George Bush, whose South Florida Task Force allegedly provided cover for drug-smuggling CIA assets entering the country on Pan Aviation and Southern Air Transport planes, among others.[103]

Mullen acknowledged spending "lots of time" with Vice President Bush's chief of drug operations, retired Admiral Daniel Murphy. By Mullen's account, Murphy set up a military-style command post in Miami and sent agents to chase Colombians in Miami, South America and the Caribbean.

Many DEA agents were given temporary duty assignments to the Bush task force and, according to Inspector Dick Salmi, learned how to bilk the system in ways never dreamed of by humble FBN agents. Salmi investigated the Bush task force and found it to be a boondoggle, with agents staying at swank hotels, figuring out how to use every penny of their expense accounts. They all knew that Reagan's war on drugs, as managed by Bush, was a mere cover for CIA drug-smuggling operations. At this point DEA agents basically gave up the fight.[104]

The farcical hypocrisy of DEA agents in flak jackets telling school kids to "just say no" was demoralizing, when they knew that Reagan and Bush were allowing the CIA to import tons of cocaine into the country. It didn't help their morale either that their anti-corruption boss, Bud Mullen, had received a home loan with the help of Reagan's Labor Secretary Raymond Donovan. Political cronyism flourished under Reagan as never before and Donovan was at center stage. Donovan valiantly fought off charges of fraud and larceny with a little help from the FBI, which failed to provide a special prosecutor and the Senate Labor and Human Resources Committee with a "set of reports that included unproved allegations by informants linking the Labor Secretary with organized crime figures."[105] For this reason Mullen remained "acting director" for four years, until the Senate cleared Donovan of corruption charges.

But in those four years, the DEA's soul was destroyed.

28

THE AGE OF NARCO-TERRORISM

FBI Agents Bud Mullen and Jack Lawn, his successor as DEA Administrator, forever changed DEA culture, infusing it with an "internal security" virus that spawned a mutant breed of managers. From 1981 onward, the DEA was an agency with an attitude. Mullen articulated the ideological tone in 1985 during Congressional Hearings "On the Role of Nicaragua in Drug Trafficking," when he declared that Cuba used "hard currency" from drug trafficking "to support revolutionary activities in Latin America."[1] At the same Hearings, Senator Charles Grassley (R-IW) quoted Reagan Administration NSC member Michael Ledeen as saying: "Running drugs is one sure way to make big money in a hurry. Moreover, the directions of the flow are ideologically attractive. Drugs go to the bourgeois countries where they are corrupt and where they kill, while the arms go to pro-Communist terrorist groups in the Third World."[2]

Ambitious DEA managers and agents were susceptible to the internal security virus and, once infected, slid effortlessly into the role of bureaucratic *suppletif* (apparatchiks), eagerly providing political cover for the Reagan Administration's imperial adventures. In one illustrative case, Customs agents in Texas arrested Francisco Guirola in February 1985 while he was carrying six million dollars. Customs said Guirola's money was "part of a terrorist-money-dope connection" and initially the DEA identified him as involved in cocaine and arms smuggling in El Salvador and Guatemala.[3] But as soon as it became known that Guirola was a fundraiser for the Reagan Administration's ally in El Salvador, Roberto d'Aubuisson, an organizer of right-wing death squads, the DEA dropped its investigation.[4]

From 1981 through 1990, Mullen and Lawn were, in turn, ultimately responsible for such decisions. But they could not have succeeded without a cadre of like-minded managers. Dave Westrate and Steve Greene will be featured in this chapter. Westrate's ascent began in 1981, when he became operations chief Frank Monastero's deputy. Greene became Monastero's executive assistant in 1982. Two years later, Mullen named Greene as his personal representative to Oliver Revell, the FBI's counter-terror chief and liaison to the CIA.[5] This was an especially critical position, given that Revell and the FBI would, during the Iran-Contra scandal, spend considerable time and energy investigating critics of Reagan's repressive policies in Central America. Whistleblowers who revealed the Reagan Administration's covert actions in Central America — especially its complicity in drug trafficking — were investigated, rather than officials like Oliver North who were involved in the trafficking.[6] By aiding and abetting the Reagan Administration in this regard, senior DEA officials played a central and largely unreported role in the Iran-Contra cover-up.

Dave Westrate in 1985 replaced Monastero as chief of operations, and was the key DEA figure during the Iran-Contra scandal. One of Westrate's first actions as chief of operations was negotiating a memorandum of understanding with the FBI, bringing the organizations into closer cooperation on a broad range of issues, including informant policies.[7] As operations chief, Westrate was also the DEA's liaison to the CIA in regard to arms and drug-dealing informants, and operations tied in to the Iran-Contra scandal.

The DEA's metamorphosis from a wolf pack to a political pork chop relied on senior executive management selecting politically correct agents for sensitive positions. This screening process was effectuated organizationally, when Mullen centralized control on the FBI model. Centralization weakened the DEA field offices. Within the United States, regional directors once were relatively free to resist intrusions by the FBI, and any but their own local political bosses. After Mullen centralized control, however, agents in charge of field offices had to comply with the wishes of an FBI-dominated management force beholden to the Reagan Administration. The same thing applied overseas, in regard to the CIA. Cynical in the extreme after 50 years of fighting a lost cause, DEA managers and agents knew they had to demonstrate their wholehearted support of Reagan's ideology, or forfeit their careers. It was that simple.

Mullen's imposition of rigid FBI procedures facilitated the political indoctrination of DEA agents. Although they faced the same bureaucratic and operational problems as their forbears, agents were unable to exercise the initiative and ingenuity the Wolf Pack had used to work around them. After 1981, DEA agents were forced to work in teams with anal FBI agents scrutinizing their every move. Some struggled to maintain their street-smart heritage, but the process of imposed assimilation gradually eroded the rugged individualism exemplified by agents like Fred Dick, who, for all his shortcomings, could calmly tell a CIA officer to "fuck off."

Another of Mullen's demoralizing edicts was having the DEA report through the FBI to the Justice Department. This put Attorney General Edwin Meese, as chairman of the National Drug Policy Board, in the chain of command and further undermined the ability of DEA managers to make apolitical decisions. Making matters worse, FBI agents immediately proved their inability to manage drug cases when they botched the "reverse sting" of auto-maker John DeLorean. DeLorean was charged with conspiring to smuggle $24 million worth of cocaine into the US, based on a videotape made of him discussing the deal with undercover agents. His attorney, however, proved that DeLorean was coerced into the deal. DeLorean was acquitted of all charges, and the DEA was greatly embarrassed. An inspector who reviewed the case found that the DeLorean team "was a den of vipers" and that the DEA supervisor and his FBI counterpart "almost came to blows" over the FBI's mismanagement of the case.[8]

The one positive outcome of Mullen's micro-management style was that the offices of intelligence and operations were compelled to work more closely together. Operations Chief Frank Monastero had ten desks, but his personal focus was organized crime, the historical area of overlap between the FBI and DEA. That happy coincidence was complimented by the ascent of female intelligence analysts within the organization. Women represented the DEA's new sensibility, in which having the muscle to kick down a door mattered less than communication skills. Intelligence Analyst Mona Ewell, for example, was instrumental in assembling, and sharing with enforcement, the crucial background documentation in the DEA's seminal Pizza Connection case.[9] Based on the field work of Agent Tom Tripodi in Italy, Ewell located fugitive Tomasso Buscetta in Brazil, where he was importing heroin from Khun Sa in Burma and channeling it to Mafia pizza parlors in the US.[10] Based on Buscetta's information and the undercover work of Agent Frank Tarallo, the DEA set an intricate trap that netted Benny Zito, the central defendant in the case.[11] The Pizza Connection Case led to the demise of several Sicilian and American Mafia chiefs, including Vince Promuto's reputed godfather in the Genovese family, "Fat Tony" Salerno.

Iran-Contra

IN THE EARLY 1980'S, LATIN American drug traffickers were visiting terrible violence upon politicians they viewed as collaborating with the US government. Reagan, in a reversal of Carter's Human Rights approach to foreign policy, responded with greater violence. He declared drug trafficking a threat to national security and the age of narco-terrorism began, dove-tailing neatly with Reagan's lawless imperial ambitions.[12]

To neutralize the threat to US security posed by Nicaragua's Sandinista government, Reagan's Director of Central Intelligence, William Casey, put Vice President George Bush (with that lean and hungry look) in charge of a secret operation to organize an insurgent group dubbed the Contras.[13] To skirt Congress, Casey, Bush, and Bush's national security advisor Donald Gregg formed and operated a "counter-terror network" of right-wing ideologues whose secret purpose was to illegally arm the Contras.[14] Among them was former DEACON I asset Felix Rodriguez, who had served as Gregg's "counter-terror team" advisor in Vietnam.[15] Assigned as an advisor to the Salvadoran Army's Civil Affairs department, Rodriguez managed the CIA's pacification effort in El Salvador and Guatemala, applying the same technique he had refined in Vietnam.[16] General Paul Gorman, who commanded US forces in Central America in the mid-1980's, defined this type of counter-terrorism as "a form of warfare repugnant to Americans ... in which non-combatant casualties may be an explicit object."[17]

Bush's central role in this secret operation was formalized on June 14, 1983, when he was picked to head an "accelerated program against drug smuggling" using CIA and military assets.[18]

Concurrent with Bush's official covert operation, Marine Lieutenant Colonel Oliver North at the NSC launched a parallel "off-the-shelf" covert operation headed by General Richard Secord at the Special Operations and Policy Group in the Pentagon.[19] As Iran-Contra investigator Lawrence Walsh noted, Secord in 1983 had "retired from the Air Force following allegations of improper dealings with former CIA agent Edwin Wilson, who was convicted of smuggling arms to Libya."[20] Adept in the craft of covert logistics, Secord established a complex web of numbered bank accounts and shell corporations worthy of any major drug-trafficking organization. Known as the Enterprise, it was designed to conceal the sale of missiles to Iran (then fighting Iraq) in exchange for US hostages. At North's direction, Secord's Enterprise diverted some of the profits to buy arms for the Contras.[21]

Secord's Enterprise included foreign agents at both the Iran and Contra ends of the operation. It also included former CIA officers Tom Clines and Ted Shackley, and several of their exile Cuban assets. According to author David Corn, "within the spook world the belief spread that Shackley was close to Bush. Raphael Quintero was saying that Shackley met with Bush every week."[22]

In November 1984, Shackley traveled to Hamburg to meet with Iranian-Jewish arms and drugs trafficker Manucher Ghorbanifar.[23] Shackley then introduced Ghorbanifar to his business partner, Michael Ledeen, the neoconservative NSC member and Reagan Administration back channel to the Israelis. As noted earlier in this chapter, Ledeen had a keen interest in connecting drug trafficking to terrorism. Ledeen and the Israelis met Ghorbanifar in Paris and recommended him as an agent to North.[24] Thus began the first official arms-for-hostages deal with Iran, with North using profits from the sales to buy arms for the Contras. North, in November 1986, even purchased $500,000 worth of weapons from Monzer al-Kassar, a notorious Syrian arms and drugs trafficker.[25] The Kassar family was "reputed to be the largest drug-and-arms-dealing family in Syria," but the DEA refused to confirm that fact."[26]

DEA agents were involved in the double-dealing as early as January 1985, when Reagan's assistant Edward V. Hickey Jr. introduced DEA Agent Bill Dwyer to North.[27] Dwyer told Hickey that Frank Tarallo, the undercover agent in the Pizza Connection case, had a contact in the Middle East who could locate William Buckley, a CIA officer held hostage in Lebanon. Dave Westrate assigned Agent Abraham Azzam, an Arabic speaker, to North's Hostage Locating Task Force as Dwyer and Tarallo's supervisor.

The entire escapade was a huge fiasco. Tarallo's source demanded $50,000, which the CIA paid. When he demanded an additional $200,000 for operating expenses and later $2 million for each hostage, Azzam voiced his concerns and refused to pay. North questioned Azzam's loyalty and Azzam responded, reportedly, by referring to Ollie as a "nutcase."[28]

At this point North side-stepped the CIA and obtained the $2,200,000 in cash from Texas industrialist Ross Perot. The money was delivered to Dwyer and Tarallo while their source ventured into Lebanon and returned with proof of Buckley's location — proof the security experts at the FBI determined was phony. CIA deputy Director for Operations, Clair George, called the whole affair "a scam."[29]

Undeterred, Dwyer and Tarallo, having looked long and deep into Perot's black bag, talked North into removing them from the CIA's supervision and placing them under his control. North agreed and he and the DEA agents schemed for a year, during which time Buckley was killed, and Dwyer developed a new source whose plan was to have the hostages taken out of Lebanon on the ship Erria, which Tom Clines brought to Cyprus.[30]

All was for naught. Not only did the second source prove unreliable, Perrot lost his money. Worse, North's "hip-pocket" DEA operation put an end to Secord's hostage initiative, and provided the hostage takers with enough cold hard cash for countless more kidnapping operations. In his defense, Agent Tarallo testified that Attorney General Meese approved the use of Perot's funds. But as we know from the Croupier and Silver Dollar cases, the DEA's own top attorney ruled it was illegal for the DEA to accept private funds for its operations.[31]

But times had changed and ethical lines had blurred. DEA operations were now indistinguishable from White House political actions, comparable to General de Gaulle's Service d'Action Civique. Westrate rationalized the situation as follows: "DEA has always had a tremendous stable of sources overseas as you know, so it is not surprising that we developed information about the hostages. This continues today in the war on terror over and over again. We have always been a community player."[32]

Mismanagement by Design

THE CONTRA RESUPPLY EFFORT RELIED on drug traffickers, as became obvious in April 1989, when Senator John Kerry's Subcommittee on Terrorism, Narcotics and International Operations released its report,

"Drugs, Law Enforcement and Foreign Policy."[33] As revealed in the report, Oliver North in July 1984 wrote in his diary that he "wanted aircraft to go to Bolivia to pick up paste, want aircraft to pick up 1,500 kilos." His July 12, 1985 entry said, "$14 million to finance [arms] Supermarket came from drugs."[34]

The DEA never launched an investigation of North, even though Congress in 1953 had enacted statutes in which anyone committing any act, no matter how small, in the furtherance of a crime was guilty of conspiracy. As an agent explained in Chapter 6, "we caught many of the major people behind the scenes by charging conspiracy, many of the conspirators never laying their hand on the contraband." But when it came to North, the DEA chose not to obey the law, even though it knew that his Contra resupply scam employed some of the DEA's most wanted traffickers. In 1983, for example, Customs informed the DEA that Juan Matta Ballesteros owned the airline SETCO in Honduras.[35] In the Customs report, SETCO was described as "a corporation formed by American businessmen who are dealing with Matta and are smuggling narcotics into the United States." The Kerry Report indicated in 1986 that SETCO was "the principal company used by the Contras in Honduras to transport supplies and personnel."[36] North obtained State Department funding for SETCO and three other Contra supply airlines, "each and every one [of which] had been set up and was run by major traffickers."[37]

Top DEA officials certainly knew all this. As early as 1980, the DEA knew that Matta and his associates Miguel Felix Gallardo and Caro Quintero were responsible for one third of the cocaine consumed in the US.[38] But instead of taking action, they closed their office in Honduras, as part of their new internal security mandate — call it mismanagement by design — in which politically incorrect information was smothered in its crib, so DEA officials could mislead Congress and the public. This was no small thing, for the DEA knew that Matta, Gallardo and Caro Quintero had helped kidnap, torture and murder DEA Agent Enrique Camarena in Mexico in 1985.[39] But because the traffickers contributed money and arms to the Contras, Matta wasn't arrested until 1988 and Gallardo until 1989, when tying up Iran-Contra loose ends became imperative for George H.W. Bush's political ascent.

In the meantime, when holes appeared in the internal-security safety net, the DEA did more than look away. For example, in 1986 DEA Agent Celerino Castillo was sent to El Salvador to investigate a pilot who parked his plane at the Ilopango airbase. While there, Castillo learned that the CIA had allocated space in one hangar to North's Contra supply operation.[40] He often saw Luis Posada and Felix Rodriguez, whom he described as "American terrorists," at Ilopango.[41] Amazed and confounded, he reported this to his bosses John Marsh, chief of the Latin American Desk, and Robert Nieves, the Agent in Charge in Costa Rica. "They wanted me to use the word 'alleged' on my reports," Castillo explained, "instead of facts."[42]

One of the facts Castillo reported was that a CIA agent was requesting a US visa for a Contra drug smuggler who was flying cocaine out of American John Hull's ranch in Costa Rica to anti-Castro Cuban miscreants in Miami. "The CIA's own station chief in Costa Rica admitted that....Hull worked with the Agency on "military supply and other operations on behalf of the Contras," besides receiving a $110,000 monthly retainer courtesy of Oliver North."[43]

Castillo's mistake was personally telling Vice President Bush about this at a party at the ambassador's house in Guatemala City. Quick as a flash, US Ambassador to El Salvador Edwin Corr, likely a member of Bush's counter-terror network, sent a "back-channel" cable to the State Department. Within days, DEA headquarters had shut down Castillo's inquiry and his reports mysteriously disappeared.[44] As Castillo noted, "we had a place up there [at DEA headquarters] called the 'Black Hole'; all these reports went in there, and they were never distributed to the right people."[45]

In February 1987, DEA investigators found "no credible information" indicating that traffickers represented any political organization, Contra or Sandinista. They said Castillo's reports never existed and harassed him into quitting in 1990.[46] They did this, despite the fact that the Contra resupply network had been revealed in 1986 when the Sandinistas shot down a Southern Air Transport plane. The plane, once owned by DEA asset Barry Seal, had made frequent trips to Colombia where a federal witness claimed to have seen cocaine loaded on board.[47] As the DEA well knew, North made arrangements for Southern Air Transport to send planes to Felix Rodriguez in El Salvador.[48]

The sad fact is that most DEA agents approved of what Reagan was doing. To this day Dave Westrate says, "I have no knowledge of drug trafficking by North or anything close to that." It's the "anything close to that" part of his statement that is unbelievable. But having accommodated the Contra drug-supply network, in what amounted to criminal negligence, the DEA lost any pretense of moral authority to fight America's war on drugs.

Community Players

GARY MATTOCKS IS MORE IN the modern "community player" mold than Celerino Castillo. Based on favors performed for the CIA while running DEACON I, Mattocks was hired back into CIA in 1977.[49] His friend, Ted Shackley, then the assistant deputy director for operations, assigned him to the CIA's narcotics unit in Peru. Mattocks was in Peru for two years operating unilaterally, undercover in the visa section of the US consulate, apart from Peruvian, DEA, and State INM officials. At the time, the DEA was pursuing Santiago Ocampo in Colombia. Ocampo was buying cocaine in Peru, and Matta Ballesteros was flying it through Honduras, Mexico and Panama to exile Cuban miscreants in Miami. One of the receivers, Francisco Chanes Rodriguez, an erstwhile DEACON asset, owned two seafood companies that served as fronts in North's Contra supply network, receiving and distributing tons of Contra cocaine.[50]

While working as the covert agent in DEACON I, Mattocks often met at Felix Rodriguez's house with Shackley's close friend Tom Clines, a member of Secord's Enterprise and Shackley's case officer to Ed Wilson. When in Florida, Clines socialized with Contra arms-and-drug dealer Chanes.[51]

Could Mattocks not have known?

After Peru, Mattocks joined the Contra support operation under Latin American Division chief Duane Clarridge. On behalf of Clarridge (indicted for lying to Congress in the Iran-Contra scandal but pardoned by president Bush), Mattocks was present in 1984 when CIA officers handed Barry Seal a camera and told him to secretly take photographs of Sandinista official Freddie Vaughan loading bags containing drugs from the Medellin cartel onto Seal's plane.[52]

As they testified to Congress in 1988, Dave Westrate and Ron Caffrey, then head of the DEA's cocaine desk, held two meetings with North and Clarridge about Seal's undercover operation against the Medellin cartel. Caffrey said that DEA asset Seal was running drugs for Jorge Ochoa Vasquez and that Ochoa was using Nicaragua as a transit point for his deliveries.[53] The DEA sent Seal to pick up a load in Nicaragua, aware that Mattocks and other CIA officers had outfitted Seal with a camera concealed in his plane.

Caffrey testified that the case agents in Miami sent him copies of the photos and that Westrate asked him to brief North. Westrate said North called the meeting. Two things of note happened at the meeting. First, North asked for DEA consent to have Seal, who was returning to Ochoa with $1.5 million in drug-sale money, to pull a fast one and instead deliver the cash to the Contras. At the meeting, North also passed around the photo of Vaughan unloading cocaine from Seal's plane. North discussed how it could be used to influence a Congressional appropriations vote. In other words, North tried to suborn the DEA agents into blowing a case against the Medellin cartel, and diverting drug money to terrorists. When Caffrey and Westrate objected, North leaked the story and the photos to the right-wing *Washington Times*.[54] North blew the DEA's biggest case at the time, and the DEA did nothing about it.

Reagan made out like a bandit, claiming on TV that the photo of Vaughan (who was said by Customs Commissioner Eric Von Raab to be working with Robert Vesco in Cuba), proved the Sandinistas were drug-dealing terrorists, thus swaying the public to support *his* drug-dealing terrorists, the Contras.[55]

Barry Seal fared less well. Once Reagan had blown his cover, Seal's value as an undercover agent abruptly ended. He was used as the main witness against Medellin cartel members Pablo Escobar, Carlos Lehder, Jorge Ochoa and Rodriguez Gacha. The smugglers (apart from Vaughan, who was actually a CIA agent in place in the Sandinista regime) were tried in absentia, and some were later captured or killed. But as DEA Administrator Jack Lawn told Senator Kerry, leaking the photos blew any further investigation and "severely jeopardized the lives" of agents.[56]

Indeed, Seal was assassinated in Louisiana in 1986.

Concerned Congressmen asked Dave Westrate if he would blow a major case for partisan political purposes. He said he would not. They asked him why he would discuss the details of an ongoing operation with political operatives and spies who could sabotage cases and, potentially, be called as witnesses in the case. Westrate said it was routine to discuss cases with the CIA and NSC, so political, espionage, and drug operations did not conflict.[57]

When there was a conflict, drug traffickers involved in US Government-sanctioned political espionage operations were protected, until the operations ended and the traffickers lost their value.

Narco-Terror

THE WHITE HOUSE AND CIA need to control the DEA, so they can control which traffickers the DEA targets. Nowadays DEA officials go along, 1: because the CIA has better technology and contacts, and helps them make big cases; or, 2: because they support or fear their political bosses. It's part of a tradition that precedes the CIA and dates back to 1934, when FBN Agent Maurice Helbrant made a case on drug-smuggling members of an American airline, TACA, that was delivering drugs from Honduras to the Mafia in New Orleans. Because the US supported the Honduran officials involved, Helbrant was forced to stop his investigation.[58] By March 1939, TACA held cargo service concessions in Costa Rica, Nicaragua, Guatemala, El Salvador and Honduras; and continued to engage in smuggling activities "virtually untouched by government action."[59]

Ironically, TACA flights from Belize to New Orleans were investigated as part of Operation Sandstorm in 1973 ... which, again, resulted in no arrests.[60] Some things never change, and as General Paul Gorman, commander of US forces in Latin America during the Iran-Contra scandal, explained, "The fact is, if you want to go into the subversion business, collect intelligence, and move arms, you deal with the drug movers."[61]

There are so many examples, one cannot list them all. Two pertinent cases, however, deserve special attention. The first involved Gary Mattocks and his DEACON I asset Guillermo Tabraue. In 1989, the CIA instructed Mattocks to testify as a defense witness at Tabraue's trial.[62] Mattocks testified that Tabraue was his informant from 1973-1977 and that the CIA paid Tabraue $1400 a week. Although Tabraue had earned $75 million from drug trafficking by 1989, the judge declared a mistrial based on Mattocks' testimony. Tabraue was released. Some people inferred that President G.H.W. Bush had personally sent Mattocks down to dynamite the case.

The second case involved DEA Agent Dick Salmi and his work as chief of a special investigative unit in New York.[63] The DEA was interested in Roberto Cabrillo, a drug smuggling member of CORU, an organization of murderous Cuban exiles formed by drug smuggler Frank Castro and Luis Posada (mentioned above) while George Bush was DCI. Castro was arrested in the DEA's Operation Tick-Talks in 1981, but released and established a Contra training camp in the Florida everglades.[64] Hired by the Bush counter-terror cabal in 1985, Posada managed resupply and drug shipments for the Contras at the Ilopango air force base in El Salvador. Charged in Venezuela with blowing up a Cuban airliner and killing 73 people in 1976, Posada was convicted in Panama in April 2004 for a bombing plot aimed at Fidel Castro.[65] Four months later, "outgoing Panamanian President

Mireya Moscoso — who lives in Key Biscayne, Florida, and has close ties to the Cuban-American community — pardoned Posada and his co-conspirators on the Panamanian bombing plot. At the time, there was press speculation that the move was a political favor to George W. Bush, who was in a tough battle for Florida's electoral votes."[66] The US Government under George Bush continued to harbor this international terrorist.[67]

Working with FBI Agent Larry Wack, DEA Agent Dick Salmi recruited Cabrillo for the purpose of penetrating CORU. In Atlanta at a closely monitored meeting, Salmi presented Cabrillo with a package of disinformation prepared by DEA Intelligence Analyst Judy Bertini. The package included documents and photographs, some real, some fake, concerning the assassination of Orlando Letelier in Washington in 1976. Salmi asked Cabrillo to pass the bundle along to CORU, prompting one member to confess that he had provided the explosives used to murder Letelier. Through Cabrillo, Agents Salmi and Wack warned CORU to stop bombing people in the US. It could maim and kill people anywhere else, just not here in the homeland.[68]

Cabrillo, notably, was simultaneously working for the CIA, which asked Salmi to recruit, through Cabrillo, CORU members willing to set up controlled drug deliveries for busts in the US. On the CIA's behalf, Cabrillo was also arranging for the defection of a colonel in Cuba's intelligence service. The CIA asked Salmi to help. The defection took place in Miami under the direction of Salmi's CIA case officer Robert McCarthy. Salmi handled three more defections with McCarthy, Cabrillo and his CORU comrades. DCI William Casey and Dewey Clarridge were personally involved in the defection of one Nicaraguan official. The official worked at a Nicaraguan port, and arranged for the CIA's special operations division to sink the Nicaraguan ship Monimbo, which was carrying arms from Taiwan to the Sandinistas. The captain and 22 crew members were killed.[69]

Salmi passed his CORU drug-trafficking reports to Steve Greene, who, like Dave Westrate, "didn't want to know." Judy Bertini and Jack Lawn, however, were eager to proceed and kept Salmi in touch with Cabrillo in order to make cases using CORU drug dealers as assets, including members of the Frank Castro organization, which flew drugs from Ilopango into Miami. By then, Salmi notes, the Justice Department had a special "grey-mail section" to fix cases involving CIA terrorists and drug dealers.[70] That would come in very handy during the Contra cover-up, discussed in the next chapter.

Going Paramilitary

IN 1985, ON BEHALF OF the Reagan Administration, Jack Lawn began the paramilitarization of federal drug law enforcement. Crack cocaine had appeared in New York, the so-called "cocaine wars" had spilled onto the streets and into the headlines, and the public was clamoring for a stronger federal effort.

Lawn's first step was convincing his friend, Reagan's chief of staff Edwin Meese, to change the system back so that the DEA no longer reported to the Justice Department through the FBI.[71] Lawn's operations chief Westrate shifted DEA resources from investigating heroin sources in Asia to investigating cocaine sources in Latin America, where the new "extraditables" were native Latin Americans, not Italians and Frenchmen.[72] Lawn then obtained more State Department funds to help source countries expand their anti-narcotics operations. State did this primarily through an air-support program managed by two consulting companies employing Corporate Jets, a private company composed of some 150 employees, many former pilots with Air America, to fly and maintain a fleet of helicopters, spray planes and transport aircraft. Based in Latin America, the air program failed to comply with numerous parts of its contract and one chief operations officer "was indicted for conspiring to smuggle drugs from Mexico before taking the State Department job."[73]

Next Congress amended the Posse Comitatus Act (10 USC 374) and Lawn conscripted the military, although the State Department's Bureau of International Narcotics Matters (INM) was responsible for coordinating joint military, State and DEA operations.[74] With Meese's backing, Lawn got Admiral Bud Zumwalt to provide Navy instructors to teach DEA agents how to patrol the jungle rivers on which cocaine was transported. "Riverine" programs were initiated in several "hot" countries using boats purchased by State INM. Lawn got the Marines to train DEA agents at Quantico, and General Steve Olmstead became the coordinator between the DEA and a military staff operating out of the US Special Operations Command at McDill Air Force Base.[75]

Finally, Lawn arranged for Meese to visit an outpost in Bolivia where DEA agents were training troops to attack cocaine labs. Many of the weapons were inoperable and the equipment second rate. Upon his return to Washington, Meese raised the subject with Reagan and logistical support quickly improved. DEA agents were soon being sent to Ranger School and taught how to establish Special Forces type A camps in the jungles as part of Operation Snowcap, a CENTAC-style project aimed at stopping the growing, processing, and transporting of cocaine into the US.[76] Almost every government agency got involved under the direction of Vice President Bush, who simultaneously served as head of the South Florida Task Force on Drugs, the National Narcotics Border Interdiction System, and Operation Alliance with the Mexicans. Bush's involvement further diluted DEA control over investigations. But the DEA soldiered on, launching innovative operations like Swordfish and Polar Cap, designed to entrap drug-money launderers. Its objective was to make big splashy cases, so it could compete with the two dozen other agencies getting money from Congress for drug law enforcement. As Westrate notes, "You're more successful if you have something to point to from a manager's point of view."[77]

Snowcap was initially billed as successful and that translated into more funding from Congress. Soon the DEA owned helicopters, and Snowcap was expanded into Peru and Colombia under the direction of Agent Steve Casteel, who in 2003 became the senior US advisor to the Iraqi Ministry of Interior.[78]

Military involvement in the drug war stirred patriotic feelings and garnered public support for DEA paramilitary operations. But the volume of cocaine smuggled into the US continued to increase, leading skeptics to conclude that drug aid was being used for political repression instead. There were even reports that Snowcap boats were used by foreign military and police officers for commercial purposes, such as delivering chemical precursors to the labs the DEA was searching for. After several DEA agents were killed in a plane crash, Snowcap was cancelled.[79] Paramilitary operations, however, did not cease; they simply became less visible and more tightly controlled by the CIA.

The Counter-Narcotics Center

THE OVERWHELMING QUESTION, ACCORDING TO Dave Westrate, was "How to play with the CIA?"[80]

The CIA's answer was the Counter-Narcotics Center, created in 1988 by the new DCI, former FBI Director William Webster. Staffed by over 100 agents, the CNC was designed to serve as a springboard for covert penetration and paramilitary operations against traffickers protected by high-tech security firms, lawyers, and well-armed private armies. The CNC brought together, under CIA control, every federal agency involved in the drug wars.[81] Many DEA managers resisted it, but some saw it as a way of obtaining better intelligence and making bigger cases. Terry Burke, then the DEA's Deputy for Operations, was allowed to send one liaison officer to the CNC.[82]

"We had a series of agents from Steve Greene's Foreign Ops shop assigned as liaison to the CNC," Burke explained, "but their main role evolved into keeping us informed of what they could learn of the CNC's activities. This was not a spy mission, but for us to make sure the CNC wasn't doing something that would get us all in a mess. (And they were, of course, doing the same with us!)"

The genesis of the CNC is rather interesting. In the late 1980s, according to Burke, the CIA had a narcotics unit under its Special Operations Division Chief John Randall, a veteran of opium-rich Laos. This was certainly the new improved version of the Twofold unit DEA Agent Joey DiGennaro had been in from 1972-77. Randall's narcotic unit was headed by an avid anti-Castro Cuban who kept sinking DEA cases. Many of the cases involved Latin American enforcement officials whom the CIA unit had trained. The Cuban CIA officer had a learning disability. No matter how many times the DEA told him, he never grasped the idea that if the CIA heard about a drug shipment via a phone tap in a foreign country, and passed the information to the DEA, the DEA would have to reveal the source if it wanted to make a case in court. Sometimes it seemed the CIA passed along such information deliberately, to sabotage a case against an important asset.[83]

As Congressional investigations into the Iran-Contra scandal climaxed, the CIA decided it needed someone with more stature and visibility to manipulate the DEA. At this point the CIA, while maintaining its secret anti-narcotics unit, formed the Counter-Narcotics Center with veteran officer Howard Hart as its first chief. Hart was a veteran of Pakistan where until 1984 he supported a "contra" mujahadeen faction led by narcotics trafficker Gulbuddin Hekmatyar, a CIA asset fighting the Soviets in Afghanistan.[84]

Late in 1988, Lawn introduced Burke to Hart. As deputy for operations, Burke was the principal liaison to the CIA and periodically met with Hart, who had been reassigned from Bonn, Germany where he'd been chief of station. Burke and Hart developed a close friendship, though Lawn worked with Hart at a higher level, as did Westrate. Hart dealt primarily with Lawn on issues of damage control and strategic intelligence, such as the production of narcotics in particular countries and the politics involved. The DEA agent assigned to the CNC asked no questions about unilateral CIA anti-narcotics operations, and formed a good working relationship with Hart. However, the DEA and CIA would ultimately clash over the CNC's unilateral operations.[85]

The CNC had a staff of analysts but, according to Burke, its main job was to motivate the CIA's field agents to be pro-active. On Hart's behalf, Burke met with the CIA's Latin American station chiefs to brief them on the DEA mission. The DEA agent-in-charge and the CIA station chief in Bogota were fighting "like alley cats," and Burke and Hart brought them into line.

Burke uses Snowcap in Peru as an example of how the DEA put CIA intelligence to good use. In that instance, the CIA discovered that Communist rebels had set up cocaine labs at their training sites. The CIA passed the information to the DEA operations center, which knew where the labs were located, but did not know they were protected by armed guerillas. The DEA mounted successful paramilitary operations against the labs under Agent Frank White, but would have lost a lot of men unless, as Burke explained, "we hadn't checked with the CIA before the raids."

If only the CIA could bring itself to wage war on the right-wing drug smugglers it supports, the supply-side effort in the war on drugs might have a chance of succeeding.

29

THE VIEW FROM THE TOP

TERRY BURKE SERVED AS A CIA paramilitary officer in Laos in 1965. He was in the country "black," without official cover, and never set foot inside the station in Vientiane. He worked with Tony Poe, the fearsome CIA officer whose tribal troops worshipped him as a god and stuck the heads of their enemies on poles around his camp at Nam Yu. There, in the heart of darkness, Poe taught Burke the laws of jungle war. Burke later won the CIA's highest honor, the Intelligence Star, for returning to a camp that had been overrun by enemy forces and attempting to rescue a downed American pilot.[1]

Burke was stationed at Nam Yu at the same time Poe was making sure the CIA's share of opium was delivered a few miles south to the old French airstrip at Houei Sai. As Poe told the author, the opium was packed in oil drums, loaded on C-47s piloted by Taiwanese mercenaries and flown to the Gulf of Siam, then dropped into the sea and picked up by accomplices in sampans waiting at specified coordinates. The opium was ferried to Hong Kong, made into heroin by Chinese chemists, and sold through established brokers to the CIA's Mafia partners from OSS days.[2]

Most of Poe's account was confirmed by CIA officer Don Wittaker at a January 1966 meeting with FBN Agent Al Habib in Vientiane. The FBN knew what the CIA was doing. Wittaker's boss,

James Lilley — whom President Bush appointed ambassador to China in 1989 — knew all this too, and more.[3] Which goes to show how deeply and for how long US officials have been covering up CIA complicity in international drug trafficking. By the time Bush became president, the "old boy" system of plausible deniability had been formally built into the DEA through layers of bureaucracy that served, essentially, no other purpose.

In 1970, Burke joined the BNDD knowing it was a growth industry. Applying the principles of jungle warfare and CIA tradecraft, he eventually became the DEA's deputy and acting administrator. His ascent began in 1982 as Agent Tom Byrne's deputy on the marijuana desk. Hoping to prove that Reagan was tough on drugs, Ed Meese ordered the DEA to spray the poisonous herbicide paraquat on a pot plantation in Georgia. The Forest Service had miscalculated its location, however, and when the plane doused a farmer's corn crop instead, the media had a field day. That night Burke did excellent damage control on a radio call-in show. Lawn recognized his poise, and potential as a DEA poster boy, but decided he needed executive management experience.[4]

At Lawn's urging, the Career Review Board selected Burke for a senior executive service appointee as deputy chief of intelligence. But Andy Tartaglino's disciple, Frank Monastero, recalling Burke's betrayal during the Jackson Hearings, blocked the appointment. ("That time Burke was out in front of the train," Tartaglino quipped in an interview with the author.) So in 1985 Lawn selected Burke as ASAC in Denver, and in 1987 named him Special Agent-in-Charge in Phoenix, Arizona. In 1988, after Monastero had retired, Lawn tapped Burke as Westrate's deputy for operations.

Lawn favored combat veteran Burke over bureaucrat Westrate, and secretly maneuvered to put his man in place. As Burke recalled, "While I was SAC in Phoenix, Lawn told me he was bringing me to DC and, when [Lawn's Deputy Administrator] Tom Kelly retired ... I would replace Kelly. All of this was in confidence. It was difficult at times working with Dave [Westrate] as his deputy, knowing he wanted to and expected to replace Kelly, but my knowing that was not the plan."[5]

Burke went to headquarters in January 1988 as deputy to Operations Chief Dave Westrate. A few months earlier, on Burke's recommendation, Lawn had named another combat veteran, Steve Greene, as head of foreign operations. The triumvirate of Greene reporting to

Burke, and Burke reporting to Westrate, operated at the highest level of DEA management. By then the Wolf Pack was extinct: Greene, Burke and Westrate were the veterans, representing an organization that, in Greene's words, had entered "the big time." The budget topped a billion dollars and Reagan had made the drugs wars a matter of national security. Westrate, Burke and Greene communicated with the White House on operations against the Colombian cartels, Manuel Noriega in Panama, Far East heroin traffickers, and Iran-Contra connected traffickers in Mexico where the DEA was investigating the murder of Agent Enrique "Kiki" Camarena. Things would happen quickly in regard to these major issues, with Burke largely in control.

"As Deputy for Ops," Burke explained, "I had the various drug desks under me: the Compliance Division, Intelligence, Foreign Ops, Training and Special Ops. I tried to make the Deputy for Ops the ombudsman for the field SACs to David, [Tom] Kelly and Lawn. I established a command system and center for crisis management, following the theory that the most senior leaders should not get bogged down in the day-to-day running of a crisis. I met routinely with FBI and CIA and other agency counterparts, but more on case specific problems. David handled similar liaison but at the next higher level. David's meetings were more strategic and long range in nature than were mine. David had a real interest in our Intel Division and provided a lot of personal direction to it. This allowed me to concentrate on the other areas."

Burke described being deputy of operations as "the toughest job" he'd ever had. "Operations is the narrow part of the hour glass," he said, and "determines what the boss needs to know." To this end he wrote to all the SACs, asking them what they considered the most critical personnel problems and where DEA was going as an agency. They were all "depressing replies."

SAC Phil Perry in Denver had the best overview, so Burke put him in charge of a team of agents that reviewed the replies and came up with a plan to change things for the better. At the top of the list was improving communications between the enforcement and intelligence divisions. Burke addressed this ingrained problem by initiating specially funded intelligence programs to put attention where it was needed. He also sought better relations with his former employer, the CIA. According to Burke, Intelligence Chief Tom Byrne was very bright and legalistic, but was trying to keep the CIA out of the DEA's data base. He was "right technically," Burke observed, "but wrong politically." So Burke moved Byrne out and put in Richard Bly, with Judy Bertini as Bly's deputy, to work with the CIA. Bly worked well with the Agency and, according to Burke, "We saw a renaissance in DEA intelligence over this period. Now people know what you're doing."

Burke also pushed for "pro-active intelligence operations." Southeast Asian heroin was a major problem and he aimed several specially funded intelligence programs and special enforcement operations in that direction. Intelligence and enforcement worked together and came up with "umbrella operations," with each division assigning 20 or 30 people. The CIA and military volunteered personnel too. Burke cites as an example a case in which the US military monitored the radio transmissions of Thai trawlers, allowing the CIA to develop operational intelligence, which the prosecutors in Hong Kong could use in court without having to reveal that the CIA was the source.[6]

Burke was a progressive, and keen on getting more women and minorities into executive management positions — a 33% increase by his estimation. "We didn't need quotas," he explained. "We had minorities, and the best person for a particular job was often a minority." Burke's efforts in this regard are partially responsible for the ascent of women into the upper regions of DEA management.

Burke also tried to improve relations with the DEA's old rival, Customs, noting that in Houston, the SACs "didn't even know each other." In a flashback to the Ingersoll-Ambrose days, Burke negotiated a memo of understanding allowing Customs to carry out drug investigations on their own, as long as they reported to the DEA. This agreement with Customs, as well as Burke's cozy relationship with the CIA, minorities, and female employees, angered some DEA veterans. According to Westrate, Burke "gave the store away."[7]

"David and I worked well together," Burke said graciously, "and I always respected his dedication to DEA."

Then came the shocker: as Burke recalled, "In October 1989, Jack Lawn jumped me over David and two other Assistant Administrators into the Deputy Administrator position. Lawn retired in March 1990 and until September 1990 I was the Acting Administrator, and concurrently Deputy. During that time I made a number of changes of senior personnel, including transferring David to be Assistant Administrator for Inspections, to provide him with a fresh challenge as well as to allow me to get some new ideas infused into the Ops area."

The First Bush Regime

TERRY BURKE'S TENURE AS ACTING DEA Administrator was marked by the invasion of Panama to arrest CIA asset Manuel Noriega for drug smuggling; the CIA's assassination of kingpin trafficker José Rodriguez Gacha; and the DEA's abduction in Mexico of a potential witness to the murder of Agent Kiki Camarena.

All of this happened during the presidency of George H.W. Bush, former head of the quicksilver CIA. During his presidency, Bush sought over $8 billion dollars to fund the drug wars.[8] Between 1989 and 1992, over 20 million Americans used illegal drugs, and around thirty-percent of Bush's budget went to treatment and prevention.[9] Ten-percent of the federal "drug supply reduction" budget went to the DEA while the military got the lion's share, with nineteen-percent (twice what the DEA got) going to the Coast Guard alone.[10]

Instead of leaving drug law enforcement in the hands of trained professionals, Bush politicized and militarized it in ways giddy Gordon Liddy never dreamed possible. In 1990 Bush tasked General Peter Pace, commander of US military activities in South and Central America (and Chairman of the Joint Chiefs of Staff under George W. Bush) to support the DEA. Through Pace, an army colonel was given an office at DEA headquarters and designated to help plan anti-drug operations with Terry Burke, David Miller at the NSC, Melvin Levitsky at State, and the usual shady CIA representatives. Burke refers to their get-togethers as "horror-group meetings."[11]

DEA headquarters was the logical place to coordinate inter-agency intelligence, but the Coast Guard objected, so in 1991 Bush created the National Drug Intelligence Center. Headed by a DEA agent, but "under the direction and control of the Attorney General," the NDIC was established in Johnstown, Pennsylvania, as an independent component of the Justice Department. Investigative reports from every agency involved in "national security and law enforcement" were sent there for analysis. The purpose was "threat assessment" — trying to predict where a problem might arise. There was no "case support," but strategic intelligence reports were sent to the attorney general and, if applicable, to places like the narcotics unit of the Chicago Police Department.[12]

Johnstown, alas, could not make agencies share intelligence. The least helpful member was the CIA, which gathered the best intelligence, but rarely gave it away. This was not an auspicious development, as President Bush relied more heavily than any of his predecessors on the CIA to ensure control over DEA targeting and foreign operations. Reflecting new regional priorities, Bush in 1990 appointed Jack Devine as head of the CNC. A veteran CIA officer, Devine from 1985-87 had headed the CIA's Afghan Task Force, working closely with Pakistan's intelligence service and the drug-smuggling muhajadeen.[13] There was a sharp rise in drug addiction in Pakistan during this period, and with CIA links to drug smugglers in Afghanistan becoming public knowledge, it was essential for Bush to have a veteran of the CIA's Central Asian campaign in charge of CIA drug operations. Ironically, the notorious CIA double agent, Aldrich Ames, worked at the CNC from 1991-94.

Insofar as the Iran-Contra scandal could have led to Bush's impeachment, managing the war on drugs was, for him, a matter of political survival. To prove his resolve, and to deflect attention from his complicity in Contra drug smuggling schemes, Bush on August 21, 1989 authorized Attorney General Richard Thornburgh to release a list of twelve Colombian drug lords Bush wanted "dead or alive."[14] Bush was intent on asserting the CIA's prominence in the war on drugs. To make that clear, a US army officer assigned to the CIA, and assisted by an elite unit of Colombian policemen firing machine guns from two American helicopters, assassinated Medellin cartel member José Rodriguez Gacha, his-17 year old son, and their bodyguards on December 15, 1989.[15] The massacre transcended any symbolic strategy ever devised by the Nixon White House. While his spokesmen initially denied any US involvement, Bush later boasted that "the mission was covert with American involvement concealed and protected by plausible deniability."[16]

The DEA played no role in the Gacha assassination, which did not put a dent in drug trafficking or diminish the violence that accompanied it. It was simply a sign of the vicious measures Bush would take in the name of drug law enforcement.

Panama

THERE IS A FAMOUS PHOTO of Donald Rumsfeld smiling broadly and pumping Saddam Hussein's hand on December 20, 1983, knowing full well "the brutal dictator" was pouring chemical weapons on the Kurds.[17] At almost the same moment, Bush was meeting with another brutal dictator, Manuel Noriega, to seal an equally devious deal.[18]

Bush's first recorded meeting with Noriega occurred in 1976, when, as DCI, he gave Noriega a tour of Langley headquarters.[19]

Noriega, at the time, was on the CIA payroll at a cool $1-200,000 a year.[20] Jimmy Carter severed that arrangement, but Reagan restored CIA relations with Noriega. Reagan was intent upon crushing nationalist uprisings in Latin America, and initially sought the assistance of Panamanian President Omar Torrijos. But Torrijos refused to help in the Contra supply effort. Shortly thereafter Torrijos perished in a plane crash, and CIA asset Noriega took over the Panamanian government and its drug organization.

Bush and Noriega met again in December 1983 to seal a deal in which Noriega allowed the Contras to set up an arms distribution network in Panama.[21] Noriega was guided in this venture by Mossad security expert Mike Harari. According to one source, Harari played a "key role in a Panama-based triangle that apparently helped put drugs from Colombia into the US, used the proceeds to buy arms (some captured from the PLO in Lebanon) from Israel or through Israeli brokers, and then sold the arms. They certainly went to US-backed contras and friendly Latin governments."[22] According to Jose Blandon, an intelligence advisor to Noriega, the Harari network "was established with Israeli citizens, Panamanians and Unites States citizens for arms-supply purposes." He said that through the Harari network, "guns would go in one shipment and drugs would come out in another."[23]

Bush publicly denied knowing about Noriega's drug dealing, but North was so pleased with Noriega's assistance that he suggested that the CIA's Office of Public Diplomacy "help clean up his image" and lift the ban on arms sales to the Panamanian Defense Force. He did this knowing that Noriega was cutting side deals with the Colombian cartels.[24]

The DEA protected Noriega too. Although Bensinger denies the charge, two DEA agents insist that Noriega's file was destroyed on his watch, with its incriminating details of the Sea Witch case, so the Panama Canal treaties could be ratified by the Senate. In any event the past was erased and, with Noriega's assistance, the DEA, through Operation Pisces, arrested 115 traffickers and seized 10,000 pounds of cocaine.[25] Bensinger, Mullen and Lawn sang his praises, and Dave Westrate wrote him thank-you letters. Westrate also went to the White House meeting where it was decided to have the 82nd Airborne serve the DEA's warrant for Noriega's arrest. The indictment made no mention of Noriega's work for the DEA, CIA, North or Bush; only his involvement with the Medellin cartel.[26]

Bush's December 1989 invasion, billed as a "Just Cause" to free the people of Panama, was typical "read my lips" double talk. While no one was freed, hundreds were killed, and thousands maimed, rendered homeless, and arrested.

The pretext for the invasion dated to October 1986, when Sandinista soldiers shot down a CIA Contra resupply plane. An American survivor blew the whistle on the CIA's arms-for-drugs operation, prompting powerful establishment forces to take aim at Bush's secret counter-terror network. The shell game commenced. North quickly shifted all drug flights from John Hull's ranch in Costa Rica to exile Cubans out of Ilopango air base in El Salvador; and Bush turned his "anti-terror" apparatus into a Homeland KGB targeting anyone who spoke ill about his illegal activities. DEA officials assisted: from the DEA agent who helped Hull escape Costa Rica after his arrest, to the SACs in every Central American country, who swore there was no evidence linking the Contras to drug trafficking.[27]

When the Christic Institute filed a RICO lawsuit against members of Secord's Enterprise, the DEA stepped in. Curious to know what evidence it had, Westrate's deputy Tom Cash in December 1986 sent Dick Salmi to investigate the Christic's allegation that Contra drug money was being laundered through a bank in Denver, with the assistance of former DEA Agent William Wanzeck, and sent to Jeb Bush (the Vice President's son and later governor of Florida) in Miami for Contra weapons. Salmi passed the information to the FBI, which decided not to investigate.[28]

The Justice Department was also involved in the cover-up and when Alan Fiers, chief of CIA's Central American Task Force, told Congressional investigators that the DEA and CIA met in July 1987 to discuss drug trafficking by the Contras, the Justice Department's Inspector General said neither the DEA nor the CIA could locate any record of any such discussions.[29]

The Bush regime could not blame itself for the CIA Contra cocaine epidemic, so it began a search for a suitable scapegoat. For federal prosecutors, it was simply a matter of ignoring any evidence related to the CIA, or its Contras and Cubans, and focusing exclusively on Noriega and the Colombians. Noriega, for example, had allowed (for a fee) Colombian cocaine smuggler Jorge Morales to fly through Panama. After his arrest, Morales was willing to testify against Noriega. But Morales did not make a great witness. To begin with, he had been resupplying the Contras through John Hull's ranch in Costa Rica, where he'd crossed paths with CORU co-founder and CIA asset Frank Castro, whom North's sidekick, Robert Owens, described to North as being "heavily into drugs."[30] Morales, obviously, had smuggled guns and drugs with the knowledge of the CIA.[31] Customs had played a role too, as "between 50 and 100 flights that had been arranged by the CIA took off from or landed at US airports during the past two years without undergoing inspections."[32]

The DEA was, typically, a community player. It was about to arrest Morales in November 1985, when CIA Officer Gary Mattocks called a meeting with DEA officials to let them know that Morales was a CIA asset.[33] For that reason, and because he worked with Contra leader-cum-Bush contributor Octaviano Cesar, Morales trafficked freely until the Iran-Contra scandal erupted in October 1986. Only then was he arrested. Despite all this double-dealing, federal prosecutors felt they could use Morales to testify against Noriega. But when Morales mentioned that he was scheduled to meet Bush at a fundraiser in May 1986, hosted by Jeb Bush, the prosecutors deemed him "not credible," and the burden of proof fell on Noriega's other Colombian controller, Floyd Carlton.[34]

Carlton's testimony also presented hurdles; his airline had received State Department funds for Contra resupply, which again cast the public's eye in the direction of CIA drug dealing.[35] So Carlton was given immunity and his testimony led to the 1988 indictment of Noriega for drug trafficking.[36]

Oliver North was also indicted in 1988 and received immunity too, in exchange for his melodramatic testimony before Congress, which led to a well-deserved career in show-biz.

The Bush administration's lies got larger in direct proportion to the percolating corruption scandal underlying the pending Noriega trial in Miami. The chief of the CIA's Central American Task Force Alan Fiers (later a member of President George W. Bush's propaganda team that paved the way for the Iraq invasion and occupation) was called as a witness before Iran-Contra prosecutor Lawrence Walsh. In his testimony to Walsh, in anticipation of the pending trial, Fiers blamed Noriega and exonerated John Hull, whose ranch in Costa Rica was used by Contra drug smugglers.[37]

President George H.W. Bush pardoned Fiers after his conviction for with-holding information from Congress.

Finally, after DEA agents arrested Noriega in January 1990, Bush did everything in his power to prevent him from receiving a fair trial.

This was no easy task, as the CIA had protected Noriega's drug dealing activities for three decades. The CIA acknowledged paying Noriega $322,000 during this period; although Noriega's defense claimed the sum was in the millions.[38] Noriega's lawyers said he had presided over an $11 million dollar CIA slush fund, and $23 million he laundered for the Medellin cartel came from the CIA. Naturally, the CIA contributed to the Noriega show trial by refusing to provide classified documents concerning him. The Bush White House went so far as to bar federal agencies from cooperating with a GAO investigation into Noriega's drug smuggling activities.[39]

Further cover came from lapdog reporters like Jeff Gerth at the *New York Times*, who blamed the DEA's failure to stop the cocaine surge from Latin America on "the CIA's over reliance on foreign security officials who assisted in the fight against Communism but themselves have been involved in drug trafficking."[40]

Not until May 1990 did Noriega's lawyers learn that he had been targeted for assassination by the US government. When they demanded to see the incriminating documents, Judge William Hoeveler ruled that the De-Feo Report was classified and thus inadmissible.[41] When Noriega's lawyers sought 700 documents to bolster their claim that his links to drug smuggling had CIA approval, Hoeveler said they too were inadmissible, as were all documents detailing Noriega's discussions with Bush, Casey and North.[42] By restricting inquiries into "classified areas," Hoeveler prevented North and CORU co-founder Frank Castro from being called as defense witnesses.

Cheered on by the exile Cuban community in Miami, the Justice Department lost DEA files showing Noriega's cooperation in several big cases. It belatedly found other files showing that Noriega's narcotics squad gave the DEA the names of Colombian money launderers, and provided intelligence on Medellin boss José Rodrigues Gacha. The only documentary evidence against Noriega, in fact, was a letter from a convicted marijuana trafficker. And yet, as preordained, Noriega was convicted and sentenced to 40 years in prison. He rightfully claimed status as a prisoner of war.

While the kangaroo court was forming, Terry Burke met in Miami with chief prosecutor Richard Gregorie. Some DEA agents were saying publicly that they didn't want to see Noriega indicted, and Gregorie was looking for more DEA support. As Burke recalled, "After hearing the evidence they had to date, I said I felt they had a long way to go to get Noriega. At the time of his arrest, the evidence was minimal and it wasn't until they started getting "cooperating witnesses" months later that they made a case for the jury."[43]

As Dave Westrate notes, "The Noriega case was weak. Tom Cash said it was 'turning water into wine.' The case was superseded several times, as new witnesses emerged. But by the time it went to trial it was a different story." According to Westrate, DEA financial intelligence analyst Lenora Sauers became the main witness and "made the case."[44]

Westrate says everyone was on "pins and needles," although Burke said, "There wasn't much impact or internal reaction at DEA as to Noriega's arrest. Just another bad guy. It was really the US Attorney's case more than it was DEA's. We just provided some investigative assistance. If there was uproar over Noriega's Agency connection, we figured that was their problem."

Noriega's trial was the equivalent of a Stalinist "show trial," and every US official who participated in it was as corrupt as Noriega and his patron saint, George H. W. Bush. As Noriega told Larry King on *Washington Weekly*, Bush "flew weapons to the Contras and flew drugs back to the United States." He said he was railroaded "to hide the dirty dealings that Bush did."

It is no mystery what those dirty dealings are. What is mysterious is why the American public tolerates such corruption on the part of its elected officials and their minions.

Kiki

MORE IMPORTANT TO THE DEA than the fairness of Noriega's trial was the murder of Agent Enrique "Kiki" Camarena.[45] After he located a huge marijuana plantation and unraveled the partnership between top Mexican officials and drug traffickers, Camarena was kidnapped in February 1985.[46] He was tortured and killed within 30 hours, but his mutilated body wasn't found until March. At that point Operations Chief Dave Westrate set up a command center, and Internal Affairs launched a murder investigation.[47] Bud Mullen, however, threw a wrench into the works by stating that Mexican DFS member José Antonio Zorilla "might be involved in the whole thing."[48] After that, Mexican, CIA, and Reagan Administration officials obstructed the case in every way possible.

Not until three years later would the US district court in Los Angeles indict five men for Camarena's murder. Three were top Mexican officials, one of whom, Armando Pavon, was on Contra supporter

Carlo Quintero's payroll. A captured tape of the torture revealed that the interrogator was a commander in the Mexican DFS. Contra supporters Felix Gallardo and Juan Matta Ballesteros, already in prison for drug smuggling, were also indicted. All of the evidence of a cover-up, however, pointed to a conspiracy between Reagan Administration, CIA and Mexican officials. DEA Agent Jamie Kuykendall went so far as to say the CIA "indirectly" had to share the blame in Camarena's murder.[49]

The CIA-Contra connection to Camarena's murder generated more bad publicity for the DEA, which had to exact revenge in order to maintain agent morale, but without implicating Reagan or Bush. Choosing a politically correct scapegoat was the only option. To this end, Mullen's successor Jack Lawn worked with Robert Mueller, chief of the Criminal Division at the Justice Department, and Robert Bonner, the US Attorney in Los Angeles. According to Terry Burke, Lawn personally directed a secret operation designed to abduct Humberto Alvarez-Machain, the doctor who allegedly kept Camarena alive during his torture. Alvarez was a potential witness in the case against the Mexican Interior Minister, Manuel Bartlett Diaz.

Burke recalled Inspector Pete Gruden calling him in April 1990 and asking "Do you remember the doctor who kept Kiki alive. Well, we got him."[50]

Steve Greene refers to the Camarena case as "the DEA's finest hour." One would think the DEA's finest hour would involve measurable success in the war on drugs, but that was impossible. On the other hand, the doctor's abduction proved that management still cared about the average agent.[51] It was a PR coup that attached a human, heroic face to the DEA. Since the era of ODALE abuses, DEA agents were viewed by many as an army of often corrupt wooden soldiers marching in ideological lock-step; suddenly they were all potential martyrs, despite the fact that their job is statistically less hazardous than a hundred blue-collar jobs in sawmills, on construction crews, fighting fires, etc.

The Alvarez abduction itself was no different from dozens the DEA had previously conducted, and relied on the same law that allowed slave owners to send bounty hunters into Mexico to retrieve runaway slaves. Under Lawn's direction, DEA agents hired a few Mexican mercenaries working under José Francisco Sosa, a former Mexican policeman. On April 2, Sosa and his gang snatched Alvarez from his office and held him overnight at a motel. The next day they flew him by private plane to El Paso, where DEA agents arrested him. He was kept in detention for three weeks until, under harsh questioning, he made what Burke refers to as "a half-assed confession." He was then transferred to Los Angeles, where he had been indicted, to stand trial. The Mexicans responded angrily, and the doctor's abduction and trial were all for naught: Alvarez was acquitted in December 1992 due to insufficient evidence. He then turned around and sued Lawn and his other abductors. The Supreme Court, however, held that the kidnapping violated no treaties and that the district court had the power to try him even though he'd been "brought within the court's jurisdiction by forcible abduction."[52] In this respect, the Camarena case can be seen as another instance in which DEA procedures paved the way for public acceptance of the extraordinary renditions that characterized George W. Bush's global war on terror, with its disregard for due process and reliance upon torture for confessions.

Bonner In, Burke Out

IN MAY 1990, PRESIDENT BUSH nominated Robert C. Bonner, the prosecutor on the Alvarez case, to be Administrator of the DEA. The Senate confirmed him in July. Bonner did not ask Terry Burke to be his deputy but instead asked Steve Greene, whom he knew from Los Angeles, where Greene had been the deputy SAC before becoming chief of operations. Bonner considered Greene absolutely "straight-laced" and non-evasive, "someone who had been an agent and would compliment me."[53]

According to Greene, Bonner was "wary" of Burke, who retired and joined Investigative Group International, heading its international division. CNC chief Jack Devine would join the company in 1999, as head of its New York office.[54]

Following in Jack Lawn's macho footsteps was no easy task, and Robert Bonner instead brought a studious style to the DEA. This was not always helpful: although well informed, intelligent, and concerned, he was reserved and uncomfortable in public. According to one senior agent, Bonner was "the smartest, but the most aloof."

Bonner's philosophy was that he had limited resources, and could best use them by focusing on the highest levels of the largest international drug trafficking organizations: what he called the "kingpin" strategy.[55] As a way of helping Operations decide how best to neutralize a kingpin, Bonner beefed up the Intelligence Division. He created a Special Operations Division to identify, largely through wiretaps

(500-1000 annually) and the gathering of financial intelligence on the kingpins and their chief financial officers.[56] The biggest kingpins were Khun Sa in Burma and the cartel bosses in Colombia. Bonner's strategy included disrupting production and transportation. He made an effort to encourage foreign governments not to provide kingpins with sanctuary, and he asked their narcotics units to coordinate more closely with the DEA. He notes with pride that the DEA operated in 55 countries, more than any federal agency other than the CIA and State Department. He considered the DEA's overseas operations and relationships in so many countries as its "crown jewel." Along with its high-tech special ops division, this vast international network, to some degree, freed the DEA from its dependence on the CIA and NSA for intelligence derived from electronic surveillance.[57]

To accentuate his strategy, Bonner made the Intelligence Division equal to operations, and he made Dave Westrate chief of intelligence. "It was a paper shuffle," Westrate notes, "that put the DEA on more of an equal footing with the CIA. Dick Bly and Judy Bertini managed most of the intelligence division." Harold "Doug" Wankel, who had served in Afghanistan and Pakistan, served as Westrate's liaison to Jack Devine at the CIA's CNC.[58] Bonner described Wankel and Devine as "like twins."[59] Described by Westrate as "forward thinking and aggressive," Wankel became deputy to the operations chief John Coleman.

Bonner's big problem was how to get CIA and DEA agents to work more closely together in embassies. He "welcomed" their assistance, but the CIA's operational role "created tensions." The CIA wanted to use drug intelligence and operations as a political hammer, while the DEA, as ever, wanted the CIA to simply gather and report on strategic intelligence, like the amount of opium production and the political attitudes of tribal chiefs in Afghanistan. And there was always a CIA-related crisis du jour.

In late 1990, Customs agents in Miami seized a huge load of pure cocaine from Venezuela. To their surprise, a Venezuelan undercover agent said the CIA had approved the delivery. DEA Administrator Robert Bonner ordered an investigation and discovered to his horror that the CIA had, in fact, shipped over a ton of pure cocaine to Miami from its warehouse in Venezuela throughout 1990. The Orwellian "uncontrolled deliveries" were managed by CIA officer Mark McFarlin, a veteran of Reagan's bloody CIA-led counter-revolution in El Salvador. Bonner wanted to indict McFarlin and General Ramon

Guillen Davila, the top Venezuelan official involved in the conspiracy. But at a "horror group" meeting in June 1991 with CNC Chief Jack Devine, Justice Department officials, and Melvin Levitsky, chief of State INM, Bonner was told to forget it: that if Guillen was indicted, the US might have to cut off assistance to Venezuela, which was in the process of fighting off a rebellion led by Hugo Chavez.[60]

As Robert Bonner learned the hard way, Bush and the CIA preferred an America flooded with drugs over a Communist ruling oil-rich Venezuela. As it was in the beginning, it is now and ever shall be: national security trumps drug law enforcement.

Clinton

ROBERT BONNER WAS ONE OF two Bush-appointed officials to remain in office after Bill Clinton defeated Bush in the 1992 elections. Bonner felt he had done his job well and, knowing that Clinton was going to reduce the DEA's budget and work force, he was ready to leave. But he wanted to wait until an attorney general had been appointed. He also wanted to prevent the FBI from realizing its secret plan to merge with the DEA.[61]

According to Dave Westrate, the FBI was plotting the merger before the election. DEA spies caught wind of the plot, and Westrate talked to sympathetic members of Congress before they drafted the FBI's proposal. Luckily for the DEA, Westrate convinced Congress to change the language from "it will be done" to "it's a good idea."[62] The proposal went to Attorney General Janet Reno the same day she took office. Bonner immediately went to her and explained that he hadn't even been consulted by the FBI. He spent his last six months in office opposing the merger, which had tentative White House approval.[63]

"Reno agonized over it," Westrate recalled. "She talked to everyone, even street agents. We had charts and graphs showing drugs are so important it deserved a single mission agency. This was the big hurdle in 1993." Reno announced her decision on a Monday morning at an IACP convention attended by several thousand policemen. When she said she wouldn't approve the merger, she got a standing ovation. "It was the best I ever felt," Westrate said, "like crossing the Rubicon."[64]

Bonner felt it was his greatest achievement as DEA Administrator.[65]

Louis Freeh became FBI Director in September 1993, and according to Westrate, "declared neutrality." In return, Bonner's replacement as Acting Administrator, Steve Greene, invited an FBI agent to be deputy at DEA intelligence.[66] Freeh reciprocated by offering the DEA access to the FBI lab. All was right with the world and having done his part to save the DEA, Westrate took a transfer to Quantico to run the training academy. Westrate's focus was that DEA agents know how to properly present cases that are scrutinized by a judge and jury. To prepare them for that inevitability, he instituted mock trials. He also developed a program in which agents were taught to debrief informants.[67]

Bonner's executive management philosophy, shared by Westrate and Greene, was simple. They felt the DEA's job was to pull the rest of the drug enforcement world together and be the backbone of the anti-drug effort. According to Westrate, it is a simple mission and cannot have two chiefs. It is a hierarchy that starts with a cop in a cruiser who has access to information at EPIC. In Stage Two, the local narcotics squad gets involved and in Stage Three, state and local task forces. Stage Four is a DEA investigation; Five is the DEA working with other federal agencies; Six is the initiation of a foreign operation and acquiring intelligence from other countries; and Seven is a major interdiction program with help from the CIA and Defense Department. In a perfect world, all these elements work together and are vested in success.[68]

But the world is a messy place. The military and CIA were not about to put their paramilitary operators under the command of a DEA agent, or their analysts under a DEA agent at the Johnstown national drug intelligence center. In 1994, the DEA still had only one representative at the CIA's CNC. There was cooperation in the field, the type that led to the CIA assassination of kingpin Pablo Escobar in Colombia in 1994. But behind the scenes the battle for sources raged and in October 1994, DEA Agent Richard A. Horn actually sued the CIA for eaves-dropping on his conversations in Burma. In his suit, Horn said the CIA had "a political and personal agenda to thwart" anti-drug missions and "to deny Burma any credit for its drug enforcement efforts."[69]

Stage Seven is where the system fails, despite what Bonner, Westrate and Greene suggest. But theirs is the view from the top, with its eternally pleasant panoramic vista. The reality on the ground is far different. On the day Joe Toft, the SAC in Bogota, finished his seven-year tour in Colombia, he said on national television that Colombia was a "narco-democracy" whose president "had accepted million of dollars in campaign contributions from the Cali drug cartel."[70]

Corruption, be it foreign or domestic, will never go away, despite the endless re-organizations and declarations of cooperation. In 1995, former DCI William Colby said, "The Latin American drug cartels have stretched their tentacles much deeper into our lives than most people believe. It's possible they are calling the shots at all levels of government."[71]

Greene to Constantine

STRAIGHT ARROW STEVE GREENE SERVED as DEA Acting Administrator until Bill Clinton appointed Tom Constantine in April 1994. Constantine remained as deputy director until 1996, by which time, Greene says, "the CIA's role was properly defined."[72] Meaning that Clinton, in 1995, nullified the memorandum of understanding that gave the CIA the "primary role in coordinating the use of foreign drug informants."[73] From then on, theoretically, the CIA would gather and provide information on kingpins to the DEA, especially in countries where the DEA had no access. The DEA would then make cases and the kingpins would be extradited and put in jail. In return, Greene, a ranking member of the elite inter-agency effort, had no qualms about putting the names of DEA informants into the CIA source registry. "We were doing good," he said. "We had people inside security for the Medellin cartel."

But, Greene added philosophically, "It's not a war on drugs, it's a problem — an extremely complex issue because of the demand for drugs, and it's not going to be resolved by simplistic law enforcement and interdiction solutions." Soberly, he said, "the key element is education and treatment."

John Coleman, DEA Operations Chief under Robert Bonner, agrees with Steve Greene. "The expression, 'war on drugs' has created problems over the years," he said. "As a metaphor, I can understand and accept the expression. However, I think it also establishes a notion of a win-lose combat-type situation rather than that of a serious and complex public health problem requiring persistent vigilance. From the multinational cartels around the world, to the subsistence farmers in Colombia, Peru, Bolivia, Afghanistan, or Laos, to the gangs inflicting terror and mayhem, to the high school kid non-medically using Ritalin to score big on the SAT — all play an important role in this.

"Progress may come when we stop thinking of this as a 'war,' and begin seeing it for what it is: namely, a difficult social, medical, health, public safety, and legal problem requiring all the wisdom we can muster just to manage. The disease model is a far more accurate depiction of what we face.

"Law enforcement plays a large and vital role in all this but it, alone, must never be viewed as the only viable strategy. The future, in my opinion, may bring greater success from the laboratory where new chemotherapies for treating drug addiction will emerge and new delivery systems and abuse-resistant formulations of controlled substances will reduce their abuse. Of course, advances in technology may bring risks that the drug culture may also find new and more potent poisons to play with."[74]

Will progressive thinking like this save the day?

EPILOGUE

GONE ARE THE DAYS OF Johnny Star, the lone-wolf FBN agent with a star tattoo on his left hand, in the fleshy part between the thumb and forefinger. Johnny had tracks on his arms from injecting heroin and carried a six-gun, even in New York City. He also kept a gun concealed in one of his cowboy boots, and when he got busted in Texas while working undercover, he used it to break out of jail.[1]

Gone are the days when Charlie Siragusa, Paul Knight and Jack Cusack were the only federal narcotic agents overseas. To save the FBN money, they traveled across the Atlantic on tramp steamers. In 1952 they spent half their time making narcotics cases and the other half working for the CIA.[2] Nowadays there are more DEA agents in New York City than there were in the entire FBN, and all foreign-based agents work for the CIA.

The nature of the Wolf Pack has changed dramatically since the days when FBN Agent Frankie Waters almost single-handedly made the French Connection case. Waters kept an American flag on his desk along with a framed copy of Kipling's poem *The Law of the Jungle*. One part says, "The strength of the Pack is in the Wolf; and the strength of the Wolf is in the Pack."

In those days the Wolf Pack consisted of a group of tough, street-smart agents who broke all the rules in the process of making under-cover cases on vicious Mafiosi and their French connections. But as Agent Marty Pera said, "Most were corrupted by the lure of the under-world. They thought they could check their morality at the door — go out and lie, cheat, and steal — then come back and retrieve it. But you can't. In fact, if you're successful because you can lie, cheat, and steal, those things become tools you use in the bureaucracy."[3]

Our current national politicians prove that every day. This book began with the formation of the BNDD in the wake of a corruption scandal involving FBN agents and their informants, some 27 of whom were allegedly murdered. It told how Andy Tartaglino fought the DEA Administrator John Bartels and the Wolf Pack in an epic battle that shaped federal drug law enforcement and ended with the DEA ceding most of its undercover duties to mercenary informants. Tartaglino's corruption probe also allowed the CIA to infiltrate the BNDD while it was expanding its intelligence and foreign operations. The CIA's influence became pervasive through the Office of Strategic Intelligence, the International Division, and Lou Conein's Special Operations unit. As early as 1974, DEA agents were being taught the rules of plausible deniability to "insulate US involvement."[4]

Tartaglino's crusade ended with congressional hearings that paved the way, five years later, for the FBI to take over the DEA's management. Under Bud Mullen, the FBI's "internal security" mentality rubbed off on ambitious DEA officials, whose priority was protecting the Reagan Administration's illegal drug operations. Under George H.W. Bush, the DEA became an adjunct of the counter-terror network that defines American foreign policy along ideological lines: investigating Allende's associates in Chile was required, as was "looking away" so Pinochet's associates could deal drugs with impunity.[5]

Today the DEA is a top-heavy bureaucracy ruled by ideologues unsullied by street work, strained through a sieve of security clearances, oblivious to their mandate and beholden only to political power brokers. They are successful because they can lie, cheat, and steal from the public and Congress. This pack of PR experts preaches the party line, but is unable to manage the metaphorical "war on drugs." Thus the war goes on and on, and the same problems loom larger than ever.

At the core of America's drug problem is the ingrained corruption in our system: the lying, cheating, and stealing epitomized by the Iran-Contra affair. The drug aspect of this corruption scandal exploded in 1996, when reporter Gary Webb published a series of articles in the *San Jose Mercury* about CIA-supported Contra drug traffickers in Los Angeles.[6] The "Dark Alliance" exposé forced CIA Director John Deutsch to crisscross the country trying to convince the African-American community that the CIA did not cause the crack cocaine epidemic. He failed, but the mainstream media pilloried Webb and his supporters for unveiling the central role the Establishment plays in perpetuating the phony war on drugs.[7] Establishment is defined as that "exclusive group of powerful people who rule a government or society by means of private agreements and decisions."[8]

Afghanistan

WHILE THE NATION WAS FOCUSED on Central American in the 1980s and 1990s, an equally explosive situation had developed in Central Asia. In 1979, the US embassy in Kabul was closed when the Soviets invaded Afghanistan. In January 1981, the DEA's former deputy country attaché in Kabul, Doug Wankel, was assigned as DEA country attaché in Islamabad, Pakistan. Wankel's assignment put him in relations with the CIA at a time when Pakistan station chief Howard Hart was supporting Islamic fundamentalists, the Mujahadeen, against the Soviets in Afghanistan. The situation in Central Asia was no different from Central America: DEA agents were expected to look away from the CIA's counter-terror network and its drug-dealing intrigues, which relied on the logistical support of Pakistan's Inter Service Intelligence (ISI) and the services of Pakistani banks.[9] As Wankel's deputy Joseph Molyneux said, "Neither the CIA nor ISI liked to work with DEA. ISI and CIA worked close together but not with DEA."[10]

DEA operations were not permitted in Afghanistan, but were conducted in the tribal areas of Pakistan's Northwest Frontier. According to Molyneux, "The job we had there was to survey poppy fields and locate heroin conversion laboratories and take them out. This most always resulted in a firefight, the farmers not giving up their lucrative business so easily. Usually, the Pakistani army had to be brought in for backup. The tribal areas and much of the Northwest Frontier simply did not submit to central government control, responding mainly to the leadership of tribal chieftains."

Wankel, Molyneux, and Agent Bob Adams were three of only seven DEA Agents in Pakistan in 1981. Molyneux and Adams were sent back to the US in 1982 for importing and selling guns, although Wankel, who allegedly supplied a shotgun to a Pakistani police officer, remained.[11] There was little drug enforcement by 1982, and the heroin trade in the Pakistan-Afghanistan borderland was booming, supplying half of US and world demand.[12] In Pakistan, the heroin-addict population soared from near zero to 300,000.[13] The reason was simple: the CIA's Mujahadeen army in Afghanistan "ordered peasants to plant opium as a revolutionary tax. Across the border in Pakistan, Afghan leaders and local syndicates under the protection of Pakistan Intelligence operated hundreds of heroin laboratories."[14]

DEA headquarters could not ignore the statistics, and in 1984, sixteen agents were assigned to Pakistan under Wankel's replacement, former CIA officer Chuck Gutensohn. Gutensohn came to Pakistan from Burma, where CIA asset "Khun Sa's army transported and refined about 80 percent of the Golden Triangle's opium harvest."[15] Gutensohn said his job was to interdict heroin coming into Pakistan from Afghanistan and that in 1985, the DEA and Pakistan's narcotics squad seized a substantial quantity.[16]

Things, however, took a turn for the worse in 1985, when Reagan signed National Security Decision Directive 166, authorizing stepped-up covert military aid to the Mujahadeen. It's unclear if Gutensohn and the DEA were subverted or simply looked away: in either case, Pakistan's opium harvest tripled and addiction rose to over one million.[17]

DEA Agent Chuck Carter arrived as country attaché in 1986. Unlike Wankel and Gutensohn, his responsibilities included operations inside Afghanistan. Carter developed a program with the CIA in which Mujahadeen would retreat into Pakistan as refugees, where they were trained to take out heroin labs. "We trained them how to use video to show they did it," Carter said. Other times they would bring back a kilogram of heroin as proof. Carter himself went on two missions. He claims the DEA took out 20 labs a year.[18]

Iranian chemists and traffickers played an important role in the regional trade. When the moon was full, a motorized drug caravan would leave from Zahedan in Iran, near the border of southern Afghanistan and western Pakistan, carrying 55 gallon drums packed with opium, and bags of money. The trucks would zigzag through the hills while Carter and the CIA tracked them by satellite. The dealers would make the rounds and then go back to Iran to supply the glut of heroin addicts, as well as outlets to Europe. Hashish from Afghanistan was also making its way to Germany in soccer balls. Carter worked closely with CIA station chief Milton Bearden, who had final approval over Carter's use of informants. "He could steal them," Carter said, "and not even tell you."[19]

Management of narcotics informants was critical, as the CIA's mission was destabilizing the Soviet Union through the promotion of militant Islam inside the Central Asian Republics. Many Islamic terrorist groups originated in this period. As part of its strategic plan the CIA chose warlord Gulbuddin Hekmatyar to command the Mujahadeen from Pakistan's drug-laden Northwest Frontier. By 1988 there were between 100-200 heroin refineries in Pakistan's Northwestern region, and Professor Al McCoy described Hekmatyar as "Afghanistan's leading drug lord."[20] Inside Afghanistan, the Mujahadeen ordered peasants on captured territory to grow poppies; the Mujahadeen supply apparatus, arranged by the CIA, was used to transport it into Pakistan.[21]

According to Michel Chossudovsky, a professor of economics at the University of Ottawa: "In 1995, the former CIA director of the Afghan operation, Charles Cogan, admitted the CIA had indeed sacrificed the drug war to fight the Cold War. `Our main mission was to do as much damage as possible to the Soviets. We didn't really have the resources or the time to devote to an investigation of the drug trade,'... `I don't think that we need to apologize for this. Every situation has its fallout.... There was fallout in terms of drugs, yes. But the main objective was accomplished. The Soviets left Afghanistan.'"[22]

Chuck Carter departed Pakistan in February 1988. Six months later US Ambassador Arnold Lewis Raphel was killed with Pakistani President Muhammed Zia when their plane exploded minutes after take-off. The next US Ambassador to Pakistan, Robert B. Oakley, had served as US Coordinator for Counter-Terrorism under President Reagan. By then Afghanistan was producing 2000 tons of opium a year, surpassing Burma. Warlord Hekmatyar in May 1992 became Prime Minister and the country descended into a civil war, and Hekmatyar allegedly entered into an alliance with Osama bin Laden.[23]

Knowing the drug trade would hasten the collapse of the Soviet Union, the CIA also facilitated the operations of anti-Soviet rebels in the republics of Uzbekistan, Chechnya, and Georgia. Criminal syndicates in Turkey and Eastern Europe formed relations with the type of "political or intelligence organizations selling drugs to promote political activity, and militant political groups selling drugs to finance terrorists," that the DEA had been investigating since 1972.[24] According to one DEA agent, Russian Jews were running the operation, and the KGB was providing security.

Calling the drug traffic "un-Islamic," Taliban leader Mullah Omar in Afghanistan ordered a ban on opium cultivation in July 2000, in a vain attempt to gain diplomatic recognition.[25] But the following year President George W. Bush used the hunt for Osama bin Laden as a pretext to invade Afghanistan and overthrow the Taliban. The opium ban was lifted, CIA-backed warlords were put in control, and

Afghanistan once again became the world's major center of opium production.

Beltway Bandits

AMERICA IS AN OLIGARCHY RULED by corporations. It is not a democracy. The corporations buy politicians from both parties, who in turn select DEA bosses based on their ability to lie, steal and cheat in order to maintain the Establishment's class and race prerogatives. Suborned DEA managers like Doug Wankel go along with the CIA, while earnest agents struggle to do their job. In 1997, the *Dallas Morning News* reported that "the CIA has formed alliances of convenience with traffickers to gather intelligence on other governments, political movements and terrorists. In fighting the drug war, the CIA also finds its methods at odds with those of law-enforcement agencies, say officials from both groups."[26]

"The CIA will block prosecutions," the newspaper reported, noting that DEA targets are often CIA informants. Agent Tom Cash was quoted as saying, "It's very dangerous to have intelligence people involved in the drug-smuggling business in any way, shape or form."[27]

In the same article, CIA Officer Duane Clarridge "dismissed charges the CIA had interfered with drug investigations," claiming they reflected "the dishonesty and insecurity of our DEA colleagues." Clarridge, notably, was indicted in 1991 on seven counts of perjury in the Iran-Contra scandal, and is not to be believed. Like Ollie North, Clarridge lied on behalf of President George H W. Bush, who later pardoned him for not blowing the whistle on their criminal conspiracy.

DEA agents must pucker up to the likes of Bush and Clarridge if they want to climb the ladder of success. This "pucker principle" became the new law of the jungle with the creation of the CIA's Counter-Narcotics Center(CNC). As Agent Doug Wankel (a former liaison to the CNC) explained, the CNC was "personality dependent" and DEA agents "look suspiciously at participants." Wankel, who worked closely with, if not for, the CIA in Pakistan, confessed, "I was not real popular within the DEA."[28]

The Iran-Contra scandal simmered through the 1990s, but Bill Clinton's sexual escapades dominated the news and in 2001, George W. Bush won the presidency through a combination of political patronage and election fraud in Florida, and a judicial coup d'etat by the Supreme Court. His paralyzed administration stank of venality until September 11, 2001, when Muslim fundamentalists came to his rescue. Since then the drug war has faded from view. Once in a while one hears about Afghanistan, where, assisted by Dyn-Corp mercenaries, Doug Wankel managed the DEA's most unsuccessful antinarcotics effort ever. In 2007 Wankel was assigned to the State Department to manage the US Government's anti-narcotics effort. Afghanistan still continues to supply about ninety per cent of the world's opium.[29]

Like many of his peers, Wankel saw beyond the war on drugs and capitalized on the narco-terror craze. The embodiment of the pucker principal, Wankel and Craig Chretien, his deputy in Afghanistan in 2007, are nowadays busy acquiring contracts from various "government entities."[30] As David G. Wilson, Executive Director of the Association of Former Federal Narcotics Agents said in an email to the AFFNA membership, "There is a lot of work to be done in Afghanistan, but Craig tells me progress is being made. There will be many years of US support needed but the vast majority of the Afghan people want our help and are working hard to make their part of the world a better place. Craig and Doug are working on several contract proposals for various USG entities, including DEA, that will need a number of DEA retirees (many of them non-1811) to work in the region; Afghanistan, the UAE, Africa, and elsewhere in that region, as well as other parts of the world."[31]

Wankel & Co. will make big money supplying DEA retirees to work in foreign nations as police trainers. There are now 500 American police trainers in Afghanistan alone.[32]

Former CIA Officer Roger Mackin, who ran the Phoenix Program in Vietnam's highlands, and managed the assassination of Colombian drug trafficker Pablo Escobar while assigned to the CNC, is another Beltway Bandit who has parlayed the narco-terror craze into a comfortable nest egg. After 9/11, Mackin became the Department of Homeland Security's Counter-Narcotics Officer-Interdiction Coordinator with the job of severing connections between drug traffickers and terrorists. Mackin got out of government and formed a company that supplies the DHS with the tools it needs to spy on innocent Americans.[33]

The Alpha Wolf of this new Pack is former DEA Agent Steve Casteel. As the DEA's SNOWCAP chief in South America, Casteel apparently gained priceless CIA connections, and in the fall of 2003, George W. Bush named him senior advisor to the Iraqi Minister of Interior, Falah al Naqib. Casteel "set policy and led the creation and operations of the

Ministry's police, Border Police, Immigration, Customs Service, Civil Defense and fire programs."[34] He managed the recruitment, training, equipping, and deployment of services and personnel. In other words, he played a central role in America's colonization of Iraq.

Casteel and Al-Naqib formed a Special Police Commando regiment that is advised and equipped by the CIA. The Commandos have the job of winning the hearts and minds of the Iraqi people through psychological warfare[35] To this end, the CIA created a self-promotional TV series about the Commandos called "Terrorism in the Grip of Justice." The CIA also advises the Commando's aptly-named "Wolf Brigade," which is famous for committing atrocities at its Nissor Square detention facility.[36]

While shaping Iraq's brutal, out-of-control police forces with the CIA, Casteel hobnobbed with American and European companies and Middle Eastern and Coalition governments like Syria and Saudi Arabia. After his government service, he used these connections to obtain a position as senior vice president of the Vance Corporation. In 2008 he managed some 600 Vance employees in northern Iraq alone, mostly guarding oil company interests. Casteel also supported Vance clients in Pakistan, Libya and Saudi Arabia.[37]

And to think that Andy Tartaglino made a federal case out of Phil Smith possibly feathering a nest for himself down the road....

Conclusion

AMERICA'S STRATEGY IN THE WAR on drugs is to accommodate its corporate Establishment bosses. To that fashionable end, President Bush appointed Karen Tandy as the DEA's first female administrator in 2003. Big deal. Someone asked her the name of the first female agent and she did not know it was Heather Campbell. Tandy did give the DEA a contemporary look, however, and she understood the need for accommodating the CIA. Her major initiative was shutting down medical marijuana clinics at a time when a TV show, *Weeds*, glorified a single mother making ends meet by dealing marijuana in an upscale California suburb. Weeds has won two Golden Globe awards.

Nothing is more absurd than America's self-delusional war on drugs. It's as absurd as the picture of Doug Wankel standing behind Afghani policemen, armed with big sticks, whacking poppy plants on some poor farmer's field in an effort to eradicate opium from Afghanistan. This scene appeared on a TV documentary and when

Wankel, surrounded by mercenaries, ordered them to whack poppies in another nearby field, the policemen refused. "'Fuck the police,' Wankel snarled, and turned and walked away."[38]

America's self-delusional war on drugs is as absurd as believing that Taliban nationalists are forcing farmers in Afghanistan to grow opium, and using the profits to fund Al Qaeda in Iraq. It's as absurd as the Pentagon putting 50 of Afghanistan's most powerful opium barons on a "kill list."[39] Apart from the fact that the CIA exempts its collaborators from such hit lists – and that formalizing assassination can only plunge American deeper into the moral abyss – the only way the US can get Afghanistan's warlords to follow the American line is to allow them to make millions growing opium and selling heroin.

It's as absurd as George Bush Sr. leaving his post as DCI to become a member of the Eli Lilly Pharmaceutical Company's board of directors.[40] Thanks to George Bush Jr., Lilly is protected from lawsuits under the Homeland Security Act.[41] Pharmaceutical drugs cause more damage to Americans than illegal drugs. Pharmaceutical companies made nearly $40 billion in 2006.[42]

It's as absurd as choosing people to become DEA agents because they are overly aggressive and deceptive, which is what it takes to be productive. Supervisors seeking entry into management cut these agents slack they shouldn't have. Thus the best agents become unmanageable and the corruption of self-promotion becomes systemic. Those who climb to the top, with a few exceptions, see their job as a stepping stone to some lucrative, post-DEA, Beltway Bandit career. On the bright side, some agents are strong enough, despite weak management, to put predatory drug traffickers in prison. But the vast majority become ideologically indoctrinated and remain unaware that prevention is not inconsistent with enforcement. To perpetuate the "war on drugs" boondoggle, their managers make statistics on prevention seem nebulous, while asserting that arrests and seizures are measurable. This deception, and the fact that its mission is undermined by politicians and spies, makes the DEA unstable, and the drug epidemic inevitable.

Kicking these bad habits, and feeling the pain, is the only solution.

The War On Drugs, declared by President Nixon forty years ago, is the longest continuous war in American history. Between the outright mayhem and the wasted lives, it may also be the one of the most deadly. Of the nation's two million prisoners, 500,000 (25%) are incarcerated for drug offenses.[43]

"The United States has less than 5 percent of the world's population. But it has almost a quarter of the world's prisoners."[44] As the New York Times noted, "Indeed, the United States leads the world in producing prisoners, a reflection of a relatively recent and now entirely distinctive American approach to crime and punishment. Americans are locked up for crimes — from writing bad checks to using drugs — that would rarely produce prison sentences in other countries. And in particular they are kept incarcerated far longer than prisoners in other nations.[45]

This is insanity. In the end, all wars must have a resolution, if you subscribe to the notion that peace is preferable. The Obama administration's stated policy is to no longer use the term "War On Drugs", stop the raids on medical marijuana facilities, and begin to reduce draconian sentencing rules. But dismantling the $44 billion a year DEA behemoth would take a courageous Act of Congress, and we all know the odds on that happening – about the same as people deciding to just say no.

ACRONYMS

AID: Agency for International Development
ASAC: Assistant Special Agent in Charge
AUSA: Assistant United States Attorney
BDAC: Bureau of Drug Abuse Control
BNDD: Bureau of Narcotics and Dangerous Drugs
BOSSI: Bureau of Special Services and Investigations
BUNCIN: Bureau of Narcotics Covert Intelligence Network
CI: Counter Intelligence
CIA: Central Intelligence Agency
CIC: Counter Intelligence Corps
CID: Criminal Investigations Division
CCINC: Cabinet Committee on International Narcotics Control
CNC: Counter Narcotics Center
DEA: Drug Enforcement Administration
DEACON: DEA Clandestine Operations Network
DEASOG: Drug Enforcement Administration Special Operations Group
DIA: Defense Intelligence Agency
DNC: Democratic National Committee
DOJ: Department of Justice
FAA: Federal Aviation Authority
FBI: Federal Bureau of Investigations
FBN: Federal Bureau of Narcotics (1930-1968)
GAO: General Accounting Office:
G-DEP: Geographical Drug Enforcement Program
GVN: Government of Vietnam
IACP: International Association of Police Chiefs
IG: Assistant Administrator for Intelligence
IGO: Special Projects in DEA Intelligence
INIS: International Narcotics Information System

INM: International Narcotics Matters
INS: Immigration and Naturalization Service
KMT: Kuomintang.
LEAA: Law Enforcement Assistance Agency
ODALE: Office of Drug Abuse Law Enforcement
OMB: The Office of Management and Budget.
NCO: Narcotic Control Officer
NDIC: National Drug Intelligence Center
NNICC: National Narcotics Intelligence Consumers Committee
NSC: National Security Council
NSA: National Security Agency
NYPD: New York Police Department
OSS: Office of Strategic Services
PEMEX: Petróleos Mexicanos [Mexican Petroleums]
RD: Regional Director
RIU: Regional Intelligence Unit
SAC: Special Agent in Charge
SAC: Service d'Action Civique
SEC: Securities and Exchange Commission
SFIP: Special Field Intelligence Project
SIO: Office of Strategic Intelligence
SIU: Special Investigations Unit
USA: United States Attorney

ENDNOTES

Chapter 1: The Shadow of the Wolf

1. Reorganization Plan No. 1, February 7, 1968, effective date April 8, 1968.
2. Patrick P. O'Carroll, "Reorganization Plan No. 1: Narcotics and Drug Abuse." University of Oklahoma, undated graduate thesis, courtesy of DEA library (hereafter known as O'Carroll Thesis).
3. FBN, BDAC and BNDD organizational charts and rosters provide by several agents, interviews with former FBN, BDAC and BNDD agents. John Finlator, *The Drugged Nation; a "Narc's" Story* (New York: Simon and Schuster, 1973).
4. Order No. 394-68 Designating John Finlator and Henry Giordano as Associate Directors of the Bureau of Narcotics and Dangerous Drugs. April 7, 1968.
5. March 9, 2005 letter from Ramsey Clark to the author.
6. Ibid.
7. Interview with John Ingersoll.
8. Hearings before the House Appropriations Committee (Washington, DC: GPO), March 10, 1970 (hereafter known as Rooney Hearings), p. 990.
9. Interview with John Warner.
10. Interviews with John Ingersoll and John Warner.
11. Interview with Richard Blum.
12. Interview with John Warner.
13. See BNDD organizational chart. [p. 463]
14. Interview with Ingersoll.
15. Interview with John Warner.
16. Correspondence with John Dean.
17. Interview with Andrew Tartaglino.
18. Interpol is the International Police association formed by the police agencies of member nations to distribute information on criminals. It is

not an operational organization and contains no enforcement or investigative agents.

19. Interview with Andrew Tartaglino.
20. Interview with Andrew Tartaglino, re: Lapham as CIA.
21. John Windham in Kansas City and Frank Pappas in Baltimore. Bowman Taylor became deputy RD in Miami under former BDAC agent William Logan.
22. Interview with Walter Panich.
23. Interview with Robert DeFauw.
24. Interview with DeFauw.
25. Interview with Colonel Tulius Acampora.
26. Interview with Paul E. Knight.
27. Interview with Paul Knight's son, Harold Knight
28. Peter Carlson, "International Man of Mystery: Ex-CIA Agent And Current Convict Has Many Stories To Tell, Some May Even Be True," *Washington Post*, June 22, 2004, p. C1.
29. Interviews with Richard Secord, Thomas Clines and Douglas M Schlachter, Jr.
30. Interview with George Gaffney.
31. John McWilliams interview with George Belk, January 7, 1987, transcript provided to the author by McWilliams.
32. Interview with John Ingersoll.
33. Federal Narcotic Enforcement, Interim Report of the Committee On Government Operations, United States Senate, Made By Its Permanent Subcommittee On Investigations, 94th Congress, 2nd Session (Washington, DC: GPO, July 19, 1976) (hereafter known as 1976 Jackson Hearings), p 75.
34. Interview with Lawrence J. Strickler.
35. Interview with Andy Tartaglino.

Chapter 2: The McDonnell Case

1. Interview with FBN Agent.
2. Jack D. Compton, Statement to US Attorney John Clark (hereafter known as Compton Affidavit). Former USA Jamie Boyd provided the author with a copy of the Compton Affidavit. The author attempted to retrieve Compton's statement through a Freedom of Information Act request filed in November 1993, but was told by the Deputy Director of the Department of Justice's Office Information and Privacy that the records were not located.
3. Tom Tripodi with Joseph P. DeSario. *Crusade: Undercover Against the Mafia & KGB*, (Washington, DC: Brassey's, 1993), p. 158.
4. Compton Affidavit, pp. 54-56.
5. Interview with Tom Tripodi. Tripodi *Crusade*.

6. Interview with David Wiser.
7. Interview with Andy Tartaglino.
8. Interviews with Ike Wurms and Tom Taylor.
9. Interview with Frank Waters.
10. Ibid.
11. Compton Affidavit.
12. Ibid.
13. Ibid.

Chapter 3: Connoisseurs of Chaos
1. Interview with John Gunn.
2. Steve Greene, Keith Shostrom and Glen Cooper, "Final Report, MKUL-TRA Cross file: AC-AI-77-FO352," to Inspector Peter L. Palatroni, December 4, 1978. In November 1993, this writer filed a Freedom of Information Act request with the CIA for documents on the Victims Task Force. After waiting nearly six years, he filed a complaint in federal district court in Springfield, Massachusetts, and in February 2000 received 96 documents. They are referred to through out this book by the number the CIA assigned them.
3. Interview with Andy Tartaglino.
4. Interview with George Gaffney.
5. Dr Sidney Gottlieb, Memorandum for the Record, January 30, 1967.
6. Interview with Art Fluhr.
7. Charles Siragusa interview by CIA officer Michie, March 24, 1977 (hereafter known as Michie Memo), document provided by Richard E. Salmi.
8. Interviews with Ike Feldman, Andy Tartaglino and other agents.
9. Interview with Larry Cohn.
10. Interview with Charlie Vopat.
11. Interview with Howard Safir.
12. Interview with BNDD agent.
13. Interview with Clarence Cook.
14. Ibid.
15. Interview with Art Fluhr.
16. Interviews with Robert Peloquin and Bruce Jensen.
17. Interview with Walter Fialkewicz.
18. Jean-Pierre Charbonneau, *The Canadian Connection* (Optimum Publishing: Ottawa, 1976), pp. 263-273.
19. Interview with John Ingersoll.
20. Interviews with Bob DeFauw, Dick Salmi, and other agents posted overseas at the time.
21. Interview with George Gaffney.
22. John McWilliams interview with George Belk, January 7, 1987, transcript provided to the author by McWilliams.

23. Interviews with several case-making agents.
24. Charbonneau, *Canadian Connection*, p. 261.
25. *Project Pilot III*, complied by DEA, CIA and Customs officers within the DEA's Office of Intelligence, International Intelligence Division, 1973 (hereafter known as *Project Pilot III*), p. 361
26. *Project Pilot III*, p. 363
27. Leonard S Schrier, "Santo Trafficante, et al," August 4, 1967.
28. *Project Pilot III*, p. 396.
29. *Project Pilot III*, pp. 11-18.
30. Nathan M. Adams, "The Hunt For André," *Reader's Digest*, March 1973 (reprint), p. 225. See *Project Pilot III*, Ricord organizational chart, p. 169.
31. Memorandum Report, Case File No NY: S 12110, Date August 14, 1968 by Anthony S. Pohl, "Interview of Louis Douheret @ Jean Claude LeFranc conducted on August 8, 1968, at the Federal Penitentiary, Atlanta, Georgia." Memorandum Report, Case File No NY: S 12110, Date August 26, 1968 by Anthony S. Pohl, "Interview of Louis Douheret conducted on August 19, 1968, at the Federal Penitentiary, Atlanta, Georgia." *Project Pilot III*, pp. 98, 192-200.
32. Adams, "The Hunt For André," p. 237. Interview with Bob DeFauw.
33. Adams, "The Hunt For André," p. 235.
34. *Project Pilot III*, pp. 124-128, 130, 133, 134, 139.
35. Ibid.
36. Adams, "The Hunt For André," p. 237.
37. Anthony S. Pohl, Memorandum Report, Case File No NY: S 12110, Date August 14, 1968, re Interview of Jean Nebbia conducted on August 7, 1968, at the Federal Penitentiary, Atlanta, Georgia
38. Ibid.
39. *Project Pilot III*, p. 189.
40. Anthony S. Pohl, Memorandum Report, Case File No NY: S 12110, Date August 26, 1968, "Interview of Louis Douheret conducted on August 19, 1968, at the Federal Penitentiary, Atlanta, Georgia."
41. *Project Pilot III*, pp. 133-151.
42. Ibid., p. 135.
43. Interview with Tony Pohl.
44. *Project Pilot III*, p. 352.
45. Ibid., pp. 354, 481-6.
46. Douglas Valentine. *The Strength of The Wolf* (New York: Verso), 2004, pp. 272-274, 361-363.

Chapter 4: Turning to Tartaglino

1. Interviews with John Ingersoll and Andy Tartaglino.
2. Interview with Andy Tartaglino.

3. Interview with John Ingersoll.
4. Interviews with John Enright, Frank Monastero, Dave Westrate and Walter Panich.
5. Interview with Frank Monastero.
6. Interview with Andy Tartaglino.
7. Tartaglino showed portions of the four memorandums to the author during an interview. The documents are referenced in the 1976 Jackson Hearings, pp. 68-72.
8. 1976 Jackson Hearings, p. 72.
9. Ibid., p. 75.
10. Ibid., pp. 74-77.
11. Interview with Andy Tartaglino.
12. Ibid. Tartaglino showed the author portions of the Greenfeld memorandum.
13. Interview with John Enright.
14. Interview with George Gaffney.
15. Interview with Dennis Dayle.
16. Interview with Dennis Dayle.
17. *New York Times*, February 1, 1970, p. 57.

Chapter 5: Symbolic Strategies
1. Edward Jay Epstein, *Agency of Fear: Opiates and Political Power in America* (New York: G. P. Putnam's Sons, 1977), p. 64.
2. Interview with John Ingersoll.
3. Title II and Title III of the Comprehensive Drug Abuse Prevention and Control Act of 1970.
4. Rooney Hearings, pp. 986, 1001.
5. Testimony by Eugene T. Rossides, Assistant Secretary of the Treasury in charge of the Customs Bureau and Secret Service, before the Senate Subcommittee to Investigate Juvenile Delinquency, on September 29, 1969.
6. Interview with Myles Ambrose.
7. Ibid.
8. Hughes; Kate Doyle, "The Dead of Tlatelolco," IRC Americas Program (Silver City, NM: International Relations Center, October 13, 2006).
9. Interview with Myles Ambrose.
10. Finlator, *Drugged Nation*, p. 100.
11. Interviews with David Ellis and Myles Ambrose.
12. Interview with Richard Dunagan.
13. *New York Times*, September 30, 1969, p. 8:1.
14. *New York Times*, January 4, 1970, p. 1.
15. Interview with Myles Ambrose.
16. Interviews with David Ellis and Myles Ambrose.

17. Interview with Myles Ambrose.
18. Interview with Richard Dunagan.
19. Interview with Tulius Acampora.
20. Finlator, *Drugged Nation*, pp. 64-65.
21. Interview with Ralph Barber.
22. Finlator, *Drugged Nation*, pp. 96-97, 136-140; according to Finlator, Jack Compton's attempt "to snatch" a major heroin supplier resulted in Compton fatally shooting five Mexican traffickers; but since Compton had no authority to shoot anyone, the incident had to be hushed up and Mexican police were given credit for killing the bandits
23. Interview with James Ludlum.
24. Ibid.
25. As detailed in *Strength of the Wolf*, Angleton used Mafia drug traffickers to assassinate, kidnap, burglarize enemy agents, and Corsicans to spy on the French intelligence service, believing it had been penetrated by the KGB.
26. Mary Walmpers was present and engaged in the interview with James Ludlum.
27. James Ludlum read from his notes of this meeting.
28. *New York Times* January 14, 1969, p. 7:1, lifts ban, March 10, 1969. p. 4:5.
29. Interview with Myles Ambrose.
30. Mary Walmpers was present and concurred with James Ludlum.
31. Interviews with Tulius Acampora, Paul Knight and George Corcoran.
32. Interview with George Corcoran.
33. Interview with James Ludlum.
34. Interview with Tony Pohl.

Chapter 6: The Big Picture

1. Interview with John O'Brien.
2. John McWilliams interview with George Belk, January 7, 1987, transcript provided to the author by McWilliams.
3. Interview with John Ingersoll
4. Interviews with Water Panich and John Ingersoll.
5. *New York Times*, May 9, 1970, 42:3. Rooney Hearings, p. 996.
6. Interview with Bowman Taylor.
7. Interviews with Water Panich and John Ingersoll.
8. Rooney Hearings, p. 987.
9. Interviews with Jerry Strickler and John Bacon.
10. Rooney Hearings, p. 988.
11. At this point Walter Panich joined inspections, replacing Irwin Greenfeld as chief of the field inspections division.
12. Interview with Ron Metcalf, Howard Safir and other agents in Special Projects.

13. *New York Daily News*, February 25, 1971, p. 1.
14. Rooney Hearings, p. 997.
15. Interviews with John Enright and Andy Tartaglino.
16. Interview with Denny Raugh.
17. Ibid.
18. Interview with John O'Brien.
19. Ibid.
20. Interview with Ted Vernier, head of the NYJTF.
21. *New York Times*, December 18, 1969, p. 43.
22. Interview with Denny Raugh.
23. Interview with Anthony S. Pohl.
24. Anthony Pohl, ""International Liaison for Director Ingersoll," chronology April 25, 1969-February 6, 1970. The following section is based on this document, interviews with Pohl, and Robert DeFauw, Deputy Regional Director, Paris, to John Ingersoll, Director, BNDD, "International Committee on Narcotics," December 3, 1969.
25. Interview with Tony Pohl.
26. Valentine, S*trength of the Wolf*, p. 524-525
27. Valentine, *Strength of the Wolf*, p, 231-232.
28. Interview with John Evans.
29. "International Committee on Narcotics."
30. Interview with James Ludlum and Mary Walmpers, AID's Turkey representative.
31. Valentine, *Strength of the Wolf*, p. 199.
32. Interviews with Myles Ambrose, John Ingersoll, and Tony Pohl.
33. Interviews with John Warner.
34. Richard E. Salmi, Report of Investigation, "Turkey Requirement No. C-DI-56003," 30 November 1971," p. 22-3.
35. Interview with Tony Pohl and Robert DeFauw. Robert DeFauw, Deputy Regional Director, Paris, to John Ingersoll, Director, BNDD, "International Committee on Narcotics," December 3, 1969, p. 4.
36. Anthony Pohl, ""International Liaison for Director Ingersoll," chronology April 25, 1969 - February 6, 1970. John E Ingersoll, Director, BNDD to Jean Dours, Director General, Police Nationale," November 13, 1969.
37. Robert DeFauw, "International Committee on Narcotics."
38. Interview with Robert DeFauw.
39. *Project Pilot III*, p. 96-7 and interview with Robert DeFauw.
40. Interview with Bob DeFauw.
41. *New York Times*, January 7, 1970.
42. Rooney Hearings, p. 988.
43. John E. Ingersoll letter to Anthony S. Pohl, February 6, 1970 (Pohl Document).

44. Correspondence with Tony Pohl.
45. The Franco-American Accords were signed a year later on February 26, 1971. House Foreign Affairs, The World Heroin Problem, Report # 92-298, 92nd Congress, 1st Session (hereafter known as World Heroin Problem), p. 8. *New York Times*, February 27, 1971.
46. Interview with Richard Salmi. Richard E. Salmi, Report of Investigation, "Turkey — Objective IV, Goal A, Target 2," February 2, 1970.
47. Salmi, "Turkey — Objective IV, Goal A, Target 2," p. 2.
48. Interview with Robert DeFauw.
49. Interview with Dick Salmi.
50. Interview with Paul Knight.
51. Felix Belair, Jr., "2 U.S. Agencies to Join in Fight on Drug Traffic," *New York Times*, July 30, 1970.
52. Ibid.
53. Hearings on Crime In America — Heroin Importation, Distribution, Packaging and Paraphernalia, Select Committee on Crime, House, 91st Congress Second Session, June 25, 26, 27, 29 and 30, 1970, New York.
54. Interview with Edward Coyne.
55. Hearings on Crime In America.
56. Ibid.
57. Ibid. Interview with Tony Pohl.
58. Interview with Myles Ambrose.

Chapter 7: A New York Narcotic Agent in Saigon

1. Christopher Hitchens, "The Case against Henry Kissinger, The Making of a War Criminal," *Harper's Magazine*, February 2001.
2. Stanley Karnow, *Vietnam: A History* (New York: The Viking Press, 1983), p. 593.
3. Alfred W. McCoy, *The Politics of Heroin: CIA Complicity in the Global Drug Trade* (Brooklyn: Lawrence Hill Books, 1991), p. 226.
4. Interviews with Fred Dick and Andy Tartaglino.
5. Charlie McDonnell in 1975 alleged that Dick had killed an informer near 125th Street on the East Side. He said that Fred hit him and he didn't wake up, so Fred and his partner Ben dropped the body off a pier. When asked about it by this author, Fred said it wasn't true. He said he did, on occasion, hang informers by their ankles over the pier — an interrogation method he learned from Hank Manfredi — and one of them may have slipped through Manfredi's hands.
6. Interview with Fred Dick.
7. *Project Pilot III*, 134, 465.
8. Interview with Fred Dick
9. Interview with Major McBee.
10. Interview with Charlie Vopat.

11. Interviews with Walt Sears and Fred Dick.
12. Albert Habib Memorandum, January 3, 1966: Production of opium and factories for conversion of opium into morphine base and heroin in Laos
13. Interview with Fred Dick.
14. Correspondence with Fred Dick.
15. Interviews with Fred Dick and Tulius Acampora.
16. McCoy, *Politics of Heroin*, p. 231.
17. Nguyen Ngoc Huy and Stephen B Young, Understanding Vietnam, The DPC Information Service, The Netherlands, 1982, p. 139, 148
18. *Chicago Sun Times*, "Find air hero guilty of piloting opium run," April 26, 1970. *New York Times*, April 26, 1970, p. 93.
19. McCoy, *Politics of Heroin*, p. 253.
20. McCoy, *Politics of Heroin*, p. 252.
21. Fraud and Corruption in Management of Military Club Systems; Illegal Currency Manipulations Affecting South Vietnam. Hearings before the Permanent Subcommittee on Investigations, Senate Committee on Government Operations, September 30, 1969, to March 17, 1971.
22. Interview with Tulius Acampora.
23. Dan Moldea. *The Hoffa Wars: The Rise and Fall of Jimmy Hoffa*. SPI Books: New York, 1993, 351. See also Jim Hougan, *Secret Agenda: Watergate, Deep Throat, and the CIA* (New York: Random House) pp. 312-313.
24. Interview and correspondence with Fred Dick.
25. Interview and correspondence with Fred Dick
26. Correspondence with BNDD Agent.
27. Interview with Fred Dick.
28. Interview with David Ellis. See also David C. Ellis, *U.S. Customs Special Agents: America's Senior Investigators* (self-published autobiography, December 2004), p. 408.
29. Ellis, *U.S. Customs Special Agents*, pp. 409-10.
30. Interview with Dave Ellis.
31. Ibid.
32. Interview with Lawrence Byrne.
33. Interview with Robert Flynn.
34. Interview with William Young. See *Strength of the Wolf*, pp. 420-22.
35. Interview with several CIA officers stationed at Savannahket.
36. Interviews with William Knierm and Robert Flynn.
37. *New York Times*, April 22, 1971, p. 1.
38. Interview with Robert Flynn.
39. Interviews with Robert Flynn and Dave Ellis.
40. Norodom Sihanouk and Wilfred Burchett, *My War With The CIA* (New York: Pantheon Books, 1972), p. 245.
41. Correspondence with Fred Dick.

42. Correspondence with Fred Dick.
43. Interview with William Young. See *Strength of the Wolf*, pp. 420-22.
44. Albert Habib Memorandum Report to Bowman Taylor, "Production of opium and factories for conversion of opium into morphine base and heroin in Laos," January 3, 1966. See also Habib to Taylor, "Heroin and morphine in Laos," January 27, 1966; "Opium Traffic between Laos and Vietnam," July 20, 1966; "Opium Traffic between Laos and Vietnam," July 28, 1966; "Opium Traffic between Laos and Vietnam," August 5, 1966; "Opium Traffic between Laos and Vietnam," September 2, 1966; "Opium Traffic between Laos and Vietnam," September 16, 1966.
45. Interview with Douglas Chandler.
46. Mc,Coy, *Politics of Heroin*, p. 227.

Chapter 8: Rude Awakenings

1. Agreement between the Bureau of Narcotics and Dangerous Drugs and the Direction Générale de la Police Nationale Française For The Co-Ordination Of Preventive and Repressive Action Against The Illicit Narcotic and Dangerous Drug Traffic, February 26, 1971.
2. Interview with Tony Pohl.
3. Definition provided by Anthony Pohl.
4. Interview with Tony Pohl.
5. Interview with Andy Tartaglino
6. Interview with John Warner
7. Interview with Dick Salmi
8. Clyde McAvoy, *The Diplomatic War on Heroin: A Southeast Asian Success Story* (US Department of State, 1974-75) (hereafter *Diplomatic War*), p. 7.
9. William Durkin, Regional Director, letter to Francis Wroblewski, Acting Assistant District Director of Investigation, INS, July 12, 1971 suggesting joint operations against Chinese nationals (Pohl document).
10. Interview with John Falvey
11. Interview with Thomas di Trinquet. Morris Kaplan, "Philippine Diplomat Seized Here As Heroin Smuggler," *New York Times*, November 12, 1971, p. 93.
12. Interview with Thomas di Trinquet.
13. Interview with Gerry Carey.
14. Interview with Jerry Strickler.
15. Interview with Jerry Strickler.
16. Ibid.
17. Ibid.
18. Interview with Dominick P. Petrossi.
19. Henrik Kruger, *The Great Heroin Coup: Drugs, Intelligence, & International Fascism* (Boston: South End Press), 1980, pp. 147-8.
20. *New York Times*, June 22, 1970, p. 1.

21. Interview with Jerry Strickler.
22. Moldea, *Hoffa Wars*, p. 7.
23. Moldea, *Of Grass and Snow*, p. 37.
24. *Project Pilot III*, pp. 239n, 626.
25. Interviews with Frangullie and Strickler.
26. Interview with Jerry Strickler.
27. Interviews with Hurney and Strickler.
28. Interview with Jerry Strickler.
29. Adams, "The Hunt for André," p. 235.
30. *Project Pilot III*, 239-52. Adams, "The Hunt for André," p. 237.
31. Adams, "The Hunt for André," p. 237.
32. *Project Pilot III*, p. 293. Interview with Gerry Carey.
33. *Project Pilot III*, pp. 293-304.
34. Adams, "The Hunt for André," pp. 238-9.
35. Ibid., p. 242.
36. Ibid., pp. 252-54.
37. Kruger, *Great Heroin Coup*, p. 122.
38. *Project Pilot III*, p. 148.
39. Interview with Jerry Strickler.
40. Kruger, *Great Heroin Coup*, p. 149—Kruger claims Trafficante was at war with the Corsicans. For the Far East connection, see also *Project Pilot III*, p. 172.
41. Everett Clark, Nicholas Horrock, *Contrabandista*, (New York: Praeger, 1973), p. 195.
42. Interviews with Victor Maria and Jerry Strickler.
43. Interviews with Vic Maria, Jerry Strickler and Tony Pohl.
44. Interview with Jerry Strickler.
45. Ibid.
46. Interview with Vic Maria.
47. Ibid., p. 189
48. Ibid., p. 451.
49. Charbonneau, *Canadian Connection*, p. 294.
50. Ralph Blumenthal, *Last Days of the Sicilians: At War with the Mafia*, (New York: Random House, 1988), p. 85.
51. Charbonneau, *Canadian Connection*, p. 295.
52. Interview with Jerry Strickler.
53. Charbonneau, *Canadian Connection*, p. 302.

Chapter 9: Espionage Intrigues

1. William Peers and Dean Brellis, *Behind the Burma Road* (Boston: Little Brown, 1963), p. 64.
2. Valentine, *Strength of the Wolf*, p. 279 re: the CIA escorting dope to its warlords.

3. Joseph Trento. *Wilmington News-Journad.* January 10, 1981. Also Warren Hinckle and William Turner, *Deadly Secrets* (New York: Thunder's Mouth Press), 1981), pp. 412-3

4. Interview with Myles Ambrose.

5. Valentine, *Strength of the Wolf*, pp. 332-4.

6. Kruger, *Great Heroin Coup*, p. 154.

7. *New York Times*, March 28. 1969, p. 16.

8. Peter Dale Scott, *Deep Politics and the Death of JFK* (Berkeley: University of California Press, 1993), p. 175.

9. Scott, *Deep Politics*, p. 175.

10. *New York Times*, January 10, 1958, p. 1.

11. Moldea, *Hoffa Wars*, p. 387, citing Charles Crimaldi.

12. See Chapter 15 Capitol Capers.

13. Scott, *Deep Politics*, p. 200.

14. Scott, *Deep Politics*, p. 174

15. Art Kunkin, Compiled by Marvin Miller. *The Breaking of a President 1974 Volume 3.* (Therapy Productions, Inc, 1974,) pp. 46-8.

16. Moldea, *Of Grass and Snow*, pp. 37-38.

17. Interviews with Jerry Strickler, Tom Hurney and John Bacon.

18. Interview with Peter Scrocca.

19. Ibid.

20. Subcommittee on Internal Security, Committee on Judiciary, US Senate, *World Drug Traffic and its Impact on US Security* (Washington, DC, GPO, August 14, 1972), p. 108-121. The section on Squella is based on interviews with the agents involved and Attorney Bierman.

21. Interview with Jerry Strickler.

22. Ibid.

23. Interview with Donald Bierman.

24. Interview with Tom Tripodi.

25. Moldea, *Hoffa Wars*, p. 127. Siragusa interview by CIA officer Michie, March 24, 1977 (hereafter known as Michie Memo), document provided by Richard E. Salmi.

26. Kruger, *Great Heroin Coup*, pp. 15, 25n 62.

27. Interview with Naomi Spatz. Mortimer Benjamin, Memorandum Reports, "Investigation into the Activities of Maurice Castellani and Joseph Irving Brown," October 11, 1965; November 17, 1965 and November 30, 1965.

28. Alain Jaubert, *Dossier D...comme Drogue* (Paris: Editions Alain Moreau, 1973), p. 46 n20.

29. Jaubert, *Dossier D*, pp. 37-40.

30. McCoy, *Politics of Heroin*, pp. 131-135.

31. Tripodi, *Crusade*, p. 185.

32. Ibid., p. 186.

33. Jill Jonnes, *Hep Cats, Narcs and Pipe Dreams: A History of America's Romance With Illegal Drugs* (New York: Scribner, 1996), p. 185.
34. Interview with Andy Tartaglino.
35. Mortimer Benjamin, Memorandum Reports, "Investigation into the Activities of Maurice Castellani and Joseph Irving Brown," 11 October 1965; 17 November 1965 and 30 November 1965.
36. Interview with Vic Maria.
37. Interview with special employee Richard Jepson. See also John L Hess, "The Fournier Case: A Faimliar Ring," *New York Times*, November 16, 1971.
38. *Project Pilot III*, 405-406.
39. Interview with Vic Maria.
40. Kruger, *Great Heroin Coup*, p 67.
41. *Project Pilot III*, pp. 8, 75-77, b85 and 363. The Staff and Editors of Newsday, *The Heroin Trail:* (New York, Holt Rinehart, Winston), 1973, pp.109-118. Tripoldi, *Crusade*, p. 187.
42. *Project Pilot III*, 189-190.
43. *Project Pilot III*, 189-190. Kruger, *Great Heroin Coup*, p. 76.
44. Interview with Tom Tripodi.
45. Interviews with George Corcoran and Tully Acampora.
46. *Project Pilot III*, 58.
47. Interview with Bob DeFauw.
48. *Project Pilot III*, 438, 440, 444, 455-460, 463, 474.
49. Tripodi, *Crusade*, 186.
50. *Project Pilot III*, 438, 440, 444, 455-460, 463, 474.
51. *Heroin Trail*, 128
52. McCoy, *Politics of Heroin*, 43-45
53. *The Heroin Trail*, 86.
54. Jaubert, *Dossier D*, 160.
55. Interview with Dick Salmi.
56. Interview with Bob DeFauw.
57. *New York Times*, 20 September 1970, 14.
58. Richard E. Salmi, Report of Investigation, "Turkey Requirement No. C-DI-56003," 30 November 1971, 11.
59. Richard E. Salmi, Report of Investigation, "Turkey – Objective IV, Goal A, Target 2," 2 February 1970, 2.
60. Interview with John Warner.
61. *Project Pilot III*, 370-76, 629; see also *World Drug Traffic and its Impact on US Security*, 82, 96-98, 157. Interviews with Wayne Valentine and author John Koehler.
62. Interview with Wayne Valentine.
63. February 12, 1971 Statement of Manuel Suarez Dominguez given in AMMOOOO5 at the San Antonio Task Force Office (hereafter known as Suarez Statement).

64. Interview with Wayne Valentine.
65. *Suarez Statement*, 4.
66. Interview with James Attie. Herbert Brean, "Crooked, Cruel Traffic In Drugs," *Life Magazine*, 25 January 1960, 94.
67. *Suarez Statement*, 7-18.
68. Ibid, 18-22.
69. Ibid, 23-37.
70. Ibid, 38-55.
71. Ibid, 56-75.
72. *Project Pilot III*, 369.
73. Ibid, 370.
74. *World Drug Traffic and its Impact on US Security*, 157.

Chapter 10: The First Infestations

1. Interview with David Wiser.
2. Paradiso was shot in the head on a pier in New York City. The author asked the accused FBN agent if he had done the dirty deed and he denied it. Other agents insist he did.
3. Interview with Tom Tripodi.
4. Interview with Phil Smith.
5. Interview with David Wiser.
6. 1976 Jackson Hearings, p. 76.
7. Report of the Attorney General (Pursuant to Attorney General's Order N. 600-75; Assigning Employees to Investigate Allegations of Fraud, Irregularity and Misconduct in the Drug Enforcement Administration), June 13, 1975: Subject: Additional Integrity Matters (hereafter known as DeFeo Report), p. 12. Portions of the DeFeo Report were leaked to the *Village Voice* in 1976 and provided to the author by journalist John Kelly.
8. Ellis, *U.S. Customs Special Agents*, pp. 293-312.
9. Interviews with Andy Tartaglino and Vernon "Iron Mike" Acree.
10. Hearings before the Permanent Subcommittee on Investigations of the Committee on Government Operations US Senate 94th Congress, First Session, June 9, 10, and 11, 1975, Part 1 (Washington, DC: 1975) (hereafter known as 1975 Jackson Hearings, p. 613.
11. *New York Times*, February 26, 1970; February 27, 1970, 1:3
12. Ibid.
13. Ibid.
14. Jack Kelly with Richard Mathison, *On the Street: The Autobiography of the Toughest US Narcotics Agent* (Chicago: Henry Regnery Company), 1974, p. 980. Interview with John Warner.
15. DeFeo Report, p. 17.

16. *New York Times*, March 3, 1970.
17. *New York Times*, April 26, 1970.
18. Interview with Andy Tartaglino.
19. DeFeo Report, p. 12.
20. 1975 Jackson Hearings, p. 613.
21. Report to the President by the Commission on CIA Activities Within the United States (Washington, DC: GPO, June 1975) (hereafter known as Rockefeller Commission Report), pp. 232-4. Nicholas M Horrock, "High-Level Backing Cited in C.I.A. Drug-Unit Spying," *New York Times*, July 10, 1975.
22. Interview with Pat Fuller.
23. Interview with Robert Medell.
24. Rockefeller Commission Report, Findings and Conclusions, p. 39; Interview with Pat Fuller.
25. Rockefeller Commission Report, p. 234.
26. DeFeo Report, p. 20 and DEA Investigative File IR-73-131-C.
27. Interview with Chuck Gutensohn.
28. Interview with Terry Burke.
29. Ibid.
30. *New York Times*, May 7, 1970, p. 1.
31. Compton Affidavit, p. 57.
32. Ibid., p. 59.
33. Interviews with John Ingersoll and John Warner.
34. John Warner, Executive Assistant to John E. Ingersoll, re: BNDD Intelligence Requirements and Organizational Structure...A request for CIA Survey, May 18, 1970.
35. E. Drexel Godfrey to John E Ingersoll, "The Intelligence Needs of the Bureau of Narcotics and Dangerous Drugs," October 26, 1970.
36. Andrew Tartaglino, Assistant Director for enforcement to John Warner, Executive Assistant, November 17, 1970, "Comments on Dr. Godfrey's Intelligence report.
37. Report of the BNDD Task Force On Intelligence, January 7, 1970 (John Warner Chairman, Walter Panich, Vice Chairman, William Ewell, Martin Kurke, PhD, avid Melocik, secretary) and Intelligence Task Force report on Domestic Regional Intelligence Function, December 22, 1970 (Task Force members: John Warner, Chairman, Walter Panich, Vice Chairman, William Ewell, Dr. Martin Kurke, Dave Melocik). (Warner Doc).
38. John Ingersoll, Director to All Assistant Directors All Domestic regional Directors, "Domestic Regional Intelligence Function," December 30, 1970; and Andrew C. Tartaglino, Assistant Director for enforcement to All Regional Directors, re: Establishment of regional Intelligence Units, January 23, 1971.

39. From William T Ewell, Special Assistant, Office of Administration to John Warner, Executive Assistant, Comments on the Study, "The Intelligence Needs of the Bureau of Narcotics and Dangerous Drugs," by E. Drexel Godfrey.

40. Interviews with John Warner and other SIO personnel. John Warner, Chief Strategic Intelligence Office to All SI Personnel, "Office Order #9 — SIO Office File and Document Control Station," February 9, 1972.

41. Intelligence Task Force Report on Operational Intelligence Functions at Headquarters, (Task Force members: John Warner, Chairman, Walter Panich, Vice Chairman, William Ewell, Dr. Martin Kurke, Dave Melocik). January 29, 1971 (Warner Doc).

42. Adrian Swain, *The Time of My Life: Memoirs Off A Government Agent From Pearl Harbor To The Golden Triangle* (Tampa Bay: Axelrod Publishing, 1995), p. 435.

43. Swain, *Time of My Life*, pp. 444-9.

44. Ibid., p. 447.

45. Interview with Terry Baldwin.

46. Swain, *Time of My Life*, p. 465.

47. Ibid., p. 466.

48. Ibid., pp. 466-7.

49. *New York Times*, June 18, 1971, p. 1.

50. Interview with John Warner.

51. Interview with Richard Bly.

52. Interview with Tom Tripodi.

53. Tripodi, *Crusade*, p. 174.

54. Interviews with Tripodi and Kobakoff.

55. Tripodi, *Crusade*, p. 175.

56. Ibid., p. 179.

57. Bart Barnes, *Washington Post*, obituary section, July 6, 1998.

58. Interview with Lou Conein.

59. DeFeo Report, p. 8.

60. Ibid.

61. Interview with John Bacon.

62. Interview with John Warner.

63. John Ingersoll, "Foreign Office Reporting To Strategic Intelligence," January 2, 1972.

64. Interview with Jim Ludlum.

65. George C Corcoran to The Commissioner of Customs, June 18, 1971.

66. Valentine, *Strength of the Wolf*, pp. 42-3, 226, 228,234,235,254-255, 316-317.

67. Siragusa, *The Trail Of The Poppy; Behind The Mask Of The Mafia* (Englewood Cliffs, NJ: Prentice-Hall, 1966), p. 108

68. Interview with Bob DeFauw.

Chapter 11: Angels and Archangels

1. World Heroin Problem.
2. World Heroin Problem, p. 36. *New York Times*, May 26, 1971, p. 14.
3. *New York Times*, June 5, 1971, p. 6 re: Laird. *New York Times*, June 7, 1971, p. 6.
4. Interview with Robert Steele.
5. Ibid.
6. World Heroin Problem, pp. 40-44.
7. Ibid., p. 8.
8. *Heroin Trail*, pp. 87.
9. Charbonneau, *Canadian Connection*, p. 100.
10. World Heroin Problem, p. 9.
11. Epstein, *Agency of Fear*, p 276.
12. Richard E. Salmi, Report of Investigation, "Turkey Requirement No. C-DI-56003," November 30, 1971, p. 6.
13. World Heroin Problem, p. 30. Interview with Richard Salmi.
14. Finlator, *Drugged Nation*, p. 264. William Shawcross, *The Shah's Last Ride: The Fate of an Ally* (New York: Simon and Schuster, 1988), p. 185
15. World Heroin Problem, p. 42.
16. Interview with Robert Steele.
17. World Heroin Problem, p. 39.
18. Interview with Robert Steele.
19. World Heroin Problem, pp. 1, 5, 19, 20.
20. See among other books and articles World Heroin Problem. *New York Times* and McCoy, *Politics of Heroin*.
21. Minutes of May 27, 1971meeting, provided by the Nixon Archive.
22. Ibid.
23. Jonnes, *Hep-Cats, Narcs, and Pipes Dream*, pp. 273-276; *New York Times*, June 11, 1971, p. 10.
24. Minutes of May 27, 1971meeting, provided by the Nixon Archive (5:56 pm), p. 61.
25. NSC member Arnold Nachmanoff, in an interview with the author, said drug matters were often handled by a security group headed by Larry Lynn in 1971.
26. Minutes of May 27, 1971meeting, provided by the Nixon Archive, p. 66.
27. Epstein, *Agency of Fear*, p. 143.
28. Ibid., p. 142.
29. Ibid., p. 143.
30. Ibid., p. 142.
31. Ibid., p. 142.
32. Ibid., p. 142.
33. Ibid., p. 144.

34. Interview with Tony Pohl.
35. Epstein, *Agency of Fear*, p. 158.
36. Interview with Walter Minnick.
37. Ibid.
38. George M Belk, Acting deputy Assistant Administrator for Intelligence to John Warner, Acting Chief Foreign Inteelligencee Division, "Foreign Intelligence programs," August 20, 1973.
39. Interview with Walter Minnick.
40. Ibid.
41. Ibid.
42. Interview with Terry Baldwin.
43. Interview with Jim Ludlum.
44. Interviews with John Ingersoll and John Warner.
45. Epstein, *Agency of Fear*, chapter 11.
46. Ibid., chapter 11.
47. Interview with Richard Blum.
48. Interviews with Lou Conein and Daniel Ellsberg.
49. McCoy, *Politics of Heroin*, p. 249.
50. Conein letter to Harper Row President Winthrop Knowlton, October 10, 1972.
51. Interview with Daniel Ellsberg.
52. McCoy, *Politics of Heroin*, pp. x (see also 134, 145).
53. Interviews with Tom Tripodi and Al McCoy.
54. McCoy, *Politics of Heroin*. p. x.
55. Ibid., pp. 239, (see 540 n 150).
56. Ibid., pp. 228.
57. Interview with Tulius Acampora.
58. McCoy, *Politics of Heroin*, pp. 229, (see also 537, n 113 and 534, n 30).
59. Ibid., pp. xii-xiii.
60. Albert Habib, "Jean Marie Le Rouzic May 1971 letter 'To the attention of Mr. Lachaud, Sûreté Nationale, Nice'" September 10, 1971 (Hereafter Le Rouzic letter).
61. McCoy, *Politics of Heroin*, p. xvi.
62. Le Rouzic letter.
63. Ibid.
64. McCoy, *Politics of Heroin*, pp. 379-380, 284-85, citing interview with BNDD agent, November 18, 1971.
65. Le Rouzic letter.
66. Interview with Jerry Strickler.
67. Blumenthal, *Last Days of the Sicilians*, p. 87.
68. Interview with Alan McClain.
69. *Operation Sandstorm* case file, FOIA Request Number 93—1896-F.

70. Info-Turk, "The Counter-Guerilla Remains Untouchable," Brussels, February 1993. See also Danielle Ganser, "Secret Warfare and NATO's Stay-Behind Armies," ECOTERRA Intl, December 17, 2004.

71. Interviews with Steve Greene and Dick Salmi.

72. Interview with Dick Salmi.

73. Interview with Dewey Clarridge.

74. George C. Corcoran Customs attaché, Paris, to Commissioner of Customs, July 10, 1971. George C. Corcoran, Customs attaché, Paris, to Commissioner of Customs, June 1, 1972. George C. Corcoran, Customs attaché, Paris, to Commissioner of Customs, "Liaison Visit to Bulgarian Customs, January 22-26, 1973," February 22, 1973.

75. Richard E. Salmi, "Operation Bruit, Target 1, Mehmet — Kulekcioglu (Kulekci) — Istanbul," December 27, 1971.

76. Interview with Dewey Clarridge.

Chapter 12: The Politics of Enforcement

1. Interview with Al Habib.

2. Ibid.

3. Ibid.

4. Correspondence with Tony Pohl citing Mortimer Benjamin report dated April 28, 1971.

5. Interviews with Al Habib, Joe Quarequio, Tony Pohl and Morty Benjamin.

6. Interviews with Myles Ambrose and Jerry Strickler.

7. Reuters November 25, 1971, "Debre Calls Drug-SDECE Case A No-Value "Confused Novel."

8. *Heroin Trail*, pp. 102-103. *Project Pilot III*, pp. 305-307.

9. *Newsweek*, "The French Connection," November 29, 1971, p. 16.

10. Morton Mills, "French Connection Plot Thickens," *Washington Post*, April 19, 1972, p. A3.

11. George C. Corcoran, Assistant Customs Attaché Enf, Paris to Office of Investigations, Bureau of Customs, "Roger Xavier Leon DELOUETTE, et al," April 27, 1971. Paul Boulad, Special Agent, to Commissioner of Customs, Attention: John A Lund, Jr, Director, Criminal Investigations Division, July 15, 1971.

12. George C. Corcoran, Assistant Customs Attaché Enf, Paris to Office of Investigations, Bureau of Customs, "Roger Xavier Leon DELOUETTE, et al," April 27, 1971.

13. *Newsweek*, "The French Connection," November 29, 1971, p. 16.

14. Ambassador Thomas Watson to Secretary of State, "Dept Pass BNDD Hqs/For Enfc And For Treasury For Customs From Cusack," April 27, 1971. Customs Agent Vernon G Pikster in a 24 October 1972 letter to

Al Seely identified Mariani's cousin, Jean Claude Marchani, as a former SDECE agent fired for bad conduct.

15. John T. Cusack, RD, to Honorable Thomas K Watson, American Ambassador, "Roger Delouette, at al," November 3, 1971.
16. Mark Lander, "German Court Seeks Arrest of 13 CIA Officers," *New York Times*, January 31, 2007.
17. *Project Pilot III*, pp. 327-328. Interview with Tony Pohl.
18. Anthony S. Pohl, AARD, to Frank Monastero, ARD, "Louis Cirillo et al, Highlights of the Conspiracy Investigation," April 25, 1972.
19. George C. Corcoran to Office of Investigations, "Roger Delouette and André Labay, et al. investigations," September 3, 1971.
20. *Project Pilot III*, p. 524.
21. George C. Corcoran to Office of Investigations, "Roger Delouette and André Labay, et al. investigations," September 3, 1971.
22. John L Hess, "US Drug Agent's Charges Anger the French Police," *New York Times*, August 26, 1971.
23. Hess, "US Drug Agent's Charges Anger the French Police."
24. November 25, 1971, L'AURORE "When Americans Judge French Justice Harshly" by Christian d'Epeneoux.
25. Correspondence with Tony Pohl.
26. *Newsweek*, "The French Connection," November 29, 1971, p. 16.
27. Tripodi, *Crusade*, pp. 188-189.
28. *Project Pilot III*, pp. 543-545.
29. Interviews with Tony Pohl and Morty Benjamin.
30. *Project Pilot III*, pp. 544-545.
31. Interview with Gerry Carey.
32. Gerard F. Carey, Group Supervisor, To the Files, September 28, 1971.
33. Interview with Tony Pohl.
34. Joseph Quarequio to Mortimer Benjamin, "C1-71-0276 Luis Ortega et al," September 28, 1971.
35. Interview with Gerry Carey.
36. Interview with DEA agent.
37. Interview with Daniel Casey.
38. Daniel P. Casey, Regional Director, to John E. Ingersoll, Director, "Cooperative Narcotics Intelligence Committee," August 11, 1972.
39. Intelligence, undated, unsigned BNDD document provided by John Warner.
40. Interview with Tony Pohl.
41. *World Drug Traffic and its Impact on US Security*, pp. 99-103; *Project Pilot III*, pp. 522-542; Interview with Tony Pohl.
42. Information on the Berdin, Preiss and Labay cases comes from *Project Pilot III*, Berdin, pp. 328, 506, 522-34, 538 and Labay, pp. 8, 327-8, 335, 491, 522-27, and 534-42; as well as interview with Tony Pohl and other agents on the case.

43. *Project Pilot III*, p. 538.
44. Ibid., pp. 493, 527. Charbonneau, *Canadian Connection*, p. 346.
45. *Project Pilot III*, pp. 534-6. *Heroin Trail*, p. 253.
46. *Project Pilot III*, p. 525.
47. Ibid., pp. 534-6.
48. Ibid., p. 529.
49. Ibid., pp. 531-533. *Heroin Trail*, p. 236.
50. *Project Pilot III*, p. 533. Interview with Tony Pohl.
51. Ibid., p. 533.
52. *Heroin Trail*, pp. 242-243.
53. Ibid.
54. *Project Pilot III*, p. 539.
55. Ibid., pp. 540-542.
56. Interview with Anthony Pohl.
57. Interview with Anthony Pohl; Anthony S. Pohl to Jerry N Jenson, Acting RD, Status Report, December 1, 1971.
58. Alex Michelini, "Feared a Connection to Death: Frenchman, *New York Daily News*, April 20, 1972.
59. Walter B Miller to John A Frost, "Disappearance of Government witness Erika Rita Bunne on October 10, 1967," October 19, 1967.
60. Lt. John J Tooth, Field Services Bureau to Major Howard J. Graff, Investigations Officer, New Jersey State Police, "Polygraph Examination conducted upon Angelo Kenneth Wedra," April 26, 1972. Anthony Mangiaracina to Mortimer Benjamin, "Information relative to possible malfeasance in office," April 6, 1972.
61. Interview with Tony Pohl.
62. Anthony S. Pohl, AARD, to Frank Monastero, ARD, "Louis Cirillo et al, Highlights of the Conspiracy Investigation," April 25, 1972.
63. Interview with Tony Pohl. Customs Agent Vernon G Pikster to Special Agent in Charge, New York, October 2, 1972.
64. Anthony S. Pohl, AARD, to The Records, "Interview of Miss Nancy Grigor," January 14, 1972.
65. Anthony S. Pohl, AARD, Special Tactical Unit #1 to The Record, "Development in the Roger Delouette Investigation," December 7, 1971.
66. Ibid.
67. Anthony S. Pohl, ARDD, Special Tactical Unit #1 to Daniel P. Casey, re: Customs Complaint Regarding the Undersigned, January 26, 1972.
68. Anthony S. Pohl, AARD, Special Tactical Unit #1, Memorandum, Cirillo Case, March 30, 1972.
69. Anthony S. Pohl, AARD, Special Tactical Unit #1 to The Records, Briefing of Associate Deputy Attorney General Harlington Wood," December 15, 1971.
70. Anthony S. Pohl, ARDD, Special Tactical Unit #1 to Daniel P. Casey, "Customs Complaint Regarding the Undersigned, January 26, 1972.

71. Anthony S. Pohl, AARD, to The Records, "Interview of Miss Nancy Grigor," January 14, 1972.
72. Bernard Vallery, "All's Okay with France: Drug Sleuth" *New York Daily News,* January 17, 1972. Francis Schull, "Mr Ingersoll's Little Remark," *L'Aurore,* January 19, 1972.
73. John T Cusack to Ambassador Thomas Watson, November 3, 1971 re: Berdin identifies Delouette.
74. *Project Pilot III,* 329-332. John J Coleman, "Investigation Conducted to Date re: Testimony of Claude Pastou, April 5 — May 14, 1973, Statement of Claude Pastou," May 15, 1973, p. 17. Commissaire Divisionnaire, Chief, Central Office for the Suppression of Illicit Narcotics Traffic to Central Director Judicial Police, "Delouette Case," December 14, 1972.
75. Anthony S. Pohl, AARD, Special Tactical Unit #1, Memorandum, Cirillo Case, March 30, 1972.
76. Ibid. Interview with Tony Pohl.
77. Anthony S. Pohl, ARDD, Special Tactical Unit #1 to Daniel P. Casey, re: Customs Complaint Regarding the Undersigned, January 26, 1972. Interview with Tony Pohl.
78. Anthony S. Pohl, AARD, to Daniel P. Casey, RD, "Investigation on Louis Cirillo's Attempt to Obstruct Justice and Jump Bail," April 20, 1972.
79. Interview with Tony Pohl.
80. Anthony S. Pohl, AARD, to Daniel P. Casey, RD, "Investigation on Louis Cirillo's Attempt to Obstruct Justice and Jump Bail," April 20, 1972.
81. *New York Post,* "Feds Find 'Mr Big's' $ Million," April 30, 1972.
82. Moldea, *Of Grass and Snow,* pp. 26-27, 33-34. See also Clarence Lusane, *Pipe Dream Blues: Racism and the War on Drugs* (Boston, MA: South End Press, 1991).
83. *Project Pilot III,* pp. 560-565.
84. Moldea, *Of Grass and Snow,* p. 44.
85. Anthony S. Pohl, AARD, to Daniel P Casey, RD, "Interview by AO Representatives," April 19, 1972.

Chapter 13: Shock Treatment

1. 1975 Jackson Hearings, p. 111.
2. Interview with Myles Ambrose.
3. See Bowman Taylor quote, early in Chapter 6. ("I used to think we were fighting the drug business. But after they formed the BNDD, I realized we were feeding it."
4. Interview with Myles Ambrose.
5. Epstein, *Agency of Fear,* prologue.

6. Epstein, *Agency of Fear*, chapter 11.
7. Interview with Myles Ambrose and other ODALE officials.
8. Ibid.
9. Interview with John Bartels.
10. Interview with John Ingersoll.
11. Interview with Ambrose and other agents.
12. Interview with Tony Pohl.
13. Interview with Mike Acree.
14. Interview with George Corcoran.
15. George c. Corcoran, Customs attaché, Paris, to Commissioner of Customs, July 10, 1972.
16. Interview with Paul Knight.
17. Interview with François Le Mouel.
18. *Project Pilot III*, pp. 393-405.
19. Interview with Paul Knight.
20. Interview with Al Habib.
21. Interview with John Ingersoll, John Warner, Andy Tartaglino and other BNDD agents.
22. John Warner, "Headquarters Reorganization, July 1, 1972."
23. Interview with Richard Bly.
24. John Parker, Acting Assistant Director for Strategic Intelligence to S. B. Bilbrough, Chief, Office of Operations Planning, "Kobakoff draft of the functional and activities statement of SIO," July 28, 1972.
25. Interviews with John Bacon and Jerry Strickler.
26. Interview with John Bacon.
27. Ibid.
28. John Warner, "Headquarters Reorganization, July 1, 1972" (including G-Dep Organizational Chart).
29. Interview with Jim Ludlum.
30. Notes (in lieu of recording) with Seymour Bolten, Intelligence Advisor on Drug Abuse Policy, Domestic Policy Staff, Room 4188, Old Executive Office Building, Washington, DC, February 4, 1981, Carter Library (hereafter known as Bolten Interview).
31. Bolten Interview and Seymour Hersh, *The Dark Side of Camelot*, Boston (Little Brown, 1997), p. 440.
32. Carl Bernstein, "The CIA and the Media," *Rolling Stone*, October 20, 1977, p. 66.
33. Burton Hersh, *The Old Boys: The American Elite and the Origins of the CIA* (New York: Charles Scribner's Sons, 1992), p. 374.
34. Bolten Interview.
35. Interview with Dewey Clarridge.
36. Interview with Jerry Strickler.
37. Interview with Tully Acampora.

38. Interview with Andy Tartaglino.
39. Interview with John Warner.
40. Philip Agee, *Inside The Company: CIA Diary* (Harmondsworth, England: Penguin Books, 1975), p. 532. Interview with John Warner and CIA sources.
41. Interview with Walter Minnick.
42. Richard Nixon, The White House, Executive order Providing for the Establishment of an Office of National Narcotics Intelligence Within the Department of Justice, July 27, 1972.
43. Interview with Walter Minnick.
44. Curt Gentry, *J Edgar Hoover, The Man and the Secrets* (New York: WW Norton & Company, 2001), p. 572.
45. Anthony Summers, *Official and Confidential: The Secret Life of J. Edgar Hoover* (New York: Pocket Books, 1994), pp. 459-462.
46. Subcommittee On Departments of State, Justice, And Commerce, The judiciary, And Related Matters, John J. Rooney, Chairman, September 28, 1972 "Legal Activities and general Administration, Salaries and expenses, general administration, Office of National Narcotics Intelligence," pp. 851-874 (hereafter known as ONNI Hearings).
47. Attorney General Richard Kleindienst, Memorandum To Department And Agencies, "Office of National Narcotics Intelligence (ONNI) December 6, 1972, including "Authorization and Mission Statement of the Office of National Narcotics Intelligence (hereafter known as Kleindienst ONNI)."
See also "Office of National Narcotics Intelligence Mission' (undated, unsigned).
48. ONNI Hearings.
49. Ibid.
50. My ONNI FOIA response.
51. Epstein, *Agency of Fear*, 219.
52. Interview with John Warner.
53. Interview with Andy Tartaglino.
54. Interview with Colonel Tulius Acampora.
55. Interview with Thomas Fox.
56. Joe Esterhaus, "Death in the Wilderness: The Justice Departments' Killer Strike Force, *Rolling Stone*, May 1973.
57. Daniel P. Casey, Regional Director, to John Ingersoll, Director, August 11, 1972, "Cooperative Narcotic Intelligence Committee."
58. Ibid.
59. "BNDD Intelligence," undated unsigned (Warner document).
60. Ibid.
61. Seven John Does v. Office of Personnel Management, MSPB Docket Nos. DA083188110337 and DC083181105596, Six Appellant's

Closing Brief, 14. In response to an FOIA request by the author, the CIA said it had no documents about the ININ.

62. Interview with CIA Officer Nelson Brickham.

Chapter 14: Chasing the Dragon

1. The author viewed the pipe at Dick's well appointed home in Tavernier, Florida.
2. McCoy, *Politics of Heroin*, pp. 203-4.
3. Conein letter to Harper Row President Winthrop Knowlton, October 10, 1972.
4. *New York Times*, August 8, 1971 re Kontum and LLDB; July 25, 1971, 51 kilos of heroin and 330 kilos opium into Cholon by Viet Navy--drug money to buy votes in national assembly. "Recently, a member of the South Vietnamese legislature, and friend of high-ranking government officials, was arrested smuggling heroin into Vietnam." June 30, 1971, Ambassador Godley attacks with AA choppers Houei Phi Lark in NW Laos, heroin refinery. Owner of the refinery is Chao La, King of the Yao tribe, supplied many recruits to Vang Pao's army clandestine. At which point lose the war. In wake of Lam Son in February 1971. July 15, 1971, NBC says President Thieu's national security chief, general Dang Van Quang, was the biggest pusher, along with his associate Admiral Chung Tan Cang. Station Chief Ted Shackley assigns deputy Ron Landreth as head of committee to investigate General Quang, whom he advises. August 1971 *New York Times* quotes director of Customs as saying "planes of SVAF were the principle carriers of dope into South Vietnam. Commander of an on Nhut where planes load is Col Phan Phung Tien, (5th Transport Wing) close to many Corsican gangsters and has been implicated in smuggling between Laos and Nam." In August 71, director general of Viet custom says Tien "Least cooperative (McCoy, p. 188)
5. McCoy, *Politics of Heroin*, pp. 239-240, 234. *New York Times*, July 18, 1971, p. 5.
6. McCoy, *Politics of Heroin*, p. 255. Interview Harry "Buzz" Johnson.
7. McCoy, *Politics of Heroin*, pp. 243-47.
8. Interviews with William Colby and Evan J. Parker.
9. Interview with Jim Ludlum re: "rice bowls."
10. *New York Times*, June 6, 1971, p. 2.
11. Jean Marie Le Rouzic May 1971 letter "To the attention of Mr. Lachaud, Sûreté Nationale, Nice."
12. Correspondence with Fred Dick.
13. John F. Sullivan, *Of Spies and Lies: A CIA Lie Detector Remembers Vietnam* (University Press of Kansas, 2002).
14. Interview with Fred Dick.

15. Interview with Tully Acampora.
16. Interview with Bill Logay.
17. Interview with Tom Polgar.
18. Interview with Bill Logay
19. Interview with Steve Greene.
20. "Search and Destroy: The War on Drugs," *Time*, September 4, 1972.
21. Interview with Steve Greene.
22. Interview with Major McBee.
23. Interview with Charlie Vopat.
24. Interview with Major McBee.
25. Ellis, *U.S. Customs Special Agents*, pp.424-427.
26. Ellis, *U.S. Customs Special Agents*, pp. 418-20.
27. Ibid., pp. 438-443. Interview with Dave Ellis.
28. Ibid., p. 443.
29. Ibid., pp. 444-46.
30. Ibid., p. 424.
31. Interview with Dave Ellis.
32. Ellis, *U.S. Customs Special Agents*, p. 426.
33. Dr. Joseph D. Douglass, Jr, Introduction by Dr. Ray S. Cline, *Red Cocaine: The Drugging of America and the West* (Atlanta GA: Clarion House, 1990; London: Edward Harle Ltd, 1999), (excerpts viewed online at http://www.freerepublic.com/forum/a388dd92874d8.htm).
34. Douglass, *Red Cocaine*, excerpts viewed online at http://www.freerepublic.com/forum/a388dd92874d8.htm.
35. Interview with Walt Minnick.
36. Interview with Dave Ellis.
37. Ibid.
38. William Young to unnamed Customs official, 8 page report on the 118A Network and related subjects (hereafter known as 118A Network Report), August 1972, p. 4.
39. 118A Network Report, p. 4.
40. Ibid.
41. Interviews with Tony Poe and Terry Burke.
42. Interviews with Tony Poe and Bill Young.
43. Ellis, *U.S. Customs Special Agents*, p. 453.
44. Ellis, *U.S. Customs Special Agents*, p. 456.
45. World Drug Traffic and Its Impact on US Security, p. 184.
46. World Drug Traffic and its Impact on US Security, p. 255.
47. Jonathan Kwitney, *The Crimes of Patriots: A True Tale of Dope, Dirty Money, and the CIA* (New York: W.W. Norton, 1987), p. 52. World Drug Traffic and its Impact on US Security, pp.147-150.
48. "Grisly Smuggling," *Time*, January 1, 1973, p. 25. Interview with US Attorney Michael E Marr

49. 118A Network Reportt, p. 1.
50. 118A Network Report, pp.1-2.
51. Ibid., pp. 2-4.
52. Ibid., p. 5.
53. Ibid., pp. 3-4.
54. Interview with Walter Minnick.
55. 118A Network Report, p. 6.
56. Ibid., p. 5.
57. World Drug Traffic and its Impact on US Security, pp. 36-48.
58. Correspondence with Fred Dick.
59. Correspondence with Fred Dick.
60. Interview with Walter Minnick.
61. *New York Times*, June 26, 1971, p. 2: while a general in Vietnam, Cushman began an antinarcotic drive in the Delta in June 1971.
62. Interviews with Bill Logay and Tully Acampora.
63. *Diplomatic War*, p. 10.
64. 118A Network Report, p. 1.
65. *Diplomatic War*, pp. 8, 11.
66. *Diplomatic War*, pp. 9-12.
67. Correspondence with Fred Dick.
68. 536 F.2d 993 UNITED STATES of America, Plaintiff-Appellee, v.Victor LEONG et al., Defendants-Appellants. Nos. 973, 981 and 972, Dockets 76-1001, 76-1006 and 76-1016. United States Court of Appeals, Second Circuit. Argued April 29, 1976.
69. Correspondence with Thomas de Trinquet.
70. Interviews with numerous sources.

Chapter 15: New York, New York
1. Gregory Wallance, *Papa's Game* (New York: Rawson, Wade Publishers, Inc., 1981), pp. 14-17.
2. Wallance, *Papa's Game*, p. 21.
3. Ibid., p. 28.
4. Ibid., p. 16.
5. Ibid., p. 111.
6. Ibid., pp. 49—50.
7. Ibid., pp. 219-222.
8. Ibid., p. 111.
9. Ibid., pp. 122-24.
10. Ibid., pp. 132-33, 222, 236.
11. Ibid., pp. 98-9.
12. Interviews with Tom Taylor and Ike Wurms.
13. "Murder of Narcotics Informants on Rise, Law Authorities Report," *New York Times*, March 3, 1970.

14. *New York Times*, April 3, April 22, June 7, 1970.
15. Interview with Andy Tartaglino.
16. Tripodi, *Crusade*, p. 205.
17. Wallance, *Papa's Game*, p. 27.
18. Interviews with Tom Tripodi, Tom Taylor and Ike Wurms.
19. Interview with Tom Taylor. *Papa's Game*, pp. 106-108.
20. Robert Leuci, *All the Centurions: A New York City Cop Remembers His Years on the Street, 1961-1981* (New York: Harper Collins, 2004). Wallance, *Papa's Game*, p. 102.
21. Interview with Tom Taylor.
22. Leuci, *All the Centurions*, pp. 217-222.
23. Interview witth Frankie Waters and other FBN agents.
24. Interview with Frankie Waters.
25. Interview with Andy Tartaglino.
26. Rockefeller Commission Report, pp. 239, 297.
27. Interview with Nelson Brickham.
28. Interview with Andy Tartaglino.
29. Charbonneau, *Canadian Connection*, p. 461.
30. Interviews with Clarence Cook and John O'Brien. 475FF.2d 832, US v Elvin Lee Bynum et al.
31. Interview with Tom Taylor.
32. Interview with John O'Brien.
33. Interview with John Thompson.
34. Interviews with several BNDD agents.
35. Interviews with Tom Taylor, Andy Tartaglino, and numerous BNDD agents.
36. Joanne Bario, *Fatal Dreams* (Garden City NY: Dial Press/Doubleday & Company, Inc., 1985) for Santo Bario's life story.
37. Interviews with Mike Picini and Andy Tartaglino
38. Interview with Ted Hunter.
39. Interview with Bill Hansen.
40. Interview with David Wiser.
41. Interview with Clarence Cook.
42. Interviews with Bob Leuci and Clarence Cook.
43. Wallance, *Papa's Game*, p. 112.
44. Interview with Tom Taylor.
45. Interview with Chares Vopat.
46. Interview with Morty Benjamin.
47. Wallance, *Papa's Game*, p. 110.
48. Interviews with agents on the scene.
49. Interview with Tom Taylor.
50. Interview with John Thompson.
51. Interview with Tom Taylor.

52. Robert Daly, *Prince of the City: the True Story of a Cop Who Knew Too Much* (Boston: Houghton Mifflin Company, 1978), p. 109.
53. Interview with Andy Tartaglino.
54. Interviews with Vincent Nardiello, James Rothstein, and Dee Fernandez.
55. Robin Moore, *The Country Team* (New York: Crown Publishers, 1967), p.114.
56. Moore, *Country Team*, p. 188-189.
57. Robin Moore with Barbara Fuca, *Mafia Wife* (New York: Macmillan Publishing Co., Inc., 1977), p. 121.
58. Interview with Mike Powers.
59. Interview with TomTripodi.
60. Interview with Tom Taylor.
61. Wallance, *Papa's Game*, pp. 222, 272.

Chapter 16: Capitol Capers

1. Keith W Olson, *Watergate: The Presidential Scandal That Shook America* (Kansas: University Press of Kansas, 2003), p. 38.
2. Olson, *Watergate*, p. 39.
3. http://www.gwu.edu/~nsarchiv/NSAEBB/NSAEBB222/family_jewels_pt3_ocr.pdf. William V Broe, IG, to William Colby, review of minutes of morning meetings, May 31, 1973.
4. Olson, *Watergate*, p. 39.
5. The June 23, 1972 Nixon-Haldeman Transcript (1:04-1:13 PM), The Staff of the *New York Times, The End of A Presidency*, (New York: Bantam Books, Inc, 1974), p. 331.
6. H.R. Haldeman with Joseph Dimona, *The Ends of Power* (New York: Times Books, 1978), p. 39.
7. Moldea, *Hoffa Wars*, 387, citing Charles Crimaldi.
8. CIA Memorandum for the Record, Subject: Report on Plots to Assassinate Fidel Castro, May 23, 1967.
9. CIA Employee Bulletin 359, "DDCI Statement About The Watergate Case," May 21, 1975.
10. Moldea, *Hoffa Wars*, 7.
11. CIA Memorandum for the Record, Subject: Report on Plots to Assassinate Fidel Castro, 23 May 1967. See also Watergate 1: The Evidence to Date, *Time*, Aug. 20, 1973. *Richard Helms, A Look Over My Shoulder: A Life in the Central Intelligence Agency* (New York: Random House, 2003).
12. Olson, *Watergate*, p. 47.
13. Peter Dale Scott, "Deep Politics: Some Further Thoughts," from the Preface to the 1996 edition of *Deep Politics and the Death of JFK* (Berkeley: University of California Press) (note 10, citing Dick Russell, *The Man Who Knew Too Much*, p. 239), p. 11.

14. Jefferson Morley, "LITEMPO: The CIA's Eyes on Tlatelolco," National Security Archive Electronic Briefing Book No. 204, Posted - October 18, 2006.

15. Valentine, *Strength of the Wolf*, 71-72: The drug conspiracy had its inception in 1939 when, at Meyer Lansky's request, Virginia Hill moved to Mexico and according to Ed Reid, *The Mistress and the Mafia: The Virginia Hill Story* (New York: Bantam Books, 1972), p. 42, seduced a number of Mexico's "top politicians, army officers, diplomats, and police officials." Hill's partner in this venture, Dr Margaret Chung, was an agent of the Kuomintang and member of the Flying Tigers, an airline used by the US to fly supplies to the opium-smuggling Nationalist Chinese in WWII. The FBN, according to Reid (Reid, *Hill*, p. 90) knew that Chung was "in the narcotic traffic in San Francisco." And yet, despite the fact that the FBN agents "kept her under constant surveillance for years," they "were never able to make a case against her." The CIA protected this network after 1947.

16. Interview with Tulius Acampora.

17. CIA Employee Bulletin 359, "DDCI Statement About The Watergate Case," May 21, 1975.

18. Haldeman, *Ends of Power*, pp. 133-5.

19. Olson, *Watergate*, pp. 39-40.

20. Interview with Janet Ray Weininger and notes provide by Weininger citing a CIA historical interview with Jacob Esterline, conducted in November 1975 upon his retirement. Esterline was the CIA operations chief who oversaw the Bay of Pigs invasion.

21. Dick Russell. *The Man Who Knew Too Much*. New York: Carroll & Graf Publishers/R. Gallen, 1992, 261 (citing a passage from Hunt's novel, *The Berlin Ending*).

22. Haldeman, *Ends of Power*, p. 109.

23. Ibid., p. 117.

24. Ibid., p. 142.

25. Interview with Ralph Frias.

26. John Ehrlichman, *Witness to Power: the Nixon Years* (New York: Simon and Schuster, 1982), note p. 399.

27. Michael C Jensen, "Chilean Break-ins Puzzle Watergate Investigators," *New York Times*, May 29, 1973.

28. E. Howard Hunt, *Undercover, Memoirs of an American Secret Agent* (New York: Berkeley Pub. Corp, 1974), p. 185.

29. Wallance, *Papa's Game*, pp. 151-158,

30. Epstein, *Agency of Fear*, p. 205.

31. Interview with Thomas Clines.

32. Peter Dale Scott and Jonathan Marshall. *Cocaine Politics: Drugs, Armies, and the CIA in Central America* (Berkeley: University of California Press, 1991), p. 220 n. 38. Interview with Thomas Clines.

33. Weininger notes citing a CIA historical interview with Esterline.
34. Interview with Thomas Clines.
35. Jonathan Marshall, "The White House Death Squad," *Inquiry*, March 5, 1979, p. 17.
36. Correspondence with Len Colodny.
37. Interview with Richard Bly.
38. George Crile III, "The Colonel's Secret Drug War," *Washington Post*, June 13, 1976, p. C1.
39. Marshall, "The White House Death Squad," p. 18.
40. Ibid., p. 17.
41. *Project Pilot III*, p. 311-324.
42. *Project Pilot III*, p. 316.
43. Executive Intelligence Review, Dope, Inc., *The Book That Drove Henry Kissinger Crazy*. June 1992, pp. 462-463 re: Ambassador, see also pp. 21, 107, 168, and 497 re Lansky and Rosenbaum.
44. DeFeo Report, citing memo from John Doyle re Customs indictment of Moises, 5-9-72.
45. Marshall, "The White House Death Squad," p. 16.
46. David Corn, *Blond Ghost: Ted Shackley and the CIA's Crusades* (New York: Simon & Schuster, 1994), p. 256.
47. Kruger, *Great Heroin Coup*, pp. 162-3.
48. Tad Sultz, *Compulsive Spy: the Strange Career of Howard Hunt* (New York: Viking Press, 1974), p. 145
49. Interview with Jerry Strickler.
50. Interviews with John Bacon and John Warner.
51. Marshall, "The White House Death Squad," p. 16. Interview with John Bacon.
52. Ibid., p. 18.
53. DeFeo Report, citing March 16, 1972 CIA cable re: Torrijos reaction to US press report re Moises, and May 23, 1972. Tartaglino to Ingersoll re Moises Torrijos.
54. S.D. Breckenridge, Memorandum for the Record, "DDI 'Trap' On Leaks of Narcotics Intelligence," May 26, 1973.
55. Corn, *Blond Ghost*, 260.
56. Jim Hougan, *Spooks: The Haunting of America* (New York: Bantam Books, 1979), pp. 215-225.
57. Ibid., p. 224.
58. Ibid., p. 224.
59. Ibid., p. 224.
60. Ibid., p. 221.
61. Jaubert, *Dossier D*, p. 163-168.
62. Hougan, *Spooks*, p. 213, see also *Project Pilot III*, p. 551-557.
63. Ibid., p. 221.
64. Ibid., p. 221.

65. Kruger, *Great Heroin Coup*, p. 183.
66. Hougan, *Spooks*, pp. 231-232.
67. *Time*, April 1, 1974.
68. Peter Brewton, *The Mafia The CIA and George Bush* (New York: S.P.I. Books, 1992), p. 297.
69. Hougan, *Secret Agenda*, pp. 312-313. cf. Scott, *Deep Politics*, p. 378.
70. Interview and correspondence with Len Colodny author with Robert Gettlin of *Silent Coup: The Removal of a president* (New York: St. Martin's Press)
71. Correspondence with John Dean.
72. Robert Stutman, and Richard Esposito, *Dead on Delivery: Inside the Drug Wars, Straight from the Street* (New York: Warner Books, 1992), p. 97.
73. Correspondence with John Dean.
74. Stanley Karnow, *Vietnam, A History* (New York: Viking Press, 1983), p. 634.
75. Finlator, *Drugged Nation*, pp. 106-109; Interview with Steve Greene.
76. Undated, unsigned document provided by John Warner.

Chapter 17: Covert Intelligence

1. Two Special Agents to Andrew Tartaglino, "Project BUNCIN: Summary, September 1972-March 1973," March 12, 1973 (hereafter known as "BUNCIN Summary"). BUNCIN, DEACON, and documents related to DEA covert intelligence operations, and complied by a DEA "study team" appointed by Henry Dogin, were obtained by the National Organization for Reform of Marijuana Laws under a Freedom of Information Act request by John Hill (The Hill Collection) and provided to the author by John Kelly.
2. Special Agents William Logay and Robert Medell to Andrew Tartaglino, Deputy Director for Operations, "Project BUNCIN — Operational Plan," November 2, 1972, p. 2 (The Hill Collection).
3. Ibid.
4. Alan A Bock and John C McWilliams "On the Origins of American Counterintelligence: Building a Clandestine Network," *Journal of Policy History*, Vl. 1, No. 4, University Park, Pennsylvania State University Press, 1989, pp. 361-369.
5. "Annex A — BUNCIN/DEACON Mission Definition (SEC-IGO-75-0003)," citing December 20, 1972 letter from John Ingersoll to DOD Chief Counsel Buzhardt (The Hill Collection). Special Agents to Andrew Tartaglino, Deputy Director for Operations, "Project BUNCIN — Operational Plan," November 29, 1972, p. 3 (The Hill Collection).
6. "BUNCIN Summary" (The Hill Collection).

7. "Development of Covert Collection Techniques in Drug Law Enforcement, The Experimental Operation" (The Hill Collection).
8. Development of Covert Collection techniques in Drug Operations, Background, 23 pages undated unsigned (but completed by the DEA "study team" appointed by Henry Dogin), plus summary of IGO Projects (The Hill Collection).
9. Interviews with John Ingersoll, Andrew Tartaglino, Robert Medell and William Logay.
10. Interview with Tom Tripodi.
11. Interviews with Rich Kobakoff and Bob Medell.
12. Interview with Rich Kobakoff.
13. Interview with Bob Medell.
14. Special Agent (redacted) to Andrew C. Tartaglino, Deputy Director for Operations, Minutes of Meeting, March 13, 1973, Re: Project BUNCIN - Summary, March 14 1973 (The Hill Collection).
15. Interview with Pat Fuller.
16. "Development of Covert Collection Techniques in Drug Law Enforcement, The Experimental Operation," p. 17 (The Hill Collection).
17. Ibid.
18. Project BUNCIN Proposed Budget for FY 1974 (The Hill Collection).
19. Special Agent (redacted) to Andrew C. Tartaglino, Deputy Director for Operations, Minutes of Meeting, March 13, 1973, Re: Project BUNCIN - Summary, March 14, 1973 (The Hill Collection).
20. "BUNCIN Summary" (The Hill Collection).
21. Interview with Bob Medell.
22. Scott, *Cocaine Politics*, p. 29. The Alvarez Cruz network later joined the contra supply apparatus for George H.W. Bush.
23. Interview with Bob Medell.
24. Interview with Grayston Lynch.
25. Interview with Bob Medell.
26. Interview with Thomas Clines.
27. Interview with Jerry Strickler. George Crile III, "The Informant Who Jumped Bail," *Washington Post*, June 13, 1976.
28. Interview with Jerry Strickler.
29. Ibid.
30. Interview with Bob Medell.
31. Interview with William Logay.
32. Interview with Tom Hurney.
33. Interviews with Howie Safir, Vic Maria and Paul Knight.
34. Interview with Paul Knight.
35. US Department of Justice, Drug Enforcement Administration, "Drug Enforcement Administration: A tradition of Excellence," 1973-2003, p. 20.

36. DeFeo Report, pp. 3-5.
37. Interview with Robert Peloquin.
38. DeFeo Report, pp. 3-5.
39. Ibid.
40. Ibid.
41. Alan A Block, *Masters of Paradise, Organized Crime and the Internal Revenue Service in the Bahamas* (New Jersey: Transaction Publishers, 1991), p. 70, see also pp. 48-9, 66-70, 81-84, 100-103, 161-179.
42. Interview with Andy Tartaglino.
43. "Comprehensive Briefing Book for the White House, Attachment 1," undated unsigned document provided by John Warner.
44. Robert W. Goe, Acting Assistant Director for Strategic Intelligence to Andrew Tartaglino, Deputy Director for Operations, "Status of Strategic Intelligence Workload," January 19, 1973; and John Warner, Assistant Director for Strategic Intelligence to Andrew C. Tartaglino, Deputy Director for operations, Status of Strategic Intelligence Workload, April 16, 1973 (Warner document).
45. "Comprehensive briefing Book for the White House" (undated, unsigned Warner document).
46. Interview with Richard Blum.
47. Interview with Andrew C. Tartaglino.
48. Interview with Richard Blum.
49. Interview with Rich Kobakoff.
50. Interview with John Warner.

Chapter 18: The Parallel Mechanism

1. Gerard F. Carrey, Group Supervisor to Daniel P. Casey, Regional Director, "Proposal of a Special South American Task Force," October 24, 1972.
2. Interview with Gerry Carey.
3. Gerry Carey, "Status Report for Operation Springboard," June 1, 1973.
4. *Project Pilot III*, pp. 180, 219, 322, 607, 630.
5. *Project Pilot III*, p. 513.
6. Interview with Jerry Strickler.
7. *Project Pilot III*, p. 579.
8. Interview with Jerry Strickler.
9. Kruger, *Great Heroin Coup*, p. 107.
10. *Project Pilot III*, pp. 180, 581. Interview with BNDD agent.
11. Ibid., p. 238.
12. Interview with Jerry Strickler.
13. Howard Marks, "Extradition, US Drug Policy and the Erosion of Individual Liberties," undated monograph, citing USA v Toscanino, No. 746, Docket No. 73-2732.

14. Interview with Jerry Strickler; *Canadian Connection*, pp. 451-454.
15. Interview with Jerry Strickler; *Heroin Trail*, pp. 153-156.
16. *Project Pilot III*, pp. 329-332; John J Coleman, "Investigation Conducted to Date re: Testimony of Claude Pastou, April 5-May 14, 1973, Statement of Claude Pastou," May 15, 1973, p. 17.
17. *Project Pilot III*, p. 180.
18. Kruger, *Great Heroin Coup*, pp. 51-56, 70.
19. Ibid., p. 108.
20. Anthony S. Pohl, Deputy Associate Regional Director to Frank Monastero Associate Regional Director "Interview of Defendant Christian DAVID," November 28, 1972. Kruger, *Great Heroin Coup*, p. 71, re CIA.
21. Anthony S. Pohl, Deputy Associate Regional Director to Frank Monastero Associate Regional Director "Interview of Defendant Christian DAVID," November 28, 1972.
22. Ibid.
23. Ibid.
24. Interview with John Bacon.
25. Interview with Jerry Strickler.
26. Ibid.
27. Ibid.
28. Ibid.
29. Ibid.
30. James Mills, *The Underground Empire: Where Crime and Governments Embrace* (New York, Doubleday & Company, Inc 1986), pp. 358, 363, 550.
31. Kruger, *Great Heroin Coup*, pp. 177-180.
32. Interview with Jerry Strickler.
33. Epsrein, *Agency of Fear*, p. 143.
34. Ibid., p. 144.
35. Ibid., p. 159.
36. Marshall, "The White House Death Squad," p. 16.
37. Interview with J Thomas Ungerleider, MD.
38. Interview with Joseph DiGennaro.
39. Ibid.
40. Ibid.
41. Interview with Joe Quarequio.
42. Interview with Joseph DiGennaro.
43. Ibid.
44. Interview with Gerry Carey.
45. Interview with Joseph DiGennaro.
46. Interview with John Ingersoll.
47. Interviews with persons knowledgeable about Seymour Bolten and his activities.

48. Interview with Tulius Acampora.
49. Ibid.
50. Interview with Paul Knight.

Chapter 19: Myles to Go
  1. Interview with Myles Ambrose.
  2. Pete Brewton, *The Mafia, The CIA and George Bush* (New York, S.P.I. Books, 1992), p. 155.
  3. Scott, *Cocaine Politics*, p. 98.
  4. Brewton, *Mafia, The CIA and George Bush*, p 155.
  5. Ibid., pp. 155-6.
  6. Ibid., p. 156.
  7. Ibid., p. 157.
  8. Interviews with Arthur Sedillo and Caesar Diosdado.
  9. Brewton, *Mafia, The CIA and George Bush*, p. 157.
 10. Interviews with Arthur Sedillo and Caesar Diosdado
 11. Brewton, *Mafia, The CIA and George Bush*, p. 157.
 12. Correspondence and interview with Arthur Sedillo.
 13. Interviews with Caesar Diosdado and David Ellis.
 14. Brewton, *Mafia, The CIA and George Bush*, p. 155.
 15. Wallance, *Papa's Game*, pp. 184-187: four SIU members of the Strike Force were selling information. *New York Times*, November 11, 1972.
 16. Interviews with Arthur Sedillo and Caesar Diosdado.
 17. Blumenthal, *Last Days of the Sicilians*, pp. 84, 87.
 18. Interview with William Hughes.
 19. Ibid.
 20. Interview with Myles Ambrose.
 21. Al Weberman, Nodule 10 (http://www.ajweberman.com/nodules2/nodulec10.htm) citing Peter Dale Scott.
 22. Brewton, *Mafia, The CIA and George Bush*, p. 158.
 23. Ibid.
 24. Interview with William Hughes.
 25. Interview with Dave Ellis. See: January 20, 1978 House Select Committee on Assassinations request for information from the CIA's Central Cover Staff for information on Caesar Diosdado, David Christ (who in 1970 went to work for the CIA proprietary company, Devenco, for whom Ambrose had worked for in the early 1950s), Louis Posada, David A. Phillips and Lucien E Conein.
 26. Interview with Walter Minnick.
 27. Interview with Customs agent.
 28. Interview with Myles Ambrose.
 29. Interview with Bill Hughes.
 30. Interview with John Ingersoll.

31. Ibid.
32. Interview with Ken Bloemker.
33. "In The Name of The Law," *Time*, 14 May 1973; 1975 Jackson Hearings, 18.
34. 563 F.2d 343, 2 Fed. R. Evid. Serv. 746 John MEINERS, Plaintiff-Appellant, Cross-Appellee, v, Dennis MORIARITY et al., Defendants-Appellees, Cross-Appellants. Nos. 76-1730, 76-1731. United States Court of Appeals, Seventh Circuit. Argued April 18, 1977. Decided Oct. 6, 1977.
35. Interview with Ken Bloemker.
36. James B Balakar and Lester Grinspoon. *Drug Control In A Free Society.* Cambridge University Press, New Ed edition 1988, pp. 110-111.
37. Interview with Walter Minnick.
38. Ibid.
39. *Bolten Interview.*
40. Interview with Anthony Pohl. See also Stephen Del Corvo, Bill Erwin, Michal Fooner, *Blue Domino.* New York: G P Putnam's Sons; Adams, "Night of the Big Drug Bust," *Reader's Digest,* for a complete account of the case.
41. Interviews with Tony Pohl and Myles Ambrose.
42. Interview with Dan Casey. "Indict 86 as Big Dope Dealers," *New York Daily News,* April 17, 19973, pp. 1, 3, 39, 42-43. John Corey, "City-US Raid Net 65 Reputed Narcotics Dealers," *New York Times,* April 17, 1973, pp. 1, 37.
43. Interview with Tony Pohl.
44. Interviews with Pat Fuller and John Warner.
45. Interview with Fred Dick.
46. Indicted in New Jersey in 1973 on tax fraud and perjury charges, Gross would resign in 1973 and be replaced by former US Ambassador to Turkey, William Handley, who was fired in 1974 and replaced by Sheldon B Vance. Gross served six months in prison in 1976 and was murdered in September 1997. Ronald Smothers, "2 Are Given Up to 30 Years In Murder of a Millionaire," *New York Tines,* October 8, 1998; and Robert Hanley, "Nelson Gross, Prominent State Republican, Is Missing," *New York Times,* September 20, 1997.
47. *New York Times,* "Drug Unit Chief Resigns, Assailing Ex-Nixon Aides," June 30, 1973.

Chapter 20: The DEA
1. Interview with John Ingersoll.
2. Interview with Myles Ambrose.
3. Interview with Walter Minnick.
4. Interview with John Bartels.

5. DEA Roster, Personnel Currently Assigned to Headquarters," December 1973.
6. Interview with Andy Tartaglino.
7. Interview with John Evans.
8. Interview with Bruce Jensen.
9. Interview with John Enright.
10. Ibid.
11. Interview with John Evans.
12. Interview with Andy Tartaglino.
13. 1975 Jackson Hearings, p. 533.
14. Interview with John Bartels.
15. Interview with Andy Tartaglino.
16. Interviews with Andy Tartaglino and George Brosan.
17. Douglas Kinder, "Bureaucratic Cold Warrior: Harry J. Anslinger and Illicit Narcotics Traffic," Pacific Coast Branch, American Historical Association, *Pacific Historical Review*, 1981, pp. 172-3.
18. A J Languth, *Hidden Terrors* (Pantheon Books, 1978). Section 660 of the Foreign Assistance Act.
19. John Warner, Chairman, Domestic Intelligence Subcommittee to John R Bartels, Chairman, DEA Intelligence Committee, Report of Domestic Intelligence Subcommittee, plus attachments: 1: Intelligence Needs and Functions; 2, Functional Operations; 3, Geographical Organization; and 4, Unresolved Issues;" plus tabs for the Office of Foreign Intelligence, a Position Paper on US Customs Intelligence Needs As Related to DEA, Intelligence Needs of the INS with Respect to Illicit Drugs, the Office of Domestic Intelligence, the Office of Special Projects, Office of Information Systems, and Operational Intelligence Module," May 15, 1973 (Warner document.)
20. Tom Peters, Deputy Chief, International Narcotics Control, Federal Drug management Division, Executive Office of the President, Office of Management and budget (OMB) to John Bartels re: DEA Intel Org. May 31, 1973. Attached were May 23, 1973 Report of the Foreign Intelligence Group of the Intelligence Subcommittee and the May 29, 1973 Report of the Foreign Intelligence Group of the Intelligence Subcommittee, Summary and Recommendations (with organizational charts) (Warner document).
21. John Warner, Assistant Director for Strategic Intelligence, "The Role of Intelligence in Narcotic and Drug Law Enforcement," April 1973.
22. Intelligence Division Roster, 1973 (Warner document)
23. Belk, acting Deputy AAI to Warner, acting chief foreign Intel, re Foreign intelligence Programs," August 20, 1973 PRC mentioned.
24. John R. Bartels, Notice, "Regional Intelligence Operations (with attachments)," February 21, 1974 (Warner document).

25. Interagency Drug Intelligence Group—Mexico (Warner document, undated, unsigned)
26. Interviews with John Warner and Richard Blum. Appendix D, Description of Special Operations and Field Support Projects (The Hill Collection).
27. Gabriel Dukas, Chief Western Section to Phillip Smith, Chief, Domestic Intelligence Division, "Subcommittee Report — Mission and Function," October 18, 1973.
28. Recommendations For the Establishment of a Special Operations Staff and Clandestine Intelligence Field units, November 19, 1973, unsigned (The Hill Collection).
29. Interviews with Morty Benjamin and George Brosan.
30. Interview with DEA Agent.
31. Interview with Jerry Strickler.
32. Interview with Tom Clines.
33. Interview with Jerry Strickler.
34. Ibid.
35. Ibid.
36. Ibid.
37. McCoy, *Politics of Heroin*, pp. 461-78.
38. Interview with Jerry Strickler.
39. John Burgess, "The Thailand Connection," *Counterspy*, Vol. 2, No. 4, 1976, pp. 31-3
40. Corn, *Blond Ghost*, p. 300.
41. Interview with Raymond I. Coffey.
42. Burgess, "The Thailand Connection," p. 33.
43. McCoy, *Politics of Heroin*, p. 341.
44. Interview with Ron Metcalf.
45. Correspondence with Fred Dick.
46. Burgess, "The Thailand Connection," p. 33.
47. John Marks, "The CIA's Corporate Shell Game," *Washington Post*, July 11, 1976, cited in Philip Agee; Louis Wolf (Ed.), *Dirty Work: The CIA in Western Europe* (New York, Lyle Stuart, 1978), p. 132.
48. Christopher Robbins, *Air America* (New York: Avon Books, 1985), p. 242.
49. Corn, *Blond Ghost*, p. 300.
50. Burgess, "The Thailand Connection," p. 33.
51. Correspondence with Joe Lagattuta.
52. Interview with Ray Coffey.
53. Agency for International Development Negotiated Contract No. AID 493-559, May 30, 1973.
54. Mills, *Underground Empire*, p. 780.
55. Interview with Ray Coffey.
56. Ibid.

57. Mills, *Underground Empire*, p. 780.
58. Interview with Gordon Young.
59. *Project Pilot III*, p. 386.
60. Staff Study of the Frank Peroff Case, Permanent Subcommittee on Investigations, March 1975, 94th Congress, first session, (Washington, DC, GAO), (Hereafter known as Peroff Staff Study), p. 35.
61. Peroff Staff Study, p. 90.
62. Ibid., p. 175.
63. Ibid., p. 176.
64. Ibid., p. iv.
65. Interview with Bruce Matre.

Chapter 21: The Dirty Dozen

1. Phillip R Smith Acting Deputy Assistant Administrator for Intelligence to George M Belk, Acting Assistant Administrator for Intelligence, July 19, 1973, "DEACON I: Drug Enforcement Administration Clandestine Operations Network (SEC-SI-73-2506)."
2. Part 1 Development of Covert Collection techniques in Drug Operations, Background, 23 pages undated unsigned, plus summary of IGO Projects.
3. Phillip R Smith Acting Deputy Assistant Administrator for Intelligence to George M Belk, Acting Assistant Administrator for Intelligence, July 19, 1973, "DEACON I: Drug Enforcement Administration Clandestine Operations Network (SEC-SI-73-2506)," p. 2.
4. Development of Covert Collection techniques in Drug Operations, Background, 23 pages undated unsigned, plus summary of IGO Projects.
5. Phillip R Smith Acting Deputy Assistant Administrator for Intelligence to George M Belk, Acting Assistant Administrator for Intelligence, July 19, 1973, "DEACON I: Drug Enforcement Administration Clandestine Operations Network (SEC-SI-73-2506)," p. 3.
6. John R Bartels, Jr, Administrator to All Personnel, 4 January 1974.
7. Development of Covert Collection techniques in Drug Operations, Background, 23 pages undated unsigned, plus summary of IGO Projects, p. 4.
8. John Bartels, DEA Notice, Special Field Intelligence Programs, March 19, 1974. Portions of the DeFeo Report were leaked to the *Village Voice* and passed to the author by John Kelly.
9. March 19, 1974, John Bartels, Notice, Special Field Intelligence Programs.
10. Development of Covert Collection techniques in Drug Operations, Background, 23 pages undated unsigned, plus summary of IGO Projects, p. 4.
11. Ibid., p. 5.

12. John Warner, NIO Program document, undated, unsigned.
14. Interview with Elias Chavez.
15. Interviews with Wes Dyckman, Lou Davis, Hugh Murray, and Chris Thompson.
16. Interviews with Gary Mattocks, Terry Baldwin and Joe Lagattuta.
17. Development of Covert Collection techniques in Drug Operations, Background, 23 pages undated unsigned, plus summary of IGO Projects, p. 9.
18. Ibid., p. 11.
19. Ibid., p. 12.
20. Ibid., p. 12.
21. Mooncake Case file, obtained April 11, 1994, through FOIA request 94-0028-F.
22. Seven John Does v. Office of Personnel Management, Merit System Protection Board Docket Nos. DA083188110337 and DC083181105596, Closing Brief.
23. Overall Assessment of Project DEACON I, December 2, 1974, unsigned 14 page report with appendices and charts.
24. DEACON I (Miami): Mission and Resource Requirements, undated, unsigned.
25. Scott, *Cocaine Politics*, p. 28.
26. Interview with a DEA agent and Robert Medell.
27. Scott, *Cocaine Politics*, p. 28, citing December 2, 1974 Overall Assessment of Project DEACON I. See also Progress Report, January 11, 1974, sabotage of Bahamian freighter M/V MEREGHAN II.
28. December 2, 1974 Overall Assessment of Project DEACON I, p. 6.
29. Interview with Bill Logay.
30. Interview with Cecilia Plicet.
31. Special Agent IGO to Lucien E Conein, Acting Chief IGO, "DEACON I — Security," June 1974.
32. Ibid., p. 12
33. Interview with Gary Mattocks. Jefferson Morley, "Barry and his city: crack in the Washington culture," *The Nation*, February 19, 1990, pp. 14-20. Frank Cerabino, "Elder Tabraue gets mistrial," *Miami Herald*, January 24, 1989, p. 3B.
34. Interview with Bob Medell.
35. Ibid., p. 4. Interview with Gary Mattocks. See also: Special Agent IGO to Narcotic Intelligence Officer, DEACON I, "Guidelines re recruitment and utilization of assets," July 1, 1974; and Special Agent IGO to Narcotic Intelligence Officer, DEACON I, "Guidelines re Duties of Narcotics Intelligence Officer," July 1, 1974.
36. Interview with Gary Mattocks.
37. Ibid.

38. Interview with Tom Clines.
39. Interview with Gary Mattocks.
40. Affidavit of Daniel P. Sheehan, filed December 12, 1986, revised January 31, 1987.
41. Overall Assessment of Project DEACON I, December 2, 1974 (undated unsigned).
42. Seven John Does v Office of Personnel Management, Initial Decision by Edward J Reidy, Administrative Law Judge, May 20, 1982, p. 5. Document provided by Eli Chavez. Interviews with Gary Mattocks and Robert Medell.
43. Interview with Gary Mattocks.
44. Lucien E. Conein to Michael D. Brom, SAIC, DEACON-I, "Role of DEACON I — Narcotics Intelligence Collection," January 22, 1975.
45. Interview with Eli Chavez.
46. George Belk, Assistant Administrator for Intelligence and Mark Moore Chief Office of Planning and Evaluation Background Establishment of a Clandestine Collection Gathering effort Within DEA, October 8, 1974 with appendixes, one listing all DEACONs.
47. Interview with Eli Chavez.
48. Interview with Barry Carew.
49. Interviews with Barry Carew, Eli Chavez and other DEA agents.
50. Interview with Eli Chavez.
51. Interview with Lou Davis.
52. Utility, Function and coordination of Intelligence undated unsigned (Warner document).
53. Lucien E Conein to files, Intelligence Collection programs, with attachment on Special Operations and Field Support Staff, February 3, 1975.
54. Interviews with Louis Davis and several other members of the Dirty Dozen.
55. Interview with Wes Dyckman.
56. Interview with Luke Benson.
57. DeFeo Report, summary, p. 9.
58. Hougan, Spooks, pp. 123-124. Lawrence Meyer, "DEA Was Offered Explosive Devices," Washington Post, January 23, 1975, p. A3.
59. Interview with John Muldoon.
60. Lawrence Meyer, "DEA Was Offered Explosive Devices," Washington Post, January 23, 1975, p. A3.
61. Kruger, Great Heroin Coup, 182.
62. Ibid., pp. 184-5.
63. Interview with Wes Dyckman.
64. Interview with Paul Knight.
65. Interview with John Bacon.
66. April 30, 1974 Smith memo to Conein, cited in DeFeo Report, p. 5.
67. Interview with Robert Medell. DeFeo Report, pp. 5-7.

68. DeFeo Report, p. 7.
69. George Belk, Assistant Administrator for Intelligence and Mark Moore Chief Office of Planning and Evaluation Background Establishment of a Clandestine Collection Gathering effort Within DEA, October 8, 1974 with appendixes, one listing all DEACONs.

Chapter 22: The Serpent in My Garden
1. Interview with George Brosan.
2. 1975 Jackson Hearings, p. 194.
3. Ibid., 191-192. Interview with George Brosan.
4. Ibid., 145. 1976 Jackson Hearings, p. 96.
5. 1975 Jackson Hearings, p. 193. Interview with George Brosan.
6. 1975 Jackson Hearings, p. 193-194. DeFeo Report, p. 12-14.
7. 1975 Jackson Hearings, p. 195.
8. Ibid., p. 196.
9. 1976 Jackson Hearings, pp. 76- 82.
10. Interview with Vincent Promuto.
11. 1976 Jackson Hearings, p. 83.
12. Interview with Carl Shoffler.
13. 1976 Jackson Hearings, p. 83.
14. Ibid., pp. 95-96.
15. Ibid., p. 85.
16. Ibid., p. 94.
17. 1976 Jackson Hearings, p. 96.
18. Ibid., p. 144.
19. 1975 Jackson Hearings, p. 146.
20. 1976 Jackson Hearings, pp. 141-142.
21. 1975 Jackson Hearings, p. 226.
22. Interview with John Bartels.
23. 1976 Jackson Hearings, p. 109.
24. 1975 Jackson Hearings, p. 153.
25. 1976 Jackson Hearings, pp. 84-87.
26. Interview with Andy Tartaglino.
27. 1975 Jackson Hearings, p. 196.
28. 1976 Jackson Hearings, p. 92.
29. Interview with Bruce Jensen.
30. 1976 Jackson Hearings, pp. 104-105.
31. Ibid., p. 102.
32. 1975 Jackson Hearings, pp. 230-231.
33. 1976 Jackson Hearings, p. 104.
34. Interview with Andy Tartaglino.
35. Interviews with George Brosan and Andy Tartaglino. 1975 Jackson Hearings, pp. 355-356.
36. 1975 Jackson Hearings, pp. 354-355.

37. 1976 Jackson Hearings, p. 88.
38. Ibid., 101-102.
39. 1976 Jackson Hearings, p. 111. 1975 Jackson Hearings, p. 566.
40. 1975 Jackson Hearings, pp. 201-202, 386, 392; 1976 Jackson Hearings, p. 113.
41. 1976 Jackson Hearings, p. 114.
42. 1975 Jackson Hearings, p. 202.
43. Ibid., p. 391.
44. Ibid., p. 147.
45. Ibid., p. 392.
46. Ibid., p. 392.
47. Ibid., pp. 207-209.
48. Ibid., pp. 116-117.
49. Ibid., pp. 388, 208-209.
50. Ibid., p. 208.
51. 1976 Jackson Hearings, p. 122.
52. Interview with Andy Tartaglino.
53. 1975 Jackson Hearings, pp. 211-212.
54. 1976 Jackson Hearings, pp. 122-3.
55. Ibid., p. 124.
56. Interview with John Bartels. 1976 Jackson Hearings, p. 126.
57. 1976 Jackson Hearings, pp. 126-7.
58. Gary Sick, *New York Times*, April 15, 1991.
59. 1975 Jackson Hearings, p. 718.
60. Ibid., pp. 721, 724-725.
61. Ibid., p. 721.
62. 1976 Jackson Hearings, pp. 128-131.
63. Ibid., p. 131.
64. Ibid., pp. 129-132.
65. Ibid., pp. 133-4.
66. Interview with Andy Tartaglino.
67. Interview with George Brosan.
68. 1975 Jackson Hearings, p. 730.
69. Ibid., pp. 726, 733.
70. 1976 Jackson Hearings, p. 134.
71. Ibid., pp. 134-136.
72. Interview with Phil Manuel.
73. Interview with George Brosan.
74. Interview with John Bartels.
75. Interview with Phil Smith.
76. 1976 Jackson Hearings, p. 162.
77. Ibid., p. 162.
78. Ibid., pp. 164-166.

79. Interview with Terry Burke.
80. 1976 Jackson Hearings, pp. 166-167.
81. Interview with Bill Logay.
82. Ibid., p. 169.
83. Ibid., p. 168.
84. Ibid., p. 165.
85. Ibid., p. 119.
86. Interview with Bill Logay.
87. Interview with Andy Tartaglino.
88. Interview with John Bartels.

Chapter 23: Political Drug Wars
1. 1975 Jackson Hearings, pp. 29-30; 1976 Jackson Hearings, p. 131. Interview with Andy Tartaglino.
2. 1976 Jackson Hearings, p. 150.
3. Ibid., pp. 159-60.
4. 1975 Jackson Hearings, pp. 57-62.
5. 1975 Jackson Hearings, p. 95.
6. Ibid.
7. S/A Michael L. Mullen to Charles D. Sherman, Inspector-in-Charge "Telephone conversation with Ms. Linda Stanier and S/A Anthony "Tony" Triponi," February 28, 1974.
8. Mullen, "Telephone conversation with Ms. Linda Stanier and S/A Anthony "Tony" Triponi." Interview with Linda Stanier.
9. Mortimer L. Benjamin, Inspector to Charles D. Sherman, Inspector-in-Charge, "Interview of Special Agent Anthony Triponi and Miss Linda Stanier," March 21, 1974.
10. Interview with Morty Benjamin.
11. Benjamin "Interview of Special Agent Anthony Triponi and Miss Linda Stanier."
12. Interview with George Brosan.
13. 1975 Jackson Hearings, p. 529. Interview with George Brosan.
14. DeFeo Report, p. 9. Rockefeller Commission Report, p. 234.
15. Richard Salmi, undated, untitled report. See also Tartaglino memorandum re: Medusa, attached to 40 page document Project Medusa, Document Control CON:SCI:71-0003-2, 1-17-75 Medusa.
16. Lawrence Meyer, "DEA Was Offered Explosive Devices," *Washington Post*, p. A3, January 23, 1975. George Crile III, "The Colonel's Secret Drug War," *Washington Post* Outlook, June 13, 1976.
17. DeFeo Report, p. 8.
18. Kruger, *Great Heroin Coup*, p. 185.
19. Peroff Staff Study, p. iii.
20. Interview with Phil Smith.

21. Interview with Luke Benson.
22. DeFeo Report, Title Page.
23. DeFeo Report, General Documents on File, listed the following people as having been interviewed: Thomas Durkin, George B Brosan, William Durkin, Dennis Dayle, Edward Jagan, Frankie Perkins, Irvin C Swank, Thomas V Cash, Carl Shoffler, William J Logay, Phillip R Smith, John Gibbons, Merle A Whittington, Bruce E Jensen, Terrance Burke, Allen Yarborough, Edwin L Stamm, Robert T Richardson, Daniel P Casey, Vincent L Promuto, John Fallon, John R Bartels, Andrew C Tartaglino, John Arntz, Robert L Latchford, John A Lund, Jr, Santo Bario, Cyril Frank, George Belk, Robert Peloquin and Lucien Conein.
24. DeFeo Report, p. 1.
25. DeFeo Report, pp. 3-7.
26. Ibid., p. 11.
27. Bolten Interview.
28. Thomas Powers, *The Man Who Kept The Secrets: Richard Helms and the CIA* (NY: Knopf, 1979), p. 379.
29. Carl Bernstein, "The CIA and the Media," *Rolling Stone*, October 20, 1977, p. 66.
30. "The CIA and the Media," p. 66.
31. Ibid., p. 66.
32. Jeffrey St Clair and Alexander Cockburn, *Whiteout: The CIA, Drugs and the Press* (New York: Verso, 1998), p. 251.
33. Interview with Andy Tartaglino.
34. DeFeo Report, p. 16.
35. Tripodi, *Crusade*, pp. 205-209, *DeFeo Report*, p. 23.
36. Interview with Ron Metcalf.
37. Interview with Dave Westrate.
38. Interview with Chuck Leya, Frank Waters, and other federal narcotics agents.
39. Tripodi, *Crusade*, p. 208.
40. Interview with Andy Tartaglino.
41. DeFeo Report, 15-16
42. DeFeo Report, 17
43. Interview with John Warner. See Jack Kelly with Richard Mathison, *On the Street: The Autobiography of the Toughest US Narcotics Agent* (Chicago: Henry Regnery Company, 1974), p. 90, regarding Patch's contacts at Fort Bragg.
44. DeFeo Report, p. 20.
45. Ibid., pp. 118, 22, 24, 255.
46. Lucien Conein to Jesse M. Gallegos, re: IGO Comments on Internal Audit Report (The Hill Collection).
47. John Kelly and Joe Conason, "Bush and the Secret Noriega Report," *Village Voice*, October 11, 1998, p. 32.
48. "Bush and the Secret Noriega Report," p. 1.

49. "Bush and the Secret Noriega Report," p. 30.
50. Lou Conein, Potential Problem Areas, undated (The Hill Collection).
51. John Kelly, *San Francisco Bay Guardian*, December 14, 1988.
52. Interview with John Bartels.
53. 1976 Jackson Hearings, p. 133.
54. Interview with Andy Tartaglino.
55. 1976 Jackson Hearings, p. 167.
56. Ibid., p. 145.
57. Ibid., pp. 147-9.
58. Ibid., p. 151.
59. Interview with Terrence Burke.
60. 1976 Jackson Hearings, pp. 152-3.
61. Ibid., p. 154. On December 31, 1974, CIA director Colby and the CIA general counsel John Warner briefed Silberman about recent *New York Times* articles on the CIA illegal activities, the so-called "family jewels." Silberman helped organize the whitewash that ensued.
62. 1975 Jackson Hearings, pp. 750-751. 1976 Jackson Hearings, p. 159.
63. 1975 Jackson Hearings, p. 750.
64. 1976 Jackson Hearings, p. 159.
65. Ibid., p. 154.
66. 1975 Jackson Hearings, pp. 543-544.
67. 1975 Jackson Hearings, p. 634. 1976 Jackson Hearings, pp. 155-6,
68. 1976 Jackson Hearings, pp. 157-158.
69. 1975 Jackson Hearings, p. 565.
70. 1976 Jackson Hearings, p. 54.
71. Ibid., p. 54. See also 1975 Jackson Hearings, p. 622.
72. Ibid., p. 55.
73. Ibid., p. 55.
74. Ibid., pp. 41-45.
75. 1975 Jackson Hearings, pp. 625-626.
76. 1976 Jackson Hearings, p. 55. See also 1975 Jackson Hearings, p. 573.
77. Ibid., p. 55.
78. 1975 Jackson Hearings, p. 569.
79. Ibid., p. 569.
80. Ibid., p. 188.
81. Hougan, *Spooks*, pp. 460-1.
82. Interview with Terry Burke.
83. Interviews with Tartaglino and Paradiso's case agents.
84. Interview with Terry Burke.
85. Ibid.
86. Ibid.
87. Interview with Bill Logay.
88. 1975 Jackson Hearings, p. 142. Interviews with Andy Tartaglino, Fred Dick, and Ed Coyne.

89. 1975 Jackson Hearings, p. 141.
90. Interview with Andy Tartaglino.
91. Interviews with numerous federal agents.
92. Interviews with Andy Tartaglino, Fred Dick, and John Enright.
93. Correspondence with Thanh Dick.
94. Interviews with Fred Dick and Cecilia Plicet.
95. Memorandum from John Lund to Domestic Intelligence Division, August 5, 1975, re termination of DEACON I and reassignment of personnel.
96. John A. Lund, Jr, Regional Director, DEA, Miami Regional Office to Domestic Intelligence Division, re: DEACON-1, August 5, 1975 (The Hill Collection).
97. Special Agent, IGO to Acting Chief, IGO, re: request by Region 5 to Utilize DEACON I Intelligence, September 26, 1975 (The Hill Collection).
98. CIA Narcotics Intelligence Collection, undated, unsigned (The Hill Collection).
99. Scott, *Cocaine Politics*, p. 30.
100. Brewton, *Mafia, The CIA and George Bush*, p. 111.

Chapter 24: If at First
1. White Paper on Drug Abuse, September 1975--A Report to the President From the Domestic Council Drug Abuse Task Force.
2. "Analysis of the Headquarters Intelligence and Enforcement Structure," by Jerry Strickler, Tom Hurney and Mark Moore, May 8, 1975.
3. 1976 Jackson Hearings, p 35.
4. Hearings Before the Permanent Subcommittee on Investigations, "Federal Drug Law Enforcement," 94th Congress, Second Session, August 23-26, 1976, p. 1292.
5. 1976 Jackson Hearings, p. 142.
6. William J. Durkin, Acting Assistant Administrator for Enforcement to All Domestic Regions, "Conspiracy Case Development," July 1, 1973. Interview with Tony Pohl.
7. James K. Balla, Personnel Director, Notification of Personnel Action, 09-23-1973 (Pohl Document).
8. Anthony S. Pohl, Special Assistant for Conspiracies to Daniel P. Casey, Chief Domestic Intelligence Division, "Tactical Unit Concept," March 2, 1974.
9. Interview with Tony Pohl.
10. Pohl documents on Centacs 1-5, undated, unsigned.
11. Daniel P Casey, Acting Assistant Administrator for enforcement to All Division Chiefs, Office off enforcement, "Central Tactical Unit #3," December 6, 1973. Anthony Pohl, Central Tactical Unit #3,

"Organization and Operation." Daniel P Casey, Chief, Domestic Investigations Division to John E Van Diver, RD LA, "Central Tactical Unit #3," December 18, 1973.

12. Douglas Chandler, Special Agent — Centac 4 to Anthony S Pohl, Special Assistant for Conspiracies, "Centac 4," March 18, 1974.

13. Larry Kerness, Special Assistant Dangerous Drugs to Daniel P Casey, Chief Domestic Intelligence Division, "Centac 5 Progress Report, March 29, 1974.

14. Interview with Tony Pohl.

15. Hearings Before the Permanent Subcommittee on Investigations, "Federal Drug Law Enforcement," 94th Congress, Second Session, August 23-26, 1976, 1308.

16. Interview with Martin Pera.

17. Ibid.

18. Hearings Before the Permanent Subcommittee on Investigations, "Federal Drug Law Enforcement," 94th Congress, Second Session, August 23-26, 1976, p. 1292.

19. Ibid., p. 1294.

20. Ibid., p. 1314.

21. Interview with Dennis Dayle.

22. Interview with John Evans.

23. Scott, *Deep Politics*, p. 167.

24. Mills, *Underground Empire, passim.*

25. Mills, *Underground Empire*, p. 362.

26. Mills, *Underground Empire*, p. 363.

27. Kruger, *Great Heroin Coup*, p. 182. Mills, *Underground Empire*, p. 362.

28. Illicit Traffic in Weapons and Drugs Across the United States-Mexican Border, Permanent Subcommittee on Investigations, 95th Congress, January 12, 1977, *passim.*

29. Mills, *Underground Empire*, 550; p. 358.

30. Illicit Traffic in Weapons and Drugs Across the United States-Mexican Border, Permanent Subcommittee on Investigations, 95th Congress, January 12, 1977.

31. Mills, *Underground Empire*, p. 385.

32. Ibid., p. 384.

33. Ibid., p. 535.

34. Ibid., p. 608.

35. Ibid., p. 386.

36. Patricia B. McRae, "Reconceptualizing the Illegal Narcotics Trade and Its Effect on the Colombian and the Mexican State," South East Conference on Latin American Studies, Savannah, GA. April 9-12, 1998.

37. Irvin Molotsky, "Physician From Mexico Arrested In '85 Slaying of U.S. Drug," *New York Times*, April 16, 1990.

38. Interview with Rich Kobakoff.
39. Richard L Kobakoff, "Narcotics Moneyflow," *Drug Enforcement*, July 1978, p. 10.
40. Bolten Interview.
41. Peter Bensinger, "Reorganization of the Office of Intelligence," March 23, 1978.
42. Hearings before the Subcommittee on Criminal Justice of the Committee on the Judiciary, US Senate, 2nd Session, July 23-24, 1980 (US GPO, 1981).
43. DEA History Website.
44. "Intelligence,' November 1975 (Warner document).
45. "Briefing outline, Quarterly Staff Meeting," July 24, 1974. (Warner Document).
46. Interview with Arthur Fluhr.
47. Ibid.
48. "Analysis of the Headquarters Intelligence and Enforcement Structure," study conducted by Jerry Strickler, Tom Hurney and Mark Moore, May 5, 1975.
49. Ibid., p. 28
50. Development of Covert Collection techniques in Drug Operations, Background, 23 pages undated unsigned (possibly by Joe Jaffe and DEA Internal Security Staff), plus summary of IGO Projects.
51. Henry S. Dogin, Acting Administrator to Office of enforcement, Office of Intelligence and Office of Inspection and Internal security, re: Request for Information from DEA Guidelines Committee, October 3, 1975.
52. Special Agent, IGO to IO Staff/DEACON I Staff, re: termination of DEACON I, August 8, 1975. See also: Development of Covert Collection techniques in Drug Operations, Background, 23 pages undated unsigned, plus summary of IGO Projects (The Hill Collection), p. 6.
53. Lucien Conein to William Lenck, the Acting Assistant Administrator for Special Projects, "IGO Input for DEA Guidelines Committee," October 7, 1975 and Lucien Conein to John Warner, chief of the international intelligence division, "IGO Position Paper," October 8, 1975 (Warner documents).
54. Lucien E. Conein to Jesse M Gallegos, Special Assistant to the Assistant Administrator for Intelligence, re IGO Comments on Internal Audit Report, March 24, 1976.
55. Lucien Conein, Acting Chief, IGO to John Warner, Chief, International Intelligence Division, Position Paper, p. 6.
56. Evaluation of Proposed Reorganization of the Office of Intelligence, February 27, 1976.
57. Conein was probably referencing a GAO report, "Problems in Slowing the Flow of Cocaine and Heroin from South America," cited in

Development of Covert Collection techniques in Drug Operations, Background, 23 pages undated unsigned, plus summary of IGO Projects (The Hill Collection).
58. Unresolved Issues. (See Chapter 20, note 19)
59. George Crile III, "The Colonel's Secret Drug War," *Washington Post*, C1, June 13, 1976.
60. Kruger, *Great Heroin Coup*, p. 181.
61. September 2, 1976 John Warner briefing paper.
62. Mansfield Amendment to the International Security Assistance and Arms Control Act of 1976.
63. DeFeo Report, CIA Narcotic Intelligence Collection, undated, unsigned.
64. CIA Narcotic Intelligence Collection (undated, unsigned, from Hill FOIA release).
65. Hinckle, *Deadly Secrets*, p. xxxvii.
67. Burgess, "The Thailand Connection."
68. Kruger, *Great Heroin Coup*, p. 173.
69. Daniel P. Casey, Assistant Administrator for Enforcement, to Peter B. Bensinger, Administrator, re: Central Intelligence Agency (date illegible). The desk chiefs were Jerry Strickler, John R Doyle, Bruce Van Matre, Gary Liming and David Westrate.
70. Ibid.
71. Jerry Strickler, Deputy Chief, Operations for Europe and Middle East to Wayne Valentine, Acting Assistant Administrator for Enforcement, re: Central Intelligence Agency, February 11, 1977.
72. Correspondence with W Gordon Fink.

Chapter 25: Going Underground
1. Jonnes, *Hep Cats, Narcs and Pipe Dreams*, p. 308.
2. Jonnes, *Hep Cats, Narcs and Pipe Dreams*, p. 314.
3. Walter Wink, "Drug Policy: The Fix We're In," *Christian Century*, February 24, 1999.
4. David Boyum and Peter Reuter, "An Analytic Assessment of US Drug Policy: American Enterprise Institute for public policy Research, Washington DC, 2005, p. 18.
5. Michael McClintock, *Instruments of Statecraft: U.S. Guerrilla Warfare, Counter-Insurgency, Counter-Terrorism 1940-1990* (New York: Pantheon Books, 1992) p. 192.
6. Ibid. p. 193
7. Ibid., p. 314.
8. National Security Archives, citing an October 1978 cable from Robert E. White, the US ambassador to Paraguay, "Second Meeting with Secretary of State Re Letelier Case."
9. Brewton, *Mafia The CIA and George Bush*, p. 304.

10. Scott, *Cocaine Politics*, p. 204.
11. McClintock, *Instruments of Statecraft*, p. 314.
12. Ibid., p. 315.
13. Ibid., p. 316.
14. Nicholas Daniloff and Cheryl Arvidson, UPI, February 15, 1978.
15. Ibid.
16. Ibid.
17. Ibid.
18. Adam Clymer, "Canal Pack Foes in Senate Lose Procedural Clash With Backers," *New York Times*, February 22, 1978, p. 1.
19. Interviews with Jerry Strickler and John Bacon.
20. Interviews with William Lenck.
21. Correspondence and interviews with Edwin Wilson.
22. Interview with Douglas Schlachter.
23. Corn, *Blond Ghost*, p. 338.
24. Ibid.
25. McCoy, *Politics of Heroin*, p. 477.
26. Robert Parry, consortiumnews.com, "Original October Surprise," October 2006. Robert Parry, *Secrecy & Privilege: Rise of the Bush Dynasty from Watergate to Iraq* (Arlington, VA: Media Consortium, 2004). Barbara Honegger. *The October Surprise*, (New York: Tudor, 1989).
27. John Warner, Briefing Outline, Quarterly Staff Meting, July 24, 1974.
28. Correspondence with BNDD Agent.
29. Interviews with DEA agents.
30. John R. Bartels, Notice, "Regional Intelligence Operations (with attachments)," February 21, 1974 (Warner document).
31. Informant nets in foreign regions (proposed dea notice to be latter incorporated in an intelligence manual) (Bacon document).
32. John R. Doyle, Deputy Regional Director, Region 16, to all SAIC, "Intelligence Nets," April 29, 1974.
33. John R. Bartels, Special Field Intelligence Programs, Attachment B, Collection guidance and intelligence Production (Foreign Regions) March 19, 1974.
34. Utility, Function and coordination of Intelligence undated unsigned (Warner document).
35. Interview with Dan Addario and other DEA agents in Thailand at the time.
36. Interview with Thomas de Triquet.
37. March 9, 1976 Assistant Attorney General for Administration report on IGO.
38. Interviews with John Evans and Tully Acampora.
39. John Jiggens, *The Sydney Connection: The CIA, drugs, Nugan Hand and the murder of Donald Mackay*. Australia: Hill End, 2004), p. 33, citing

Al McCoy, *Drug Traffic: Narcotics and Organized Crime in Australia.* (Sydney: Harper & Row, 1980), pp. 261-266.

40. Jiggens, *Sydney Connection*, p. 34.

41. The FBN knew the CIA had been using this methodology at last since 1962, when Etienne Tarditi named Irving Brown, the International Confederation of Free Trade Unions' representative to the UN, in connection with L'affaire Rosal. Through a routine background check, FBN agents learned that Brown was a CIA agent, that he had port privileges in New York (meaning his baggage was not checked by Customs), and that his wife was a secretary for Carmel Offie, a former CIA agent then managing an import-export business in Manhattan. In 1965, Brown accompanied known Corsican drug trafficker Maurice Castellani to New York. The CIA obstructed the FBN's investigations of Brown's connections with Rosal and Castellani.

42. Interview with John Evans.

43. Interviews with Mort Benjamin and John Enright. "Aussies arrested in Hong Kong" *New York Times*, January 31, 1967, 28:2; July 18, 1967, p. 34.

44. The Commonwealth-New South Wales Joint Task Force on Drug Trafficking Report, volumes 2, 4, Nugan Hand (hereafter known as Joint Task Force on Drug Trafficking) (Canberra, 1982, 1983), p. 654 re: 1975-1980 and p. 661 re: quote.

45. Interviews with Colby, Shackley, Clines and Secord.

46. Joint Task Force on Drug Trafficking, pp. 689-692

47. Jiggens, *Sydney Connection*, 37, citing Toohey, Brian and Wilkinson, Marian, "Nugan Hand spies guns drugs fall into place," *National Times*, February 21, 1982, p. 12.

48. Interview with Buzz Johnson.

49. McCoy, *Politics of Heroin*, pp. 355-361.

50. Interview with Richard Secord.

51. Ibid.

52. Joint Task Force on Drug Trafficking, p. 90.

53. McCoy, *Politics of Heroin*, p. 464.

54. Ibid., p. 464.

55. Royal Commission of Inquiry into the Activities of the Nugan Hang Group, Final Report, Vol. 2 (hereafter known as Stewart Report), June 1985, p. 698. McCoy, *Politics of Heroin*, p. 480.

56. Jiggens, *Sydney Connection*, p. 69.

57. Ibid., p. 69.

58. McCoy, *Politics of Heroin*, p. 466.

59. Jiggens, *Sydney Connection*, p. 43.

60. McCoy, *Politics of Heroin*, p. 469.

61. Jiggens, *Sydney Connection*, p. 47. McCoy, *Politics of Heroin*, p. 468.

62. Ibid., p. 47.
63. Ibid., p. 77.
64. Correspondence with Clive Small.
65. Interviews with several DEA agents in Thailand at the time.
66. Jiggens, *Sydney Connection*, p. 93.
67. Kwitney, *Crimes of Patriots*, p. 219.
68. Jiggens, *Sydney Connection*, p. 80.
69. Ibid., p. 81.
70. McCoy, *Politics of Heroin*, p. 477, and Interview with Wilson employee Douglas Schlachter.
71. Joint Task Force on Drug Trafficking, pp. 736-7.
72. Joint Task Force on Drug Trafficking, p. 735.
73. McCoy, *Politics of Heroin*, p. 473.
74. Kwitney, *Crimes of Patriots*, pp. 56-63.
75. McCoy, *Politics of Heroin*, p. 462.
76. Joint Task Force on Drug Trafficking, p. 737.
77. Corn, *Blond Ghost*, p. 350.
78. McCoy, *Politics of Heroin*, pp. 475-6.
79. Ibid., p. 476.
80. Stewart Report, p. 751.
81. McCoy, *Politics of Heroin*, p. 476.
82. Ibid., p. 474.
83. Ibid., p. 657.
84. Joint Task Force on Drug Trafficking, p. 793.
85. Interview with Paul Knight.
86. Dispatch from Chief of Station (deleted) to William Harvey, October 11, 1960, included within "QJ/WIN," 1977 HSCA Staff Report, provided by the National Archives Assassination Records Review Board as part of CIA Historical Review Program, 1994.
87. Interviews with Hal Fiedler and Sal Vizzini.
88. Kwitney, *Crimes of Patriots*, p. 207.
89. Ibid., p. 215.
90. Ibid., p. 216.
91. Interviews with Powers and Addario.
92. Joint Task Force on Drug Trafficking, p. 731. McCoy, *Politics of Heroin*, pp. 466-7.
93. Ibid., pp. 712-5.
94. Terence C Lee, "The Causes of Military Insubordination: Explaining Military Organizational Behavior In Thailand," University of Washington, March 2005, p. 22.
95. Joint Task Force on Drug Trafficking, p. 709.
96. Kwitney, *Crimes of Patriots*, p. 214.
97. Lee, "The Causes of Military Insubordination," p. 34.

98. Joint Task Force on Drug Trafficking, pp. 714-15.
99. Ibid., pp. 212-213.
100. Ibid., p. 488.
101. Ibid., p. 102.
102. John Warner, Briefing Outline, Quarterly Staff Meting, July 24, 1974.
103. Interview with Howard Safir.
104. Interview with Bruce Van Matre.
105. Interview with Walter Sears and January 17, 1980 transcript of Oscar Skinner interview of Charles Seaver, p. 21.
106. Guillermo X. Garcia and D Weyermann, "DPS agent's killer claims entrapment," *Arizona Daily Star*, April 13, 1984, pp. A1, 17A.
107. Garcia, "DPS agent's killer claims entrapment," p. 17A.
108. Interview with Hugh Murray.
109. Garcia, "DPS agent's killer claims entrapment," p. 17A.
110. Ibid.
111. Ibid.
112. Transcript of December 3, 1980 interview by US Attorney Don Overall of Hugh Murray at the Pima County Attorney's office.
113. Garcia, "DPS agent's killer claims entrapment," p. 17A.
114. Garcia, "DPS agent's killer claims entrapment," insert on Celeya's work to help US firms tap Mexico's oil wealth.
115. Ibid.
116. Interview with Genaro Celeya.
117. Garcia, "DPS agent's killer claims entrapment," insert on Celeya's work to help US firms tap Mexico's oil wealth.

Chapter 26: George White's Ghost
1. Interview with Ted Hunter.
2. Interview with George Brosan.
3. DEA roster, Personnel Currently Assigned to Headquarters," December 1973.
4. Letter from Charles Ruff to Joseph Krueger, December 31, 1975.
5. Interview with Ted Hunter.
6. Interview with John Evans.
7. Ibid.
8. Interview with Morty Benjamin. Mortimer Benjamin to Charles Ruff, "Summary of Review of Closed Internal Security Files 1969 — June 1975, from June 9 to July 2," July 24, 1975. The infamous 35 were: Joe Baca, George Belk, Joe Catale, Carl Cipriani, Dennis Dayle, Fred Dick, Bill Durkin, Joe Ferro, Art Fluhr, John Gallagher, Steve Georgio, Pete Gruden, James Guy, Al Habib, George Halpin, Richard Holborrow, Jim Hunt, Carl Jackson, Jerry Jensen, Leonard Katz, Bob Manning, Walter Miller, Tom O'Grady, Jack Peterson, Susan Rice, Pete Scrocca, Rey

Sepulveda, Ron Swanson, Peter Wilkochi, Tom Zepeda, Clarence Cook, John Griffen, Vernon Meyer, Bill Olivanti, and Vinnie Lozowicki.

9. Interview with Morty Benjamin, "Summary of Review of Closed Internal Security Files 1969 — June 1975, from 9 June to 2 July."

10. Interview with William Coonce.

11. Interview with Carl Shoffler

12. Interview with Ted Hunter.

13. Interviews with Jaime Boyd and Jack Compton.

14. Garland Roarke, *The Coin of Contraband: The True Story of United States Customs Investigator Al Scharff* (Garden City: Doubleday & Company, Inc., 1964), pp. 392-5.

15. Interviews with Boyd and Compton. Jamie C Boyd, US Magistrate to John E Clark, US Attorney, April 11, 1976, regarding official records furnished last August.

16. Compton Affidavit. The others were Herbert E. Hailes, R. N. Staton, Phillip M. DeHoyos and Joseph Beurer. Jamie C Boyd, US Magistrate to John E Clark, US Attorney, April 11, 1976, regarding official records furnished last August.

17. Undated Letter from James Kerr to Jamie Boyd re Investigation of Secret Recordings of Conversations between DEA Special Agents and Assistant USA's. See also: AUSA James W Kerr to USA Jamie C Boyd, "Investigation of Secret Recordings of Conversations between DEA Special Agents and Assistant US Attorneys;" USA Jamie Boyd to file, "August 1 Meeting with Ervin C Swank, DEA," August 3, 1977. USA Boyd to Swank, August 3, 1977 Boyd to Frangullie; AUSA Leroy Morgan Jahn to Jamie Boyd, "Freeze," August 1, 1977; USA Boyd to all Assistant US Attorneys, "Freeze," August 3, 1977. Magistrate Jamie Boyd to USA John Clark, "Letter of April 1 Pertaining to DEA Personnel," April 12, 1976.

18. Interview with Jamie Boyd.

19. May 31, 1978 letter from Jamie Boyd to Benjamin R. Civiletti. In response to a FOIA request from the author for this document and Compton's affidavit (both of which the author possesses), the Department of Justice advised on November 14, 1994 "that no responsive records were located..."

20. Rockefeller Commission Report, p. 226.

21. Joseph B Treaster, "Ex-C.I.A. Aide Says Scientist Who Died Knew About LSD Tests," *New York Times*, July 18, 1975. p. 1.

22. Hearings before the Subcommittee On Health And Scientific Research of the Committee On Human Resources, "Human Drug Testing By The CIA," U.S. Senate, 95th Congress, 1st Session on S. 1893 To Amend the Public Health Service Act To Establish The President's Commission for the Protection of Human Subjects of Biomedical and Behavioral

Research, and for Other Purposes (Hereafter known as Kennedy Hearings), GPO, August-September 1977, p. 125.

23. John Marks, *The Search for the Manchurian Candidate*, (New York: Times Books, 1979), *passim.*

24. Marks, *Manchurian Candidate*, p. 63.

25. Ibid., pp. 106, 99.

26. Ibid., p. 183.

27. Kennedy Hearings, p. 159.

28. Turner to Bell, Jan 10, 1979.

29. Lauren Paine, *The CIA at Work* (London: Robert Hale, 1977), pp. 164-5.

30. Ibid., pp. 150 and 169.

31. Martin A. Lee and Bruce Shlain, *Acid Dreams: The Complete Social History of the LSD, the Sixties, and Beyond* (New York: Grove Press, 1992), pp. 3-4.

32. Alan W. Scheflin and Edward M. Opton Jr, *The Mind Manipulators* (New York & London: Paddington Press Ltd, 1978), p. 135.

33. Interview with Andy Tartaglino. Robert Wiltse, Memorandum for the Record, "MKULTRA Subprojects 3, 14, 16, 42, 132, 149 and MKSEARCH (deleted) — Bureau of Narcotics," final report and history of FBN involvement in MKULTRA.

34. William Howard Moore, *The Kefauver Committee and the Politics of Crime, 1950-1952* (Columbia: University of Missouri Press, 1974), p. 124.

35. Portions of George White's Diary were provided by Alan Block, others were obtained from the CIA through three Freedom of Information Act Requests (F-1993-02381, F-1998-01108, and F-1998-01939) filed by the author: all are hereafter collectively referred to as *White's Diary.* Robert Wiltse, Memorandum for the Record, "MKULTRA Subprojects 3, 14, 16, 42,132, 149 and MKSEARCH (deleted) — Bureau of Narcotics," final report and history of FBN involvement in MKULTRA.

36. Marks, *Manchurian Candidate*, pp. 91-97.

37. Interview with John Bartels.

38. Kennedy Hearings, p. 116.

39. Interview with Andy Tartaglino.

40. Kennedy Hearings, p. 117.

41. Ibid., p. 118.

42. Ibid., p. 118.

43. Ibid., p. 118.

44. Ibid., p. 119.

45. Ibid., p. 119.

46. Ibid., p. 120.

47. Interview with Art Fluhr.

48. Dr Sidney Gottlieb, Memorandum for the Record, January 30, 1967.

49. Interview with Andy Tartaglino.
50. Interview with Ike Feldman. MKULTRA Document Doc 87, "Richard Salmi and Frank Laubinger Interview with Feldman." Richard Salmi and Glennon Cooper also provided the author with numerous documents concerning the Victims Task Force. One, titled Michie Memo, was an interview CIA officer Michie did with Siragusa prior to the Kennedy Hearings in which Feldman's safe house activities in New York were discussed.
51. Interview with George Gaffney.
52. Interview with Larry Cohn.
53. Interview with Howie Safir.
54. Interview with Morty Benjamin.
55. Interview with DEA Agent Tom Sheehan.
56. Corn, *Blond Ghost*, 331, and CIA Memorandum For the Record, Subject: Report on Plots to Assassinate Fidel Castro, May 23, 1967 (hereafter known as 1967 IG Report).
57. Mel Ayton, "The Assassination of Robert F. Kennedy and the Girl in the Polka Dot Dress," History News Network, May 7, 2007.
58. Interviews with Richard Salmi and Gene Wheaton.
59. Interview with Richard Salmi.
60. FOIA 993-1863-F, MKULTRA and the Victims Task Force, plus the following documents provided by Richard Salmi: Thank you letter from Stansfield Turner to Peter Bensinger, July 6, 1979, expressing appreciation for Salmi's work on "our search for unwitting subjects of MKUL-TRA drug research...;" thank you letter from Stansfield Turner to Griffin B. Bell, July 6, 1979 expressing appreciation for Salmi's work on the search for MKULRA victims; Anthony A. Lapham, General Counsel via Deputy Director of Central Intelligence for Director of Central Intelligence, "MKULTRA — Program to Identify Subjects of Agency-Sponsored Drug Testing," July 24, 1978; Richard E Salmi, Staff Investigator, to File, "MK-ULTRA AC-AI-77-FO342," May 7, 1979; Frank Laubinger via Robert H Wiltse, Special Assistant/DDA, Memorandum for Deputy Director for Administration, March 9, 1979; Richard E Salmi, Staff Investigator, to File, "MK-ULTRA AC-AI-77-FO342, February 27, 1979; Larry A Hammond, Acting Assistant Attorney General, Office of Legal Counsel, Memorandum for The Attorney General, "Assistance to CIA to identify unwitting subjects of drug testing," January 24, 1979.
61. Interview with Dick Salmi.
62. Interviews with Steve Greene, Keith Shostrom and Glen Cooper and their "Final Report, MKULTRA Cross file: AC-AI-77-FO352," to Inspector Peter L. Palatroni, December 4, 1978.
63. Interview with Steve Greene.
64. Ibid.

65. Steve Greene, Keith Shostrom and Glen Cooper and their "Final Report, MKULTRA Cross file: AC-AI-77-FO352," to Inspector Peter L. Palatroni, December 4, 1978.
66. Interview with John Evans.
67. Interview with John Evans.
68. The information about Bario derives from many sources, including his widow Joanne Bario, her book *Fatal Dreams*, as well as interviews with Kiere, DEA inspectors and other individuals and journalists involved in the investigation of Bario's death.

Chapter 27: Enter the FBI

1. Gary Cartwright, *Dirty Dealing* (New York: Atheneum, 1984), pp. 1, 33.
2. Cartwright, *Dirty Dealing*, pp. 3, 80.
3. Cartwright, *Dirty Dealing*, pp. 30-32, 45-61. Interview with Ken Bloemker, ref DEA file M7-74-0139.
4. Interview with former Customs Agent Joseph Price.
5. Cartwright, *Dirty Dealing*, p. 34. Interview with Jack Compton.
6. Compton Affidavit, p. 72.
7. Cartwright, *Dirty Dealing*, pp. 61, 67.
8. Ibid., p. 67. Interviews with Chris Thompson and with Carl Shoffler.
9. Interview with Carl Shoffler.
10. Interviews with Chris Thompson and Customs Agent Joe Price. Sally Denton, *The Bluegrass Conspiracy* (New York: Avon Books, 1990), p. 73.
11. Interviews with Chris Thompson and DEA Agent Ken Bloemker.
13. Denton, *Bluegrass Conspiracy*, p. 72. Cartwright, *Dirty Dealing*, p. 87. Interview FBI Agent and federal prosecutor.
14. Interview with Dennis Dayle and other Centac agents.
15. Cartwright, *Dirty Dealing*, pp. 73-77.
16. Richard J Connolly and Jim Calogero, ""Raymond Patriarca Dies at 76, Reputedly Ruled N.E. Organized Crime," *Boston Globe*, July 12, 1984.
17. Interview with federal prosecutors John Durham and Jeff Averhahn.
18. Brewton, *Mafia, The CIA and George Bush*, pp. 199-202.
19. Ibid., p. 285.
20. Cartwright, *Dirty Dealing*, p. 83.
21. Ibid., pp. 117, 149, 157.
22. Ibid., pp. 106-108, 129. Interview with Ken Bloemker.
23. Cartwright, *Dirty Dealing*, p. 130.
24. Ibid., p. 126.
25. Ibid., p. 126.
26. Matthew Brelis, "Taped Reminiscences Used At Winter Hearings," *Boston Globe*, January 28, 1992, 17; "Ask The Globe," January 23, 1980, 60; "Slain Gunman is Identified By The Police," *Boston Globe*, December 19, 1983; Richard J Connelly, "Two In Drug Case Linked to Blackfriars

Victim" *Boston Globe*, June 5, 1983; Robert Kenney, "5 Murdered with Shotguns a Blackfriars," *Boston Globe*, September 22, 1980.

27. Cartwright, *Dirty Dealing*, p. 127.

28. Bill Mintz, "Wood shooting still a mystery," *San Antonio Express*, November 28, 1978, 1, 4-A. The author worked as a private investigator on the Charles Harrelson case and amassed information on the Wood assassination from reports and interviews with federal agents, police officers, prosecutors, criminal defense attorneys, witnesses involved in the case, as well as from Harrelson's statements to his attorney (referred to hereafter as *Confidential Sources*).

29. Cartwright, *Dirty Dealing*, pp. 132-33.

30. US Attorney Jamie Boyd to Philip B Heymann, Assistant Attorney General, Criminal Division, "Attempted Assassination of AUSA James Kerr," December 5, 1979.

31. Cartwright, *Dirty Dealing*, pp. 172-176. *Confidential Sources*.

33. Ibid., p. 141.

34. "Wood shooting still a mystery," pp. 1, 4-A.

35. Chronology of Kerr—Wood investigation from November 21, 1978 to February 11, 1980, provided by Jamie Boyd.

36. Cartwright, *Dirty Dealing*, pp. 170-171; *Bluegrass Conspiracy*, pp. 73-75.

37. Cartwright, *Dirty Dealing*, p. 171. Chronology of Kerr—Wood investigation.

38. Cartwright, *Dirty Dealing*, p. 183.

39. "Trial draws friends and lovers," *The San Antonio News*, 26 October 1982, p. 3A.

40. Cartwright, *Dirty Dealing*, p. 184; *Confidential Sources*.

41. Interview with attorneys Bruce Green and William Habern.

42. Cartwright, *Dirty Dealing*, pp. 184-5.

43. Ibid., pp. 290, 320.

44. W.R. Deener, "Painstaking investigation allowed FBI to fill in pieces of slaying puzzle," *Dallas Morning News*.

45. Michael Webster, "Cash is King," *Paso del Norte*, p. 26.

46. Cartwright, *Dirty Dealing*, p. 317.

47. Ibid., p. 318.

48. *Confidential Sources*.

49. Chronology of Kerr—Wood investigation

50. Ibid.

51. Interview with Jamie Boyd.

52. Chronology of Kerr—Wood investigation.

53. Information and photograph provided to the author by Jamie Boyd.

54. Interview with John Evans.

55. Interviews with John Evans and Terry Baldwin.

56. William Clifford Breen letter to William Webster.
57. Harris Country District Attorney, "Information Regarding Charles Harrelson," June 6, 1979, document provided by Jamie Boyd. Interview with Gordon Fink.
58. Cartwright, *Dirty Dealing*, p. 203.
59. Interview with Jamie Boyd.
60. Interview with Jamie Boyd.
61. Interviews with Jack Compton, Jamie Boyd, Chris Thompson and Hank Washington.
62. Interviews with Jack Compton and Jamie Boyd.
63. Chronology of Kerr—Wood investigation.
64. US Attorney Jamie Boyd to Philip B. Heymann, Assistant Attorney General, Criminal Division, "Attempted Assassination of AUSA James Kerr," December 5, 1979.
65. Interview with Jamie Boyd.
66. US Attorney Jamie Boyd to Philip B. Heymann, Assistant Attorney General, Criminal Division, December 7, 1979. US Attorney Jamie Boyd to Philip B. Heymann, Assistant Attorney General, Criminal Division, December 12, 1979. US Attorney Jamie Boyd to Attorney General Benjamin R. Civiletti, December 19, 1979. US Attorney Jamie Boyd to Philip B. Heymann, Assistant Attorney General, Criminal Division, December 20, 1979. US Attorney Jamie Boyd to Philip B. Heymann, Assistant Attorney General, Criminal Division, January 17, 1980.
67. Chronology of Kerr—Wood investigation from November 21, 1978 to February 11, 1980, provided by Jamie Boyd. Interview with Jack Compton.
68. US Attorney Jamie Boyd to Attorney General Benjamin R. Civiletti, February 8, 1980; US Attorney Jamie Boyd to Philip B. Heymann, Assistant Attorney General, Criminal Division, "Investigation into the Murder of United States District Judge John H Wood, Jr, February 8, 1980. See also US Attorney Jamie Boyd to Attorney General Benjamin R Civiletti, February 7, 1980. US Attorney Jamie Boyd to Philip B. Heymann, Assistant Attorney General, Criminal Division, "Investigation into the Murder of United States District Judge John H. Wood, Jr," February 7, 1980.
69. Jamie Boyd, "Position of the United States Attorney general for the Western District of Texas on Negotiations for Information in Kerr/Wood cases, February 21, 1980; see also US Attorney Jamie Boyd to Charles B Renfrew, Deputy Attorney General, June 2, 1980.
70. US Attorney Jamie Boyd to Philip B. Heymann, Assistant Attorney General, Criminal Division, June 24, 1980.
71. Scott, *Deep Politics*, pp. 131, 138.
72. Interview with Jamie Boyd.

73. Interview with Carl Shoffler.
74. Cartwright, *Dirty Dealing*, pp. 213, 214.
75. Interview with Mike Taylor.
76. Federal Public Defender C Larry Mathews to Philip B. Heymann, Assistant Attorney general, criminal Division, "Robert Riojas," February 29, 1980 and Riojas Proffer, documents provided by Jamie Boyd.
77. Telephone log off calls between Brown, Culbreath and other suspects on May 29, 1979, provided by Jamie Boyd.
78. Cartwright, *Dirty Dealing*, p. 217. Interview with Mike Taylor.
79. Interviews with Mike Taylor and Jamie Boyd. *Confidential Sources.*
80. Interview with Jack Lawn.
81. Ibid.
82. Ibid.
83. Cartwright, *Dirty Dealing*, p. 316.
84. Interview with Jack Lawn.
85. Interview with Bud Mullen.
86. Ibid.
87. Ibid.
88. Michael Shaheen Jr, Counsel, Office of Professional responsibility to Francis M Mullen, Jr., Acting Administrator Drug Enforcement Administration, "Jerry N. Jensen, George R.. Halpin, Charles E. Hill, and William F. Alden," September 1, 1981. Joseph E. Krueger, Chief Inspector to Francis M. Mullen, Jr, Acting Administrator, "Response to Office of professional Responsibility memorandum of September 15, 1981 entitled "Jerry N. Jenson, George R. Halpin, Charles Hill and William F. Alden," (AF-R1-80-Ao277, October 26, 1981.
89. Francis M. Mullen, Acting Administrator to Michael E Shaheen, Jr., Counsel, Office of professional responsibility, Department of Justice, "Annual Report to the Attorney General — 1980 Office off Professional responsibility," December 8, 1981. Ronald J. Ostrow, "Drug Agency Called Lax in Self-Policing," *Los Angeles Times*, November 10, 1981.
90. Interview with Gordon Fink.
91. Interview with Bud Mullen.
92. Ibid.
93. USDOJ/OIG Special Report: The CIA-Contra-Crack Cocaine Controversy: a Review Of The Justice Department's Investigations And Prosecutions, December, 1997, (hereafter known as USDOJ/OIG Special Report). See also Robert Parry, "Contra-Cocaine: Evidence of Premeditation," *IF Magazine*, July-August 1998.
94. Interview with Bud Mullen.
95. Interview with Carl Jackson.
96. Interview with Carl Jackson and other African American agents.

97. Interview with Steve Greene and other non-African American agents.
98. Interview with Clarence Cook.
99. Interview with Bud Mullen.
100. Michael Levine, *The Big White Lie: The Cia and the Cocaine/Crack Epidemic: An Undercover Odyssey*, (New York: Thunder's Mouth Press, 1993), p. 76.
101. Ibid.
102. Interview with John Evans.
103. Interviews with Joe Price and Bradley Ayers.
104. Interview with Dick Salmi.
105. "Less Than Full Disclosure," *Time*, May 10, 1982.

Chapter 28: The Age of Narco-Terrorism

1. Subcommittee On Children, Family, Drugs and Alcoholism, 99th Congress, "Role of Nicaragua in Drug Trafficking," April 19, 1985, p. 5.
2. "Role of Nicaragua in Drug Trafficking," p. 5.
3. Craig Pyes and Laurie Becklund, "Inside Dope in El Salvador," *The New Republic*," cited in "Role of Nicaragua in Drug Trafficking," p. 10.
4. Ibid.
5. Interviews with Dave Westrate, Steve Greene, and Frank Monastero.
6. Senate Committee on Foreign Operations, Subcommittee on Terrorism, Narcotics and International Operations, Report, Drugs, Law Enforcement and Foreign Policy (hereafter Kerry Report) 100th Congress, 2nd Session (Washington, DC, GPO, 1989), 1017; Deposition of Robert Owen, 6 May 1987; and Owen memo to North, March 17, 1986.
7. Interview with Dave Westrate.
8. Interview with DEA Inspector.
9. Blumenthal, *Last Days of the Sicilians*, pp. 123-4, 192-5, 229-30, 285-6.
10. Ibid., pp. 80-83, 123-4, 153, 194.
11. Ibid., pp. 172, 216, 276.
12. David M Malone, Unilateralism and US Foreign Policy (Center on International Cooperation Studies in Multilateralism, 2003), p. 134, n21, Re NSCDD-221.
13. John Cummings and Ernest Volkman, "Snowbound," *Penthouse*, July 1989, p. 66.
14. Interviews with Rudy Enders, Donald Gregg, and other CIA sources. Lee H Hamilton and Daniel K. Inouye, Report of the Congressional Committees Investigating the Iran/Contra Affair (November 13, 1987, Washington, 1987) (hereafter Iran/Contra Report), 100th Congress, 1st Session; House Report No. 100-433, Senate Report No 100-216, pp. 11, 22, and 71 (footnote 144).
15. Interviews with Donald Gregg and Rudy Enders.

16. Douglas Valentine, *The Phoenix Program* (New York, William Morrow, 1990), pp. 424-5.
17. *Boston Globe*, July 10, 1984.
18. *New York Times*, June 14-15, 1983.
19. Interview with Richard Secord. Richard V. SECORD, Plaintiff, v Leslie COCKBURN, et al., Defendants. Civil Action No. 88-0727-GHR. United States District Court, District of Columbia. Aug. 27, 1990.
20. Final Report Of The Independent Counsel For Iran/Contra Matters Volume I: Investigations and Prosecutions Lawrence E. Walsh Independent Counsel (August 4, 1993 Washington, DC) Chapter 9, US Vs Richard Secord (Hereafter Walsh Report).
21. *Shaking Hands with Saddam Hussein: The U.S. Tilts toward Iraq*, 1980-1984 National Security Archive Electronic Briefing Book No. 82, February 25, 2003.
22. Corn, *Blond Ghost*, p. 358.
23. Iran/Contra Report, p. 164.
24. Ibid., p. 169.
25. Iran-Contra Report, Chapter 8; *Boson Globe*, "Alleged terrorist linked to arm sales," April 20, 1986, 5. Sadegh Tabatabai, arrested in West Germany with more than 3 pounds of opium in 1983, was a hostage broker for the Carter Administration (*San Jose Mercury News*, February 23, 1983).
26. *Boston Globe*, "Alleged terrorist linked to arms sales," April 20, 1987, p. 5.
27. Iran/Contra Report, pp. 361-366.
28. Interviews with several knowledgeable DEA agents.
29. Iran/Contra Report, p. 363.
30. Ibid.
31. Ibid.
32. Correspondence with David Westrate.
33. The Oliver North File: His Diaries, E-Mail, and Memos on the Kerry Report, Contras and Drugs, National Security Archie Electronic briefing Book No. 113, February 26, 20044.
34. Ibid.
35. US Customs Service investigative report, "Guy Penilton Owen, et al., N90201," file NOGGBDO30036, New Orleans, May 18, 1983, pp. 6-8.
36. Oliver North File
37. Jonnes, *Hep-Cats, Narcs, and Pipes Dreams*, p. 361.
38. Scott, *Cocaine Politics*, p. 41.
39. Camarena knowledge
40. Celerino Castillo with David Harmon, *Powder Burns, Cocaine, Contras and The Drug War*. (Toronto: Mosaic Press, 1994).

41. Correspondence with Celerino Castillo.

42. Correspondence with Celerino Castillo.

43. Scott, *Cocaine Politics*, p. 13, citing Kerry Report, 2, p. 134.

44. Castillo, *Powder Burns.*

45. Ibid.

46. Ibid.

47. Rob Nordland, "Is There a Contra Drug Connection," *Newsweek*, January 2, 1987, p. 26.

48. Oliver North memo to Felix Rodriguez, September 20, 1985, declassified by the House-Senate Iran-Contra committee.

49. Interview with Gary Mattocks

50. CIA IG Report, note 20; and the more reliable Scott, *Cocaine Politics*, pp. 105, 111, 119 (citing Kerry Report, pp. 414-19, 365-70), 131 (citing Robert Owen depositions and Iran/Contra Report, Appendix B, Vol. 20, 799, 733).

51. Affidavit of Shirley A. Brill," July 15, 1988, Mary D. Hopkins, Notary Public, p. 8.

52. Interview with Gary Mattocks.

53. Enforcement Of Narcotics, Firearms, And Money Laundering Laws: Oversight Hearings before the Subcommittee on Crime of the Committee on the Judiciary, House of Representatives, One Hundredth Congress, Second Session, July 28, September 23, 29, and October 5, 1988. Washington : US G.P.O. 1989, pp. 56-67, 72, 74-78.

54. Ibid.

55. "The Role of Nicaragua in Drug Trafficking," p. 18.

56. *Kerry Report*, p. 135

57. Narcotics, Firearms, And Money Laundering Laws, Oversight Hearings before the Subcommittee on Crime of the Committee on the Judiciary, House of Representatives, One Hundredth Congress, Second Session, July 28, September 23, 29, and October 5, 1988,

58. Maurice Helbrant, *Narcotic Agent* (New York, The Vanguard Press, 1941), pp. 273-281.

59. Douglas Clark Kinder and William O. Walker III, "Stable Force in a Storm: Harry J. Anslinger and United States Narcotic Policy, 1930-1962," *The Journal of American History*, vol. 72, no. 4, March 1986, p. 919 n. 33.

60. DEA Operation Sandstorm case file, FOIA Request.

61. Jonathan Marshall, *Drug Wars* (Forestville, CA, Cohan & Cohen, 1991), p. 54.

62. Interview with Gary Mattocks. Jefferson Morley, "Barry and his city: crack in the Washington culture," *The Nation*, February 19, 1990, pp. 14-20. Frank Cerabino, "Elder Tabraue gets mistrial," *Miami Herald*, January 24, 1989, p. 3B.

63. Interview with Richard Sami.
64. Scott, *Cocaine Politics*, p. 111.
65. Andrew O Selsky, "Link found to bombing," Associated Press, May 4, 2007.
66. Robert Parry, "Bush, Posada and Terrorism Hypocrisy," Consortium-News.com, May 10, 2005.
67. Carlos J Williams, "Luis Posada Carriles, a terror suspect abroad, enjoys a coming-out in Miami," *Los Angeles Times*, May 7, 2008.
68. Interview with Dick Salmi.
69. Ibid. Arthur Liman questioning of North at Senate Iran-Contra Hearings, pp. 375-6.
70. Interview with Dick Salmi.
71. Interviews with Jack Lawn.
72. Interview with Dave Westrate.
73. Jeff Gerth, "Management Woes Hobble US Air Fleet in Drug War," *New York Times International*, June 13, 1990.
74. Gerth, "Management Woes Hobble US Air Fleet in Drug War." Correspondence with Norm Rosnor at INM in 1988; excerpt from INM publication "US Efforts and The International Situation."
75. Interviews with Dave Westrate and Jack Lawn.
76. Interview with Dave Westrate.
77. Ibid.
78. Ibid.
79. Stephen G Trujillo, "Corruption and Cocaine in Peru," *New York Times*, April 7, 1972.
80. Interview with Dave Westrate.
81. Michael Isikoff, "CIA Creates Narcotics Unit to help in Drug Fight," *Washington Post*, May 28, 1989, pp. C1A, A13.
82. Interview and correspondence with Terry Burke.
83. Ibid.
84. Howard Hart, Chief of the CIA's Counter Narcotic Center, Notes From An Off-The-Record Talk At Harvard, November 13, 1990, .
85. Interview and correspondence with Terry Burke.

Chapter 29: The View from the Top
1. Interview with Terry Burke.
2. Interview with Tony Poe.
3. Albert Habib, Memorandum Report, January 27, 1966.
4. Interview with Terry Burke.
5. Ibid.
6. Ibid.
7. Interview with Dave Westrate.

8. Bernard Weintraub, "President Offers Strategy for United States on Drug Control," *New York Times*, September 6, 1989. p. A1.

9. Jonathan Harris, *Drugged America* (New York, Four Winds Press, 1991), p. 156.

10. ONDCP stats provided by Fred Dick.

11. Interview with Terry Burke.

12. National Drug Intelligence Center website.

13. Association of Former Intelligence Officers, Weekly Intelligence Notes #46-05 dated November 28, 2005.

14. Knute Royce, "Behind Colombia Raid: US Got Gacha," *Newsday*, May 4, 1990, p. 1.

15. Royce, "Behind Colombia Raid," p. 1.

16. Ibid., p. 22.

17. Shaking Hands with Saddam Hussein: The U.S. Tilts toward Iraq, 1980-1984 National Security Archive Electronic Briefing Book No. 82 Edited by Joyce Battle February 25, 2003.

18. Jim McGee and David Hoffman, "Rivals Hint Bush Understates Knowledge of Noriega Ties," *Washington Post*, May 8, 1988.

19. Robert A Pastor, "The Memoirs of Manuel Noriega, America's Prisoner," *Washington Monthly*, June 1997. Stephen Engleberg and Jeff Gerth, "Bush and Noriega: Their 20 Year Relationship," *New York Times*, September 28, 1988.

20. *Newsweek*, January 15, 1990.

21. Bernard Weintraub, "Former Spy Chief Talks for Dukakis," *New York Times*, October 2, 1988.

22. Richard H. Curtiss, "What You Won't Read About Michael Harari, Noriega's Israeli Adviser Who Got Away," *Washington Report On Middle East Affairs*, February 1990, p. 5.

23. *Cocaine Politics*, p. 74.

24. Oliver North, August 23, 1986 email to John Poindexter, declassified by the House-Senate Iran-Contra Committee.

25. Philip Shenon, US Officials Praised Drug Effort by Noriega," *New York Times*, February 9, 1988.

26. Interview with Dave Westrate.

27. Hull escapes.

28. Richard E Salmi, Chief, Special Investigative Support Unit to Thomas V Cash, Deputy Assistant Administrator for Operations, "Alleged Conspiracy Involving Narcotic Distribution in the US to Finance Contras in Nicaragua," December 17, 1986.

29. US Department of Justice Office of the Inspector General, Special Report, "The CIA-Crack Cocaine Controversy: A Review of the Justice Department's Investigations and Prosecutions" (December 1997)

Chapter XI, DEA Headquarters' Review of Allegations of Contra Drug Trafficking.

30. *Cocaine Politics*, p. 113.
31. Rob Nordland, "Is There a Contra Drug Connection," *Newsweek*, January 2, 1987, 26.
32. Stephen Kurkjian, "US probing drug links to CIA's flights," *Boston Globe*, April 26, 1987, pp. 1, 27.
33. Interview with Gary Mattocks.
34. *Cocaine Politics*, p. 115.
35. Ibid., p. 110.
36. Larry Rother, "Victory in Noriega Case Stunned Even Prosecutors," New York Times, April 17, 1992.
37. *Cocaine Politics*, p. 116.
38. January 16, 1990 that (16:1) and January 19, 1990 (I, 14:5)
39. Jeff Gerth, "C.I.A. Shedding Its Reluctance To Aid in Fight Against Drugs," *New York Times*, 25 March 25, 1990, p. 1.
40. Gerth, "C.I.A Shedding," p. 1.
41. Ibid., p. 1.
42. *New York Times*, September 7, 1990, Section I, 11.
43. Interview with Terry Burke.
44. Interview with Dave Westrate.
45. See Elaine Shannon's book, *Desperados.*
46. Jerry Meldon, "Did the CIA coddle Camarena's killers?" *Boston Globe*, July 29, 1990, p. 58.
47. Interview with Dave Westrate.
48. "The C.I.A. and the Drug War," p. 22.
49. William Branigin, "Trial in Camarena Case Shows DEA Anger at CIA." *Washington Post*, July 16, 1990.
50. Interview with Terry Burke.
51. Interview with Steve Greene.
52. United States v. Alvarez-Machain, 504 U.S. 655, 669, 112 S. Ct. 2188, 119 L. Ed. 2d 441 (1992).
53. Correspondence with Robert Bonner.
54. Interviews with Steve Greene and Terry Burke.
55. Correspondence with Robert Bonner.
56. Ibid.
57. Ibid.
58. Interview with Dave Westrate.
59. Correspondence with Robert Bonner.
60. November 20, 1993 *New York Times*; US 11th Circuit Court of Appeals US v FERNANDEZ, United States Court of Appeals, Eleventh Circuit, Nos. 94-4021 and 96-4878, March 17, 1998.
61. Correspondence with Robert Bonner.

62. Interview with Dave Westrate.
63. Correspondence with Robert Bonner.
64. Interview with Dave Westrate.
65. Correspondence with Robert Bonner.
66. Interview with Steve Greene.
67. Interview with Dave Westrate.
68. Ibid.
69. Tim Weiner, "Suit by Drug Agent Says U.S. Subverted His Burmese Effort," *New York Times International,* October 27, 1994.
70. Steve Gutkin, "DEA Agent Attacks Colombia as `Narco-Democracy," *Washington Post,* October 1, 1994.
71. Catherine Austin Fitts, "Solari Rising," Philadelphia citypaper.net, November 15-22, 2001.
72. Interview with Steve Greene.
73. Gerth, "CIA Shedding."
74. Interview with John Coleman.

Epilogue
1. Interview with FBN Agent.
2. Interview with Paul Knight.
3. Interview with Marty Pera.
4. John R. Doyle, Deputy Regional Director, Region 16, "To all SAICs re intelligence nets," April 29, 1974.
5. Kruger, *Great Heroin Coup,* p. 166.
6. Gary Webb, "Dark Alliance," *San Jose Mercury News,* August 18, 19, 20, September 16, 1996.
7. Peter Kornbluh, "The Storm Over Dark Alliance," *Columbia Journalism Review,* January/February 1997.
8. *The American Heritage Dictionary,* New College Edition (Boston, Houghton Mifflin Company, 1969).
9. McCoy, *Politics of Heroin,* p. 11.
10. Interview with Joseph Molyneux.
11. Interview with DEA Inspector.
12. McCoy, *Politics of Heroin,* p. 447.
13. Michel Chossudovsky, "Who Is Osama Bin Laden?" University of Ottawa Centre for Research on Globalisation (CRG), Montréal, September 12, 2001.
14. Chossudovsky, "Who Is Osama Bin Laden?"
15. McCoy, *Politics of Heroin,* p. 434.
16. Interview with Chuck Gutensohn.
17. Ann B. Wrobleski, Acting Assistant Secretary for International Narcotics Matters, "Statement before the Task Force on International Narcotics Control of the House Foreign Affairs Committee on May 13, 1986,

Narcotics trafficking in Southwest Asia," transcript, US department of State Bulletin, September 1986.
18. Interview with Charles Carter.
19. Ibid.
20. McCoy, *Politics of Heroin*, p. 450.
21. Chossudovsky, "Who Is Osama Bin Laden?"
22. Ibid.
23. Gary Leupp, "Meet Mr Blowback: Gulbuddin Hekmatyar, CIA Op and Thug," *CounterPunch*, February 14, 2003.
24. John R. Doyle, Deputy Regional Director, Region 16, to all SAIC, "Intelligence Nets," April 29, 1974, cited in Chapter p. 25.
25. Luke Harding, "Taliban to lift ban on farmers growing opium if US attacks," *Guardian*, September 25, 2001.
26. David LaGesse, George Rodriguez, "Drug war often finds CIA at odds with DEA," Washington Bureau of *Dallas Morning News*, February 16, 1997, p. 1J.
27. Ibid.
28. LaGesse, "Drug war often finds CIA at odds with DEA."
29. Jon Lee Anderson, "The Taliban's Opium War," *The New Yorker*, July 9, 2007.
31. David G. Wilson, Executive Director of the Association of Former Federal Narcotics Agents, email to membership, August 27, 2007.
32. World Security Institute, "The EU Police Mission in Afghanistan: Marching to a Slow Drum?" Brussels, February 6, 2008.
33. CRA Inc Website (http://cra-usa.net/1mackin.htm), biography of Roger Mackin.
34. Vance Global Website (http://www.vanceglobal.com/whoweare/leadership/showleader.asp?LID=2) Casteel Biography.
35. Peter Maass, "The Way of the Commandos," *New York Times*, May 1, 2005.
36. Max Fuller, "Crying Wolf: Media Disinformation and Death Squads in Occupied Iraq," *Global Research*, November 10, 2005.
37. Vance Global Website (http://www.vanceglobal.com/whoweare/leadership/showleader.asp?LID=2) Casteel Biography.
38. Anderson, "The Taliban's Opium War."
39. Jason Straziuso, "U.S. targets 50 drug lords in Afghanistan," *Chicago Sun Times*, August 11, 2009.
40. Annette Fuentes, "Eli Lilly and Thimerosal," *In These Times*, November 11, 2003.
41. Bruce Levine, "Eli Lilly, Zyprexa & the Bush Family," *Z Magazine* online, May 2004.
42. Henry A Waxman, Ranking Minority Member, Committee on Government Reform, September 19, 2006. Analysis Pharmaceutical Industry

Profits Increase by Over $8 Billion After Medicare Drug Plan Goes Into Effect.

43. Darryl Fears (http://projects.washingtonpost.com/staff/email/darryl+fears/): "Racial Shift in Drug-Crime Prisoners; Fewer Blacks and More Whites, Says Sentencing Project," *Washington Post*, April 15, 2009.

44. Adam Liptak, "U.S. prison population dwarfs that of other nations," *New York Times*, April 23, 2008

BIBLIOGRAPHY

Books

Agee, Philip. *Inside The Company: CIA Diary.* Harmondsworth, England: Penguin Books, 1975.

Agee, Philip, Louis Wolf (Editor), *Dirty Work: The CIA in Western Europe.* New York: Lyle Stuart, 1978.

Balakar, James B., and Lester Grinspoon. *Drug Control in a Free Society.* Cambridge: Cambridge University Press, New Ed edition 1988.

Bario, Joanne. *Fatal Dreams.* Garden City, NY: The Dial Press/Doubleday & Company, Inc. 1985.

Blumenthal, Ralph. *Last Days of the Sicilians: At War with the Mafia.* New York: Random House, 1988.

Brewton, Peter. *The Mafia The CIA and George Bush.* New York, S.P.I. Books, 1992.

Castillo Celerino with David Harmon. *Powder Burns, Cocaine, Contras and The Drug War,* Toronto, Mosaic Press, 1994.

Charbonneau, Jean-Pierre. *The Canadian Connection.* Montreal: Optimum Publishing Company Limited, 1976.

Clark, Everett, Nicholas Horrock, *Contrabandista.* New York: Praeger, 1973.

Stephen Del Corvo, Bill Erwin and Michal Fooner, *Blue Domino.* New York: Putnam, 1978.

Corn, David. *Blond Ghost: Ted Shackley and the CIA's Crusades.* New York: Simon & Schuster, 1994.

Daly, Robert. *Prince of the City: the True Story of a Cop Who Knew Too Much,* Boston: Houghton Mifflin Company, 1978.

Denton, Sally. *The Bluegrass Conspiracy.* New York: Avon Books, 1990.

Douglass, Dr. Joseph D. Jr. *Red Cocaine: The Drugging of America and the West.* Atlanta, GA: Clarion House, 1990; London: Edward Harle Ltd., 1999.

Ehrlichman, John. *Witness To Power: The Nixon Years*. New York: Simon and Schuster, 1982.

Ellis, David C. *U.S. Customs Special Agents: America's Senior Investigators*. Whitman Communications, 2004.

Epstein, Edward Jay. *Agency of Fear: Opiates and Political Power in America*. New York: Putnam, 1977.

Executive Intelligence Review, *Dope, Inc.: The Book That Drove Henry Kissinger Crazy*. 1992.

Finlator, John. *The Drugged Nation; a "Narc's" Story*. New York: Simon and Schuster, 1973.

Gentry, Curt. *J Edgar Hoover, The Man and the Secrets*. New York: W W Norton & Company, 2001.

Hinckle, Warren and William Turner. *Deadly Secrets*. New York: Thunder's Mouth Press, 1981.

Hougan, Jim. *Spooks, The Haunting of America*. New York: Bantam Books, 1979.

Hunt, E. Howard. *Undercover, Memoirs of an American Secret Agent*, New York: Berkley Pub. Corp, 1974.

Huy, Nguyen Ngoc and Stephen B Young. *Understanding Vietnam*. The Netherlands: The DPC Information Service, 1982.

Jaubert, Alain. *Dossier D ... comme Drogue*. Paris: Editions Alain Moreau, 1973.

Jiggens, John. *The Sydney Connection: The CIA, drugs, Nugan Hand and the murder of Donald Mackay*. Australia: Hill End, 2004

Jonnes, Jill. *Hep-Cats, Narcs, and Pipes Dreams: A History of America's Romance with Illegal Drugs*. New York: Scribner, 1996.

Kelly, Jack with Richard Mathison, *On the Street: The Autobiography of the Toughest US Narcotics Agent*. Chicago: Henry Regnery Company, 1974..

Kruger, Henrik. *The Great Heroin Coup: Drugs, Intelligence, & International Fascism* Boston: South End Press, 1980.

Kwitny, John. *Crimes of Patriots*. New York: WW Norton 1987

Lee, Martin A., and Bruce Shlain. *Acid Dreams: The Complete Social History of the LSD, the Sixties, and Beyond*. New York: Grove Press, 1992.

Leuci, Robert. *All the Centurions: A New York City Cop Remembers His Years on the Street, 1961-1981*. New York: Harper Collins.

Marks, John. *The Search for the Manchurian Candidate*. New York: Times Books, 1979

Mills, James. *The Underground Empire: Where Crime and Governments Embrace*, New York, Doubleday & Company, Inc 198

Moldea, Dan. *The Hoffa Wars*. New York: SPI Books, 1993.

McCoy, Alfred W. *The Politics of Heroin: CIA Complicity in the Global Drug Trade*. Chicago: Lawrence Hill Books, 1991.

Messick, Hank. *Of Grass and Snow: The Secret Criminal Elite.* Englewood Cliffs, NJ: Prentice-Hall, 1979.

Moore, Robin. *The Country Team,* New York: Crown Publishers, 1967

Moore, Robin with Barbara Fuca, *Mafia Wife.* New York: Macmillan Publishing Co., Inc., 1977.

The Staff and Editors of Newsday. *The Heroin Trail.* New York: Holt Rinehart, 1973.

Olson, Keith W. *Watergate: The Presidential Scandal That Shook America.* Kansas: University Press of Kansas, 2003.

Paine, Lauren. *The CIA at Work.* London: Robert Hale, 1977.

Peers, William and Dean Brellis. *Behind the Burma Road.* Boston: Little Brown, 1963.

Roarke, Garland. *The Coin of Contraband: The True Story of United States Customs Investigator Al Scharff.* Garden City: Doubleday & Company, Inc., 1964.

Robbins, Christopher. *Air America.* New York: Avon Books, 1985.

Russell, Dick, *The Man Who Knew Too Much.* New York: Carroll & Graf Publishers/R. Gallen, 1992.

Scott, Peter Dale and Jonathan Marshall. *Cocaine Politics: Drugs, Armies, and the CIA in Central America.* Berkeley: University of California Press, 1991.

Scott, Peter Dale. *Deep Politics and the Death of JFK.* Berkeley: University of California Press, 1993.

Sihanouk, Norodom as related to Wilfred Burchett. *My War With The CIA.* New York: Pantheon Books, 1972.

Shawcross, William. *The Shaw's Last Ride: the fate of an ally.* New York: Simon and Schuster, 1988.

Siragusa, Charlie with Robert Wiedrich. *On the Trail of the Poppy: Behind the Mask of the Mafia.* New Jersey: Prentice Hall Inc., 1966.

Sullivan, John F. *Of Spies and Lies: A CIA Lie Detector Remembers Vietnam.* University Press of Kansas, 2002

Sultz, Tad. *Compulsive Spy: the Strange Career of Howard Hunt.* New York: Viking Press, 1974.

Summers, Anthony. *Official and Confidential: The Secret Life of J Edgar Hoover.* New York: Pocket Books, 1994.

Swain, Adrian. *The Time of My Life: Memoirs Off A Government Agent From Pearl Harbor To The Golden Triangle.* Tampa Bay: Axelrod Publishing, 1995.

Tripodi, Tom with Joseph P. DeSario. *Crusade: Undercover against the Mafia and KGB.* Washington: Brassey's, 1993.

Valentine, Douglas. *The Strength of The Wolf.* New York: Verso, 2004.

Wallance, Gregory. *Papa's Game.* New York: Rawson, Wade Publishers, Inc., 1981.

Articles

Adams, Nathan M. "Night of the Big Drug Bust." *Reader's Digest.*

Adams, Nathan M. "The Hunt For André." *Reader's Digest.* March 1973 (reprint).

Anderson, Jack. "Altering the Muckraker's Behavior." *Washington Post.* September 9, 1977. p. D15.

Anderson, Jon Lee. "The Taliban's Opium War." *The New Yorker.* July 9, 2007.

Belair, Felix Jr. "2 U.S. Agencies to Join Fight on Drug Traffic." *New York Times.* July 30, 1970.

Bart Barnes. Conein obituary. *Washington Post.* July 6, 1998.

Belair, Felix Jr. "2 U.S. Agencies to Join in Fight on Drug Traffic." *New York Times.* July 30, 1970.

Boston Globe. "Ask The Globe." January 23, 1980. 60; "Slain Gunman is Identified by The Police." December 19, 1983; "Alleged terrorist linked to arm sales." April 20, 1986. p. 5.

Brean, Herbert. "Crooked, Cruel Traffic In Drugs." *Life.* January 25, 1960. p. 94.

Brelis, Matthew. "Taped Reminiscences Used At Winter Hearings." *Boston Globe.* January 28, 1992.

Branigin, William. "Trial in Camarena Case Shows DEA Anger at CIA." *Washington Post.* July 16, 1990.

Cerabino, Frank. "Elder Tabraue gets mistrial." *Miami Herald.* January 24, 1989. p. 3B.

Clymer, Adam "Canal Pack Foes in Senate Lose Procedural Clash with Backers." *New York Times.* February 22, 1978. p. 1.

Connolly, Richard J. and Jim Calogero. "Raymond Patriarca Dies at 76, Reputedly Ruled N.E. Organized Crime." *Boston Globe.* July 12, 1984.

Crile, George III. "The Colonel's Secret Drug War." *Washington Post.* June 13, 1976 (picture off Ellsberg), p. C1.

Crile, George III. "The Informant Who Jumped Bail." *Washington Post.* June 13, 1976.

Conason, Joe and John Kelly. "Bush and the Secret Noriega Report." *Village Voice.* October 11, 1983.

Connelly, Richard J. "Two In Drug Case Linked to Blackfriars Victim." *Boston Globe.* June 5, 1983.

Cummings, John. "Work for us Or Die." *Penthouse.* December 1989. p. 58-68.

Daily Hampshire Gazette. "Reagan's contra policy said to hurt war on dugs." April 13, 1989.

d'Epeneoux, Christian. "When Americans Judge French Justice Harshly." *L'Aurore.* November 25, 1971.

Dettmer, Jamie. "DEA Drives Off the Old Guard." *Washington Times, Insight.* August, 17, 1998.

Fuentes, Annette. "Eli Lilly and Thimerosa." *In These Times.* November 11, 2003.

Fuller, Max. "Crying Wolf: Media Disinformation and Death Squads in Occupied Iraq." *Global Research.* November 10, 2005.

Garcia, Guillermo X. and Weyermann, D. "DPS agent's killer claims entrapment," *Arizona Daly Star,*" April 13. 1984. pps. 1A, 17A

Gerth, Jeff. "CIA Shedding Its Reluctance to Aid in Fight Against drugs." *New York Times.* March 25, 1990. p. 1.

Gerth, Jeff. "Management Woes Hobble US Air Fleet in Drug War." *New York Times International.* June 13, 1990.

Greve, Frank. "Contra Advisers in Peru." *Philadelphia Inquirer.* May 30, 1990.

Hanley, Robert. "Nelson Gross, Prominent State Republican, Is Missing." *New York Times.* September 20, 1997.

Hess, John L. "US Drug Agent's Charges Anger the French Police." *New York Times.* August 26, 1971.

Hinckle, Warren. "Thornburgh joins drug-secrets game." *San Francisco Examiner.* May 30, 1990.

Hitchens, Christopher. "The Case against Henry Kissinger, The Making of a War Criminal." *Harper's* magazine. February 2001.

Horrock, Nicholas M. "High-Level Backing Cited in C.I.A. Drug-Unit Spying." *New York Times.* July 10, 1975.

Isikoff, Michael. "CIA Creates Narcotics Unit to help in Drug Fight." *Washington Post.* May 28, 1989. p. A13.

Kelly, John. "Bush: Covering up for the CIA." *San Francisco Bay Guardian.* December 14, 1988

Kenney, Robert. "5 Murdered with Shotguns a Blackfriars." *Boston Globe.* September 22, 1980.

Kinder, Douglas. "Bureaucratic Cold Warrior: Harry J. Anslinger and Illicit Narcotics Traffic." Pacific Coast Branch, American Historical Association, *Pacific Historical Review,* 1981. p. 172-3.

Kurkjian, Stephen. "US probing drug links to CIA's flights." *Boston Globe.* April 26, 1987. p. 1, 27.

L'Aurore. "Mr Ingersoll's Little Remark." January 19, 1972.

LaGesse, David and George Rodriguez. "Drug war often finds CIA at odds with DEA." Washington Bureau of *Dallas Morning News.* February 16, 1997. p. 1J.

Marks, Howard. Extradition, US Drug Policy and the Erosion of Individual Liberties.

Marks, John. "The CIA's Corporate Shell Game." *Washington Post.* July 11, 1976.

Marshall, Jonathan. "The White House Death Squad." *Inquiry*. March 5, 1979.

Maass, Peter, "The Way of the Commandos," *New York Times*. May 1, 2005.

Meyer, Lawrence. "DEA Was Offered Explosive devices," *Washington Post*. November 23, 1975. p. A3, 23.

Michelini, Alex. "Feared a Connection to Death: Frenchman." *New York Daily News*. April 20, 1972.

Michelini, Alex. "Cirillo Guilty In Hein Plot; May Do 60 Yrs," *New York Daily News*. April 26, 1972.

Mintz, Bill. "Wood shooting still a mystery," *San Antonio Express*. November 28, 1978, p. 1, 4-A

Morley, Jefferson. "Barry and his city: crack in the Washington culture," *The Nation*, February 19, 1990.

New York Times, "Drug Unit Chief Resigns, Assailing Ex-Nixon Aides," June 30, 1973.

Nordland, Rob. "Is There a Contra Drug Connection." *Newsweek*. January 2, 1987. p. 26.

Ostrow, Ronald J. "Drug Agency Called Lax in Self-Policing." *Los Angeles Times*. November 10, 1981.

Parry, Robert. "Contra-Cocaine: Evidence of Premeditation." *IF Magazine*. July-August 1998.

Parry, Robert. ConsortiumNews.com. "Original October Surprise." October 2006.

Reuters. November 25, 1971, "Debre Calls Drug-SDECE Case a No-Value Confused Novel."

Ring, Wilson. "US Looks at Honduras As Drug Transfer Point," *Washington Post*. p. 1, A31.

Rother. Larry. "Victory in Noriega Case Stunned Even Prosecutors." *New York Times*. April 17, 1992.

Rothberg, Donald M. "Police Agencies Build Up 'Private' Files in Computer." *Washington Star*. May 14, 1975.

Royce, Knute. "Behind Colombia Raid US Got Gacha." *Newsday*. May 4, 1990.

San Antonio News. "Narcotics chief says informers may get $50,000," May 8, 1970.

Selsky, Andrew O. "Link found to bombing." Associated Press, May 4, 2007.

Smothers, Ronald. "2 Are Given Up to 30 Years in Murder of a Millionaire," *New York Times*, October 8, 1998.

Stein, Nancy and Michael Klare. "Merchants of Repression." *NACLA's Latin America and Empire Report* (North American Congress on Latin America). July-August 1976, 31-33. *Time*. "Search and Destroy: The War on Drugs." 4 September 1972; "Grisly Smuggling." January 1, 1973. p. 25.

Trujillo, Stephen G. "Corruption and Cocaine in Peru." *New York Times.* April 7, 1972.

Vallery, Bernard. "All's Ok with France: Drug Sleuth." *New York Daily News.* January 17, 1972.

Washington Post. "CIA Used Drug Ranch in Training, Report Says," citing *Los Angeles Times.* July 5, 1990.

Webster, Michael. "Cash is King." Paso del Norte.

Weiner, Tim. "Suit by Drug Agent Says U.S. Subverted His Burmese effort." *New York Times International.* October 27, 1994. p. A9.

Williams, Carlos J. "Luis Posada Carriles, a terror suspect abroad, enjoys a coming-out in Miami." *Los Angeles Times.* May 7, 2008.

Personal Sources: Interviews and Correspondence

Acampora, Tulius
Acree, Vernon D
Addario, Daniel
Alexander, Frank
Ambrose, Myles J
Arntz, John
Arpaio, Joseph
Aruslan, Russ
Ashcraft, William
Ayers, Bradley
Bacon, John E
Baker, Robert
Baker, Robert
Baldwin, Terry
Barber, Emmett R
Bario, Joanne
Bartels, John
Bax, John
Belin, David
Benjamin, Mortimer L
Benson, Luke
Bierman, Donald
Block, Alan
Bloemker, Kenneth
Blum, Richard
Bly, Richard P
Bonner, Robert
Borquez, Sergio
Boureguat, Ali

Briggs, Francis
Brosan, George
Brigs, Frank
Boyd, Jamie
Burke, Terrence
Byrne, Larry
Campbell, Heather
Carew, Barry
Carey, Gerald F
Carter, Charles
Casey, Daniel P
Castillo, Celerino
Celeya, Genaro
Chaminadas, Claude
Chandler, Douglas
Charbonneau, Jean
Chavez, Elias
Clark, Ramsey
Clarridge, Duane R
Clines, Thomas
Coffey, Raymond
Cohn, Larry
Colby, William E.
Compton, Jack
Conein, Lucien
Cook, Clarence
Coonce, William
Cooper, Glennon
Corcoran, George C
Costa, David W
Cowan, Candace
Coyne, Edward
Cruciani, Joseph P
Dayle, Dennis
Dean, John W
DeFauw, Robert
De Triquet, Thomas
Diaz, Raul J
Dick, Fred
Dietrich, Joseph
DiGennaro, Joe
Diosdado, Caesar
Downey, Arthur

Dunagan, Rick
Durham, John
Dyckman, Wesley
Ellis, David
Ellsberg, Daniel
Enders, Rudy
Enright, John R
Evans, John G
Falvey, John
Feldman, Ira
Fialkewicz, Walter S
Fink, William G
Flipse, Joseph
Flynn, Robert
Fluhr, Arthur
Fox, Thomas D
Frangullie, George C
Freeman, William
Freeman, J R
Frias, Ralph
Fuller, Patrick W
Furey, Bob
Gaffney, George H
Giordano, Henry
Green, Bruce
Green, Ronald (Rocky)
Greene, Stephen H
Gregg, Donald
Griswold Erwin N (8 March 1994 letter)
Gunn, John W Jr
Gutensohn, Chuck
Guy, James
Habern, William
Habib, Albert
Hansen, William
Hughes, William F
Hunt, E Howard
Hunter, Ted
Hurley, Michael
Hurney, Tom
Ingersoll, John
Jackson, Carl
Jensen, Bruce

Kiere, Jack
King, Joseph
Knierm, William
Knight, Paul E.
Koehler, John
Krogh, Egil
Krueger, Joseph E
Kvoriak, Joseph R.
Lagattuta, Joseph
Lansdale, Phoebe
Larkworthy, Frank
Laubinger, Frank
Lawn, Jack
LeMouel, Francois
Lenck, William M
Leuci, Robert
Levergeois, Andre
Levine, Michael
Leya, Charles
Lloyd, Jack
Logay, William J
Ludlum, James H
Lynch, Greyston
Maduro, Reynaldo
Manfredi, Doris
Mangiaracina, Anthony
Maria, Victor
Marr, Michael A
Mattocks, Gary
McBee, Major
McClain, Allan C
McCracken, Robert
Medell, Robert
Metcalf, Harold R
Meyer, Jack
Michel, Werner
Milano, Morino H
Minnick, Water C
Missud, Guy
Missud, Michele
Monastero, Frank V
Moore, Melvin
Morris, Walter

Mullen, Francis
Murphy, David
Murray, Hugh
Nachmanoff, Arnold
Navarro, Nick
Niblo, Peter
O'Brien, John J
Panich, Walter
Patin, Harold
Peloquin, Robert
Pera, Martin
Petrossi, Dominic
Picini, Michael
Plicet, Cecelia
Pohl, Anthony
Poissant, Gilles
Polgar, Thomas
Pool, Tom
Poshepny, Anthony
Powers Michael
Price, Joseph
Pringle, Allan
Promuto, Vincent
Quarequio, Joe
Quinn, Donald
Raugh, Dennis
Redd, Bernard
Rieux Sicart, Georges
Riley, Ross
Rinehart, Jerry
Robinson, J T
Roemer, William
Rosnor, Norman
Ross, Ralph
Rothstein, James
Safir, Howard
Salmi, Richard E
Schlachter, Douglas
Scrocca, Peter
Secord, Richard
Sedillo, Arthur
Seely, Al
Seifer, Matthew

Sears, Walter E
Schrier, Leonard
Scrocca, Peter M
Selvaggi, Frank
Shackley, Theodore
Shanley, Wallace
Sheppard, Jeffrey
Shirley, Jack
Shoffler, Carl
Smith, Phillip R
Spatz, Naomi.
Stanier, Linda
Steele, Robert
Strickler, Lawrence J
Stutman, Robert
Swain, Adrian
Swank, Irvin
Tartaglino, Andrew
Tarallo, Frank
Taylor, Bowman
Taylor, Thomas
Thompson, Chris
Thompson, John
Tobin, Mickey
Toft, Joseph
Tripodi, Thomas
Ungerleider, J Thomas, MD
Unkefer, Dean
Valentine, Wayne
Van Diver, John
Vernier, Theodore
Vizzini, Salvatore
Vopat, Charles
Walmpers, Mary E
Waniewski, Michael A
Wanzeck, William
Warner, John
Washington, Hank
Westrate, David
Waters, Francis
Wheaton, Gene
White, Francis E
Wilson, Charles

Wilson, Edwin P
Wiser, David R
Wurms, Ivan
Young, Gordon
Young, William

INDEX

Made in the USA
Monee, IL
21 November 2020